INDIANA AUTHORS
and
THEIR BOOKS
1816-1916

INDIANA AUTHORS
and their
BOOKS

1816-1916

Biographical sketches of authors
who published during the first
century of Indiana statehood
with lists of their books.

Compiled by R. E. Banta

Published as a contribution to institutional libraries by

WABASH COLLEGE
Crawfordsville, Indiana

1949

Composed, Printed and Bound by
The Haddon Craftsmen, Inc., Scranton, Pa.

The Editorial Committee wishes to make grateful acknowledgment of the assistance rendered in compiling this volume by Margaret K. Husting, Annie C. Leavenworth and Eunice Henley; by Indiana librarians, students of Indiana letters, and friends and relatives of the authors listed.

The Committee also wishes to acknowledge its debt to the unpublished Master of Arts theses of Thomas J. Barry—*A Bibliographical and Biographical Dictionary of Indiana Authors* and of Ora Cole Briscoe—*Indiana Fiction Before 1870* and to the authors, editors and publishers of hundreds of books, encyclopedias, newspapers and periodicals who thoughtfully noted facts about Indiana authors and their works during the century and a half just past.

A WORD ABOUT INDIANA AUTHORS

WE REALIZED that we were undertaking a task of large proportions when we began the compilation of a biographical and bibliographical list of Hoosiers who had published books during the first century of Indiana's statehood. We knew that it was a forbidding project even after we had decided to exclude textbooks, newspaper articles, contributions to periodicals or serials, state or federal publications, and printings of speeches except when they were discourses presumably intended as much for the printed page as for the platform.

We had always heard that every Hoosier had a book ready-outlined in his head and that literature grew as naturally and as luxuriantly as the horseweed along the banks of the quiet Indiana streams. But still we failed to realize the extent of the flowering of the art of letters in our state.

We knew that Coggeshall, early celebrator of the Midwestern muse, had quoted some thirty Indiana writers of verse in his *Poets and Poetry Of The West*, published in 1860; and that a contributor to the CINCINNATI GAZETTE for Dec. 7, 1876, who signed himself "D. S. A.," had remarked upon the abundance of Indiana letters at that date. We knew that Meredith Nicholson had devoted a large part of a successful book to the subject; we knew that the New York and Philadelphia and Boston newspapers (whose destinies were often enough guided by transplanted Hoosiers) frequently turned their eyes westward and commented on the literary fertility of Indiana soil. We knew that even the eastern literary magazines observed Indiana, in the strange midlands, and expressed wonder from time to time. Still we did not comprehend the magnitude of the task we had planned.

Now we have reached the end of our journey. But we fear that much Indiana literary territory remains unexplored. Later there must be supplements and additions, and even then the story will be far from told. For there has been and there still remains something in this rich, imperturbable Middle West—always doing more than its duty in combating such far away annoyances as wars, plagues, international politics and the unpleasant situation of the natives of Borrioboola Gha, but always realizing that those matters are not of real primary importance—which causes its true citizen to contemplate the things which interest him, and to cherish a desire to put his observations on paper. This desire to communicate is but one aspect of the noticeable friendliness of the Hoosier character.

There has been a truly enormous amount of writing done in Indiana. Some of it is masterly, a great deal of it is average, and some of it is bad and colorless, with a depressing kind of badness which also sometimes comes from places other than Indiana and often with great names signed to it. We are glad to note, however, that there is also another kind of badness which appears in Hoosier literature now and then: it is *inspired* badness, of a kind which we sometimes find almost as charming as excellent writing. Stephen Leacock says, "It is the work of people who would undoubtedly have been poets if they had had education and academic background."

We have excluded nothing (except those categories mentioned before) which comes in the form of book or pamphlet. Private printing, far from being frowned upon, rather has been sought for. In that field there is nothing to prevent even the most inept from printing whatever he may write provided he can meet the printer's price; and we have listed some of that inept production. But there have been many other instances in which a writer had something important to say and said it extremely well, but could find no publisher who would accept his work; perforce, he resorted to self-financed publication. That is the sort of private publishing which gets into literary essays, booksellers' catalog notes, appreciations, memorials, et cetera. We have found some of that sort of private printing, also.

We have probably made errors of omission, and possibly other errors which will appear uncomfortably obvious, but we have made a start. Our sincere hope is that others will correct, amend and expand in the future.

Probably the principal claim to virtue in Indiana letters lies in the field of fiction. Some effete Easterner has intimated that the people of Indiana turn to fiction as an escape from the desolation of the midwestern scene. That, of course, is absurd. Hoosiers need no escape, psychological or physical. Did any Hoosier, author or other, ever leave the state except to make more money or as a sort of missionary to the benighted seaboards, east or west?

Indiana's first novelist (he was also one of the first west of the Alleghenies) is believed to have based part of his one novel on his father's reminiscences, thus setting the Hoosier pattern of successful writing even before Indiana emerged from territorial status. He was Jesse Lynch Holman and he settled near the present site of Aurora in 1811. It is true that his novel, *The Prisoners Of Niagara, Or Errors Of Education*, was written in Kentucky and published there the year before he came to Indiana; but, since he lived out his life as one of Indiana's leading citizens, he may be claimed by both states with equal justice.

A few current authorities might hold Theodore Dreiser and one or two others to be the great artists of the state. But who is to say that the phenomenal group of fairly recent best sellers, though early of their kind—David Graham Phillips, George Barr McCutcheon, Meredith Nicholson, Booth Tarkington, George Ade—may not eventually be placed in a higher category of art as well as material success by some future critic? Such a revival of popularity has happened before.

Even these were not the first of the Indiana writers whose books sold in impressive figures. Lew Wallace's *Ben-Hur*, Maurice Thompson's *Alice Of Old Vincennes*, and Charles Major's *When Knighthood Was In Flower*, all made substantial fortunes for their authors and brought fame to the state of Indiana.

The fact is that the works of Indiana authors have sold more extensively during the past half century than those of the authors of any other state except New York—and New York's margin of superiority is small. The study which resulted in this information was made by a new arrival in the state who wondered if the place of Hoosiers in literature could be even a fraction of what it was claimed to be. This new arrival was John H. Moriarity, then recently appointed librarian of Purdue University, who knew how to establish the facts. After making a careful analysis of the data in Alice Payne Hackett's *Fifty Years Of Best Sellers*, Mr. Moriarity reported:

"For each year since 1895, Mrs. Hackett lists the ten novels which lead in nation-wide sales in order of their popularity.

"We took the period from the turn of the century to the beginning of World War II, and assigned the score of ten for each top best seller during those years. The second novel on the list was scored as nine, the third as eight and so on. The birthplace of each author was then ascertained (foreign-born authors were ignored as not of interest for this study and co-authors were divided equally if two states were involved). The various states were then credited with the total score of the authors born in them. And Indiana, during the forty years checked, was second state in the Union, and a fighting second at that. The top ten were:

1. New York, with a score of 218
2. Indiana, with a score of 213
3. Pennsylvania, with a score of 125
4. Virginia, with a score of 102
5. Kentucky, with a score of 94
6. Missouri, with a score of 80
7. Ohio, with a score of 73
8. Michigan, with a score of 70
9. Minnesota, with a score of 67
10. California, with a score of 64

—rather an amazing result in view of the fact that New York's population—and therefore the potential authors of best sellers—averaged almost four times that of Indiana during the forty-year period analyzed."*

*INDIANA QUARTERLY FOR BOOKMEN, Vol. III, No. 1, Jan. 1947, as revised by the author.

Customarily only fiction titles make the best seller lists, and there Indiana has been amazingly well represented. But Hoosiers have written in the non-fiction fields, with similar facility and distinction.

In the writing of history, Indiana need only show her list of names. It begins with Judge John Law of Vincennes and John Brown Dillon—a competent scholar by any standard and a tragic character worthy of a biography of his own. It proceeds through the Nineteenth and Twentieth centuries with John Clark Ridpath (most prolific, if not most scholarly), James Albert Woodburn, Wilbur Cortez Abbott, Frederic Austin Ogg, Claude Bowers, Charles Austin Beard and his wife Mary Ritter Beard, and so on to a younger group, the members of which cannot be recorded here, brilliant as they are. There are, besides, dozens who were not historians by profession but whose one or two books or pamphlets, written on subjects timely in their day, were so well executed as to have become valuable history collectors' items. Any student of book auction records will immediately recognize the names of William H. Winter, Overton Johnson, Joel Palmer, Daniel Mc-Donald, Sandford Cox, Isaac Reed and Isaac McCoy.

A similar distinction attends Hoosier writing in the field of science, even from the earliest days. In the New Harmony group were Thomas Say, David Dale Owen, Charles Alexandre LeSueur, and, for a time, Josiah Warren, not to mention those whose residence was ephemeral but who took notes while they visited the New Harmony community—John James Audubon, Constantine Samuel Rafinesque and Prince Maximilian von Neuweid. Their work was of permanent and world-wide significance. More recently there were, in the field of natural sciences, Willis Stanley Blatchley, Samuel Record, John Merle Coulter and George Brown Goode. And, though we may reluctantly concede that other states hold prior claim to his citizenship by reason of longer residence, it remains a fact that David Starr Jordan came to his intellectual maturity during his period as teacher in various Indiana institutions and as president of Indiana University.

Apparently the first work published in Indiana relating to the physical sciences had to do with the engineering problems involved in raising the roads out of what was then held to be the bottomless Indiana mud. It was Robert Dale Owen's *A Brief Practical Treatise On The Construction And Management Of Plank Roads*, published in New Albany in 1850. There was little writing on the pure sciences of mathematics, physics, and chemistry (since we exclude textbooks) before the last decade of the Nineteenth century. At that time the Indianians who had studied these sciences at Hanover, Wabash, DePauw, Franklin, Earlham and other Indiana colleges, and at Indiana University, began to put their findings and conclusions into books and pamphlets. Within another decade or two they were joined by the graduates of the more recently founded Purdue University and Rose Polytechnic Institute.

The first serious Indiana work on any phase of agriculture was published in 1826. Its title, after the fashion of the day, is fully explanatory: *The American Vine-*

Dresser's Guide, Being A Treatise On The Cultivation Of The Vine And The Process Of Wine Making: Adapted To The Soil And Climate Of The United States: By John James Dufour, Formerly Of Switzerland, And Now An American Citizen, Cultivator Of The Vine From His Childhood, And For The Last Twenty-Five Years, Occupied In That Line Of Business, First In Kentucky, And Now On The Borders Of The Ohio, Near Vevay, Indiana.

Soon there was more writing on agriculture. Most of the settlers in the state had been lured here by the glowing descriptions of Indiana lands which appeared in the "emigrant guides"; but these works had been written for the most part by Easterners who had an economic interest in undeveloped Indiana farmland—just as Indianians in later decades wrote alluringly of Kansas, Iowa, Texas, California and, even within the memory of living man, of Florida.

One such book was written about Indiana in the early days by a New Englander who had some Indiana land in his family holdings and who eventually became a distinguished citizen of the state. He was Henry W. Ellsworth; and his book, *The Valley Of The Upper Wabash*, published in New York in 1838, certainly sold his land very profitably. Incidentally it was good land and well worth the price.

Solon Robinson, of wide reputation among students of the history of agriculture, did much of his most important writing and research while a resident of Crown Point. He was a tireless contributor to newspapers and agricultural periodicals and his name or initials appear over sound, sensible writing on many phases of farm life and farm improvement.

A somewhat different form of agricultural literature appeared in the Eighties, which saw the flowering of the County History Era. The pioneer who had come to new Indiana as a young man was now a prosperous old gentleman and ready to pay the necessary five or ten dollars to see himself immortalized by the followers of this school of historical writing. He believed his agricultural opinions and successes to be of interest and value, if he was a farmer, and he usually managed to work them into the notes he supplied for his biographical sketch.

In another field of literature Indiana appears, perhaps unfortunately, to have led the way—the juvenile "series" novels.

Mrs. J. R. Hibbard, a Richmond doctor's wife who wrote under the name of Faith Wynne, seems to have made a beginning at one of those long juvenile series when she published two books before 1876—*Flossy Lee* and *Flossy Lee At The Mountains*. Had she written two or three decades later she would have seen the "series" fad off to a good start, and a continuing source of expense to the parents of youthful fans who followed the repetitious doings of their little heroes and heroines. Did Indiana have a part in this? Indiana had practically a monopoly. Elsie Dinsmore, The Little Colonel, the Bobbs Hill Boys, the Twins series, the myriad Brownie books, Raggedy Ann—their creators were all Hoosier born or Hoosier seasoned. These enjoyed phenomenal success and, far from being out-dated by the decades which have passed since their first publication, many of them are still in demand in the children's section of every public library.

Evaleen Stein wrote, illustrated and decorated truly beautiful little books for children. They did not have the benefit of wide circulation but they will be rediscovered one of these days.

A great deal of Indiana writing has been devoted to one sort or another of social reform. Dreaming in the broader fields began in Robert Owen's New Harmony with plans for making every citizen happy, for reducing the working day to the vanishing point, illuminating children's minds without bothersome letters and figures, and feeding one and all a bountiful diet magically produced by cooperative effort. At about the same period, the Quakers around Centerville and Richmond were thinking and writing on the problems of how best to secure an opportunity for their own and their neighbors' children to learn to read and write, how to improve farming methods and, later, what to do toward helping eliminate the national evil of slavery, which they saw all too plainly as a coming threat to the welfare of the whole country.

Two brief years brought the New Harmony social visionaries to a rude awakening; but the anti-slavery movement, even though half of the State's influential citizens had moved to Indiana from slave-holding territory, continued and was voluminously written of in newspapers, books and pamphlets.

Much writing on the subject of religion resulted from the evangelical wave which washed the Middle West and South in the Twenties and Thirties. It was almost all of a rabid sectarian nature. The writing was not particularly creditable either to religion or to letters, but it has a significance. There was a lull in religious writing after the Forties, and when it began again in Indiana it was more restrained, broader in view, and in many cases of considerable importance.

The first tide of religious writing waned around the Mexican War period, but soon a new and different evangelical wave struck the state and the country; someone in England had discovered in the Thirties that alcohol, used in its various forms as a beverage, was sometimes associated with trouble, domestic, economic, legal, physical and moral. Word of this eventually reached the United States and, in due time, filtered through to Indiana. A great army of speakers, pleaders and exhorters deserted their previous subjects and took up the cause of Temperance. It could not be Prohibition, in that day, for whiskey was one of the chiefest of the doctor's prescriptions and a staple article in every grocery. Naturally, writing in pamphlet and book form followed the pleadings and exhortations: exhortation alone was insufficient; the audience needed to be sold or given something to take home to read and mull over at moments of temptation and to use as a reference work in debates with the neighbors. It was exciting stuff and it continued to attract readers for many years. Luther Benson's *Fifteen Years In Hell*, published and republished in Indianapolis in the Seventies and Eighties, must have outsold many an American classic in its day.

There were other evils crying for suppression. Gambling, for instance. Jonathan H. Green, who made his headquarters in Lawrenceburg for some time and who frequented many brawling river towns along the Ohio and Mississippi, had a peculiar literary experience in connection with a book which he expected to discourage gambling. In his book, *Jonathan H. Green: The Reformed Gambler*, he went into such minute detail in describing the means by which the professional sharper mulcted his victims that the work became the foremost text for ambitious young men who wished to learn the lucrative trade which Mr. Green sought to destroy. The book had a remarkable sale.

In Terre Haute in the Seventies some writing began to appear about a new sort of reform. Terre Haute was the principal city in the western Indiana coal area, then beginning to be worked on a large scale, and it was also something of a railroad center. Coal miners and railroad men were early among those who organized their trades into unions. Terre Haute was also the town in which Eugene Victor Debs had been born in 1855. The result of these two factors was unavoidable: Terre Haute became a center of the modern labor movement in thought and writing. It is probable that this movement influenced the works of other Terre Haute citizens—William Riley Halsted, Robert Wiles Hunter, Ida Husted Harper, and Orlando J. Smith—whether they realized it or not.

But it is in the composition of poetry that the Hoosier, to use a rural Indiana phrase, runs hog-wild. In this compilation of Indiana writers who published during and prior to the year 1916 we have probably missed some writers of fiction, biography, history, scientific works and so on; but due to the astronomical numbers of its perpetrators within the confines of the state, now and in the past, we have undoubtedly omitted dozens of writers of book-published poetry.

It may be that the success of the folksy and easy-flowing verse of James Whitcomb Riley inspired his fellow citizens with the illusion that they could relax from their vocational duties and do likewise. However, a glance at the compilations of Venable, of Coggeshall, and of Parker and Heiney demonstrates that there was an inordinately great proportion of poets in Indiana long before Riley had learned his alphabet. Perhaps it is the soil, perhaps it is the climate, with its wide and unfavorably known extremes, perhaps it is a virus transmitted from Indiana weeds to Indiana citizens by Indiana cows —as in the notorious "milk-sick" of the early Nineteenth century—but it is unquestionably there. For some reason, about one Hoosier in ten writes what he believes to be poetry, whether or not he admits it to his friends and associates.

The writer of the before-mentioned article in the CINCINNATI GAZETTE for Dec. 7, 1876, said of the Indiana poets in the book collection which he described:

"Poems that never saw the type until 1871 were written when two-thirds of Indiana was a howling wilderness. Miss Chitwood died in 1855. Mrs. Bolton was born in 1820 [sic] and when fourteen years old excited the envy of her fellow-pupils in Madison by the excellence of her composition. *A Few Poems* of Judge Biddle's attracted the attention of Washington Irving in 1842, and in 1830, John Finley . . . wrote 'The Hoosier's Nest'. . . . Indiana has no reason to be ashamed of her poets. . . ."

There were poetry pages in the newspapers, poetry societies, poetry clubs, poetry associations and poetry annuals, anthologies and collections, the latter not always above suspicion of venal aims. There were poetry prizes, poetry contests and poetry days, evenings, afternoons, and mornings. Besides those versifiers of sufficient merit to have had their works purchased and published by recognized houses, there was always a lush crop of the less talented awaiting the oily advances of the "vanity publisher." Many an elderly gentleman, or lady, with time on his hands finally got around to writing the verse he had always felt competent to write since he first heard Jim Riley read his things at the Baptist Church benefit in 1897. And he had the result privately printed by the local printer and bound for distribution among the children and the nieces and the nephews. Strangely enough, there is occasionally in this twilight endeavor some rather well written verse, often the result of a tranquil and pleasant sort of thought of which this world could use a great deal more.

Between the paid and the self-published poets there is another and an interesting class. This third variety of Indiana poet paid for printing, it is true, but he bargained the local printer down to the ultimate dime. When an edition of the book came out he peddled it from door to door and from street corner to street corner and sold it with every art known to salesmanship. Not infrequently, if the work descended to a really remarkable literary depth, these people made respectable profits.

Such, to a superlative degree, was James Buchanan Elmore, "The Bard of Alamo," unofficial Poet Laureate of Indiana, who combined farming, poesy inspired by a genius of perfectly hopeless and unbelievable ineptitude, and a keen sense of personal publicity values. Elmore, author of such classics as "The Monon Wreck," died in his eighties possessed of five hundred acres of Montgomery County land, the fruit of his pen and his plow about equally.

Be the motives, the method and the results of authorship what they may, whatever could be located of the books of poems published before the end of 1916 are listed here. Indiana need make no apologies: Hoosiers have produced much poetry which is likely to live—even including "Curfew Must Not Ring Tonight"!

*   *   *

So the speculation ends and the biographies and bibliographies begin. There are a considerable number of them. Never again need a native Hoosier be embarrassed, as apparently was D. S. A., the author of the CINCINNATI GAZETTE article quoted before, by any such episode as this which he reports in 1876:

"Several months ago Mr. Evans, the very urbane custodian of the Indianapolis library, spoke 'of the paucity of Indiana authors.' Said he, 'I'm preparing a list of our authors for the Boston Library, and I've been unable to learn of more than *Seventy!* Mr. Hough replied that 'he had the works of more than one hundred in his own library, and he presumed there had been many more than this. . . .' "

Let not, henceforth, an Indiana librarian, urbane or otherwise, so underestimate the role of the Hoosiers in print!

The compilation of this work has been a long task but a pleasant one. We hope that it will prove useful to librarians and collectors, to students and teachers, and that it will serve as a start toward a more careful keeping of the records in the future.

R. E. BANTA, *for*
The Editorial Committee

A Note on the Scope and Use of This Work

1. The compilers have endeavored to include all writers of books (other than textbooks, purely technical works, and contributions to periodical or serial publications) who published prior to 1916, the centennial of Indiana's statehood.

2. Writers are included who (a) were born in Indiana, (b) were reared and educated in Indiana, (c) whose literary work began during residence in Indiana and was obviously influenced by Indiana residence, or (d) who chose Indiana as a place in which to spend a major portion of their lives.

3. Writers are listed, in so far as the knowledge of the compilers extends, by name and, in the case of women, by married name.

4. The abbreviation "n.p." indicates that no place of publication appears on the title page. If the place is known the name of the city appears in brackets. The same applies to date of publication (abbreviated "n.d."). When no information is given as to place or date it is due to the fact that while the book is stated upon good authority to have been published, no copy was available for examination.

5. The Wabash College Library and the Indiana State Library have on file the original notes for this work plus sketches and bibliographies of some hundreds of Indiana writers who were discovered, upon research, to be ineligible because of insufficient residence, absence of published works before 1916 or other reasons. These institutions will welcome correspondence correcting errors in this publication or furnishing additional material upon writers included or not included herein.

A

ABBOTT, RUSSELL BIGELOW: 1823–?

Russell Bigelow Abbott, son of Joseph Jackson and Mary Osborn Abbott, was born near Brookville, Ind., on Aug. 8, 1823. He was educated at Indiana University, receiving the A.B. degree in 1847 and the A.M. in 1850. For a number of years he was principal of the public schools of Muncie and New Castle, Ind., and of the Whitewater Presbyterian Academy. Following his ordination as a Presbyterian minister in 1857 he was pastor of churches in Brookville and Knightstown, Ind., and in Albert Lea, Minn. He was a founder and for several years president of Albert Lea College.

Information from *Who's Who in America* and the Indianapolis Public Library.

* * *

Bible History. 2 vols.
History and Analysis of the Books of the Bible.
History of the Winona Presbytery.
A Chapter of Autobiography. n.p., n.d.

ABBOTT, WILBUR CORTEZ: 1869–1947.

Wilbur Cortez Abbott, one of the foremost historians of the Twentieth century, was born in Kokomo, Ind., on Dec. 28, 1869. His parents were Thomas W. and Eleanor L. Holliday Abbott.

He was educated at Wabash College, where he received the A.B. degree in 1892 and the A.M. in 1904. He continued graduate study at Cornell and Oxford universities and received advanced and honorary degrees from Wabash College and Yale University.

Beginning in 1893, Dr. Abbott was for a time an instructor in Indiana high schools. He then began a career as professor of history at various leading educational institutions, including Cornell, Michigan, Dartmouth, Kansas, Yale and Harvard. At the same time he carried on an exhaustive study of the Cromwellian period in England, on the continent, and in the United States. He became the acknowledged authority on the subject. He retired from teaching in 1941 and devoted the remainder of his life to research and writing.

In his youth Dr. Abbott wrote a great deal of poetry which was published in periodicals and in the INDIAN-

APOLIS NEWS, for which he acted as correspondent while teaching in Indiana.

Dr. Abbott married Margaret E. Smith on Sept. 6, 1899. He died on Feb. 3, 1947.

Information from Wilbur Cortez Abbott.

* * *

Colonel Thomas Blood, Crown-Stealer, 1618-1680. *Rochester, N. Y., 1910.*

The Expansion of Europe. A History of the Foundations of the Modern World. *New York, 1918.* 2 vols. (Also published under other titles.)

Colonel John Scott of Long Island, 1634 (?)-1696. *New Haven, 1918.*

Conflicts with Oblivion. *New Haven, 1924.*

The New Barbarians. *Boston, 1925.*

A Bibliography of Oliver Cromwell. A List of Printed Materials Relating to Oliver Cromwell, Together with a List of Portraits and Caricatures. *Cambridge, Mass., 1929.*

New York in the American Revolution; Illustrations by Victor H. Paltsits. *New York, 1929.*

An Introduction to the Documents Relating to the International Status of Gibraltar, 1704-1934. *New York, 1934.*

Index to Periodicals, Publications of Societies, Series, etc. [of material on Oliver Cromwell]. *Cambridge, Mass., 1934.*

Adventures in Reputation, with an Essay on "Some New History and Historians." *Cambridge, Mass., 1935.*

The Writings and Speeches of Oliver Cromwell; with an Introduction, Notes and a Sketch of his Life . . . with the Assistance of Catherine D. Crane. *Cambridge, Mass., 1937, 1939, 1945.* 3 vols.

ADAMS, ANDY: 1859–1935.

Andy Adams, writer of popular Western fiction, was the son of Andrew and Elizabeth Elliot Adams. Born in Whitley County, Ind., on May 3, 1859, he was reared on the family farm and attended the country schools—probably for not more than the five or six years customary at that time.

Evidently affected by the epidemic of Texas fever which well nigh depopulated the Middlewest of male youths in the Seventies, Adams made his way to that state and spent ten years as a cowhand. At the end of that period he went to the Cripple Creek country in Colorado in order to try his hand at mining. Through some strange transition he eventually took up writing and produced several successful books.

In his later years he made his home at Colorado Springs, Colo. He died on Sept. 26, 1935.

Information from *Who's Who in America* and Burke and Howe—*American Authors and Books, 1640–1940.*

* * *

The Log of a Cowboy: A Narrative of the Old Trail Days; Illustrated by E. Boyd Smith. *Boston, 1903.*

A Texas Matchmaker. *Boston, 1904.*

The Outlet. *Boston, 1905.*

Cattle Brands. A Collection of Western Camp-fire Stories. *Boston, 1906.*

Reed Anthony, Cowman: An Autobiography. *Boston, 1907.*

Wells Brothers; the Young Cattle Kings. *Boston, 1911.*

The Ranch on the Beaver; A Sequel to 'Wells Brothers, the Young Cattle Kings'; with Illustrations by Edward Borein. *Boston, 1927.*

Golden Tales of the Far West.

North Platte.

The Western Himalayas and Cashmere.

ADAMS, ESTELLA: ?–

Estella Adams, a resident of Kokomo, Ind., was the author of children's books. She also compiled several books of quotations not listed here.

Information from the Federal Writers Project— *Indiana Authors*, 1937.

* * *

Indiana for Little Children. *Indianapolis, 1915.*
Pioneer Life for Little Children. *Indianapolis, 1916.*

ADDINGTON, THOMAS: 1829–?

Thomas Addington, born in Wayne County, Ind., in 1829, attended local schools, the Union Literary Institute, and Liber College, in Jay County, Ind. He married Martha Ann Hughes in 1851 and was ordained to the Christian ministry in 1858.

According to Tucker's *History of Randolph County*, "Elder Thomas Addington is ready with the pen as well as fluent in speech, and has contributed many valuable articles to the press upon important subjects pertaining to religion and morality."

His one recorded book purports to be the true story of a runaway slave who attended Union Literary Institute with the author.

Information from Tucker—*History of Randolph County (1882)* and the Indiana State Library.

* * *

Jim Baker. *Winchester, Ind., 1898.*

ADE, GEORGE: 1866–1944.

George Ade was an author who proved that writing as a profession would pay a handsome living to a man with the right combination of human sympathy, good craftsmanship and steady application. His *Fables In Slang*, published in periodicals, syndicated and collected in several books, brought him fame as a humorist, a classification he never quite accepted for himself.

His musical comedies and plays brought him a larger income and international fame. His poetry was undistinguished. His travel sketches gave him satisfaction but added little to his luster. He lives on as a "warmhearted satirist," the title given him by his biographer, Fred C. Kelly. (*George Ade: Warmhearted Satirist*, by Fred C. Kelly, 1947.)

Born in Kentland, Ind., Feb. 9, 1866, George Ade had a happy childhood and later a gay youth at Purdue University, where he graduated in 1887 without having displayed any interest in either engineering or agriculture but where he shone modestly in the literary field. He did journalistic work in Lafayette until June, 1890, when he went to Chicago and started work on the CHICAGO DAILY NEWS (which became the CHICAGO NEWS RECORD, then THE CHICAGO RECORD). For ten years he was a prolific writer and was closely associated with his friend, John T. McCutcheon, the cartoonist. It was in his daily column, captioned "Stories of the Streets and of the Town," that his "Pink Marsh," "Doc' Horne," and "Artie" stories appeared, as well as his earliest fables. Scattered through the column were embryonic plays, "playlets" and dialogue, all containing shrewd observations, brevity of wit and entertainment.

His reports of the Columbian Exposition in 1893 had made him aware of the foreign world and had given him a thirst to travel. In 1895 and 1898 he visited the strange places he had seen in miniature at the Chicago Fair. Throughout his life he enjoyed trips around the world and particularly cruises to the West Indies.

In 1900 his fables were syndicated. By this time several books had appeared, collected from his newspaper column, and he started his play-writing career in earnest. The first decade in the Twentieth Century saw them written, produced and published; later Ade received further dividends when they were in demand for motion pictures.

His summer home near Brook, Ind., called "Hazelden," was built in 1903, and his hospitality brought him more fame. Here he entertained political rallies and community parties, as well as his friends and brothers in Sigma Chi. His private golf course became

a regional club under his fine organizing ability. From December to May he was usually at home in Miami Beach, Fla., the most agreeable spot for winter-living that he found in his travels. He never married.

Why is George Ade's name generally placed with Booth Tarkington's, next to James Whitcomb Riley's, at the top of the list of Indiana's literary men? Good writing and hard work and a sincere love for his fellow man must be the answer. He touched more lives than most of us because he was not content to meet people and pass on; he kept them as friends up to his death on May 16, 1944, and on beyond. His personal correspondence approached literary production, for he never neglected it, and when it became too much for individual response he issued mimeographed "news bulletins." The quality of friendship is therefore proved to be a good companion to literary ability and effort, in the life and work of George Ade.

Dorothy R. Russo.

* * *

Stories of the Streets and of the Town [First Series]. *Chicago*, 1894.

Stories of the Streets and of the Town: Second Series. *Chicago*, 1894.

Stories of the Streets and of the Town: Third Series. *Chicago*, 1895.

Stories of the Streets and of the Town: Fourth Series. *Chicago*, 1895.

What a Man Sees Who Goes Away from Home. *Chicago*, 1896.

Circus Day. *Chicago* and *New York* [1896].

Stories from History. (pseudonym, John Hazelden) *Chicago* and *New York* [1896].

Artie. *Chicago*, 1896.

Pink Marsh. *Chicago* and *New York*, 1897.

Stories of the Streets and of the Town: Fifth Series. *Chicago*, 1897.

Stories of the Streets and of the Town: Sixth Series. *Chicago*, 1898.

Stories of the Streets and of the Town: Seventh Series. *Chicago*, 1899.

Doc' Horne. *Chicago* and *New York*, 1899.

Fables in Slang. *Chicago* and *New York*, 1900 (sic).

Stories of the Streets and of the Town: Eighth Series. *Chicago*, 1900.

More Fables. *Chicago* and *New York*, 1900.

Forty Modern Fables. *New York*, 1901.

Grouch at the Game. [*Madison, Wis.*, 1901].

The Girl Proposition. *New York*, 1902.

The Sultan of Sulu. *New York, Chicago*, etc., 1902. (Musical comedy.)

Peggy from Paris. *New York, Chicago*, etc., 1903. (Musical comedy.)

People You Know. *New York*, 1903.

The Sultan of Sulu. *New York*, 1903. (Play.)

In Babel. *New York*, 1903.

The Rolling Peanut. *Detroit, Mich.*, n.d.

Handsome Cyril. (*Phoenix, Ariz.*, 1903.) (Strenuous Lad's Library, No. 1)

Clarence Allen. (*Phoenix, Ariz.*, 1903.) (Strenuous Lad's Library, No. 2)

Rollo Johnson. (*Phoenix, Ariz.*, 1904.) (Strenuous Lad's Library, No. 3)

Breaking into Society. *New York* and *London*, 1904.

The Sho-Gun. *New York, Chicago,* etc., 1904. (Comic opera.)

True Bills. *New York* and *London*, 1904.

In Pastures New. *New York*, 1906.

The Slim Princess. *Indianapolis* [1907].

The Fair Co-ed. *New York, Chicago*, etc., 1908. (Musical comedy.)

Chapter Houses, with Particular Reference to Purdue University. [*Lafayette, Ind.,* n.d.].

I Knew Him When—. *Chicago*, 1910.

Hoosier Hand Book and True Guide for the Returning Exile. *Chicago*, 1911.

Verses and Jingles. *Indianapolis* [1911].

A Picture Book for Purdue Sigs. n.p., n.d. [*Lafayette, Ind.,* 1912.]

The Revised Legend of One Who Came Back. *New York*, 1912.

Knocking the Neighbors. *Garden City, N. Y.*, 1912.

Ade's Fables. *Garden City, N. Y.*, 1914.

An Invitation to You and Your Folks from Jim and Some More of the Home Folks. *Indianapolis* [1916].

Marse Covington. *Washington, D. C.*, 1918.

The Fable of the Hostess and the Hikers and the Party Under the Trees. Issued by the American Red Cross, 1918.

Not a Fable. *New York,* n.d.

Hand-Made Fables. *New York*, 1920.

Fred Stone Jingles for Good Little Girls and Good Little Boys, n.p., n.d. [1921].

Single Blessedness and Other Observations. *Garden City, N. Y.*, 1922.

The Mayor and the Manicure. *New York* and *London*, 1923.

Nettie. *New York* and *London*, 1923.

Speaking to Father. *New York* and *London*, 1923.

The College Widow. *New York* and *London*, 1924.

Father and the Boys. *New York* and *London*, 1924.

The County Chairman. *New York* and *London*, 1924.

Just Out of College. *New York* and *London*, 1924.

L'Opera La Veuve Academie, n.p., n.d. [*Chicago*, 1924.]

Thirty Fables in Slang. *New York*, 1926.

Bang! Bang! *New York* [1928].

John Hertz: An Appreciation. *Miami, Fla.*, 1930.

The Old-Time Saloon Not Wet—Not Dry Just History. *New York*, 1931.

Revived Remarks on Mark Twain. (Compiled by George Hiram Brownell) *Chicago*, 1936.

One Afternoon With Mark Twain. *Chicago*, 1939.

Notes & Reminiscences. (with John T. McCutcheon) *Chicago*, 1940.

Stories of the Streets and of the Town. (Edited by Franklin J. Meine) *Chicago*, 1941.

ALBERTSON, CHARLES CARROLL: 1865–

Charles Carroll Albertson was born at Plainfield, Ind., Feb. 11, 1865. His parents were Benjamin and Martha Bowman Albertson. Originally educated for the law, he turned to the ministry, studied theology in the Garrett Bible Institute, and received the D.D. degree from Allegheny College in 1899.

From 1888 to 1892 he was pastor of the Presbyterian Church in Goshen, Ind. He then held pastorates in several cities in Pennsylvania and New York until 1928, at which time he became a lecturer at Biblical Seminary in New York.

He was twice married—first to Florence Edith Romer, who died in 1926, then, in 1928, to Permelia Hogg Lindridge. In addition to his books, he wrote poems and essays and edited and compiled several works.

Information from *Who's Who in America* and the Indianapolis Public Library.

* * *

Safe Counsel and Sweet Comfort: Messages for the Young. *New York*, 1891.

The Gospel According to Christ. 1898.

Verba Consolantes for the Use of Ministers in Pastoral Visitation and at Funerals; Containing Appropriate Scriptural Selections, Prayers, Poems, and the Burial Service: Also Three Funeral Addresses. *Buffalo, N. Y.*, 1901.

Probationer's Book. *Buffalo, N. Y.*, 1900.

Many Voices. *Philadelphia*, 1904.

Death and Afterwards. 1907.

Lincoln the Lawyer. Dr. Charles C. Albertson's Address at the Annual Dinner of the Bar Association, at Genesee Valley Club, January Twenty-first, Nineteen Hundred and Eight. [*Rochester, N. Y.,* 1908.]

College Sermons. *Philadelphia*, 1909.

Joint Debate Hubbard-Albertson. Question: Resolved That Christianity Is Declining. *East Aurora, N. Y.*, 1909.

The Distinctive Ideas of Jesus. *Philadelphia*, 1914.

Chapel Talks: A Collection of Sermons to College Students. *New York* [1916].

The Prophets and the War. *New York* (1917).

The Reality of Religion. *New York* [1928].

Prayers and Reflections of a Modern Disciple. *London*, 1933.

Voices in the Night; Poems of the Nazi-Conquered Peoples. *New York*, 1943.

ALERDING, HERMAN JOSEPH: 1845–?

"Herman Joseph Alerding was born in Westphalia, Germany, April 13, 1845, a son of B. Herman and Theresa (Schrameier) Alerding. He was too young to remember the voyage which brought his parents to America and to a new home at Newport, Ky. At Newport he attended the parochial school of Corpus Christi Church . . . and from 1858 until 1859 attended the Diocesan Seminary at Vincennes, Ind. The next year he was a student in the old St. Thomas Seminary at Bardstown, Ky., and in the fall of 1860 entered St. Meinrad's Abbey of the Benedictine Fathers in Spencer County, Ind. There under Bishop de St. Palais he received his . . . priesthood Sept. 22, 1868. Following that for three years he was assistant at St. Joseph's Church at Terre Haute and also had charge of neighboring missions. Oct. 18, 1871, he became pastor of St. Elizabeth's Church at Cambridge City, where he remained until August, 1874 . . .

"In the summer of 1874 Father Alerding was transferred to Indianapolis as procurator for the newly established St. Joseph's Seminary, and was also pastor of the congregation that worshipped in the Seminary chapel. After a year the Seminary was abandoned and Father Alerding was directed to build a new church. St. Joseph's Church of Indianapolis was dedicated July 4, 1880 . . .

"Father Alerding was consecrated Bishop of the Diocese of Fort Wayne Nov. 30, 1901 . . . both his work and personal character have earned him a high place among the Catholic dignitaries of America."

> Condensed from Dunn—*Indiana and Indianans*, Vol. 4.

* * *

A History of the Catholic Church in the Diocese of Vincennes. *Indianapolis*, 1883.

Plymouth Rock and Maryland. 1886.

The Diocese of Fort Wayne, 1857—September 2, 1907; A Book of Historical Reference, 1669–1907. *Fort Wayne, Ind.*, 1907.

ALEXANDER, GRACE CAROLINE: 1872–

Grace Caroline Alexander was born in Indianapolis in 1872. She attended the Indianapolis public schools and was employed in them as a teacher for many years.

From 1891 to 1903 she acted as music critic and as an editorial writer for the INDIANAPOLIS NEWS and, after 1904, as a reader for the Bobbs-Merrill Company.

> Information from the Indianapolis Public Library.

* * *

Judith: A Story of the Candle-Lit Fifties; with Illustrations by George Wright. *Indianapolis*, 1906.

The Camden Circle.

Prince Cinderella. *Indianapolis*, 1921.

ALEXANDER, JOHN D.: 1839–1931.

Born in Bloomington, Ind., on Feb. 6, 1839, John D. Alexander moved with his parents to Greene County, Ind., in 1843. He graduated from Indiana University in 1861.

On Aug. 18, 1862, he volunteered as a private in Company E, 97th Indiana Volunteer Infantry and before the end of the war had advanced to captain of Company D of the same regiment.

Following his discharge from the service he entered the law school of the University of Michigan. He practiced law in Bedford and Bloomfield, Ind.

At the time of his death, which occurred on Feb. 27, 1931, he was the oldest living graduate of Indiana University and the oldest living member of Beta Theta Pi fraternity.

> Information from the INDIANAPOLIS STAR, June 8, 1925 and Feb. 28, 1931.

* * *

History of the 97th Regiment of Indiana Volunteer Infantry. *Terre Haute, Ind.*, 1891.

ALEXANDER, MATILDA GREATHOUSE (MRS. ANDREW): 1842–1892.

Matilda Greathouse, youngest child of George Washington and Martha Harshman Greathouse, was born in Mount Vernon, Ind., on June 14, 1842. She was married to Andrew Alexander in 1864.

According to Leffel, *Posey County Indiana, 1913*: "Mrs. Alexander was a woman of broad education, possessed intellectual ability of a high order and gained extended reputation as an author."

She founded and liberally endowed the Alexandrine Library of Mount Vernon.

Mrs. Alexander died on April 22, 1892.

> Information from Leffel—*Posey County Indiana, 1913.*

* * *

Going West: or, Homes for the Homeless. A Novel. *Indianapolis*, 1881.

Worth Wins: A Novel. *St. Louis*, 1882.

[The following titles are listed as works of the author on the title page of Worth Wins. No other data is available]:

The Outcast Reclaimed.

A Widow's Life.

Christianity and Infidelity.

From the Hovel to the Hall. (5 act drama about Lincoln).

Married, Not Mated.

ALEY, MAXWELL: 1889–

Born at Vincennes, Ind., in 1889, Maxwell Aley, son of Robert Judson and Nellie Archer Aley, was educated at Indiana University, from which he received the A.B. degree.

He was managing editor of CENTURY MAGAZINE (1921-22), fiction editor of WOMAN'S HOME COMPANION (1922-29), and, beginning in 1932, an editor for Longman's Green & Company. He also acted as literary advisor to Bobbs-Merrill Publishing Company, Indianapolis, and lectured on the short story at New York University. His short stories have been published in numerous periodicals, including GOOD HOUSEKEEPING, DELINEATOR, WOMAN'S HOME COMPANION, PICTORIAL REVIEW, McCALLS, and COLLIER'S.

> Information from *Who's Who Among North American Authors* and the Indianapolis Public Library.

* * *

The Story of Indiana and Its People. (with Robert Judson Aley) *Chicago* [1912].

The Barnstormers . . . *New York*, 1914.

ALEY, ROBERT JUDSON: 1863–1935.

Robert Judson Aley, son of Jesse J. and Paulina Moyer Aley, was born May 11, 1863, at Coal City, Ind. In 1882 he received the B.S. degree from Valparaiso College, in 1888 and 1890, respectively, the A.B. and A.M. degrees from Indiana University, the A.M.

from Stanford University in 1895, and the Ph.D. from the University of Pennsylvania in 1897. He also received LL.D. degrees from Franklin College (1909), the University of Pennsylvania (1917) and Butler University (1922).

His career as an educator includes time spent as a teacher and administrator in public schools and as professor of mathematics at various universities. From 1910 to 1921 he was president of the University of Maine and, from 1921 to 1931 president of Butler University.

He wrote, edited and revised several text books and contributed many articles on biography, education, history, and mathematics to educational journals.

Dr. Aley died in Indianapolis, Nov. 18, 1935.

> Information from *Who's Who Among North American Authors*; *Who Was Who in America*; and the Indianapolis Public Library.

* * *

Graphs, a Monograph. *Boston*, 1902.

The Story of Indiana and Its People. (with Maxwell Aley) *Chicago* [1912].

ALFORD, LOYAL ADOLPHUS: 1814–1883.

Loyal Adolphus Alford, physician and minister, was born in Ferrisburg, Vt., on May 29, 1814.

He first studied medicine and began to practice in 1835, but he soon turned to the ministry, to which he was ordained in 1844, and became pastor of the First Baptist Church at Erie, Pa. After serving as pastor of churches in Rollins and Litchfield, Mich., during the 1850's he came to Elkhart, Ind., where he established the First Baptist Church. In 1863 he moved to Logansport, Ind. There he was a minister as well as a physician and there began the writing of his books.

Dr. Alford established the Commercial Publishing Company and published the SUNDAY SCHOOL VISITOR, a semi-monthly paper, using the profits to assist destitute Sunday Schools and churches. He was a member of scientific societies in Europe and America and wrote much on religious and semi-scientific subjects.

He died at Logansport on Dec. 20, 1883.

> Information from Powell—*History of Cass County* and Mrs. W. A. Bicker, granddaughter of Dr. Alford.

* * *

Masonic Gems; Consisting of Odes, Poem and Dirge. Being a Miniature Sketch of Esoteric and Exoteric Masonry. *Cincinnati*, 1867.

The Great Atonement Illustrated. A Poem Concerning a Plea of all the Subsidiary Attributes of Deity, Before the Grand Council in Heaven—the Seven Spirits of God—the Seal of the Eternal Covenant. *Cincinnati,* 1868.

The Biblical Chart of Man. 1868.

Mystic Numbers of the Word: or, Five Hundred Important Theological and Scientific Questions Answered; Also, the Existence of the Mystic Numbers, as Revealed in the Sciences of Geology, Botany, Chemistry and Anthropology. *Logansport, Ind.,* 1870.

A Trip to the Skies. The Stars! The Stars! Ecce Cœlum. *Logansport, Ind.,* 1884.

ALLEN, ALBERT J.: 1856–

Albert J. Allen was born a slave in Tennessee in 1856. He came to Logansport, Ind., as a young man some years after the Civil War and made that place his home for most of the remainder of his life.

> Information supplied by the Logansport Public Library.

* * *

John's Message to Christ and Other Poems. *Fairland, Ind.,* 1906.

ALLEN, ROBERT: 1815–1886.

There is no information available on the life of Robert Allen, except for the facts that he was born in Ohio in 1815, resided in Tippecanoe County, Ind., and died in 1886.

> Information from Federal Writers Project—*Indiana Authors,* 1937.

* * *

Letters of an Old Methodist to His Son in the Ministry. *New York,* 1904.

The Life, Times, and Travels of Abraham.

The Words of Christ.

ALLISON, GEORGE WILLIAM: 1887–

George William Allison, son of John W. and Eva May Shimmin Allison, was born in Reddick, Ill., on Dec. 26, 1887. He graduated from Hanover College in 1910, receiving the A.M. degree in 1916 and the D.D. in 1926. Following his graduation he was a student at McCormick Theological Seminary, Auburn Theological Seminary, from which he received the B.D. degree in 1913, and the University of Chicago. On Aug. 26, 1913, he married Edna C. Kunkel.

Ordained to the Presbyterian ministry in 1913, in the same year he organized Hope Church at South Bend, Ind., and served as its pastor until 1918. From 1919 to 1930 he was a pastor in Indianapolis, from 1930 to 1935 in Topeka, Kan., and after 1935 in Fort Wayne, Ind. During the first World War he was a chaplain with the A.E.F.

> Information from *Who's Who in America.*

* * *

A Place in the Sun. *South Bend, Ind.,* 1916.

Out of the Ashes, and Other Sermons. *Nashville, Tenn.,* 1928.

With Christ in Kansas. 1935.

Our Heritage, an Historical Address Delivered . . . February 7, 1943. *Fort Wayne, Ind.* [1943].

The Fort in the Forest. [1944].

Forest, Fort and Faith. Historical Sketches of the Presbytery of Fort Wayne, Organized January 1, 1845. [*Fort Wayne, Ind.,* 1945.]

ALTER, JAMES LEANDER: ?–

No biographical information on James Leander Alter has been located. Obviously, from the titles of his two books, he was a citizen of Indiana whose books were published prior to 1916; obviously, also, he must have spent some time outside the limits of Hoosierdom.

> Information from the Indiana State Library.

* * *

Books of Poems; Tales of the Hoosier Traveler Embracing the Following Subjects: Travels Through the United States and Mexico, Canada, Alaska, West Indies and the Philippines; the Inferno and Essays on Astronomy. *Remington, Ind.,* 1904.

Book of Song Poems; the Hoosier Rambler. *Remington, Ind.,* 1905.

ALTER, JOHN E.: 1853–1934.

On Nov. 13, 1934, the RENSSELAER [Ind.] REPUBLICAN carried an article on the death of John E. Alter, which stated, in part:

"John E. Alter a picturesque figure in the daily life of Rensselaer and farming community, a man whose interesting career reached far back into the county's history, died at his farm home north of Rensselaer at 8:30 this morning . . .

"Mr. Alter . . . was born in this county on Feb. 14, 1853, a son of Isaac and Eliza Willet Alter.

"After completing his district school training, Mr.

Alter kept his mind active by turning to . . . the study of principles of civil engineering, in the meanwhile spending his winters in teaching school. He served three terms as surveyor . . . Although thus engaged, he never neglected his farm interests and accumulated 200 acres of land in Union Township where he lived . . .

"Mr. Alter loved Nature to an intense degree. His was the typical Hoosier home of song and story, wholesome, hospitable, inviting, with the pleasant atmosphere of the early pioneer days. He was associated with all phases of community life and county interests.

"He has written for the local press many interesting stories of pioneer days and reminiscences of his boyhood days."

> Clipping from the files of the Rensselaer Public Library.

* * *

Hoosier Hunting Grounds or the Beaver Lake Trail. (Bill Bat, pseud.) *New York* and *Washington*, 1904.

ANDERSON, CARL: 1875–1943.

Carl Anderson was born in Brooklyn, Ind., on Sept. 1, 1875. His parents—John Wesley and Lide Spaulding Anderson—took him to Spencer, Ind., in 1877, and there he maintained residence until his death.

He attended local schools and De Pauw University. He founded and edited the OWEN LEADER, taught commercial art in Indianapolis and traveled as a lecturer and chalk-talk artist.

He died in May, 1943.

> Information from the Indiana State Library.

* * *

Owen County Centennial Pageant. *Spencer, Ind.,* 1916.
With Pad and Pencil. *Spencer, Ind.,* n.d.
The Wagons: A Story of Owen County. *Spencer, Ind.,* 1935.

ANDERSON, DAVID WILSON: ?–

David Wilson Anderson, a teacher, spent his entire life in LaFayette, Ind. No facts as to his date of birth, his education or his death are available. His one known book is a juvenile.

> Information from de Hart—*Past and Present of Tippecanoe County,* 1909.

* * *

Oliver and His Friends. *Terre Haute, Ind.,* 1897.

ANDREEN, GUSTAV ALBERT: 1864–1940.

Gustav Albert Andreen was born in Porter, Ind., on Mar. 13, 1864, the son of the Rev. Andrew and Hilda Esping Andreen.

Following graduation from Augustana College in 1881, he studied law for a brief time, then taught at Augustana College for two years. The next two years he spent in study at various European universities. From 1886-1900 he was a professor at Bethany College (Kan.), in 1900-01 he taught at Yale, and from 1901 to 1935 he was president of Augustana College. He died Oct. 1, 1940.

> Information from *Who Was Who in America* and the Indianapolis Public Library.

* * *

Det Svenska Språket I Amerika. *Stockholm* [1900].
Studies in the Idyl in German Literature. *Rock Island, Ill.,* 1902.
History of the Educational Work of the Augustana Synod. 1910.
L. P. Esbjörn and the Pilgrim Fathers of 1849. [*Rock Island, Ill.,* 1925.]
The Early Missionary Work of the Augustana Synod in New York City (1865-66). 1932.
History of Augustana College at Its Seventy-Fifth Anniversary. 1935.

ANDREWS, ALBERT CHARLTON: 1878–1939.

Charlton Andrews, son of Albert Munson and Marie Louise Newland Andrews, was born in Connersville, Ind., on Feb. 1, 1878. His mother was a writer, a leader in the woman's suffrage movement, and a founder of the Western Association of Writers. She died in 1891.

Charlton Andrews (he preferred to use this name) was educated in private schools and entered De Pauw University, where he graduated with the Ph.B. degree in 1898. The next two years he spent in France, studying at the University of Paris, writing, and engaging in newspaper work. After his return to the U.S. he taught in various high schools and colleges, and in 1914 he was on the editorial staff of the NEW YORK TRIBUNE. He died Aug. 13, 1939.

Besides the titles listed he translated several works from the French.

> Information from Dunn—*Indiana and Indianans,* and *Who's Who in America.*

* * *

A Parfit Gentil Knight. *Chicago,* 1901.

The Drama Today. *Philadelphia*, 1913.

The Technique of Play Writing; Introduction by J. Berg Esenwein. *Springfield, Mass.* [1915].

The Lady of Gestures. *New York* [1927].

Don't Believe It; A One-Act Farce. *Chicago*, 1930.

The Butterfly Murder. *New York* [1932].

Chin-Music; A One Act Play. *New York*, 1935.

He Got the Job; A Comedy in One Act. *New York*, 1935.

A Night at Valley Forge; A Play in One Act. *New York*, 1935.

The Affair of the Malacca Stick. *New York* [1936].

The Affair of the Syrian Dagger. *New York* [1937].

Murder at the Class Reunion; A Farce in One Act. *Chicago*, 1938.

The Interrupted Revels. 1910.

His Majesty the Fool. (A play; produced in Philadelphia, 1913.)

Get Me in the Movies. (With Philip Dunning) (A play; produced in 1927.)

Ladies' Night. (collaborator) 1920.

The Golden Age. (With Lester Lonergan) (A play; produced 1928.)

ARMSTRONG, DWIGHT LE ROY: 1854–1927.

Le Roy Armstrong was born in Plymouth, Ind., on May 13, 1854, the son of Augustus G. and Ara Strong Armstrong. He was educated in the local schools, entered Indiana University and studied law for a time but gave up study in his seventeenth year to take a newspaper job.

Armstrong left newspaper reporting at Ladoga, Ind., to become editor of the LAFAYETTE [Ind.] MORNING JOURNAL in 1896 and continued with it and with the LAFAYETTE DEMOCRAT until 1905, when he removed to Salt Lake City, where he edited the HERALD-REPUBLICAN. Mr. Armstrong was also connected with the daily papers of Chicago for many years.

He died at Salt Lake City on Mar. 29, 1927.

> Information from de Hart—*Past and Present of Tippecanoe County*, 1909, and *Who Was Who in America.*

* * *

An Indiana Man. *Chicago*, 1890.

Washington Brown, Farmer. *Chicago*, 1893.

Byrd Flam in Town; Being a Collection of that Rising Young Author's Letters, Written at Chicago . . . *Chicago*, 1894.

Dan Gunn, the Man from Mauston: A Countryman Who Did Up the Town. *Chicago* [1898].

Pictorial Atlas Illustrating the Spanish-American War:

Comprising a History of the Great Conflict of the United States with Spain. *Washington, D. C.* [1898].

The Outlaws: A Story of the Building of the West. *New York*, 1902.

Theodore Roosevelt, Twenty-sixth President of the United States: A Typical American; Introductory Chapters by Gen. Joseph Wheeler and Opie Read (with Charles Eugene Banks). *Chicago*, 1902.

John Haliday's Work. 1909.

Financial California: An Historical Review of the Beginnings and Progress of Banking in the State (with J. O. Denny). *San Francisco*, 1916.

Field Book of Western Wild Flowers.

Sergeant Gore.

ARTHUR, JOSEPH CHARLES: 1850–1942.

Joseph Charles Arthur, son of Charles and Ann Allen Arthur, was born in Lowville, N. Y., on Jan. 11, 1850, and moved with his parents to Iowa at the age of six. He graduated with the first class from Iowa State College in 1872, receiving the M.S. degree in 1877 and the Sc.D. in 1920. Following his education at Iowa State College he engaged in post-graduate work at Johns Hopkins, Harvard, the University of Bonn, and Cornell, receiving the Sc.D. from the last-named institution in 1886. He was also awarded honorary degrees by the University of Iowa and Purdue. On June 12, 1901, he married Emily Stiles Potter, who died in 1935.

After serving as an instructor of botany at the universities of Wisconsin and Minnesota, from 1884 to 1887 he was connected with the Experimental Station at Geneva, N. Y., and in 1887 became professor of botany at Purdue. The following year he was made the first botanist of the Indiana Agricultural Experiment Station and held both positions until his retirement in 1915. He was one of the founders and twice president of the Botanical Society of America, as well as a member and officer of other scientific organizations. In addition to his books Dr. Arthur was the author of many scientific bulletins and articles, and several text books.

He died at Brook, Ind., on Apr. 30, 1942.

> Information from the Purdue University Libraries and from *Who's Who in America.*

* * *

Contributions to the Flora of Iowa; A Catalogue of the Phaenogamous Plants. *Charles City*, 1876.

Living Plants and Their Properties: A Collection of Essays (with Daniel Trembly MacDougal). *New York*, 1898.

The Plant Rusts (with others). *New York, 1929.*
Manual of the Rusts in United States and Canada. *Lafayette, Ind., 1934.*

ARTMAN, ADELIA COBB (MRS. SAMUEL R.): 1869–1936.

Adelia Cobb was born in Marion township, Boone County, Ind., in 1869. She was the daughter of Capt. Thomas and Julia Cobb. On May 1, 1889, she married Samuel Artman, then a Boone County teacher but later circuit judge and Indiana legislator.

Mrs. Artman was an active church worker and club woman both in Lebanon and Indianapolis, where the couple spent their last years.

She died on May 2, 1936.

Information from the Indiana State Library.

* * *

Glimpses of the Sunny South. *New York, 1903.*
Flower in the Rain. *Kansas City, Mo., 1931.*

ARTMAN, SAMUEL R.: 1866–1930.

Samuel R. Artman was born near New Augusta, Ind., on May 15, 1866. Educated in the New Augusta schools, he later attended Indiana State Normal College at Terre Haute and taught school for four years. He married Adelia Cobb on May 1, 1889.

After his teaching experience he studied law, was admitted to the Boone County bar and, after practicing in Lebanon, Ind., for a time, was elected judge of the local circuit court. He also served in the Indiana State Legislature, on the State Industrial Board and on the State Public Service Commission. His later years were spent in Indianapolis.

He retired in 1929 and died in June, 1930, as the result of a fall.

Information from the Indiana State Library.

* * *

Legalized Outlaw. *Indianapolis, 1908.*
Within the Length of the Cable Tow. *Indianapolis, 1918.*

ATKINS, GAIUS GLENN: 1868–

Gaius Glenn Atkins, son of Thomas Benjamin and Caroline Morris Atkins, was born in Mt. Carmel, Ind., on Oct. 4, 1868. He graduated from Ohio State University in 1888 and from the Cincinnati Law School in 1891 and attended Yale Divinity School. In 1904 he received the D.D. degree from the University of Vermont, in 1906 another D.D. from Dartmouth College, in 1923 the L.H.D. from the University of Vermont, and in 1933 the Litt.D. from Ohio State University.

He married Adaline Haynes on Aug. 25, 1892.

After spending three years as head of the history department at Mt. Hermon Fitting School, in 1895 he was ordained to the Congregational ministry. From 1895 until 1927 he served as pastor of churches in Greenfield, Mass., Burlington, Vt., Providence, R. I., and Detroit, Mich. He was professor of homiletics and sociology at Auburn Theological Seminary from 1927 to 1939. From 1942 to 1945 he acted as interim pastor of the First Congregational Church at Fall River, Mass. He edited and compiled several religious works.

Information from *Who's Who in America.*

* * *

Things That Remain: Sermons. *Detroit, 1910.*
Pilgrims of the Lonely Road. *New York* [1913].
The Maze of the Nations and the Way Out. *New York, 1915.*
The Godward Side of Life. *Boston, 1917.*
Jerusalem, Past and Present; the city of Undying Memories. *New York, 1918.*
The Undiscovered Country, and Other Addresses. *New York, 1922.*
Modern Religious Cults and Movements. *New York, 1923.*
Craftsmen of the Soul, and Other Addresses. *New York, 1925.*
Rendezvous with Life. *New York, n.d.*
The Making of the Christian Mind. *New York, 1928.*
Reinspecting Victorian Religion; A Back to Normal Critique; Being the Samuel Harris Lectures on Literature and Life Given at Bangor Theological Seminary in 1928. *New York, 1928.*
The Procession of the Gods. *New York, 1930.*
Life of Cardinal Newman. *New York, 1931.*
Religion in Our Times. *New York, 1932.*
Preaching and the Mind of Today. *New York, 1934.*
Throne Rooms. *New York, 1935.*
From the Cross—A Study of the Seven Last Words. *New York, 1937.*
Resources for Living: A Plain-man's Philosophy. *New York, 1938.*
Christianity and the Creative Quests. *Nashville, Tenn., 1939.*
History of American Congregationalism. (with F. L. Fagley) *Boston, 1942.*

ATKINSON, ELEANOR STACKHOUSE (MRS. FRANCIS B.): 1863–

Eleanor Stackhouse, daughter of Isaac and Margaret Smith Stackhouse, was born in 1863 in Rensselaer, Ind., where her father conducted a mercantile business.

She was graduated from the Indianapolis Normal Training School, taught for four years in the Indianapolis and Chicago public schools and became a special writer on the staff of the CHICAGO TRIBUNE in 1889, using the pen name Nora Marks.

On Mar. 14, 1891, she married Francis Blake Atkinson of Chicago.

In 1900 she became editor of THE LITTLE CHRONICLE and continued in this post until 1907.

During the latter part of her writing career Mrs. Atkinson made her home in Manhasset, L. I.

Information from the Rensselaer Public Library.

* * *

Mamzelle Fifine; A Romance of the Girlhood of the Empress Josephine on the Island of Martinique. *New York*, 1903.

The Boyhood of Lincoln. *New York*, 1908.

Lincoln's Love Story. *New York,* 1909.

The Story of Chicago and National Development, 1534–1910; Edited and Extended by the Editorial Staff of the Little Chronicle Company. *Chicago* [1909].

A Loyal Love. *Boston* [1912].

Greyfriars Bobby. *New York*, 1912.

The "How and Why" Library: Little Questions that Lead to Great Discoveries . . . *Chicago*, 1913.

Johnny Appleseed; the Romance of the Sower; with Illustrations by Frank T. Merrill. *New York*, 1915.

Hearts Undaunted; A Romance of Four Frontiers. *New York*, 1917.

Poilu, a Dog of Roubaix. *New York*, 1918.

AULLS, JOSEPH A.: ?–

No biographical facts regarding Joseph A. Aulls are available except that he was a resident of South Bend, Ind. Judging from the dedication of his book, "To all Railroad Men in General and to the Telegraphic Fraternity in Particular," he was probably a railroad telegrapher.

Information from the Indiana State Library.

* * *

Sparks and Cinders. *South Bend, Ind.*, 1876.

AYDELOTTE, FRANK: 1880–

Frank Aydelotte, who was to become one of America's leading educators, was born Oct. 16, 1880, in Sullivan, Ind., the son of William E. and Matilda Brunger Aydelotte.

He was educated at Indiana University (A.B., 1900), Harvard (A.M., 1903), and at Oxford University (B.Litt., 1908), where he was a Rhodes Scholar. He received honorary doctorates from Allegheny College, Yale, Indiana University, New York University, Dickinson College, Pomona College, University of Iowa, University of California, University of Pennsylvania, University of Pittsburgh, Oberlin, and Oxford.

In 1900 he began his teaching career as instructor in English at Southwestern State Normal School, California, Pa. The following year he taught at Indiana University and the next two years at Louisville Boys' High School. He returned to Indiana University in 1908 as associate professor of English. From 1915 until 1921 he was English professor at Massachusetts Institute of Technology, a position he left in 1921 to become president of Swarthmore College. While at Swarthmore he became a convert to the Society of Friends, joining formally after he had resigned as head of Swarthmore. In 1939 he was appointed director of the Institute for Advanced Study, Princeton, N. J.

He married Marie Jeannette Osgood, of Cambridge, Mass., on June 22, 1907.

Information from *Who's Who in America*; *Current Biography*, 1941; and the Indianapolis Public Library.

* * *

Elizabethan Rogues and Vagabonds and Their Representation in Contemporary Literature. *Oxford*, 1913.

The Oxford Stamp, and Other Essays; Articles from the Educational Creed of an American Oxonian. *New York,* 1917.

Oxford of Today; A Manual for Prospective Rhodes Scholars. (Joint editor with L. A. Crosby) *New York*, 1922.

Swarthmore College. Adventure in Education. *New York*, 1941.

The City of Man; A Declaration on World Democracy, Issued by Herbert Agar, Frank Aydelotte, G. A. Borgese (and others) . . . *New York, 1941.*

Breaking the Academic Lock Step; the Development of Honors Work in American Colleges and Universities. *New York* [1944].

The American Rhodes Scholarships; A Review of the First Forty Years. *Princeton, N. J.*, 1946.

B

BABCOCK, AUGUSTUS DWIGHT: 1852–

Born in Jasper County, Ind., in 1852, Augustus Dwight Babcock was a resident of Goodland, Ind., during his later years.

Information supplied by the Indianapolis Public Library.

* * *

The Silver Oar and Other Poems. *Goodland, Ind.*, 1914.

BABER, JACK: 1821–?

In his one published work—a historical pamphlet now quite scarce in its original form—Jack Baber describes himself thus:

"Uncle Jack Baber is a bachelor, on the shady side of fifty years of boyhood, and was born in Richland township, Greene county, Ind., on Saturday, the 10th day of Feb., 1821, at dinner time! He was raised in Clay County, on the old Baber farm, at the Coffee postoffice place, fifteen miles from Worthington. Uncle Jack has had two brothers and two sisters, and one of the brothers died in 1855, and one of the sisters died many years ago. His brother, William W. Baber, and his sister, Mrs. Emiline Fires, both live in Greene county. Uncle Jack Baber is a common farmer and market gardener, and has recently established a first-class agricultural fair ground and exchange trade, for all kinds of choice poultry, fine hogs, evergreen shrubbery, and ornamental trees, at Worthington, Greene county, Indiana."

From the title described below.

* * *

The Early History of Greene County, Indiana. As Taken from the Official Records, and Compiled from Authentic Recollections, by Pioneer Settlers. Embracing All Matters of Interest Connected with the Early Settlement of the County. From 1813 to 1875, Including Brief Sketches of Pioneer Families, Giving Marriages, Births and Deaths, with Names of Creeks, Roads, Ferries, etc., etc., by Uncle Jack Baber. *Worthington, Ind.*, 1875.

BACON, ALBION FELLOWS (MRS. HILARY E.): 1865–1933.
(See also sketch of Annie Fellows Johnston.)

Some of the spirit which had moved Robert Owen and his associates in the founding and operation of the New Harmony community in the 1820's must still have lingered in the southern Indiana "pocket" country in the 1860's. At Evansville, Ind., on Apr. 8, 1865, was born to the Rev. Albion and Mary Erskine Fellows a daughter who, as Albion Fellows Bacon, was to become one of the Middlewest's most active women in the field of social reform.

Albion Fellows was graduated from the Evansville high school in 1883 and five years later married Hilary E. Bacon. The Bacons became the parents of four children, but Albion Fellows Bacon's duties as mother and housekeeper did not interfere with either her activities as a reformer or as a writer. During the forty-five years after her marriage she found time to organize the Flower Mission and to act as leader of it for five years; she helped to organize the Anti-Tuberculosis League; she organized and became president of the Working Girls' Association and the Indiana Housing Association. She eventually became a director of the National Housing Association and a member of the Public Health Nursing Association, and she harassed the probably none-too-enthusiastic Indiana State Legislature into passing the state tenement law of 1913 and the state housing law of 1917. She wrote and lectured on tenement reform during all these years and in 1931 was appointed a member of President Hoover's conference on Home Building and Home Ownership.

She died at her home in Evansville on Dec. 10, 1933.

Information from the Evansville Public Library.

* * *

Songs Ysame (with Annie Fellows Johnston). *Boston*, 1897.

The Awakening of a State. 1911.

A Tale of the Tenements. *Indianapolis* [1912].

Beauty for Ashes. *New York*, 1914.

Soldier's Book of Worship (with Albert Hallett). *New York*, 1917.

State's Centennial Pageant. 1917.

What Bad Housing Means to the Community; with a Prefatory Note by Lawrence Veiller. *Boston*, 1917.

Housing—Its Relation to Social Work. *New York*, 1918.

Child Welfare Legislation; Work of the Indiana Sub-Commission on Child Welfare of the Commission on Child Welfare and Social Insurance (with Edna Hatfield Edmondson). *Bloomington, Ind.*, 1921.

Consolation; A Spiritual Experience. *Boston*, 1922.

Citizenship Day Program, July 4, 1923. *Washington, D. C.*, 1923.

After Care of a Housing Law. *New York*, n.d.

There Ain't No Law. *New York*, n.d.

The Path to God. *New York*, 1928.

The Charm String. *Boston*, 1929.

The Housing Problem of Indiana. *Indianapolis*, n.d.

BACON, RAYMOND FOSS: 1880–

Raymond Foss Bacon, son of the Rev. Charles and N. V. Wiggs Bacon, was born in Muncie, Ind., on June 29, 1880, and graduated from De Pauw University in 1899, receiving the A.M. degree in 1900 and the D.Sc. in 1919. He also received the Ph.D. degree from the University of Chicago in 1904 and the D.Sc. from the University of Pittsburgh in 1918. On Aug. 4, 1905, he married Edna Hine.

From 1905 to 1910 he was associated with the United States Bureau of Science in Manila, P. I., in 1910-11 with the Bureau of Chemistry in Washington, D. C., and from 1912 to 1914 with the University of Pittsburgh. From 1912 to 1921 he was with the Mellon Institute of Industrial Research, University of Pittsburgh, as associate director and later as director. He then became a consulting engineer in New York. During the first World War he served as a colonel in the Chemical Warfare Service of the U.S. Army.

Information from *Who's Who in America*.

* * *

Object and Work of the Mellon Institute. *Pittsburgh*, 1915.

American Petroleum Industry (with W. A. Hamor). *New York*, 1916. 2 vols.

Problems in the Utilization of Fuels. *London*, 1919.

American Fuels (with W. A. Hamor). *New York*, 1922. 2 vols.

BAILEY, JOHN WILLIAM: 1873–

John William Bailey, son of James Perry and Virginia Caroline Coker Bailey, was born on May 5, 1873, in Scott County, Ind. He was educated at Franklin College (A.B., 1898) and at the Divinity School, University of Chicago (B.D., 1901; Ph.D., 1904). He received the D.D. degree from Franklin College in 1941.

In 1905 he was ordained in the Baptist ministry and began his work as pastor in Fairbury, Ill. He later held pastorates at Oshkosh, Wis., and Pella, Ia. From 1914 to 1917 he was president of Central College and from 1918 to 1923 president of Colorado Woman's College. In 1923 he became a professor at Berkeley Baptist Divinity School.

Dr. Bailey was twice married: first to Celestine Marcella Wood, who died in 1938, then, in 1940, to Louise White Herron.

Information from *Who's Who in America* and the Indianapolis Public Library.

* * *

Does Hellenism Contribute Constituent Elements to Paul's Christology? *Chicago*, 1905.

Temporary Reign of Messiah in Early Judaism. 1934.

Read It Again—A Series of Studies of Papyri.

BAKER, FRANK TARKINGTON: 1878–1924.

Frank Tarkington Baker, newspaperman, was born at Vincennes, Ind., on Aug. 6, 1878. His youth and most of his adult life was spent in Indianapolis.

For a time Mr. Baker was a newspaper owner in Colorado, but he returned to Indianapolis as editor of the INDIANAPOLIS SENTINEL and later served as dramatic and literary critic for the INDIANAPOLIS NEWS. Still later he was associated with the INDIANAPOLIS STAR as dramatic editor, a position he held until 1918, when he went to New York as director of publicity for a film company. He died in New York on Jan. 1, 1924.

Besides his one book Mr. Baker wrote many magazine articles on gardening and architecture.

Information from the Indianapolis Public Library.

* * *

Yard and Garden. 1908.

BAKER, ORLANDO HARRISON: 1830–1913.

Orlando Harrison Baker, son of Jacob and Mary Chesney Baker, was born in Union County, Ind., near Brownsville, on Sept. 13, 1830. He graduated from De Pauw University in 1858, receiving the A.M. degree in 1861. In 1906 he received the LL.D. degree from Simpson College, Ia. Mr. Baker was married first to Mary Catherine Ridley in 1858 and, after her death, to Mrs. Rachael Halton Beach in 1895.

For ten years he served as principal of various seminaries and academies, in 1868 he became professor of ancient languages at Simpson College, and in 1871 he was made president of Algona College, serving until 1875. From 1880 to 1886 he was editor of the INDIANOLA [Ia.] HERALD.

Mr. Baker served as U.S. Consul at Copenhagen (1892-94), at Sydney, Australia (1900-1908), and at Sandakan, North Borneo (1908-12).

He died in Nagasaki, Japan, on Aug. 6, 1913.

Information from De Pauw University's *Alumnal Record, 1920*, and *Who Was Who in America*.

* * *

Who Are the Robbers?

BALDWIN, DANIEL PRATT: 1837–1908.

Daniel Pratt Baldwin was born in the state of New York in 1837 and moved to Cass County, Ind. in 1860. He was graduated from Madison University in 1856 and from Columbia University Law School in 1860.

After moving to Indiana he became a member of the law firm of Pratt and Baldwin and was one of the leading attorneys of Cass County. He was appointed judge of the Common Pleas Court in 1870 and in 1888 was elected Attorney General of Indiana. He died Dec. 13, 1908.

Information from Powell—History of Cass County, 1913.

* * *

A Lawyer's Readings in Evidence of Christianity; An Address. *Logansport, Ind.*, 1875.

How States Grow.

Christ's Credentials. *Logansport, Ind.*, n.d.

Manners.

Real Facts Touching the Claims of the State to the Beaver Lake Lands Together with Some Reasons Why the Senate Bill No. 269 Should Not Pass (with others). *Indianapolis, Ind.*, 1881.

Personality, a Sunday College Chapel Address. *Logansport, Ind.*, 1889.

The Wastes of Life. *Logansport, Ind.*, 1891.

Christ's Limitations.

The Seeing Eye. An Address Delivered at the Graduating Exercises at Cazenovia (N. Y.) Seminary, June 20, 1906. *Cazenovia, N. Y.*, n.d.

Oratory and Orators. An Address. *Cazenovia, N. Y.*, n.d.

BALDWIN, JAMES: 1841–1925.

James Baldwin was born in Hamilton County, Ind., on Dec. 15, 1841, the son of Isaac and Sarah Clayton Baldwin. Although he had some instruction in the district schools, he was largely self-taught. After teaching for three years in his native county, he became, in 1869, superintendent of city graded schools in Indiana, a position he held until 1887 when he accepted a post with Harper & Brothers publishing house in New York. From 1894 to 1924 he was editor of school books for the American Book Company. He died Aug. 30, 1925.

Besides the titles listed here, Baldwin was the author, editor and compiler of dozens of textbooks in the fields of literature, history and mathematics.

Information from *Who Was Who in America.*

* * *

The Story of Siegfried. *New York*, 1882.

The Story of Roland. *New York*, 1883.

The Book Lover; A Guide to the Best Reading. *Chicago*, 1885.

A Story of the Golden Age. *New York*, 1887.

A Guide to Systematic Readings in the Encyclopaedia Britannica. *Chicago*, 1895.

The Horse Fair. *New York*, 1895.

Fifty Famous Stories Retold. *New York*, 1896.

Old Stories of the East. *New York*, 1896.

Social and Ethical Interpretations in Mental Development: A Study in Social Psychology. *New York*, 1897.

Four Great Americans: Washington, Franklin, Webster, Lincoln. *Chicago*, 1897.

Our New Possessions: Cuba, Puerto Rico, Hawaii, Philippines. *New York*, 1899.

The Discovery of the Old Northwest and Its Settlement by the French. *New York*, 1901.

The Conquest of the Old Northwest and Its Settlement by Americans. *New York*, 1901.

The Wonder Book of Horses. *New York*, 1903.

Hero Tales Told in School. *New York*, 1904.

Abraham Lincoln, a True Life. *New York* [1904].

Thirty More Famous Stories Retold. *New York*, 1905.

The Golden Fleece; More Old Greek Stories. *New York* [1905].

An American Book of Golden Deeds. *New York*, 1907.

Gulliver's Travels; Retold for Children. *Chicago*, 1908.

Stories of the King. *Chicago*, 1910.

The Sampo: Hero Adventures from the Finnish Kalevala. *New York*, 1912.

Fifty Famous People: A Book of Short Stories. *New York*, 1912.

Stories from English History for Young Americans. *New York*.

John Bunyan's Dream Story: the Pilgrim's Progress Retold for Children and Adapted to School Reading. *Chicago*, 1913.

In My Youth, from the Posthumous Papers of Robert Dudley. *Indianapolis* [1914]. (Reissued in 1923 as In the Days of My Youth; An Intimate Personal Record of Life and Manners in the Middle Ages of the Middle West.)

Fifty Famous Rides and Riders. *New York*, 1916.

The Story of Liberty. *Chicago* [1919].

Sailing the Seas; the Log of Tom Darke (with William W. Livengood). *New York*, 1920.

BALDWIN, MARY H.: 1841–

Mary H. Baldwin, born in Crawfordsville, Ind., in 1841, is believed to have been the posthumous daughter of the Rev. Elihu Whittlesey Baldwin and his wife,

Julia C. (Baldwin) Baldwin. Dr. Baldwin, first president of Wabash College, died late in 1840.

> Information from Federal Writers Project—*Indiana Authors*, 1937, and Hatfield—*Patient Continuance in Well-Doing: A Memoir of Elihu W. Baldwin.*

* * *

Speech and Song.
Voice-Placing for Elocution.

BALL, TIMOTHY HORTON: 1826–1913.

Timothy H. Ball, Lake County, Ind., historian and minister, was born in Agawam, Mass., in 1826. Coming to northern Indiana as a young man, he took an active part in the cultural and religious activities of the section, appearing as its first historian in the early Seventies.

During the latter part of his eighty-seven years he made his home at Crown Point, Ind., where he died in 1913.

His historical writing was sound, and several of his books have become items of interest both to collectors and to historical libraries.

> Information from the Gary Public Library.

* * *

Scripture Teaching on the Immortality of the Human Soul. By Y. N. L. (T. H. Ball). *Boston*, 1861.

Lake County, Indiana, from 1834 to 1872. *Chicago*, 1873.

Principles of Church Government. Authority, the New Testament. By Y. N. L. (T. H. Ball). *Crown Point, Ind.*, 1877.

The Lake of the Red Cedars; or Will It Live? Thirty Years in Lake. Record of the First Thirty Years of Baptist Labors in the County of Lake, State of Indiana. *Crown Point, Ind.*, 1880.

A Glance into the Great South-East, or Clarke County, Alabama, and Its Surroundings, from 1540-1877. *Grove Hill, Ala.*, 1882.

Lake County, Indiana, 1884. An Account of the Semi-Centennial Celebration of Lake County, September 3 and 4, with Historical Papers and Other Interesting Records. *Crown Point, Ind.*, 1884.

A Dream of Hell. By an Orthodox Dreamer. *Crown Point, Ind.*, 1886.

Poems and Hymns. *Crown Point, Ind.*, 1888.

Notes on Luke's Gospel. *Crown Point, Ind.*, 1889.

The Sunday Schools of Lake. An Account of the Commencement and Growth of the Sunday Schools of Lake County, Indiana, from about 1840 to 1890. A Semi-Centennial Volume. *Crown Point, Ind.*, 1891.

Annie B., the Dying Girl. *Crown Point, Ind.*, 1893.

The Creek War of 1813 and 1814. (with H. S. Halbert) *Chicago*, 1895.

Origin of the Nations . . . An Ethnological Study of the Tenth Chapter of Genesis. *Crown Point, Ind.*, 1897.

The Home of the Redeemed and Other Discourses. *Crown Point, Ind.*, 1899.

Northwestern Indiana from 1800 to 1900; or a View of Our Region Through the Nineteenth Century. Crown Point, Valparaiso, LaPorte, Knox, Winamac, Monticello, Rensselaer. *Kentland, Ind.*, 1900.

Francis Ball's Descendants; or, the West Springfield Ball Family, from 1640 to 1902. *Crown Point, Ind.*, 1902.

Genealogical Records of the Dinwiddie Clan of Northwestern Indiana. *Crown Point, Ind.*, 1902.

Inspired Scriptures. *Crown Point, Ind.*, 1903.

Two Greek Particles. An Exegetical Study. *Hammond, Ind.*, 1905.

Old Truth in a New Setting. *Crown Point, Ind.*, 1906.

Nature, Providence, Grace. *Crown Point, Ind.*, 1908.

A Memorial of Mrs. C. C. Ball of Crown Point, Indiana. By Her Husband . . . *Crown Point, Ind.*, 1912.

BALLANTINE, ELISHA: 1809–1886.

Elisha Ballantine was a member of the Indiana University faculty, at least during the Seventies, and the father of another Indiana University professor, William Gay Ballantine. His wife was the former Betsy Ann Watkins.

Prof. Elisha Ballantine died in Bloomington, Ind., on Mar. 31, 1886.

> Information from *Indiana University, 1820–1904*, and from his son's biography in *Who Was Who in America.*

* * *

Christ, His Own Witness; or the Words of Jesus Concerning Himself. *New York*, 1877.

Old Age; Two Discourses Delivered at Bloomington, Indiana. *Bloomington, Ind.*, 1879.

BALLARD, EVA F. CLODFELTER: ?–

Eva F. Clodfelter was reared in the southwestern part of Montgomery County, Ind., attended the Alamo Academy and later enrolled in De Pauw University.

She married Emerson Ballard, a De Pauw graduate and a lawyer of Crawfordsville, Ind., where she resided throughout her life.

Mrs. Ballard was one of the disciples of Mary Hannah Krout, Indiana writer and worker in the cause of women's suffrage.

Information from friends of Mrs. Ballard in Crawfordsville, Ind.

* * *

She Wanted to Vote; or, Home Influences. *Crawfordsville, Ind.,* 1901.

BALLARD, GRANVILLE MELLEN: 1833–1926.

Born on Mar. 30, 1833, in Westport, Ky., Granville Mellen Ballard was the son of Dr. Chester Ballard, and Helda Simonds Ballard. The family later moved to Greencastle, Ind., where Dr. Ballard was associated with the administration of Asbury Institute, now De Pauw University.

Following his graduation from Indiana Asbury (now De Pauw) University in 1851, he served for a time as private secretary to Gov. Joseph A. Wright of Indiana. He married Martha Stilwell of Indianapolis in 1865.

He was a teacher at the Indiana School for the Blind and, until fifteen years before his death, engaged in the real estate business in Indianapolis, being forced to retire because of illness.

He died in Indianapolis on July 20, 1926.

Information from the INDIANAPOLIS STAR, July 21, 1926, and Parker & Heiney—*Poets and Poetry of Indiana.*

* * *

Blood for Blood. A Legend of the "Big Elm Tree." *Indianapolis,* 1906.
Legend of the Big Elm Tree, and Other Poems.

BANTA, DAVID DEMAREE: 1833–1896.

David Demaree Banta was born on a farm in Johnson County, Ind., on May 23, 1833. He was the son of Jacob and Sarah Demaree Banta, who in the fall of 1832 had moved to Indiana from Henry County, Ky.

David's father died a few years after coming to Indiana, but his mother remained on the farm. The boy attended a local school, taught school for a while, then spent some time in Iowa, where he began reading law. In the spring of 1853 he returned to Indiana and entered Franklin College and the following year became a student at Indiana University. Upon completion of the liberal arts course he entered the law school, took his degree in law in 1857, and began practicing the same year in Franklin, Ind. In 1856 he married a widow, Mrs. M. E. Perrin, the daughter of James Riddle of Covington, Ky.

After practicing law successfully for many years and serving on the bench and in various capacities as a governmental appointee, he became dean of the Indiana University School of Law in 1889. His historical writing—a hobby—is still considered a model in style and form for local history interpretation. He contributed to FIELD AND STREAM and to Indianapolis and Chicago newspapers.

Judge Banta died April 9, 1896.

Information from Dunn—*Indiana and Indianans* and the Indianapolis Public Library.

* * *

A Historical Sketch of Johnson County, Indiana. *Chicago,* 1881.
Making a Neighborhood; An Address Delivered at the Shiloh Reunion, May 26, 1887. *Franklin, Ind.* [1887].
A History of the Presbyterian Church of Franklin, Indiana.

BANTA, GEORGE: 1857–1935.

Born in Covington, Ky., on July 16, 1857, George Banta, son of David Demaree and Melissa E. Riddle (Perrin) Banta, was reared in Franklin and Bloomington, Ind., and graduated from Indiana University in 1876. He married Ellen Lee Pleasants in 1886.

After graduation from college he was admitted to the Indiana bar but did not practice. He entered the insurance business and, for twenty-eight years, was the state agent in Wisconsin for the Phoenix Insurance Company of Brooklyn.

Mr. Banta was president of the Banta Publishing Company in Menasha, Wis., and served as mayor of Menasha for three terms. He was the first national president of Phi Delta Theta and the founder of BANTA'S GREEK EXCHANGE, an interfraternity magazine which he edited until his death on Sept. 27, 1935.

Information from The University Libraries, Indiana University, and by George Banta, Jr.

* * *

Flying Leaves: Being a Collection of Poems, Stories, Articles, etc., of Various Members of the Banta and Pleasants Families. *Menasha, Wis.*

BANTA, MELISSA ELIZABETH RIDDLE: 1834–1907.

Melissa Elizabeth Riddle, daughter of James and Elizabeth Riddle, was born near Cincinnati, O., on Mar. 27, 1834. In 1852 she married J. J. Perrin, who died the following year, and in 1856 she married David Demaree Banta of Indiana. She published one book of poetry and wrote some prose which was published in magazines. She died in 1907.

> Information from Parker & Heiney—*Poets and Poetry of Indiana* and Dunn—*Indiana and Indianans*, Vol. III.

* * *

Songs of Home. *Menasha, Wis.*, 1895.

BANTA, NATHANIEL MOORE: 1867–1932.

Nathaniel Moore Banta, son of Henry and Mary Jane Robinson Banta, was born in Rensselaer, Ind., on Dec. 3, 1867. He was educated at Valparaiso University, National Normal School (Fenton, Mich.), and the University of Chicago. From 1890 to 1906 he taught in the public schools of Indiana and Illinois, from 1906 to 1921 he was a trade agent in Chicago for subscription book publishers, and from 1921 until his death on Feb. 5, 1932, he was editor and manager of the publication department of A. Flanagan & Company, book publishers of Chicago. Besides the titles listed, he adapted, edited and compiled dozens of books for children.

> Information from *Who's Who in America*.

* * *

The Brownie Primer (with Alpha Banta Benson). *Chicago*, 1905.
The Second Brownie Book (with Alpha Banta Benson). *Chicago*, 1911.
Peter Rabbit, and Other Stories. *Chicago*.
The Brownies and the Goblins (with Alpha Banta Benson). *Chicago*, 1915.
Ten Little Brownie Men (with Alpha Banta Benson). *Chicago*, 1918.
The Robin Redbreast Book. *Chicago*, 1922.
Once Upon a Time Stories (with Julia Darrow Cowles). *Chicago*, 1922.
Chickadee Book. *Chicago*, 1922.
Jenny Wren Book. *Chicago*, 1922.
The Bluebird Book. *Chicago*, 1923.
Bluest of the Bluebirds. *Chicago*, 1923.
Busy Little Brownies. *Chicago*, 1923.
Fairies of the Nine Hills. *Chicago*, 1923.
Four-and-Forty Fairies (with Alpha Banta Benson). *Chicago*, 1923.
Old Tales of the East. *Chicago*, 1924.
Brownies at Work and Play. *Chicago*, 1926.
Brownies in the Greenwood. *Chicago*, 1927.

Who Stole the Bird's Nest, and Other Bird Poems. *Chicago*.

BARNES, JAMES A.: ?–

James A. Barnes was a resident of Michigantown, Ind., when, on Aug. 11, 1862, he enlisted for the Civil War in the 86th Regiment, Indiana Volunteer Infantry. He served as a private, being mustered out on June 6, 1865. He lived in Indiana at least until 1895.

> Information from The Eighty-Sixth Regiment, Indiana Volunteer Infantry.

* * *

The Eighty-Sixth Regiment, Indiana Volunteer Infantry. A Narrative of Its Services in the Civil War of 1861–1865 (with James R. Carnahan and Thomas H. B. McCain). *Crawfordsville, Ind.*, 1895.

BARNS, WILLIAM EDDY: 1853–1915.

William Eddy Barns, son of Rezin M. and Susan Smead Barns, was born in Vevay, Ind., on Aug. 29, 1853, and graduated from Illinois Wesleyan University in 1872. On Nov. 1, 1875, he married Mattie M. Rowe, who died in 1877, and on Oct. 26, 1880, he married Louise Goode Gillett.

He began newspaper work as city editor of the DAILY REPUBLICAN in Decatur, Ill., in 1874 was a correspondent for CHICAGO INTER-OCEAN, and from 1875 to 1884 was associate editor of the CENTRAL CHRISTIAN ADVOCATE in St. Louis. After 1886 he served as editor of the ST. LOUIS LUMBERMAN and THE AGE OF STEEL. He was also president of the Journal of Commerce Company.

Mr. Barns died in 1915.

> Information from *Who Was Who in America*.

* * *

Nobody Knows. 1889.
The Utilization of Wood Waste by Distillation. 1907.
"The Lumber Octopus." 1911.

BARTLETT, CHARLES H.: 1853–1937.

Charles H. Bartlett was born in South Bend, Ind., on Dec. 11, 1853. According to an article in the SOUTH BEND TRIBUNE for Nov. 26, 1929, on the occasion of an address by Mr. Bartlett at the celebration of the quarto-millennial anniversary of LaSalle's landing at the St. Joseph-Kankakee Portage:

"Mr. Bartlett, living here as a boy, took a great interest in the history of the locality, often walking out over the old Portage trail and exploring the wonder of the Kankakee swamps. His books, 'Tales of the Kankakee Land' and 'LaSalle in the Valley of the St. Joseph' attest his fondness for the chronicles of the region.

"He was graduated with the first class from the South Bend High School in 1872. He attended Williams College 1872-73 and Wabash College 1873-77, after which he came back to South Bend, serving as principal of the high school from 1878 to 1905. Following his resignation from this position he was for many years New England manager of the educational department of Charles Scribners' Sons.

"His father, Joseph Greely Bartlett, was one of the prominent pioneer merchants of South Bend . . ."

He died on Sept. 2, 1937.

> Clipping from the South Bend Public Library; other information from the INDIANA HISTORY BULLETIN, February, 1938.

* * *

LaSalle in the Valley of the St. Joseph: An Historical Fragment (with Richard H. Lyon). *South Bend, Ind.,* 1899.

Tales of Kankakee Land. *New York,* 1904.

BASS, FLORENCE: 1860–1938.

Florence Bass was born near Columbus, Ind., in 1860. In 1872 she accompanied her family to Indianapolis, where she spent the remainder of her life.

After graduating from the Indianapolis High School and Indianapolis Normal School, she taught in the public schools until her retirement in 1928. Her interest in her profession is evidenced by her books, which were written for elementary grade use. She was also author of several textbooks. Miss Bass died in 1938.

> Information from the Indianapolis Public Library.

* * *

Nature Stories for Young Readers. *Boston,* 1892.

Nature Stories for Young Readers. Animal Life. *Boston,* 1892. (Reissued in 1912 as Stories of Animal Life.)

Nature Stories for Young Readers. Plant Life. *Boston,* 1897. (Reissued in 1912 as Stories of Plant Life.)

Stories of Pioneer Life, for Young Readers. *Boston,* 1900.

Child's First Book for Home and School. *Boston,* 1911.

Stories of Early Times in the Great West for Young Readers. *Indianapolis,* 1927.

Stories of Early Times in Indiana.

BATES, FRANK GREENE: 1868–

Frank Greene Bates, son of Caleb Greene and Sally Frances Matteson Bates, was born in Warwick, R. I., on Sept. 22, 1868. Following a preparatory education at the English and Classical School in Providence, he studied at Cornell University, the Boston University Law School, and Columbia University. He taught history and political science at Alfred University and the University of Kansas, was state librarian of Rhode Island, and was librarian of the Rhode Island Historical Society. In 1912 he became a professor of political science at Indiana University.

> Information from *Who's Who in America.*

* * *

Rhode Island and the Formation of the Union. *New York,* 1898.

Civics of Kansas. *Boston,* 1910.

The Commission Plan of City Government. *Lawrence, Kan.* [1910].

City Planning and Zoning. *Bloomington, Ind.,* 1923.

A City Planning Primer (with George Edward Lommel). *West Lafayette, Ind.,* 1925.

State Government (with Oliver P. Field). *New York,* 1928.

BATES, MARGARET HOLMES ERNSPERGER (MRS. CHARLES A.): 1844–?

Born at Fremont, O., Oct. 6, 1844, Margaret Holmes Ernsperger began school at Fremont and completed her education at Rochester, Ind. She taught school in Ohio and Indiana. In 1865 she was married to Charles Austin Bates of Indianapolis, where she lived for the next twenty-five years.

Mrs. Bates began her literary career by contributing local reports and book reviews to Indianapolis newspapers and stories and poems to Eastern publications. Later she wrote novels while continuing her book reviewing. She compiled two books of recitations, other than those listed.

After leaving Indianapolis she lived in New York.

> Information from *Who's Who in America* and the Indianapolis Public Library.

* * *

Manitou. *Indianapolis,* 1881.

The Chamber Over the Gate. *Indianapolis*, 1886.

Little Dialogues for Little People. *Indianapolis*, 1887.

The Price of the Ring. *Chicago*, 1892.

Shylock's Daughter: A Novel. *Chicago*, 1894.

Select Readings and Recitations for All Year Round. *Indianapolis*, 1896.

Jasper Fairfax. *New York*, 1897.

In the First Degree. *New York*, 1907.

Silas Kirkendown's Sons. *Boston*, 1908.

Paying the Piper. *New York*, 1910.

Only a Dream. 1911.

Hildegarde and Other Lyrics. *New York*, 1911.

Shame. 1919.

Browning Critiques. *Chicago*, 1921.

My Little Neighbor.

Robin's Egg Blue.

In Quiet Hours.

Nineveh.

BATES, WILLIAM OSCAR: 1852–1924.

William Oscar Bates was born at Harrisburg, Ind., Sept. 19, 1852. He attended the public schools of Harrisburg, Norwestern Christian (now Butler) University, and received the Ph.B. degree from Cornell University in 1875.

From 1877 to 1899 he worked on newspapers—the INDIANAPOLIS JOURNAL, CINCINNATI NEWS-JOURNAL, ST. PAUL PIONEER PRESS, NEW YORK WORLD, and the NEW YORK COMMERCIAL ADVERTISER—and in 1900 he returned to Indianapolis to devote his time to playwriting. He died Oct. 29, 1924.

> Information from *Who's Who in America*; Dunn —*Indiana and Indianans*; and the Indianapolis Public Library.

* * *

Our Foreign Correspondent. 1888. (Play.)

Parlor Plants and Window Gardening . . . *London* and *New York* [1895].

Uncle Rodney. (Play; produced 1896.)

Recitations and How to Recite . . . *London* and *New York* [1895].

Dogs, Cats and Other Pets. *London* and *New York*, 1896.

Jacob Leisler; A Play of Old New York; With an Introductory Note by Mrs. Schuyler Van Rensselaer. *New York*, 1913.

The Black Bokhara. *New York*, n.d. [1917]. (Play; produced in Indianapolis in 1907.)

Polly of Pogue's Run; A One Act Play of the Civil War. *New York*, 1917.

Asaph; A Comedy. *New York,* n.d. (Produced in Indianapolis in 1918.)

Dryad and the Deacon. *New York*, n.d. (Play; Produced in Indianapolis in 1920.)

Tea.

Baby Angeline.

The Indianapolis Centennial Pageant, Coliseum, June 8th, 1920; The Book of Words by William O. Bates . . . [*Indianapolis*], 1920.

BAUMGARTNER, SAMUEL HENRY: 1860–1936.

Samuel Henry Baumgartner was born in French Township, Adams County, Ind., Mar. 2, 1860, the sixth of nine children born to Samuel and Verena Welty Baumgartner, emigrants from Switzerland. Instructed only in reading, spelling, writing, and arithmetic as a youth, in his eighteenth year he attended the graded school in Linn Grove, Ind., for two sessions of six months each, and from 1880 to 1882 he attended summer sessions at the Adams County Normal School at Decatur, Ind., and taught in the school of his native township.

In January, 1881, he joined the Evangelical Association at Vera Cruz, Ind., and upon the death of his father in March he was elected to succeed him as "class leader" in the local church. He continued in this position until he entered Northwestern College, Naperville, Ill., in 1883. While in college he decided to enter the Christian ministry, and after graduation in 1887 he began his active ministry. In 1886 he had married Kezzie Keiper in Naperville.

During forty years as a pastor and presiding elder he held numerous appointments in the Indiana Conference of his church and was active for many years in promoting and managing camp-meetings and young people's conventions.

Following his retirement from the active ministry the Baumgartners removed to Connecticut where Mrs. Baumgartner died in 1930 and Samuel Henry Baumgartner on Nov. 18, 1936.

> Information from Hope L. Baumgartner, son.

* * *

Brief Historical Sketches of Seven Generations; Descendants of Deacon David Baumgartner, who was born 1735. 1908.

Brief Historical Sketches of Eight Generations; Descendants of Ulrich Welty, Born 1728. 1926.

BAYLOR, ADELAIDE STEELE: ?–1935.

Adelaide Steele Baylor, daughter of James Craig and Susannah Steele Baylor, was born in Wabash, Ind.

Although no birth date is available, it is presumed that she was born about 1860, since she graduated from high school in 1878.

From 1893 to 1895 she was a student at the University of Michigan. She received the Ph.B. degree from the University of Chicago in 1897 and the M.A. from Columbia in 1918. During her career as an educator she was a teacher in Indiana public schools, superintendent of the city schools of Wabash, Ind., assistant State Superintendent of Public Instruction, and state supervisor of home economics. In 1923 she became associated with the federal education service in Washington, D. C. Miss Baylor died in 1935.

> Information from *Who Was Who in America* and the Carnegie Library, Wabash, Ind.

* * *

Adventures of Miss Tabby Gray. *Chicago*, 1913.
Young America's First Book (with Emma Colbert). *New York,* 1919.

BEADLE, JOHN HANSON: 1840–1897.

John Hanson Beadle was born in Liberty Township, Parke County, Ind., on Mar. 14, 1840. He was a son of James Ward and Elizabeth Bright Beadle, and a brother of William Henry Harrison Beadle.

According to Dunn—*Indiana and Indianans*, Vol. V.: "He was a precocious child, frail physically but strong mentally. His parents removed to Rockville when he was eight years old, and he was then far ahead of schoolmates of his age. At that time the Sunday Schools of Indiana were conducted on an educational basis, with memorizing the Scriptures as a prominent feature; and when ten years old young Beadle could recite the entire New Testament."

He attended Rockville Seminary until 1857, when he went with his brother to the University of Michigan. In the summer of 1861 he joined Company A, 31st Indiana Regiment, as a private, but he was discharged as an incurable consumptive after the battle of Fort Donelson. In 1864, his health improved, he re-enlisted, again as a private, in the 133rd Regiment and served until the end of the war. Intending to become a lawyer, he settled in 1868 in Evansville, where he wrote editorials for the EVANSVILLE JOURNAL; however, his health failed again and he went to California as correspondent of the CINCINNATI COMMERCIAL.

Indiana and Indianans says further: "He had found his calling. It was the day of the newspaper correspondent, and Beadle ranked among the best. Most of this stay in the West was passed in Utah, where he became editor of the SALT LAKE REPORTER. It was a time when animosity between Mormons and Gentiles was at its height, and the evils of Mormonism struck Beadle with great force. He not only called a spade a spade, but if the emergency seemed to demand it, called it a spade and a rake. In consequence he was attacked by Mormons and severely wounded. The tactical mistake of his assailants was that they did not kill him, for he did more to form the popular American estimate of Mormonism than any other one man."

In 1869 he returned home, and the next ten years saw five of his books published. (*Life in Utah* sold 80,000 copies.) On Dec. 25, 1872, he married Jennie Cole of Evansville. In 1879 he became owner and editor of the ROCKVILLE TRIBUNE, which did not turn out to be a financial success, principally because of Beadle's proclivity for stating his views and disregarding other considerations. While in the employ of a news syndicate in 1886 he made a winter trip by dog sledge to Manitoba and Saskatchewan, and the same syndicate sent him to England and France "with instructions to write his letters 'just as he would if he were doing it for the ROCKVILLE TRIBUNE and the people of Parke County.' " In 1893 Mr. Beadle covered the Columbian Exposition in Chicago, and he was in Washington, D. C., as congressional correspondent until 1896.

He died at Rockville, Ind., on Jan. 15, 1897.

> Information from Dunn—*Indiana and Indianans,* Vol. V.

* * *

Life in Utah: or, the Mysteries and Crimes of Mormonism. Being an Exposé of the Secret Rites and Ceremonies of the Latter-Day Saints, with a Full and Authentic History of Polygamy and the Mormon Sect from Its Origin to the Present Time. *Philadelphia* [1870].

Brigham's Destroying Angel: Life, Confession, and Startling Disclosures of Notorious Bill Hickman, Danite Chief of Utah; Edited by J. H. Beadle. *Philadelphia,* 1872.

The Undeveloped West; or, Five Years in the Territories . . . *Philadelphia,* 1873.

Women's War on Whisky: Its History, Theory, and Prospects . . . *Cincinnati,* 1874.

Western Wilds, and the Men Who Redeem Them: *Cincinnati,* 1878.

Polygamy; or, the Mysteries and Crimes of Mormonism, Being a Full and Authentic History of This Strange Sect from Its Origin to the Present Time . . . By J. H. Beadle . . . Assisted by Hon. O. J. Hollister . . . *Philadelphia* [1904].

BEADLE, WILLIAM HENRY HARRISON: 1838–1915.

"William Henry Harrison Beadle (Jan. 1, 1838-Nov. 13, 1915), educator, was born in a log cabin, built by his father, close to the Wabash River in Parke County, Ind. His parents, James Ward Beadle and Elizabeth Bright, had moved after their marriage from Kentucky to the frontier in western Indiana. . . . He learned to use the axe, plow, and rifle, got his education in a log schoolhouse and later in the graded school in the county seat . . . His father offered him a farm, but he chose to take instead a thousand dollars for a college education. Entering the University of Michigan in the fall of 1857, he specialized in civil engineering. After his graduation in June, 1861 he entered the Union army as first lieutenant of Company A, 31st Indiana Volunteer Infantry. He was repeatedly promoted, and was given the rank of brevet brigadier-general when he was discharged, Mar. 26, 1866. During the war, on May 18, 1863, he had married Ellen S. Chapman at Albion, Mich. Beadle attended the University of Michigan Law School for a year after his discharge and received his LL.B. in March 1867. After practising law in Evansville, Ind., and Boscobel, Wis., he was appointed, March 1869, surveyor general of Dakota territory . . . In the next four years he became acquainted with the country and early settlers. As secretary of the commission which drew up the code of 1877, he gained valuable experience in clear exposition of complicated ideas. The responsibility for passing the code through the legislature fell largely on Beadle through his chairmanship of the judiciary committee in the House. He accepted the superintendency of public instruction in 1879 with the condition that he 'should stand strongly for the principle that no school lands should ever be sold for less than their appraised value, and never for less than ten dollars an acre' . . . when statehood was attained. For the next six years Beadle was busily engaged in organizing new schools necessitated by the rapid expansion of settlement, in introducing the township unit of administration, and in holding teachers' institutes . . . Beadle continued his educational service by his able and inspiring presidency of the Madison State Normal School from 1889 to 1906 and as professor of history until his retirement in 1912. He died [1915] in San Francisco, while on a visit to his daughter . . ."

Condensed from R. G. W., *Dictionary of American Biography*, Vol. II.

* * *

Dakota; Its Geography, History, and Resources. *St. Paul, Minnesota*, 1888.

The Natural System of Teaching Geography (with A. F. Bartlett). *Chicago*, 1899.

Autobiography. 1906.

BEARD, CHARLES AUSTIN: 1874–1948

Charles Austin Beard, distinguished American historian, son of William Henry and Mary Payne Beard, was born in Knightstown, Ind., on Nov. 27, 1874.

He was educated in the local schools and graduated from De Pauw University in 1898. He studied at Oxford and Cornell and received his A.M. from Columbia in 1903, and his Ph.D. in 1904. On Mar. 8, 1900, he married Mary Ritter of Indianapolis, who had been graduated from De Pauw one year before him. Mary Ritter Beard became not only the mother of his two children but also his fellow worker in the field of American social and political history and joint-author of several of his most significant works.

From 1910 to 1917 Charles Austin Beard was a member of the Columbia University faculty. In 1917 he became director of the Training School for Public Service, New York, and continued there until 1922. In that year he became adviser to the Institute of Municipal Research at Tokyo, and after the earthquake of 1923 he became adviser to Count Geto, Japanese Minister of Home Affairs.

In later years the Beards resided at New Milford, Conn. He spent this period mainly in research and writing in his field. He died on Sept. 1, 1948.

Besides the titles listed, Dr. Beard edited and compiled many works on history and government and was the author and co-author of many textbooks.

Information from *Who's Who in America.*

* * *

The Industrial Revolution, with a Preface by F. York Powell. *London*, 1901.

The Office of Justice of the Peace in England in Its Origin and Development. *New York*, 1904.

An Introduction to the English Historians. *New York*, 1906.

The Development of Modern Europe. An Introduction to the Study of Current History (with J. H. Robinson). *Boston*, 1907-08. 2 vols.

Readings in Modern European History; A Collection of Extracts from the Sources Chosen with the Purpose of Illustrating Some of the Chief Phases of the Development of Europe During the Last Two Hundred Years (with J. H. Robinson). *Boston*, 1908-09. 2 vols.

European Sobriety in the Presence of the Balkan Crisis. *New York*, 1908.

Politics. (A Lecture). *New York*, 1908.

American Government and Politics. *New York*, 1910.

Modern European History. *New York*.

Party Government in the United States. *New York*.

Expansion of the United States. *New York*.

Industrialism and Democracy. *New York*.

English History to the Tudors. *New York*.

English History from James I. *New York*.

City Manager Plan of Municipal Government.

Documents on the State-Wide Initiative, Referendum and Recall (with Birl Earl Shultz). *New York*, 1912.

The Supreme Court and the Constitution. *New York*, 1912.

American City Government; A Survey of Newer Tendencies. *New York*, 1912.

An Economic Interpretation of the Constitution of the United States. *New York*, 1913.

Contemporary American History, 1877-1913. *New York*, 1914.

American Citizenship (with Mary Ritter Beard). *New York*, 1914.

Outlines of European History (with J. H. Robinson). *Boston*, 1914. Vol. 2.

Economic Origins of Jeffersonian Democracy. *New York*, 1915.

Six Years' Experience with the Direct Primary in New York.

National Governments and the World War (with F. A. Ogg). *New York*.

History of the American People (with W. C. Bagley). *New York*, 1920.

History of Europe, Our Own Times, the Eighteenth and Nineteenth Centuries: The Opening of the Twentieth Century and the World War (with J. H. Robinson). *Boston*, 1921.

Our Old World Background (with W. C. Bagley). *New York*, 1922.

Cross Currents in Europe To-day. *Boston*, 1922.

The Economic Basis of Politics. *New York*, 1922.

The Administration and Politics of Tokyo; A Survey and Opinions. *New York*, 1923.

Government Research, Past, Present and Future. *New York*, 1926.

The Rise of American Civilization (with Mary Ritter Beard). *New York*, 1927. 2 vols.

The American Party Battle. *New York*, 1928.

The Balkan Pivot—Yugoslavia; A Study in Government and Administration (with George Radin). *New York*, 1929.

The American Leviathan; The Republic in the Machine Age (with William Beard). *New York*, 1930.

Charter for the Social Sciences in the Schools. *New York*, 1932.

The Myth of Rugged American Individualism. *New York*, 1932.

The Navy: Defense or Portent. *New York*, 1932.

The Future Comes; A Study of the New Deal (with G. H. E. Smith). *New York*, 1933.

The Nature of the Social Sciences in Relation to the Objectives of Instruction. *New York*, 1934.

The Idea of National Interest; An Analytical Study in American Foreign Policy (with G. H. E. Smith). *New York*, 1934.

The Open Door at Home; A Trial Philosophy of National Interest (with G. H. E. Smith). *New York*, 1934.

The Recovery Program (1933-1934). A Study of the Depression and the Fight to Overcome It (with G. H. E. Smith). *New York*, 1934.

The Presidents in American History. *New York*, 1935.

Schools in the Story of Culture (with William G. Carr).

The Discussion of Human Affairs; An Inquiry into the Nature of the Statements, Assertions, Allegations, Claims, Heats, Tempers, Distempers, Dogmas, and Contentions Which Appear When Human Affairs Are Discussed and into the Possibility of Putting Some Rhyme and Reason into Processes of Discussion. *New York*, 1936.

Annual Guide to American Government and Politics. *New York*, 1936.

The Devil Theory of War; An Inquiry into the Nature of History and the Possibility of Keeping Out of War. *New York*, 1936.

Jefferson, Corporations and the Constitution. *Washington, D. C.*, 1936.

Unemployment and Adult Education.

The Making of American Civilization (with Mary Ritter Beard). *New York*, 1937.

History of Civilization; Our Own Age (with J. H. Robinson and D. V. Smith). *Boston*, 1937.

America Today (with W. C. Bagley and R. F. Nichols). *New York*, 1938.

America Yesterday (with W. C. Bagley and R. F. Nichols). *New York*, 1938.

America Yesterday and Today (with W. C. Bagley and R. F. Nichols). *New York*, 1938.

America in Midpassage (with Mary Ritter Beard). *New York*, 1939. (Vol. 3 of The Rise of American Civilization.)

Giddy Minds and Foreign Quarrels; An Estimate of American Foreign Policy. *New York*, 1939.

A Foreign Policy for America. *New York*, 1940.

The Old Deal and the New (with G. H. E. Smith). *New York*, 1940.

American Party Battle. *New York*, 1941.

Public Policy and the General Welfare. *New York*, 1941.

The American Spirit; A Study of the Idea of Civilization in the United States (with Mary Ritter Beard). *New York*, 1942. (Vol. 4 of The Rise of American Civilization.)

The Republic; Conversations on Fundamentals. *New York*, 1943.

Basic History of the United States (with Mary Ritter Beard). *Garden City, N. Y.,* 1944.

President Roosevelt and the Coming of the War 1941. *New Haven*, 1948.

BEARD, MARY RITTER (MRS. CHARLES A.): 1876–

Mary Ritter, daughter of Eli Foster and Narcissa Lockwood Ritter, was born in Indianapolis on Aug. 5, 1876. She received the Ph.B. degree from De Pauw University in 1897 and later studied at Columbia University, in Europe, and in the Orient. She married Charles Austin Beard on Mar. 8, 1900 and became, with him, editor and joint author of some of the most significant historical writing of the Twentieth century, as well as a writer of distinction on her own account.

Information from *Who's Who in America.*

* * *

American Citizenship (with Charles A. Beard). *New York*, 1914.

Woman's Work in Municipalities. *New York*, 1915.

A Short History of the American Labor Movement. *New York*, 1920.

History of the United States (with Charles A. Beard). *New York*, 1921.

The Rise of American Civilization (with Charles A. Beard). *New York,* 1927. 2 vols.

The American Labor Movement: A Short History. *New York*, 1931.

On Understanding Women. *New York*, 1931.

A Changing Political Economy as It Affects Women. *Washington, D. C.,* 1934.

The Making of American Civilization (with Charles A. Beard). *New York*, 1937.

America in Midpassage (with Charles A. Beard). *New York*, 1939. (Vol. 3 of The Rise of American Civilization.)

The American Spirit: A Study of the Idea of Civilization in the United States (with Charles A. Beard). *New York*, 1942. (Vol. 4 of The Rise of American Civilization.)

Basic History of the United States (with Charles A. Beard). *Garden City, N. Y.,* 1944.

Woman as Force in History: A Study in Traditions and Realities. *New York*, 1946.

BEARD, REED: 1862–1939.

According to Beard's statement, printed under his portrait frontispiece in his book, *The Battle of Tippe-*

canoe: "I was born in Iowa, Aug. 31, 1862, and in infancy became totally blind. During the same year my parents removed to Indiana. At the age of ten, I entered the Indiana Institution for the Education of the Blind, from which I graduated eight years later . . ." He resided in Lafayette during most of his life.

Information from Beard—*The Battle of Tippecanoe.*

* * *

Brief Biographies of American Presidents. *Lafayette, Ind.,* 1886.

The Battle of Tippecanoe. Historical Sketches of the Famous Field Upon Which General William Henry Harrison Won Renown That Aided Him in Reaching the Presidency. Lives of the Prophet and Tecumseh with Many Interesting Incidents of Their Rise and Overthrow. The Campaign of 1888 and Election of General Benjamin Harrison. n.p. [*Chicago*], n.d. [1889].

BECK, FRANK ORMAN: 1872–

Born in Wayne County, Ind., in 1872, Frank Orman Beck was educated at Indiana, Boston, Chicago and Edinburgh universities, receiving the A.B., A.M., S.T.B., and Ph.D. degrees. He married Daisy Woodward of Bloomington, Ind.

A Methodist clergyman and college teacher, his last position before his retirement was in the School of Theology, Northwestern University. He served as a minister in New Albany and Indianapolis, Ind., and in Evanston and Chicago, Ill. He was one of the founders of the Methodist Federation of Social Service.

In addition to the book listed below, Dr. Beck was the author of numerous articles in the AMERICAN JOURNAL OF RELIGION and the METHODIST REVIEW and had a number of writings published by the Department of Public Welfare, Chicago, and the Indiana State Board of Charities and Corrections.

Information from Indiana University.

* * *

Marching Manward: A Study of the Boy. *New York*, 1913.

BEHARRELL, THOMAS G.: 1824–?

The Rev. Thomas G. Beharrell was born in Huntingdonshire, England, on Dec. 17, 1824, the son of H. Beharrell, a Wesleyan minister. The latter emigrated to American in 1837 and settled in Evansville, Ind. Later he became the Wesleyan minister in New

Albany, Ind. Thomas Beharrell was educated in the common schools and for two years at a private school in New Albany. Although at first interested in medicine, he soon turned to the ministry, studying while teaching school.

He was pastor of churches in several Indiana towns and cities—Shelbyville, Madison, Jeffersonville, and Indianapolis. In 1849, in Indianapolis, he married Miss Sarah Ellen Hughes. He received the honorary A.M. degree from Indiana Asbury (now De Pauw University) in 1860, and the LL.D. degree from Indiana University in 1877. In addition to his work as a minister, he was an active member of the Independent Order of Odd-Fellows and of the Masons and was also an enthusiastic temperance worker.

Information from *Representative Men of Indiana*, Vol. I.

* * *

The Brotherhood: Being a Presentation of the Principles of Odd-Fellowship: With a Brief History of Bible Men and Women, Who Developed the Principles That Have Been Adopted by the Fraternity in Their Several Lives. *Cincinnati*, 1860.

A Complete Alphabetically Arranged Biblical Biography, Containing a Full History of Bible Men and Women, with an Appendix Embracing a Biography of Unnamed Persons. *Indianapolis*, 1867.

History of Odd-Fellowship in Indiana.

The New I.O.O.F. Monitor and Guide, Containing History of the Degrees of Rebekah, and Its Teachings. *Indianapolis*, 1898.

Hannah, the Odd-Fellow's Orphan.

BELL, WILLIAM MELVIN: 1860–1933.

William Melvin Bell, son of Isaac H. and Nancy E. Ihrig Bell, was born in Whitley County, Ind., on Nov. 12, 1860. He graduated from Roanoke (Ind.) Classical Seminary in 1879. Following his ordination in the United Brethren ministry, he was pastor of churches at LaGrange, Lafayette, Ligonier, and Elkhart, Ind. From 1890 to 1893 he was president and superintendent of the Indiana Sunday School Association and from 1893 to 1905 he was general secretary of the Department of Home and Foreign Missions. He was made a Bishop in 1905 and was appointed Senior Bishop in 1921 in charge of the Eastern District. He died Oct. 6, 1933.

Information from *Who Was Who in America*.

* * *

The Love of God. *Dayton, O.*, 1902.
The Social Message of Our Lord. *Dayton, O.*, 1909.

Torches Aloft. *Dayton, O.*, 1915.
Life of Bishop Nicholas Castle. *Dayton, O.*, 1923.

BELLAMY, ORLANDO ROLLINS: 1856–

Orlando Rollins Bellamy was born in Vevay, Ind., in 1856. No other information is available.

Information from the Indianapolis Public Library.

* * *

Songs of the Wayside.

BENDER, JOHN S.: 1827–?

John S. Bender was born near Carlisle, Pa., in 1827. As a boy of eleven he was taken to Wayne County, O. He moved to Indiana as a young man and became a teacher in a country school.

After teaching for a time he attended and was graduated from Northwestern Christian (now Butler) University. He resumed teaching in South Bend, but ill health forced him to take outdoor employment after only two terms.

His health regained, he took up law and practiced in Plymouth, Ind., was auditor of Starke County from 1854 to 1860, published and owned a Republican newspaper from 1868 to 1875, then resumed his law practice successfully.

Information from Plymouth, Ind., Public Library.

* * *

Money: Its Definition, Tests. Being an Argument Showing That Money Is Such by Decree of the Government, Not Made to Hoard, but to Be Used as a Tool of Commerce, and a Sufficient Volume Thereof Is Indispensable to the Progress of Civilization . . . *Plymouth, Ind.*, 1879.

A Hoosier's Experience in Western Europe with Notes on the Way. *Plymouth, Ind.*, 1880.

BENHAM, EMMA CAROLINE KING (MRS. JOHN S.): 1857–1942.

Emma Caroline King was the daughter of Isaac and Emily Carrington King of Lincolnville (now Benham), Ind. She was born on Dec. 11, 1857.

She married John S. Benham, a teacher and onetime Congressman. The couple had two sons, both of whom died in infancy, and, after the death of the second, she divorced her husband and devoted the rest of her life to writing and art.

Styling herself "Emma King Benham, author-poet-artist," she published only two books but left many short stories, poems and sketches in manuscript form to the Ripley County, Ind., Historical Society.

Mrs. Benham died on June 23, 1942.

Information from Violet E. Toph, Versailles, Ind.

* * *

Wayside Flowers. *Indianapolis*, 1902.

Memorial Volume to the Boy, Pioneer-Poet-Printer, Ross Alley, n.p., 1929.

BENSON, LUTHER: 1847–1898.

Since the usual county history biographical sketch is designed to conceal any small derelictions of conduct on the part of the subject—and since this office is usually performed so thoroughly that each sketch seems to recount the experiences of a candidate for beatitude —it is a relief to find one in which the most is made of the subject's slips from grace. Here, as a brilliant exception to an otherwise well-nigh fast rule, is the sketch of the life of Luther Benson in the *Encyclopedia of Biography of Indiana, 1899*:

"This sketch purports simply to recount a few chief and interesting facts of an already familiar subject; for the name of Luther Benson, like that of John B. Gough, is well known throughout the country in connection with the noble cause of temperance. Any biography of this man is necessarily a record of one of the greatest triumphs ever achieved by mortal in his life-and-death struggle with abnormal appetite. This appetite was undoubtedly inherited from his maternal grandfather and was fostered and strengthened by the customs of the day, spiritous liquors being kept and freely used by every family. Luther Benson was one of a family of nine children, seven of whom were boys. His father, John Harley Benson, was born Mar. 2, 1802 . . . In 1835 he left Kentucky with his family and located in Rush County, Ind. . . .

"Here his son Luther, destined to become so singularly distinguished, was born Sept. 9, 1847, and grew to manhood assisting with the work of his father's farm. He obtained the rudiments of an education in two little log school-houses—one standing by a stream called Hood's Creek, the other on the site of the present Ammon's mill. When sixteen years of age he began attending school at the little village of Fairview . . . His education was completed at Moore's Hill College near Cincinnati, after which he began the study of law; but the time had come when the onward current of his expanding young life was to receive a fearful check and its sweet and wholesome waters be turned to bitterness. His passion for drink had come upon him;

and, although he afterward entered college, his attendance was of short duration. Henceforth his best efforts must be expended in fighting the fiend that threatened his destruction. Of his moral sense and moral stamina his later years of triumph gave abundant proof; but that triumph came only after a long season of misery and humiliation to himself, his family and friends.

"On Jan. 21, 1877, he experienced a profound revulsion to his manner of life and determined to raise above his weakness. This seeming conversion occurred at Jeffersonville, Ind., and was the forerunner of his permanent conquest of a few months later at Fowler, although a period of relapse to his pitiful thralldom intervened. During the ten years prior to this time he had been engaged in the practice of law, a vocation to which in some ways he was admirably adapted, having, when not under the influence of liquor, a logical intelligence and eloquent flow of language. He had begun his legal studies in the office of Hon. John S. Reid, at Connersville, and had subsequently opened one on his own account at Rushville, where he practiced with good success until, himself released from the tyranny of strong drink, he felt impelled to devote his remaining days to the rescuing of like victims. Imbued with the moral courage of a lofty purpose, the chosen scene of his first lecture was Raleigh, whose inhabitants had been eye-witnesses to his most reckless dissipations. After this he proceeded from one to another of the principal towns of Indiana until, within three years, he had delivered nearly five hundred lectures in his home State. Subsequently he made a tour in the East . . . his efforts meeting everywhere with much appreciation and enthusiasm . . .

"In 1883 or '84 Mr. Benson received the Democratic nomination for Congress from the Sixth District, but in a manly letter declined the nomination, not wishing actively to enter into political life . . . In 1884 Mr. Benson was married to Anna C. Slade. His domestic life was made beautiful by a wealth of affection, and his death which occurred June 21, 1898, was deeply and widely deplored . . .

"Not only with oral eloquence did Mr. Benson labor for the cause of temperance; he toiled with pen as well. *Fifteen Years in Hell* is the significant title of a book of which he is the author and which has had a phenomenal sale throughout the country; and Mrs. Benson holds for publication the manuscript of her husband's autobiography, completed shortly before his death . . ."

Condensed from the *Encyclopedia of Biography of Indiana*, 1899. Vol. 2.

* * *

Fifteen Years in Hell. Autobiography. *Indianapolis*, 1877.

The Ribbon Workers (with James M. Hiatt). *Chicago*, 1878.

Luther Benson's Struggle for Life. *Boston*.

Book of Remarkable Trials and Notorious Characters. *New York*.

BENTLEY, ARTHUR FISHER: 1870–

Born at Freeport, Ill., in 1870, Arthur F. Bentley was educated at Johns Hopkins University, receiving the A.B., A.M. and Ph.D. degrees. He lives near Paoli, Ind.

Information from the Indianapolis Public Library.

* * *

The Condition of the Western Farmer, as Illustrated by the Economic History of a Nebraska Township. *Baltimore*, 1893.

The Process of Government: A Study of Social Pressures. *Chicago*, 1908.

Relativity in Man and Society. *New York*, 1926.

Linguistic Analysis of Mathematics. *Bloomington, Ind.*, 1932.

Behavior, Knowledge, Fact. *Bloomington, Ind.*, 1935.

BERGENGREN, ANNA FARQUHAR (MRS. RALPH W.): 1865–

Anna Farquhar, who sometimes wrote under the pseudonym of Margaret Allston, was born in Brookville, Ind., in 1865, and was educated in Indianapolis, Boston, and Europe. She studied music and trained her voice for the concert stage, but overwork—singing in churches, practicing, and teaching—ruined her voice. During her musical career she began to write for the BOSTON TRANSCRIPT, the DETROIT FREE PRESS, and the SPRINGFIELD REPUBLICAN, and after the abandonment of that career she devoted all of her time to writing. For some time previous to 1902 she was assistant editor of the NATIONAL MAGAZINE. She married Ralph Wilhelm Bergengren, also a writer.

Information from *Who's Who in America* and the Indianapolis Public Library.

* * *

A Singer's Heart. *Boston*, 1897.

The Professor's Daughter. *New York*, 1899.

Her Boston Experiences: A Picture of Modern Boston Society and People. *Boston*, 1900.

The Devil's Plough: The Romantic History of a Soul Conflict. *Boston*, 1901.

Her Washington Experiences as Related by a Cabinet Minister's Wife in a Series of Letters to Her Sister. *Boston*, 1902.

An Evans of Suffolk. *Boston*, 1904.

BEVERIDGE, ALBERT JEREMIAH: 1862–1927.

"Albert Jeremiah Beveridge, senator, historian, was born on a small farm in Highland County, O., the son of Thomas H. and Frances Parkinson Beveridge. In 1865 the father, after the loss of his property, moved the family to a farm in Illinois. Young Beveridge's early life was one of privation and hardship. He was a plowboy at twelve, a railroad hand with a section gang at fourteen, a logger and teamster at fifteen. Before he was sixteen, however, he managed to enter a high school ... With a loan of $50 from a friend, in the fall of 1881 he entered Asbury College, now De Pauw University, at Greencastle, Ind. During his college course he won inter-state oratorical honors and prizes sufficient to provide for two of his college years. He graduated in 1885. He was twice married: in 1887 to Katherine Langsdale of Greencastle, Ind., who died June 18, 1900; in 1907 to Catherine Eddy of Chicago. Admitted to the bar in 1887, for twelve years Beveridge practiced law in Indianapolis. Meanwhile he had become well known in his state as a political orator. In every campaign for fifteen years ... he had stumped the state from end to end. In a deadlock among the leading senatorial candidates in 1899 the Republican legislative caucus turned to him as a compromise candidate, and he was elected to the United States Senate at the age of thirty-six, being among the youngest members ever to sit in that body. In 1905 he was reelected without opposition within his party, but in 1911, chiefly because of party schism, he was defeated for a third term, after which he never again held public office ...

"With this senatorial experience and his democratic disposition it was easy and natural for him to go with Roosevelt into the Progressive party in 1912. In the Progressive National Convention in Chicago in that year it was Beveridge, as temporary chairman, who sounded the 'keynote' in a campaign address, entitled 'Pass Prosperity Around.' During the same year he was nominated by the Progressive party of Indiana as its candidate for governor. He received 10,000 more votes than the Republican candidate, but was defeated by the Democratic candidate, Samuel M. Ralston. In 1914, after the adoption of the Seventeenth Amendment, the Indiana Progressives nominated Beveridge as their candidate for the United States Senate, but

Progressive support had fallen away, and he came in third in the popular vote ... In 1922 he was nominated for the United States Senate by the Republicans of Indiana in a state-wide popular primary, defeating Harry S. New, the sitting senator, but in the ensuing election he was again defeated by Samuel M. Ralston, the Democratic nominee. This closed his political career.

"He was a pronounced nationalist, suspicious of foreign countries, with some anti-British feeling, a stout opponent of America's having anything to do with the League of Nations; at times disposed toward jingoism in speech ... He was somewhat temperamental, but his finer qualities greatly overtopped his minor defects. ...

"But he was even more distinguished as a historical writer than as a politician ... Beveridge's greatest work ... was his biography of Chief Justice John Marshall, designed as an historical and political interpretation of the Supreme Court and of Marshall's part in giving that court its place in American history. This task he accomplished in a way that gained the universal approval of scholars and critics. As a biographer Beveridge showed his characteristic industry in gathering his materials, a discriminating mind in sifting and evaluating, a painstaking care in revising and rewriting until the facts took on their right relations and proportionate importance ... he produced an outstanding historical biography ... Beveridge then turned his attention to what he considered a harder and more important task, a similar biography of Lincoln in four volumes. At the time of his death two of these volumes had been substantially completed ... He had a horror of mistakes and his completed chapters had been read in manuscript by many historical scholars and were carefully revised and rewritten, some of them as many as fifteen times. His death was regretted on many accounts, but above all because of the loss to the world of his uncompleted Lincoln."

Senator Beveridge died on Apr. 27, 1927, in Indianapolis.

> Condensed from J. A. W., *Dictionary of American Biography*, Vol. II.

* * *

The "March of the Flag," Beginning of Greater America. Endorsement of the War Administration Issue. American Voters to Stand by Their Government—Effect of This Election on Other Nations ... Speech ... Opening the Indiana Republican Campaign, at Tomlinson Hall.

For the Greater Republic, Not for Imperialism. An Ad-

dress ... at the Union League of Philadelphia, February 15, 1899.

Conservatism: The Essential in American Character and Policy; Address ... At Chicago ... February 22d, 1902. *Chicago*, 1902.

The Philippine Situation ... *Washington, D. C.,* 1902.

Republicanism: The Spirit of Conservative Progress. Issues of the Campaign of 1902, Speech of Senator Beveridge, as Chairman of the Indiana State Republican Convention, at Indianapolis, Ind., April 23d, 1902 ...

The Russian Advance. *New York,* 1903.

Address of Albert J. Beveridge ... At the Dedication of Indiana's monuments on the Battlefield of Shiloh, Tennessee, April 6, 1903. *Indianapolis* [1903].

"All Is Well with the Republic." n.p.

The Young Man and the World. *New York,* 1905.

The Bible as Good Reading. *Philadelphia,* 1907.

Employment of Child Labor. Speech ... in the Senate of the United States, January 23, 28, and 29, 1907. *Washington, D. C.,* 1907.

The Meaning of the Times, and Other Speeches. *Indianapolis,* 1908.

Americans of To-day and To-morrow. *Philadelphia,* 1908.

Work and Habits. *Philadelphia,* 1908.

Tariff Commission. *Washington, D. C.,* 1908.

The Invisible Government. 1912.

"Pass Prosperity Around," Speech. *New York,* 1912.

Accepting the Nomination for Governor by the Progressive Party at the Indiana State Convention August 1, 1912. n.p., 1912.

What Is Back of the War. *Indianapolis,* 1915.

The Life of John Marshall. *Boston,* 1916-19. 4 vols.

Address at the Celebration of the 299th Anniversary of the Landing of the Pilgrims, Delivered at Plymouth, Massachusetts, December 22nd, 1919. *Plymouth, Mass.,* 1919.

Address of Hon. Albert J. Beveridge at the McKinley Day Celebration of the Detroit Republican Club. Detroit, Michigan, January 29, 1920. n.p.

The Assault Upon American Fundamentals ... [Address at the Annual Meeting of the American Bar Association, St. Louis, August 26, 1920]. n.p. [1920].

Address Delivered ... on February 22, 1921, at the Second Washington's Birthday Celebration of the Sons of the Revolution and Other Patriotic Societies at Carnegie Hall, New York and at the Thirty-Ninth Banquet of the Sons of the Revolution at the Hotel Plaza, New York. *New York* [1921].

Address ... at Evansville, Indiana, September 26th, 1922. n.p. [1922].

"An Appeal to Plain Americans"; Address ... at the Annual Banquet of the Indiana Society of Chicago, December 9, 1922, and Introductory Remarks by Carroll Shaffer. n.p., 1922.

Courts and the People. *New York,* 1923.

The State of the Nation. *Indianapolis,* 1924.

The Art of Public Speaking. *Boston,* 1924.

Lincoln an Example to Young Men. *Tarrytown, N. Y.,* 1926.

Sources of the Declaration of Independence; An Address Delivered Before The Historical Society of Pennsylvania, June 2, 1926.

Abraham Lincoln, 1809-1858. *Boston,* 1928. 2 vols.

History of the World War.

Tribute to the American Woman, Frances E. Willard.

Personal Recollections of Abraham Lincoln.

BEVIN, PHILIP: 1811–1890.

Philip Bevin was born in New Port, England, Feb. 27, 1811, where records in his diary reveal that he was apprenticed at the age of seventeen to learn the carpenter trade and architecture. However, he did not like this work and in the year 1834 he sailed for the United States and arrived in Philadelphia. Soon after his arrival he made a trip down the Ohio River to Natchez and stopped at New Orleans and Cincinnati for a short time.

In the year 1836 he returned to England and married Elizabeth Ablard, the daughter of the man to whom he had been apprenticed.

In the year 1843, Bevin, with his wife and son, sailed from Liverpool to America. After arriving he was attracted by the opportunities offered by the new West and on Oct. 24 he arrived in Jackson County, Ia. He lived there two years, during which time he was engaged in farming and was also a minister of a newly organized church.

After the death of his wife he decided to devote his entire life to the ministry. During 1846 he entered Lane Theological Seminary in Cincinnati to prepare himself for his chosen profession. He was graduated from the Seminary in June, 1849. The rest of his life was spent in Indiana in the service of the Presbyterian Church in Southern Indiana. He lived during this period in Jefferson County, Jeffersonville, Byrnsville, Leavenworth, and Martinsburg, where he died Apr. 3, 1890.

In addition to the four known publications listed below, he left approximately twenty manuscripts (preserved in the Americana collection of W. E. Wilson), some of which may have been published but not recorded. During the period of twenty-five years of his residence in Indiana, he was a regular contributor of poems to local newspapers and religious magazines.

Information supplied by W. E. Wilson.

* * *

America. A Poem. *Cincinnati,* 1848.

Woman, Lost and Gained; or, The Island of the Innocent. *Cincinnati,* 1875.

Songs of the War for the Union, The Mystic Isle . . . *Cincinnati,* 1887.

Adalia: The Sinless World. n.p., n.d.

BIDDLE, HORACE PETERS: 1811–1900.

Horace P. Biddle, who was to become one of the chief disseminators of culture in the early Indiana scene, was born in what is now Hocking County, O. His parents, Benjamin and Abigail Converse Biddle, had come to Ohio from New England.

Young Biddle attended such subscription schools as were available in Ohio in his youth and eventually he began to read law under the guidance of Hocking H. Hunter of Lancaster, O. "Reading law" in those days, unless the reader was able to pay tuition to the learned barrister who supervised his studies, involved far more than academic pursuits: the student was expected to (and had better, if he wished to continue his preparations for the acquisition of fame and fortune) keep the fire in the fireplace in a state likely to satisfy the expectation of the waiting client with real money to pay as a retainer (splitting the wood if that proved necessary), to maintain a supply of sharp quills, to see to the ink (boiling poke-berries as a last expedient) and to copy all documents which passed through the office in a legible hand and with absolute accuracy. Biddle performed these services to the satisfaction of his mentor, Attorney Hunter, and acquired a little knowledge of the law to boot. In 1839 he was admitted to the Ohio bar.

Either Ohio was becoming too crowded with lawyers or young Biddle believed that possible lacunae in his learning would be less noticeable in a new country, because in October of the same year he went to Logansport, Ind., and announced himself ready to receive clients in need of advice or assistance.

He soon acquired a profitable practice and, by investing his fees wisely, was in middle age one of the most prosperous citizens of the community. In 1846 he was elected presiding judge of the eighth Indiana district, and, while his service was adequate in every respect, it did little to add lustre to his name except for the fact that he was thereafter "Judge" Biddle to the title-loving Hoosiers. He later served, from 1874 to 1881, as a judge of the Supreme Court of Indiana. After 1881 he devoted his time entirely to writing, reading and research.

It was not as a jurist, nor as the very competent

business man which he was, that Judge Biddle is remembered; it is as a patron, a student and a scholarly commentator of letters, science, philosophy and music. At his beautiful home on Biddle's Island in the Wabash River he found time not only to hunt and fish but also to collect one of the largest private libraries of its day in Indiana, to read, to translate from the French, German, Spanish, Portuguese and Italian, to study, and to play and enjoy music, and to write with authority on a great many subjects. Judge Biddle was able to live in this fashion, not only in the nineteen years of his life after his retirement but during his active career as well, while he was amassing a respectable estate entirely by his own efforts. Obviously, he was a master at organizing and utilizing his time to the best possible advantage. It is in no way remarkable that Indiana writers who knew him in their impressionable years invariably spoke of his culture and his manner of living with awe; he must have furnished an ideal for every ambitious and educated young man of the state.

Judge Biddle died on May 13, 1900.

Information from notes compiled by the late Esther U. McNitt, of the Indiana State Library.

* * *

My Cabin Home. 1839.

A Few Poems. 1849. (No copy located but referred to by D. S. A. in an article in the CINCINNATI GAZETTE of Dec. 7, 1876, as having attracted the attention of Washington Irving.)

A Discourse on Art . . . on the Occasion of George Winter's Annual Distribution of Oil Paintings at . . . Lafayette, December 30, 1854. *Lafayette, Ind.*, 1855.

A Few Poems. *Cincinnati*, 1858. (Apparently enlarged from the edition of 1849.)

The Musical Scale. *Cincinnati*, 1860.

My Island Home. 1860.

Poems. *New York*, 1868.

A Review of Prof. Tyndall's Work on Sound. *Cincinnati*, 1872.

Biddle's Poems. *New York*, 1872.

The Definition of Poetry: An Essay. *Cincinnati*, 1873.

Glances at the World. n.p., 1873.

My Scrap Book. *Logansport, Ind.*, 1874.

The Analysis of Rhyme: An Essay. *Cincinnati*, 1876.

American Boyhood. *Philadelphia*, 1876.

An Essay on Russian Literature. *Cincinnati*, 1877.

The Tetrachord: A New Musical Instrument. *Cincinnati*, 1877.

Amatories by an Amateur. *Cincinnati*, 1878. (Edition of 10 copies.)

The Elements of Knowledge. *Cincinnati*, 1881.

Prose Miscellany. *Cincinnati*, 1881.

Last Poems. *Cincinnati*, 1882.

The Eureka: A New Musical Instrument. *Logansport, Ind.*, 1886.

Life and Services of John B. Dillon (with John Coburn). *Indianapolis*, 1886.

The Dictionary of Music.

BIEDERWOLF, WILLIAM EDWARD: 1867–1939.

William Edward Biederwolf was born at Monticello, Ind., in 1867. He attended local schools and received the A.B. degree from Wabash College. He then graduated from the Princeton Theological Seminary and won a fellowship which gave him two years of study in Germany and France.

In 1897 Mr. Biederwolf was ordained a minister of the Presbyterian Church and accepted the pastorate of the Logansport Broadway Church. He enlisted as chaplain of the 161st Indiana Regiment in the Spanish-American War and saw six months service each in the U. S. and Cuba. He returned to his church in 1899 but resigned to take up evangelistic work and later the editorship of THE FAMILY ALTAR. As dean of the Winona Bible Conference he achieved a nation-wide reputation. He made his permanent home in Monticello, Ind. He died in 1939.

Information from *Who's Who in America*.

* * *

History of the One Hundred and Sixty-First Regiment, Indiana Volunteer Infantry. *Logansport, Ind.*, 1899.

Hell; Why, What, How Long. *Chicago* [1900].

The White Life: A Plea for Personal Purity. *Chicago*, 1900.

Christian Science: What Do Revelation, Philosophy, Medicine Say of Its Claim? *Boston*, 1901.

The Growing Christian. *Chicago* and *New York*, 1901.

A Help to the Study of the Holy Spirit. *Boston*, 1902.

How Can God Answer Prayer? Being an Exhaustive Treatise on the Nature, Conditions and Difficulties of Prayer. *Chicago*, 1906.

Mormonism Under the Searchlight. *Chicago*, 1908.

The Unvarnished Truth About Christian Science. 1908. (Reissued in 1914 as The Unvarnished Facts About Christian Science.)

Spiritualism: Divine or Devilish? *Chicago*, 1908.

The Christian and Amusements: Is Dancing Sinful? Is Card-Playing Wrong? Is Theater-Going Harmful? *Chicago*, 1909.

Russellism Unveiled. *Chicago*, 1909.

Seventh Day Adventism. *Chicago*, 1910.

Christian Science Tested by Philosophy, Medicine and Revelation. *Chicago*, 1910.

The Evangelistic Situation. 1917.

Mormonism. *Chicago*, 1920.

The Man God Tried to Kill, and Other Sermons. *Chicago, 1921.*

Evangelism, History and Method. 1921.

Evangelism: Its Justification, Its Operation and Its Value. *Chicago*, 1921.

Biederwolf's Evangelistic Sermons. *Chicago*, 1922.

How to Build a Tabernacle; For Union Gospel Meetings and Assemblies in General (with others). *Chicago*, 1922.

The Millennium Bible; Being a Help to the Study of the Holy Scriptures in Their Testimony to the Second Coming of Our Lord and Saviour Jesus Christ. *Chicago*, 1924.

Later Evangelistic Sermons. *Chicago*, 1925.

What About So-Called Christian Evolution? *Chicago,* 1926.

"They Have Taken Away My Lord." *Chicago*, 1926.

Illustrations from Mythology. *Chicago*, 1927.

After the Revival; A Simultaneous Campaign of Individual Evangelism. *Chicago*.

Great Evangelistic Sermons on the Fundamental Doctrines of Christianity. *Chicago*.

Make Christ King (with Edwin O. Excell). *Chicago*.

When the Song of the Lord Began and Other Sermons. *Chicago*, 1928.

Why I Know the Bible Is the Word of God. *Louisville*, 1929.

The Great Tribulation and the Second Coming. 1929.

Illustrations from Art. *New York*, 1930.

The Visible God. 1930.

The Adventure of the Hereafter. *New York*, 1930.

Frozen Assets; Twelve Evangelistic Sermons. *Grand Rapids, Mich.*, 1933.

Whipping Post Theology; or, Did Jesus Atone for Disease. *Grand Rapids, Mich.*, 1934.

The Coming Dictator, and Is Jesus Coming Back? *Hoytville, O.* [1934].

The New Paganism, and Other Sermons. *Grand Rapids, Mich.*, 1934.

The Man Who Said He Would and Other Sermons. *Grand Rapids, Mich.*, 1935.

The Man Nobody Missed and Other Sermons. *Grand Rapids, Mich.*, 1936.

The Wonderful Christ. *Grand Rapids, Mich.*, 1937.

Awake, O America! *Grand Rapids, Mich.*, 1937.

The Kiss of Judas. *Grand Rapids, Mich.*, 1939.

The World's Saturday Night, and Other Sermons. *Grand Rapids, Mich.*, 1939.

BIGGER, FINLEY: 1807–

Finley Bigger, son of John Bigger and brother of Samuel Bigger, Indiana governor in 1840, was born near Lebanon, O., on Sept. 29, 1807.

He had a limited formal education as a boy, read law, and was admitted to the bar in 1834 or 1835. In 1836 he moved to Rushville, Ind., and began the practice of law. From 1853 to 1861 he served as register of the U. S. Treasury.

A writer on political and social topics, he contributed articles to the JACKSONIAN, a Rushville paper, and acted at times as its editor. Another of his interests was mathematics, in which he displayed unusual skill.

He married Nancy Wilson of Warren County, O., on Mar. 6, 1827.

Information from *Representative Men of Indiana*, Vol. I.

* * *

Five of the Most Useful and Practical Rules in Arithmetic—to Wit, Simple Proportion, Compound Proportion, Simple and Compound Interest, and Percentage —Unified and Solved by One Simple Formula; One Formula for Either, or for Any Problem in Either. Original Mathematical Formulas. *Indianapolis*, 1874.

BILLINGS, JOHN SHAW: 1838–1913.

"John Shaw Billings [Apr. 12, 1838-Mar. 11, 1913] descended from William Billings of Somersetshire who migrated to New England about the middle of the Seventeenth Century. In the course of six generations the family removed through New York State to Switzerland County in southeastern Indiana, where John was born to James Billings and his wife, Abby (Shaw) Billings . . .

"As a boy John read voraciously, learned Latin with a little aid from a clergyman of the neighborhood, and later made an agreement with his father to waive all claim to an inheritance in favor of the other child, a sister, if the father would help him through college. He prepared himself, and at the age of fourteen entered the sub-freshman class of Miami University . . . Five years later he received the degree of B.A. with honors and in the fall of the following year began his professional studies at the Medical College of Ohio. In the spring of 1860 he obtained his M.D. and in the fall was appointed demonstrator of anatomy in the medical college at which he had studied. A year later he went before the medical examining board of the regular army, then being rapidly enlarged to meet the demands at the opening of the war, and passed at the top of the list. He received his commission the following spring and was put in charge of a hospital. At the end of the summer he became executive officer of a Philadelphia hospital filled with thousands of sick and wounded, and at that post developed a facility in disposing of official business by which he was ever after characterized. In Apr. 1864 he was assigned to duty with the medical director of the Army of the Potomac . . . In July he was invalided back to Washington and in December he was transferred to the surgeon-general's office, where he remained until his retirement from active duty thirty years later. During the first few years of this period his time was occupied largely with routine departmental duties in connection with the closing of many great army hospitals and the discharge of civilian physicians and surgeons.

"During his student years in the Medical College Billings had been aroused to the need of a great medical library in the U. S. His graduating thesis had been on *The Surgical Treatment of Epilepsy*. The six months which he spent in writing it, ransacking the while the libraries of Cincinnati and of eastern cities for material, showed him that there were more than 100,000 printed volumes of medical books and journals to search, that no medical library in the United States possessed the majority of these books . . . This experience led him after peace came 'to try to establish for the use of American physicians a fairly complete medical library and in connection with this to prepare a comprehensive catalogue and index.'

"Soon after beginning his Washington life Billings was put in charge of the Surgeon-General's Library and much of his time thereafter was devoted to fostering its growth. A sum of $80,000, turned in from the army hospitals after the war, was made available, and, energetically using this opportunity, he increased the library from 600 entries in the catalogue of 1865 to more than 50,000 entries in that of 1873. After he had seen the Surgeon-General's Library thus grow under his hands, he printed in 1876 *A Specimen Fasciculus of a Catalogue* and submitted it to the medical profession for suggestions. It was well received and four years later Congress provided for printing Billings's monumental work, the *Index Catalogue*, in the preparation of which he was ably assisted by Dr. Robert Fletcher. The first volume appeared in 1880 . . . One volume of the *Index Catalogue* including about one thousand pages royal octavo appeared each year thereafter until 1895, when the sixteen volumes had been printed and Billings, retiring from the service, left his successors to produce a second series, 1896-1916, even

more voluminous, and to begin upon a third. In 1879 the *Index Medicus*, planned by Billings and Fletcher as a monthly guide to current medical literature and a companion publication to the *Index Catalogue*, began to appear, and it was continued without a break until after the retirement of Billings in 1895 . . .

"As Billings in 1873 was beginning his work at cataloguing and indexing the Surgeon-General's Library, Johns Hopkins of Baltimore died, leaving a generous endowment for a great hospital. The trustees asked five experts in hospital construction to submit sketch plans for the construction, heating, ventilation, and administration of the proposed group of buildings. The plans of Billings were accepted . . .

"Perhaps the greatest change in medicine during the present generation has been a shift in emphasis from curative to preventive medicine, from caring for the individual patient to caring for community health; in this change Billings was a pioneer. He was one of the original members of the American Public Health Association which was formed in 1872 and to that organization he gave much time and energy. In 1878 a report which it received about the recent alarming epidemics of yellow fever was referred to a committee of which he was chairman . . . A few months later the wide alarm over the ravages of yellow fever resulted in the creation of a National Board of Health mainly to aid localities menaced or decimated by that pestilence. Billings was made its vice-chairman and proved most efficient first in confining the disease to Memphis, where it had gained headway, and then in crushing it at that focal point. This victory was a main cause of his election the following year to the presidency of the American Public Health Association . . .

"Five years before the date upon which Billings was to retire from active duty in the army, the University of Pennsylvania with the permission of the Surgeon-General appointed him director of its University Hospital and professor of hygiene; after his retirement he removed to Philadelphia to give himself more fully to these duties. One year later, however, after securing the reluctant consent of the University authorities, he resigned to accept a greater and more congenial task in New York City where the remaining seventeen years of his life were spent. Three libraries and library endowments in that city, the Astor, Lenox, and Tilden foundations, were consolidated in 1895 by common agreement and with the hope that a library worthy to be compared with the best in Europe might result from the union . . . Of the New York Public Library as it stands to-day he was 'in a very real sense the creator.'

It now contains more than 3,000,000 books and pamphlets.

"In his last eleven years Billings was active in the organization and guidance of the Carnegie Institution of Washington, designed to encourage research, especially in the fields of pure and applied science . . .

"Billings was married on Sept. 3, 1862, at Georgetown, D. C. to Katharine Mary Stevens . . ."

He died on Mar. 11, 1913.

> Condensed from W. F. W., *Dictionary of American Biography*, Vol. II.

* * *

A Report on Barracks and Hospitals, with Descriptions of Military Posts. *Washington, D. C.,* 1870.

Report on the Hygiene of the U. S. Army. *Washington, D. C.,* 1875.

Johns Hopkins Hospital. Reports and Papers Relating to Construction and Organization. [Baltimore, 1876.]

Medical Education. Extracts from Lectures Delivered Before the Johns Hopkins University, Baltimore, 1877-8. *Baltimore,* 1878.

Medical Bibliography. *Baltimore,* 1883.

The Principles of Ventilation and Heating, and Their Application. *New York,* 1884.

Description of the Johns Hopkins Hospital. *Baltimore,* 1890.

BINFORD, JOHN H.: 1844–1912.

Born in 1844, John H. Binford was a teacher and later a lawyer in Greenfield, Ind. He died in 1912.

> Information from the Greenfield Public Library.

* * *

History of Hancock County, Indiana, from Its Earliest Settlement by the "Pale Face," in 1818, Down to 1882 . . . *Greenfield, Ind.,* 1882.

BINGHAM, KATE BOYLES (MRS. ?): 1876–

Kate Boyles, daughter of Judge Samuel A. and Martha Jane Dillin Boyles of Dubois County, Ind., was born in 1876.

In collaboration with her brother, Virgil Dillin Boyles, she wrote several successful novels.

> Information from the Indianapolis Public Library.

* * *

Langford of the Three Bars (with Virgil Boyles). *Chicago,* 1907.

The Homesteaders (with Virgil Boyles). *Chicago,* 1909.

The Spirit Trail (with Virgil Boyles). *Chicago,* 1910.

The Hoosier Volunteer (with Virgil Boyles). *Chicago,* 1914.

A Daughter of the Badlands (with Virgil Boyles). *Boston,* 1922.

BIRGE, EDWARD BAILEY: 1868–

Edward Bailey Birge, son of Edward and Cornelia M. Day Birge, was born in Northampton, Mass., on June 12, 1868, and graduated from Brown University in 1891. In 1904 he received the Mus.B. degree from Yale University. He married Mary Thompson on June 20, 1901.

From 1896 to 1901 he was supervisor of music for the state normal schools at New Haven and New Britain, Conn. He came to Indianapolis in 1901 as director of public school music, a position he held until 1921, when he became professor of music at Indiana University. From 1911 to 1921 he was also superintendent of the American Institute of Normal Methods at Evanston, Ill.

He organized the People's Chorus at Indianapolis in 1912 and served as director until 1921. He was editor of the school music department of MUSICIAN and chairman of the editorial board of MUSIC EDUCATOR'S JOURNAL. In addition to the books listed below, he was the composer of concert overtures, choruses, etc., and an editor and compiler of song books.

> Information from *Who's Who in America.*

* * *

W. Birge Earhart. *Boston,* 1915.

Progressive Music Series (with Osbourne McConathy and W. O. Miessner). *New York,* 1924.

Music Hour Series (with Osbourne McConathy). *New York,* 1927. 8 vols.

History of Public School Music in the United States. *Boston,* 1928.

BLACK, ANNA ROBINSON: ?–

Anna Robinson Black was a resident of Terre Haute, Ind., in the Nineties and early Nineteen Hundreds.

> Information from the Emmeline Fairbanks Memorial Library, Terre Haute, Ind.

* * *

Hoosier Girl Abroad; A Diary of Seventy-Seven Days Attending the World's Fourth Sunday School Convention in Jerusalem, 1904. *Terre Haute, Ind.,* 1904.

BLACK, WILLIAM HENRY: 1854–1930.

William Henry Black, son of the Rev. Felix G. and Lydia K. Frederick Black, was born at Centerville, Ind., on Mar. 19, 1854. He graduated from Waynesburg (Pa.) College in 1876, receiving the A.M. degree in 1879, and graduated from Western Theological Seminary in 1878. In 1888 he received the D.D. degree from Cumberland University, in 1903 the LL.D. from Westminster College, and in 1915 the Litt.D. from Waynesburg College. He married Mary Ella Henderson on Apr. 3, 1879.

Ordained to the Presbyterian ministry in 1876, he served as pastor at Pittsburgh from 1877 to 1881 and at St. Louis from 1881 to 1890. After 1890 he was president of Missouri Valley College.

Dr. Black died on June 22, 1930, at Marshall, Mo.

Information from *Who Was Who in America.*

* * *

Sermons for the Sabbath School. 1886.
God Our Father. *Nashville, Tenn.,* 1891.
Womanhood. *Nashville, Tenn.,* 1891.
Outline Life of Paul. 1894.
The Life and Times of Moses. 1901.
The Hebrew Monarchy—a Harmony. 1902.
The Life of Jesus: Tripaschal. 1906.
The Division and Fall of the Hebrew Monarchy—A Harmony. 1910.

BLACKALL, EMILY LUCAS (MRS. CHRISTOPHER R.): 1832–1892.

Emily Lucas was born in Salem, Ind., in 1832. She became the second wife of Christopher Rubey Blackall, a newspaper editor, in 1873. She died in New York in 1892.

Information from sketch of Christopher Rubey Blackall in *Who Was Who in America.*

* * *

Superior to Circumstances. *Boston,* 1889.
Stories About Jesus (with C. R. Blackall). *Philadelphia,* 1890.
Won and Not One. *Philadelphia,* 1891.

BLACKBURN, WILLIAM MAXWELL: 1828–1898.

"William Maxwell Blackburn, author and educator, was born at Carlisle, Ind., Dec. 30, 1828, son of Alexander and Deliah (Polk) Blackburn . . . He re-

ceived his early education in district schools and in an academy at La Porte, Ind., and taught at similar institutions previous to entering . . . Hanover College, where he was graduated, June, 1850. He then studied for the Presbyterian ministry at Princeton Theological Seminary from 1850 to 1854, and after completing his course held pastorates at Three Rivers, Mich., Erie, Pa., Trenton, N. J., Chicago, Ill., and Cincinnati, O. Beginning in his early ministry by contributions to the PRINCETON REVIEW, he occupied his leisure continuously with writing; and while preaching and administering the affairs of his pastorates he became known both in America and England, first, as a successful author of Sunday-school books, and later for works on subjects of wider interest. In 1868, the position was offered him of professor of biblical and ecclesiastical history in what is now McCormick Theological Seminary at Chicago . . . He accepted and filled the chair until 1881. From 1884 until 1886, he was president of the Territorial University of North Dakota, and later was appointed president of Pierre University, at East Pierre, S. D., which, in 1898, was removed to Huron, S. D.

"He received the honorary degree of D.D., from Princeton in 1870 and that of LL.D. from Wooster University . . .

"Dr. Blackburn was married in 1854 at Valparaiso, Ind., to Elizabeth Powell . . ."

Dr. Blackburn died at Huron, S. D., on Dec. 29, 1898.

Condensed from *The National Encyclopedia of American Biography,* Vol. 9.

* * *

Uncle Alick's Stories. (A series of juveniles listed separately below) *Philadelphia.*
The Early Watermelons; or, Alick Never Afraid of the Truth.
Alick and His Blind Uncle.
Cherry-Bounce; or, Wise Management of Human Nature.
My Dog Rover, and Some Good That He Did in the World.
Teddy, the Bill-Poster, and How He Became Uncle Alick's Right-Hand Man.
Uncle Alick's Sabbath School.
Aonio Palearío and His Friends. *Philadelphia.*
The Holy Child: or, Early Years of Jesus Christ. *Philadelphia.*
Exiles of Madeira. *Philadelphia,* 1862.
Judas the Maccabee and the Asmonian Princess. *Philadelphia,* 1864.

The Rebel Prince, or, Lessons from the Career of the Young Man Absalom. *Philadelphia* [1864].

William Farel, and the Story of the Swiss Reform. *Philadelphia,* 1865.

The Crime Against the Presidency. A Sermon, Delivered Sunday, April 16, 1865, in the Fourth Presbyterian Church, Trenton, New Jersey . . . *Trenton, N. J.,* 1865.

The College Days of Calvin. *Philadelphia,* 1866.

Young Calvin in Paris, and the Little Flock That He Fed. *Philadelphia,* 1866.

Geneva's Shield: Story of the Swiss Reformation. *New York,* 1868.

The Nevers, a Numerous Family. *Boston,* 1868.

Ulrich Zwingli, the Patriotic Reformer. *Philadelphia,* 1868.

St. Patrick and the Early Church of Ireland. *Philadelphia,* 1869.

Admiral Coligny and the Rise of the Huguenots. *Philadelphia* [1869]. 2 vols.

The Theban Legion. *Philadelphia,* 1871.

The Ancient Schoolmaster, and the Greatest School of Old Times. *Philadelphia.*

The Curious Chapter, and How Its Prophecies Were Fulfilled by the Young King Josiah. *Philadelphia.*

The Benefits of Christ's Death.

Vow at the Bars. *New York.*

History of the Christian Church from Its Origin to the Present Time. *New York,* 1880.

Colleges of the New West . . . Introduction by Herrick Johnson. *Chicago,* 1896.

BLAICH, LYDIA REBECCA: 1870–1933.

Lydia Rebecca Blaich was born in Indianapolis in 1870. She was educated in the local schools and at the University of Chicago, with graduate work and advanced degrees from several other institutions. She studied German educational methods on a fellowship at Jena in 1909-10.

Miss Blaich served as a teacher and administrator in the Indianapolis public schools throughout most of her career. She died in that city in February, 1933. Besides the works listed she was the author of at least one textbook.

Information from the Indiana State Library.

* * *

A Report on Observations of Education in Germany, Made in the Winter of 1909-10. *Indianapolis,* 1910.

Three Industrial Nations; An Industrial Geography of England, Germany, and the United States. *New York,* 1915.

BLAKE, MARY KATHARINE EVANS (MRS. WILLIAM MCKENDREE): 1859–1923.

Born in Rockport, Ind., in 1859, Mary Katharine Evans, daughter of Joseph Smith and Mary Catherine Cotton Evans, was educated at Rockport Collegiate Institute. She married William McKendree Blake on Aug. 28, 1876. For a number of years she was engaged in newspaper work in Washington, D. C., and later lived in Minneapolis, Minn. She died in Indianapolis in 1923.

Information from *Who's Who in America.*

* * *

Heart's Haven. *Indianapolis,* 1905.

The Stuff of a Man. *Indianapolis,* 1908.

BLAND, THOMAS AUGUSTUS: 1830–?

Thomas Augustus Bland, son of Thomas Bland, was born in Bloomfield, Ind., on May 21, 1830. His father came to Indiana in 1817 and farmed until 1850, when he moved to Illinois. Young Thomas was educated in the county schools and studied medicine at the Eclectic Medical College in Cincinnati. In 1852 he married Mary Cornelia Davis.

During the Civil War he served as a surgeon in the Union Army, in 1864 became editor of the HOME VISITOR, a literary weekly published at Indianapolis, and in 1865 established the NORTHWESTERN FARMER. He sold the latter paper in 1871 and moved to Chicago, where he became editor of the SCIENTIFIC FARMER. Two years later he moved the magazine to New York. In 1878 he located in Washington, D. C. His wife assisted him in editing the magazines and herself established and edited the LADIES OWN MAGAZINE.

Information from *Representative Men of Indiana,* Vol. I.

* * *

Farming as a Profession. *Boston,* 1870.

History of New England (joint author). *Boston,* 1875.

The Spartan Band. *Washington, D. C.,* 1879.

Life of General B. F. Butler. *Boston,* 1879.

How to Grow Rich. *Washington, D. C.,* 1881.

The Reign of Monopoly. *Washington, D. C.,* 1881.

Life of Alfred B. Meacham. *Washington, D. C.,* 1883.

People's Party Shot and Shell. *Chicago,* 1892.

Esau; or, The Banker's Victim. *Washington, D. C.,* 1892.

How to Get Well and How to Keep Well. *Boston,* 1894.

"In the World Celestial." *New York,* 1901.

The Great Thinkers.

American Medical Union, a History of Its Origin, Principles, Purposes and Progress. *Chicago, 1902.*

Pioneers of Progress. *Chicago, 1906.*

BLATCHLEY, WILLIS STANLEY: 1859–1940.

Willis Stanley Blatchley, scientist and author, was born at North Madison, Conn., in 1859. In 1860 his family came to Hendricks County, Ind., where he received his early education. He graduated from Indiana University in 1887 with the A.B. degree and received the A.M. degree from the same institution in 1891 and the LL.D. in 1921. In 1882 he married Clara A. Fordice of Russellville, Ind.

Before becoming state geologist of Indiana (1894-1911), he taught in the Terre Haute High School. Mr. Blatchley was the author of hundreds of papers on geology and entomology. From 1911 until his death he traveled extensively, was a member of scientific expeditions, and wrote many books on geology and natural history.

He died on May 28, 1940.

> Information from *Who's Who in America;* Dunn —*Indiana and Indianans,* and from the Indianapolis Public Library.

* * *

Gleanings from Nature. *Indianapolis, 1899.*

A Nature Wooing at Ormond by the Sea. *Indianapolis, 1902.*

The Petroleum Industry of Southeastern Illinois. *Urbana, Ill., 1906.*

Boulder Reveries. *Indianapolis, 1906.*

Mineral Production of Illinois in 1908. *Urbana, Ill., 1909.*

Coleoptera of Indiana. *Indianapolis, 1910.*

The Indiana Weed Book. *Indianapolis, 1912.*

Woodland Idyls. *Indianapolis, 1912.*

Rhynchophora or Weevils of North Eastern America (with Charles W. Lang). *Indianapolis, 1916.*

Orthoptera of Northeastern America; With Especial Reference to the Faunas of Indiana and Florida. *Indianapolis, 1920.*

Heteroptera or True Bugs of Eastern North America; With Especial Reference to the Faunas of Indiana and Florida. *Indianapolis, 1926.*

Blatchleyana; A List of Published Writings . . . Together with a Chronology of His Life: The Fixation of Types of New Genera and Species Described by Him. *Indianapolis, 1930.*

My Nature Nook; or, Notes on the Natural History of the Vicinity of Dunedin, Florida. *Indianapolis, 1931.*

In Days Agone; Notes on the Fauna and Flora of Subtropical Florida in the Days When Most of Its Area Was a Primeval Wilderness. *Indianapolis, 1932.*

South America as I Saw It; The Observations of a Naturalist on the Living Conditions of Its Common People; Its Topography and Products; Its Animals and Plants. *Indianapolis, 1934.*

Fishes of Indiana, with Descriptions, Notes on Habits and Distribution in the State. *Indianapolis, 1938.*

BOBBITT, JOHN FRANKLIN: 1876–

Born in southern Indiana on Feb. 16, 1876, John Franklin Bobbitt graduated from Indiana University in 1901 and received the Ph.D. degree from Clark University in 1909. He married Mabel Deiwert.

From 1893 to 1902 he was a teacher in rural and village schools, from 1902 to 1909 in the Philippine Normal School at Manila, and after 1909 was associated with the University of Chicago, serving as professor of education from 1918 to 1941. Mr. Bobbitt was a director of numerous school surveys.

> Information from *Who's Who in America.*

* * *

Growth of Philippine Children. *Worcester, Mass., 1909.*

San Antonio Public School System: A Survey. *San Antonio, Tex., 1915.*

What the Schools Teach and Might Teach. *Cleveland, O., 1915.*

The Curriculum. *Boston, 1918.*

Curriculum-Making in Los Angeles. *Chicago, 1922.*

How to Make a Curriculum. *Boston, 1924.*

Curriculum Investigations (with others). *Chicago, 1926.*

Patty, William L. Study of Mechanism in Education. *New York, 1938.*

The Curriculum of Modern Education. *New York, 1941.*

BOETCKER, WILLIAM JOHN HENRY: 1873–

William J. H. Boetcker was born in Altona (Elbe), Germany, on July 17, 1873, the son of William M. E. and Wilhelmina Christlieb Boetcker. He was educated in the local gymnasium, the Royal Christianeum at Altona and the theological seminary at Brecklum, Germany. After coming to the U. S. he attended the Chicago Theological Seminary, a seminary at Bloomfield, N. J. and New York University. He became a Presbyterian minister, later devoting himself to adult educational pursuits.

On Nov. 6, 1899, he married Anna Emilie Albrecht. They made their home in Shelbyville, Ind.

He had published his first book in Germany when he was sixteen, and he continued writing in the U. S. Not listed here are his numerous pamphlets, titled

Mental Antidote and designed to be of an inspirational nature, which are signed "T. I. A. Nutshell."

Information from *Indianapolis and Vicinity.*

* * *

Raeselshatz. (*Germany*) 1889.
Picturesque Shelbyville. *Shelbyville, Ind.,* 1902.
Sermon and Text Register.

BOLLMAN, LEWIS: 1811–1888.

Born in Williamsport, Pa., on May 11, 1811, Lewis Bollman graduated from Indiana University in 1831 and received the LL.B. degree in 1846. A lawyer, reporter, and farmer, he originated the plan for the Ohio & Mississippi Railroad and the P.V. & C.R. Railroad. He died in Bloomington, Ind., on Oct. 3, 1888.

Information from The University Libraries, Indiana University.

* * *

The Industrial Colleges. n.p., n.d.
The State University of Indiana; The Causes of Its Want of Prosperity Considered. *Indianapolis,* 1882.
A Month at Mr. Johnstone's.

BOLTON, NATHANIEL: ?–1858.

Because of his own modesty in the matter of signing his newspaper stories and because of the fame of his wife as a pioneer Indiana writer, Nathaniel Bolton was doomed to be known chiefly as "Sarah T. Bolton's husband." That he had distinguished attributes of his own is attested by John Henry Byrne Nowland's sketch of his career in the book, *Sketches of Prominent Citizens of 1876.*

The INDIANAPOLIS GAZETTE, of which Bolton was co-owner, was the first newspaper published in Indianapolis and operated the first job printing establishment. It began publication in January, 1822, the month after Bolton arrived in the town. Nowland says of Bolton:

". . . He was born in Chillicothe, O., and came to this place with his step-father and partner, George Smith, in December, 1821, when quite a young man. After Mr. Smith had retired from the GAZETTE, Mr. Bolton continued the paper alone and then with different partners for some time. In the meantime he was married to Miss Sarah T. Barrett, of Madison, now well known as one of Indiana's most gifted daughters. Although a very talented lady, she lost nothing in that way by her connection with Mr. B., but had a great deal to gain . . . He was a ready writer, and wrote most of the articles for the GAZETTE over fictitious signatures, besides writing the leading editorials.

"About the second year of the administration of President Pierce he was appointed Consul to Geneva, and remained there until President Buchanan's administration, when he was compelled on account of his health to resign and return home. He arrived at home in May, and died the next November . . ."

Nathaniel Bolton also occupied the position of State Librarian for a time, was a member of the Indiana legislature, and was a leader in the early development of Indianapolis almost from its beginning.

Information from Nowland—*Sketches of Prominent Citizens of 1876* and the Indianapolis Public Library.

* * *

A Lecture Delivered Before the Indiana Historical Society, on the Early History of Indianapolis and Central Indiana . . . the 31st of January, 1853. *Indianapolis,* 1853. (Reissued in 1897 as The Early History of Indianapolis and Central Indiana.)

BOLTON, SARAH TITTLE BARRETT: 1814–1893.

Born in Newport, Ky., Dec. 18, 1814, the daughter of Jonathan Belcher and Esther Pendleton Barrett, Sarah T. Barrett as a child moved with her family to Madison, Ind. She began to write poetry at an early age, and her contributions to the Madison newspaper led to her acquaintance with its editor, Nathaniel Bolton, and their subsequent marriage.

A year later they moved to Indianapolis, where he was founder of the INDIANAPOLIS GAZETTE. Mrs. Bolton continued to write poetry, contributing to newspapers and to the HOME JOURNAL. She also had a number of songs published. During the Forties and Fifties she was poet laureate of Indiana. She also engaged actively in public affairs, assisting Robert Dale Owen in his campaign for women's property rights. During the administration of President Pierce she accompanied her husband to Geneva, where he was United States Consul.

About five years after Nathaniel Bolton's death, which occurred in 1858, Sarah T. Bolton married Judge Addison Reese of Missouri, but she used the name of Reese only for business purposes. She died in Indianapolis on Aug. 4, 1893.

Information from the *Dictionary of American Biography*, Vol. II; Dunn—*Indiana and Indianans;* Esarey—*History of Indiana;* THE INDIANA MAGAZINE OF HISTORY, Vol. 8; Kunitz and Haycraft—*American Authors 1600-1900;* and the Indianapolis Public Library.

* * *

Poems. *New York,* 1865.

The Life and Poems of Sarah T. Bolton. *Indianapolis,* 1880.

Songs of a Life-Time. Edited by John Clark Ridpath. With an Introduction by General Lew Wallace and a Poem by James Whitcomb Riley. *Indianapolis,* 1892.

Paddle Your Own Canoe, and Other Poems. *Indianapolis.,* n.d. [1897].

BOOK, JOHN WILLIAM: 1850–?

John William Book was born near Starlight, Ind., on Oct. 21, 1850. He was the son of William and Mary Engel Book, emigrants to Clark County, Ind., from Germany in 1846.

John William Book was educated in local schools, St. Meinrad's Academy and St. Joseph's College (Ky.). He was ordained a priest of the Roman Catholic Church in 1873 and later had charge of churches in Rockport and Cannelton, Ind.

Information from the *National Cyclopedia of American Biography,* Vol. 7.

* * *

Short Lines to the Roman Catholic Church, 1888.

Side Switches of the Short Line (with Rev. Thomas J. Jenkins). 1892.

Thousand and One Objections to Secret Societies. 1893.

Mollie's Mistake; or Mixed Marriages. n.p. 1894.

The Book of Books.

BOOK, WILLIAM FREDERICK: 1873–1940.

William Frederick Book, son of Christian Henry and Mary Elizabeth Bussdicker Book, was born in Princeton, Ind., on June 10, 1873. He graduated from Indiana University in 1900, receiving the Ph.D. degree from Clark University in 1906. He also studied at the University of Chicago and at Columbia. After the death of his first wife, Mary Roach Cougle, whom he married in 1907, he married Clara D. King, on June 3, 1926.

From 1906 to 1912 he was a professor of psychology at the University of Montana, in 1912-13 he was pro-

fessor of educational psychology at Indiana University, and from 1913 to 1917 he was director of vocational education in Indiana. After 1917 he was a member of the faculty of Indiana University as professor of psychology and director of the Psychological Laboratory. He lectured at other universities and was editor of the JOURNAL OF APPLIED PSYCHOLOGY.

Information from *Who Was Who in America.*

* * *

The Psychology of Skill with Special Reference to Its Acquisition in Typewriting. *Missoula, Mont.,* 1908.

Suggestions for the Study of Vocational Education in Township Institutes. *Indianapolis,* 1914.

The Intelligence of High School Seniors as Revealed by a State-Wide Mental Survey of Indiana High Schools. *New York,* 1922.

The Will to Learn. 1925.

Learning to Typewrite—With a Discussion of the Psychology and Pedagogy of Skill. *New York,* 1925.

How to Succeed in College. *Baltimore,* 1927.

Learning How to Study and Work Effectively; A Contribution to the Psychology of Personal Efficiency. *Boston,* 1926.

Economy and Technique of Learning. *Boston,* 1932.

BOOK, WILLIAM HENRY: 1863–1946.

William Henry Book was born at Newcastle, Va., in 1863.

He attended Milligan College (Tenn.) and received the A.B. and A.M. degrees. He held various pastorates in the Church of Christ, concluding his active career in the pulpit with twenty years of service as pastor of the Tabernacle Church of Christ, Columbus, Ind.

During these twenty years he acted as editor and contributor to several religious publications. After leaving his charge in Columbus he became an evangelist but continued to make his home in that city. For a time he was a trustee of Butler University.

Information from William Book (his son).

* * *

Real Life and Original Sayings of William Henry Book. *Cincinnati,* 1900.

The Columbus Tabernacle Sermons. *Cincinnati* [1909-1913]. 2 vols.

Where Are Our Dead? *Columbus, Ind.* [1910].

Sermons for the People. *Cincinnati,* 1918.

BOOKWALTER, JOHN WESLEY: 1837–1915.

Born in Rob Roy, Ind., in 1837, John Wesley Bookwalter was reared on a farm and taught in the country schools. He married a daughter of James Leffel, manufacturer of turbine engines, and became his partner and later principal owner of the business. He was an unsuccessful candidate for the governorship of the state of Ohio. A resident of Springfield, O., Mr. Bookwalter was the owner of a famous art collection.

Information from *Who's Who in America.*

* * *

If Not Silver, What? *Springfield, O.,* 1896.
Siberia and Central Asia. *Springfield, O.,* 1899.
Rural Versus Urban; Their Conflict and Its Causes. *New York,* 1910.

BOONE, RICHARD GAUSE: 1849–1923.

Born at Spiceland, Ind., on Sept. 9, 1849, Richard Gause Boone, son of Driver and Elizabeth Cooper Boone, was graduated from the Spiceland Academy in 1871 and later received degrees from De Pauw University and from Ohio University. During his career as an educator he was superintendent of schools at Frankfort, Ind., professor at Indiana University, president of Michigan Normal College, superintendent of schools at Cincinnati; and a lecturer on education at the University of California. He married Mary E. Stanley in 1874. He died in 1923.

Information from *Who Was Who in America* and the Indianapolis Public Library.

* * *

Education in the United States; Its History from the Earliest Settlements. *New York,* 1889.
Outline to Accompany "Leonard and Gertrude." *Boston,* 1891.
A History of Education in Indiana. *New York,* 1892.
Science of Education. *New York,* 1904.

BOOTH, NEWTON: 1825–1892.

Newton Booth, son of Beebe and Hannah Pitts Booth and uncle of Booth Tarkington, was born in Salem, Ind., on Dec. 25, 1825. He was educated in the common schools and graduated from Indiana Asbury (now De Pauw) University in 1846.

After studying law at Terre Haute, he was admitted to the bar in 1850 and in the same year went to California, where he located at Sacramento and was in the wholesale grocery business until 1857. He then returned to Terre Haute and practiced law until 1860, when he returned to California and opened a law office there.

He was interested in literature and history and in 1862 began to contribute articles to the SACRAMENTO UNION. His support of the Union cause and devotion to the Republican Party led to his election to the state senate in 1863. He helped carry California for Grant in 1868. In 1871 he was elected governor of California on an independent ticket, but he resigned the office in 1875 after his election to the U. S. Senate. Following his term in the Senate he engaged in commercial occupations in California.

He married Mrs. J. T. Glover on Feb. 29, 1892, and died at Sacramento on July 14, 1892.

Information from Dunn—*Indiana and Indianans*; Appletons' *Cyclopaedia of American Biography,* Vol. I; and the *Dictionary of American Biography,* Vol. II.

* * *

Spiritual; A Lecture Delivered in . . . Sacramento, October 28, 1863. *Sacramento, Calif.,* 1865.
Newton Booth of California, His Speeches and Addresses (Edited by Lauren E. Crane). *New York,* 1894.

BORNTREGER, JOHN E.: 1837–1930.

John E. Borntreger, northern Indiana Amish teacher and minister, was born in Somerset County, Pa., on Oct. 9, 1837. His parents brought him to the northern Indiana Amish colony while he was a small child.

He received his education in the local schools (with, perhaps, some time in educational institutions maintained by the church) and taught in public schools. He married Barbara Mishler.

In 1871, at the age of thirty-four, he was ordained a minister of the Old Order Amish Mennonite Church, which he served until his death in 1930.

Information from Eli J. Bontreger [sic], son, and Goshen College.

* * *

Eine Geschichte der Ersten Ansiedlung der Amischen Mennoniten und Die Gründung Ihrer Ersten Gemeinde im Staate Indiana, Nebst Einer Kurzen Erklaerung Über Die Spatung Die in Dieser Gemeinde Geschehen Ist. *Elkhart, Ind.,* 1907.
Was der Einflusz Einer Mutter Vollbringen Kann. 1914.

BOWERS, CLAUDE GERNADE: 1878–

Claude Gernade Bowers, ambassador and author, was born in Hamilton County, Ind., on Nov. 20, 1878, the son of Lewis and Juliet Bowers. He was educated in the public schools and under private tutors and received honorary degrees from various colleges and universities.

In 1901 and 1902 he was an editorial writer for the INDIANAPOLIS SENTINEL, from 1903 to 1906 for the TERRE HAUTE STAR, and from 1917 to 1923 he served as editor of the FORT WAYNE JOURNAL GAZETTE. In 1923 he went to New York as an editorial writer for the NEW YORK WORLD, a position he held until 1931, when he became a political columnist for the NEW YORK JOURNAL.

While a resident of Terre Haute, Ind., Mr. Bowers became interested in politics. He was a candidate for Congress from the Terre Haute district, a member of the Bureau of Public Improvements, and a delegate to the 1908 Democratic National Convention. From 1911 to 1917 he served as secretary to Senator John W. Kern. He delivered the keynote address at the Democratic National Convention at Houston, Tex., in 1928. From 1933 to 1939 he was ambassador extraordinary and plenipotentiary to Spain, and in 1939 he became ambassador to Chile.

Information from *Who's Who in America.*

* * *

The Democracy of Woodrow Wilson. *Washington, D. C.*
The Irish American. *Washington, D. C.*
Irish Orators; A History of Ireland's Fight for Freedom. *Indianapolis, 1916.*
Life of John Worth Kern. *Indianapolis, 1918.*
The Party Battles of the Jackson Period. *Boston, 1922.*
Jefferson and Hamilton—The Struggle for Democracy in America. *Boston, 1925.*
Founders of the Republic. *Chicago, 1927.*
The Tragic Era—The Revolution After Lincoln. *Boston, 1929.*
Civil and Religious Liberty; Jefferson; O'Connell. *Worcester, Mass., 1930.*
Beveridge and the Progressive Era. *Boston, 1932.*
Jefferson in Power—The Death Struggle of the Federalists. *Boston, 1936.*
Spanish Adventures of Washington Irving. *Boston, 1940.*
The Young Jefferson. *Boston, 1945.*

BOWLES, JANET PAYNE (MRS. J. M.): ?–

Mrs. Janet Payne Bowles, member of the faculty of Shortridge High School, Indianapolis, was born in Indianapolis and graduated from Shortridge High School. For a time she studied piano in Boston, then married J. M. Bowles of Indianapolis, founder of the magazine, MODERN ART. She became interested in metal jewelry and began to teach its design, metal-smithing and pottery-making.

Information from the Indianapolis Public Library.

* * *

Complete Story of the Christmas Tree. *New York, 1916.*
Gossamer to Steel. *New York, 1917.*

BOYD, JACKSON: 1861–1920.

Jackson Boyd was born in Putnam County, Ind., in 1861. He was a lawyer, a widely known writer, and a member of the Indiana State Legislature. He died at his home in Greencastle, Ind., on Mar. 16, 1920.

Information from the Greencastle Public Library and the Indiana State Library.

* * *

The Unveiling; A Poetic Drama in Five Acts. *New York, 1915.*
The Human Situation in Nature. *Chicago, 1921.*

BOYD, LOUISE ESTHER VICKROY (MRS. SAMUEL S.): 1827–?

Louise Esther Vickroy was born in Urbana, O., on Jan. 22, 1827. She began to write at an early age, and by the middle of the Nineteenth century she was a popular contributor, especially of verse, to GRAHAM'S MAGAZINE, APPLETON'S JOURNAL, THE KNICKERBOCKER MAGAZINE, and other currently popular periodicals.

Shortly after the Civil War she married Dr. Samuel S. Boyd, and they removed to Dublin, Ind., making their home in this state for more than twenty-five years.

Her popularity as a writer continued, and she added the CENTURY and SCRIBNER'S MAGAZINE, HARPER'S YOUNG PEOPLE, THE WOMAN'S JOURNAL, COUNTRY LIFE IN AMERICA and others to the list of periodicals to which she contributed. Before her death she returned to Ohio.

Information from Parker and Heiney—*Poets and Poetry of Indiana.*

* * *

Twelve Portraits of the French Revolution.

Twilight Stories for Little People. 1869.
Poems of Louise Vickroy Boyd (Edited by Esther Griffin White). *Richmond, Ind., 1911.*
Alabama in the Fifties.
Women Citizens.

BOYLES, VIRGIL DILLIN: 1872–

Virgil Dillin Boyles, son of Judge Samuel A. and Martha Jane Dillin Boyles, of Dubois County, Ind., was born in 1872.

With his sister, Mrs. Kate Boyles Bingham, he wrote several successful novels.

Information from the Indianapolis Public Library.

* * *

Langford of the Three Bars (with Kate Boyles Bingham). *Chicago, 1907.*
The Homesteaders (with Kate Boyles Bingham). *Chicago, 1909.*
The Spirit Trail (with Kate Boyles Bingham). *Chicago, 1910.*
The Hoosier Volunteer (with Kate Boyles Bingham). *Chicago, 1914.*
A Daughter of the Badlands (with Kate Boyles Bingham). *Boston, 1922.*
Where the Sod Shanty Stood. *Mitchell, S. D., 1926.*

BRANHAM, ADELIA POPE: 1861–1917.

Adelia Pope Branham was born in Greenfield, Ind., in 1861 and spent her entire life in that community, dying there in January, 1917. She wrote verse, short stories and essays for the periodical press.

Information from the Greenfield Public Library.

* * *

Grandma Tales and Others. *Greenfield, Ind., 1899.*
April Showers.
Daughter of April. *New York, 1903.*

BRANIGIN, ELBA L.: 1870–

Elba L. Branigin, son of William D. and Nancy Lash Branigin, was born in Johnson County, Ind., on Nov. 12, 1870.

He attended local schools and entered Franklin College in 1886, graduating with the class of 1892. His family, meanwhile, had moved to Franklin.

He taught in county schools and read law. In 1894 he married Zula Francis.

In 1896 he was admitted to the Johnson County bar and formed a partnership with Thomas W. Woollen. He was active in civic and political affairs and served as a trustee and attorney for Franklin College.

Information from Branigin—*History of Johnson County.*

* * *

History of Johnson County, Indiana. *Indianapolis, 1913.*

BRANNON, MELVIN AMOS: 1865–

Melvin Amos Brannon, son of James and Eleanor Foster Brannon, was born in Lowell, Ind., in 1865. He was educated at Wabash College, receiving the A.B. degree in 1889 and the A.M. in 1890, and was a student at the Marine Biological Laboratory, Woods Hole, Mass., from 1891 to 1894. In 1912 he received the Ph.D. degree from the University of Chicago.

After teaching at Wabash College and in the Fort Wayne (Ind.) High School, he went to the University of North Dakota in 1894 as professor of biology. In 1905 he organized the School of Medicine at the university, and in 1911 he became dean of the College of Liberal Arts. From 1914 to 1917 he was president of the University of Idaho, from 1917 to 1923 president of Beloit College, and from 1923 to 1933 chancellor of the University of Montana.

Information from *Who's Who in America* and the Wabash College archives.

* * *

The Influence of Heat Upon the Maturation of Vegetables and Fruits.
The Salton Sea: The Action of Salton Sea Water on Vegetable Tissues . . . *Chicago, 1914.*
Some Biological Phenomena of a Dying Lake.
Effect of Growth Substances on Green Algae.

BRAY, JEREMIAH WESLEY: ?–

The only information available on Jeremiah Wesley Bray is that he was born in Nora, Ind., received the A.B. and A.M. degrees from Indiana University and was, for a time, principal of Plymouth (Ind.) High School.

Information from Federal Writers Project—*Indiana Authors, 1937.*

* * *

A History of English Critical Terms. *Boston, 1898.*
Dramatized Themes with Tableaux. *Chicago, 1899.*

BRAYTON, ALEMBERT WINTHROP: 1848–1926.

Alembert Winthrop Brayton, son of Elijah F. and Helen Parker Brayton, was born in Avon, N. Y., on Mar. 4, 1848. He was reared on a farm in Illinois and attended Chicago Normal School, from which he was graduated in 1869. In 1871-72 he was a student at Cornell University. After receiving the B.S. and M.S. degrees from Butler University and the M.D. from the Indiana Medical College, he served as a professor at the latter institution for many years. From 1892 to 1911 he was editor of the INDIANA MEDICAL JOURNAL. Dr. Brayton died in 1926.

Information from *Who Was Who in America.*

* * *

Fishes of the Southern Allegheny Region, with 20 Species New to Science (with David Starr Jordan).
Birds of Indiana. 1885.
Mammals of Ohio. 1886.

BREITWIESER, JOSEPH VALENTINE: 1884–

Joseph Valentine Breitwieser, son of John Conrad and Katherine Elizabeth Baitz Breitwieser, was born in Jasper, Ind., on Mar. 31, 1884, and graduated from Central Normal (now Canterbury) College in 1904. He received the A.B. and A.M. degrees from Indiana University in 1907 and 1908 and the Ph.D. from Columbia University in 1911. In 1910 he married Ruth Fowler.

After spending two years as a teacher in the public schools of Tipton, Ind., and another two years as an assistant in the psychology department at Indiana University, in 1910 he joined the faculty of Colorado College as an assistant professor of psychology and education, becoming a full professor in 1911 and serving until 1918. From 1918 to 1927 he was an associate professor of education at the University of California and after 1927 professor of education, director of the graduate division, director of summer sessions, and dean of the School of Education at the University of North Dakota.

Information from *Who's Who in America.*

* * *

Attention and Movement in Reaction Time. *New York,* 1911.
Psychological Experiments. *Colorado Springs,* 1914.
Psychological Advertising. *Colorado Springs,* 1915.
Psychological Effects of Altitude. 1917.

Psychological Education; A Presentation of the Principles and Applications of Educational Psychology. *New York,* 1926.

BRENGLE, SAMUEL LOGAN: 1860–1935.

Born at Fredericksburg, Ind., in 1860, Samuel Logan Brengle graduated from De Pauw University in 1883 and studied theology at Boston University. He married Elizabeth R. Swift in May of 1887. She died in 1915.

After serving as pastor of a Methodist Episcopal Church in South Bend, Ind., he joined the Salvation Army and in 1887 was sent to England to be trained. He returned to the U. S. in November and began his work at Taunton, Mass., later serving in Danbury, Conn., Boston, Portland, Me., Chicago, and New York. In 1926 he was appointed commissioner, being the first American to attain this rank.

He retired in 1931 and died at Scarsdale, N. Y., on May 20, 1935.

Information from The Salvation Army.

* * *

Heart-Talks on Holiness. *New York,* 1897.
Helps to Holiness. *New York,* 1901.
The Way of Holiness. *New York,* 1902.
The Soul-Winners Secret. *New York.*
When the Holy Ghost Is Come. *Chicago,* 1906.
Love-Slaves. 1923.
The Resurrection Life and Power. 1925.
Ancient Prophets. 1929.
Fifty Years Before and After.
The Consolation Wherewith He Was Comforted.
Save Little Children.
Retired.
The Atonement.
A Helpful Testimony.
God's Love and Understanding. *Grand Rapids, Mich.*
Guest of the Soul. *London,* 1936.

BRENNEMAN, DANIEL: 1834–1919.

Born near Bremen, O., on June 8, 1834, Daniel Brenneman began his ministry in the Mennonite Church in 1856.

He married Susanna Keagy, of Virginia, and after living about six years in Ohio, they moved to Elkhart County, Ind.

Daniel Brenneman was living in Goshen, Ind., at the time of his death in 1919.

Information from Brenneman—*Thoughts in Rhyme.*

* * *

Thoughts in Rhyme Consisting of Sacred Memories of Loved Ones Gone Before, to Which Are Added Reflections and Exhortations Upon Various Subjects. *Goshen, Ind.,* 1911.

BRENNEMAN, HENRY B.: 1831–1887.

Born in Fairfield County, O., on Aug. 12, 1831, Henry B. Brenneman served as a deacon in the Mennonite Church for twenty-three years. For several years, as "Brother Henry," he conducted the "Children's Column" in the HERALD OF TRUTH, a church publication. He married Matilda Blosser in 1850 and died at Elkhart, Ind., on Sept. 28, 1887.

Information from the Goshen College Library.

* * *

Gems of Truth for Children. A Series of Religious Instructions on Different Subjects: and Is Intended to Impress Upon the Minds of the Young, the Truths of the Scriptures. Written in Simple Language. *Elkhart, Ind.,* 1873.

The Little Visitor. A Holiday Paper for the Children. *Elkhart, Ind.*

BRIDGES, ALBERT FLETCHER: 1853–1926.

Albert Fletcher Bridges, son of Dillon Bridges, was born near Poland, Ind., on Aug. 22, 1853. He married Ada Craycraft on Dec. 25, 1870.

Following his graduation from De Pauw University in 1874, he entered the itinerant ministry of the Methodist Episcopal Church, retiring in 1881 to become editor and publisher of the BRAZIL REGISTER. The Rev. Mr. Bridges was a contributor to the NORTH AMERICAN REVIEW and other magazines. He and his wife endowed the chair of Romance Languages at De Pauw.

The latter part of his life was spent in Colorado Springs, Colo. He died in November, 1926.

Information from De Pauw University's *Alumnal Record, 1920* and an article in the BRAZIL ENTERPRISE, December 2, 1926.

* * *

History of St. Paul's Methodist Episcopal Church.

John B. Craft, Jr.; True Story of a Remarkable Reformation. *Brazil, Ind.,* 1889.

A Soldier's Farewell to His Old Flag. *Brazil, Ind.,* 1889.

A History of Brazil.

Poems. *Colorado Springs,* 1898.

History of Hendrix Chapel Methodist Episcopal Church.

The Epic of Life; Poems of a Lifetime. *Cincinnati,* n.d.

BRINGHURST, THOMAS HALL: 1819–1899.

Thomas Hall Bringhurst, son of Robert R. and Mary Wood Bringhurst, was born in Philadelphia on Aug. 20, 1819. After serving a five-year apprenticeship to a cabinet maker, he practiced his trade in Alabama and in Dayton, O., before moving to Logansport, Ind., in 1845, where he spent the remainder of his life.

In Logansport he engaged in the manufacture of lumber for several years. His business was interrupted, however, by one year's service in the Mexican War. In 1848 he established the LOGANSPORT JOURNAL, which he edited until 1870. During the Civil War he served as colonel of the 46th Indiana Infantry from 1861 until the close of the war.

From 1870 to 1876 he was a special agent in the Post Office Department, and in 1877 he became a partner in the Logansport Manufacturing Company, which manufactured spokes and other wood materials for wagons and carriages.

Mr. Bringhurst served as mayor of Logansport for three terms. He was married twice. He died on May 23, 1899.

Information from Powell *History of Cass County,* 1913, and THE INDIANIAN, Vol. IV, No. 6.

* * *

A History of the Forty-Sixth Regiment Indiana Volunteer Infantry. September, 1861, September, 1865. Compiled by Order of the Regimental Association (with Frank Swigart). n.p., 1888.

BRITAN, HALBERT HAINS: 1874–

Halbert Hains Britan, son of George Whitney and Mary Arbella Taylor Britan, was born in Bethlehem, Ind., on Oct. 8, 1874. He graduated from Hanover College in 1898, receiving the A.M. degree in 1902 and the Ph.D. degree from Yale University in 1902. On Aug. 1, 1907, he married Mary Edith Fisher. After 1905 he was professor of philosophy at Bates College. In addition to his books, he contributed articles to philosophical magazines.

Information from *Who's Who in America.*

* * *

Philosophy of Music: A Comparative Investigation into
the Principles of Musical Aesthetics. *New York, 1911.*
Affective Consciousness. *New York, 1931.*

BRITTS, MATTIE DYER (MRS. JAMES H.): 1842–?

Mattie Dyer, daughter of the Rev. Sidney M. Dyer,
was born on Nov. 23, 1842, in New York City and
was educated at the Baptist Seminary in Indianapolis.
For a time she taught school in Ladoga, Ind., but she
spent most of her married life in Crawfordsville, Ind.
She married James H. Britts in 1860. Mrs. Britts
was an author of juvenile books and of poetry and was
a writer for periodicals and newspapers.

Information from *Appletons' Cyclopaedia of
American Biography* and the Indianapolis Public
Library.

* * *

Edward Lee. *Philadelphia, 1865.*
Harry Henderson. 1880.
Honest and Earnest; or, Fred Norman's Trials. *Philadelphia, 1883.*
Boys and Girls of Deep Glen. *Philadelphia, 1884.*
Better Than Gold: A Temperance Story. *Philadelphia, 1885.*
Chryssie; or, Standing Alone. *Philadelphia, 1886.*
Earle Armstrong. *Philadelphia, 1886.*
Marcia; or Cross Purposes. *Chicago* [1886].
Nobody's Boy; or, How Good Goes On. *Philadelphia, 1888.*
Cosy's Resolve; or, My Brother's Keeper. *Philadelphia, 1889.*
Riches Without Wings. *Philadelphia, 1889.*
Roy Kennedy's Reward; or, The Way to Win. *Philadelphia, 1893.*
Rush-Lights. *Philadelphia, 1894.*
House Full of Girls.
Halford's Luck; or, Which Is the Better. *Philadelphia.*
Mrs. Middleton's Girls. *Philadelphia.*
Today and Tomorrow. *Philadelphia.*
Love's Prayer.
Council of Three. *Philadelphia.*
Hannah. *Philadelphia.*

BROOKS, MARIE SEARS: ?–1893.

Marie Sears was born in Springfield, Mass., probably within the first three decades of the Nineteenth
century. She was educated in Springfield and at nineteen married and moved west with her husband.

At the beginning of the Civil War she was living in
Missouri, and her earliest writing was concerned with
anti-slavery and rebellion trouble in that state. In 1862
she moved to Madison, Ind., where she became an active contributor of poems, short stories and articles to
newspapers and periodicals.

She was elected vice-president of the Western Association of Writers in 1889 and served as secretary in
1890. She died in 1893.

Information from Parker and Heiney—*Poets and
Poetry of Indiana.*

* * *

In His Name. 1882.
Vanquished.
A Vision of the Mistletoe . . . n.p. [*Buffalo, N. Y.*] n.d.

BROOKS, SAMUEL: ?–

Mr. Brooks was evidently a Hoosier of long stand-
ing in 1881, for lines from his autobiographical verses
read:
"We lived within the Hoosier State"
Another:
"I lived in Jefferson [presumably county] before I
came here . . ."
And a couplet which is descriptive of housing short-
ages in the middle of the Nineteenth century reads
[again it is the county to which the author refers]:
"I came to Hancock in the year thirty-two,
The houses were scarce and the people were few."

Information from Brooks—*Poems, Ballads and
Songs.*

* * *

Poems, Ballads and Songs. *Greenfield, Ind., 1881.*

BROTHERTON, ALICE WILLIAMS (MRS. WILLIAM E.): ?–1930.

Alice Williams, daughter of Alfred Baldwin and
Ruth Hoge Johnson Williams, was born in Cambridge
City, Ind. After her marriage to William Ernest
Brotherton on Oct. 18, 1876, she lived in Cincinnati,
O. She was a lecturer on Shakespeare and a contribu-
tor to CENTURY and other periodicals. She died on
Feb. 9, 1930.

Information from *Who Was Who in America.*

* * *

Beyond the Veil. *Chicago, 1886.*

The Sailing of King Olaf, and Other Poems. *Chicago,* 1887.

What the Wind Told to the Treetops. 1888.

The Orchard Path and Other Poems, 1917.

BROWN, DEMARCHUS CLARITON: 1857–1926.

"Demarchus C. Brown was born at Indianapolis June 24, 1857, son of Philip and Julia (Troester) Brown . . . Philip Brown was born in Butler County, Ohio, in 1800, and in 1852 moved to Indianapolis . . . His wife, Julia Troester, was a native of Reutlingen, Wuertemberg, Germany, where she was born in 1832. She died in 1874 . . .

"Demarchus C. Brown attended the public schools of Indianapolis and later the Northwestern Christian University, now Butler College, from which he was graduated A.B. in 1879 . . . In 1880 he received his Master's degree, and the years 1882-83 he spent abroad in the University of Tuebingen, Germany, and the British Museum at London. He returned to become instructor in Greek and secretary of the board of directors of Butler College. In 1884 he was elected to fill the chair of Greek Language, and it was from that position that he was called to his present [1919] post as state librarian in September 1906 . . .

"In March 1881 Mr. Brown married Miss S. Anna Rudy of Paris, Ill. She died in April, 1891. On Sept. 1, 1897, Mr. Brown married Jessie Lanier Christian . . ."

Besides the works listed Mr. Brown translated several books.

Demarchus C. Brown died in Indianapolis on Aug. 22, 1926.

> Condensed from Dunn—*Indiana and Indianans,* Vol. V.

* * *

Indiana Legislature and State Manual. 1907.

Government of Indiana. *New York,* 1912.

Brief Sketch of Harvey W. Wiley.

BROWN, HILTON ULTIMUS: 1859–

Hilton Ultimus Brown, son of Philip and Julia Troester Brown, was born in Indianapolis on Feb. 20, 1859, and graduated from Butler University in 1880, receiving the A.M. degree from Butler in 1882 and an honorary LL.D. from Indiana University in 1935. On Oct. 30, 1883, he married Jennie Hannah, who died in 1939.

For one year (1880-81) he served as principal of the Oaktown (Ind.) Seminary, and after 1881 he was associated with the INDIANAPOLIS NEWS as, successively, reporter, city editor, receiver, managing editor, and general manager. He is now (1947) secretary-treasurer and member of the Associated Press for the NEWS.

> Information from *Who's Who in America* and Mr. Brown.

* * *

"Fifty-Four Forty or Fight." *Indianapolis,* 1912.

Hilton U. Brown, Jr., One of Three Brothers in Artillery. *Indianapolis,* 1920.

Irvington, Indianapolis; Fortieth Anniversary and Home Coming, 1912. *Irvington,* n.d.

BROWN, JULIA: ?–

Julia Brown, daughter of Henry L. and Sallie A. Bush Brown, was born in Lawrenceburg, Ind., and was educated at Wesleyan College in Cincinnati, O. As a resident of London, England, she contributed to American newspapers and magazines. Her first story, "Pink Topaz," was published in ST. NICHOLAS MAGAZINE in 1909.

> Information from *Who's Who in America.*

* * *

The Enchanted Peacock, and Other Stories. *Chicago,* 1911.

The Mermaid's Gift, and Other Stories. *Chicago,* 1912.

BRUMBLAY, ROBERT: 1876–

No information has been located regarding the Rev. Robert Brumblay—except that he was born in Lawrenceburg, Ind., in 1876.

* * *

> Information from the Barry Ms.

Lee Jason, Oregon's Path-Finder.

Experiences in the Home Mission Field of the Northwest.

BRYAN, CHARLOTTE AUGUSTA LOWE: 1867–1948.

Charlotte Augusta Lowe of Indianapolis graduated from Indiana University in 1888 and married William Lowe Bryan on July 13, 1889. She collaborated with him in editing and translating three works. She died on Aug. 28, 1948.

Information from The University Libraries, Indiana University, and Dunn—*Indiana and Indianans,* Vol. III.

* * *

Studies in Plato's Republic (with William Lowe Bryan). *New York,* 1898.

BRYAN, ENOCH ALBERT: 1855–1941.

Enoch Albert Bryan, son of the Rev. John and Eliza Jane Philips Bryan, was born in Bloomington, Ind., in 1855, and graduated from Indiana University in 1878, receiving the A.M. degree in 1885. He also received the A.M. degree from Harvard University in 1893 and honorary degrees from various other institutions. In 1881 he married Hattie E. Williams.

He was superintendent of the public schools of Grayville, Ill., from 1878 to 1882, president of Vincennes University from 1882 to 1893, president of Washington Agricultural College and School of Sciences (now State College of Washington) from 1893 to 1916, and commissioner of education for Idaho from 1917 to 1923. From 1923 to 1939 he served as research professor of economics and economic history at State College of Washington.

He died on Nov. 6, 1941.

Information from *Who Was Who in America.*

* * *

The Mark in Europe and America: A Review of the Discussion of Early Land Tenure. *Boston,* 1893.

A National System of Education. Presidential Address . . . *Berkeley, Calif.,* 1915.

The Legal Status of the Functions of the State College of Washington and the University of Washington. n.p., n.d. [1916].

Historical Sketch of the State College of Washington, 1920-1925. *Spokane, Wash.,* 1928.

Orient Meets Occident; The Advent of the Railways to the Pacific Northwest. *Pullman, Wash.,* 1936.

BRYAN, WILLIAM LOWE: 1860–

William Lowe Bryan, president of Indiana University for thirty-five years, was born near Bloomington, Ind., on Nov. 11, 1860, a son of the Rev. John and Eliza Jane Philips Bryan. Following his graduation from Indiana University in 1884 he taught at the University and studied for the A.M. degree, which he received in 1886. He also studied in Berlin, Paris, and Wurzburg, and in 1892 he received the Ph.D. from Clark University. He was later the recipient of honor-

ary degrees from numerous colleges and universities.

He married Charlotte Augusta Lowe of Indianapolis, on July 13, 1889. Dr. Bryan was professor of philosophy at Indiana University from 1885 to 1902, acted as vice-president from 1893 to 1902 and served as president from 1902 to 1937. Besides the works listed in this sketch he was the author of numerous contributions to periodicals, translations and occasional addresses.

During President Bryan's administration Indiana University grew phenomenally in enrollment, standing and physical property.

Information from *Who's Who in America* and Indiana University.

* * *

On the Development of Voluntary Motor Ability; With a Preface on the Requirements of Work in Experimental Psychology . . . *Worcester, Mass.,* 1892.

Capital in Nerves . . . *Indianapolis,* n.d. [1893].

Studies in Plato's Republic . . . (with Charlotte Lowe Bryan) *New York,* 1898.

He Knew What Was in Man . . . *Indianapolis,* n.d. [1913].

The Spirit of Indiana; Commencement Addresses, 1902-1917 . . . *Bloomington, Ind.,* 1917.

The Wisdom of a Race. *Bloomington, Ind.,* 1921.

Youth in Revolt? n.p., n.d.

Paradise. *Bloomington, Ind.,* 1927.

Have You Ever Made a First-Rate Success at Anything? n.p. [*Bloomington, Ind.*], 1930.

The President's Column. *Bloomington, Ind.,* 1934.

Farewells. *Bloomington, Ind.,* 1938.

Wars of Families of Minds. *New Haven, Conn.,* 1940.

On the Psychology of Learning a Life Occupation (with E. H. Lindley and Noble Harter). *Bloomington, Ind.,* 1941.

The Measured and the Not-Yet-Measured. The Seer . . . *Bloomington, Ind.,* n.d. [1947].

A Better World or None. n.p. [*Bloomington, Ind.*], n.d. [1947].

BRYANT, WILLIAM MCKENDREE: 1843–?

William McKendree Bryant, son of Eliphalet W. and Esther Eliza Brown Bryant, was born in Lake County, Ind., on Mar. 31, 1843. He was educated at Ohio Wesleyan University, receiving his A.B. degree in 1869 and his A.M. in 1871. During the Civil War he served as a private in the 3rd Iowa Infantry and spent the last few months of the war as assistant to the adjutant general of his brigade. On Aug. 8, 1867, he married Sarah Augusta Shade.

He was superintendent of schools in New Lisbon, O., and in Burlington, Ia.; a teacher in the St. Louis public schools; and from 1881 to 1912 taught psychology, ethics, and history in St. Louis Normal and Central High School. In 1912 he retired from teaching and engaged in literary work exclusively until his death. In addition to titles listed here he translated, edited and wrote textbooks.

Information from *Who Was Who in America*.

* * *

Philosophy of Landscape Painting. *St. Louis,* 1882.

World-Energy and Its Self-Conservation. *Chicago,* 1890.

Ethics and the New Education. *Chicago,* 1894.

Hegel's Educational Ideas. *Chicago,* 1896.

Life, Death and Immortality; With Kindred Essays. *New York,* 1898.

American Scheme of State Education and Other Works.

Modern Education.

Fundamental Syntheses of History.

Philosophy and Immortality.

BRYER, JAMES T.: 1828–1895.

James T. Bryer, son of Robert and Dorcas Bryer, was born in Fountain County, Ind., on Aug. 4, 1828. In 1833 he moved to Logansport where he lived until his death on Mar. 11, 1895.

On May 15, 1852 he married Sarah E. Hensley. They had two sons and seven daughters. He held numerous state and county governmental offices. From 1861 until his death he was editor of the LOGANSPORT JOURNAL.

Information from Powell—*History of Cass County,* 1913.

* * *

History of Logansport. *Logansport, Ind.,* 1889.

Pioneers and Old Residents of Logansport. *Logansport, Ind.,* 1892.

BUCHANAN, BENJAMIN FRANKLIN: ?–

B. F. Buchanan was a native of Ohio County, Ind., who operated a drug store in the village of Rising Sun for many years. The following is, as far as is known, his only literary effort to appear in book form.

Information from the Rising Sun Public Library.

* * *

Bogus Hollow, a Tale of Blue Jean's Town and Vicinity. *Dayton, O.,* 1901.

BURCHENAL, ELIZABETH: 1877–

Born in Richmond, Ind., in 1877, Elizabeth Burchenal received the B.L. degree from Earlham College and graduated from the Sargent College of Physical Education. She taught physical education at Horace Mann School, Barnard College, and Columbia University from 1902 to 1905 and was then employed by the New York Public Schools until 1916. She began her researches in folk dances and folk dance music in 1904.

In 1916 she organized the American Folk Dance Society and in 1929 became permanent director of the organization, promoting interest in the folk arts through writing and lecturing. Besides the titles listed Miss Burchenal compiled and edited at least a half dozen collections of folk dances and games.

Information from *Who's Who in America* and Burke and Howe—*American Authors and Books, 1640-1940.*

* * *

Folk-Dance Music. *New York,* 1908.

May Day Celebrations. *New York,* 1914.

Folk Dancing as a Social Recreation for Adults. *New York,* 1920.

Folk-Dancing as a Popular Recreation; A Handbook. *New York,* 1922.

Folk-Dances from Old Homeland. *New York,* 1922.

Three Old American Quadrilles. 1926.

Four Folk Games. 1928.

Five Folk Dances. 1929.

Athletics for Girls.

German Folk Dances.

Folk Dances of Germany; Containing Twenty-Nine Dances and Singing Games; Collected and Provided with Full Directions for Performance; Accompaniments Arranged and Edited by Emma Howells Burchenal. *New York,* 1938.

American Country Music. 1941.

BURGHALTER, DANIEL: 1867–

Born in Geneva, Ind., Oct. 16, 1867, Daniel Burghalter, son of Christian and Mary Hartman Burghalter, had his preparatory education at Mission House College in Plymouth, Wis., and graduated from Heidelberg College in Tiffin, O. After graduating from Heidelberg Theological Seminary in 1895 he was ordained to the ministry of the Reformed Church in the U. S. He held pastorates in Germantown, Dayton, and Galion, O.; edited the CHRISTIAN WORLD for two years; and after 1911 was field secretary of the Board of Foreign Missions of the Reformed Church.

Information from *Who's Who in America*.

* * *

The History of the First Reformed Church of Galion, Ohio. 1910.
Dawning and Turning in Japan and China. 1923.
The History of Central Ohio Classics. 1939.

BURK, JAMES H.: ?–

D. S. A., writing of Daniel Hough's collection of books by Indiana authors, in the CINCINNATI GAZETTE for Dec. 7, 1876, refers to James H. Burk as an Indiana novelist.

Information from the CINCINNATI GAZETTE, Dec. 7, 1876.

* * *

First Quarrels and First Discords in Married Life. *Cincinnati*, 1860.

BURNETT, WILLIAM GREEN: 1833–1906.

William Green Burnett was born in Edgar County, Ill., in 1833, received the A.B. and A.M. degrees from De Pauw University, and is recorded by that university as having died in 1906.

The subject matter of his books seems sufficient to indicate continued Indiana residence after his college career.

Information from Federal Writers Project—*Indiana Authors*, 1937.

* * *

History of Clinton County, Indiana.
Monograph of Steuben County, Indiana.

BURNS, JAMES ALOYSIUS: 1867–1940.

James Aloysius Burns was born in Michigan City, Ind., on Feb. 13, 1867, the son of Patrick and Bridget Connolly Burns. Following his graduation from the University of Notre Dame in 1888, he joined the Congregation of the Holy Cross, and in 1889-90 he taught at Sacred Heart College in Watertown, Wis. In 1893 he was ordained in the Roman Catholic Church. He was a professor at the University of Notre Dame 1893-

1900; president and professor at Holy Cross College 1900; and president of the University of Notre Dame 1919-22. From 1927 until 1938 he was provincial superior of the Congregation of the Holy Cross in the U. S. He died Sept. 9, 1940.

Information from the University of Notre Dame Library.

* * *

Catholic School System in the United States: Its Principles, Origin and Establishment. *New York*, 1908.
Growth and Development of the Catholic School System in the United States. *New York*, 1912.
Catholic Education: A Study of Conditions. *New York and London*, 1917.

BURTON, ALMA HOLMAN (MRS. GEORGE W.): 1855–?

Born in Noblesville, Ind., in 1855, Alma Holman graduated from De Pauw University in 1877 and received the A.M. degree in 1880.

From 1877 to 1879 she was principal of the high school at Huntington, Ind. She studied in Europe from 1880 to 1882 and again from 1883 to 1884. In 1882 she was an instructor in modern languages at Stanford Female Seminary in Kentucky. From 1882 to 1885 she was connected with De Pauw University as professor of modern languages and literatures.

She married George W. Burton on Nov. 26, 1885. He died in 1900.

From 1909 to 1920 Mrs. Burton was dean of the Girls' School, Malolos, Dulacan, P. I., but in 1920 resigned to devote herself to literary work and to study in France.

Information from De Pauw University's *Alumnal Record, 1920*.

* * *

Massasoit: A Romantic Story of the Indians of New England. *New York*, 1896. (Also issued in the same year as Historical Reader: Story of the Indians of New England and in 1899 as Massasoit: A Historical Romance of the "Land of the Bays.")
Four American Patriots: Patrick Henry, Andrew Jackson, Alexander Hamilton, and Ulysses S. Grant. *Chicago*, 1898.
Lafayette, the Friend of American Liberty. *Chicago*, 1898.
History of the United States. *Chicago*, 1899.
Story of Our Country. *Chicago*.
Builders of Our Nation. *Chicago* [1905].

BURTON, CHARLES PIERCE: 1862–

Charles Pierce Burton, born in Anderson, Ind., on Mar. 7, 1862, lived there only three months. He is qualified by birth for inclusion here, and, when he once expressed doubt as to his eligibility to be known as an Indiana author, he was assured by Booth Tarkington that "three months was long enough for inoculation."

His mother died when he was ten months old, and he lived with his grandmother and a maternal aunt until 1873, when his father re-married and brought him to Aurora, Ill., where the senior Burton was editor and publisher of a weekly newspaper. With the exception of three years in Valparaiso and Gary, Ind., 1912-16, Charles Pierce Burton remained in Aurora as newspaper and trade paper editor, contributor to periodicals and writer of juvenile fiction.

Information from Charles Pierce Burton.

* * *

The Bashful Man and Others. *Chicago, 1902.*

The Boys of Bob's Hill. *New York, 1905.*

The Bob's Cave Boys. *New York, 1909.*

The Bob's Hill Braves. *New York, 1910.*

The Boy Scouts of Bob's Hill. *New York, 1912.*

Camp Bob's Hill. *New York, 1915.*

Raven Patrol of Bob's Hill. *New York, 1917.*

The Trail Makers. *New York, 1919.*

Bob's Hill Trails. *New York, 1922.*

Treasure Hunters of Bob's Hill. *New York, 1926.*

Bob's Hill Meets the Andes; Doings of the Band in South America as Told in the Minutes of the Meetin'. *New York, 1929.*

Bob's Hill Boys in the Everglades. *New York, 1932.*

Bob's Hill on the Air; Some Adventures That the Secretary Failed to Record in the Minutes of the Meeting. *New York, 1934.*

Moving the Earth. *New York, 1936.*

Bob's Hill Boys in Virginia. *New York, 1939.*

BUSKIRK, CLARENCE AUGUSTUS: 1842–?

Born at Friendship, Allegany County, N. Y., on Nov. 8, 1842, Clarence A. Buskirk was the youngest of four sons of Andrew C. Buskirk, tailor and merchant. As a boy he attended the public schools and Friendship Academy and then taught for a time before going to Kalamazoo, Mich., where an older brother lived. In Michigan he farmed, taught, and read law, subsequently enrolling in law school at Ann Arbor. He was admitted to the bar in 1865, and in June of

1866 he came to Princeton, Ind., where he practiced law for the remainder of his life.

Mr. Buskirk was a civic leader in Princeton. In 1872 he was elected Gibson County representative in the State Legislature and in 1874 was elected Attorney General of Indiana.

Information from *Representative Men of Indiana,* Vol. I; Stormont—*History of Gibson County, Indiana;* and Tartt—*History of Gibson County, Indiana.*

* * *

Christian Science: Its Religious Philosophy. *Boston.*

Cavern for a Hermitage: A Poem. *New York, 1889.*

BUTLER, AMOS WILLIAM: 1860–1937.

Amos William Butler, son of William Wallace and Hannah Wright Butler, was born in Brookville, Ind., on Oct. 1, 1860. He was graduated from Indiana University in 1894 with the A.B. degree and received the A.M. degree in 1900. On June 2, 1880, he married Mary I. Reynolds. In 1896-97 he was ornithologist in the Department of Geology and Resources of Indiana; from 1897 to 1923 he was secretary of the Indiana Board of State Charities; and in 1928-29 he was senior sociologist in the U. S. Bureau of Efficiency.

Mr. Butler was a member of various commissions and boards and was a delegate from the U. S. to international conferences on prisons. He was the author of many books and papers on sociology, zoology, agriculture, and economics. He died on Aug. 5, 1937.

Information from Dunn—*Indiana and Indianans* and *Who Was Who in America.*

* * *

Indiana: A Century of Progress.

The Development of Public Charities and Corrections.

Birds of Indiana. *Indianapolis, 1891.*

A Century of Changes in the Aspects of Nature.

Government and Municipal Pensions. *Fort Wayne, Ind., 1906.*

Burden of Feeble Mindedness. *Fort Wayne, Ind., 1907.*

Statistics (with others). *Fort Wayne, Ind.*

Feeble-Minded: The Need of Research. *Fort Wayne, Ind., 1916.*

Indeterminate Sentence and Parole Law; A Study of Eighteen Years' Operation in Indiana. *Indianapolis, 1916.*

Official Outdoor Relief and the State. *Fort Wayne, Ind., 1916.*

Treatment of the Misdemeanant. *Fort Wayne, Ind., 1916.*

BUTTERFIELD, SEYMOUR ATTWOOD: 1819–?

Seymour Attwood Butterfield, son of John Butterfield, was born in Jefferson County, N. Y., on July 30, 1819, and moved with his parents to Connersville, Ind., in the same year. Two years later the family moved to Morgan County, Ind., where John Butterfield became a successful farmer. Young Seymour attended the county schools and helped his father on the farm.

After studying medicine under a Mooresville doctor, he practiced his profession in the neighborhood of his father's farm for thirteen years. On June 6, 1843, he married Araminta D. Utter. He became a resident of Indianapolis in 1862.

> Information from Nowland—*Sketches of Prominent Citizens of 1876.*

* * *

Poems . . . In Attestation of My Gratitude for Their Uniform, and I Fear Oft Unmerited, Kindness, and as a Keepsake When I Am in My Grave, This Little Volume Is Inscribed and Presented to My Friends. *Indianapolis,* 1880.

Amusement of Idle Hours. The Poems of S. Attwood Butterfield, M.D. *Indianapolis,* 1887.

BYFORD, HENRY TURMAN; 1853–1938.

Henry Turman Byford, son of Dr. William Heath and Anne Holland Byford, was born in Evansville, Ind., on Nov. 12, 1853, and graduated from Williston Seminary in 1870. He received the M.D. degree from Chicago Medical College in 1873. On Nov. 8, 1882, he married Lucy Larned.

Dr. Byford practiced medicine in Chicago and from 1892 to 1913 was on the faculty of the College of Medicine of the University of Illinois (Chicago) as professor of gynecology. He was the author and co-author of several medical textbooks.

He died on June 5, 1938.

> Information from *Who Was Who in America.*

* * *

To Panama and Back. *Hammond, Ind.,* 1908.

BYRUM, ENOCH EDWIN: 1861–

Enoch Edwin Byrum was born in Randolph County, Ind., in 1861. He studied at Ridgeville College, Valparaiso University, Otterbein College, and the North American Institute at Chicago. His wife was the former Isabel Coston, of Chicago.

His life was spent in religious work, travel, especially in South and Central America, and writing. He made his residence in Anderson, Ind., during his later years.

> Information from *Who's Who Among North American Authors.*

* * *

The Boy's Companion: Personal Tales. *Moundsville, W. Va.,* 1892.

Divine Healing of Soul and Body. *Moundsville, W. Va.,* 1894.

The Secret of Salvation, How to Get It and How to Keep It. *Moundsville, W. Va.,* 1896.

The Great Physician and His Power to Heal. *Moundsville, W. Va.,* 1900.

Behind the Prison Bars: A Reminder of Our Duties Towards Those Who Have Been So Unfortunate as to Be Cast Into Prison. *Moundsville, W. Va.,* 1901.

What Shall I Do to Be Saved? Words of Advice, Warning, and Encouragement to the Unsaved, Pointing Out the Way of Salvation, and the Requirements Necessary to Obtain It. *Anderson, Ind.,* 1903.

Ordinances of the Bible. *Anderson, Ind.,* 1904.

Travels and Experiences in Other Lands. *Anderson, Ind.,* 1905.

How We Got Our Bible. *Anderson, Ind.,* 1905.

Man of Galilee. *Anderson, Ind.,* 1907.

Riches of Grace. *Anderson, Ind.,* 1912.

Secret of Prayer: How and Why We Pray. *Chicago* and *New York.*

Startling Incidents and Experiences in the Christian Life; Narratives of the Wonderful Dealings of the Lord with Those Who Put Their Trust in Him and of Their Deliverances in Time of Adversity, Trial, and Temptation. *Anderson, Ind.,* 1915.

Miracles and Healing. *Anderson, Ind.,* 1919.

Life Experiences; Containing Narratives, Incidents, and Experiences in the Life of the Author. *Anderson, Ind.,* 1928.

Peter, The Fisherman Preacher. *Anderson, Ind.,* 1931.

BYRUM, ISABEL COSTON (MRS. ENOCH E.): 1870–1938.

Isabel Coston Byrum, wife of Enoch Edwin Byrum, was born in Chicago in 1870 and was a resident of Anderson, Ind., for many years. She died in 1938.

> Information from the Barry Ms. and *Who's Who Among North American Authors.*

* * *

Beautiful Stories From the Good Old Book. *Anderson, Ind.,* 1904.

Favorite Stories From the New Testament. *Anderson, Ind., 1905.*

Our Darlings' A B C Book. *Anderson, Ind., 1908.*

The Guardian Angel. *Anderson, Ind., 1910.*

The Value of a Praying Mother. *Anderson, Ind., 1911.*

Bed-Time Stories From the Old Testament For the Children. *Anderson, Ind., 1911.*

Twilight Talks With the Children. *Anderson, Ind., 1913.*

Happy Hours at Home. *Anderson, Ind., 1914.*

Child's Picture Gallery. *1914.*

The Pilot's Voice; Words of Warning to the Youth and Enlightenment for Parents. *Anderson, Ind., 1916.*

How John Became a Man; Life Story of a Motherless Boy. *Anderson, Ind., 1917.*

The Manger Babe. *1917.*

The Troubles of Biddy. *1917.*

The Poorhouse Waif and His Divine Teacher. *Anderson, Ind., 1919.*

Harry the Newsboy, and Other Children's Hour Stories. *Anderson, Ind., 1926.*

Arabella's Hen, and Other Children's Hour Stories. *Anderson, Ind., 1927.*

Cripple Willie, and Other Children's Hour Stories. *Anderson, Ind., 1927.*

Tiny Tots in Story Town. *1929.*

Mr. Noah's A B C Zoo. *1933.*

Our Darlings' Bible A B C Book. *Cincinnati, 1934.*

Tread of Years. *Anderson, Ind., 1938.*

Grandmother's Lily, and Other Children's Hour Stories.

C

CAIN, JOHN: 1805–1867.

"Capt. John Cain was a native of the Old Dominion, born in Culpepper County in the year 1805. He there learned the book-binding business, but ere he had attained his majority came west, and for a short time worked at his trade in Hamilton, Ohio.

"In the year 1826 he came to Indianapolis, when its whole population did not exceed eight hundred souls. He immediately opened the first book-bindery in the place. In 1832 he published a book of miscellaneous poems, the first book of any kind, with the exception of the laws of the State, published in the place; he also opened the first bookstore about that time. Shortly after his arrival here he wooed and won the hand of Miss Eliza Jenison, the only daughter of the late Rufus Jenison, one of the prominent farmers of the county . . .

"After the election of Gen. Jackson, and in the spring of 1829, he was appointed postmaster, which position he held through his eight years administration, and four years of Mr. Van Buren's . . .

"After he quit the post office the second time, he engaged in merchandising. About the year 1847 he sold out his entire property and removed to one of the lower Ohio river counties in Kentucky, bought a farm and mill, and commenced merchandising again. His farm was stocked with negroes, and although he was raised in a slave State he did not understand the managing of them; he thought, in order to keep them under subjection, it was necessary to flog them occasionally . . . In consequence of this rigorous course the negroes set fire to his mill and store, and almost burned him out of house and home. He then, with his family, returned to Indianapolis, and for a while kept the Capital House, which was noted for its fine table . . .

"In 1853 he was appointed by President Pierce Indian agent for Washington Territory, and with his eldest son, Andrew J. Cain, went there and remained some years, and somewhat recuperated his damaged fortune . . . He died suddenly and unexpectedly in 1867 . . ."

> Condensed from Nowland: *Sketches of Prominent Citizens of 1876.*

* * *

Miscellaneous Poems. *Indianapolis, 1832.*

The Officer's Guide and Farmer's Manual. *Indianapolis, 1837.*

CALDWELL, FRANK: 1867–?

Frank Caldwell was born in Boone County, Ind., in 1867. No information as to his education is available; it is known only that he contributed juvenile stories to periodicals. He is believed to have died in 1938.

> Information from Federal Writers Project—*Indiana Authors, 1937.*

* * *

Wolf the Storm Leader. *New York, 1910.*

CALDWELL, OTIS WILLIAM: 1869–

Otis William Caldwell, son of Theodore Robert and Belle Caldwell, was born in Lebanon, Ind., on Dec. 18, 1869, and graduated from Franklin College in 1894. He received the Ph.D. degree from the University of Chicago in 1898 and was awarded the LL.D. by Franklin in 1917. He married Cora Burke on Aug. 25, 1897.

From 1899 to 1907 he was professor of biology at Eastern Illinois State Normal School, from 1907 to 1917 he taught botany at the University of Chicago, and from 1917 to 1935 he was on the faculty of Columbia University, serving as professor of education in Teachers College until 1927 and as director of the Institute of School Experimentation after 1927.

In addition to his books, Dr. Caldwell was a contributor to scientific and educational journals and author of a number of textbooks and manuals.

Information from Franklin College and *Who's Who in America.*

* * *

Suggestions to Teachers . . . Designed to Accompany "Plant Structures"; A Second Book of Botany by J. M. Coulter. *New York,* 1900.

Gary Public Schools: Science Teaching. *New York,* 1919.

Biology in the Public Press. 1923.

Then and Now in Education 1845-1923; A Message of Encouragement From the Past to the Present (with S. A. Courtis). *Yonkers-on-Hudson, N. Y.,* 1924.

Open Doors to Science (with W. H. D. Meier). *Boston,* 1925.

Biological Foundations of Education (with C. E. Skinner and J. W. Tietz). *Boston,* 1931.

Experimental Study of Superstitions as Related to Certain Units of General Science (with G. E. Lundeen). *New York,* 1932.

Do You Believe It (with G. E. Lundeen). *New York,* 1934.

Description of the Science Laboratories, Lincoln School of Teachers College (with E. R. Glenn and C. W. Finley).

CALKINS, HARVEY REEVES: 1866–

Harvey Reeves Calkins was born in Valparaiso, Ind., in 1866. He received the A.B. degree from Northwestern University in 1888, the A.M. degree from the same institution three years later, and the B.D. from Garrett Bible Institute in 1890. He spent the following year in travel and study in Europe, returning in 1896 for further study.

In 1892 he was ordained a minister in the Methodist Episcopal Church and held pastorates in Castle Rock and Denver, Colo., and in Chicago from 1894 to 1898. He acted as a missionary field evangelist from 1898 to 1900 and spent the following ten years as a missionary in India, returning to this country after 1910.

Information from *Who's Who in America.*

* * *

Victory of Mary Christopher. *New York,* 1903.

Mind of Methodism. *New York,* 1905.

Man and His Money. *New York,* 1914.

Stewardship Starting Points; An Introduction. *Chicago,* 1916.

Ganga Dass, a Tale of Hindustan. *New York,* 1917.

The Centenary At Old First. *New York,* 1919.

Ten Weeks; The Journal of a Missionary. *New York,* 1920.

CALLAHAN, JAMES MORTON: 1864–

James Morton Callahan, son of Martin I. and Sophia Tannehill Callahan, was born in Bedford, Ind., on Nov. 4, 1864. He graduated from Indiana University with the A.B. degree in 1894, received his A.M. from the same institution in 1895, and received the Ph.D. degree from Johns Hopkins in 1897.

After teaching history and political science in various colleges and universities for a number of years, in 1900 he became associated with the University of West Virginia as director of the bureau of historical research. From 1902 to 1929 he was professor and head of the department of history and political science, and from 1916 to 1929 he acted as dean of the College of Arts and Sciences, becoming research professor in 1929. A lecturer and an authority on the foreign policy of the U. S., Mr. Callahan was the author of many books on the subject and contributed articles to magazines and encyclopedias; he also wrote a number of textbooks.

Information from *Who's Who in America* and Dunn—*Indiana and Indianans,* Vol. V.

* * *

A Guide to Actual Work in Practical Physiology With Methods. *Chicago,* 1893.

The Northern Lake Frontier During the Civil War. *Washington, D. C.,* 1897.

The Neutrality of the American Lakes, and Anglo-American Relations. *Baltimore,* 1898.

Cuba and International Relations: A Historical Study in Diplomacy. *Baltimore,* 1899.

American Relations in the Pacific and the Far East, 1784-1900. *Baltimore,* 1901.

Great Heroes and Leaders. *New York,* 1901.

Diplomatic History of the Southern Confederacy. *Baltimore,* 1901.

Central America and the American Foreign Policy. *Washington, D. C.,* 1902.

The American Expansion Policy. *Baltimore,* 1904.

Introduction to American Foreign Policy, Vol. 1—The Monroe Doctrine and Inter-American Relations. 1904.

Alaska Purchase and Americo-Canadian Relations. *Morgantown, W. Va.,* 1908.

An Introduction to American Expansion Policy. *Morgantown, W. Va.,* 1908.

Russo-American Relations During American Civil War. *Morgantown, W. Va.,* 1908.

Evolution of Seward's Mexican Policy. *Morgantown, W. Va.,* 1909.

Genealogical and Personal History of the Upper Monongahela Valley, West Virginia . . . With an Account of the Resources and Industries of the Upper Monongahela Valley. *New York,* 1912. 3 vols.

Semi-Centennial History of West Virginia; With Special Articles on Development and Resources. *Charleston, W. Va.,* 1913.

History of West Virginia. *Chicago,* 1923. 3 vols.

Americo-Canadian Relations Concerning Annexation, 1846-1871. *Bloomington, Ind.,* 1925.

History of the Making of Morgantown, West Virginia; A Type Study in Trans-Appalachian Local History. *Morgantown, W. Va.,* 1926.

American Foreign Policy in Mexican Relations. *New York,* 1932.

American Foreign Policy in Canadian Relations. *New York,* 1937.

The United States and Canada: A Study in International History.

American Northern Frontier Development.

Early American Continental Policy.

CAREY, MRS. ANGELINE PARMENTER: 1854–1934.

On Nov. 20, 1934, the INDIANAPOLIS STAR carried the following:

"Mrs. Angeline Parmenter Carey, 80 years old, retired English teacher of Shortridge [Indianapolis] High School, died yesterday in her home, 34 W. Joseph St., after an illness of three years.

"Mrs. Carey was born in Troy, N. Y. After graduating from the Emma Willard Seminary for Girls in Troy she took a summer course at Oxford University, England, and returned to this country and taught in Greenfield (Mass.) schools. She came to the Indianapolis school to join the faculty when May Wright Sewell resigned [in the early Eighties]. At that time Shortridge was known as the Indianapolis High School . . ."

Condensed from the INDIANAPOLIS STAR, Nov. 20, 1934.

* * *

Guide to the Study of Literary Criticism. *Indianapolis,* 1895.

The Reader's Basis. *Indianapolis,* 1908.

CARNAHAN, JAMES RICHARDS: 1840–1905.

James Richards Carnahan, son of the Rev. James Aikman and Martha A. Carnahan, was born at Tippecanoe, Ind., on Nov. 18, 1840.

He enrolled in Wabash College but left in 1861 to enlist as a private in the 11th Indiana Infantry. After serving throughout the war, he was mustered out as a captain in 1865, returned to Wabash, and graduated in 1866. In 1867 he graduated from Indiana Law School. He married Susan Elizabeth Patterson on Nov. 7, 1867.

Mr. Carnahan was a resident of Indianapolis at the time of his death in 1905.

Information from *Who Was Who in America.*

* * *

Tactics and Manual for the Uniform Rank Knights of Pythias. *Cincinnati,* 1883.

Pythian Knighthood: Its History and Literature. *Cincinnati,* 1888.

Camp Morton; Reply to Dr. John A. Wyeth. *Indianapolis,* n.d. [1892].

The Eighty-Sixth Regiment, Indiana Volunteer Infantry. A Narrative of its Services in the Civil War of 1861-1865 (with James A. Barnes and T. H. B. McCain). *Crawfordsville, Ind.,* 1895.

CARR, JOHN WESLEY: 1859–?

John Wesley Carr, son of James Newton and Laura E. Stallings Carr, was born in Lawrence County, Ind., on Dec. 13, 1859, and graduated from Indiana University in 1885, receiving the A.M. degree in 1890. He also studied at Columbia and at New York University, receiving the Ph.D. degree from the latter institution in 1913. On Oct. 7, 1878, he married Rachel Ashcraft, who died in 1927, and on Apr. 21, 1928, he married Mary Willia Moss.

He was connected with the public schools of Indiana from 1877 to 1905, serving as teacher in Greene County, principal of the high schools in Bloomington and Muncie, and superintendent in Anderson. He was superintendent of the public schools of Dayton, O., from 1905 to 1908 and of Bayonne, N. J., from 1909 to 1916. He was then principal of Friends' Central School at Philadelphia for two years. During the first World War he was in War Camp Community Service. After spending two years as director of the Division of Hygiene for the Educational Department of Kentucky, in 1923 he organized and became first president of

Murray State Teachers College in Kentucky, serving as its dean and president until 1940.

Information from *Who's Who in America*.

* * *

Taxation and Teachers' Salaries in Indiana. 1904.

A System of School Support—New Jersey. 1913.

Course in Physical Education for the Common Schools of Kentucky. 1920.

Factors Affecting Distribution of Trained Teachers Among Rural White Elementary Schools of North Carolina. *New York, 1927.*

CARR, MICHAEL W.: 1851–1922.

Born in County Leitrim, Ireland, in 1851, Michael Carr came to the U. S. in 1861 and settled in Toledo, O., where his father had established a home. He was educated in the Toledo schools and at the University of Notre Dame.

From 1873 to 1879 he acted as editor of the TOLEDO REVIEW. In 1881 he came to Indianapolis, where he was biographical correspondent for the INDIANAPOLIS SENTINEL and later editor of the PEN, an early monthly magazine. He died in Indianapolis on Apr. 30, 1922.

Information from Cyril S. Carr, of Indianapolis.

* * *

History of Catholicity and Catholic Institutions in Indianapolis with Sketches of Bishop Chatard and His Four Predecessors. *Indianapolis, 1887.*

History of Catholicity and Catholic Institutions in Evansville. *Indianapolis, 1888.*

Catholicity in Terre Haute and Vigo County, Indiana—A Short History. *Indianapolis, 1888.*

History of Catholicity in Richmond and Wayne County, Indiana. *Indianapolis, 1889.*

History of Catholicity in New Albany and Jeffersonville and Floyd and Clark Counties, Indiana. *Indianapolis, 1890.*

Catholicity in Tipton, City and County, Indiana. *Indianapolis, 1890.*

Criticism of Fanatical Temperance. *Indianapolis, 1895.*

History of Catholicity in Indiana. Volume 1 (with others). *Logansport, Ind., 1898.*

History of Catholicity in Northern Ohio and in the Diocese of Cleveland. *Cleveland, 1903.* 2 vols.

CARROLL, PATRICK JOSEPH: 1876–

Patrick Joseph Carroll was born in 1876 in Ballingrame, Ireland. Coming to the U. S. as a youth, he at-tended the University of Notre Dame, receiving the A.B. degree; he later received the Litt.D. from the Catholic University of America.

He began to contribute poetry to periodicals in the late Nineties, and later added biography, fiction, and drama to his literary production. He has been professor of poetry at the University of Notre Dame.

Information from the Barry Ms.

* * *

Round About Home, Irish Scenes and Memories. *Notre Dame, Ind., 1914.*

Songs of Creelabeg. *New York, 1916.*

The Ship in the Wake. *South Bend, Ind., 1916.*

The Saving of Pug Halley; A Boy's Play in Three Acts. *South Bend, Ind., 1918.*

Memory Sketches. *South Bend, Ind., 1920.*

Ted, A Play for Boys. *South Bend, Ind., 1920.*

The Man-God; A Life of Jesus. *Chicago, 1927.*

Heart Hermitage, and Other Poems. *Chicago, 1928.*

Patch; Sketches of Irish Life. *Notre Dame, Ind., 1930.*

The Bog; A Novel of the Irish Rebellion of Nineteen Sixteen and After. *Notre Dame, Ind., 1934.*

Mastery of Tess. *Notre Dame, Ind., 1935.*

Vagrant Essays. *Notre Dame, Ind., 1936.*

Many Shall Come. *Notre Dame, Ind., 1937.*

Smoking Flax. *Notre Dame, Ind., 1939.*

Michaeleen. *Notre Dame, Ind., 1940.*

Patch of Askeaton Days. *Notre Dame, Ind., 1943.*

CASE, CLARENCE MARSH: 1874–

Clarence Marsh Case, son of Elon Ervin and Pamelia Marsh Case, was born in Indianapolis on Jan. 18, 1874. He received the A.B. degree from Earlham College in 1905, the A.M. from Brown University in 1908, and the Ph.D. from the University of Wisconsin in 1915. In 1908-09 he took graduate work at Harvard.

He was teacher and ward principal of the Noblesville, Ind., public schools; pastor of the South 8th Street Meeting of Friends, Richmond, Ind.; and resident minister of the Moses Brown School in Providence, R. I. From 1910 to 1917 he was professor and head of the department of history and social sciences at Penn College, Oskaloosa, Ia., and from 1917 to 1923 he was associate professor of sociology at the University of Iowa. In 1923 he became professor of sociology at the University of Southern California.

Information from *Who's Who in America*.

* * *

Banner of the White Horse; A Tale of the Saxon Conquest. *New York*, 1916.

Non-Violent Coercion; A Study in Methods of Social Pressure. *New York*, 1923.

Social Process and Human Progress. *New York*, 1931.

Essays in Social Values. *Los Angeles*, 1944.

CATHERWOOD, MARY HARTWELL (MRS. JAMES STEELE): 1847–1902.

Any history of Middle Western literature must include mention of the prolific writer, Mrs. Mary Hartwell Catherwood. Although she was born in Ohio (Dec. 16, 1847), was a resident of Indiana only from 1877 to 1882, and lived thereafter mainly in Hoopeston and Chicago, Ill., Mrs. Catherwood became during her Hoosier years an intimate and influential part of the literary circle centering in Indianapolis and she kept a close relationship with it all the rest of her life. In her writing, although she derived contemporary fame chiefly from a series of popular but rather unsubstantial historical romances produced between 1888 and 1902, she turned out two groups of regional short stories that have won her a permanent place in American local color literature. The first group, written largely during her Indiana years, memorializes the corn belt from central Ohio west to the Illinois prairies. The second, written in the Nineties, dealt with the French-border country from Mackinac to the Gulf of St. Lawrence.

Mrs. Catherwood was born in Luray, Licking County, O. When she was about ten, the family migrated to Milford, Iroquois County, Ill., where the father, Dr. Marcus Hartwell, died in 1857 and the mother, Phoebe Thompson Hartwell, in 1858. The three orphaned children, of whom Mary was the oldest, returned to Ohio where they were reared by the maternal grandparents in Hebron. Autobiographical reflections of the early trip on the National Road through Ohio and Indiana to Illinois are to be found in *Old Caravan Days* and *On Indiana Roads*, juveniles published in 1880. Details of an unhappy girlhood in an Ohio village at the intersection of the National Road and the Ohio Canal fill the background of her novel *Craque-O'-Doom*, written in Indianapolis and published in 1881.

At fourteen she was teaching country schools, and two years later she was publishing her first poetry and stories in the Newark, O., NORTH AMERICAN. In 1865 she entered the Granville, O., Female College and completed a four-year course in three, graduating in 1868. She was "the first important woman writer of any prominence in American literary ranks to acquire a college education," Prof. Fred Lewis Pattee points out, "graduating not in the East, as one might suppose, but from a new college in the new West." Pattee also notes that she was the first woman novelist of the period born west of the Alleghenies. It can be added that in her self-supported struggle toward a literary career and national recognition she was the pioneer woman writer of the Middle West.

From 1868 until 1874, she taught schools in Granville, O., and in Danville, Ill. At the latter place in 1871, she won a $100 prize for a short story in WOOD'S HOUSEHOLD MAGAZINE and shortly afterward became a regular contributor to WOOD'S and various other popular periodicals.

These successes led her in 1874 to give up teaching entirely for free-lance writing, first in Newburgh, N. Y. (1874-1875), then in Cincinnati (1875-1877). A voluminous output of pot-boilers during this period included her first novel, *A Woman in Armor* (1875) first serialized in HEARTH AND HOME. This writing was anything but distinctive, but she managed to support herself by it most of the time from 1874 to 1877, not a common accomplishment for young, unknown free-lance women writers in the Seventies.

In December, 1877, she married James Steele Catherwood of Hoopeston and went to live over the railway station (still standing) in Oakford (Fairfield), Howard County, Ind. Released from the pressure of self-support, she began taking stock of Middle Western life and translating it into sketches, poems, and stories for various Indiana papers. Notably literary conscious in these decades, Indiana's newspapers were soon aware of her and her writing. There were two important results: a long and stimulating acquaintance with James Whitcomb Riley and the perfection of Mrs. Catherwood's style in her first significant, nationally-recognized local color writing.

Mrs. Catherwood and Riley met in Kokomo in February, 1879. Riley, whose work had not yet won him hope of literary success, was going through a period of deep discouragement. Mrs. Catherwood had given up thoughts of a literary career for married life in an isolated country village and was not completely happy with the results. Friendship warmed quickly and there was a mutually inspired burst of creative work. Among other writing they were collaborating in 1879 on *The Whittleford Letters*, a romance based upon the lives of two young writers whose careers and meeting very closely resembled their own. The project was never completed, chiefly, Mrs. Catherwood has said, because the substance of the fictional romance suddenly became too real for both.

In December, 1879, the Catherwoods moved to Indianapolis. The month before, Riley had taken a permanent post on the JOURNAL. Mrs. Catherwood became at once an intimate part of the city's literary group and from October, 1880, until her removal to Hoopeston in 1882 was drama critic for and regular contributor to George C. Harding's SATURDAY REVIEW.

Her production during these Indianapolis months was enormous. In addition to her reviews, she turned out three book-length serials (including her second novel, *Craque-O'-Doom*, named for a poem by Riley), two book-length and numerous shorter juveniles, at least seven short stories including some of her finest local color narratives, and a large miscellany.

Now as always she was writing too much, but she was perfecting her best skills. Such stories as *The Career of a Prairie Farmer* (LIPPINCOTT's, June, 1880) describing life on Illinois farms, *Mallston's Youngest* (LIPPINCOTT's, Aug., 1880), utilizing her recent background in Oakford, *Serena* (ATLANTIC, June, 1882) and *Queen of the Swamp* (HARPER's, Dec., 1882), both of the latter giving scenes from her girlhood region in Ohio, mark a culmination of her attempts to record realistic details of rural life in the Middle West. Riley, too, it is interesting to note, was just on the verge of recognition.

From 1882 until 1899, Mrs. Catherwood lived in Hoopeston. Her greatest fame began in 1888 with the publication of *The Romance of Dollard*, an historical novel based upon old French-American themes popularized by the writings of Francis Parkman. Both the manuscript and the writer were introduced to Richard Watson Gilder, CENTURY's editor, by letters from Riley who by now had full access to Eastern editorial attention. *The Story of Tonty, The Lady of Fort St. John*, and a long line of other historical romances followed, most of which were serialized first in either the CENTURY, HARPER's, or the ATLANTIC.

Mrs. Catherwood's forte was in recording a multitude of realistic human-interest details of manners, customs, speech, and every-day incidents. On the other hand, she was never a skillful contriver of plots, a weakness that, together with her tendency toward extremes of romantic escape, made her novels too thin for any continuing attention today.

Within the compressed scope of the short story, however, she was able to integrate form and color with highly artistic results. Her successes with corn-belt material in the Eighties were matched in the Nineties

by other craftsmanlike work with French-border themes, in such fine tales as *The Windigo* (ATLANTIC, Apr., 1894) and *The Mothers of Honoré* (HARPER's, June, 1899). Various of these French-border short stories have been the most widely reprinted of her works.

A few of her better earlier cornlands tales Mrs. Catherwood revived in *The Queen of the Swamp and Other Plain Americans* in 1899. But some of the finest of her early Middle Western local color lies uncollected in the magazines of the Eighteen-eighties. The best of her French-border tales Mrs. Catherwood collected in *The Chase of Saint-Castin and Other Stories* (1894) and *Mackinac and Lake Stories* (1899).

Mrs. Catherwood's personal relationships with Middle Western authors were many and vital. At Indianapolis in 1886, for example, she helped organize, with Riley, Maurice Thompson, and others, the Western Association of Writers and was active in the work of this influential organization the rest of her life.

After 1890, Mrs. Catherwood traveled much—to Mackinac Island for her summers, to French Canada, and in 1891 and 1894 to Europe, the latter trip to gather material for her fictional life of Jeanne d'Arc published in 1897.

From 1899 until her death (Dec. 26, 1902), she resided in Chicago. Her writing here, more voluminous than ever, included her most popular success *Lazarre*, a historical romance based upon the career of Eleazar Williams, the supposed "Lost Dauphin." Its popularity was enhanced by a stage version with Otis Skinner in the leading role. Its chief interest today, however, lies in an episodic contribution that it has made to the nationally-accepted folk myth of Johnny Appleseed.

Almost completely forgotten for a time, the permanent values in Mrs. Catherwood's short tales were first pointed out by Prof. Pattee in 1915. Now, no representative collection of American local color stories is considered complete without some of her work.

By Robert Price, Professor of English at Otterbein College, O.

* * *

A Woman in Armor. *New York*, 1875.

The Dogberry Bunch. *Boston*, 1879.

Old Caravan Days including Over Indiana Roads. *Boston*, 1880.

Craque-O'-Doom. *Philadelphia*, 1881.

Rocky Fork. *Boston*, 1882.

The Secrets at Roseladies. *Boston*, 1886.

The Romance of Dollard. *New York*, 1889.

The Story of Tonty. *Chicago, 1890.*

The Lady of Fort St. John. *Boston, 1891.*

Old Kaskaskia. *Boston, 1893.*

The White Islander. *New York, 1893.*

The Chase of Saint-Castin and Other Stories of the French in the New World. *Boston, 1894.*

The Days of Jeanne D'Arc. *New York, 1897.*

The Spirit of an Illinois Town, and The Little Renault: Two Stories of Illinois at Different Periods. *Boston, 1897.*

Bony and Ban, the Story of a Printing Venture. *Boston, 1898.*

Heroes of the Middle West. *Boston, 1898.*

Mackinac and Lake Stories. *New York, 1899.*

The Queen of the Swamp and Other Plain Americans. *Boston, 1899.*

Spanish Peggy. *Chicago, 1899.*

Lazarre. *Indianapolis, 1901.*

CAUTHORN, HENRY SULLIVAN: 1828–1905.

Henry Sullivan Cauthorn was born in Vincennes, Ind., on Feb. 23, 1828. His father, Gabriel T. Cauthorn, was a Virginian, educated at the University of Virginia. He came west in 1823 and located in Lawrenceville, Ill., where he practiced medicine until his death. Henry S. Cauthorn's mother was a daughter of Elihu Stout, founder of Indiana's first newspaper, the Vincennes WESTERN SUN.

After the death of his father, in 1834, young Cauthorn, with his mother, lived in the home of his grandfather and entered the printing office of the WESTERN SUN. In 1840 he enrolled in St. Gabriel School, Vincennes, and remained until 1845, when he matriculated at Indiana Asbury (now De Pauw) University, from which he graduated in 1848.

In 1851 he began the study of law with Benjamin F. Thomas, then United States District Attorney for Indiana. He was admitted to the bar in 1853 and the next year was elected district attorney for Knox, Daviess, Pike, and Martin counties. In 1855, upon the organization of city government, he, as city attorney, framed the series of local ordinances. After filling the office of city clerk for two terms, in 1870 he was elected state representative, being reelected in 1872, 1878, and 1880.

In 1868 he married Margaret C. Bayard. He was active in the Catholic Church throughout his life. He died on Nov. 15, 1905.

Information from Goodrich—*History of Knox and Daviess Counties.*

* * *

Brief Sketch of the Past, Present and Prospects of Vincennes. *Vincennes, Ind., 1884.*

St. Francis Xavier Cathedral at Vincennes, Indiana. n.p., 1892.

History of the City of Vincennes, Indiana, from 1702 to 1901. *Vincennes, Ind., 1902.*

CAVANAUGH, JOHN WILLIAM: 1870–1935.

John William Cavanaugh, son of Patrick and Elizabeth O'Connor Cavanaugh, was born in Leetonia, O., on May 21, 1870, and graduated from the University of Notre Dame in 1890. He studied theology at Notre Dame, received the D.D. degree from Ottawa University, and in 1921 was awarded the LL.D. by Notre Dame.

Ordained a priest in 1894, from 1894 to 1905 he was an associate editor of AVE MARIA MAGAZINE, from 1898 to 1905 rector of Holy Cross Seminary, and from 1902 to 1906 professor of English literature at Notre Dame. He served as president of Notre Dame from 1905 to 1919. After spending one year teaching at Holy Cross College, he returned to Notre Dame in 1920 as professor of English, a position he held until 1931.

He died on Mar. 22, 1935.

Information from *Who Was Who in America.*

* * *

St. Paul, the Apostle of the World. *New York, 1895.*

Priests of the Holy Cross. *Notre Dame, Ind., 1905.*

The Modesty of Culture. *Notre Dame, Ind., n.d.*

Conquest of Life. *Notre Dame, Ind., n.d.*

CHAMBERS, DAVID LAURANCE: 1879–

David Laurance Chambers, son of David Abbot and Elizabeth Keyser Fracker Chambers, was born in Washington, D. C., on Jan. 12, 1879. Following his graduation from the Columbian Preparatory School in 1895, he entered Princeton University, receiving the A.B. degree in 1900 and the A.M. in 1901. In 1937 he was granted a Litt.D. degree by Wabash College. He married Nora Taggart on Apr. 29, 1910.

After serving as secretary to Dr. Henry van Dyke (1900-03) and as a member of the editorial staff of the Curtis Publishing Company in Philadelphia (1903), in 1903 he joined the Bobbs-Merrill Publishing Company of Indianapolis, becoming a member of the firm in 1907 and later its president.

Information from *Who's Who in America.*

* * *

The Metre of Macbeth, Its Relation to Shakespeare's Earlier and Later Work. *Princeton, N. J., 1903.*

Indiana, a Hoosier History. *Indianapolis, 1933.*

CHAPIN, ELDEN STEDMAN: 1809–?

Elden S. Chapin was born in Baltimore, Vt., in 1809. In 1836 he came to what was shortly to be Whitley County, Ind., of which he became one of the organizers. He removed to Kosciusko County, where he was an early settler, and in 1874 settled in Plymouth, Ind., where he remained until his death.

He was a student of theology, mathematics and linguistics, was ordained a Baptist minister in 1842, and was for many years editor of a periodical published by that denomination.

Information from the Plymouth Public Library.

* * *

Return of the Jews to Palestine.

Sketches of the Early Settlement of the Northwest Territory.

Israel and Jerusalem.

Reminiscences and Episodes.

Past-Present-Future.

CHAPMAN, JOHN WILBUR: 1859–1918.

John Wilbur Chapman, son of Alexander H. and Lorinda McWhinney Chapman, was born in Richmond, Ind., on June 17, 1859. He was graduated from Lake Forest College in 1879 and from Lane Theological Seminary in 1882, being ordained to the Presbyterian ministry in the latter year.

From 1884 to 1893 he was pastor of churches in Albany and Philadelphia and from 1893 to 1896 engaged in evangelistic work, traveling to Asia, Australia, and Great Britain and achieving an international reputation in his field. After 1903 he acted as executive secretary of the General Assembly's Committee on Evangelistic Work for the Presbyterian Church.

In addition to his professional duties, he wrote a great many books, nearly all of which concerned his life interest, evangelism. Overwork caused him to suffer several breakdowns in health. He died on Dec. 25, 1918.

His first wife, Irene Stedden Chapman, died in 1886; his second, Agnes Strain Chapman, died in 1907; and on Aug. 30, 1910, he married Mable Cornelia Moulton.

Besides his books, the Rev. Mr. Chapman compiled several hymnals.

Information from *Who Was Who in America* and the *Dictionary of American Biography*, Vol. IV.

* * *

The Ivory Palaces of the King. *New York, 1893.*

The Way and the Walk (with Rev. F. B. Meyer). *New York, 1893.*

Received Ye the Holy Ghost? *New York, 1894.* (Reissued in 1912 as Power.)

. . . "And Peter." *New York, 1895.*

Kadesh-Barnea; or, the Power of a Surrendered Life. *New York, 1897.*

The Lost Crown. *Chicago, 1898.*

Answered! Remarkable Instances of Answered Prayers (with others). *Chicago, 1898.*

Conversion. *New York, n.d.*

Life of Blessing. *Dayton, 1899.*

Revivals and Missions. *New York, 1899.*

The Secret of a Happy Day: Quiet Hour Meditations. *Chicago, 1899.*

The Spiritual Life of the Sunday School. *Chicago, 1899.*

The Surrendered Life: Quiet Hour Meditations. *Chicago, 1899.*

The Life and Work of Dwight L. Moody. *Philadelphia, 1900.*

Present-Day Parables. *Cleveland, 1900.*

And Peter and Other Sermons. *Chicago, 1900.*

Bible Readers Aids. *n.p., 1900.*

From Life to Life; Illustrations and Anecdotes for the Use of Religious Workers and for Private Meditation. *Chicago, 1900.*

Day by Day; or, Meditations for the Morning Watch. *Chicago, 1901.*

The Man Who Said He Would. *Chicago, 1902.*

Present-Day Evangelism. *New York, 1903.*

Fishing for Men. *Chicago, 1904.*

S. H. Hadley of Water Street. *New York, 1906.*

Another Mile, and Other Addresses. *New York, 1908.*

And Judas Iscariot, with Other Evangelistic Sermons. *Chicago, 1906.*

Chapman's Pocket Sermons. *New York, 1910.*

Revival Sermons. *New York, 1911.*

Problem of the Work. *New York, 1911.*

The Personal Touch: Inspiration for Christian Workers. *New York, 1912.*

Present Day Evangelization. *New York, 1912.*

Alaska's Great Highway. *Hartford, Conn., n.d.*

The Personal Worker's Guide. *New York, 1915.*

MacLean, J. K. Chapman and Alexander. *New York, 1915.*

When Home Is Heaven. *New York, 1917.*

Old Fashioned Home. *Philadelphia, 1917.*

The Minister's Handicap. *New York, 1918.*

Day After Day; a Manual of Devotions for Individual and Family Use. *Philadelphia, 1919.*

Awakening Sermons; Compiled and Edited by Edgar Whitaker Work. *New York, 1928.*

Authentic Life of D. L. Moody. *Chicago.*

Worker's Testament (with R. C. Norton). *New York.*

CHARLES, EMILY THORNTON (MRS. ?): 1845–?

Emily Thornton, who wrote under the pseudonym of Emily Hawthorne, was born in Lafayette, Ind., on Mar. 21, 1845, and attended the Indianapolis public schools. At the age of sixteen she became a teacher.

After the death of her husband (a Mr. Charles, whose given name is unknown) in 1874, she began to write for the Indianapolis papers. She later moved to Washington, D. C., where she was managing editor of the WASHINGTON WORLD and where she later died.

> Information from Parker and Heiney—*Poets and Poetry of Indiana.*

* * *

Hawthorn Blossoms. *Philadelphia, 1876.*

Lyrical Poems, Songs, Pastorals, Roundelays, War Poems, Madrigals. *Philadelphia, 1886.*

CHARLES, JAMES: ?–

James Charles was born in the vicinity of Ridgeville, Ind., and apparently spent his early years in that community, serving in the Eighties as cashier of a Ridgeville bank. Toward the end of the Eighties he removed to Richmond, Ind., where his one recorded book was written, under the pen name of Charles J. Wayne.

> Information from Melvin B. Stratton, of Indianapolis.

* * *

Caddo, or Cupid in the Gas Belt. *Richmond, Ind., 1889.*

CHATARD, FRANCIS SILAS MAREAN: 1834–1918.

"Francis Silas Chatard (Dec. 13, 1834-Sept. 7, 1918), Roman Catholic bishop of Indianapolis, was a grandson of Pierre Chatard. The latter . . . had settled in Baltimore, married the daughter of a fellow emigrant, and won local prestige by writing and practising medicine, in which he had been trained in Paris. His son, Ferdinand, had studied medicine in Paris, London, and Edinburgh, practised in Baltimore, and married Eliza Anne, daughter of Silas Marean of Brookline, Mass., who had served in the War of 1812 and as consul in Martinique, where he had married an Irish widow of an English gentleman. Francis Chatard, son of Ferdinand and Eliza Anne . . . expecting to follow the paternal profession, on his graduation from Mount St. Mary's, Emmitsburg, in 1853, studied medicine under Dr. Donaldson of Baltimore and in the University of Maryland where he obtained his medical degree. After serving two years as an interne in the Baltimore infirmary and as physician of the city almshouse, he heard the religious call and enrolled under Archbishop Kenrick . . .

"For six years Chatard pursued courses in philosophy and theology in the Urban College of the Propaganda at Rome before he was ordained (1862) and awarded the D.D. (1863). He was then named vice-rector of the American College at Rome under Dr. W. G. McCloskey, later bishop of Louisville. Succeeding to the rectorship in 1868, he headed the College for ten interesting years during which the Vatican Council of 1870 was held . . .

"Named by Pope Pius to the See of Vincennes, he was consecrated (1878) by Cardinal Franchi . . . Vincennes welcomed in him a man of polished appearance, a good linguist, an attractive conversationalist, an inspiring preacher, and a deep student of foreign politics . . . In 1898, on removal of his See to Indianapolis, he built a new cathedral, St. Vincent's Hospital, schools, and a convent. On his twenty-fifth anniversary, he was honored by the whole state in ceremonies in which Cardinal Gibbons, forty archbishops and bishops, and three hundred priests took part. Although seven years later Joseph Chartrand was appointed coadjutor, the aged bishop continued active . . . he passed away in 1918 . . ."

Besides the books listed Chatard was translator of several religious works.

> Condensed from R. J. P., *Dictionary of American Biography,* Vol. IV.

* * *

Sermon. *Rome, 1872.*

Christian Truths. Lectures. *New York, 1881.*

St. Thomas and Our Day. *Notre Dame, Ind., 1882.*

Discourse on the Occasion of the Entombment of Mgr. Celestin de La Hailandiere. *Indianapolis, 1882.*

Ordo Divini Officii Recitandi Sacrique Peragendi, in Usum Cleri Diocesis Vincennopolitanal . . . *Indianapolis, 1884.*

Tenure of Land and Eminent Domain. *Indianapolis, 1887.*

Occasional Essays. *New York, 1894.*

Symbolism of Early Christianity from the Catacombs of Rome. *New York,* 1899.

CHEEVER, REV. WILLIAM MAXEN: 1818–1878.

"The Rev. William Maxen Cheever . . . was born at North Vernon, Ind., Sept. 23, 1818. He graduated from Hanover College in 1838, and from Lane Theological Seminary in 1843 . . .

"During Mr. Cheever's residence in Monticello, on July 8, 1844, he was married to Margaret L. Jackson, the youngest daughter of Mrs. Lyman Beecher and step-sister of Mrs. Harriet Beecher Stowe . . . She died at Rockville soon after their removal. He remained pastor of the 2nd Presbyterian church there until 1850, when he removed to Terre Haute . . .

"In 1866 he became Secretary of the Northwest for the American Board of Foreign Missions, with headquarters at Boston . . .

"In December, 1871, he was installed pastor of the 2nd Presbyterian Church at Kansas City, Mo., where his ministry was ended by his death in 1878 . . ."

* * *

Condensed from the MONTICELLO HERALD, Aug. 25, 1921.

Practical Evangelism; or, Bible Christianity Enforced. *Boston,* 1856.

CHENOWETH, CAROLINE VAN DUSEN (MRS. BERNARD PEEL): 1846–?

Caroline Van Dusen, daughter of Charles Van Dusen, was born on the Indiana side of the Ohio River, not far from Louisville, Ky., on Dec. 29, 1846.

When quite young she married Col. Bernard Peel Chenoweth, who died while serving as U. S. consul at Canton, China. After his death Mrs. Chenoweth settled the affairs of the consulate and returned to the U. S. She lectured on English literature at Smith College in 1883-84 and became associate editor of the MEDICO-LEGAL JOURNAL, published in New York.

* * *

Information from *A Catalog of Authors.* Houghton Mifflin, 1899.

Stories of the Saints. *Boston,* 1880.
History of the Second Church in Leicester, Massachusetts. *Leicester, Mass.,* 1908.
Child Life in China.
An Undistinguished Citizen.

CHITWOOD, MARY LOUISA: 1832–1855.

Born near Mt. Carmel in Franklin County, Ind., on Oct. 29, 1832, Mary Louisa Chitwood was educated in the common schools. Her first poem was published in a Connersville paper, and she became familiar to literary America through the columns of the LOUISVILLE JOURNAL, the LADIES' REPOSITORY, the TEMPERANCE WREATH, and other papers. She was an editor of the TEMPERANCE WREATH. Miss Chitwood died in Mt. Carmel on Dec. 19, 1855.

Information from Dunn—*Indiana and Indianans.*

* * *

Poems. Selected by George D. Prentiss. *Cincinnati,* 1857.

CLARK, JAMES L.: 1855–1933.

James L. Clark was born in Cartersburg, Hendricks County, Ind., in 1855 and was educated at Central Normal (now Canterbury) College and at Valparaiso University. He practiced law in Danville, Ind., and was serving as a professor of law at Central Normal College, Danville, in 1895. He also served as judge of the Hendricks County Circuit Court and as a member of the state utilities commission. He died on Feb. 15, 1933.

Information from Taylor—*Biographical Sketches and Review of the Bench and Bar of Indiana,* 1895, and the Indiana State Library.

* * *

A Mixed Question of Law and Fact.
Finding of Facts and Outlines of Conclusions of Law. *Danville, Ind.,* n.d.

CLARK, LINDLEY DANIEL: 1862–

Lindley Daniel Clark, son of Daniel and Mary Robinson Clark, was born in Carthage, Ind., on June 26, 1862, and graduated from Earlham College in 1886. He also studied at De Pauw University, Maryville College (from which he received the A.M. degree in 1890), the University of Michigan, and Columbian (now George Washington) University (from which he received the LL.B. degree in 1897 and the LL.M. in 1898). On Dec. 29, 1886, he married Maria E. Young, and on Dec. 1, 1898, he married Dora J. Bradshaw.

From 1893 to 1927 Mr. Clark was with the U. S. Department of Labor, from 1924 to 1927 he served as economist in charge of industrial and economic law, and from 1927 to 1932 he was with the U. S. Employees Compensation Commission.

In addition to his book he was the author of numerous articles and bulletins and contributed to encyclopedias and periodicals. He was also a minister of the Society of Friends.

Information from *Who's Who in America*.

* * *

The Law of the Employment of Labor. *New York,* 1911.

CLARK, THOMAS CURTIS: 1877–

Thomas Curtis Clark, son of Thomas J. and Emma Rose Jennings Clark, was born in Vincennes, Ind., on Jan. 8, 1877. After graduating from Indiana University in 1899 with the A.B. degree, he studied at the University of Chicago in 1901-02.

From 1907 to 1911 he was on the editorial staff of the Christian Board of Publications and from 1912 to 1940 was on the staff of the CHRISTIAN CENTURY in Chicago. In 1920 he became an associate editor of the CHRISTIAN CENTURY PULPIT and in 1919 editor of the TWENTIETH CENTURY QUARTERLY. A member of the publishing firm of Willett, Clark & Co., a lecturer and a composer as well as an author, he also contributed to and compiled many anthologies and was a syndicate writer. Mr. Clark married Hazel P. Davis in June, 1910.

Information from *Who's Who in America*.

* * *

Poems and Songs. *St. Louis,* 1909.
Friendly Town. 1915.
Love Off to the War, and Other Poems. *New York,* 1918.
Lincoln and Others. *New York,* 1923.
It Shall Not Be Again. *New York,* 1931.
Abraham Lincoln: Thirty Poems. *Chicago,* 1934.
Home Roads and Far Horizons; Songs and Sonnets. *Chicago,* 1935.
Fifty Lincoln Poems. *Herrin, Ill.,* 1943.

CLARKE, GRACE GIDDINGS JULIAN (MRS. CHARLES B.): 1865–1938.

Born in Centerville, Ind., on Sept. 11, 1865, Grace Julian came of a family of abolitionists. Her father was George W. Julian, and her grandfather was Joshua R. Giddings of Ohio. In 1872 her parents moved to Irvington, Ind., where she attended the Mt. Zion district school and subsequently enrolled in But-

ler University, graduating in 1884 with the Ph.B. degree and receiving the Ph.M. degree in 1885. She was married to Charles B. Clarke, an Indianapolis attorney, in 1887.

For eighteen years Mrs. Clarke conducted a weekly column for the INDIANAPOLIS STAR and also, for eight years, edited a woman's page for the same paper. She was an active club woman—from 1909 to 1911 she was president of the Indiana Federation of Clubs and she was a director of the General Federation of Women's Clubs. She was an ardent advocate of women's suffrage. Mrs. Clarke died on June 18, 1938.

Besides the two biographical works listed, Mrs. Clarke also edited George W. Julian's speeches and papers.

Information from Dunn—*Indiana and Indianans,* Vol. III, and the Indiana State Library.

* * *

George W. Julian, Some Impressions. *Indianapolis,* n.d.
George W. Julian. *Indianapolis,* 1923.

CLIFTON, THOMAS A.: 1859–1935.

Thomas A. Clifton, son of Housen and Permelia Seeley Clifton, was born in Iroquois County, Ill., on Dec. 15, 1859. The family had lived in Indiana before the birth of Thomas and returned to the state before he was of school age.

Thomas was educated in the Fountain County, Ind., schools and attended De Pauw University, receiving the A.B. degree in 1885. He became a teacher and was sent to India, while still a young man, to establish a boys' high school. Returning to the U. S., he continued to teach for several years.

Shortly after the beginning of the century he became editor of the weekly COVINGTON (Ind.) REPUBLICAN, continuing in newspaper work until his death in June, 1935.

Information from Roll—*History of Indiana*.

* * *

Past and Present of Fountain and Warren Counties . . . *Indianapolis,* 1913.

CLODFELTER, NOAH J.: 1853–1901.

What could be a more appropriate recognition than a biographical sketch, perhaps composed or at least partially dictated, by the man himself, from a contemporary county history? Mr. Clodfelter's reads:

"Noah J. Clodfelter, a Poet:
   'Blessings be with them, and eternal praise,
   Who gave us nobler loves and nobler cares,
   The poets, who on earth have made us heirs,
   Of truth and pure delight by heavenly lays.'

"It is with the utmost satisfaction that the biographer places before the reader of this record a brief notice of the talented gentleman whose name appears at the opening of this article. In these practical days the poetic fire with the gentle, dreamy temperament belonging to it, comes too seldom to the notice of the world. When among us is born one of the gifted, the life of this individual holds superior interest, as the existence of a different kind of being.

"The subject of the present sketch was born in Alamo, Ind., Dec. 14, 1853, and he has been affectionately and proudly named 'The Wabash Poet.' He is scarcely conscious of the time when his thoughts did not run in rhythm, some of his published poems having been the emanations from the pen of a lad of only seventeen years. Perhaps the best known and most ambitious book of poems is the one entitled *Early Vanities*. This is to be found in the most of the larger libraries, and although it has received slashes from the critics, Mr. Clodfelter can point even now to the critics of Shakespeare.

"Our subject has not confined his pen to poetry, his novel, *'Snatched from the Poor House,'* having been kindly received, and having had a sale of over four hundred thousand copies. His first publication took place in 1886, since which time he has contributed to the papers and periodicals over the country. His residence is at 'Knoll Cottage,' a beautiful home erected at a cost of over $20,000.

"Probably more will be heard from this western poet in the future. Inspiring themes are not lacking, and the valley of the Wabash has many spots beautiful enough to encourage the poetic flame."

(The reader may, if he wishes, consider the "four hundred thousand copies" of the novel *Snatched from the Poor House,* to be a misprint or a mis-quotation of Mr. Clodfelter.)

> From *Portrait and Biographical Record of Montgomery, Parke and Fountain Counties,* 1893.

* * *

The Fates, or, the Dance on the Lethe. By Formose Puer [pseud.]. *New York,* 1882.

Early Vanities. *New York,* 1886.

Snatched from the Poor House. *Philadelphia,* 1888.

In Stony Places: A Story of the Mines in the Great Coal-Mining Region of Pennsylvania. *Philadelphia,* 1892.

The Gotham of Yasmar: A Satire. *Buffalo, N. Y.,* 1897.

COBURN, JOHN: 1825–1908.

John Coburn, son of Henry P. and Sarah Mallott Coburn, was born in Indianapolis on Oct. 27, 1825. He was educated in the public schools, at the old Marion County Seminary, and at Wabash College, from which he was graduated in 1846. After studying law, he was admitted to the bar in 1849 and began to practice in Indianapolis. For one term, 1850-51, he was a member of the Indiana State Legislature, and from 1859 to 1861 he was Judge of the Court of Common Pleas.

On Mar. 9, 1852, he married Miss Caroline Test of Centerville, Ind.

When the Civil War broke out, he was commissioned colonel of the 33rd Regiment, Indiana Volunteer Infantry. During his service he was for two months a prisoner in Libby Prison, and in September of 1864 he was in command of the reconnaissance force to which the city of Atlanta was surrendered. He was brevetted brigadier-general in 1865 at the close of the war.

Elected to Congress in 1866, he served four terms. He was chairman of the Military Committee and a member of other important committees. Following his period in Congress he resumed the practice of law in Indianapolis. General Coburn was a public-spirited man, long active in the promotion of improved public schools, parks and similar works in Indianapolis.

He died on Jan. 28, 1908.

> Information from Sulgrove *History of Indianapolis and Marion County; Representative Men of Indiana,* Vol. 11; and *Commemorative Biographical Record of Prominent Men of Indianapolis and Vicinity.*

* * *

Life and Services of John B. Dillon (with Horace P. Biddle). *Indianapolis,* 1886.

COCKRUM, WILLIAM MONROE: 1837–1924.

William Cockrum was born on Dec. 8, 1837, on the family farm, now the site of Oakland City, Ind.

He was almost entirely self-educated. While still a very young man he and his brother, James M. Cockrum, operated a general store and produce business which dealt mainly in pork and tobacco, shipped to the New Orleans market. After the Civil War Cockrum became a farmer and fruit grower.

He married Lucretia Harper on Oct. 5, 1856; they became the parents of nine children.

Cockrum became active in Underground Railroad activities in southwestern Indiana when the Fugitive Slave Law of 1850 gave an impetus to slave-hunting in free territory. When the Civil War was declared he enlisted in Company F, 47th Indiana Volunteer Infantry, and rose, during the course of the war, from lieutenant to lieutenant-colonel. He was wounded at Chickamauga, was captured and taken to Libby Prison, where he was held for eight months. This experience impaired his health permanently.

Cockrum's life on a pioneer farm, and his later adventures in the Underground Railroad service, gave him resources of information which he put to good use in the writing which occupied his later years.

Information from the Princeton Public Library.

* * *

Pioneer History of Indiana, Including Stories, Incidents and Customs of the Early Settlers. *Oakland City, Ind.,* 1907.

History of the Underground Railroad, as It Was Conducted by the Anti-Slavery League. *Oakland City, Ind.,* 1915.

COFFIN, CHARLES EMMET: 1849–1934.

Charles Emmet Coffin, born in Salem, Ind., on July 13, 1849, spent his early life on a farm and moved with his family to Bloomington, in 1862. When he was twenty years old he came to Indianapolis, where he was in the real estate business for many years.

In 1911 he became secretary-treasurer of the Indianapolis Star Publishing Company. His public service began in 1899 as a member of the Park Board and later he was president of the Board of Public Works. He became president of the Indiana Savings and Investment Company in 1899 and held the office until he died in Indianapolis on Oct. 15, 1934.

Information from the Indianapolis Public Library.

* * *

The Gist of Whist. *New York,* 1894.
Multum in Parvo. *New York.*
The Gist of Auction Bridge. *Chicago,* 1917.

COFFIN, CHARLES FISHER: 1823–1916.

"Charles Fisher Coffin . . . Quaker minister, was descended from Tristram Coffyn, Massachusetts colonist (1642) and one of the original settlers of Nantucket . . . Elijah Coffin (1798-1862) was a man of distinction and influence. He was a school teacher in

his youth in North Carolina, where he married Naomi Hiatt, a highly gifted woman of an important Quaker family. With her and his one-year-old son, Charles Fisher Coffin, he migrated to Indiana in 1824 . . . Charles Fisher Coffin was educated at first by his father and later in the early Quaker schools of the pioneer period. He began his career in the Richmond Bank, a branch of the State Bank of Indiana, when he was twelve years old, continuing his education during the evenings . . . In 1847, he was married to Rhoda M. Johnson of Waynesville, O. . . . Charles succeeded his father in the Richmond Bank in 1859, in which position he had a distinguished business career until 1885, when he retired and removed to Chicago . . . He was recorded a minister of the Gospel in the Society of Friends in 1866, and continued to preach, with effect and charm and power, until his death at the age of ninety-three . . . He and his wife were leaders in the creation of the Indiana Reform School and he was first president of the board of control of the Indiana House of Refuge for Juvenile Offenders, a position which he held from 1867 to 1880. He spent the last thirty years of his life in Chicago with the exception of two years in London, England."

Condensed from R. M. J., *Dictionary of American Biography,* Vol. IV.

* * *

Elijah Coffin. Life. With a Reminiscence by C. F. Coffin. Edited by Mary Coffin Johnson. *Cincinnati,* 1863.

Capital Punishment; A Discourse Delivered . . . May 26, 1878. *Richmond, Ind.,* 1878.

Our Prisons: an Address . . . Before the Indiana Social Science Association at Indianapolis, June 9, 1880.

British and American Prisons: an Address Delivered Before the National Prison Congress. n.p., 1891.

COFFIN, CHARLES FRANKLIN: 1856–1935.

Born in Marion County, Ind., on June 2, 1856, Charles Franklin Coffin, son of Benjamin Franklin and Emily Jane Harlan Coffin, graduated from De Pauw University in 1881, receiving the A.M. degree in 1884. He married Sarah I. Dowling on Oct. 26, 1887.

He was a teacher and administrator in the public schools of Indiana from 1881 until 1885, when he began the practice of law. From 1887 to 1893 he practiced in Wichita, Kan., in 1893-94 he acted as dean of the law school of De Pauw University, and in 1894 he became a member of an Indianapolis law firm. From 1898 to 1900 he was a lecturer at the Indianapolis

Law School. Mr. Coffin was active in the Indianapolis Chamber of Commerce for many years.

He died on Dec. 16, 1935.

Information from *Who Was Who in America* and De Pauw University's *Alumnal Record, 1920.*

* * *

Ten Years Tax Harvest from Policy-Holders' Funds. *New York, 1916.*

COFFIN, LEVI: 1789–1877.

Although his published works were limited to his *Reminiscences*, which came out the year before his death, and to the probable authorship of some ephemeral and necessarily anonymous anti-slavery pamphlets, Levi Coffin was a figure of sufficient importance in the pre-Civil War scene in the middle west to warrant an exhaustive sketch here.

The *Dictionary of American Biography* says of him, in part:

"Levi was born on a farm at New Garden, N. C., the youngest of the seven children of Levi and Prudence (Williams) Coffin. His mother's family was of Welsh descent. Both of his parents were Quakers. The boy, who was the only son, could not be spared from necessary work on the farm except for short intervals at the district school. He was mainly taught by his father at home. When he was twenty-one, he left for a session at a distant school . . . then taught for a winter, attended school the following year, and taught at intervals for several years thereafter. In 1821, together with his cousin Vestal Coffin, he organized at New Garden a Sunday-school for negroes. This succeeded for a time but eventually the masters, becoming alarmed at Coffin's methods, kept their slaves at home, and the school was closed. On Oct. 28, 1824, Coffin was married to Catharine White, a Quaker. Two years later, he moved to Newport (now Fountain City), Wayne County, Ind.—a village of about twenty families—where he was to live for more than twenty years. Here Coffin opened a store. Very soon after he came to Newport, he found that he was on a line of the Underground Railroad through which slaves often passed. Coffin let it be known that his house would be a depot and immediately fugitives began to arrive . . . The Railroad was attended with heavy expenses. These Coffin could not have borne had he not been prosperous. Journeys had to be made at night, often through deep mud and bad roads and along seldom-traveled by-ways. A week seldom passed without his receiving passengers . . . Coffin was also at this time a member of a Committee on Concerns of People of Color to look after their educational interests, treasurer of a fund raised to sustain schools and aid the poor and destitute, and an active participant in the temperance movement. Almost twenty years after he had gone to Newport to live, he became interested in the free labor question. In 1847, he agreed to go experimentally to Cincinnati for five years and open a wholesale free-labor goods store. A Quaker Convention at Salem, Ind., had voted in 1846 to raise $3,000 to begin such a project. A year after the outbreak of the Civil War, Coffin began his work for the freedmen and devoted his entire time to this for the rest of his life. In May, 1864, he went to England for this purpose, and an English Freedmen's Aid Society was formed . . . In 1867, Coffin was appointed delegate to the International Anti-Slavery Conference in Paris . . . The last ten years of his life were passed in retirement . . ."

Condensed from M. A. K., *Dictionary of American Biography,* Vol. IV.

* * *

Reminiscences of Levi Coffin, the Reputed President of the Underground Railroad; Being a Brief History of the Labors of a Lifetime in Behalf of the Slave, with the Stories of Numerous Fugitives. *Cincinnati, n.d.* [1876].

COFFMAN, JOHN S.: 1848–1899.

John S. Coffman, son of Bishop Samuel Coffman, was born in Rockingham County, Va., on Oct. 16, 1848, and was educated in the public schools and at the Normal School in Bridgewater, Va. He married Elizabeth J. Heatwole on Nov. 11, 1869.

After teaching school for six years, in 1879 he moved with his family to Elkhart, Ind., where he was assistant editor of the HERALD OF TRUTH, a Mennonite publication, until his death on July 22, 1899. He also engaged in evangelistic work, having been ordained to the ministry in 1875, and from 1890 to 1899 edited SUNDAY SCHOOL LESSON HELPS. He was influential in the establishment of Elkhart Institute in 1893—known as Goshen College since 1896.

Information from the Goshen College Library.

* * *

Infant Lesson Book; a Series of Bible Lessons, with Questions and Answers for Very Young Learners. For the Use of Sunday Schools. *Elkhart, Ind.,* 1880.
Confession of Faith and Ministers' Manual, Containing the Confession of Faith Adopted at Dortrecht in 1632—the Shorter Catechism—Forms for Baptism, the Lord's

Supper, Marriage, Ordination of Bishops and Ministers —Funeral Lessons, Texts, etc. (with John F. Funk). *Elkhart, Ind.,* 1890.

Fundamental Bible References. *Elkhart, Ind.,* 1891.

COFFMAN, LOTUS DELTA: 1875–1938.

Lotus Delta Coffman, son of Mansford E. and Laura E. Davis Coffman, was born in Salem, Ind., on Jan. 7, 1875, and graduated from Indiana State Normal School in 1896. He received the A.B. and A.M. degrees from Indiana University (in 1906 and 1910, respectively) and the Ph.D. degree from Columbia University in 1911. Honorary degrees were conferred upon him by other colleges and universities. On Dec. 28, 1899, he married Mary Emma Farrell.

From 1896 to 1907 he served as principal and superintendent of various schools in Indiana, from 1907 to 1909 and again from 1911 to 1912 he was supervisor of the Training School at Charleston, Ill., and from 1909 to 1911 he studied and lectured at Columbia University. After spending three years as a professor of education at the University of Illinois, in 1915 he became dean of the College of Education at the University of Minnesota and in 1920 was made president of the university. Coffman was the author of many textbooks besides the works listed below.

He died on Sept. 22, 1938.

Information from *Who Was Who in America.*

* * *

Reading in Public Schools (with T. H. Briggs). *Chicago,* 1908.

Social Composition of the Teaching Population. *New York,* 1911.

Teacher Training Departments in Minnesota High Schools. *New York,* 1920.

The State University: Its Work and Problems; a Selection from Addresses Delivered Between 1921 and 1933. *Minneapolis,* 1934.

Land Utilization in Minnesota—a State Program for the Cut-Over Lands (with others). *Minneapolis,* 1934.

Freedom Through Education. *Minneapolis,* 1939.

COHN, MORRIS M.: 1852–1922.

Morris M. Cohn, son of Mathias A. and Therese Koebner Cohn, was born in New Albany, Ind., on Mar. 14, 1852, and was educated privately and in the Cincinnati schools. On Aug. 19, 1883, he married Addie M. Ottenheimer.

He studied law and was admitted to the bar in 1873.

He spent two years as city attorney of Little Rock, Ark., three years as a school director, and several years as professor in the law school of the University of Arkansas.

Mr. Cohn died on Apr. 3, 1922.

Information from *Who Was Who in America.*

* * *

Essay on Religion, from a Historical and Philosophical Standpoint. *Cincinnati,* 1876.

Essay on the Growth of Law. *Chicago,* 1882.

Admiralty Jurisdiction, Law, and Practice, with Appendix Containing Rules, Statutes, and Forms. *Boston,* 1883.

An Introduction to the Study of the Constitution: a Study Showing the Play of Physical and Social Factors in the Creation of Institutional Law. *Baltimore,* 1892.

COLEMAN, CHRISTOPHER BUSH: 1875–1944.

Christopher Bush Coleman was born at Springfield, Ill., on Apr. 24, 1875. He received the A.B. degree from Yale University in 1896; B.D., University of Chicago, 1899, and University of Berlin, 1903-04, and Ph.D. from Columbia in 1914.

He came to Indianapolis in 1900 and for eighteen years was professor of history at Butler University. In 1920-24 he was head of the department of history and political science at Allegheny College. In 1924 he was named director of the Indiana State Historical Bureau; he was secretary of the Indiana Historical Society; and from 1936 to 1942 he was acting director of the Indiana State Library.

Dr. Coleman died in Indianapolis on June 25, 1944.

Information from *Who's Who in America* and the Indianapolis Public Library.

* * *

Church History in the Modern Sunday School. *St. Louis,* 1911.

Constantine the Great and Christianity; Three Phases: the Historical, the Legendary, and the Spurious. *New York,* 1914.

Memoirs of Louis Harrison Coleman. *Springfield, Ill.,* 1920.

Treatise of Lorenzo Valla on the Donation of Constantine; Edited and Translated by Christopher Coleman. *New Haven, Conn.,* 1922.

The Undying Past and Other Addresses. *Indianapolis,* 1946.

COLEMAN, LIZZIE DARROW: ?–?

Lizzie D. Coleman, daughter of Jonce and Mary Darrow Coleman, was born in Mitchell, Ind.

Her only known book—now quite rare—describes Indiana's largest Indian massacre of whites, that of the Pigeon Roost Community. Miss Coleman was residing in Bedford, Ind., at the time her book was published. She later married a Terre Haute physician and is believed to have died in childbirth while still a young woman.

> Information from Elizabeth Hayward, Ridgewood, N. J. and the Bedford Public Library.

* * *

History of the Pigeon Roost Massacre. *Mitchell, Ind.,* 1904.

COLERICK, EDWARD FENWICK: 1822–1905.

Edward Fenwick Colerick was born at Mount Vernon, O., in 1822. His father was Charles Colerick. Brought to Fort Wayne, Ind., as a child in 1828, he was educated privately, read law, and became a practicing attorney. In 1851 he married Margaret Forsyth. Three children were born to this union.

Mr. Colerick moved to Indianapolis in 1875 and remained a resident of that city until his death in 1905. Besides his one book he was also the author of a great number of newspaper and magazine articles. He spent most of his life in reading, study, and writing.

> Information from The Public Library of Fort Wayne and Allen County, Ind.

* * *

Adventures of Pioneer Children. *Cincinnati,* 1888.

COLFAX, SCHUYLER: 1823–1885.

"Schuyler Colfax (Mar. 23, 1823-Jan. 13, 1885), vice-president of the United States, was born in New York City . . . His father, Schuyler Colfax, who married (Apr. 15, 1820) Hannah Stryker of New York, died Oct. 30, 1822, and in 1834 his mother married George W. Matthews of Baltimore. In 1836 the family removed to New Carlisle, Ind., where Matthews, who became auditor of St. Joseph County in 1841, appointed his stepson deputy auditor at South Bend, an office which he held for eight years. Colfax found time to serve as assistant enrolling clerk of the state Senate (1842-44) and as correspondent of the INDIANA STATE JOURNAL (Indianapolis), and also studied law, but was never admitted to the bar. Having bought an interest in the South Bend FREE PRESS in 1845, he changed the name of the paper to ST. JOSEPH VALLEY REGISTER, made it the Whig organ of northern Indiana, and retained his interest in it until shortly after he became speaker of the House of Representatives. His political activities began early . . . When the Republican party was formed he joined it, and took an active part in organizing the new party in Indiana. In December 1855, he entered the House of Representatives of the Thirty-fourth Congress (1855-57) as a Republican, and served continuously until the end of the Fortieth Congress (Mar. 3, 1869). From the Thirty-eighth to the Fortieth Congress, inclusive (1863-69), he was speaker of the House . . . On Apr. 8, 1864, he left the speaker's chair to move the expulsion of Alexander Long of Ohio, who had spoken in favor of recognizing the Confederacy. The resolution was later changed to one of censure.

"His position as speaker, together with his 'advanced ideas on Negro suffrage' . . . , commended Colfax as a candidate for vice-president in 1868, and at the Chicago convention, after the fifth ballot, when he received 541 votes, his nomination was made unanimous . . . , and he was later elected . . . He was implicated in the Crédit Mobilier scandal, the investigation showing that he had agreed to accept twenty shares of stock in the company and had received a considerable sum in dividends. His denial of the charge was not convincing, and in his examination before the committee 'it is impossible to believe that he told the truth' (Rhodes, VII, 13-15). He escaped formal censure on the ground that his misconduct, if any, had been committed before he became vice-president, but although he claimed to have been 'fully exonerated' . . . , his political standing was ruined . . . He died suddenly at Mankato, Minn., and was buried at South Bend. His first wife, Evelyn Clark of New York, whom he married Oct. 10, 1844, died at Newport, R. I., July 10, 1863. On Nov. 18, 1868, he married Ellen W. Wade, a niece of Benjamin F. Wade of Ohio . . ."

> Condensed from W. M., *Dictionary of American Biography,* Vol. IV.

* * *

Life and Services of Gen. U. S. Grant (with Henry Coffin).

Life and Principles of Abraham Lincoln . . . Delivered in the Court House Square, South Bend, April 24, 1865. *Philadelphia,* 1865.

Education of the Heart . . . *New York,* 1868.

The Mormon Question. Being a Speech of Vice-President

Schuyler Colfax, at Salt Lake City, a Reply Thereto by Elder John Taylor; and a Letter of Vice-President Colfax Published in the "New York Independent," with Elder Taylor's Reply. *Salt Lake City*, 1870.

Example and Effort, an Address, Delivered Before the Congressional Temperance Society, at Washington, D. C. *New York*, 1872.

Landmarks of Life; to Be Found on a New Year's Day Journey. *New York*, 1883.

COLLIER, JOHN SAMUEL: 1876–

John Samuel Collier was born in Tipton, Ind., in 1876. He received the B.S. and M.S. degrees from De Pauw University and was apparently a pioneer in county agricultural agent work.

Information from Federal Writers Project— *Indiana Authors*, 1937.

* * *

What County Agent Collier Has Done for Cows in Kankakee.

Plows and Plowing Machines (with C. O. Reed). *Kankakee, Ill.*, n.d.

COLLINS, ANGELINA MARIA LORRAINE (MRS. JAMES): 1820–?

Angelina Maria Lorraine was born near Cumberland Gap, Va., in 1820. She married James Collins of New Albany, Ind., where the couple resided for a while before moving to Pekin, Ind., and later to Salem. Her second book was a temperance novel.

Information from Briscoe—unpublished ms., *Indiana Fiction Before 1870*.

* * *

Table Receipts Adapted to Western Housewifery. *New Albany, Ind.*, 1851.

Mrs. Ben Darby, or the Weal and Woe of Social Life. *Cincinnati*, 1853.

COLLINS, ARCHIE FREDERICK: 1869–

Apparently the honor of being one of Indiana's most prolific writers (if honor it be) with more than one hundred titles recorded, is Archie Frederick Collins, physicist and author of many scientific books, who was born in South Bend, Ind., on Jan. 8, 1869, and was educated in the public schools and at the University of Chicago. His achievements in his field include: invention of the wireless telephone, 1909; discovery of the effect of electric waves on brain cells, 1902; and form-

ulation of the neutron theory of the ether, 1937. He was a lecturer for the New York Board of Education, a technician for the Collins Wireless Telephone Company, editor of the COLLINS WIRELESS BULLETIN, and scientific correspondent for the NEW YORK HERALD.

Information from *Who's Who in America*.

* * *

Wireless Telegraphy, Its History, Theory and Practice. *New York*, 1905.

Manual of Wireless Telegraphy. *New York*, 1906.

The Electric Telegraph (with Charles Thom). *Chicago*, 1908.

The Design and Construction of Induction Coils. *New York*, 1909.

Plans and Specifications for Wireless Telegraph Sets, Complete and Detailed Instructions for Making an Experimental Set, Also a One to Five Mile Set. *New York*, 1912.

The Design and Construction of Wireless Sets. *New York*, 1914.

The Book of Stars; Being a Simple Explanation of the Stars and Their Uses to Boy Life, Written to Conform to the Tests of the Boy Scouts. *New York*, 1915.

The Book of Wireless; Being a Clear Description of Wireless Telegraph Sets and How to Make and Operate Them, Together with a Simple Explanation of How Wireless Works. *New York*, 1915.

The Book of Magic, Being a Simple Description of Some Good Tricks and How to Do Them, with Patter. *New York*, 1915.

The Book of Electricity, Written to Conform to the Tests of the Boy Scouts. *New York*, 1916.

Inventing for Boys. *New York*, 1916.

Short Cuts in Figures; to Which Is Added Many Useful Tables and Formulas Written So That He Who Runs May Read. *New York*, 1916.

How to Keep Your Motor Car in Repair. *New York*, 1917.

Easy Lesson in Wireless; a Practical Course of Instruction on the Principles, Construction and the Workings of Wireless Apparatus, for the Use of Students, Experimenters, and Operators. *New York*, 1917.

Home Handy Book; a Compendium of Useful Things to Do Around the Average House and How to Keep It in Repair. *New York*, 1917.

How to Fly. *New York*, 1917.

Keeping Up with Your Motor Car; Written So That He Who Reads May Ride, Also for the Car Owner to Whom Money Is an Object. *New York*, 1917.

Magic of Science; a Book of Scientific Amusements Which Can Be Performed with Simple Apparatus. *New York*, 1917.

Money Making for Boys; It Tells the Boy Who Wants to Make Money How to Do It and What to Do with His Money After He Has Made It. *New York*, 1917.

Shooting for Boys. *New York*, 1917.

The Boys' Book of Submarines; With Numerous Illustrations and Diagrams (with Virgil Dewey Collins). *New York*, 1917.

The Boys' Book of Engine Building; How to Make Steam, Hot Air and Gas Engines and How They Work, Told in Simple Language and by Clear Pictures; With Drawings by the Author. *Boston*, 1918.

Handicraft for Boys; With 185 Illustrations and Diagrams. *New York*, 1918.

The Amateur Mechanic. *New York*, 1918.

The Boys' Book of the War. *New York*, 1918.

Boys' Book of Chemistry. *New York*, 1918.

Gas, Gasoline and Oil Engines. *New York*, 1919.

The Amateur Chemist; an Extremely Simple and Thoroughly Practical Chemistry for the Home, Office, Shop and Farm. *New York*, 1919.

The Girls' Handy Book (with Mlle. Marthé Ducretet). *New York*, 1919.

Jack Heaton, Wireless Operator. *New York*, 1919.

The Boys' Airplane Book; With Numerous Illustrations, Working Drawings and Diagrams. *New York*, 1919.

Motor Car Starting and Lighting. *New York*, 1920.

Farm and Garden Tractors; How to Buy, Run, Repair, and Take Care of Them; With Numerous Illustrations and Diagrams. *New York*, 1920.

How to Take Care of an Automobile at Small Expense, with Complete Instructions for Operating Repairs and How to Make Them. *New York*, 1920.

Jack Heaton, Oil Prospector. *New York*, 1920.

Putnam's Handbook of Buying and Selling; Telling in a Simple and Practical Way How to Succeed in Business (with Virgil Dewey Collins). *New York*, 1920.

Through the Telescope. *New Haven, Conn.*, 1920.

Under the Microscope. *New Haven, Conn.*, 1920.

Spinning Tops and Gyroscopes. *New Haven, Conn.*, 1920.

Wonders of Natural History; a Comprehensive Account of Man in the Making and of Prehistoric and Present Day Animals; With a Frontispiece in Color and Eighty-Eight Illustrations in Black and White (with Virgil Dewey Collins). *New York*, 1920.

Jack Heaton, Gold Seeker. *New York*, 1921.

The Boys' Book of Physics. (Under the name of James Ramsey Clark.) *New York*, 1921.

Electrical Toys and Tricks. *Chicago*, 1921.

Mysto Card Magic. *Chicago*, 1921.

Magnetic Fun and Facts. *Chicago*, 1921.

Wonders of Chemistry. *New York*, 1922.

Radio Amateur's Handbook; a Complete, Authentic and Informative Work on Wireless Telegraphy and Telephony. *New York*, 1922.

Book of Wireless Telegraph and Telephone. *New York*, 1922.

The Boy Magician. (Under name of Raymond Dixie.) *Boston*, 1922.

The Book of the Microscope. *New York*, 1923.

The Boy Astronomer. *Boston*, 1923.

Everybody's Wireless Book. *London*, 1923.

Experimental Wireless. *London*, 1923.

The Boy Chemist. *Boston*, 1924.

The Amateur Electrician's Handbook; a Book for the Boy or Man Who Wants to Make and Do Things Electrical. *New York*, 1924.

The Amateur Photographer's Handbook. *New York*, 1925.

The Boy Scientist. *Boston*, 1925.

A Bird's Eye View of Invention. *New York*, 1926.

The Amateur Entertainer. *New York*, 1926.

The Boys' Book of Experiments. *New York*, 1927.

The Book of Puzzles. *New York*, 1927.

Boys' Book of Amusements. *New York*, 1927.

Boys' and Girls' Book of Indoor Games. *New York*, 1928.

Fun with Figures. *New York*, 1928.

Boys' and Girls' Book of Outdoor Games. *New York*, 1929.

Aviation and All About It; an Extremely Simple and Thoroughly Practical Exposition of All the Various Branches of Aviation. *New York*, 1929.

Experimental Science; Being a Series of Simple and Surprising Experiments in Mechanics, Sound, Heat, Light, Magnetism and Electricity. *New York*, 1929.

Going Somewhere; How to Travel by Land and Sea. *New York*, 1929.

Boys' and Girls' Book of Travel. *New York*, 1929.

Experimental Chemistry; Being a Series of Simple and Spectacular Experiments in Chemistry Together with Some Home-Made Chemical Apparatus. *New York*, 1930.

Mirth and Mystery; a Potpourri of Joyous Entertainment. *New York*, 1931.

Experimental Mechanics; Being a Series of Simple and Useful Experiments with Mechanical Movements and How to Make Them of Pasteboard. *New York*, 1931.

How to Understand Chemistry; Being a Simple, Clear and Concise Explanation of the Principles and Laws of Chemistry. *New York*, 1932.

Experimental Television; a Series of Simple Experiments with Television Apparatus; Also How to Make a Complete Home Television Transmitter and Television Receiver. *Boston*, 1932.

Motor Boating and All About It. *New York*, 1932.

The Metals; Their Alloys, Amalgams and Compounds. *New York*, 1932.

Experimental Optics; Being a Series of Simple and Brilliant Experiments with Light, and How to Make All Kinds of Optical Instruments. *New York*, 1933.

The Amateur Machinist; Being a Simple and Complete Guide for Using Machinists' Hand and Bench Tools, the Common Lathe and Back-Geared Screw Cutting Engine Lathe, with Chapters on Mechanical Drawings,

Fits and Fittings, and Finishing Metal Work. *New York,* 1934.

The New World of Science. *Philadelphia,* 1934.

Making Things for Fun; a How-to-Make Book for Boys and Girls of All Ages. *New York,* 1934.

How to Understand Electricity. *Philadelphia,* 1935.

How to Ride Your Hobby. *New York,* 1935.

The March of Chemistry. *Philadelphia,* 1936.

Motor Car Trailers; How to Build, Equip, and Furnish Them; Complete Specifications and Detailed Drawings for Making an Inexpensive Trailer and a Luxurious Trailer. *Philadelphia,* 1936.

Collecting Stamps for Fun and Profit. *New York,* 1936.

Fun with Electricity; a How-to-Make-It Book of Simple and Startling Experiments with Direct, Alternating, and High Frequency Electric Currents. *New York,* 1936.

Building Things for Fun. *New York,* 1936.

Amateur Power Working Tools. *Philadelphia,* 1937.

Working with Tools for Fun and Profit. *New York,* 1937.

Money-Making Hobbies. *New York,* 1938.

Photography for Fun and Money. *New York,* 1939.

Simplified Household Mechanics; Being a Simple Explanation of How the Mechanical and Electrical Equipment of Your Home Is Made, How It Works, and How It Is Serviced. *New York,* 1939.

Gardening For Fun, Health and Money. *New York,* 1940.

Science on Parade. *New York,* 1940.

Keeping Your House in Repair. *New York,* 1941.

Science for the Air Age. *New York,* 1941.

The Greatest Eye in the World; Astronomical Telescopes and Their Stories. *New York,* 1942.

There's Millions in It. *New York,* 1942.

The Royal Road to Knowledge; a Simplified Explanation of the Basic Sciences from the Beginning of the Universe Down to the Present Time. *New York,* 1942.

Time and Money Saving Gadgets. *New York,* 1943.

Inventing for Fun and Profit. *New York,* 1943.

Harlem Flats Are Falling Down. *New York,* 1944.

Science for Young Men. A Handbook for Young Men Interested in Entering Any Branch of Aviation. *New York,* 1946.

COLLINS, CHARLES WILLIAM: 1880–

Charles William Collins, son of Smith and Mary Luella Wood Collins, was born in Madison, Ind., on Nov. 19, 1880. Following his graduation from the University of Chicago in 1903, he was a reporter on the CHICAGO RECORD-HERALD for four years, then was dramatic critic, successively, for the CHICAGO INTER-OCEAN, CHICAGO EVENING POST, THE CHICAGOAN, and CHICAGO TRIBUNE. From 1909 to 1912

he acted as press representative for the Chicago Theatre Society. In 1938 he became editor of the column, "A Line o' Type or Two," in the CHICAGO TRIBUNE. In addition to his newspaper writing and his books, Mr. Collins has contributed articles and fiction to magazines.

Information from Who's Who in America.

* * *

Great Love Stories of the Theatre: a Record of Theatrical Romance. *New York,* 1911.

Natural Law; Based on the Drama of Howard Hall and C. Summer. *New York,* 1916.

The Sins of St. Anthony—Tales of the Theatre. *Chicago,* 1925.

The Dark Island (with Gene Markey). *Garden City, N. Y.,* 1928.

COMPARETTE, THOMAS LOUIS: 1868–1922.

Thomas Louis Comparette, son of Alexander Charles and Mary Jane Forder Comparette, was born in Dekalb County, Ind., on Apr. 9, 1868. He attended the University of Wooster, graduated from the University of Michigan in 1893, and received the Ph.D. degree from the University of Chicago in 1901. He also studied in Rome and in Germany.

From 1893 to 1897 he was professor of Greek and Latin at Texas Christian University, in 1905 was an assistant in Latin at the University of Missouri, and after 1905 served as curator of the Numismatic Collection of the U. S. Mint at Philadelphia.

He died on July 3, 1922.

Information from Who Was Who in America.

* * *

Debasement of the Silver Coinage Under the Emperor Nero. 1914.

Aes Signatum. *New York,* 1919.

Descriptive Catalog Selected Greek Coins. 1921.

COMSTOCK, DANIEL WEBSTER: 1840–?

Daniel Webster Comstock, son of Dr. James and Mary Wade Comstock, was born in Germantown, O., on Dec. 16, 1840. He attended local schools, graduated from Ohio Wesleyan University in 1860 and began the study of law.

In September, 1860, he located in New Castle, Ind., was admitted to the bar and began the practice of law —a practice soon to be interrupted by his enlistment in the 9th Indiana Cavalry for Civil War service. He was assistant adjutant general of the 1st Brigade at the close of the war.

In 1866 he settled in Richmond, Ind., and the next year married Miss Josephine A. Rohrer, of Germantown, O. In Richmond he practiced law, was elected to the state Senate in 1878 and was elected judge of the Seventh Judicial Circuit in 1884, serving two terms without opposition.

> Information from Taylor—*Biographical Sketches and Review of the Bench and Bar of Indiana.*

* * *

9th Cavalry, 121st Regiment Indiana Volunteers. *Richmond, Ind.,* 1890.

CONARD, JESSE: ?–?

"Jesse Conard, of Terre Haute, has written and published two novels . . . neither of which has ever been seen by Mr. [Daniel] Hough [Indianapolis collector of books by Indiana authors in 1876]. He desires to become a purchaser."

Mr. Conard began the practice of law in Terre Haute in 1838 and was elected probate judge of Vigo County in 1839. In 1841 he purchased the WABASH COURIER and published it as a Whig paper for many years.

> From D. S. A. in the CINCINNATI GAZETTE, Dec. 7, 1876 and Bradsby—History of Vigo County.

* * *

Stephen Moreland.
Mt. Echo or the Mother's Mystery.

CONDIT, BLACKFORD: 1829–1903.

Blackford Condit was born Aug. 6, 1829, in Sullivan County, Ind. The family moved to Terre Haute in 1831. He was educated at Wabash College—in both the preparatory and collegiate departments—receiving his degree in 1854. He then studied at Lane Theological Seminary in Cincinnati, graduated and was ordained in 1859.

Besides his church work and his research in history and religion he found time to keep up an active and most useful connection with his college throughout his entire life, most of which, after graduation, he spent in Terre Haute.

He acquired a large collection of early printings of the Bible and his most important scholarly work resulted from his studies in this field.

He died on Mar. 27, 1903.

> Information from Emmeline Fairbanks Memorial Library, Terre Haute, Ind.

* * *

Historic Discourse Delivered at the Quarter Century Anniversary of the Second Presbyterian Church, Terre Haute, Indiana, December 27, 1873. *Cincinnati,* 1874.

History of the English Bible, Extending from the Earliest Saxon Translation to the Present Anglo-American Revision. *New York,* 1882.

Short Studies of Familiar Bible Texts, Mistranslated, Misinterpreted and Misquoted. *New York,* 1898.

History of Early Terre Haute. *New York,* 1900.

CONDO, SAMUEL SALEM: ?–?

Samuel Salem Condo spent most of his life in Lafayette, Ind., (where he was residing before 1874) and in Marion, Ind. He was married to Sarah Ann Pottorf.

> Information from his son's biography in *Who's Who in America.*

* * *

Our Flag and the Red Flag; Their History, Meaning, Use and Abuse. *Marion, Ind.,* 1915.

CONES, FRANCIS MARION: 1836–1917.

Francis Marion Cones was born in New Palestine, Ind., in 1836. He received the A.B. and A.M. degrees from Indiana Asbury (now De Pauw) University and served as associate principal of the Thorntown (Ind.) Academy and as chaplain of the Indiana Soldiers' Home at Lafayette, Ind. He died in 1917.

> Information from Federal Writers Project—*Indiana Authors,* 1937.

* * *

History of Thorntown Academy, Thorntown, Indiana.

CONKLIN, JULIA STOUT: 1854–?

Born in Hamilton County, Ind., on Apr. 27, 1854, Julia Stout Conklin was educated at Friends' Academy, Westfield, Ind., and was a resident of Westfield. She was a trustee of the Indiana Soldiers' Orphans Home.

Information from *Who's Who in America.*

* * *

The Young People's History of Indiana. *Indianapolis,* 1899.

Indiana Soldiers' and Sailors' Monument. *Indianapolis,* 1900.

CONRAD, ARCTURUS Z.: 1855–1937.

Born in Shiloh, Ind., on Nov. 26, 1855, Arcturus Z. Conrad, son of Jacob E. and Margaret E. Slagle Conrad, was a graduate of Carleton College (A.B., 1882; A.M., 1885) and of Union Theological Seminary. In 1885 he was ordained to the Presbyterian ministry and became pastor of the Ainslie Street Presbyterian Church in Brooklyn. From 1890 to 1902 he was pastor of the First Congregational Church, Worcester, Mass. From 1905 until his death, on Jan. 22, 1937, he was pastor of the Park Street Congregational Church in Boston. Mr. Conrad spent some summers preaching in London and Glasgow.

Information from *Who Was Who in America.*

* * *

Religion of Jesus as Exemplified in the Life and Sermons of Bishop Phillips Brooks. *Worcester, Mass.,* 1893.

Jesus Christ at the Cross Roads. *New York,* 1924.

Comrades of the Carpenter. *New York,* 1926.

The Seven Finalities of Faith. *Philadelphia,* 1926.

The Gospel for an Age of Thought. *New York,* 1928.

Secret of the Life Sublime. *New York,* 1929.

Radiant Religion. *New York,* 1930.

You Must Go Right On. *New York,* 1931.

Flashes from My Forge.

The Park Street Centennial.

COOKE, MARJORIE BENTON: 1876–1920.

Marjorie Benton Cooke, dramatic reader and monologist, was born in Richmond, Ind., in 1876, the daughter of Joseph Henry and Jessie Benton Cooke. After her graduation from the University of Chicago in 1899, she began writing for magazines, then, in 1902, she became a monologist, touring the U. S. and reciting original sketches and monologues. She spent her leisure time writing stories, plays, and poetry. Miss Cooke died on Apr. 26, 1920.

Information from *Who Was Who in America* and Dunn—*Indiana and Indianans.*

* * *

Modern Monologues. *Chicago,* 1903.

Dramatic Episodes. *Chicago,* 1904.

Plays for Children. 1905.

First Thanksgiving Dinner; a Play for 6th to 12th Grade Schools. *Chicago,* 1906.

Roll Call of Heroes: Decoration Day Entertainment. *Chicago,* 1906.

When the Knights Were Bold: Play in One Act. *Chicago,* 1906.

More Modern Monologues. *Chicago,* 1907.

The Girl Who Lived in the Woods. *Chicago,* 1910.

Dr. David. *Chicago,* 1911.

To Mother. *Chicago,* 1911.

Twelfth Christmas : the Christ Child's Revelation. *Chicago,* 1911.

The Redemption of Anthony. *Indianapolis,* 1911.

In the Good Green Wood: Play. *Chicago.*

At Mme. Newberry's: Monologue. *Chicago.*

Case of Sophronia: Play. *Chicago.*

Christmas Benefit: Play. *Chicago.*

Cupid Plays Coach: Monologue. *Chicago.*

Dark-Brown Diplomat: Monologue. *Chicago.*

Fairy Ring: Play for Children. *Chicago.*

Finer Shades of Honor: Play. *Chicago.*

Her Day at Home: Monologue. *Chicago.*

In the Merry Month of May: Monologue. *Chicago.*

On Woman's Rights: Monologue. *Chicago.*

Optimist: Monologue. *Chicago.*

Page from the Past: Play. *Chicago.*

Suburbanites: Monologue. *Chicago.*

Tit for Tat: Play for Children. *Chicago.*

What the Janitor Heard: Monologue. *Chicago.*

Who's Afraid? Monologue. *Chicago.*

Springtime Fantasy: Easter Play. *Chicago.*

Bambi. *Garden City, N. Y.,* 1914.

Dual Alliance. *Garden City, N. Y.,* 1915.

The Incubus. 1915.

Cinderella Jane. *Garden City, N. Y.,* 1917.

Clutch of Circumstance. *New York,* 1918.

Threshold. *Garden City, N. Y.,* 1919.

Cricket. *Garden City, N. Y.,* 1919.

Married? *New York,* 1923.

Home, a Play in Three Acts. *New York,* 1933.

COOLIDGE, MARY ELIZABETH BURROUGHS ROBERTS (MRS. DANE): 1860–?

Mary Elizabeth Burroughs Roberts, daughter of Isaac Phillips and Margaret Jane Marr Roberts, was born in Kingsbury, Ind., on Oct. 28, 1860. She was educated at Cornell, receiving the Ph.B. in 1880 and the M.S. in 1882.

After teaching history for four years in Washington, D. C., and Cincinnati, O., she became associated in 1886 with Wellesley College as instructor in history and economics. From 1896 to 1903 she taught sociology at Stanford University, from 1904 to 1908 she was research assistant to the Carnegie Institute in Washington, and from 1918 to 1927 she was professor of sociology at Mills College. She was a member of the California State Board of Education from 1928 to 1932. Her first husband was Albert Smith, whom she married in 1890. On July 30, 1906, she married Dane Coolidge, novelist, who died in 1940.

Information from *Who's Who in America* and Dunn—*Indiana and Indianans.*

* * *

Almshouse Women. *Palo Alto, Calif.,* 1896.
Chinese Immigration. *New York,* 1909.
Why Women Are So. *New York,* 1912.
The Rain Makers; Indians of Arizona and New Mexico. *Boston,* 1929.
Navajo Indians (with Dane Coolidge). *Boston,* 1930.
The Last of the Seris (with Dane Coolidge). *New York,* 1939.

COONEY, JOHN MICHAEL: 1874–1946.

Born in Louisville, Ky., in 1874, John Michael Cooney graduated from St. Mary's College in Baltimore in 1895, receiving the A.M. degree in 1896 and the Ph.D. from the University of Notre Dame in 1917.

He returned from Baltimore to Kentucky and became owner and editor of the NELSON RECORD and special correspondent for the LOUISVILLE HERALD. In 1905 he was an instructor at St. Mary's College, from 1906 to 1911 president of Columbia College in Kentucky, and in 1911 joined the faculty of the University of Notre Dame, where he remained until his death in 1946. At the time of his death he was head of the department of journalism.

Information from The University Library, University of Notre Dame.

* * *

A Lecture on Parallel Lives. *New York,* 1915.
A Lecture on the Composers. *New York,* 1916.
Hills of Rest. *St. Meinrad, Ind.,* 1926.

COOPER, HOMER H.: 1868–

Born in Ligonier, Ind., on Dec. 22, 1868, Homer H. Cooper, son of Hiram P. and Margaret Simpson

Cooper, was educated at Indiana University (A.B., 1891; A.M., 1893). In 1891-92 he was principal in the schools of Cortland, Ind., from 1892 to 1901 he was a teacher and principal in the high school and superintendent of schools in Knightstown, Ind., and from 1901 to 1916 he taught in and was superintendent of Spiceland Academy. For two years he was a bookseller in New Castle, Ind. and in 1920 he entered the real estate and insurance business. Mr. Cooper married Mary Baily, of Spiceland, on May 31, 1900.

Information from *Who's Who in America.*

* * *

Right Living; Messages to Youth from Men Who Have Achieved. *Chicago,* 1914.
Among Friends. 1916.

COOPER, HORATIO C.: ?–1864

Horatio C. Cooper, son of John Cooper, a farmer and teacher, was probably of English birth. He was a member of one of the families which purchased farms in the so-called English Prairie, Edwards County, Ill., during the development of those lands for sale to English middle-class farmers and tradesmen by Richard Flower and Morris Birkbeck in the early 1820's.

The Cooper family was one of those which were attracted from the English Prairie to New Harmony by the Utopian community which Robert Owen proposed to set up there in 1825. The Coopers, with other English families, withdrew from Owen's community shortly before its dissolution and leased and later purchased lands about a mile east of the town, where they set up a cooperative farming project which was soon divided into private holdings.

Horatio C. Cooper married Laura Moore and had, at one time, substantial business interests in New Harmony and served in the Indiana Legislature. About 1860 he moved to St. Paul, Minn., where he died in 1864.

Beginnings of Printing in Indiana; and *History of Posey County, Indiana.*

* * *

The Adventures of a Foreigner; a Poem. In Addition Are a Number of Incomplete Patriotic Songs. *New Harmony, Ind.,* 1843.

CORBY, WILLIAM: 1833–1897.

Born in Detroit, Mich., Oct. 2, 1833, William Corby entered the University of Notre Dame at the age of nineteen. One year later he joined the Congregation of the Holy Cross, in 1859 was appointed Prefect of Discipline of the institution, and in 1860 was ordained to the priesthood.

During the Civil War he served as chaplain to the 88th New York Regiment of the Irish Brigade. After the war he returned to Notre Dame, where he taught and served a term as president. He was elected to the office of Provincial-General of the Congregation of the Holy Cross in the U. S. and was subsequently chosen First Assistant General for the Order in all parts of the world. He died in 1897.

> Information from the University of Notre Dame Library.

* * *

Memoirs of Chaplain Life. *Notre Dame,* 1894.

CORY, HARRY THOMAS: 1870–

Harry Thomas Cory, son of Thomas and Carrie Stoney Cory, was born in Lafayette, Ind., on May 27, 1870, and graduated from Purdue University in 1887 with the B.M.E. degree. In 1889 he received the B.C.E. degree and in 1929 the Dr. Engring. From Cornell University he received the M.C.E. and M.M.E. degrees. On Oct. 4, 1911, he married Ida Judd Hiller.

In his career as an engineer Mr. Cory served as assistant city engineer for Lafayette, Ind., and deputy county engineer for Tippecanoe County, taught at the University of Missouri and the University of Cincinnati, was employed by numerous railway companies, and was a consulting engineer for the U. S. Reclamation Service. After 1928 he was a consulting engineer in Los Angeles.

> Information from *Who's Who in America.*

* * *

Manual of United States System of Land Surveying (with Thomas Cory). 1888.
Atlas of Boone County, Indiana. 1888.
Atlas of Clay County, Indiana. 1890.
Atlas of Tippecanoe County, Indiana. 1892.
Imperial Valley and the Salton Sink. *San Francisco,* 1915.
Opportunities in the South. *New Orleans,* 1918.
Democratization of Family Planning; Practical Solution. *Washington, D. C.,* 1940.

COTTMAN, GEORGE STREIBE: 1857–1941.

George Streibe Cottman, son of John and Julia Wilkins Cottman, was born in Indianapolis, Ind., on

May 10, 1857. In his youth he lived on a farm near Beech Grove and attended the district school. Later (1873-1876) he served as an apprentice in the printing trade on the INDIANAPOLIS SENTINEL.

In 1888 he moved to Irvington, a suburb of Indianapolis, where he set up a printing office. In 1900 he married Vida C. Tibbott. He wrote in his spare time and founded the INDIANA QUARTERLY MAGAZINE OF HISTORY (in 1905), which he edited and printed at his own home until 1907, when the Indiana Historical Society came to his assistance. Indiana University took over its publication in 1913. He contributed to this magazine, and to other periodicals, numerous articles on Indiana history and biographical sketches of prominent citizens. In addition to his historical writing, he also was the author of several books and articles on nature study.

Mr. Cottman died at the home of his son in Madison, Ind., on May 18, 1941.

> Information from the Indianapolis Public Library and the INDIANA HISTORY BULLETIN, Mar. 1942.

* * *

Hours with Nature. *Irvington, Ind.,* 1890.
Four Hoosier Holiday Stories. *Irvington, Ind.,* 1891.
Vacation Gleanings. *Irvington, Ind.,* 1893.
Love, the Sovereign. *Irvington, Ind.,* 1900.
First Thoroughfares of Indiana. *Indianapolis,* 1906.
Canals of Indiana. *Indianapolis,* 1907.
My Lake and a Sermon from the Lily. *Irvington, Ind.,* 1907.
Early Railroads of Indiana. *Indianapolis,* 1907.
A Centennial History and Handbook of Indiana; the Story of the State from Its Beginning to the Close of the Civil War, and a General Survey of Progress to the Present Time (with Max Robinson Hyman). *Indianapolis,* 1915.
Under Three Flags. *Indianapolis,* 1916.
Irvington's Pageant for 1916. *Indianapolis,* 1916.
Pageant of Old Vincennes. *Vincennes, Ind.,* 1916.
Jefferson County in the World War. *Madison, Ind.,* 1920.
Hamilton County Pageant. *Indianapolis,* 1923.
Indiana, Its History, Constitution, and Present Government. *Indianapolis,* 1925.
Clifty Falls State Park; Its Attractions and Adjacent Points of Interest, Scenic and Historical. *Indianapolis,* 1925.
James F. D. Lanier Home; an Indiana Memorial, Madison. *Indianapolis,* 1927.
Pokagon State Park and Steuben County; a Description of Indiana's Most Picturesque Lake Region. *Indianapolis,* 1927.
Indiana Dunes State Park; a History and Description. *Indianapolis,* 1930.

Corydon State-House; a Hoosier Shrine. *Indianapolis,* n.d. [1930].

River Navigation in Indiana. *Indianapolis,* n.d.

Internal Improvement in Indiana. [*Indianapolis*], n.d.

List of the Indiana Newspapers on File in the Indiana State Library. [*Indianapolis*], n.d.

Wabash and Erie Canal. [*Indianapolis*], n.d.

Wild Animals of Indiana. [*Indianapolis*], n.d.

COTTOM, CHARLES W.: ?–?

No information regarding Charles W. Cottom has been located except for the facts that he was a newspaper man and that he was a resident of Indianapolis in the middle Fifties and of New Albany, Ind., in the early Seventies.

On Mar. 2, 1855, he purchased THE INDIANA SENTINEL in partnership with John C. Walker. They sold it on Dec. 4, following. On Jan. 24, 1856, Cottom repurchased the paper, this time in partnership with William C. Larrabee. Cottom sold his interest several months later.

He appears to have removed to New Albany, where his only known separate publication—a promotional booklet regarding the town—appeared in 1873.

> Information from Holloway—*Indianapolis. A Historical and Statistical Sketch . . . 1870.*

* * *

New Albany, Indiana: Its Material Interests and Manufacturing and Commercial Advantages. *New Albany,* 1873.

COTTON, ALFRED JOHNSON: 1800–1858.

Little biographical information is available on Alfred Johnson Cotton, Indiana pioneer, other than the few facts that can be found in county histories and in the autobiographical sketch appended to his book, *Cotton's Keepsake* (which is now a rare book of considerable value). In the latter sketch Reverend Judge (he used the titles in conjunction) Cotton gives a clear picture of himself as an individual but omits many details of his life necessary to a complete biography.

Born in Cumberland County, Me., on Apr. 20, 1800, he was the fourth of nine children. He had two or three months schooling each during several winters in the schools of the county. In 1818 he came to Dearborn County, Ind., where he erected a cabin in the wilderness, taught school, and in 1825 was ordained a preacher. He entered politics in 1828 and was an unsuccessful candidate for several offices. For a brief time he edited the NEWCASTLE BANNER, but he returned to Dearborn County, where he served as associate judge for six years and probate judge for four years.

> Information from *Cotton's Keepsake;* Shaw—*History of Dearborn County Indiana* and Walker—*Beginnings of Printing in the State of Indiana.*

* * *

Cotton's Keepsake: Poems on Various Subjects, by Rev. Judge A. J. Cotton, Philom. To Which Is Appended a Short Autobiographical Sketch of the Life of the Author, and a Condensed History of the Early Settlements, Incidents, and Improvements of the Country, from the Early Settlers Themselves, and from Observation and Experience in It, for the Space of Forty Years Last Past. *Cincinnati,* 1858.

Cotton's Sketch-Book; Autobiographical Sketches of the Life, Labors, and Extensive Home Travels of . . . in Short, Convenient Chapters. *Portland, Me.,* 1874.

COTTON, FASSETT ALLEN: 1862–1942.

Fassett Allen Cotton, son of Marion Irwin and Rachel Amanda Wright Cotton, was born in Nineveh, Ind., on May 1, 1862. From 1882 to 1889 he taught school and in 1888-89 was enrolled as a student at Terre Haute State Normal. He was county superintendent of schools (1889-95) and deputy state superintendent of public instruction (1895-1901). He received the A.B. degree from Butler University and the Ph.B. from Chicago in 1902.

From 1903 to 1909 he was Indiana State Superintendent of Public Instruction, from 1909 to 1924 president of State Normal, LaCrosse, Wis., and in 1924 became president of Northern Arizona Teachers College. He was twice married: first to Florence N. Wright in 1885, then to Lena L. Dobson in 1903.

> Information from *Who's Who in America.*

* * *

Education in Indiana; an Outline of the Growth of the Common School System Together with Statements Relating to the Condition of Secondary and Higher Education in the State and a Brief History of the Educational Exhibit. Prepared for the Louisiana Purchase Exposition, Held at St. Louis May 1 to November 30, 1904. *Indianapolis,* 1904.

Township High-School System of Indiana. *Chicago,* 1904.

Agriculture for Common Schools (with Martin L. Fisher). *New York,* 1909.

Consolidation of School Districts (with Michael V. O'Shea and Walter E. Larson). *Madison, Wisconsin,* 1912.

Education in Indiana, 1793-1934. *Bluffton, Ind.,* 1934.

COULTER, JOHN MERLE: 1851-1928.

"John Merle Coulter . . . botanist, was born at Ningpo, China, the son of missionary parents, Moses Stanley and Caroline E. (Crowe) Coulter. He graduated with the A.B. degree from Hanover College in 1870. In 1872 he was assistant geologist on the Hayden Survey. While the expedition was waiting in the mountains for Hayden, the rest of the party whiled away the time playing cards; but since young Coulter did not know how to play, he collected plants. When Hayden arrived, he was so impressed by Coulter's collections that he appointed him botanist of the expedition. The object of the expedition was to look for the rumored hot springs and geysers of what is now Yellowstone Park. When they found the geysers, each member was assigned one of the holes for study. Since Coulter was the youngest member of the party, they assigned him one of the smaller holes. It turned out to be Old Faithful.

"The study of his botanical collections took him to Washington, where he met Asa Gray. The meeting was the beginning of a life-long friendship. Coulter became Gray's most distinguished pupil and with Sereno Watson he edited (1890) the sixth edition of Gray's famous Manual. In 1873 he received the A.M. degree from Hanover College and was professor of natural sciences there, 1874-79, and professor of biology in Wabash College, 1879-91. During this period (in 1884) he received the degree of Ph.D. from Indiana State University. He was a life-long friend of David Starr Jordan, and when Jordan resigned from the presidency of Indiana State University (1891), he persuaded Coulter to succeed him. The politics of a state university and the worry about securing funds from politicians were so distasteful that Coulter resigned in 1893 and became president of Lake Forest University, which he thought was so well endowed that there would be no financial problems. Even at Lake Forest, however, administrative duties interfered seriously with his chosen work and he went to the University of Chicago (1896), where he was able to devote nearly thirty years to building up a strong department and to training young men and women for teaching and research. After retiring from active teaching in 1925 he became adviser to the Boyce Thompson Institute for Plant Research at Yonkers, N. Y., for the foundation of which he was largely responsible . . .

"In 1875, while at Hanover College, he founded the BOTANICAL GAZETTE, which he not only edited, but also managed and often financed. It has become the leading botanical journal of America. Reviews of the critical type, as distinguished from the colorless type of abstracting journals, have always been a feature of the GAZETTE, and Coulter's reviews are models of this kind of writing . . . What would have been his greatest contribution, a history of botany, will probably never be completed. For years he had been gathering material, and, occasionally, in lectures he had given glimpses of what the work might be. He had just completed a collection of biographical sketches when he died.

"Coulter's greatest influence was not through his books and papers, however, numerous and good as they were, but through the men and women he trained. No other American botanist has so many students holding high positions. He belonged to botanical organizations at home and abroad and received all the major honors his fellow botanists could bestow upon him. Before his death, his students had already established the John M. Coulter Research Fellowship in Botany, to support exceptional students engaged in research . . ."

He was the author of a great number of government publications, textbooks and contributions to learned journals and serials not eligible for listing here.

Condensed from the *Dictionary of American Biography*, Vol. IV.

* * *

Catalogue of the Plants of Indiana (with C. R. Barnes). *Crawfordsville, Ind.,* 1881.

Manual of the Botany of the Rocky Mountain Region. *New York,* 1885.

Handbook of Plant Dissection (with Joseph C. Arthur and C. R. Barnes). *New York,* 1886.

Manual of the Botany of the Northern United States (with Asa Gray and Sereno Watson). *New York,* 1889.

Practical Education. *Indianapolis,* 1891.

Manual of Texan Botany. 1893.

The Botanical Outlook. *Lincoln,* 1895.

Plants in Their Environment. *Chicago,* 1896.

Evolution. *Chicago,* 1897.

Mission of Science in Education. An Address Delivered at . . . University of Michigan. *Ann Arbor, Mich.,* 1900.

An Analytical Key to Some of the Common Wild and Cultivated Species of Flowering Plants. *New York,* 1900.

Morphology of Spermatophytes. Part 1, Gymnosperms (with Charles J. Chamberlain). *New York,* 1901.

The Polity of the Y. M. C. A. *Chicago,* 1901.

The Student Y. M. C. A. as It Relates to the Entire Association Movement. *Chicago,* 1901.

Organic Evolution as Illustrated by Plants. *Chicago,* 1902.

Phylogeny of Angiosperms. *Chicago, 1903.*

Morphology of Angiosperms (with Charles J. Chamberlain). *New York, 1903.*

New Manual of Botany of the Central Rocky Mountains. (Revised by Aven Nelson.) *New York, 1909.*

Practical Nature Study and Elementary Agriculture (with John Gaylord Coulter and Alice Jean Patterson). *New York, 1909.*

Morphology of Gymnosperms. *Chicago, 1910.*

Elementary Studies in Botany. *New York, 1913.*

Evolution of Sex in Plants. *Chicago, 1914.*

Fundamentals of Plant Breeding. *New York, 1914.*

Evolution, Heredity and Eugenics. *Bloomington, Ill., 1916.*

Record of the Doctors in Botany of the University of Chicago, 1897-1916 (with Charles J. Chamberlain). *Chicago, 1916.*

Plant Genetics (with Merle Crowe Coulter). *Chicago, 1918.*

Where Evolution and Religion Meet (with Merle Crowe Coulter). *New York, 1924.*

Botanical Research as a Career. *Washington, D. C., 1925.*

COULTER, STANLEY: 1853–1943.

Stanley Coulter, brother of John Merle Coulter, was born in Ningpo, China, on June 2, 1853. He was the son of Moses Stanley and Caroline E. Crowe Coulter, missionaries for the Presbyterian Church. After the death of his father, the family settled at Hanover, Ind., where young Stanley entered Hanover College, founded by his grandfather, and graduated in 1871, receiving the A.M. degree in 1874 and the Ph.D. in 1889. He was married in Logansport, Ind., on June 21, 1877, to Lucy E. Post, who died in 1942.

Following his graduation from college he taught for one year at Franklin, Ind., spent the years 1873-1885 as principal of the Logansport High School, and from 1882 to 1885 practiced law. In 1887 he joined the faculty of Purdue University, where until his retirement in 1926 he served as professor of biology and director of the biological laboratory. He became the first dean of the School of Science in 1907, dean of men in 1919, and acting chairman of the faculty in 1921.

Dr. Coulter was a member of the Indiana State Board of Forestry, the Conservation Commission of Indiana, and various scientific societies. Recognized nationally as a scientist, he was well known also for his work in behalf of the conservation of public resources, prevention of tuberculosis, religion, and world peace. He was often spoken of as "The Dean" or "the grand old man of Purdue" and was the friend and counselor of thousands of Purdue students during his years on the campus.

He died on June 29, 1943.

Information from the Purdue University Libraries, Dunn—*Indiana and Indianans,* and *Who's Who in America.*

* * *

A Catalogue of the Flowering Plants and of the Ferns and Their Allies Indigenous to Indiana. *Indianapolis, 1900.*

What Experience Has Taught Me Concerning Nature Study. *Lafayette, Ind., n.d.* [1901].

A Key to the Genera of the Native Forest Trees and Shrubs of Indiana, Based Chiefly Upon Leaf Characters (with Herman B. Dorner). *Lafayette, Ind., 1907.*

COVERT, WILLIAM CHALMERS: 1864–1942.

William Chalmers Covert, son of Albert Newton and Susan Elizabeth Magill Covert, was born in Franklin, Ind., on Oct. 4, 1864. After graduating from Hanover College (A.B., 1885; A.M., 1888) and from the Presbyterian Theological Seminary in Chicago (1888), he was ordained to the Presbyterian ministry in St. Paul in 1888. He was pastor of churches in St. Paul, Saginaw, and Chicago, and, from 1924 to 1934, was general secretary of the Board of Christian Education of Presbyterian Churches. In 1890 he married Alice Brown Hudson. He died on Feb. 4, 1942.

Information from *Who Was Who in America.*

* * *

Story of the Redemption From Paradise Lost to Paradise Restored. *Mountain View, Calif., 1898.*

Glory of the Pines; a Tale of the Ontonagon. *Philadelphia, 1914.*

Wild Woods and Waterways. *Philadelphia, 1914.*

New Furrows in Old Fields; a Present Day Outlook on the Opportunities for Faith and Work. *New York, 1920.*

Religion in the Heart, and Other Addresses. *New York, 1926.*

Comrades of the Christian Church; a Pageant of the Spirit of the Centuries. *Philadelphia, 1922.*

For the Land's Sake. *Philadelphia, n.d.*

Our Stainless Flag. *Philadelphia, n.d.*

Christ and Culture. *New York, 1930.*

Facing Our Day. *New York, 1934.*

With Cross and Crown in Every Land. 1937.

COX, JOHN E.: 1850–1932.

John E. Cox was born near New Harmony, Ind., on Oct. 14, 1850. His parents were Joshua and Caroline Cox.

Young Cox enlisted in the regular army in 1872 and served five years—being a member of Maj. Walker's expedition to the Black Hills in 1873; he was present at the surrender of the Sioux at Standing Rock Agency in the fall of 1876.

His enlistment over, he began to prepare himself for the Baptist ministry. In 1878 he was ordained and the same year married Mary E. Weare of Mt. Vernon, Ind.

He held pastorates in North and South Carolina, West Virginia, Ohio, Michigan, Illinois and Indiana during his active life and he contributed short stories and articles to newspapers and to the GENERAL BAPTIST MESSENGER. He died at Evansville, Ind., on Dec. 5, 1932.

> Information from Miss Grace Cox, Evansville, his daughter.

* * *

Sketches, Sermons and Sayings by Sister Skraggs. *Owensville, Ind.,* 1891.

Five Years in the United States Army. *Owensville, Ind.,* 1892.

Memorial Services. Burial Services of the National Corps, Regular Army and Navy Union. *Leavenworth, Kan.,* 1893.

A Time to Laugh or Fun Among the Preachers. *Owensville, Ind.,* 1893.

Job and Deb in Yourope. *Owensville, Ind.,* 1901.

Sang Sammy, a Story of the Mountain People. *Owensville, Ind.,* 1903.

Foot Washing. Is It an Ordinance. Different Views. *Owensville, Ind.,* 1906.

General Baptists and Foreign Missions. Island of Guam. *Owensville, Ind.,* 1913.

Reminiscences. Experiences and Incidents in the Life of Rev. John E. Cox. *Owensville, Ind.,* 1915.

The Second Coming of Christ and Related Subjects. *Owensville, Ind.,* 1919.

Thomas Price and His Descendants. A History and Genealogy. *Owensville, Ind.,* 1926.

John E. Cox. His Observations and Experiences. An Autobiography. *Owensville, Ind.,* 1928.

A History of the Cox Pioneers of Posey County Indiana. *Owensville, Ind.,* 1931.

COX, MILLARD F.: 1856–1914.

Born near Noblesville, Ind., on Feb. 25, 1856, Millard F. Cox, son of Aaron and Mary A. Cox, was educated in the public schools of Noblesville and Tipton, Ind. As a boy he learned the printer's trade on the TIPTON TIMES, and he later taught one term in a country school. After studying law at Indianapolis, he was admitted to the bar in 1880. From 1890 to 1894 he served as judge of the Criminal Court of Indianapolis, and he later served as judge of the Superior Court. On June 15, 1892 he married Hattie Pressly Weed. He wrote under the pseudonym of Henry Scott Clark.

> Information from Dunn—*Indiana and Indianans* and *Who's Who in America.*

* * *

The Legionaries, a Story of the Great Raid. *Indianapolis,* 1899.

COX, SANDFORD C.: ?–?

Sandford C. Cox arrived in Crawfordsville, Ind., with his parents and their other children, in the fall of 1824, at the very peak of the land speculation excitement and of the only turbulent period that city ever enjoyed. Sandford saw everything: land speculators with phenomenal watch-chains and plug hats, mud, overflowing taverns, recently retired Indian fighters and more mud.

Also the Cox family had stopped at the Falls of Fall Creek in their wagon emigration from Wayne County, Ind., in the Whitewater Valley, long enough for young Sandford to see four men awaiting what was soon to be a multiple hanging for three of them: probably the sole occasion in Indiana on which white men were hanged for the casual misdemeanor of killing Indians.

Cox must have received a reasonable amount of schooling before he came to Eastern Indiana, for within two years he began teaching school and continued the business in Montgomery, Fountain, Warren and Tippecanoe counties during most of his life.

Unlike some of his contemporaries in that profession—whose traditional first interest was tuition money and second and last the jug—Cox always cherished literary ambitions. He wrote long—and most interesting—descriptive letters to his old friends, and by 1833 he had begun to contribute verse to local newspapers. Such contribution indicates a faithful and disinterested wooing of the muse: newspaper editors did not pay for poems then, any more than they do today, and there was more likely to be discredit than glory for the poet in the eyes of his neighbors and patrons.

In October and November, 1859, most of the first

of the pioneers having gone on to fairer fields, it occurred to Cox that his own reminiscences of people and events in West-central Indiana might make interesting reading. He had associated with most of the leading men in the four counties in which he had taught and his keen interest in human frailties had prompted him to become acquainted with those citizens at the other extreme of the social scale. Besides, he had seen the "Indian Murderers," as they were called, with his own eyes, and his grandfather, Richard Rue, had told him the otherwise unrecorded story of the captivity of himself, Irvin Hinton and George Holman by a party of Indians under Simon Girty.

The historical contributions he made to the LAFAYETTE DAILY COURIER that fall were published over the signature "In cog." and they aroused sufficient interest to encourage the author to have a small edition of them printed in book form the next year. The book was good; far better, probably, than either Cox or his contemporary readers suspected.

This publication terminated his career as a writer except that, seven years later, he gathered together the best of his poems and published them. The two books are the total output, as far as is recorded, of as observing and as entertaining a writer as could be found in the U. S. of his day.

Cox's *Recollections of the Early Settlement of the Wabash Valley*, on account of its wealth of detail, pleasing style and the breadth of subjects covered— the "Indian Murderers," middle western settlement, an excellent account of an early Indian captivity, the Black Hawk War, etc.—has long been collected. It is becoming increasingly scarce and is increasing greatly in value.

His book of poems, far more scarce than the *Recollections*, has attracted interest only as an association item.

> Information from Cox—*Recollections* and deHart —*Past and Present of Tippecanoe County.*

* * *

Recollections of the Early Settlement of the Wabash Valley. *Lafayette, Ind., 1860.*
The Evangelist and Other Poems. *Cincinnati, 1867.*

COY, SIMEON: 1851–?

Born in Greensburg, Ind., on Oct. 13, 1851, Simeon Coy came to Indianapolis in 1863 and lived there for the rest of his life.

He entered the employ of the Shaw Carriage Works in 1866 as an apprentice in the painter's trade. At the age of twenty-four he went into the liquor business. Still later Mr. Coy entered politics, serving on the city council. At one time he served a prison sentence for election fraud, but at the expiration of that sentence he was re-elected to the city council.

> Information from the Indianapolis Public Library.

* * *

The Great Conspiracy. *Indianapolis, 1899.*

CRECRAFT, EARL WILLIS: 1886–

Earl Willis Crecraft, son of Albert Newton and Mary Tyner Crecraft, was born at Brookville, Ind., on Jan. 27, 1886, and graduated from Franklin College in 1907. From Columbia University he received the A.M. degree in 1911 and the Ph.D. in 1915, and Franklin College awarded him an LL.D. in 1934. He married Lucy Ann Guthrie on Aug. 19, 1914.

From 1908 to 1910 he was principal of the high school at Shelbyville, Ind., from 1912 to 1913 an instructor in politics at Columbia, from 1913 to 1919 an instructor and lecturer in government at New York University, and from 1919 to 1938 professor of political science at the University of Akron. In 1938 he became dean of the College of Liberal Arts and professor of political science at Kent State University.

> Information from *Who's Who in America* and Franklin College.

* * *

Government of Hudson County, New Jersey. *Jersey City, N. J., 1915.*
Government and Business: a Study in the Economic Aspects of Government and the Public Aspects of Business. *Yonkers-on-Hudson, N. Y., 1928.*
Freedom of the Seas. *New York, 1935.*

CROOKE, CHARLES WALTER: 1863–

Charles Walter Crooke, born at Odon, Ind., in 1863, received the A.B. degree from De Pauw University. He became the pastor of an Indianapolis Methodist Church and an active worker for prohibition of liquor traffic.

> Information from the Federal Writers Project— *Indiana Authors, 1937.*

* * *

Texas Prohibition Laws.
Bottles and Rags.
Texas Prohibition Prohibits.

CROOKS, JAMES: 1825–1908.

James Crooks, son of Dr. William B. and Martha Johnson Crooks, was born in Butler County, O., on Oct. 6, 1825. His parents' home was built on the state line between Franklin County, Indiana, and Butler County, O., and young James was born on the Ohio side.

In 1826 the family moved to Parke County, where they lived for five years, and in 1831 they located in Montgomery County, nine miles west of Crawfordsville, in a community called Middletown—later Waynetown. For a few months in 1834 they lived at Michigan City, then for four years were residents of Lake County, but in 1838 they returned to Parke County.

Young James began his education in Montgomery County and attended school in Michigan City and in Parke County. In 1845 he began to read medicine. He married Sarah Jane Ward on Jan. 13, 1850, and they lived with his family while he was starting the practice of medicine. In 1856 he purchased a home in Bridgeton, Ind. From 1855 to 1859 he was a student at the Eclectic Medical College of Cincinnati, from which he graduated in May of 1859.

In addition to practicing medicine, Dr. Crooks engaged in the mercantile business and in the manufacture of patent medicines. He also traveled extensively and wrote articles which were printed in the ROCKVILLE REPUBLICAN and other local papers. For a brief time he was a newspaper editor.

On Dec. 13, 1891, his first wife died, and on Mar. 15, 1893, he married Lila F. Martin. Dr. Crooks died at Bridgeton, Ind., on Feb. 1, 1908.

> Information from *The Autobiography of James Crooks* and Mrs. Claude Crooks of Rockville, Ind.

* * *

The Autobiography of James Crooks, A.M., M.D. *Terre Haute, Ind.,* 1900.

CROWE, NELSON KENDALL: 1830–?

Born at Princeton, Ind., on Dec. 15, 1830, Nelson Kendall Crowe graduated from Indiana University in 1851 and received the A.M. degree in 1854. He had studied at Princeton Academy before attending Indiana University. He was a minister at Morissa, Ill., Walton, N. Y., Savannah, O., Radnor, O. and Delaware, O.

> Information from The University Libraries, Indiana University.

* * *

A History of the Freedmen's Mission of the Reformed Presbyterian Church.

CRULL, ADAM ULLERY: ?–1915.

Adam Ullery Crull, son of Norris and Christina Ullery Crull, was born near Mishawaka, Ind. He was principal of Huntington High School for a number of years and later taught in Duluth, Minn.

> Information from the South Bend Public Library.

* * *

Ballads from the St. Jo. *South Bend,* 1894.

CUBBERLEY, ELWOOD PATTERSON: 1868–1941.

Elwood Patterson Cubberley, son of Edwin Blanchard and Kate Coryell Cubberley, was born in Andrews, Ind., on June 6, 1868. He graduated from Indiana University in 1891, received the A.M. (1902) and the Ph.D. (1905) degrees from Columbia University and was awarded an LL.D. degree by Indiana University and the University of Iowa. He married Helen Van Uxem on June 15, 1892.

From 1891 to 1896 he was professor and president at Vincennes University, from 1896 to 1898 superintendent of schools at San Diego, and from 1898 to 1933 taught at Stanford University. He served as dean of the school of education at Stanford from 1917 to 1933. For two years he was a department editor of *Monroe's Cyclopedia of Education*.

He died on Sept. 15, 1941.

> Information from *Indiana University, 1820–1904,* and *Who Was Who in America*.

* * *

A Key for Determinative Mineralogy. *Vincennes, Ind.,* 1895.

Report of the Public Schools of San Diego, Cal., with Courses of Study. *San Diego,* 1897.

Courses of Study for the Public Schools of San Francisco. *San Francisco,* 1900.

A Syllabus of School Management. *Boston,* 1901.

A Syllabus of Lectures on the History of Education, with Selected Bibliographies. *New York,* 1902. 2 vols.

School Funds and Their Apportionment. *New York,* 1905.

Changing Conceptions of Education. *Boston,* 1909.

The Improvement of Rural Schools. *Boston,* 1912.

Rural Life and Education: a Study of the Rural-School Problem as a Phase of the Rural-Life Problem. *Boston,* 1914.

State and County School Administration Source Book (with E. C. Elliott). *New York, 1915.*

Public School Administration; a Statement of the Fundamental Principles Underlying the Organization and Administration of Public Education. *Boston, 1916.*

School Organization and Administration; a Concrete Study Based on the Salt Lake City School Survey (with others). *Yonkers-on-Hudson, N. Y., 1916.*

Public Education in the United States; a Study and Interpretation of American Educational History. *Boston, 1919.*

Readings in the History of Education; a Collection of Sources and Readings to Illustrate the Development of Educational Practice, Theory, and Organization. *Boston, 1920.*

A History of Education; Educational Practice and Progress Considered as a Phase of the Development and Spread of Western Civilization. *Boston, 1920.*

A Brief History of Education. *Boston, 1922.*

The Principal and His School; the Organization, Administration, and Supervision of Instruction in an Elementary School. *Boston, 1923.*

The Cost of Education in California . . . (with J. B. Sears). *New York, 1924.*

The School Textbook Problem. *Boston, 1927.*

State School Administration. *Boston, 1927.*

CULTER, MARY NANTZ McCRAE (MRS. BRADFORD M.): 1858–

Born in New Albany, Ind., on Apr. 12, 1858, Mary Nantz McCrae was the daughter of the Rev. John and Catherine H. Shields McCrae, representatives of a pioneer New Albany family. After her graduation from Western College for Women in 1877, she taught school in Indiana and later in Kansas. On Oct. 19, 1882 she was married to Bradford M. Culter of Illinois. She began writing in 1894 and contributed poems and songs, short stories, and serials to numerous publications.

> Information from Dunn—*Indiana and Indianans* and *Who's Who in America.*

* * *

What the Railroad Brought to Timken. 1897.

Four Roads to Happiness: a Story of Hoosier Life. *Philadelphia, 1900.*

Unspeakable Gift. *Philadelphia, 1900.*

Girl Who Kept Up. *Boston, 1903.*

Prodigal Daughter. *Cincinnati, 1908.*

Jolly Half Dozen. *Cincinnati, 1910.*

A Real Aristocrat. 1917.

Ships That Pass in the Day.

Gates of Brass.

CUMBACK, WILL: 1829–1905.

Born in Franklin County, Ind., on Mar. 24, 1829, Will Cumback, son of John and Elsie Cumback, was reared on a farm and educated in the country schools. He attended Miami University and the Cincinnati Law School and began the practice of law in Greensburg, Ind., in 1853. When he was barely twenty-five years old, he was elected to Congress and was the youngest member of the 34th Congress. During the Civil War he served as paymaster of the army. His other public offices included state senator, lieutenant governor, and collector of internal revenue. He died in 1905.

> Information from *Representative Men of Indiana,* Vol. I; Dunn—*Indiana and Indianans,* and the Barry Ms.

* * *

Address Delivered by Hon. Will Cumback, at the Annual Reunion of the Miami and Whitewater Valley Pioneer Association, at Hunt's Grove, O., Saturday August 4, 1888; Also, the Presentation Speech by William Carson. *Harrison, Ohio, 1888.*

Lectures and Addresses. *Cincinnati, 1892.*

Men of Progress (with J. B. Maynard). *Indianapolis, 1899.*

CUPPY, HAZLITT ALVA: 1863–1934.

Hazlitt Alva Cuppy, son of the Rev. W. T. and Martha Ann Cuppy, was born in Shelburn, Ind., on Oct. 3, 1863. After graduating from Franklin College in 1888, he spent a year at both Oxford and Berlin universities, received an M.A. degree from Heidelberg, and was awarded Ph.D. degrees by Heidelberg and by the University of Paris. He returned to the U. S. in 1893 to become founder and editor of THE ALTRUISTIC REVIEW. From 1895 to 1897 he was editor of the BAPTIST UNION, from 1896 to 1898 director of the University of Chicago Press, and from 1898 to 1906 publisher and editor of PUBLIC OPINION. He was also, from 1893 to 1895, an associate editor of the WOMAN'S HOME COMPANION and at one time was correspondent for the LONDON ILLUSTRATED NEWS SKETCH.

Mr. Cuppy eventually left the editorial field to manufacture chocolate in Lititz, Pa., where he remained for several years. During the first World War he was a director and American representative of a large German corporation. He later started a factory of his own in San Francisco, where he died in 1934. Mr. Cuppy married Elizabeth Overstreet in 1895.

Information from *Who Was Who in America*; the Barry Ms.; and the INDIANAPOLIS NEWS, Jan. 27, 1934.

* * *

Knick-Knacks. *Indianapolis,* 1892.
Rise of the Anglo-Indian Empire.
Our Own Times—History of the Twentieth Century. (Author and editor.) 10 vols.

CUPPY, WILLIAM JACOB: 1884–

William Jacob Cuppy was born in Auburn, Ind., on Aug. 23, 1884, the son of Thomas Jefferson Cuppy and Mary Frances Stahl Cuppy.

"In spite of our funny name," says Mr. Cuppy, "the Cuppys were of some consequence as pioneers of Whitley County, Ind. My paternal grandfather, Abram Cuppy, died as long ago as 1847, while serving as state senator at Indianapolis. I was named after my uncle, Captain William Henry Cuppy, of the 44th Indiana Infantry, who died in 1862, having been wounded at Fort Donelson. We all came originally from South Carolina—French Huguenot stock.

"My happiest childhood days were spent at the Cuppy farm near South Whitley, Ind., where my widowed grandmother was the rallying point of G.A.R. activities, and where the small Will acquired his first knowledge of the birds, the flowers, and other annoying aspects of animate nature. It was there, too, that I went thru a threshing machine by mistake.

"My mother was straight Pennsylvania Dutch, and a school teacher to boot. I am very proud of my Pennsylvania Dutch strain. I think that is the best way to feel about it. Anyway, mother had most of the family sense. She was a singer of great talent, and I used to pump the organ while she sang in the choir in the Presbyterian Church in Auburn—a circumstance that finally led to my membership in the Guild of Former Pipe Organ Pumpers. By the way, my sister played the organ. When necessary, I substituted for either of them, my little brother pumping at such times.

"I attended the Auburn High School, graduating in 1902. I was out of school a good deal, having what passed for recurrent attacks of appendicitis; I now think that this was merely my way of attracting attention and getting out of work. Nevertheless, to my lasting regret, I was considered bright enough to skip the eighth grade, so that I missed all tuition in grammar, punctuation, and that sort of thing. As a result, I have always been wobbly in such matters.

"I entered the University of Chicago in 1902 and was graduated therefrom in 1907, with the degree of Ph.B. . . .

"The rest of my academic career is quite incredible. Deciding, after graduation, that I knew nothing whatever about anything, I hung about the campus for the next seven years, taking courses in practically everything, with or without credit, as the spirit moved me. For three mortal years I studied the Elizabethan prose writers in the graduate English library, and at one time had almost completed a doctor's thesis on the subject. One day I decided that all that would never do, so I cut the thesis in half, took the degree of Master of Arts in English and hopped a train for New York.

"So you see, I am really rather an erudite person. I try not to let it show in my writing. It isn't everybody that spends twelve years in college—and then writes the sort of thing I do!

"My first experience in authorship was equally fantastic. A publisher asked me to write a book of University of Chicago college stories, and I did. After purchasing and reading all the books of college stories available, I almost immediately produced a sizeable volume entitled *Maroon Tales*, as much like the others as possible but worse . . . Mercifully, most of the first edition was drowned in a flood which visited the cellar of the university press shortly thereafter.

"That was in 1909. My next book, *How to Be a Hermit*, appeared in 1929, just twenty years later. I used the twenty years between my first and my second book in trying to achieve the first faint glimmerings of how to write English . . .

"I do a little magazine writing. Most of *How to Tell Your Friends from the Apes* was first published in the NEW YORKER.

"For some years I have conducted a weekly column called Mystery and Adventure in 'Books', the literary supplement of the NEW YORK HERALD TRIBUNE. That is by no means because I prefer detective stories and Westerns to other books—it just happened so. Occasionally, I also review real, or honest-to-goodness books."

Will Cuppy is unmarried, maintains an apartment in New York, but spends most of his time, the year around, in a "shack" on one of the sandy reefs off the south shore of Long Island, where he develops the recipes that led the Library of Congress to classify his book of humor, *How to Be a Hermit*, under "culinary arts" . . .

Condensed from *Authors Today and Yesterday.*

* * *

Maroon Tales. *Chicago,* 1910.

How to Be a Hermit. *New York,* 1929.

How to Tell Your Friends from the Apes. *New York,* 1931.

How to Become Extinct. *New York,* 1941.

CURTIS, EMMA GHENT (MRS. JAMES): 1860–1918.

Emma Ghent, born in Frankfort, Ind., on May 18, 1860, was the daughter of Ira Keith and Mary Elizabeth Palmer Ghent. She graduated from the Frankfort High School in 1877.

A writer of both poetry and prose, she contributed to CENTURY MAGAZINE, ATLANTIC, YOUTH'S COMPANION and other periodicals, was an associate editor of *Funk and Wagnalls Standard Dictionary* and edited the ROYAL GORGE REVIEW of Canon City, Col. Mrs. Curtis was active in the organization of the Populist Party and worked for reform movements, including women's suffrage.

She died in Canon City, Col., in February of 1918.

Information from the Frankfort Public Library.

* * *

The Fate of a Fool. *New York,* 1888.

The Administratrix. *New York,* 1889.

CURTISS, GEORGE LEWIS: 1835–1898.

George Lewis Curtiss, son of Lewis and Mary Curtiss, was born in Columbia, Lorain County, O., on Nov. 21, 1835. Following his graduation from what is now Baldwin University in Berea, O., in 1854, he came to Indiana to teach mathematics at Moore's Hill College. He studied law for a time, then turned to the ministry and was pastor of churches in many Indiana communities—Charlestown, Madison, Greensburg, Connersville, Indianapolis, and Shelbyville. While in Madison he served one year as editor of the EVENING COURIER. In June of 1876 he was awarded the D.D. degree by Indiana Asbury (now De Pauw) University, and in the same year he graduated from the Indiana Medical College, where he lectured in 1877 and 1878. Dr. Curtiss married Matilda J. Smith in 1858. He died in 1898.

Information from *Representative Men of Indiana,* Vol. I.

* * *

History of the Methodist Episcopal Church in Shelbyville, 1823-1878. *Shelbyville, Ind.,* 1878.

Tragic Trio. *Indianapolis,* 1882.

Sketches from the Romance of American History. n.p., n.d. [1886].

Evolution of Christian Doctrines, or, Outline Lectures on the History of Christian Doctrines. *Terre Haute, Ind.,* 1891.

Interrogatory Studies in Bible History. *Greencastle, Ind.,* 1892.

Manual of Methodist Episcopal Church History, Showing the Evolution of Methodism in the United States of America; for the Use of Students and General Readers. *New York,* 1893.

Arminianism in History; or the Revolt from Predestinationism. *Cincinnati,* 1894.

A Study of the Constitution of the Methodist Episcopal Church. *New York.*

D

DAILY, WILLIAM MITCHELL: 1812–1877.

Born at Coshocton, O., in 1812, William Mitchell Daily was educated in the country schools and graduated from Indiana University in 1836, receiving the D.D. degree in 1851. He also received honorary degrees from Augusta College and the University of Louisville. He married Permelia A. Northcraft, of Madison, Ind., about 1843.

Dr. Daily was president of Indiana University from 1853 to 1859. He died at New Orleans on February 5, 1877, and was buried at Madison, Ind.

Information from The University Libraries, Indiana University.

* * *

Funeral Discourse Delivered in the Chapel of Indiana University, November 13, 1851, Over the Remains of the Late Rev. Andrew Wylie, President of Indiana University. *Indianapolis,* 1852.

Inaugural Address as President of Indiana University, August 2, 1854. *Indianapolis,* 1854.

The Heroic Men: a Baccalaureate to the Graduating Class of the Indiana University at the Commencement of 1855. *Bloomington, Ind.,* 1855.

Our Banner: a Baccalaureate to the Graduating Class of Indiana University, 1856. *Bloomington, Ind.,* 1856.

Zaph-Nath Pa-A-Ne-Ah: a Baccalaureate to the Graduating Class of Indiana University, 1857. *Bloomington, Ind.,* 1857.

Urim and Thummin: a Baccalaureate to the Graduating Class of Indiana University, 1858. *Bloomington, Ind.,* 1858.

The Powerful Pen and the Eloquent Tongue . . . *Bloomington, Ind.,* 1859.

The Great Rebellion. *Madison, Ind.,* 1862.

Discourses from the Pulpit. *Cincinnati,* 1865.

DAUGHERTY, HARVEY HARRISON: 1841–1919.

Harvey Harrison Daugherty was born in Kentucky in 1841. During the Civil War he served in the Confederate Navy, and in 1865 he came to Indianapolis to study and practice law. Two years later he moved to Shelbyville, Ind., married Mary R. Wilson, and served as city clerk and city attorney. He spent the last years of his life in Indianapolis, where he died in 1919.

Information from the Barry Ms.

* * *

Young Lawyer; and Another Essay. *Indianapolis,* 1907.
Conglomerate; With a Sketch of the Author's Life. *Indianapolis,* 1912.

DAUGHTERS, FREEMAN: 1873–

Freeman Daughters, son of William Turpen and Sarah Elmira Heaton Daughters, was born at Lawrenceburg, Ind., on February 13, 1873, and graduated from Kansas Normal College in 1896 and the Philadelphia Divinity School in 1899. He received the S.T.B. (1903) and A.M. (1915) degrees from Columbia University and the Ed.D. from Intermountain Union College.

After teaching in Bronson, Kan., and engaging in social work in Philadelphia, in 1899 he was made a deacon of the Protestant Episcopal Church and in 1900 a priest. He served as rector in Idaho and Pennsylvania from 1899 to 1906, but in 1907 he withdrew from the ministry. He engaged in newspaper work from 1906 to 1909, was principal of a high school in Idaho from 1909 to 1914, and was professor of education at the University of Montana from 1915 to 1943, serving as dean of the school of education after 1930.

Information from *Who's Who in America.*

* * *

Ann Boleyn (joint author). 1913.

DAVIS, CLARKSON: 1833–1883.

Clarkson Davis, son of Willis and Ann Coggshall Davis, was born in Wayne County, Ind., on Jan. 7, 1833, and moved with his family to Grant County in 1838. He attended the district schools of Grant County, was a student for one term at Bloomingdale Academy, and spent five months at Earlham College. Private study led to the conferring of the A.M. degree upon him by Earlham College in 1868.

From 1857 to 1863 he was in charge of the mathematical department at Earlham, and from 1863 to 1873 he was in charge of Spiceland Academy, resigning to work for Harper & Brothers, publishers, as their special agent for Iowa and Minnesota. In 1876 he returned to Spiceland Academy as principal.

Clarkson Davis married Hannah E. Brown of Wayne County on Sept. 4, 1862.

Information from *Representative Men of Indiana,* Vol. I.

* * *

Poems, Papers and Addresses . . . Published in Memoriam . . . (with Hannah E. Brown Davis). *Richmond, Ind.,* 1898.

DAVIS, ELMER HOLMES: 1890–

"The reputation of a thorough student of history and politics, a story writer and a novelist who has won popular acclaim stands behind Elmer Holmes Davis, Indiana-born, well-traveled, shrewd and tolerant news analyst. His life interests follow the two traditional Hoosier industries, politics and literature; in his most recent career as radio commentator he achieves a synthesis of both. He was engaged by the Columbia Broadcasting Company Aug. 23, 1939, just as the big war news was breaking, when its ace commentator, H. V. Kaltenborn . . . was in Europe. For some time his essays on a number of things had been appearing in HARPER'S, FORUM, SATURDAY REVIEW OF LITERATURE and other periodicals. In March, 1940, about a dozen of these were collected in one volume, *Not to Mention the War.*

"Elmer Holmes Davis was born Jan. 13, 1890 in Aurora, Ind., the son of a banker, Elam H., and Louise (Severin) Davis. He took his B.A. at Franklin College in 1910, his M.A. was awarded a year after he left, for courses taken while in residence. In 1910 he won a Rhodes Scholarship to Oxford, where he was elected president of the American Club. While studying at Oxford he began cultivating an interest in foreign affairs and politics, and spent his summers traveling abroad. It was in Paris that he met Florence MacMillan of Mt. Vernon, New York. They were married Feb. 5, 1917 and have two children: Robert Lloyd and Caroline Ann. They live at Mystic, Conn., in the summer, during the winter in New York City.

"His first job was teaching at the Franklin, Ind. High School from 1909 to 1910. Then for a year he was on the editorial staff of ADVENTURE. As a boy he had been printer's devil on the AURORA

BULLETIN. Ten years later, 1914, he became a cub reporter on the NEW YORK TIMES, rising in another ten years to become feature man on American politics, expert correspondent and editorial writer. He acquired a reputation by creating, during the 1920 Democratic Convention in San Francisco, a character named Godfrey Gloom from Amity, Ind. Godfrey (Davis) was sent for 16 years to conventions, until Davis finally killed him off, and Arthur Krock of the TIMES solemnly wrote his obituary.

"Apart from his newspaper career, Elmer Davis found time to do considerable writing, both fiction and non-fiction . . .

"Davis has won in a short time nationwide repute an an analyst . . . His scholarly background and his broad, liberal viewpoint (although one writer says that 'today he would barely qualify as a liberal'), no less than his skeptical mind, enable him to plow through propaganda and rumor in an effort to find the real truth in a report. Even in times of war crises Davis keeps his calm, unhurried manner, sorting conflicting reports, carefully checking all information. When asked recently, however, if he still had 'mike fright,' he said: 'I haven't yet lost the fear that some day I will go insane at the mike and begin spouting treason, blasphemy and (worse) libel.' But so far his manner has been so quiet and casual that he has been called 'a master of understatement.'

"It is likely that Elmer Davis prefers to be known as a scholar and observer, rather than a public figure or celebrity, since he avoids anything in the way of 'showing-off.' . . . A great deal may be learned about the real Elmer Davis from his book of essays, *Not to Mention the War*. Having to talk about the War every day, he found considerable pleasure and release in writing these non-War sketches, and published them with the hope that people may like to read about things not immediately connected with these troubled times. But he discovered that he was unable to avoid the War or Hitler, or other current topics even when writing of quite different matters—about Thucydides, cats, music, the world of 1913 or bridge.

"He likes nothing better than to see today in terms of history; he is something of an authority on the decline and fall of the Roman Empire, as his essay, *The Logic of History* shows. As a student of the classics, he believes that reading Thucydides, for example, will help us understand the times we live in better than all the works of moderns. His knowledge of history and politics breaks out in shrewdly drawn parallels when he writes on such matters, for instance, as cats and music . . .

"His style is both pungent and friendly; he is blunt, candid, witty—a person of broad sympathies and tolerance. Critics are generally delighted with his well-balanced prose, rich with allusion, classical or otherwise, and find he has the indispensable light touch.

"It may be no paradox, in this day of paradox, that an analyst of contemporary politics and events should claim Horace and Catullus (read in the original) as his favorite poets and list the Bible as the greatest book ever written, without a runner-up. And it is comforting to hear from a student of history:

" 'With an irrational optimism befitting an alumnus of the absurd age in which I came to the surface, I still believe that higher peaks of human felicity may be ahead; that our race, if it keeps on trying, might make quite a habitable place of the planet on which it resides.' "

During World War II Elmer Davis was director of the Office of War Information.

Condensed from *Current Biography*, 1940.

* * *

The Princess Cecilia. *New York,* 1915.

History of the New York Times, 1851-1921. *New York,* 1921.

Times Have Changed. *New York,* 1923.

I'll Show You the Town. *New York,* 1924.

Friends of Mr. Sweeney. *New York,* 1925.

The Keys of the City. *New York,* 1925.

Show Window. *New York,* 1927.

Strange Woman. *New York,* 1927.

Giant Killer. *New York,* 1928.

Morals for Moderns. *Indianapolis,* 1930.

White Pants Willie. *Indianapolis,* 1932.

Bare Living (with Guy Holt). *Indianapolis,* 1933.

Love Among the Ruins. *Indianapolis,* 1935.

Not to Mention the War. *Indianapolis,* 1940.

War Information. *Washington, D. C.,* 1943.

DAVIS, HANNAH E. BROWN (MRS. CLARKSON): 1841–1898.

Hannah E. Brown was born near Richmond, Ind., on Nov. 5, 1841, and was educated in the country schools and at Earlham College. In 1862 she married Clarkson Davis and began her career as a teacher at Spiceland Academy when her husband became principal the following year. She taught at the Academy for twenty-eight years.

After her husband's death in 1883 she studied art and languages in Europe. She died in North Dakota on March 24, 1898.

Information from Parker and Heiney—*Poets and Poetry of Indiana* and *Representative Men of Indiana,* Vol. I.

* * *

Poems, Papers and Addresses . . . Published in Memoriam (with Clarkson Davis). *Richmond, Ind.,* 1898.

DAVIS, SYDNEY BRIAN: 1842–?

Sydney Brian Davis was born in Parke County, Ind., on July 21, 1842, the son of Eli and Nancy McGinnis Davis.

Young Davis attended local grammar schools and was graduated from the Waveland (Ind.) Collegiate Institute in 1861. He had begun the study of law in 1858, and in 1865 he resumed his reading and was admitted to practice in the Montgomery County bar in 1867.

In 1869 he removed to Terre Haute, where he practiced law and held several public offices. He was interested—as were many of his Parke County contemporaries—in reform; his particular fields were child welfare and prison reform. The date of Mr. Davis' death is not available.

Information from the Indiana State Library.

* * *

Immortality, Reason and Revelation. *Plainfield, Ind.,* 1904.

DAVIS, THEODORE P.: 1855–1907.

Theodore P. Davis was born at Westfield, Ind., on Jan. 5, 1855. His parents were Newton J. and Louisa Pearson Davis. Davis attended school near Sheridan, Ind., where his father had purchased a farm, studied for a year at the National Normal School, Lebanon, O., and became a teacher.

He read law with the Noblesville, Ind., firm of Moss and Trissal and was admitted to the Hamilton County bar in 1874. He practiced law in Noblesville and married Miss Anna F. Gray, of Piqua, O., in 1887. He became a judge of the Appellate Court in 1892 and died in 1907.

Information from Taylor—*Biographical Sketches of the Bench and Bar of Indiana.*

* * *

Upholding the Honor of the Profession.

DEBS, EUGENE VICTOR: 1855–1926.

"Eugene Victor Debs (Nov. 5, 1855-Oct. 20, 1926), Socialist advocate, was one of the ten children of Jean Daniel and Marguerite Marie (Bettrich) Debs and was born in Terre Haute, Ind. The parents, who were married in New York City on Sept. 13, 1849, were both natives of Colmar, Alsace, and had come to America in that year. After some wandering they settled in Terre Haute in the fall of 1854. Young Debs attended school until the middle of his fifteenth year, when he went to work in the shops of the Terre Haute and Indianapolis Railway, later becoming a locomotive fireman. Four years later (1874) he quit his fireman's job and took a clerkship in a wholesale grocery house. In February of the following year he participated in the organization in his city of a lodge of the Brotherhood of Locomotive Firemen, of which he was made secretary, and in 1878 he was appointed associate editor of the FIREMEN'S MAGAZINE. He continued with the grocery firm (doing his work for the labor-union at night) until September 1879, when he was elected city clerk. In 1880 he was appointed (and later in the year elected) national secretary and treasurer of the Brotherhood and editor of its magazine. By working incredibly long hours he contrived to fill all three offices until the close of his term as city clerk in 1883, thereafter for ten years giving most of his time to his union. On June 9, 1885, he was married to Katherine Metzel of Pittsburgh, Pa., and in the fall of the year was elected to the lower house of the Indiana Legislature. In 1892 he resigned his offices in the union, but against his protest was unanimously re-elected.

"From an early day he was an opponent of the organization of labor by crafts and an advocate of organization by industries. In June 1893, he took part in the formation of a labor society of the 'industrial' type, the American Railway Union, of which he was chosen president. In several minor contests with employers the new union won considerable prestige, and it came into nationwide prominence through the strike for higher wages (Apr. 13, 1894) against the Great Northern Railroad. Eighteen days later the employees returned to work with most of their demands granted. In June the employees of the Pullman Company, at South Chicago, went out, and an appeal was made to the A.R.U. to aid them by a sympathetic strike. Debs opposed the move as inexpedient, but at a hastily called convention of the union a boycott on the moving of Pullman cars was ordered, and he at once took energetic charge of the campaign. Against the protest of Governor Altgeld, President Cleveland ordered federal troops to Chicago; Judges Grosscup and Woods issued a sweeping injunction against the strikers, and on July 10 a federal grand jury, charging conspiracy to obstruct the mails, indicted Debs and three others, who were immediately arrested, and were again arrested on July 17 for contempt of court in violating the injunction. The trial before Judge Grosscup, Feb. 6-12, 1895, resulted in a discontinuance because of the illness of a juror, but on the charge of contempt Debs and six others were sentenced by Judge Woods to six months in the McHenry County jail at Woodstock. Here Debs spent much of his time in reading, with the result that he avowed himself a convert to Socialism. Released on Nov. 22, he returned to Chicago, where he was accorded one of the most remarkable demonstrations in the history of the city, and thence to Terre Haute.

"In 1896 he campaigned for Bryan, but, in June, 1897, brought about the transformation of what was left of the A.R.U. into the Social Democratic Party of America. Three years later a tentative combination was made with the faction of the Socialist Labor party that had seceded in 1899, and Debs, as the fusion candidate for president, polled 96,116 votes. In the following year the two wings were formally united under the name of the Socialist Party of America, and in 1904 Debs was again nominated for president, polling 402,321 votes. About this time he became associate editor of the Socialist weekly, the APPEAL TO REASON, of Girard, Kan., and for five or six years gave his time to editorial work and to lecture tours in behalf of the APPEAL and the Socialist party. At Chicago, June 27-July 8, 1905, he aided in founding the Industrial Workers of the World, but after a time became dissatisfied with the organization and withdrew, though frequently thereafter defending its members from charges he deemed unjust. In 1908 he was again the Socialist candidate, and in a train known as the 'Red Special' made a speaking canvass of the entire country; but though he drew large crowds, his vote (420,973) showed only a slight gain over that of 1904. In 1912 he was nominated for the fourth time, and he again made a general canvass. The year was one of an unparalleled social ferment; and though the liberal platform of Wilson and the specifically progressive platform of Roosevelt were expected to diminish the Socialist vote, it increased to 901,062, or nearly six per cent of the total. In 1916 Debs declined to be a candidate.

"The manifesto of the St. Louis convention of the party (April, 1917), denouncing the war and counseling party members to oppose it by all means in their power, was warmly approved by Debs, though later in the year he favored some modification of the language of the party's policy. But in the following year, stirred no doubt by resentment over the many convictions for sedition, he took more extreme ground. At the Socialist state convention in Canton, Ohio, June 16, 1918, he delivered a speech in which he bitterly assailed the administration for its prosecution of persons charged with sedition. Four days later, at Cleveland, he was indicted by a federal grand jury for a violation of the Espionage Act, and on Sept. 14, after a four-days trial, was sentenced to ten years' imprisonment on each of two counts, the sentences to run concurrently . . .

"He returned to his home, but the following year spent several months in the Lindlahr Sanitarium, at Elmhurst, near Chicago . . . In 1924 the Socialist party, with Debs's approval, joined the LaFollette forces. In the following year it established in Chicago a national weekly organ, the AMERICAN APPEAL, of which Debs was made editor. His health declining, early in 1926 he went to Bermuda. In April he returned home, but in September again became an inmate of the sanitarium at Lindlahr, where a month later he died . . ."

Condensed from W. J. G., *Dictionary of American Biography*, Vol. V.

* * *

The American Movement. *Terre Haute, Ind.,* 1904.

The Federal Government and the Chicago Strike. *Terre Haute, Ind.,* 1904.

Unionism and Socialism; a Plea for Both. *Terre Haute, Ind.,* 1904.

Class Unionism . . . Speech Delivered at Chicago, November 24, 1905. . . . *Chicago,* 1909.

Craft Unionism . . . Speech Delivered at Chicago, November 23, 1905. *Chicago,* 1909.

Revolutionary Unionism . . . Speech Delivered at Chicago, November 25, 1905. *Chicago,* 1909.

The Growth of Socialism. *Chicago,* n.d.

Liberty. *Chicago,* n.d.

You Railroad Men. *Chicago,* n.d.

Industrial Unionism: an Address Delivered at Grand Central Palace, New York, Sunday, Dec. 10, 1905. *New York,* 1911.

Danger Ahead for the Socialist Party in Playing the Game of Politics (with Charles E. Russell). *Chicago,* 1912.

Labor and Freedom. *St. Louis,* 1916.

Eugene V. Debs Canton Speech. *Chicago,* n.d.

Walls and Bars. *Chicago,* 1927.

Speeches of Eugene Debs. *New York,* 1928.
Economics, Labor and Capital.

DE HART, RICHARD P.: ?–

Richard P. De Hart served as colonel of the 128th
Ind. Regiment in the Civil War (in which he was
severely wounded) and resided in Lafayette, Ind.,
after the war. In later life he bore the title General—
probably in the Indiana state militia—was elected
judge of the Tippecanoe County Circuit Court in 1902
and was still on the bench in 1909 at the time his one
known book was published.

> Information from *The Soldier of Indiana in the
> War for The Union,* Vol. 2, and from de Hart—
> *Past and Present of Tippecanoe County, Indiana.*

* * *

Past and Present of Tippecanoe County, Indiana. *Indianapolis,* 1909. 2 vols.

DEHEY, ELINOR TONG (MRS. THOMAS J.): ?–

Elinor Tong, daughter of Lucius G. and Cecilia
Ball Tong, was born in South Bend, Ind., where her
father was a lawyer and cashier of the St. Joseph
County Bank. Her mother was a native of Lafayette,
Ind. Elinor Tong married Thomas J. Dehey and at
present (1946) lives in Lafayette.

> Information from the South Bend Public Library
> and from *Representative Men of Indiana,* Vol. II.

* * *

New Manual of Catholic Devotions. *Baltimore* and *New
York,* 1901.
South Bend Blue Book for 1909-1910. *South Bend, Ind.,*
1908.
Religious Orders of Women in the United States: Accounts of Their Origin and of Their Most Important
Institutions, Interwoven with Brief Histories of Many
Famous Convents. *Hammond, Ind.,* 1913.

DE LA HUNT, THOMAS JAMES: 1866–1933.

Thomas de la Hunt—"Tommy Dellyhunt" to the
majority of his tolerant but faintly derisive fellow
citizens in Cannelton—was a character (in both the
actual and the Hoosier colloquial sense) of a sort
common to New England and the southeastern seaboard but rarely found in Indiana except in the southern river towns. There is (in Indiana, at least) usually

only one to the community: he or she lives entirely in
the past, dwelling upon the glories of a mighty family
or a titled ancestor.

Sometimes there is an estate in escrow to be proved;
sometimes there is a book to be written in evidence of
the true worth of an ancestor, or the securing of some
credit for him, which has been unjustly given to
another—but always there is preoccupation with the
past; always there is a total unawareness of the present.
They are usually gentle people—although occasionally
a female of the breed who has inherited a competence
and a handsome old home has a tendency to lord it
over the neighboring rabble—and they are gently
treated by their fellow citizens. They are smiled at
but never laughed at; seldom held in high regard but,
also, never hurt intentionally.

Thomas de la Hunt was one of these people: his
name, according to his fellow citizens, had been Delahunt for at least several generations before his romantic
researches gave him evidence to support his own more
aristocratic rendering of it. He was small and quiet
and self effacing: in a neat, rusty-black suit which gave
ready evidence of its age, black tie, black hat, one
could, in the Indiana phrase, "tell him a mile off" for
what he was.

According to the Cannelton Public Library, the
facts of his life are these:

"He was the son of Maj. T. J. and Isabelle Huckeby de la Hunt and was born Nov. 9, 1866, in
Cannelton, Ind. He attended grade and high school in
his home town and finished his education at Sewanee
College (now The University of the South), Tenn.

"He contributed a column on local history to the
EVANSVILLE COURIER. This column, called the
'Pocket Periscope,' was authentic, witty and entertaining. He wrote the script and also produced the
Perry County pageant commemorating the first centennial of Indiana's statehood.

"He was president of the Perry County Historical
Society in 1931 and 1932, and he was very active in
securing historical data pertaining to the pioneer days."

Mr. de la Hunt passed away July 3, 1933.

> Information from interviews with Mr. de la Hunt
> and from the Cannelton Public Library.

* * *

Perry County; a History. *Indianapolis,* 1916.

DE MOTTE, JOHN BREWER: 1848–1907.

Born in Waveland, Ind., in 1848, John Brewer
De Motte graduated from Indiana Asbury (now De

Pauw) University in 1874, received the A.M. degree in 1877, and was awarded the Ph.D. degree in 1887. In 1878 he married Lelia Washburn, who died in 1910.

From 1874 to 1884 he was principal of the preparatory department of Indiana Asbury (now De Pauw) University and from 1875 to 1891 served as professor of mathematics and physics at the same institution.

He died at Greencastle, Ind., on Sept. 1, 1907.

Information from De Pauw University's *Alumnal Record, 1920.*

* * *

The Secret of Character Building. *Chicago, 1893.*

DENBY, CHARLES: 1830–1904.

Charles Denby, son of Nathaniel and Jane Harvey Denby, was born in Virginia in 1830 and was educated at Georgetown University and Virginia Military Institute. For three years he taught tactics at the Masonic University in Selma, Ala.

He moved to Evansville, Ind., where he served as editor of the DAILY INQUIRER and in 1855 was admitted to the bar. In 1856 he was a member of the state Legislature. He married Martha Fitch of Logansport in September, 1858.

During the Civil War Charles Denby was a colonel of the 42nd and later the 80th Indiana Regiment. For thirteen years, from 1885 to 1898, he was U. S. Minister to China. In 1899 he was a member of the U. S. Philippine Commission.

Mr. Denby died at Jamestown, N. Y. on Jan. 13, 1904.

Information from Powell—*History of Cass County*, 1913, and supplied by the Evansville Public Library.

* * *

China and Her People. *Boston, 1906.* 2 vols.

DENNIS, CHARLES: 1844–1919.

Born in Lawrenceburg, Ind., on Sept. 4, 1844, Charles Dennis lived in Indianapolis after 1852, where he was educated in the grade schools. He learned the drug business but in 1875 turned to newspaper work. He was a partner of George C. Harding in the SATURDAY REVIEW OF INDIANAPOLIS and was a reporter on the INDIANAPOLIS JOURNAL and the INDIANAPOLIS NEWS.

Information from Parker and Heiney—*Poets and Poetry of Indiana.*

* * *

Ten Days with Francis Murphy: the Man and the Plan. *Indianapolis,* 1889.

Names of Indiana Counties. *Indianapolis,* 1917-18.

DENNIS, DAVID WORTH: 1849–1916.

David Worth Dennis, son of Nathan and Evalina Worth Dennis, was born in Economy, Ind., on Apr. 8, 1849. He attended the county schools and prepared himself for college admission at the Spiceland Academy. Entering Earlham College, he received the A.B. degree in 1873 and the A.M. in 1876. He took his Ph.D. degree at Syracuse University in 1886, and in 1889-90 studied at the universities of Bonn and Edinburgh.

His entire life was spent as an educator, first as a teacher in the Richmond, Ind., high school and for thirty-two years as professor of biology at Earlham College. For two years he served as president of Wilmington (O.) College, and for two years he was principal of Bloomingdale (Ind.) Academy.

His first wife was Martha Curl, by whom he had one son, William Cullen Dennis; after her death he married Emma Zeller. Dr. Dennis died on May 13, 1916.

Information from *Who Was Who in America* and the Morrisson-Reeves Library, Richmond, Ind.

* * *

An Analytical Key to the Fossils of the Vicinity of Richmond, Indiana. *Richmond, Ind.,* 1878.

Notes and Tables for Twenty Weeks in Experimental Chemistry and Qualitative Analysis. *Richmond, Ind.,* 1885.

Capital Punishment! What the Scriptures Teach Regarding It. *Richmond, Ind.,* 1886.

Nature Study; One Hundred Lessons About Plants. *Terre Haute, Ind.,* 1903.

DENNIS, MARTHA CURL (MRS. DAVID WORTH): ?–1897.

Born in Parke County, Ind., Martha Curl was educated in the county schools, attended Bloomingdale Academy and the Normal School at Lebanon, O., and graduated from Indiana State Normal at Terre Haute in 1874.

On June 22, 1876, while teaching at Bloomingdale Academy, she was married to David Worth Dennis, principal of the school. In 1884-85 she was an instructor in English at Earlham College. She organized the "History Class" of Richmond, Ind., in 1890 and remained its leader until her death.

Mrs. Dennis was the author of many essays and articles. Her only book, a collection of her poems and essays, was published after her death by the "History Class."

She died in Richmond, Ind., on Feb. 4, 1897.

Information from Earlham College and the Rockville Public Library.

* * *

In Memoriam . . . Published by the History Class. *Richmond, Ind.*, n.d.

DICKEY, JOHN MCELROY: 1789–1849.

John McElroy Dickey, son of David and Margaret Stephenson Dickey, was born in South Carolina in 1789. Going to Kentucky with his family, he studied with a cousin, the Rev. William Dickey, and afterwards at a school opened by the Rev. N. H. Hall at Hardin's Creek Church. In 1813 he married Nancy W. McCleskey.

He was licensed to preach by the Muhlenberg Presbytery in 1814 and moved to Washington, Ind., in 1815. To support his family he supplemented his pastoral work by farming, teaching, surveying, and other occupations. After his first wife's early death, in 1818 he married Margaret Osborn Steele.

He organized several churches in southern Indiana, becoming known as "the father of the Presbyterian Church in Indiana." After many years of ill health he died on Nov. 21, 1849.

Information from the Indiana State Library.

* * *

A Brief History of the Presbyterian Church in the State of Indiana. *Madison, Ind.*, n.d. [1828].

DILLON, JOHN BROWN: 1808?–1879.

John Brown Dillon, facile writer and able historian, was born in Wellsburg, W. Va. (then Virginia), in 1807 or 1808. Little is known of his youth or, for that matter, of his later life. He was respected by his contemporaries, and something tragic in his bearing and manner apparently elicited their sympathy, but no one seemed to be in his confidence; no one seemed to be on terms better than acquaintanceship with him.

He lived alone, in bachelor quarters reported to be more notable for the books, papers and notes with which they were strewn than for order or comfort. Lonely in life, he left no relative or close friend to search out the details or to fill in the outline of his biography.

An orphan at nine, he learned the printing trade and worked for some time in Cincinnati. There the episode probably occurred which is supposed to have prompted the writing of a poem, "The Burial of the Beautiful," which first earned Dillon regard as a writer and which was thought to be the key to the mystery of his lonely life: it was written in his eighteenth year and printed in the CINCINNATI GAZETTE, on which he was working.

Before 1834 Dillon went to Logansport, Ind. He read law—became, indeed, an authority on American colonial law and legislation—and was admitted to the bar but did not practice. Instead he and Stanislaus Lasselle (supposed to have furnished extra capital to match Dillon's technical knowledge) founded the newspaper CANAL TELEGRAPH, of which Dillon acted as editor.

It was during this period that he completed and published the most important historical work relating to the Old Northwest Territory up to his day and for at least a century following. *Historical Notes on the Discovery and Settlement of the Territory . . . Northwest of the River Ohio* was published in Indianapolis in 1843 and was immediately recognized for what it was—a sound, scholarly, readable compilation of the facts of settlement gathered from original sources which had been carefully checked in many cases with the men who took leading parts in the events described.

The authorship of this work probably had much to do with John B. Dillon's appointment to the post of Indiana State Librarian in 1845. Although the possibilities of profit in a newspaper published in a town as thriving as Logansport of that day were certainly greater than those offered by the library post, Dillon accepted; income necessary to maintain anything beyond the most Spartan existence was not likely to be of much interest to him.

During the rest of his life Dillon held various minor appointments—assuring an existence and time to write —and he carried out his duties with meticulous care for detail. He served as secretary of the State Board of Agriculture for a few years, was Assistant Secretary of State for two years and held a clerkship in the United States Department of the Interior in Washington from 1863 to 1875. He used these years in Washington to good advantage; two important books resulted from his easy access to documents and publications there.

In 1875 he left Washington and returned to Indianapolis, where he had lived as a state employe from 1845 to 1863, and remained there until his death in 1879.

The History of Indiana, from Its Earliest Exploration by Europeans, to the Close of the Territorial Government in 1816: with an Introduction Containing Historical Notes of the Discovery and Settlement of the Territory of the United States Northwest of the River Ohio. *Indianapolis, 1843.*

An Address Delivered Before the Editorial Convention, Assembled at Indianapolis, on the Ninth of December, 1846. *Indianapolis, 1847.*

Notes on Historical Evidence in Reference to Adverse Theories of the Origin and Nature of the Government of the United States of America. *New York, 1871.*

Oddities of Colonial Legislation in America as Applied to the Public Lands, Primitive Education, Religion, Morals, Indians, Etc. *Indianapolis, 1879.*

National Decline of the Miami Indians. *Indianapolis, 1897.*

DOBBINS, DOUGLAS: 1860–1927.

Douglas Dobbins, teacher, attorney and writer, was born in Shelby County, Ind., in 1860. After attending Franklin College he taught school, was superintendent of Shelby County schools from 1883 to 1887, and for a time edited the GREENWOOD NEWS. He later took up the practice of law. He wrote under the name of Stephen Arnold Douglas. Mr. Dobbins died in 1927.

Information from the Barry Ms.

* * *

Quarrytown. *Westerville, Ohio, 1915.*
Heart Echoes from Old Shelby, and Other Poems. *Franklin, Ind., 1916.*
When the Old Flag Goes By and Other Poems.
Those Old Home Scenes.

DONNAN, LAURA: 1854–1930.

Laura Donnan was born in Indianapolis in 1854. She received her education in the Indianapolis public schools, the Indianapolis Normal School, the University of Michigan, and Columbia University.

Before joining the staff of Shortridge High School (Indianapolis) in 1883, she taught in the public schools of Knightstown and Cambridge City, Ind. At Shortridge and in educational circles throughout the country she is principally remembered for her organization of the Shortridge Senate—a revolutionary step in student government.

She died in Indianapolis in 1930.

Information from the Indianapolis Public Library.

* * *

Our Governments. *Indianapolis, 1900.*

DONNAN, MAY WINTERS (MRS. WALLACE): 1859–1913.

May Winters Donnan was born in Indianapolis in 1859 and died there in 1913. She was the wife of Wallace Donnan. In addition to her poetry and juvenile fiction she wrote literary criticism which appeared in the INDIANAPOLIS JOURNAL and in the INDIANAPOLIS PRESS. For many years she conducted private classes in English literature and history at her home and gave readings and lectures at the literary clubs throughout the state.

Information from Parker and Heiney—*Poets and Poetry of Indiana* and the Indianapolis Public Library.

* * *

Various Verses. *Cambridge, 1914.*

DOOLEY, A. H.: ?–1903.

As a young man A. H. Dooley was a bookseller in Terre Haute, Ind. He became owner and publisher of the INDIANAPOLIS HERALD, was editor of the KANSAS CITY STAR, and later was identified with other Indianapolis newspapers. According to Nicholson—*The Hoosiers:* "He has found time to preach the doctrine of sweetness and light through the Indianapolis press." Mr. Dooley died in 1903.

Information from Nicholson—*The Hoosiers.*

* * *

History of Elizaville (Boone County) Baptist Church. *Lebanon, Ind., n.d.*

DOREMUS, JENNIE BROWN: ?–?

No data on the life of Jennie Brown Doremus, except for the tradition that she was a resident of Kokomo, Ind., has been found.

The title of her book—apparently biographical or reminiscent—suggests Indiana residence.

Information from the Kokomo Public Library.

* * *

Jennette Browning; or, a Hoosier Girl's Victory, a True History of a Remarkable Life. *Winona, Minn.* [1889].

DRAKE, DEAMOR R.: 1874–

Deamor R. Drake was born in LaGrange County, Ind., Aug. 12, 1874, the son of Reason R. and Salina Ann Stone Drake. He attended the common schools, graduated from LaGrange High School in 1893, and from the Valparaiso Normal College in 1894. He taught school several years in Bloomfield Township, LaGrange County. Several of his poems have been set to music.

Information from the LaGrange Public Library.

* * *

Country Chimes and Other Rhymes.
Glimpses of Hoosierdom. *Chicago,* 1903.

DRAPER, WILLIAM COLUMBUS: 1850–?

Born at Bloomington, Ind., in 1850, William Columbus Draper was educated in the Bloomington public schools and graduated from Indiana University in 1867. As a resident of Trinidad, Colo., he managed a saw-mill and was a lumber merchant.

Information from The University Libraries, Indiana University.

* * *

Esmeralda, and Other Stories. *Trinidad, Colo.,* 1902.

DREISER, THEODORE: 1871–1945.

Theodore Dreiser, a controversial literary figure in American letters, was born in Terre Haute, Ind., on Aug. 27, 1871.

His parents were John Paul and Sarah Schanab Dreiser. The father was the object of Theodore Dreiser's extreme dislike; for his mother he held an admiration amounting to worship. His book, *A Hoosier Holiday,* says: "He [the senior Dreiser] was a crank, a tenth rate Saint Simon of Assisi . . . He worked, ate, played, slept and dreamed religion."—And of his mother: "I certainly had one of the most perfect mothers ever a man had . . . an open, uneducated, wondering, dreamy mind, none of the customary, conscious principles with which so many conventional

souls are afflicted. A happy, hopeful, animal mother . . . A pagan mother . . . A great poet mother . . . A great hearted mother . . ."

Throughout his autobiographical writing, long passages of which are introspective, Dreiser refers constantly to the poverty of his family and appears to boast of the difficulties in which its members became involved. There are mentioned in *A Hoosier Holiday,* besides the father and mother: sisters, several of whom "ran away and (in seemingly, only in so far as the beliefs of my father were concerned) went to the bad. They did not go to the bad actually . . . although I might disagree with many as to what is bad . . ."; a brother, Paul (Dresser, author and composer of "On the Banks of the Wabash Far Away") who "got into jail"; a brother who "finally died of drunkenness," his brother Rome, who followed the family on one of its many moves to a new town only "to get drunk and disgrace us"; a ne'er-do-well uncle and his wife who had four children, "one of whom, the eldest, became a thief (but a very clever one, I have heard); the second a railroad brakeman; the third the wife of an idle country loafer . . . the fourth, a hunchbacked boy, was to me, at least, a veritable sprite of iniquity . . ."; and "a half uncle . . . a stingy, greedy, well meaning Baptist . . ."

In addition to these relatives, Dreiser reports most of the friends and acquaintances of his youth as eventually becoming bar-flies, odd-job men, women of ill repute (or wives of lawyers, doctors or tradesmen—a status which he regarded as less fortunate than that preceding), as having been imprisoned, killed by accidental violence, or, in the happier cases, as having disappeared leaving no trace.

The bare facts of the Dreiser family's history, shorn of his colorful trimming, seem to be these:

The father had owned a woolen mill in Sullivan, Ind. Fire had destroyed it, and its loss had taken his home and whatever other assets he may have held. The family (there would eventually be ten children) then removed to Terre Haute, where Dreiser senior became either foreman or superintendent of another woolen mill. There Theodore was born.

By the time Theodore was seven some of the older children were working (Paul had become a minstrel show man and had changed his name to the supposedly more appropriate "Dresser"), but hard times, or perhaps the difficulties to peace inherent in the life of a strict Catholic father and a "pagan . . . animal mother," caused Mrs. Dreiser to take the younger children back to the town of Sullivan.

At Sullivan the monetary situation grew so difficult

that after two years Paul Dresser—always to be patronized by the younger, more intellectual Theodore —brought his mother and her children to Evansville, where he supported the brood for two years.

After this period the family moved to Warsaw, Ind., where John Dreiser had apparently found employment. Theodore certainly attended a parochial school in Evansville, probably some sort of school in Sullivan, and possibly in Terre Haute. Now he entered the public school at Warsaw and continued there through high school. After working in Chicago for a time, he was enrolled at Indiana University, where he remained through his eighteenth year.

In 1891 he began newspaper work on the CHICAGO GLOBE, going to St. Louis the next year, where he was employed until 1894. In 1895 he became editor of the magazine EVERY MONTH, leaving after a year to do various assignments for HARPER'S, MCCLURE'S, CENTURY, COSMOPOLITAN and MUNSEY'S magazines until 1905-06, when he edited SMITH'S MAGAZINE. In 1906-07 he edited BROADWAY MAGAZINE and from 1907 to 1910 served as editor-in-chief of the Butterick Publications (DELINEATOR, DESIGNER, NEW IDEA, etc.). Later he became editor of the AMERICAN SPECTATOR, continuing until January, 1934.

Dreiser was twice married—his first wife, Sarah Osborne White Dreiser, died in 1942, and his second wife, Helen, survived him.

The first of his novels, *Sister Carrie,* appeared in 1900, when he was experienced as a periodical contributor and editor but was by no means well known. The book was startlingly frank in its treatment of delicate subject matter, and Dreiser's publishers withdrew it almost immediately, but the notoriety it acquired by its suppression was sufficient to gain a recognition of sorts for its author. Other fairly successful books followed, and in 1916 Dreiser produced *The Genius,* which enjoyed the benefits of being banned in several cities with resulting publicity. His next books sold widely, and, after a suitable period, another sensational and frequently banned novel, *An American Tragedy,* added a stimulant to his fame, which lasted to within a few years of his death on Dec. 28, 1945.

A half century or so—during which the sensationalism which marked his best known novels will have had time to mellow—should give some clear decision as to Theodore Dreiser's contribution to Twentieth century literature. During his life he was, to transplanted Hoosier critic George Jean Nathan, "the most important American author"; to many a reader of sound but less exotic taste he was only a gloomy and dirty-minded man whose prose was tortuous. To

Llewelyn Powys, he was possessed of "great lumbering imagination, full of divine curiosity . . . I never fail to feel awe at the struggles of this ungainly giant, whose limbs are still half buried in clay." H. L. Mencken said of him, "He reached heights of unintelligence as great as any of the heights of intelligence that Aristotle achieved." To many a Midwesterner he seemed to be only a writer who could find a rotten spot in every apple. Jacob Piatt Dunn, ardent Hoosier, was admittedly irritated by Dreiser's rumbling philosophical wanderings and cavalier treatment of his Indiana friends and relatives in *A Hoosier Holiday.* Putting the common plaint in words, Dunn wrote: "He was afflicted with the Marie Bashkirtseff idea that it is fine to bare your soul to the world, unconscious of the fact that the average soul is more presentable in a fig-leaf— much more so in pajamas."

Information from *Who's Who in America*; Dunn —*Indiana and Indianans*; Dreiser—*A Hoosier Holiday; Dictionary of American Biography; Living Authors*; etc., etc.

* * *

Sister Carrie. 1900.

Jennie Gerhardt: a Novel. *New York,* 1911.

The Financier. *New York,* 1912.

A Traveler at Forty. *New York,* 1913.

The Titan. *New York,* 1914.

Plays of the Natural and the Supernatural. *New York,* 1916.

A Hoosier Holiday. *New York,* 1916.

The Genius. *New York,* 1917.

The Bulwark. *New York,* 1917.

Free and Other Stories. *New York,* 1918.

The Hand of the Potter; a Tragedy in 4 Acts. *New York,* 1918.

Twelve Men. *New York,* 1919.

Hey, Rub-a-Dub-Dub; a Book of the Mystery and Wonder and Terror of Life. *New York,* 1920.

A Book About Myself. *New York,* 1922. (Reissued in 1931 as Newspaper Days.)

The Color of a Great City. *New York,* 1923.

An American Tragedy. *New York,* 1926. 2 vols.

Moods, Cadenced and Declaimed. *New York,* 1926.

Chains; Lesser Novels and Stories. *New York,* 1927.

Dreiser Looks at Russia. *New York,* 1928.

A Gallery of Women. *New York,* 1929.

My City. *New York,* 1929.

Epitaph; a Poem. *New York,* 1930.

Fine Furniture. *New York,* 1930. 6 vols.

Dawn; a History of Myself. *New York,* 1931.

Tragic America. *New York,* 1932.

America Is Worth Saving. *New York,* 1941.

The Bulwark. *New York, 1946.*

Best Short Stories. (Edited by Howard Fast.) *Cleveland, O., 1947.*

The Stoic. *New York, 1947.*

DRIVER, LEEOTIS LINCOLN: 1867–

Leeotis Lincoln Driver, son of Joab and Mary Ellen Burres Driver, was born in Stony Creek Township, Randolph County, Ind., on Feb. 22, 1867, and graduated from Central Normal (now Canterbury) College at Danville, Ind., in 1883. He received the A.B. degree from Indiana University in 1919, the A.M. from Earlham College in 1919, and an LL.D. from Wabash in 1921. On Apr. 15, 1886, he married Carrie Ann Wood.

From 1883 to 1887 he was a teacher in the elementary schools of Randolph County, from 1895 to 1907 in the Winchester (Ind.) High School, serving as principal after 1900, and from 1907 to 1920 superintendent of schools in Randolph County. He moved to Pennsylvania in 1920, where from 1920 until 1937 he was associated with the Department of Public Instruction for that state.

Mr. Driver was the author of many articles on rural school consolidation.

Information from *Who's Who in America.*

* * *

Past and Present of Randolph County, Indiana (with John L. Smith). *Indianapolis, 1914.*

The Organization of Public Education for Service in the New Democracy . . .

DRURY, AUGUSTUS WALDO: 1851–1935.

Augustus Waldo Drury, son of Morgan Shortridge and Elizabeth Lambert Drury, was born in Madison County, Ind., on Mar. 21, 1851. After graduating from Western (now Coe) College in Iowa in 1872 he taught Greek and Latin there for one year. He then entered Bonebrake Theological Seminary at Dayton, O., from which he graduated in 1877 and was ordained to the United Brethren ministry. After 1880 he was associated with the Seminary, first as professor of church history and after 1892 as professor of systematic theology. He died Feb. 18, 1935.

Information from *Who Was Who in America.*

* * *

Life of Rev. Philip William Otterbein, Founder of the Church of the United Brethren in Christ. *Dayton, 1884.*

Life of Bishop J. J. Glossbrenner. *Dayton, 1889.*

Disciplines of the United Brethren in Christ. *Dayton, 1895.*

Otterbein Birthday Book. *Dayton.*

Baptism, Its Place in the Church Visible. *Dayton, 1902.*

History of the City of Dayton and Montgomery County, Ohio. *Chicago, 1909.* 2 vols.

Outlines of Doctrinal Theology, With Preliminary Chapters on Theology in General and Theological Encyclopedia. *Dayton, 1914.*

History of the Church of the United Brethren in Christ. *Dayton, 1924.*

DRURY, MARION RICHARDSON: 1849–1939.

Marion Richardson Drury, son of Morgan S. and Elizabeth Lambert Drury, was born at Pendleton, Ind., on Dec. 27, 1849, and graduated from Western (now Coe) College in 1872, receiving the A.M. degree in 1875. In the latter year he also graduated from Union Biblical (now Bonebrake Theological) Seminary. He married Lucinda Denny on June 20, 1872.

Ordained to the United Brethren ministry in 1875, he served as pastor of churches in Iowa, Ohio, and California until 1910, when he became president of Philomath College in Oregon. From 1913 to 1916 he was president of Leander Clark College in Iowa, from 1917 to 1919 pastor at Cedar Rapids, from 1912 to 1922 student secretary of Coe College, and after 1922 missionary in Puerto Rico. He was editor or compiler of several books besides those listed.

He died on Feb. 21, 1939.

Information from *Who Was Who in America.*

* * *

At Hand: a Pocket Vocabulary of Daily Duty and Privilege for the Use of Christian Young People. *Dayton, O., 1895.*

Life of Bishop J. W. Hott. *Dayton, O., 1902.*

Our Catechism. *Dayton, O., n.d.*

After Eighty Years. 1930.

Reminiscences of Early Days in Iowa. 1931.

Life of Augustus Waldo Drury. 1936.

DUFOUR, JOHN JAMES: 1763–1827.

"John James [christened Jean Jacques] Dufour . . . pioneer viticulturist and founder of the Swiss vineyards in America, eldest child of Jean Jacques [Rudolf] Dufour, a Swiss vinedresser, was born in the commune of Chatelard, district of Vevay, Canton de Vaud, Switzerland. He came to America in 1796 with the definite purpose of founding a grape colony to cultivate the grape for wine. After an extensive search for a suitable situation for the vineyard, he arrived at Lexington, Ky., on Aug. 28, 1798, where he organized a vineyard association. A tract of 630 acres, called the First Vineyard, was purchased on the Kentucky River about twenty-five miles from Lexington. After the vineyard was well started, Dufour sent for his brothers and sisters in Switzerland. They, with relatives and friends, a little band of seventeen, arrived at the First Vineyard in the summer of 1801. They were full of hope but their efforts were doomed to failure, as a fatal disease soon attacked the vines. Some members of the colony then started the Second Vineyard . . . at . . . Vevay, Ind. The subscribers to the Vineyard Association having become disheartened, the association was dissolved and the full burden of carrying on the vineyards rested on the Swiss colony. In 1806 Dufour was obliged to return to Europe. He left the vineyards in the hands of his younger brothers. The second war with England broke out in his absence and he was delayed in returning until 1816. In the meantime his brothers abandoned the First Vineyard and joined the other colonists at Vevay. Here Dufour joined them on his return to America and here he wrote his book, *The American Vine-Dresser's Guide* . . . He died at Vevay at the age of sixty-four, a few months after his book was published. He was a man of unusual intelligence, forethought, and perseverance. While his grape colony experiments ended in failure, he contributed an important chapter to the history of grape growing in America."

> Condensed from C. R. B., *Dictionary of American Biography*, Vol. V.

* * *

The American Vine-Dresser's Guide, Being a Treatise on the Cultivation of the Vine and the Process of Wine Making; Adapted to the Soil and Climate of the United States . . . *Cincinnati*, 1826.

DUMONT, JULIA LOUISA CORY (MRS. JOHN L.): 1794–1857.

Julia Louisa Cory (also "Corey" and sometimes "Carey"), daughter of Ebenezer and Martha D. Cory [?] was born in Marietta, O., in October, 1794, a few months after her father's death, presumably at the hands of Indians. Her parents had come to Ohio from New York, and after her husband's death Mrs. Cory returned with her infant daughter to New York the following spring. She supported herself and baby by

doing tailoring, then married R. Manville (or Mandville), a widower with six children. After his death she again became a tailoress.

Julia Cory grew up in New York, attended Milton Academy, and taught school for two years. In August, 1812, she married John L. Dumont and accompanied him to Cincinnati, O., where he became a land agent for William Henry Harrison. In 1814 they came to Vevay, Ind., where they reared their family (eleven children were born to them, several of whom died in childhood) and where Mrs. Dumont, about 1820, began her teaching career. John Dumont was admitted to the Indiana bar in 1818, filled various local offices in Vevay, and was Switzerland County's representative in the first Indiana Legislature. He also ran for governor of the state in 1837 but was defeated.

Mrs. Dumont is probably best known for having taught the Eggleston brothers—Edward and George Carey—both having praised her highly in their writings. Her literary reputation is principally based on the fact that she was Indiana's first short story writer and the first widely known woman writer of the Middle West. She wrote during the era of the first successful American literary magazines, and her contributions did much to encourage new and struggling ones. Among the publications in which her stories appeared were THE CINCINNATI LITERARY GAZETTE, THE CINCINNATI MIRROR, THE WESTERN GEM AND CABINET OF LITERATURE, THE LADIES' REPOSITORY, and THE SOUTHWESTERN JOURNAL AND MONTHLY REVIEW. One of the earliest of her writings to be published in the West was "Theodore Harland," which won a contest sponsored by the CINCINNATI CHRONICLE in 1827 and was republished in other papers. Although she attempted to write realistically of the western scene, she could not divorce herself entirely from the romantic style of her day. In 1856 her stories were collected and published in one volume, *Life Sketches from Common Paths*.

Mrs. Dumont died at Vevay on Jan. 2, 1857.

> Information from Briscoe—unpublished ms. *The Hoosier School of Fiction* and the INDIANA MAGAZINE OF HISTORY, Vol. 34.

* * *

Life Sketches from Common Paths: a Series of American Tales. *New York*, 1856.

DUNGAN, DAVID ROBERTS: 1837–?

David Roberts Dungan, son of James and Mary Ann Johns Dungan, was born in Noble County, Ind., on May 15, 1837. In 1859 he was ordained to the Christian (Disciples) ministry and from 1861 to 1867 was a missionary in Nebraska. He was regent of the University of Nebraska from 1868 to 1872. In 1884, while professor of exegesis and history at Drake University, Ia., he received his A.M. He was president of Cotner University (1890-96), president (1900-02) and dean of the Bible Department (1902-05) of Christian University, and, after 1905, professor of sacred literature at Drake University.

Information from *Who's Who in America.*

* * *

On the Rock; or, Truth Stranger Than Fiction. *St. Louis,* 1872.

Prohibition vs. License. *Oscaloosa, Iowa,* 1875.

Modern Revivalism. *Oscaloosa, Iowa,* 1876.

Our Plea and Our Mission; or, Is There Sufficient Reason for Our Existence as a Separate Religious Body? *Oscaloosa, Iowa,* 1876.

Modern Phases of Skepticism. 1877.

Rum and Ruin; the Remedy Found. *Oscaloosa, Iowa,* 1879.

Chang Foo; or, the Latest Fashions in Religion. *Cincinnati,* 1885.

Mistakes of Ingersoll about Moses. *St. Louis,* n.d.

Sabbath or Lord's Day? *St. Louis,* n.d.

Moses, the Man of God. *St. Louis,* 1899.

Rosa Gray. *Cincinnati,* 1904.

Tour Through Bible. 1908.

Outline Studies in the Life of Christ. *Des Moines,* 1909.

DUNN, JACOB PIATT: 1855–1924.

Born in Lawrenceburg, Ind., in 1855, Jacob Piatt Dunn graduated from Earlham College in 1874 and attended the University of Michigan.

For about ten years he engaged in newspaper work in Colorado, being connected with various papers in that state. In 1888 he returned to Indiana, where he was associated with the INDIANAPOLIS JOURNAL and the literary bureau of the Democratic State Central Committee. He became Indiana State Librarian in 1891, and during this service wrote regularly for the INDIANAPOLIS SENTINEL. He was also an editorial writer for the INDIANAPOLIS STAR.

Mr. Dunn died in Indianapolis in 1924.

Information from Dunn—*Indiana and Indianans* and the Indianapolis Public Library.

* * *

Massacres of the Mountains: History of the Indian Wars of the Far West. *New York,* 1886.

Indiana, a Redemption from Slavery. *New York,* 1888.

Manual of the Election Law in Indiana. *Indianapolis,* 1889.

New Tax Law of Indiana and the Science of Taxation. *Indianapolis,* 1892.

Libraries of Indiana. *Indianapolis,* 1893.

Slavery Petitions and Papers. *Indianapolis,* 1894.

Documents Relating to the French Settlements on the Wabash. *Indianapolis,* 1894.

The World's Silver Question (with Mrs. S. A. Wrigley). *Indianapolis,* 1894.

Fallacy and Fraud of the Overstreet Bill. *Indianapolis,* 1898.

The Mission to the Ouabache. *Indianapolis,* 1902.

Negro Issue. *Indianapolis,* 1904.

Father Gibault, the Patriot Priest of the Northwest. *Springfield, Ill.,* 1905.

The Word Hoosier; and John Finley (with Mrs. S. A. Wrigley). *Indianapolis,* 1907.

True Indian Stories, with Glossary of Indiana Indian Names. *Indianapolis,* 1908.

Greater Indianapolis: the History, the Industries, the Institutions, and the People of a City of Homes. *Chicago,* 1910. 2 vols.

Proposed Constitution of Indiana. *Indianapolis,* 1911.

Memorial and Genealogical Record of Representative Citizens of Indiana. *Indianapolis,* 1912.

Memorial Record of Distinguished Men of Indianapolis and Indiana. *Chicago,* 1912.

The Unknown God, and Other Orthodox Essays. *Indianapolis,* 1914.

History of Indiana. Supplement to Gordy's History of the United States. *New York,* 1916.

Indiana and Indianans, a History of Aboriginal and Territorial Indiana and the Century of Statehood. *Chicago,* 1919. 5 vols.

Constitutional Amendments and the Democratic Party. *Greenfield, Ind.,* 1921.

DYE, CHARITY: 1849–1921.

Born in Mason County, Ky., in 1849, Charity Dye spent most of her life in Indiana. She was educated in the county schools, May's Lick Academy (Ky.), and the McClain Institute at Indianapolis. She graduated from the Normal School at Indianapolis and received the Ph.B. degree from the University of Chicago in 1900.

Miss Dye taught in the public schools of Indianapolis and was a member of the Indiana Historical Commission. She edited and compiled several books besides those listed.

Miss Dye died in Indianapolis in 1921.

Information from Dunn—*Indiana and Indianans* and the Indianapolis Public Library.

* * *

The Story Teller's Art: a Guide to the Elementary Study of Fiction. *Boston, 1898.*

Letters and Letter Writing as Means to the Study and Practice of English Composition. *Indianapolis, 1903.*

Historical Pageant, Closing the Centennial Celebration, June 6-13, 1914, of the Founding of New Harmony, Indiana, in 1814 . . . *Indianapolis, 1914.*

Pageant Suggestions for the Indiana Statehood Centennial Celebration. *Indianapolis, 1916.*

Some Torch Bearers in Indiana. *Indianapolis, 1917.*

DYE, JOHN T.: 1835–1913.

John T. Dye, Indianapolis attorney, was born in Kentucky in 1835. A member of the firm of Dye and Harris, from which he later withdrew to enter railway practice, he was the first president of the Indianapolis Bar Association (1878). His wife was Annie Glenn Holton Dye.

Mr. Dye was the author of some works on law, besides the book listed here.

He died in 1913.

Information from the Indianapolis Public Library.

* * *

Ideals of Democracy: Conversations in a Smoking Car. *Indianapolis, 1908.*

DYER, SIDNEY M.: 1814–1898.

Sidney M. Dyer, father of Mattie Dyer Britts, was born in Cambridge, N. Y., on Feb. 11, 1814. Although he attended Amity Street Classical School in New York City for a time, he was chiefly self-taught. In 1836 he began the study of theology, and he was ordained to the Baptist ministry in 1842.

After serving as a missionary among the Choctaw Indians and as secretary of the Indian Mission Board in Louisville, he came, in 1852, to Indianapolis as pastor of the First Baptist Church. He remained there for about seven years before going to Philadelphia as district secretary of the American Baptist Publication Society. He died in 1898.

He is principally remembered for his songs—he composed the lyrics for a great many—but he was also the author of several books.

Information from *Appletons' Cyclopaedia of*
American Biography, Vol. II, and Parker and Heiney—*Poets and Poetry of Indiana.*

* * *

Voices of Nature, and Thoughts in Rhyme. *Louisville, 1849.*

Dyer's Psalmist; a Collection of Hymns and Sacred Songs for the Use of Baptist Churches. *Louisville, 1851.*

An Olio of Love and Song Delivered Before the Athenian Society of Indiana University, July 31, 1855. *Indianapolis, 1855.*

Songs and Ballads. *New York, 1857.*

The Drunkard's Child. *New York, 1865.*

Home and Abroad; or, the Wonders of Familiar Objects. *Philadelphia, 1872.*

Black Diamonds; or, the Curiosities of Coal. *Philadelphia, 1873.*

Great Wonders in Little Things. *Philadelphia, 1874.*

Boys and Birds; or, Miss Truat's Mission. *Philadelphia, 1874.*

Hoofs and Claws. *Philadelphia, 1875.*

Ocean Gardens and Palaces; or, the Tent on the Beach. *Philadelphia, 1876.*

Elmdale Lyceum; or, God's Mighty Workers. *Philadelphia, 1877.*

The Beautiful Ladder; or, the Two Students. *Philadelphia, 1881.*

DYER, W. LINCOLN: ?–

Mr. Dyer was a resident of Cloverdale, Ind. The introduction to his book of verse (written by John Clark Ridpath) refers to it as "the work of a beginner, whose mind, without the discipline of learning, seeks expression for its moods and emotions and hopes in the form of verse."

Information from the Greencastle Public Library and the Indiana State Library.

* * *

Rhymes of a Radical. *Indianapolis, 1890.*

E

EAGLESFIELD, CARINA CAMPBELL (MRS. JAMES T.): 1856–1925.

Carina Campbell was born in Monroe, Mich., in 1856. In 1879 she was graduated from the University of Michigan, later receiving her A.M. degree. Following graduation she taught Greek in the University of Kansas. She was also an accomplished musician.

In Indianapolis she was active in literary and cultural organizations. She died in Indianapolis in 1925.

Information from the Indianapolis Public Library.

* * *

Books Triumphant; Essays on Literature. *New York,* 1901.

EARLY, SAMUEL STOCKWELL: 1827–?

Samuel Stockwell Early, only child of Jacob D. and Mary Stockwell Early, was born in Flemingsburg, Ky., on July 12, 1827. His mother died a few months after his birth, and he was reared by his grandmother. He was educated at an academy in Flemingsburg and entered Indiana Asbury (now De Pauw) University in 1841 and graduated in 1844, at the age of seventeen.

After spending two or three years working for his father in Terre Haute, Ind., he went to Europe in 1849 and spent fifteen months visiting different countries. His interest in art led him to all the famous art galleries in Europe. During this time he also contributed a series of letters to the WESTERN CHRISTIAN ADVOCATE of Cincinnati.

On his return he went into partnership with his father and from 1856 to 1862 he served as president of the Prairie City Bank of Terre Haute and from 1864 to 1871 as a director of the National State Bank. He was also president of St. Agnes Hall, a female seminary in Terre Haute, from 1864 to 1868. In 1872 he moved to Baltimore, where he was editor and proprietor of the BALTIMORE BULLETIN, a weekly literary and art journal, but he returned to Terre Haute in 1876 and in 1878 became secretary of Rose Polytechnic Institute, serving until 1884.

Information from De Pauw University's *Alumnal Record, 1920,* and *Representative Men of Indiana,* Vol. II.

* * *

The Early Family: a History of the Family of Early in America; Being the Ancestors and Descendants of Jeremiah Early, Who Came from the County Donegal, Ireland, and Settled in What Is Now Madison County, Virginia, Early in the Eighteenth Century; Arranged for Publication by Robert Stockwell Hatcher. *Albany, N. Y.,* 1896.

EDGERTON, WALTER: 1806–1879.

Walter Edgerton was born in Ohio in 1806 and removed to Henry County, Ind., in 1829. He farmed there and in 1836 taught school.

A conservative Quaker, he was a sharp critic of current fads, such as phrenology, and of changes in the Quaker faith. He was a noted and an active abolitionist, and he was active in the intra-church discussion over slavery, which resulted in the separation in the Indiana Society of Friends in 1832.

His writings were widely read and exercised considerable influence. He died in Minneapolis in 1879.

Information from the Spiceland Public Library and the Earlham College Library.

* * *

A Brief Review of Certain Phrenological Works of O. S. Fowler. *Newport, Ind.,* 1848.

A History of the Separation in Indiana Yearly Meeting of Friends . . . *Cincinnati,* 1856.

Modern Quakerism Examined and Contrasted with That of the Ancient Type. *Indianapolis,* 1876.

Walter Edgerton's Disownment by Spiceland Monthly Meeting, Within Indiana Yearly Meeting. 1877.

EDSON, HANFORD A.: 1837–1920.

Hanford A. Edson, son of Dr. Freeman Edson and descendant of an old New England family, was born in Scottsville, N. Y., on Mar. 14, 1837. He was educated at home and in the district school before he entered Williams College, from which he graduated in 1855. After graduation, he taught for three years, then studied at Union Theological Seminary and at the University of Halle in Germany.

In 1861 he returned to the U. S. and took up his duties as a minister, coming to Indianapolis in 1864 as pastor of the Second Presbyterian Church. He was married on July 16, 1867, to Helen M. Rockwood of Indianapolis. Hanover College conferred upon him the honorary degree of Doctor of Divinity in 1873.

Information from *Representative Men of Indiana,* Vol. I, and the Indianapolis Public Library.

* * *

The Church God's Building; a Historical Discourse, Delivered December 22, 1867, at the Opening of the New Chapel of the Second Presbyterian Church, Indianapolis, Indiana. *Indianapolis,* 1868.

Contributions to the Early History of the Presbyterian Church in Indiana; Together with Biographical Notices of the Pioneer Ministers. *Cincinnati,* 1898.

EGGLESTON, EDWARD: 1837–1902.

"Edward Eggleston (Dec. 10, 1837-Sept. 2, 1902), novelist, historian, was born at Vevay, Ind. His father, Joseph Cary Eggleston, lawyer and politician, was a graduate of the College of William and Mary and belonged to a family of some importance in Virginia from colonial times; his mother, Mary Jane Craig, was the daughter of Capt. George Craig, Western frontiersman and Indian fighter. Before his father's death, in 1846, the family spent much time at the Craig farm, several miles from Vevay, so that the future author of *The Hoosier Schoolmaster* early attended a country school. Some three years in Vevay followed, and then young Eggleston was sent for a long visit in Decatur County, where he enriched his knowledge of uncouth Hoosier dialect and backwoods manners. Meantime, on Dec. 25, 1850, his mother had married Williamson Terrell, a Methodist preacher, and Eggleston returned home in March 1851, not to Vevay, but to New Albany. There the family remained a half year, then spent some two years at Madison, then returned to Vevay, in 1853. Here Eggleston liked the high school and flourished under the special favor of the locally famed Mrs. Julia Dumont, who pleased him with the assurance that he was destined to be an author. In June 1854, he was off for thirteen months in Virginia, spent partly with relatives and partly at the Amelia Academy where his accidental discovery of *The Sketch Book* began the slow process of liberation from his almost fanatical devotion to a narrow religious creed (FORUM, August 1887). Meantime his growing hatred of slavery caused him to refuse the offer of a course at the University of Virginia; indeed, ill health prevented his attending any college, and his formal schooling was now at an end.

"After his return to Indiana he was employed for some time as a Bible agent; but his health, always precarious, was soon completely broken. Fearing death from consumption, he set out westward, but suddenly changed his course for Minnesota, where during the summer of 1856 he restored his health by vigorous labor in the open air; then, after an abortive attempt to reach Kansas and aid the anti-slavery cause, he returned home. Some six months (November 1856-April 1857) on a Methodist circuit in southeastern Indiana wrought, however, new disaster to his health, and he was back in Minnesota the following spring, this time for nine years: he was Bible agent (1858-59); he was pastor of small churches at Traverse and St. Peter (1857-58), St. Paul (1859-60 and 1862-63), Stillwater (1860-61), and Winona (1864-66); and he tried a variety of other occupations, always frequently interrupted by ill health (Forty-third Annual Report of the American Bible Society, 1859; Minutes of the Annual Conferences of the Methodist Episcopal Church, 1857-66; and Eggleston Papers). Early in

1866 he gave up the ministry for journalism and removed to Evanston, Ill. He was associate editor . . . June 1866-February 1867 . . . of the LITTLE CORPORAL of Chicago. In February 1867, he became editor of the SUNDAY SCHOOL TEACHER, soon renamed the NATIONAL SUNDAY SCHOOL TEACHER; and even after he had left the West he continued as its corresponding editor, until December, 1873. Meantime, as early as 1868, he was announced as 'a contributor to all the leading juvenile periodicals in the United States' (SUNDAY SCHOOL TEACHER, vol. III, no. 12); and *Mr. Blake's Walking-Stick* (1870) was the first of several small volumes of fantastic fairy lore or moral tales of too sentimental children.

"Migrating eastward, Eggleston began in May 1870 a period of about fourteen or fifteen months on the INDEPENDENT (New York), of which he had for some time been Western correspondent (INDEPENDENT, May 12, 19, 1870; and SCRIBNER'S MONTHLY, September 1873). His editorial connection from August 1871, with the then moribund HEARTH AND HOME . . . seems to have lasted only a year, but served both to revive the magazine and to start Eggleston on his career as a popular novelist destined to have an important influence in turning American literature toward realism. His first novel *The Hoosier Schoolmaster* (HEARTH AND HOME, Sept. 30-Dec. 30, 1871), was already marked by the sentimental quality as well as by the realism of his later writings . . . The Ohio River country is the setting of *The End of the World* (HEARTH AND HOME, Apr. 20-Sept. 7, 1872), a story of religious fanaticism and racial prejudice. In *The Mystery of Metropolisville* (HEARTH AND HOME, Dec. 7, 1872-Apr. 26, 1873) he turned to the Minnesota frontier and made, apparently, some use of Dickens's method in his humorous character portrayals. *The Circuit Rider* (CHRISTIAN UNION, Nov. 12, 1873-Mar. 18, 1874), with its setting in southern Ohio at the beginning of Madison's administration, pictures the devoted members of a religious fraternity of which Eggleston himself was once a member. Of the later novels, *Roxy* (SCRIBNER'S MONTHLY, November 1877-October 1878) dealt with unusual frankness, for the period, with the problem of marital infidelity against a background of old Vevay life; *The Hoosier Schoolboy* (ST. NICHOLAS, December 1881-April 1882) preached a sentimental sermon against the harshness of rural schools . . .

"Eggleston's religious enthusiasm, long since waning, finally spent itself entirely during his pastorate (1874-79) of the non-sectarian Church of Christian Endeavor, in Brooklyn (NEW YORK TRIBUNE, Dec. 27, 1877;

NEW YORK TIMES, Dec. 27, 1879). At the same time with the end of his religious zeal came also the change of his main literary interest from fiction to history. He had, indeed, early come to look upon the novel as a means of making 'a contribution to the history of civilization in America' . . .

"From 1870 until his first voyage to Europe, late in 1879, Eggleston's home was in Brooklyn; from 1881 until his death he lived at Joshua's Rock, on Lake George, but usually spent his winters in New York or other cities and delivered many lectures. His first wife, Lizzie Snider, whom he had married at St. Peter, Minn., Mar. 18, 1858, died in 1889 (Eggleston Papers), and on Sept. 14, 1891, he married Frances Goode, of Madison, Ind. (NEW YORK TIMES, Sept. 15, 1891). His last years, like his earlier life, were troubled with serious illness. Some three years before his death he suffered a stroke of apoplexy from which he never really recovered. Another stroke in August 1902 was followed by his death on Sept. 2 of that year."

Condensed from R. L. R., *Dictionary of American Biography*, Vol. VI.

* * *

Sunday-School Conventions and Institutes; With Suggestions on County and Township Organization. *Chicago*, 1867.

Improved Sunday-School Record. *Chicago*, 1869.

The Manual: a Practical Guide to the Sunday-School Work. *Chicago*, 1869.

Mr. Blake's Walking-Stick: a Christmas Story for Boys and Girls. *Chicago*, 1870.

Tracts for Sunday School Teachers. *Chicago*, n.d.

Book of Queer Stories and Stories Told on a Cellar Door. *Chicago, 1870.* (No copy is known to be in existence— the book was destroyed, plates and all, in the Chicago Fire of 1871. It is listed in the Library of Congress Catalog.)

The Hoosier School-Master. A Novel. *New York, n.d.* [1871].

The End of the World. A Love Story. *New York, n.d.* [1872].

The Mystery of Metropolisville. *New York, n.d.* [1873].

The Circuit Rider: a Tale of the Heroic Age. *New York,* 1874.

The Schoolmaster's Stories for Boys and Girls. *Boston,* 1874.

Roxy. *New York,* 1878.

FAMOUS AMERICAN INDIANS series:

Tecumseh and the Shawnee Prophet. Including Sketches of George Rogers Clark, Simon Kenton, William Henry Harrison, Corn Stalk, Black Hoof, Bluejacket, the Shawnee Logan, and Others Famous in the Frontier Wars of Tecumseh's Time (with Elizabeth Eggleston Seelye). *New York*, n.d. [1878].

Pocahontas. Including an account of the Early Settlement of Virginia and of the Adventures of Captain John Smith (with Elizabeth Eggleston Seelye). *New York*, n.d. [1879].

Brant and Red Jacket. Including an Account of the Early Wars of the Six Nations, and the Border Warfare of the Revolution (with Elizabeth Eggleston Seelye). *New York*, n.d. [1879].

Montezuma and the Conquest of Mexico (with Elizabeth Eggleston Seelye). *New York*, n.d. [1880].

The Hoosier School-Boy. *New York*, 1883.

Queer Stories for Boys and Girls. *New York*, 1884.

The Graysons. A Story of Illinois. *New York*, n.d. [1888].

A History of the United States and Its People. *New York,* 1888.

A History of the United States and Its People for the Use of Schools. *New York*, 1888. (Virtually the same as the preceding book—it was reissued in 1889 as The Household History of the United States and Its People for Young Americans.)

A First Book in American History, with Special Reference to the Lives and Deeds of Great Americans. *New York*, 1889.

The Faith Doctor. A Story of New York. *New York,* 1891.

Duffels. *New York,* 1894.

Stories of American Life and Adventure. *New York*, n.d. [1895].

Stories of Great Americans for Little Americans. *New York*, n.d. [1895].

Sister Tabea. *New York*, 1896.

The Beginners of a Nation. A History of the Source and Rise of the Earliest English Settlements in America with Special Reference to the Life and Character of the People. *New York*, n.d. [1896].

The Transit of Civilization from England to America in the Seventeenth Century. *New York*, 1901.

The New Century History of the United States. *New York*, n.d. [1904].

EGGLESTON, GEORGE CARY: 1839–1911.

"George Cary Eggleston (Nov. 26, 1839-Apr. 14, 1911), journalist, novelist, was born at Vevay, Ind., the son of Joseph Cary Eggleston and Mary Jane Craig. After an early youth of play and reading guided by his mother . . . he went to school at Madison (Ind.) and was for something over a year at Indiana Asbury (now De Pauw) University. Straitened circumstances, however, forced him when only sixteen to teach school at Riker's Ridge and to meet those amusing and trying experiences that inspired *The Hoosier Schoolmaster,* of his brother Edward. When seventeen, having inherited his family's plantation in Amelia County, Va., he was whisked into an aristocratic, genial, and leisurely life that astonished and charmed him. He then studied law at Richmond College and made friends with the Richmond literary group, especially with John Eston Cooke. In 1861, with many other gentlemen horsemen he saw service in northern Virginia in the 1st Virginia Cavalry, first under Col. J.E.B. Stuart and later under Gen. Fitzhugh Lee. In the autumn he transferred to the field artillery on the South Carolina coast, but in 1863, he was back north in Longstreet's artillery ... In 1864 his battery served as sharpshooters through the bloody siege of Petersburg; and Eggleston, with his brother Joseph as second in command, was in charge of a mortar fort.

"Immediately after the war he went to Cairo, Ill., to take a position with a banking and steamboating firm; and there on Sept. 9, 1868, he married Marion Craggs. Later he practised law in Mississippi. The work in both places, however, was uncongenial; accordingly, in 1870, with his wife and one child, he went to New York. Here he began a newspaper and editorial career that lasted, except for short intervals, for twenty years. After a year first as a reporter and later as an editorial writer on the BROOKLYN DAILY UNION under the guidance of Theodore Tilton, and after a brief period of free-lance writing, he joined his brother Edward in securing good writers for the HEARTH AND HOME, bringing among others Frank R. Stockton to the staff. He was editor-in-chief in 1874 when the magazine was sold. A free-lance again, he wrote for the ATLANTIC MONTHLY, GALAXY, APPLETON'S JOURNAL, and other periodicals. In 1875 he became a member of the editorial staff of the NEW YORK EVENING POST, and a chat with William Cullen Bryant soon thereafter brought him the POST's literary editorship ... In 1889, after eight years in which he had been literary adviser to Harper & Brothers, and literary editor and later editor-in-chief of the COMMERCIAL ADVERTISER, he was called to the editorial staff of the NEW YORK WORLD and there for eleven years he wrote under Joseph Pulitzer's inspiring guidance, being his mouthpiece in many of the WORLD's political campaigns.

"In the quieter periods of his New York life, Eggleston had written excellent non-moralizing boys' stories with his own boys as critics ... and he had done much magazine writing and miscellaneous book-making. Now, refusing to yield further to the 'call of the wild,' as he termed the lure of journalism and retiring to his Lake George home every summer, he zestfully

wrote a score or more of works: boys' stories, history, biography, autobiography, and especially novels. Some of the latter he based upon experience in Indiana, on the Mississippi, and in South Carolina. His most glamorous memories, however, were of pre-war Virginia ... The characters in these books are too perfect to seem real, but Eggleston always denied having idealized them ..."

Mr. Eggleston died on Apr. 14, 1911.

Condensed from A. L. H., *Dictionary of American Biography*, Vol. VI.

* * *

How to Educate Yourself. *New York, 1872.*

A Man of Honor. *New York, n.d.* [1873].

A Rebel's Recollections. *New York, 1874.*

How to Make a Living. *New York, 1875.*

The Big Brother; a Story of Indian War. *New York, 1875.*

Captain Sam; or, the Boy Scouts of 1814. *New York, 1876.*

The Signal Boys; or, Captain Sam's Company. *New York, 1878.*

Red Eagle and the Wars with the Creek Indians of Alabama. *New York, 1878.*

Dream of Charlotte. *New York, 1879.*

The Wreck of the Redbird: Story of the Carolina Coast. *New York, 1882.*

Joe Lambert's Ferry. *Boston, n.d.* [1883].

Strange Stories from History for Young People. *New York, 1886.*

Juggernaut, a Veiled Record (with Dolores Marbourg). *New York, 1891.*

Southern Soldier Stories. *New York, 1898.*

The Last of the Flatboats: a Story of the Mississippi and Its Interesting Family of Rivers. *Boston, 1900.*

A Carolina Cavalier: a Romance of the American Revolution. *Boston, 1901.*

Camp Venture: a Story of the Virginia Mountains. *Boston, 1901.*

Dorothy South: a Love Story of Virginia Just Before the War. *Boston, 1902.*

American Immortals: the Record of Men Who by Their Achievement in Statecraft, War, Science, Literature, Art, Law and Commerce Have Created the American Republic and Whose Names Are Inscribed in the Hall of Fame. *New York, 1902.*

The Bale Marked Circle X; a Blockade Running Adventure. *Boston, 1902.*

The Master of Warlock; a Virginia War Story. *Boston, 1903.*

The First of the Hoosiers: Reminiscences of Edward Eggleston, and of That Western Life Which He, First of All Men, Celebrated in Literature and Made Famous. *Boston, 1903.*

History of the Confederate War; Its Causes and Its Conduct: a Narrative and Critical History. *Boston,* 1903. 2 vols.

Home and School Stories (with others). *Akron, O.,* 1904.

Little Lads: Stories and Poems (with others). *Akron, O.,* 1904.

Captain in the Ranks. *New York,* 1904.

Running the River. *New York,* 1904.

Evelyn Byrd. *Boston,* n.d. [1904].

A Daughter of the South. *Boston,* 1905.

Life in the Eighteenth Century. *New York,* 1905.

Our First Century. *New York,* 1905.

Blind Alleys. *Boston,* n.d. [1906].

Jack Shelby, a Story of the Indiana Backwoods. *Boston,* n.d. [1906].

Long Knives. *Boston,* n.d. [1906].

Love Is the Sum of It All. *Boston,* 1907.

Two Gentlemen of Virginia. *Boston,* 1908.

The Warrens of Virginia. *New York,* 1908.

Irene of the Mountains. *Boston,* n.d. [1909].

Recollections of a Varied Life. *New York,* 1910.

Westover of Wanalah. *Boston,* 1910.

What Happened at Quasi; the Story of a Carolina Cruise. *Boston,* 1911.

Our Colonial Story . . . (Revised and edited by Clarence H. McClure.) *Chicago,* 1921.

EHRMANN, MAX: 1872–?

Max Ehrmann, son of Max and Margaret von Ehrmann, was born at Terre Haute, Ind., on Sept. 26, 1872, and was educated at De Pauw University (Ph.B., 1894) and Harvard. An internationally known writer of poetry, fiction, and drama, he was also a contributor to DRAMA, CAXTON'S, WOMAN'S JOURNAL, PROGRESSIVE MAGAZINE, OUTLOOK, PHYSICAL CULTURE, EDUCATOR, and BIRTH CONTROL REVIEW. He died in Terre Haute.

Information from *Who's Who in America.*

* * *

A Farrago. *Cambridge, Mass.,* 1898.

The Mystery of Madeline Le Blanc. *Cambridge, Mass.,* n.d. [1900].

A Fearsome Riddle. *Indianapolis,* n.d. [1901].

Breaking Home Ties. *New York,* n.d. [1904].

A Prayer, and Other Selections. *New York,* 1906.

Max Ehrmann's Poems. *Terre Haute, Ind.,* 1906.

Who Entereth Here, and Other Selections. *New York,* 1907.

The Poems of Max Ehrmann. *New York,* n.d. [1910].

The Wife of Marobius: a Play. *New York,* 1911.

Jesus: a Passion Play. *New York,* n.d. [1915].

Paul Dresser, Composer of "On the Banks of the Wabash." *Terre Haute, Ind.,* 1924.

The Gay Life. *Terre Haute,* n.d. [1925].

Scarlet Sketches. *Terre Haute,* n.d. [1925].

A Goose with a Rose in Her Mouth, and Other Stories. *Terre Haute,* n.d. [1925].

His Beautiful Wife, and Other Stories. *Terre Haute,* n.d. [1925].

Be Quiet, I'm Talking; Being Conversations Set Down by Edna Smith. *Terre Haute,* 1926.

Love From Many Angles. *Girard, Kan.,* 1926.

Farces: the Bank Robbery; the Plumber. *Terre Haute,* n.d. [1927].

Desiderata. *Terre Haute, Ind.,* 1927.

A Virgin's Dream and Other Verses of Scarlet Women. *Terre Haute, Ind.,* 1928.

Worldly Wisdom. *Girard, Kan.,* 1934.

ELLERBE, ALMA MARTIN ESTABROOK (MRS. PAUL): 1871–

Alma Martin, daughter of Samuel Marsh and Florence Howard Martin, was born in Greenfield, Ind., on Apr. 7, 1871. She was educated at Oxford Female College in Ohio. Later a resident of New York, Mrs. Ellerbe contributed novelettes and short stories to magazines, sometimes in collaboration with her husband, Paul Ellerbe, writer and lecturer.

Information from *Who's Who in America.*

* * *

The Rule of Three. *Boston,* 1909.

Stories of Here and Now.

ELLIOTT, ERNEST EUGENE: 1878–

Ernest Eugene Elliott, born in Indianapolis on Oct. 15, 1878, was, successively, general manager of the Illinois Car Service Association, Peoria, Ill. (1898-1909); national secretary of the Brotherhood of Disciples of Christ, Kansas City, Mo. (1909-14); and transportation and publicity secretary for the International Convention of Disciples of Christ (1914-20). Besides his connections with various boards and societies, he was also a special correspondent and contributed feature articles and children's stories to the KANSAS CITY STAR and other newspapers. He died in Kansas City.

Information from the Indianapolis Public Library.

* * *

Making Good in the Local Church. *New York,* 1913.

Problem of Lay Leadership. *New York,* 1914.
How to Fill the Pews. *Cincinnati,* 1917.
How to Advertise a Church. *New York,* 1920.
Hints That Help in Business.

ELLIOTT, JOSEPH PETER: 1815–?

Joseph Peter Elliott was born in Lynchburg, Va., on Apr. 3, 1815, the son of Peter and Ann Brown Elliott.

In 1824 the family moved to Lexington, Ky., where young Elliott supplemented the tutoring of his sister, Elizabeth, with brief attendance at the local school.

In 1836 he went to Louisville, Ky., moving on the next year to Evansville, Ind., where he became a saddler and harness maker. He married Mary Ann Harrison in 1838.

He quit the saddlery business after making harness and saddles for Indiana regiments during the Civil War and subsequently engaged in the manufacture of plows, pork packing and the real estate business. He served as a member of the Evansville council almost from its organization and took a leading part in civic affairs.

After the death of his first wife he was twice married.

Information from Elliott—*A History of Evansville and Vanderburgh County, Indiana.*

* * *

A History of Evansville and Vanderburgh County, Indiana, n.p., 1897.

ELLIOTT, JOSEPH TAYLOR: 1837–1916.

Born in Butler County, O., on Jan. 24, 1837, Joseph Taylor Elliott came with his family to Indianapolis when he was about thirteen years old. His father, William J. Elliott, was in the hotel business in Indianapolis from 1850 until 1863. After receiving a common school education, young Joseph clerked for a time in his father's hotels, went to Colorado in 1859, and in 1860 worked in a hotel in Montgomery, Ala.

He served in the Civil War, first in the 11th Indiana Zouaves, under Lew Wallace, and later in the 124th Indiana Infantry. In 1864 he was taken prisoner in Tennessee and spent some time in various Confederate prisons before being released on parole in March of 1865. He was one of the survivors of the burning and sinking of the *Sultana,* in which more than two thousand Union soldiers lost their lives, near Memphis, Tenn., in April, 1865.

From 1866 to 1900 Mr. Elliott engaged in the abstract business in Indianapolis, from 1899 to 1904 he served as president of the Marion Trust Company, and after 1904 he was in the investment business.

He married Annetta Langsdale on May 15, 1867, and died in Indianapolis on Aug. 4, 1916.

Information from Dunn—*Indiana and Indianans.*

* * *

The Sultana Disaster. *Indianapolis,* 1913.

ELLIOTT, LYDIA LANDON: ?–

Except for the fact that she was a long-time resident of Terre Haute, Ind., no information upon the life of Lydia Landon Elliott has been located.

Information from the Emmeline Fairbanks Memorial Library, Terre Haute, Ind.

* * *

The Skeleton's Message and Other Poems. *Terre Haute, Ind.,* 1896.

ELLISON, ALFRED: 1854–1934.

Born at Charleston, W. Va., on Feb. 1, 1854, Alfred Ellison was the son of an itinerant Baptist minister, who moved to Madison County, Ind., in 1860. He studied law, was admitted to the bar in 1884, and practiced law in Anderson, Ind. In 1890 he was elected judge and served one term.

Information from Parker and Heiney—*Poets and Poetry of Indiana.*

* * *

Poems. *Anderson, Ind.,* n.d.

ELLSWORTH, HENRY WILLIAM: 1814–1864.

"Henry William Ellsworth . . . lawyer, diplomat, was a grandson of Chief Justice Oliver Ellsworth and a son of Henry Leavitt Ellsworth and his wife, Nancy Allen Goodrich. Born at Windsor, Conn., where his father was practicing law, he received his early education at the Ellington School at Windsor and at Hartford, Conn. In 1830 he proceeded to Yale, where he graduated in 1834, subsequently studying for a short time in the law school there. In 1836 he went to Lafayette, Tippecanoe County, Ind., in which neighborhood his father had acquired large tracts of land from the government. Opening a law office in Lafayette, the younger Ellsworth also became a member of the firm of Curtiss and Ellsworth, general land agents, specializing in Wabash and Maumee Valley lands, and, on his father's removal to Washington, D. C., to become commissioner of patents, assumed charge of the latter's extensive Western interests. In 1838 he published *Valley of the Upper Wabash, Indiana, with Hints on Its Agricultural Advantages,* etc., embodying much information obtained from his father's paper, and this work, combined with his influential Eastern connections, helped to stimulate active interest in northwestern lands on the part of both speculators and bona fide settlers. He also . . . was an occasional contributor to the KNICKERBOCKER MAGAZINE. At the same time he participated in the political struggles of the time, was prominent among the supporters of Polk in the election campaign of 1844, and was a presidential elector in that year. On Apr. 19, 1845, he was appointed by President Polk charge d'affaires to Sweden and Norway. The duties of this position he performed with ability for over four years, but his diplomatic career was brought to a close by an episode the implications of which are even today doubtful. Early in 1849 charges were made in the European and home press that in Dec. 1848 Ellsworth had connived at an attempt to smuggle British goods into Sweden, and the facts disclosed in an ex parte investigation prima facie supported the allegation. In consequence Secretary of State Clayton recalled him as of Apr. 23, 1849, the 'President believing that the public service requires a change in the Swedish mission.' Ellsworth protested and vigorously defended himself, and a rather pathetic appeal was made to President Taylor by influential public men on his behalf, but in vain; and following a stern letter from Clayton his appointment was terminated July 25, 1849. On returning to the U. S. he resumed law practice at Lafayette and later at Indianapolis. A large circle of acquaintances evinced their unimpaired belief in his integrity, and he was retained by his father's intimate friend, S. F. B. Morse . . . , in the actions which Morse took to protect his patent rights. His health, never good, broke down, and he was compelled to relinquish his practice, retiring to New Haven, Conn., where he died at the early age of fifty. He was married on Jan. 11, 1844, to Mary E. West of Salem, Mass. . . ."

> Condensed from H. W. H. K., *Dictionary of American Biography,* Vol. VI.

* * *

The Valley of the Upper Wabash, Indiana, with Hints on Its Agricultural Advantages. *New York,* 1838.

The American Swine Breeder, a Practical Treatise on the Selection, Rearing and Fattening of Swine. *Boston,* 1840.

ELMORE, JAMES BUCHANAN: 1857–1942.

At the time of his death in 1942, the Crawfordsville JOURNAL AND REVIEW, newspaper in which many of his poems had been first published, had the following to say about James Buchanan Elmore, "The Bard of Alamo":

"James B. Elmore, Ripley township octogenarian who in the Gay Nineties and for some years thereafter delighted Hoosier folk with his rustic poems, died at his 900-acre farm home near Alamo at four A.M. He had been suffering for the past six months with the infirmities of age.

"Once the Bard bountiful whose pen was never still, he had foresworn verse in recent years, devoting his entire interest to his farming properties. But to his many friends, particularly of the older generations, he was still affectionately remembered as the man who fashioned couplets about earthy things such as sassafras and turnip greens and railroad wrecks.

"The 85-year-old former sonneteer was born on the same farm where death occurred, on Jan. 25, 1857, the son of Mathias and Mary Ann Willis Elmore and on Feb. 14, 1880, he was married to Mary Ann Murray, who, according to an autobiography of the bard, came from Nevada City, Mo. He later dedicated one of his poems, 'My Mary of Missouri', to her.

"He graduated from the Alamo Academy, where he studied with a large class which also included Noah J. Clodfelter, William Humphrey, once president of Cornell, and Eva Ballard, novelist.

"He taught school for twenty years, spending the summer months at farming. He wrote occasional poems for the newspapers of Indianapolis and Crawfordsville and in 1898 he published a volume of his poems. Three other volumes of his prose and poetry were published in later years by Mr. Elmore.

"The pastoral scenes with which he was familiar inspired most of the writings of the benign bard from Ripley township. Few older people in western Indiana have not repeated to their children and grandchildren passages from 'The Monon Wreck' with its climactic 'Cut, Oh cut my leg away!' petition; have not chuckled over his 'Shoe Cobbler', or have not recalled that song of spring from the bard's 'Sassafras, Oh Sassafras!'

"The mellifluous singer of rural roundelays was given his name—the 'Bard of Alamo'—by Jesse Green, a Crawfordsville newspaperman.

"The Alamo poet wrote hundreds of verses before he put his pen aside, and most of his songs were of a rural theme as attested by his poems 'Sugar Making', 'When the Pawpaws are Ripe', 'The Frog', 'The Old Sawmill', 'Katie Gathers Greens' and 'The Good Old Sheep-Sorrel Pie.'

"On other occasions he wrote on politics, on Wabash College and on crime. He toured the nation early in the century to read his compositions.

"Mr. Elmore was a life-long member of the Alamo Christian church and belonged to the Knights of Pythias lodge of Waynetown, and for some years to the Odd Fellows lodge at Alamo. He was prominent in Democratic politics . . ."

A few days later appeared, in the same paper:

"The widow and three children of the late James B. Elmore are to receive his $50,000 estate, under the terms of a will admitted to probate in the Montgomery circuit court.

"A son, Roscoe, was named administrator of the estate, with will annexed. Court papers revealed that the personal property owned by the 'Bard of Alamo' was estimated to be worth $15,000 and real estate was valued at $35,000.

"The will was dated May 8, 1935."

And shortly after, Frank E. Burk, of Valparaiso, Ind., who had been a Wabash College student in the Bard's palmiest days, contributed the following to the WABASH COLLEGE BULLETIN:

"I can remember the Bard, just as well as if it were yesterday, standing on Crawfordsville's Main Street opposite the Court House steps.

"It is Saturday or circus day or a fiesta or gala day of some kind. He has one of those little satchels with patent leather finish, made especially for carrying diapers . . . it was fastened around his neck with a strap. It lay open like he was selling peanuts and in it nestled at least 50 anemic looking red books about the size of a McGuffey Primer.

"This book contained the current sampling of his poetic works, unexpurgated and including, maybe, the pathetic little story about the poor little gel who had so much trouble working in the overalls factory and the far greater troubles she had with the unprincipled roues who worked in the overalls.

"The book sold for 75¢ and I don't think that James B. had to work those stony acres of his very hard, for many's the time I've seen him start on the long trip back to Alamo with his moth eaten horse and buggy and his diaper compact innocent of a single immortal tome. And I often wondered who was the smarter, the wise guy who laughed at his poesy, or the Bard, with

his pocket full of bucks, jogging homeward his dusty way laughing at the suckers who bought his books?"

Of the many thousands of copies of the many editions of his four titles which James B. Elmore had printed during his productive years, few may be found on the markets today; it is much less difficult to assemble a set of the first issues of Gen. Lew Wallace's books than to gather the four Elmore works in any edition: every Crawfordsville book store, library or other conceivable source of a possible purchase is constantly besieged by hopeful would-be acquisitors of the Bard's works from all over the English speaking world —with a decreasing modicum of success. No fabulous prices are paid but the works of James Buchanan Elmore, once collected, are read and re-read—which is a tribute not always paid to many volumes of more intrinsic worth.

Although most of his books were reprinted many times, some years of careful study have led to the conclusion that the first editions of Elmoriana are as described below.

Information from the CRAWFORDSVILLE JOURNAL AND REVIEW and the WABASH COLLEGE BULLETIN.

* * *

Love Among the Mistletoe, and Poems. *Alamo, Ind.,* 1899.

Poems. *Alamo, Ind.,* 1901.

A Lover in Cuba, and Poems. *Alamo, Ind.,* 1901.

Supplement to a Lover in Cuba, and Poems. *Nashville, Tenn.,* 1902.

Twenty-Five Years in Jackville, a Romance in the Days of "The Golden Circle," and Selected Poems. *Alamo, Ind.,* 1904.

Autumn Roses. *Alamo, Ind.,* 1907.

EMBREE, CHARLES FLEMING: 1874–1905.

Charles Fleming Embree, son of David F. and Mary Fleming Embree, was born in Princeton, Ind., on Oct. 1, 1874. His parents were members of pioneer southern Indiana families.

Young Embree was educated in the Princeton public schools and entered Wabash College in the fall of 1892. After three years he left college to devote his time to writing. In writing he achieved immediate success, his first novel being published in 1897. On Jan. 18, 1898, he married Virginia Broadwell.

He was awarded an honorary A.M. degree by Wabash College in 1903 in recognition of the distinguished place among American novelists which he had already achieved.

Charles Fleming Embree died in 1905, in his thirty-first year.

> Information from *Who Was Who in America* and the Wabash College Archives.

* * *

For the Love of Tonita, and Other Tales of the Mesas. *Chicago, 1897.*

A Dream of a Throne: the Story of a Mexican Revolt. *Boston, 1900.*

A Heart of Flame: the Story of a Master Passion. *Indianapolis, 1901.*

EMSWILER, GEORGE P.: 1830–?

George P. Emswiler was born in York, Pa., on Jan. 15, 1830. His parents were Dr. J. P. and Elizabeth Mitchell Emswiler.

He began his education in York, and, when the family came to Indiana in 1846, he continued in the Wayne County schools for a year or so.

Mr. Emswiler moved to Richmond, Ind., in 1847 and eventually set himself up as a merchant there. He was twice married, first to Martha A. Finley in 1855, and second to Attilia R. Goodrich.

> Information from the Richmond, Ind., Public Library.

* * *

Poems and Sketches; Consisting of Poems and Local History; Notes of Travel; a Long List of Wayne County's Pioneer Dead . . . *Richmond, Ind., 1897.*

ENGLE, WILLIS DARWIN: 1846–1925.

Willis D. Engle, who was born at Niles, Mich., on Oct. 22, 1846, came to Indianapolis on Apr. 1, 1865. Besides his career as a railroad man, business man, and editor, he also had an extensive record of service as a member of the Episcopal ministry. He was an active worker and held many offices in the Masonic Lodge. He died on Nov. 2, 1925.

> Information from the Indianapolis Public Library.

* * *

The Eastern Star in Indiana. *Indianapolis, 1899.*

A General History of the Order of the Eastern Star. *Indianapolis, 1901.*

ENGLISH, WILLIAM EASTIN: 1854–1926.

William Eastin English, son of William Hayden and Emma Mardulia Jackson English, was born at the family home, Englishton Park, in Scott County, Ind., on Nov. 3, 1854. He was educated at Northwestern Christian (now Butler) University, received his LL.B. from the law school in 1877, and practiced law in Indianapolis. In 1879-80 he served a term in the Indiana House of Representatives, being the youngest member of that body; was a member of the 48th Congress (1883-85); and, from 1916 to 1928, served in the Indiana State Senate. In 1925-26 he practiced law with his daughter, Rosalind Orr English, under the firm name of English & English.

Mr. English spent several years in foreign travel. During the Spanish-American War he was aide-de-camp to Gen. Joseph Wheeler during the Cuba campaign, and he was seriously injured during the bombardment of El Paso Hill when his horse was shot and fell on him. From 1899 to 1920 he served on the staff of the governor of Indiana. He made the seconding speech at the nomination of Cleveland in 1892 and was a Democrat until the party division in 1896. He died on Apr. 29, 1926.

> Information from Dunn—*Indiana and Indianans* and *Who Was Who in America.*

* * *

History of Early Indianapolis Masonry and of Center Lodge. *Indianapolis, 1895.*

History of Masonry in Indianapolis. *Indianapolis, 1901.*

Letters from Europe.

ENGLISH, WILLIAM HAYDEN: 1822–1896.

"William Hayden English . . . congressman, Democratic candidate for the vice-presidency, historian, was born at Lexington, Scott County, Ind., the son of Elisha G. and Mahala Eastin English. On his mother's side he was descended from Jost Hite, one of the first white settlers of the Shenandoah Valley. His parents removed from Kentucky to Indiana in 1818, and there Elisha English, a Democrat, took a prominent part in politics, being at different times sheriff of Scott County, a representative and also a senator in the Indiana Legislature, and United States marshal.

"Young English attended Hanover College for three years, studied law, and was admitted to the bar at the early age of eighteen. The same year, 1840, he was a delegate to the Democratic state convention at Indianapolis. When Tyler succeeded to the presidency after the death of Harrison, he appointed the young Democrat postmaster of Lexington. In 1843 English was elected clerk of the Indiana House of Representatives, and a year later he received an appointment in the

Treasury Department at Washington, a position he held until shortly before the end of Polk's presidency, becoming, soon after, clerk of the U. S. Senate committee on claims during the historic session of 1850. He next became secretary of the convention that framed the Indiana constitution of 1851, and as speaker, during part of the session of the next House of Representatives, played a leading part in re-adjusting the laws and machinery of government to the conditions created by the new constitution.

"In 1852 he was elected to represent the second Indiana district in the Thirty-third Congress. As a member of that body he voted for the Kansas-Nebraska Bill and was one of the few Northern Democrats so voting who survived the next congressional election. He was re-elected . . . in 1856 and again in 1858. In the latter year he stood with Douglas in opposing the effort of Buchanan of the South to bring Kansas into the Union under the Lecompton constitution, which had been ratified in an election in which the voters of the Territory had not been given a fair chance to express their views. A conference committee became necessary, and as a member of this committee English played a leading part in framing the compromise known as the English Bill. This measure, which ultimately became a law, in effect offered the people of Kansas a bribe of public land if they would ratify the pro-slavery constitution, a thing which as English had foreseen, they refused to do.

"In 1860 he declined to stand for reelection and in March 1861 retired to private life. He opposed secession, and denied that the election of a Republican president justified an attempt to break up the Union. In a speech in the House he warned his Southern associates that his constituents would only 'march under the flag and keep step to the music of the Union.' Upon the outbreak of war, Gov. Morton offered him command of a regiment but he declined it. He supported the Union cause, however, and opposed the Knights of the Golden Circle in Indiana.

"In 1863 he removed to Indianapolis, and there helped to organize the First National Bank, of which he became president, holding that position until 1877. He played a prominent part in the business life of the city and ultimately became a millionaire. In 1880 geographical and other reasons led the National Democratic Convention to nominate him for the vice-presidency as the running mate of Gen. Hancock. Throughout his life he was interested in scientific and literary matters. While a congressman he was a regent of the Smithsonian Institution, and in later life he was long president of the Indiana Historical Society. For

many years he collected material bearing upon the early history of the old Northwest . . . In 1847, while a clerk at Washington, English married Emma Mardulia Jackson of Virginia . . . He died Feb. 7, 1896."

Condensed from P. L. H., *Dictionary of American Biography*, Vol. VI.

* * *

Conquest of the Country Northwest of the River Ohio, 1778-1783, and Life of Gen. George Rogers Clark. *Indianapolis,* 1896. 2 vols. (Re-issued, 1897, under binder's title History of Indiana.)

ESAREY, LOGAN: 1873–1942.

Logan Esarey was the leading scholar of his day in the field of Indiana history and one of the leading scholars in the country in Middle Western history and historical method. In his teaching he was equally interested in the non-intellectual freshman and in the scholarly graduate student. His published historical writings, often completed to meet a particular need at a particular time, did not do justice to his scholarship. Aside from his influence in the training of students, his most important work lay in the collecting, preservation, and study of historical materials for the Library of Indiana University.

He was an individual of the type referred to in a certain era of American history as "rugged": he believed some truths to be self-evident; he had, and in others honored, "horse-sense," and he was a great teacher of American history—perhaps the greatest of his day in the Middle Western field. Impatient of politic ritual, he aspired to no executive or administrative position; once he had reached his maturity, he wished only to teach, and that he did for the last thirty years of his life.

Son of John Clark and Barbara Ewing Esarey, he was born on Jan. 3, 1873, near Branchville, Ind. His youth was spent on a farm, a farm not prosperous or currently modern but operated in the style of a half century earlier. This experience enabled him to portray in his lectures, and to write in his posthumously published essays, *The Indiana Home,* of the true day-to-day life of the midwestern pioneer.

He attended local schools and received his higher education at Central Normal (now Canterbury) College and Indiana University. He received the A.B., A.M. and Ph.D. degrees from the latter institution.

He married Laura Pearson on May 20, 1897, and served as superintendent of schools for Perry County, Ind., from 1897 to 1903. Between 1907 and 1909 he was principal of the high schools in Vincennes and Bloomington and from 1909 to 1912 acted as dean of Winona College. He became a member of the Indiana University faculty in 1912 and continued until his retirement in 1941.

He died on Sept. 24, 1942.

In addition to his published works listed below, Esarey contributed to publications of the Indiana Historical Society and Indiana University.

> Information from *Who's Who in America* and Buley—*Logan Esarey, Hoosier.*

* * *

A History of Indiana. *Indianapolis,* 1915-1918. 2 vols. (Abridged edition in 1922.)

The Government of Indiana (with Charles E. Finch). *New York,* 1927.

The Indiana Home (Edited by R. Carlyle Buley). *Crawfordsville, Ind.,* 1943.

ESTEY, JAMES ARTHUR: 1886–

James Arthur Estey, son of Henry Guilford and Emma Louisa Spurden Estey, was born at Fredericton, N. B., Canada, on July 16, 1886, and graduated from Acadia University in 1907. A Rhodes scholar, he was awarded the A.B. degree by Oxford University in 1909 and received the Ph.D. degree from the University of Wisconsin in 1911. On June 7, 1910, he married Emma Grey Murray.

From 1911 to 1913 he was an associate professor of economics and history at Dalhousie University in Nova Scotia. He came to the U. S. in 1913 and for one year taught at the University of Wisconsin. In 1914 he joined the faculty of Purdue University, serving as professor of economics after 1920 and as head of the department of history, economics and government after 1929. He became a citizen of the U. S. in 1932.

> Information from *Who's Who in America.*

* * *

Revolutionary Syndicalism. *London,* 1913.

The Labor Problem. *New York,* 1928.

Business Cycles; Their Nature, Cause, and Control. *New York,* 1941.

EVANS, MADISON: 1834–1866.

Madison Evans was born in Warrick County, Ind., on Oct. 24, 1834.

He received the A.B., A.M. and LL.B. degrees from Indiana University and became, successively, a tutor at the University of Wisconsin, principal of a New Albany, Ind., school, and a professor at Northwestern Christian (now Butler) University. He resigned the last position to study law but died on Mar. 5, 1866, at the age of thirty-two.

> Information from Wylie—*Indiana University, Its History from 1820 to 1890.*

* * *

Biographical Sketches of Pioneer Preachers of Indiana. *Philadelphia,* 1862.

EVERTS, ORPHEUS: 1826–1903.

Orpheus Everts, son of Dr. Sylvanus and Elizabeth Heywood Everts, was born in Liberty, Ind., on Dec. 18, 1826. He belonged to a family of physicians—his father, uncle, and three brothers were all doctors. He was educated in the schools of his native county and received his M.D. degree from the Medical College of Indiana in 1846. During the Civil War he served as a surgeon with the 20th Regiment of Indiana Volunteers from 1861 to 1865. From 1868 to 1879 he was superintendent of the Indiana Hospital for the Insane, and from 1880 on he was superintendent of the Cincinnati Sanitarium. He died in 1903.

Dr. Everts was one of the earliest Indiana-born writers. He was also an amateur painter, an editor, and author of medical literature.

> Information from *Representative Men of Indiana,* Vol. I, and *Who Was Who in America.*

* * *

O-Na-We-Quah, and Other Poems. *Laporte, Ind.,* 1856.

The Spectral Bride and Other Poems. *Laporte, Ind.,* 1857.

The American Idea. An Oration . . . Delivered at Buchanan, Michigan, July 4, 1867. *Buchanan, Mich.,* 1867.

Giles & Co., or, Views and Interviews Concerning Civilization. *Indianapolis,* 1878.

Constancy, a Midsummer Night's Idyl. *Indianapolis,* 1881.

What Shall We Do for the Drunkard? A Rational View of the Use of Brain Stimulants. *Cincinnati,* 1883.

Facts and Fancies. *Cincinnati,* 1896.

The Cliffords; or, "Almost Persuaded." *Cincinnati,* 1898.

Address: Delivered at the Annual Meeting of "Old Settler" Society of Laporte County, Indiana, June 21, 1900. *Cincinnati,* 1900.

Lost Poet. *Cincinnati,* 1901.

F

FELLOW, HENRY COFFIN: 1856–?

Born in Henry County, Ind., in 1856, Henry Coffin Fellow was educated at Earlham College (Ph.B., 1886; M.S., 1891), Kansas State University (A.M., 1891), and Nebraska Wesleyan University (Ph.D., 1893). In addition to the titles listed he wrote a text-book or two and had poems published in various anthologies.

Information from the Barry Ms.

* * *

A Study in School Supervision and Maintenance. *Topeka, Kan.,* 1896.

Rhymes of the Yesteryear. *Richmond, Ind.,* 1914.

Odes of Worship and Service. *Boston,* 1926.

Bella Vista Lyrics and Other Poems. *Bella Vista, Ark.,* 1928.

Maumewa, an Indian Lyric of the Ozarks. *Wichita, Kan.,* n.d. [1930].

Ozark Reveries; Daisies, Dog Fennel and Dust, by Uncle Henry. *Wichita, Kan.,* n.d. [1931].

Chimes at Eventide. *Wichita, Kan.,* 1935.

Mountain Melodies and Other Poems. *Wichita, Kan.,* 1937.

Kiddom Reveries in Hoosierdom and Otherwheres. *Wichita, Kan.,* n.d. [1938].

Autumn Lays. *Wichita, Kan.,* n.d. [1939].

FERRIS, DR. EZRA: 1783–1857.

Ezra Ferris, a native of Connecticut, was born in 1783 and was brought west by his parents when he was six years old. He was educated in the East and was licensed as a Baptist preacher. While preaching in Baptist churches around Lawrenceburg, Ind., he also practiced medicine and had a drug store in the town. In 1816 he was a member of the Dearborn County delegation at the state constitutional convention. According to Dunn—*Indiana and Indianans,* Vol. I (p. 297): "He was the backbone of the Baptist church in the county, and wrote the best account we have of the early settlement of the region."

Information from Dunn—*Indiana and Indianans.*

* * *

The Early Settlement of the Miami Country. *Indianapolis,* 1851.

FIDLAR, CHESTER L.: 1858–1933.

Chester L. Fidlar, born in 1858, was educated in the Terre Haute, Ind., public schools and began his teaching career as a supply teacher in the local schools while attending Terre Haute Normal (now Indiana State Teachers College). He graduated from that institution in 1902.

Mr. Fidlar was appointed supervisor of music in the Terre Haute public schools and continued in this capacity for more than thirty years. He died in New York in August, 1933, while carrying on graduate study at Columbia University.

Information from the Indiana State Library.

* * *

The Old Indian Orchard. A Legend. *Terre Haute, Ind.,* 1896.

FIELD, ISOBEL OSBOURNE STRONG: 1858–?

Isobel Osbourne was born in Indianapolis in 1858. Her mother (the former Fanny Van de Grift) divorced her husband, Samuel Osbourne, and left Indianapolis, taking her son, Samuel Lloyd Osbourne, and Isobel when the latter was about four years old.

They went to Paris, where Isobel attended Julian's Atelier des Dames.

Her mother met and married Robert Louis Stevenson, and Isobel was a member of the Stevenson household and assisted him to some extent in his writing. She accompanied him and her mother on his search for health in the U. S. and in the Pacific isles.

In 1879 she married J. D. Strong and, in 1914, Salisbury Field. Some of her writing was published under each name.

Information from the Barry Ms. and from biographies of Robert Louis Stevenson.

* * *

Memories of Vailima (with Lloyd Osbourne). *New York,* 1902.

The Girl from Home; a Story of Honolulu. *New York,* 1905.

Robert Louis Stevenson. *New York,* 1911.

This Life I've Loved; an Autobiography. *New York,* 1937.

FIELD, NATHANIEL: 1805–1888.

Born in Jefferson County, Ky., on Nov. 7, 1805, Nathaniel Field graduated from Transylvania Medical School in Lexington, Ky., and practiced for three years in Alabama and for a time in Kentucky before settling in Jeffersonville, Ind., in 1829. His father, a veteran of the Revolutionary War, had emigrated to Kentucky in 1784.

In 1838-39 Dr. Field was a member of the Indiana Legislature. Despite his birth in a slave state and in a slave-holding family, he was a strong abolitionist— he was president of the first anti-slavery convention held in Indiana, and in 1834 he voted against his entire township on a proposition to expel free negroes.

During the Civil War he acted as surgeon of the 66th Regiment of Indiana Infantry. In 1868 he was president of the Indiana State Medical Society. Dr. Field founded two churches in Jeffersonville and, in addition to his medical duties, acted as pastor of them for fifty-seven years without salary or other compensation. He died in Jeffersonville on Aug. 28, 1888.

Information from *Representative Men of Indiana*, Vol. I, and *Appletons' Cyclopaedia of American Biography*, Vol. II.

* * *

Debate on the State of the Dead, Between Rev. Thomas P. Connelly and Nathaniel Field . . . *Louisville*, 1854.

A Genealogy of the Pope Family of Kentucky. *Jeffersonville, Ind.*, 1879.

Arts of Imposture and Deception Peculiar to American Society, n.d. [1858].

FINLEY, JOHN: 1797–1866.

John Finley, known for many years as "The Hoosier Poet" until that name was given to James Whitcomb Riley, was born in Brownsburg, Va., on Jan. 11, 1797. His father, Andrew Finley, was a merchant in the town, but the family lived on a farm near the Blue Ridge Mountains. During the War of 1812, when John was sixteen years old, his father suffered financial reverses, and John had to give up schooling and take a job in his uncle's tanning business. He educated himself, however, by diligent reading.

In 1816 he started west and, after a short stay in Cincinnati, settled, in 1820, in Richmond, Ind. For the remainder of his life he was engaged in public affairs—in 1822 he served as Justice of the Peace, from 1828 to 1831 he was a member of the state Legislature, from 1837 to 1845 he was clerk of the Wayne County Courts (he lived at Centerville, the county seat, during this time), and from 1852 until his death he was mayor of Richmond. From 1831-34 he edited and owned the controlling interest in the RICHMOND PALLADIUM.

Mr. Finley is supposed to be the first to use the word "Hoosier" in print. In 1830 the RICHMOND PALLADIUM printed his poem, "The Hoosier's Nest," which was reprinted in the INDIANAPOLIS JOURNAL in 1833. In these printings the word was spelled "Hoosher," but Mr. Finley changed it to the present spelling in later editions of the poem. He contributed many poems to newspapers and had one volume of his works published. He was twice married and died on Dec. 23, 1866.

Information from Dunn—*Indiana and Indianans*, Vols. II and V.

* * *

The Hoosier's Nest, and Other Poems. *Cincinnati*, 1860.

FINLEY, MARTHA: 1828–1909.

Martha Finley, Nineteenth century writer of best-sellers, whose books mirror much of the conventions, moral code, and religious philosophy of her time, was born in Chillicothe, O., on Apr. 26, 1828. She was the daughter of Dr. James Brown and Maria Theresa Brown Finley, first cousins.

When she was eight years old, the family moved to South Bend, Ind., where Martha was educated in private schools and later conducted a school of her own. After the death of her father the family returned East in 1854.

She lived in New York and Philadelphia and supported herself by teaching school and writing newspaper stories and Sunday-school books, the latter published by the Presbyterian Board of Publications in Philadelphia. In her early writing she used the name of Farquharson, the original Gaelic of Finley.

During the Civil War Miss Finley, physically incapacitated by a back ailment, began the writing of the first book of her most famous series, *Elsie Dinsmore*, and from its publication in 1867 until four years before the author's death in 1909, the demands of her public and publishers were met with a steady output of books about Elsie or her relative, Mildred Keith. Miss Finley attempted at various times to end the series but was persuaded to continue—the result is a list of more than two dozen titles which may properly be identified as "Elsie Books" with Elsie, as lass, matron and oldster having a part in many others.

In 1876 Miss Finley moved to Elkton, Md., where she built a home and spent the remainder of her life. She died at Elkton on Jan. 30, 1909.

Miss Finley has suffered greatly in the light of present-day criticism. Much of her disrepute results from the passage of time and a changing of manners and morals, as well as a shift from the romantic to the realistic school of writing. On top of that she was anything but an expert craftsman, and her lack of literary style, her poor character development and the sameness of her plots are technical faults which have all contributed to her lack of present-day regard. However, she is important for having been widely read in her day and for the influence she exerted on youthful readers of the late Nineteenth and early Twentieth centuries.

> Information from *The Dictionary of American Biography,* Vol. VI; *The University of Buffalo Studies,* Vol. 17, No. 3; and the South Bend Public Library.

* * *

Marion Harvie, a Tale of Persecution in the Seventeenth Century. *Philadelphia,* 1857.

Willie Elton, the Little Boy Who Loved Jesus. *Philadelphia,* 1864.

Black Steve, or, The Strange Warning. By Martha Farquharson. *Philadelphia,* 1865.

Elsie Dinsmore. *New York,* 1867.

Elsie's Holidays at Roselands. *New York,* 1868. (Reissued 1898 as Holidays at Roselands.)

DO-GOOD LIBRARY. *Philadelphia,* 1868. 9 vols.
   Anna Hand, the Meddlesome Girl
   Grandma Foster's Sunbeam
   Little Patience
   Little Helper
   Little Dick Positive
   Loitering Linus
   Maud's Two Homes
   Milly, the Little Girl Who Tried to Help Others
   Stupid Sally.

Caselia; or, the Children of the Valleys. *Philadelphia,* 1869.

Lilian: or, Did She Do Right. *Philadelphia,* 1871.

An Old-Fashioned Boy. *Philadelphia,* 1871.

Wanted—a Pedigree. *Philadelphia,* 1871.

Elsie's Girlhood. *New York,* 1872.

Our Fred; or, Seminary Life at Thurston. *New York,* 1874.

Elsie's Womanhood. *New York,* 1875.

Elsie's Motherhood. *New York,* 1876.

PEWIT'S NEST SERIES. 1876. 12 vols.
   Pewit's Nest
   Harry's Fourth of July
   Harry's Ride
   Harry's Walks
   Harry's Little Sister
   Harry's Christmas
   Harry and His Chickens
   Aunt Kitty's Fowls
   Harry's Grandma
   Rose and Robbie
   Harry at Aunt Jane's
   Harry and His Cousins.

Signing the Contract, and What It Cost. *New York,* 1879.

Elsie's Widowhood. *New York,* 1880.

Allan's Fault. *Philadelphia.*

HONEST JIM SERIES. *Philadelphia,* 6 vols.
   Honest Jim
   Contented Jim
   How Jim Did It
   The Twin Babies
   Noll, the Beggar Boy
   Noll in the Country.

LITTLE BOOKS FOR LITTLE READERS. *Philadelphia,* 6 vols.
   The White Dress
   The Broken Basket
   Jamie by the Lake
   Bertie Page
   Amy and Her Kitten
   Jane Hart.

Mysie's Work and How She Did It. *Philadelphia.*

Annandale: a Story of the Twins of the Covenanters. *Philadelphia.*

Aunt Ruth; or, Persecuted, Not Forsaken. *Philadelphia.*

Brookside Farmhouse from January to December. *Philadelphia.*

Cares and Comforts. *Philadelphia.*

Clouds and Sunshine. *Philadelphia.*

Ella Clinton; or, By Their Fruits Ye Shall Know Them. *Philadelphia.*

Eva Merton; or, the Blue Morocco Shoes. *Philadelphia.*

Hugo and Franz. *Philadelphia.*

Lame Letty; or, Bear Ye One Another's Burdens. *Philadelphia.*

Little Joe Carter, the Cripple; or, Learning to Forgive. *Philadelphia.*

Nursery Tales for Her Little Friends. *Philadelphia.*

Peddler of La Grave. *Philadelphia.*

Robert and Daisy; or, "Thou Shalt Not Covet." *Philadelphia.*

Rufus the Unready. *Philadelphia.*

The Shannons; or, From Darkness to Light. *Philadelphia.*

Try: Better Do It Than Wish It Done. *Philadelphia.*

Week in Lilly's Life. *Philadelphia.*

Mildred and Elsie. *New York,* 1881.

Grandmother Elsie. *New York,* 1882.

Mildred's Married Life and a Winter with Elsie Dinsmore. *New York,* 1882.

Elsie's New Relations, What They Did and How They Fared at Ion. *New York,* 1883.

Elsie at Nantucket. *New York,* 1884.

Mildred at Home. *New York,* 1884.

The Two Elsies. *New York,* 1885.

The Thorn in the Nest. *New York,* 1886.

Elsie's Kith and Kin. *New York,* 1886.

Mildred's Boys and Girls. *New York,* 1886.

Elsie's Friends at Woodburn. *New York,* 1887.

Christmas with Grandmother Elsie. *New York,* 1888.
Elsie and the Raymonds. *New York,* 1889.
Elsie Yachting with the Raymonds. *New York,* 1890.
Elsie's Vacation and After Events. *New York,* 1891.
Elsie at Viamede. *New York,* 1892.
Elsie at Ion. *New York,* 1893.
Tragedy of Wild River Valley. *New York,* 1893.
Elsie at the World's Fair. *New York,* 1894.
Mildred's New Daughter. *New York,* 1894.
Elsie's Journey on Inland Waters. *New York,* 1895.
Elsie at Home. *New York,* 1897.
Elsie on the Hudson and Elsewhere. *New York,* 1898.
Twiddledetwit; a Fairy Tale. *New York,* 1898.
Elsie in the South. *New York,* 1899.
Elsie's Young Folks in Peace and War. *New York,* 1900.
Elsie's Winter Trip. *New York,* 1902.
Elsie and Her Loved Ones. *New York,* 1903.
Elsie and Her Namesake. *New York,* 1905.
Elsie in Florida.

FISHBACK, WILLIAM PINCKNEY: 1831–1901.

William Pinckney Fishback was born at Batavia, O., on Nov. 11, 1831. He was educated at Miami University and Farmer's College (O.).

He studied law with his father and was associated with him in practice for a time, then removed to Indianapolis, where he opened a law office in 1857. From 1870 to 1872 he acted as editor of the INDIANAPOLIS JOURNAL. In 1872 he became a member of the staff of the ST. LOUIS DEMOCRAT but returned to Indianapolis in 1874 and resumed the practice of law.

Mr. Fishback died at Indianapolis on Jan. 15, 1901.

Information from the Indiana State Library.

* * *

A Plea for Honest Elections. *Indianapolis,* 1886.
The Lawyer in Literature. *Indianapolis,* 1892.
Recollections of Lord Coleridge. *Indianapolis,* 1895.

FISHER, DANIEL WEBSTER: 1838–1913.

"Daniel Webster Fisher . . . for twenty-eight years president of Hanover College, Ind., was born at a place called Arch Spring, in Sinking Valley, then a part of Huntingdon County, Pa. His father, Daniel, was a well-to-do farmer of German descent who had married a woman of Dutch ancestry, Martha Middleswarth. When he was fourteen years of age young Daniel entered Milnwood Academy, located at Shade Gap, and

later finished his preparation for college at Airy View Academy. He graduated from Jefferson College in 1857, and from the Western Theological Seminary three years later. In Apr. 1860, having been accepted by the Presbyterian Board of Foreign Missions for service and appointed to Siam, he was ordained by the Presbytery of Huntingdon. On the 25th of the same month he married Amanda D. Kouns, daughter of Michael Kouns of Ravenswood, Va. (now W. Va.). The illness of his wife as they were about to sail for their foreign station caused them to postpone the journey, and ultimately led him to resign his appointment. In the autumn of 1860 he took charge of the Thalia Street Church, New Orleans, but owing to the outbreak of the Civil War, he returned North in June of the following year. From 1861 to 1876 he was pastor of the First Presbyterian Church, Wheeling, W. Va. A trip abroad followed. Upon his return he supplied various churches, and had been ministering for a year and a half to the Second Presbyterian Church, Madison, Ind., when on July 8, 1879, he was elected president of Hanover College. The institution was financially embarrassed and its existence in jeopardy, but under his administrative skill it was kept alive through the crisis, and as the years went on it increased in endowment, buildings, and efficiency. During the twenty-eight years of his presidency, he continued active in the affairs of his denomination . . . After his resignation as president of Hanover he lived at Washington, D. C., and engaged in writing . . ."

Condensed from H. E. S., *Dictionary of American Biography,* Vol. VI.

* * *

A Human Life, an Autobiography with Excursuses. *New York,* 1909.
The Unification of the Churches: a Present Day Study. *New York,* 1911.
Calvin Wilson Mateer, Forty-Five Years a Missionary in Shantung, China: a Biography. *Philadelphia,* 1911.

FLETCHER, JAMES COOLEY: 1823–1901.

"James Cooley Fletcher . . . missionary, the son of Calvin and Sarah (Hill) Fletcher . . . was born in Indianapolis. He prepared for college at the Indianapolis Seminary, and at Phillips Exeter Academy, Exeter, N. H., and graduated from Brown University in 1846 . . . he entered Princeton Theological Seminary and took the full course there . . . he was licensed to preach by the Presbytery of New Brunswick, N. J. He spent the following year in theological study at Paris, France, and Geneva, Switzerland, and married, on Aug. 28, 1850, in Geneva, Henrietta, daughter of the Rev. Dr. César and Jenny Malan ... He was ordained on Feb. 13, 1851, by the Presbytery of Muncie, Ind., and at the close of the same year went to Brazil as missionary of the Christian Union and chaplain of the Seaman's Friend Society. During the year 1852-53 he was first secretary *pro tem.* and then acting secretary of the United States legation at Rio de Janeiro, a position which brought him into intimate relations with the Emperor Dom Pedro II. In 1854, after a visit to Chile, he returned to the United States for several months ... From 1856 to 1862 he lived in Newburyport, Mass., engaged in writing, preaching, and lecturing ...

"In 1862-63 he was agent in Brazil of the American Sunday School Union, cooperating with the American Bible Society. He made a journey of 2,000 miles up the Amazon to the borders of Peru, gathering natural history specimens for Prof. Louis Agassiz—a journey which led to an expedition by Agassiz himself in 1865 ... In 1868-69 he was Brazilian agent of the American Tract Society. From 1869 to 1873 he resided in Portugal as U. S. consul at Oporto for the full period and during the year 1870 acted also as United States charge d'affaires at Lisbon. On Oct. 22, 1872, he married at the consulate in Oporto his second wife, Fredrica Jane Smith. From 1873 to 1890, save for a brief visit to the United States, he resided in Naples, Italy, engaging in voluntary missionary work with the Waldenses and the Free Church of Scotland; and contributing numerous articles to American newspapers and magazines ... He returned to the U. S. in 1890 and took up his residence in Los Angeles, Calif., serving as stated supply of the Presbyterian Church at Wilmington, Calif., during 1892, and at La Crescenta, Calif., from 1893 until his death. On Jan. 2, 1897, he married Mrs. Elizabeth (Murton) Curryer of Oakland, Calif. During the last six years of his life he was president of the Los Angeles School of Art and Design. He died and was buried at Los Angeles. He was survived by his third wife and by a son and daughter of his first marriage ..."

> Condensed from J. C. A., *Dictionary of American Biography*, Vol. VI.

* * *

Brazil and the Brazilians (with the Rev. D. P. Kidder). *Philadelphia,* 1857.
Our Commercial Relations with South America.
Pompeii.

FLORY, AARON M.: 1833–1893.

Aaron M. Flory, a prominent lawyer of Logansport, Ind., was born in 1833 and died at Emporia, Kan., in 1893. He married Elizabeth Funston of Cass County; they had three children. During the Civil War Mr. Flory served with the 46th Indiana Regiment and rose to the rank of lieutenant colonel. He was captured at Sabin Pass., La., in 1863, and escaped from a rebel prison in Texas. His one published work is an entertaining account of his experience in prison and his escape.

> Information from Powell—*History of Cass County 1913.*

* * *

Prison Life in Texas. *Logansport,* 1865.

FORREST, JACOB DORSEY: 1866–1930.

Jacob Dorsey Forrest, son of Andrew Jackson and Emily Louise Dorsey Forrest, was born in Baltimore, Md., on July 21, 1866, and graduated from Hiram College, receiving the A.M. degree in 1892. He also studied at Ohio State University and in 1900 received the Ph.D. degree from the University of Chicago. On Aug. 17, 1893, he married Albertina May Allen, who died in 1904, and in 1915 he married Cordelia Kautz.

From 1897 to 1909 he was professor of sociology and economics at Butler College in Indianapolis. While on leave of absence from the college in 1907 he was one of the promoters of the Citizens Gas Company of Indianapolis, which he later organized and managed. During the first World War he converted this company into a producer of high explosives.

He died on Nov. 7, 1930.

> Information from *Who Was Who in America* and from Dunn—*Indiana and Indianans.*

* * *

The Development of Western Civilization. *Chicago,* 1907.
Church and Social Problems. *Chicago,* n.d.

FOSTER, JOHN WATSON: 1836–1917.

"John Watson Foster (Mar. 2, 1836-Nov. 15, 1917), lawyer, soldier, editor, diplomat, secretary of state, professor, was born in Pike County, Ind., where his father, Matthew Watson Foster, was a successful farmer. His mother, Eleanor Johnson, came of a Virginia family. Foster attended the Indiana University (B.A., 1855), where through study and in debate he developed the anti-slavery convictions implanted by his father. After a year at the Harvard Law School he spent another year in a law office in Cincinnati before he associated himself in the practice of law at Evansville with Conrad Baker, one of the ablest lawyers of Indiana. In 1859 he married Mary Parke McFerson . . . When the Civil War broke out Foster's zeal for the anti-slavery cause and for the Union led him to enlist. Gov. Morton sent him a commission as major. For his share in the capture of Fort Donelson he was promoted lieutenant-colonel, and for his meritorious service at Shiloh he was made a colonel. He commanded a brigade of cavalry in Burnside's expedition into East Tennessee and was the first to occupy Knoxville in 1863 . . .

"After the war Foster became editor of the EVANSVILLE DAILY JOURNAL, the most influential paper in Southern Indiana. In 1872, he served as chairman of the Republican state committee. As such he was instrumental in bringing about the reëlection of Oliver P. Morton to the United States Senate and of Gen. Grant to the presidency. The next year President Grant designated him as minister to Mexico. He served there during the transition from the Lerdo to the Diaz régime and under trying circumstances succeeded in making himself highly agreeable to the Mexican government.

"Early in 1880, President Hayes transferred him to St. Petersburg. He remained there a year and had little to do except to attend ceremonies and to plead for leniency in the treatment of American Jews. He returned to Washington and set up in the practice of law. In 1883, President Arthur offered him the appointment as minister to Spain. Foster accepted. He negotiated a reciprocity treaty affecting the trade with Cuba, but the treaty failed to meet the approval of the Senate. During Cleveland's first administration Foster practised law. Harrison appointed him on a special mission to Madrid to negotiate another reciprocity treaty. This treaty became effective and for two years greatly facilitated American trade with Cuba and Porto Rico.

"During the latter part of Harrison's administration Foster became the agent for the U. S. in the Bering Sea or fur-seal arbitration . . .

"For about eight months during 1892 and 1893 and partly overlapping the period of the fur-seal arbitration Foster served as secretary of state. As such he negotiated a treaty of annexation with the Republic of Hawaii. This negotiation took place so shortly after the establishment of the republic under the domination of American citizens there and under such questionable circumstances that when Cleveland succeeded to the presidency he withdrew the treaty from the Senate . . .

"At the close of the Chino-Japanese War, December, 1894, the Chinese foreign office invited Foster, then a private citizen, to join the Chinese commissioners in the negotiation of peace with Japan. He accepted, and performed a creditable service in bringing about an agreement between Li Hung Chang and Marquis Ito. Later, in 1907, Foster represented China at the Second Hague Conference. In 1903 Great Britain and the U. S. agreed to arbitrate their differences about the Alaska-Canadian boundary. The U. S. designated Foster as agent to take charge of the preparation of the case. Greatly to his credit, the tribunal sustained substantially his arguments and conclusions. As a lawyer in Washington Foster represented various governments, notably the Mexican . . .

"Foster delivered numerous lectures on various phases of international relations which found their way later into periodicals and pamphlets. He was especially interested in foreign missions and in arbitration . . ."

Condensed from C. E. H., *Dictionary of American Biography*, Vol. VI.

* * *

International Awards and National Honor. *Washington, D. C.,* 1886.

Treaties and Conventions Between the United States and Other Powers. 1889.

Visit to Foreign Mission Lands. *New York,* 1895.

Biographical Sketch of Matthew Watson Foster, 1800-1863. *Washington, D. C.,* 1896.

The Civilization of Christ. *Philadelphia,* n.d.

A Century of American Diplomacy; Being a Brief Review of the Foreign Relations of the United States, 1776-1876. *Boston,* 1900.

The Alaskan Boundary Tribunal. *Washington, D. C.,* 1903.

American Diplomacy in the Orient. *Boston,* 1903.

Arbitration and the Hague Court. *Boston,* 1904.

What the United States Has Done for International Arbitration.

Proper Grade of Diplomatic Representatives. *Washington, D. C.,* 1904.

The Practice of Diplomacy as Illustrated in the Foreign Relations of the United States. *Boston,* 1906.

Armaments and the "Next War." *Washington, D. C.,* 1906.

The Relation of Diplomacy to Foreign Missions. *Sewanee, Tenn.,* 1906.

Present Conditions in China. *Washington, D. C.,* 1906.

Diplomatic Memoirs. *Boston,* 1909. 2 vols.

War Not Inevitable. *Boston,* 1911.

Hawaiian Islands. *Washington, D. C.*

Limitation of Armament on the Great Lakes. *Washington, D. C., 1914.*

War Stories for My Grandchildren. *Cambridge, Mass., 1918.*

Las Memorias Diplomaticas de Mr. Foster Sobre Mexico, con un Prologo de Genaro Estrada. *Mexico, 1929.*

FOULKE, ELIZABETH ELLEN (MRS. ?): ?–?

Mrs. Foulke, whose maiden name has not been learned, was born in Richmond, Ind., educated in the public schools, the Friends Academy and in Earlham College and was a teacher in Richmond schools for many years.

She was long interested in writing, and her published works include a book of short stories for children and a collection of verse. She died about 1943.

Information from the Richmond Public Library.

* * *

Twilight Stories. *Boston, 1895.*
Braided Straws. *Boston, 1896.*

FOULKE, WILLIAM DUDLEY: 1848–1935.

William Dudley Foulke (pseudonym—Robert Barclay Dillingham), son of Thomas and Hannah Shoemaker Foulke, was born in New York City on Nov. 20, 1848. His father was a minister of the Society of Friends and at one time was principal of Friends Seminary in New York City, from which young Foulke graduated in 1863. In 1869 he received the A.B. degree from Columbia University, in 1871 he graduated from Columbia Law School, and in 1872 he was awarded the A.M. degree.

He practiced law in New York City from 1871 to 1876, when he came to Richmond, Ind., and entered into a law partnership with Jesse P. Siddall, representing the Pennsylvania Railroad. For a time in the late Seventies he was part owner and an editor of the RICHMOND PALLADIUM. From 1883 to 1885 he was a member of the Indiana State Senate. Mr. Foulke was a strong advocate of civil service reform. In 1885, while he was president of the Indiana Civil Service Reform Association, he, Oliver Morton, and Louis Howland were members of a committee to investigate abuses in the State Hospital for the Insane, and their report led to corrective legislation. Theodore Roosevelt appointed him to the United States Civil Service Commission in 1901, following outstanding work on his part as chairman of a special committee of the National

Civil Service Reform League which conducted investigations of the civil service. Mr. Foulke was also interested in woman's suffrage. He was president of the American Woman's Suffrage Association for a number of years (until 1890).

In 1890 he retired from active law practice to devote himself to reform movements and literary pursuits. From 1909 to 1912 he served as editor of the Richmond EVENING ITEM. He was a contributor to the ATLANTIC MONTHLY, FORUM, CENTURY, and CURRENT HISTORY. In 1872 Mr. Foulke married Mary Taylor Reeves of Richmond. He died May 30, 1935.

Besides the titles listed he edited, translated and compiled several works.

Information from *Who's Who in America* and the INDIANAPOLIS STAR, May 31, 1935.

* * *

Slav or Saxon: a Study of the Growth and Tendencies of Russian Civilization. *New York, 1887.*

The Theory and Practice of Civil Service Reform. *New York, 1894.*

Biography of Arthur Middleton Reeves and Correspondence. *New York, 1895.*

Life of Oliver P. Morton, Including His Important Speeches. *Indianapolis, 1899.* 2 vols.

Maya: a Story of Yucatan. *New York, 1900.*

Civil Service in Our Own New Dependencies. *Philadelphia, 1902.*

Protean Papers. *New York, 1903.*

The Reasons for Civil Service Reform. *New York, 1904.*

The Quaker Boy; a Tale of the Outgoing Generation As It Appears Chronicled in the Autobiography of Robert Barclay Dillingham. *New York, 1910.*

Dorothy Day. *New York, 1911.*

Maya: a Drama. *New York, 1911.*

A German City Worthy of Emulation: a Study of Frankfort-on-the-Main as an Example in Municipal Administration—Taxing the Unearned Increment—Industrial and Public Service Enterprises of the City; Reprinted From the American City. *Washington, D. C.*

Lyrics of War and Peace. *Indianapolis, 1916.*

Fighting the Spoilsmen; Reminiscences of the Civil Service Reform Movement. *New York, 1919.*

To-Day and Yesterday; Sonnets and Other Verses. *New York, 1920.*

A Hoosier Autobiography. *New York, 1922.*

Is Our Civilization Really Declining? *Indianapolis, 1923.*

Roosevelt and the Spoilsmen. *New York, 1925.*

A Random Record of Travel During Fifty Years. *New York, 1925.*

Songs of Eventide; Heloise; Maya. *Indianapolis, 1928.*

Earth's Generations Pass; to Which Is Added an Anthology from Lyrics of War and Peace, Some Love

Songs of Petrarch, To-day and Yesterday, and Songs of Eventide. *New York,* 1930.
Lucius B. Swift, a Biography. *Indianapolis,* 1930.

FOWLER, WILLIS WILFRED: ?–

According to Parker and Heiney—*Poets and Poetry of Indiana,* 1900, "Willis Wilfred Fowler is a young man of Shelbyville, Ind., who has in the last few years attracted much attention by contributions of verse to the newspapers, and by two or three little collections or dainty leaflets of verse that he has caused to be printed for the delight of his friends . . ."

Information from Parker and Heiney—*Poets and Poetry of Indiana,* 1900.

* * *

Poems. *Martinsville, Ind.,* 1890.
Buds and Blossoms. *Martinsville, Ind.,* 1897.

FOX, HENRY CLAY: 1836–1920.

The son of Levi and Rebecca Inman Fox, Henry Clay Fox was born near West Elkton, O., on Jan. 20, 1836.

The family moved to Wayne County, Ind., and Fox attended the county schools, Whitewater College, at Centerville, and finally read law in the office of George W. Julian. He was admitted to the bar in 1861.

In the same year he married Helen S. Linsley and shortly enlisted in the 57th Regiment, Indiana Volunteer Infantry with which he served during the Civil War. After the war he resumed his law practice in Richmond, and in 1896 he was appointed county judge. He died in 1920.

Information from the Morrisson-Reeves Library, Richmond, Ind.

* * *

Adventures of a Philosopher, a Dun Mule and a Brindle Dog. By an Indiana Man. *Richmond, Ind.,* 1888.
Uncle Zeke and Aunt Liza; a Tale of Episodes. *Boston,* 1905.
Memoirs of Wayne County and the City of Richmond, (Indiana.) *Madison, Wis.,* 1912. 2 vols.

FRANK, HENRY: 1854–1933.

Born in Lafayette, Ind., on Dec. 21, 1854, Henry Frank, son of Jacob H. and Henrietta Auerbach Frank, graduated from Chicago High School in 1871 and from Phillips Academy, Andover, Mass., in 1874.

He was a student at Harvard in 1874. In 1876-77 he was professor of literature and history at Cornell College in Iowa. After serving for a number of years as a Methodist minister, in 1886 he became pastor of the Congregational Church in Jamestown, N. Y., and in 1888 he renounced orthodoxy and originated the Independent Congregational Church at Jamestown. In 1897 he founded the Metropolitan Society of New York. He went to San Francisco in 1917, where he founded and was a leader of the People's Liberal Church. He died on July 31, 1933.

Information from *Who Was Who in America.*

* * *

The Skeleton and the Rose, and Gems by the Wayside. *New York,* 1886.
His Bold Experiment. *New York.*
The Doom of Dogma and the Dawn of Truth. *New York,* 1901. (Reissued in 1911, as *The Doom of Dogma and the Triumph of Truth.*)
The Shrine of Silence: a Book of Meditations; with Some Embellishments by H. B. Reissman. *New York,* 1901.
The Scientific Demonstration of the Soul's Existence and Immortality. *New York,* 1903.
Kingdom of Love. *New York,* 1907.
The Mastery of Mind in the Making of a Man. *New York,* 1908.
Modern Light on Immortality. *Boston,* 1909.
The Tragedy of Hamlet: a Psychological Study. *Boston,* 1910.
Psychic Phenomena, Science and Immortality. *Boston,* 1911.
The Story of America Sketched in Sonnets. *Boston,* 1911.
The Clash of Thrones; a Series of Sonnets on the European War. *Boston,* 1915.
The Challenge of the War; Can Science Answer the Riddle of the Grave? *Boston,* 1919.
The Last Enigma; a Philosophical Poem. 1924.
Optimism or Pessimism: Which Is the More Reasonable Philosophy of Life? *Girard, Kan.,* 1924.
Jesus: a Modern Study. *New York,* 1930.

FRANKLIN, BENJAMIN: 1812–1876.

Benjamin Franklin was senior member of the printing firm of Franklin & Smith of Milton, Ind. They were publishing a newspaper, the MILTON TIMES, as early as 1847 (no copies are recorded as being preserved, and the extent of publication is not known), and in 1848 their imprint appears upon a report of a religious debate published by them.

Franklin also edited and the firm published the

WESTERN REFORMER, A MONTHLY PUBLICATION, DEVOTED TO THE CAUSE OF CHRISTIANITY. The volumes of this preserved in the Indiana University Library are Vol. 6 and Vol. 7, 1847 to 1849. Vols. 1 to 5 of this paper, under the title of THE REFORMER, had been published at Centerville, Ind.

> Information from Ms. notes of R. E. Banta, Walker—*Beginnings of Printing in the State of Indiana,* and the Indiana State Library.

* * *

An Oral Debate on the Coming of the Son of Man, Endless Punishment, and Universal Salvation. Held in Milton, Ind., Oct. 26, 27, and 28, 1847. Between Erasmus Manford, Editor of the Western Universalist, and Benjamin Franklin, Editor of the Western Reformer. *Indianapolis,* 1848.

Gospel Preacher; a Book of Twenty Sermons. *Cincinnati,* 1869.

Oral Debate Between Benjamin Franklin and J. A. Thompson, Held at Reynoldsburg, Ohio . . . On I. Remission of Sins . . . II. Quickening of the Sinner . . . III. Baptism . . . IV. Eternal Salvation. *Franklin,* 1874.

FRENCH, WILLIAM M.: 1817–1886.

William M. French was born in Dearborn County, Ind., in 1817 and spent his youth in the town of Rising Sun, Ind. A Methodist preacher, he served as steward of an insane asylum for some years and during the Civil War was employed by Governor Morton to take sanitary stores to the soldiers and bring back pay to their families. He was also a trustee of Indiana University from Clark County. He died in April, 1886, and was buried at Rising Sun.

> Information from the Indiana State Library.

* * *

Life, Speeches, State Papers and Public Service of Gov. Oliver P. Morton. *Cincinnati,* 1864.

FRITSCH, WILLIAM AUGUST: 1841–?

The only information available establishes William August Fritsch as having been born in 1841 and having spent his mature years in Evansville, Ind.

> Information from the Evansville Public Library.

* * *

Zur Geschichte Des Deutschthums in Indiana. *New York,* 1896.

Aus Amerika, Alte und Neue Heimat. *Stargard,* 1905.

German Settlers and German Settlements in Indiana; a Memorial for the State Centennial, 1916. *Evansville, Ind.,* 1915.

FRYBERGER, AGNES MOORE (MRS. W. O.): 1868–

Agnes Moore was born at Madison, Ind., on May 30, 1868. She was the daughter of Benjamin Franklin and Florence Virginia Wilber Moore.

Miss Moore studied at the University of Minnesota and Northwestern and Columbia Universities, majoring in music.

In 1891 she married Dr. W. O. Fryberger but continued her work as a public school music supervisor and, eventually, as an instructor in music appreciation at the University of Minnesota.

> Information from the Madison, Ind., Public Library.

* * *

Listening Lessons in Music. *Boston,* 1916.

Kiddie Canticles. 1925.

Creative Listening.

FULLER, HECTOR: 1864–1934.

Hector Fuller, Indianapolis journalist, was born in England on Oct. 17, in either 1864 or 1865. Since he was a younger son, the family estate went to an older brother, and Hector took to the sea. After traveling over a large part of the world, he finally came to the U. S. and, in 1891, to Indianapolis, where he was shortly employed as a reporter by the INDIANAPOLIS NEWS.

He was with the NEWS for twenty years. During the Russo-Japanese War, which he covered for the NEWS, he was captured by the Russians after slipping into Port Arthur and was almost shot as a spy. After he left the NEWS, he spent some time as a dramatic critic for the INDIANAPOLIS STAR, was a columnist for five years on the WASHINGTON HERALD, and served as Sunday editor of the BUFFALO NEWS.

Mr. Fuller eventually went to New York, where he became spokesman and personal representative of Mayor James J. Walker. He accompanied Walker to Europe and later wrote a book about the trip. He was press representative for many interests and, according to Hilton U. Brown, of the INDIANAPOLIS NEWS, "became internationally known as an irrepressible and delightful entertainer."

He died in New York on Oct. 3, 1934, and was survived by his wife, two sons, and a daughter.

Information from Hilton U. Brown, of the INDIANAPOLIS NEWS, and from the INDIANAPOLIS STAR, Dec. 4, 1934.

* * *

Roach & Co.—Pirates, and Other Stories. *Indianapolis,* 1898.

Abroad with Mayor Walker, Being a Veritable Account of the Voyage, as Unofficial Ambassador, of the Hon. James J. Walker, Mayor of New York, on His Hardworking Vacation to the Charming Cities of London, Dublin, Castlecomer, Berlin, Munich, Baden-Baden, Venice, The Lido, Rome and Paris. *New York,* 1928.

FUNK, JOHN FRETZ: 1835–1930.

John Fretz Funk was born in Bucks County, Pa., on Apr. 6, 1835. Shortly before the Civil War he moved to Chicago to engage in the lumber business but soon abandoned his original plans and established a publishing enterprise for the special benefit of the Mennonite people. In 1864 he founded the HERALD OF TRUTH and its German counterpart, the HEROLD DER WAHRHEIT. A few years later he moved his printing establishment to Elkhart, Ind., where it eventually became known as the Mennonite Publishing Company, although still privately owned. He died in Elkhart in 1930.

Information from the Goshen College Library.

* * *

Warfare. Its Evils, Our Duty. *Chicago,* 1863.

The Mennonite Church and Her Accusers. *Elkhart, Ind.,* 1878.

A Biographical Sketch of Bishop Christian Herr. Also a Collection of Hymns Written by Him in the German Language. *Elkhart, Ind.,* 1887.

Confession of Faith and Ministers' Manual, Containing the Confession of Faith Adopted at Dortrecht in 1632 —the Shorter Catechism—Forms for Baptism, the Lord's Supper, Marriage, Ordination of Bishops and Ministers—Funeral Lessons, Texts, Etc. (with John S. Coffman). *Elkhart, Ind.,* 1890.

Biographical Sketch of Preacher John Geil, Pastor of the Mennonite Church at Line Lexington, Bucks County, Pennsylvania. *Elkhart, Ind.,* 1897.

An Address by John F. Funk on the Occasion of the Ninety-Second Anniversary of His Birth, at the Mennonite Church, Elkhart, Indiana. n.p., n.d.

G

GADDIS, ALFRED: ?–?

Alfred Gaddis was a resident of Tippecanoe County, Ind., who served as major of the Third Indiana Cavalry during the Civil War.

Information from de Hart—*Past and Present of Tippecanoe County,* 1909.

* * *

Three Years of Army Life. *Lafayette,* 1896.

GAGE, MOSES D.: 1828–?

Moses D. Gage, a native of Madison County, N. Y., was a minister of the gospel, aged thirty-four years, and a resident of Lebanon, Ind., when he enlisted as a sergeant in Company B, 89th Regiment, Indiana Infantry, on Aug. 8, 1862. In the following November he was transferred to the 12th Indiana Regiment and appointed chaplain. He was mustered out on June 8, 1865.

Information from Terrell—*Civil War Records,* Vols. 2 and 6, and D. S. A. in the CINCINNATI GAZETTE, Dec. 7, 1876.

* * *

From Vicksburg to Raleigh; or, a Complete History of the Twelfth Regiment Indiana Volunteer Infantry . . . *Chicago,* 1865.

GARNETT, LOUISE AYRES (MRS. EUGENE H.): ?–1937.

Louise Ayres, daughter of Lafayette and Sallie Munday Ayres, was born in Plymouth, Ind., and was educated at St. Mary's Hall in Indianapolis, Dearborn Seminary in Chicago and Northwestern University. On June 14, 1900, she was married to Eugene H. Garnett. In addition to writing poetry, plays, and juvenile verse, she collaborated in the writing of oratorios and cantatas. She died on Oct. 31, 1937.

Information from *Who Was Who in America.*

* * *

The Muffin Shop. *Chicago,* 1908.

The Rhyming Ring. *Chicago,* 1910.

Creature Songs: Humorous Jingles. *Boston,* 1912.

Master Will of Stratford; a Midwinter Night's Dream; in Three Acts, with a Prologue and an Epilogue. *New York,* 1916.

The Merrymakers. *Chicago, 1918.*

Forest Rondo; Shakesperian Fantasy for Children's Voices and Orchestra. *Boston, 1919.*

New Earth; an Ode for Mixed Chorus, Soli and Orchestra. (Music by Henry Hadley.) *Boston, 1919.*

The Courtship; a Dramatization of Longfellow's Poem "The Courtship of Miles Standish." *Chicago, 1920.*

Resurgam. (Music by Henry Hadley.) *Boston, 1922.*

Three to Make Ready; Hilltop, Muffins, the Pig Prince; Three Plays for Young People. *New York, 1923.*

Eve Walks in Her Garden. *New York, 1926.*

Mirtil in Arcadia. *1927.*

The Joyous Pretender. *New York, 1928.*

A Fairy Wedding.

Belshazzar.

Adeste Fidelis, a Christmas Processional. *Boston, 1936.*

GAUSE, FRANK ALES: 1874–

Frank Ales Gause, son of Amos W. and Margaret Morrow Gause, was born in Westfield, Ind., on Mar. 1, 1874. He graduated from Friends' Academy in Westfield in 1891 and from Indiana University in 1904, receiving the A.M. degree from the latter school in 1905. He also had two years of graduate work at the University of Chicago.

From 1892 to 1894 he was a district school teacher; in 1894 assistant principal of Friends' Academy; from 1897 to 1903 superintendent of schools at Cicero, Ind.; from 1905 to 1909 superintendent at Salem, Ind.; from 1909 to 1913 superintendent of U. S. government schools in Panama and after 1914 superintendent of the Bay City, Mich., schools. He married Rose Carey in 1896.

Information from *Who's Who in America.*

* * *

The Story of Panama: the New Route to India (with Charles Carl Carr). *New York, 1912.*

An Isthmian Idyl. *1913.*

Business Methods Applied in School Administration. *1915.*

GAVIN, FRANK E.: 1854–?

Frank E. Gavin, son of James and Martha E. Tucker Gavin, was born at Greensburg, Ind., on Feb. 20, 1854. He received the A.B. degree from Harvard University in 1873 and was admitted to the bar at Greensburg in February, 1875. There he practiced until 1892, when he was elected judge of the Appellate Court for a four-year term.

Frank E. Gavin married Miss Ella B. Lathrop in November, 1875. They were the parents of three children.

Information from Taylor—*Biographical Sketches and Review of the Bench and Bar of Indiana.*

* * *

Mutability of Social Institutions.

GHENT, WILLIAM JAMES: 1866–1942.

William James Ghent, son of Ira Keith and Mary Elizabeth Palmer Ghent, was born in Frankfort, Ind., on Apr. 29, 1866, and was educated in the public schools. On July 17, 1909, he married Amy Louise Morrison.

Entering the newspaper profession, he worked as a compositor and proofreader in various cities and as sub-editor of trade papers in New York. In 1899 he was an aide to Samuel M. Jones of Toledo, acting as literary manager of the mayoralty and gubernatorial campaigns of that year. He was an occasional contributor to various publications, a regular contributor to THE INDEPENDENT and THE WEEKLY REVIEW, editor of the AMERICAN FABIAN, and editor of the CALIFORNIA OUTLOOK. From its founding in 1906 until 1909 he served as secretary of the Rand School of Social Science, acting as president from 1909 to 1911. Mr. Ghent was also one of the founders of the Social Reform Club of New York, in 1894. In 1911-12 he was secretary to Victor L. Berger. He edited several works on Socialism besides those listed.

He died on July 10, 1942.

Information from *Who's Who in America.*

* * *

Our Benevolent Feudalism. *New York, 1902.*

Mass and Class: a Survey of Social Divisions. *New York, 1904.*

Socialism and Success: Some Uninvited Messages. *New York, 1910.*

The Reds Bring Reaction. *Princeton, N. J., 1923.*

The Road to Oregon; a Chronicle of the Great Emigrant Trail. *New York, 1929.*

The Early Far West. *New York, 1931.*

Broken Hand; the Life Story of Thomas Fitzpatrick (with Le Roy R. Hafen). *Denver, 1931.*

GIBSON, LOUIS HENRY: 1854–

Born in Aurora, Ind., in 1854, Louis Henry Gibson studied at Massachusetts Institute of Technology and in Paris. In 1879 he married Emily S. Gilbert.

An Indianapolis architect, Mr. Gibson wrote, in addition to his books, articles for magazines and newspapers.

Information from *Who Was Who in America.*

* * *

Gradual Reduction Milling. A Treatise on the Art of Modern Milling. *Minneapolis, 1885.*

A Romance of the Milling Revolution; or, the History of a Typical Modern Mill. By "Cereal." *Kansas City, 1886.*

Convenient Houses; with Fifty Plans for the House-keeper. *New York, 1889.*

Beautiful Houses. *New York, 1895.*

GIFFE, WILLIAM THOMAS: 1848–1926.

William Thomas Giffe, son of William and Deborah Hughes Giffe, was born in Portland, Ind., on June 28, 1848, and was educated in the local schools and at Liber College in Portland.

When he was sixteen years old, he enlisted in the 34th Indiana Infantry and served during 1864-65. After spending two years as principal of Portland School, he resigned to study law but later turned to music. He lived in Indianapolis from 1875 to 1879, when he moved to Logansport and served as supervisor of public school music for six years. From 1887 to 1896 he was the proprietor of a book and music store, and he was president of the Home Music Company of Logansport. He later engaged in the real estate and insurance business.

Mr. Giffe married Nancy Jane Booth in 1889 and died in 1926.

He wrote a number of music textbooks and compiled many song collections not listed here.

Information from the Logansport Public Library.

* * *

The Helping Hand, Extended and Dedicated to Sunday-Schools and Praise Meetings (with J. H. Rosecrans). *Cincinnati, 1878.*

The Teacher's Manual of Explanations and Instructions for Using Giffe's Vocal Drill Charts. *Philadelphia, 1884.*

My Indiana Home; Words and Music. *Logansport, Ind., 1898.*

Song for Indiana: Words and Music. *Logansport, Ind., 1899.*

Onward and Upward, No. 2. *Logansport, Ind., 1900.*

Shepherd, Lead Me On; Words and Music. *Logansport, Ind., 1906.*

GIGNILLIAT, LEIGH ROBINSON: 1875–

Leigh Robinson Gignilliat, son of William Robert and Harriet Heyward Gignilliat, was born in Savannah, Ga., on July 4, 1875, and graduated from Emerson Institute (Washington) in 1891. He graduated from Virginia Military Institute in 1895, received the A.M. degree from Trinity College in 1915, and was awarded honorary degrees by Colgate University and Kenyon College. On Aug. 2, 1898, he married Mary Seddon Fleet.

After spending a year as an assistant engineer working on the boundary line location of Yellowstone National Park, in 1897 he became commandant of cadets at Culver Military Academy in Indiana, serving in this capacity until 1910 when he became superintendent of the Academy. He spent twenty-nine years as superintendent and from 1939 to 1942 served as president of the Culver Educational Foundation. During the first World War he was on the General Staff of the A.E.F.

Information from *Who's Who in America.*

* * *

Arms and the Boy; Military Training in Schools and Colleges; Its Value in Peace and Its Importance in War; with Many Practical Suggestions for the Course of Training; and with Brief Descriptions of the Most Successful Systems Now in Operation. *Indianapolis, 1916.*

GILBERT, FRANK M.: 1846–1916.

Frank M. Gilbert, son of Samuel E. and Cordelia Manson Gilbert, was born in Mobile, Ala., on July 1, 1846, and went with his parents in 1852 to Evansville, Ind., where he was educated in the public schools and where he lived most of his life.

From the age of sixteen to twenty-five he was a traveling salesman. He began writing humor for the SATURDAY HERALD of Evansville and later was employed as river editor of the EVANSVILLE COURIER. In 1877 he went West—during the Colorado mineral excitement—and worked for a time for the LEADVILLE CHRONICLE, the DENVER TRIBUNE and the ROCKY MOUNTAIN NEWS.

On his return to Evansville he established the ARGUS and soon became well known for his humorous writings and poems. He purchased the EVENING TRIBUNE in 1885.

Mr. Gilbert married Annie Hudspeth in 1880 and died in Florida on Dec. 1, 1916.

Information from the Evansville Public Library.

* * *

Plunkett's Troubles. *New York,* 1882.

Pigeons and All About Them. *Boston,* 1898.

Pigeon Queries. *Milwaukee,* n.d.

History of the City of Evansville and Vanderburgh County. *Chicago,* 1910. 2 vols.

GILES, FREDERICK REED: 1864–1897.

Frederick Reed Giles was born in Evansville, Ind., in 1864. He attended De Pauw University, receiving the Ph.B. degree. He died in New York in 1897.

Information from the Federal Writers Project— *Indiana Authors,* 1937, and the Indiana State Library.

* * *

The Mysterious Mr. Jarvis. *New York,* 1892.

GILLIOM, PETER: 1847–1934.

Peter Gilliom was born in Wayne County, O., on Oct. 24, 1847, the son of Abraham and Anna Hofstetter Gilliom, natives of Switzerland. In 1869 he moved with his parents to a farm near Elkton, Hickory County, Mo., in the foothills of the Ozarks, where in 1872 he married Rachel, daughter of the Rev. Peter S. and Verena Sprunger Lehman, also natives of Switzerland. During their residence in Missouri twelve children were born to them, three of whom died in infancy.

In the early Nineties the family moved to a farm near Berne, Ind., where two more children were born. After twenty-one years of farming they moved into Berne, where they resided until the death of Mrs. Gilliom in 1933 and that of Mr. Gilliom in the following year.

With little formal education, Peter Gilliom was well read, observant and well posted. He had some native literary ability and for many years served as church correspondent to the Mennonite Church paper, DER BUNDESBOTE.

Information from the Berne, Ind., Public Library.

* * *

A Short History of the Lehman Family (with Peter S. Lehman). *Berne, Ind.,* 1914.

A Brief History and Record of the Gilliom Relationship. *Berne, Ind.,* 1922.

GINGER, SAMUEL: ?–?

Samuel Ginger was a gunsmith who settled in Ridgeville, Ind., in the early 1850's and remained there until his death, sometime after 1905. He served during the Civil War and contributed articles on local pioneer history to local newspapers.

Information from Melvin B. Stratton, Indianapolis.

* * *

Reminiscences of Ridgeville and the Mississinewa. *Union City, Ind.,* 1905.

GIVEN, ABRAHAM: 1825–1895.

Born in Juniata County, Pa., on Feb. 28, 1825, Abraham Given married Rebecca J. Smith, of Wooster, O., on June 10, 1858, and settled in Frankfort, Ind., in 1860.

Here, in partnership with his brother Alex, he opened a general store, which was sold in 1867. Mr. Given then went into partnership with three other men to organize the International Bank, which in 1871 was merged into the First National Bank, of which he later became president, serving until 1885 when he resigned because of ill health.

He died on Dec. 1, 1895, and was buried at Frankfort.

Information from the Frankfort Public Library.

* * *

Overland Trip to California in 1850. *Frankfort, Ind.,* n.d.

GLASCOCK, WILL H.: 1857–1901.

Born in Hancock County, Ind., in 1857, Will H. Glascock received his education at Central Normal (now Canterbury) College in Danville, Ind., and also studied at Indiana University and the University of Chicago. He began teaching at Woodbine School, Hancock County. For four years he was superintendent of the Hancock County Schools and for two years of those of Greenfield, Ind. In 1891 he was made chief deputy in the office of the State Superintendent of Public Instruction. From 1894 to 1898 he acted as superintendent of the Indiana State School for the Blind, and from 1900 until his death in 1901 he was superintendent of schools in Bloomington, Ind.

Information from the Barry Ms.

* * *

The Stories of Columbia. *New York,* 1895.
Young Folks' Indiana. *Chicago,* 1898.

GOODE, GEORGE BROWN: 1851–1896.

George Brown Goode, one of Indiana's several distinguished biological scientists, was born in New Albany, Ind., on Feb. 13, 1851. His parents were Francis Collier and Sarah Woodruff Crane Goode.

His parents removed to Dutchess County, N. Y., in 1857. He was prepared for college in New York state, graduated from Wesleyan University and entered Harvard University for graduate study. There he met Louis Agassiz and, returning to Wesleyan in 1871, he also met Spencer F. Baird, commissioner of the U. S. Department of Fish and Game. Acquaintance with these two men seems to have set the pattern for his career. He served under Baird during summer vacations and continued his work at Wesleyan until 1877, when he accepted a full-time appointment with Baird at the Smithsonian Institution, where he remained until his death on Sept. 6, 1896. He was survived by his wife, Sarah Lamson Ford Judd, and by four children.

Besides the titles listed, he was the author of dozens of contributions to learned publications and books published by governmental agencies and learned societies.

Information from the *Dictionary of American Biography,* Vol. VII.

* * *

A List of the Fishes of Essex County (with T. H. Bean). *Salem, Mass.,* 1879.

Game Fishes of the United States (with S. A. Kilbourne). *New York,* 1879.

American Fisheries: a History of the Menhaden. *New York,* 1880.

A Review of the Fishery Industries of the United States. *London,* 1883.

Beginnings of Natural History in America. 1886.

Britons, Saxons and Virginians. 1887.

Virginia Cousins: Study of the Ancestry and Posterity of John Goode, of Whitby, a Virginia Colonist of the 17th Century; with Preface by R. A. Brock. *Richmond, Va.,* 1887.

American Fishes: a Popular Treatise Upon the Game and Food Fishes of North America, with Especial Reference to Habits and Methods of Capture. *New York,* 1888.

GOODWIN, THOMAS AIKEN: 1818–1906.

The son of one of Indiana's early settlers, Thomas Aiken Goodwin was born in Brookville, Ind., Nov. 2, 1818. During his youth he worked on the farm in summer and attended country schools in winter. He was the first student at Indiana Asbury (now De Pauw) University and was in its first graduating class in 1840. On Sept. 13, 1842, he married Content L. Craft.

Following his graduation he was ordained by the Indiana Methodist Conference and was in pastoral work until 1844 when he opened the Madison Female College. In 1853 he left teaching to edit the INDIANA AMERICAN, a Whig paper at Brookville, which he turned into a vigorous anti-slavery and temperance journal. While editing his paper he continued to preach, delivering about one hundred sermons a year for more than twenty years and doing his work without remuneration in the form of salary or payment for traveling expenses.

In 1857 he moved the paper to Indianapolis and continued to edit it until ill health forced his retirement to the farm. He continued to write, however, after his retirement and contributed voluminously to magazines and religious periodicals. He also wrote frequent letters to newspapers—especially the Indianapolis JOURNAL —using the signature U. L. C. Besides his work as an abolitionist, he was a temperance radical and championed a campaign for the introduction of theological curricula into colleges.

At one time—following the publication of *The Mode of Man's Immortality*—he was tried for heresy by the Methodist Church, but the case was dropped, and he continued to be a member of the church all of his life. Early sources refer to him as "Parson Goodwin," evidently the name by which he was usually known. He died in Indianapolis on June 19, 1906.

Information from Dunn—*Indiana and Indianans,* Vol. II; *Representative Men of Indiana,* Vol. I; De Pauw University's *Alumnal Record, 1920;* and the Indianapolis Public Library.

* * *

The Perfect Man. *Cincinnati,* 1869.

The Mode of Man's Immortality; or, the When, Where and How of the Future Life. *New York,* 1874.

Ministry of Angels, a Sermon. *Indianapolis,* 1876.

Duty of Literary Men . . . *New York,* 1878.

A Brother's Inquest Over a Brother's Grave; or the Question, Who Murdered Dr. John R. Goodwin? Candidly Considered; an Appeal to the People of Brookville. *Indianapolis,* 1880.

Seventy-Six Years Tussle with the Traffic: Being a Condensation of the Laws Relating to the Liquor Traffic in Indiana from 1807 to 1883 Inclusive, and All the Points Decided by the Supreme Court on More Than 400 Appeals. *Indianapolis,* 1883.

Then and Now, and the Duty of Now; a Tract for the

Times in View of the Threatened Hereafter. *Indianapolis, 1885.*

The Heroic Women of Early Indiana Methodism. An Address Delivered Before the Indiana Methodist Historical Society at De Pauw University, June 16, 1889. *Indianapolis, 1889.*

The Constitution of the Methodist Episcopal Church as Seen by a Layman. (Anonymous) *Cincinnati, 1894.*

Prohibition Impossible Through a Separate Party and Why . . . It Ought Never to Be Obtained Through Any Party, and Why . . . What Then? *Indianapolis, 1894.*

Lovers Three Thousand Years Ago as Indicated by the Song of Solomon. *Chicago, 1895.*

Tentative Constitution . . . *Indianapolis, 1896.*

Does It Pay? Whom Does It Pay? Two Companion Questions in the Correct Answer to Which Every Man, Woman and Child Is Interested, with a Few Facts, Figures and Suggestions in Aid of Those Who Wish to Investigate . . . *Indianapolis, 1899.*

Then and Now; of Indianapolis as It Was Under Prohibition; Contrasted with Indianapolis as It Is Under a Wide-Open Policy, with a Few Reflections and Suggestions in Relation Thereto; Published by the Indiana Anti-Saloon League. *Indianapolis, 1899.*

The Prohibitory Law of 1855; How It Was Obtained, How It Worked, Why and How It Was First Annulled Then Repealed; with a Preachers Suggestion or Two. *Indianapolis, 1904.*

Return of Prayers, the Tidings of Peace, and the Folly of Relapsing. *Philadelphia, n.d.*

Is It Well with the Child? A Few Pertinent Facts Relating to Education and Protection of Children in Indianapolis, with a Suggestion or Two. *Indianapolis, n.d.*

Methodist Episcopal Churches and Organized Labor. (Anonymous.) n.p., n.d.

Facts and Figures, Showing That State Universities Are Needlessly Expensive . . . *Indianapolis, n.d.*

How the Indiana University, a Strictly Private Corporation, Became a State School . . . *Indianapolis, n.d.*

Hypocrisy and Cowardice of Pilate Less Objectionable Than the Hypocrisy and Cowardice of Many Men of Our Day Who Are Called Both Brave and Good, a Temperance Sermon. n.p., n.d.

GOOKINS, SAMUEL BARNES: 1809–1880.

Samuel B. Gookins was born in Rupert, Vt., May 30, 1809. His parents were William and Rhoda Gookins. The family emigrated to Rodman, N. Y., in 1812, where William Gookins died in 1814.

In 1823 the mother, an older brother and young Samuel set out for the Wabash Valley, where they planned to make their home. Instead of the conventional routes overland through central Pennsylvania or by way of the even more popular Ohio River they took the course which the French had used in the original white settlement of the Wabash.

The mother had nine children older than Samuel and probably a considerable number of grandchildren. The older son who came west was twenty-three and Samuel was fourteen. The three went by steamboat on Lake Ontario from Sackett's Harbor to Lewiston, around Niagara Falls by wagon, to Buffalo by open boat, across Lake Erie to Detroit by schooner and again by schooner to Fort Meigs, at the mouth of the Maumee. Here they purchased a canoe and poled, paddled and portaged up the Maumee and down the Wabash to Terre Haute.

In 1826 young Gookins apprenticed himself to John W. Osborn, owner of the WESTERN REGISTER, Terre Haute's first newspaper. By 1832 Gookins had become the paper's editor but, upon the sale of the paper, he took the advice of a friend and began to study law.

He was admitted to the bar in 1836 and practiced successfully in Indiana and Illinois until 1850, when he was appointed judge of the Indiana Circuit, which included the counties between Knox and Vigo, of which the chief town was Vincennes. The appointment was not ratified by the Legislature.

Gookins was, himself, soon elected a state representative and, within four years, a judge of the Indiana Supreme Court. He retired after three years and practiced law in Chicago from 1858 to 1875.

It was during these years that Judge Gookins' chief contributions to periodicals were made. In 1875 he returned to Terre Haute and completed his history of Vigo County only a few days before his death on June 14, 1880.

> Information from S. B. Gookins' own notes in Beckwith—*History of Vigo and Parke Counties* . . .

* * *

An Address Delivered Before the Graduating Class of the Law Department of the Indiana University, February 28, 1856. *Bloomington, Ind., 1856.*

History of Vigo County [in Beckwith, H. W.—History of Vigo and Parke Counties]. *Chicago, 1880.*

GORDON, JONATHAN W.: 1820–1887.

Jonathan W. Gordon, son of William and Sarah Walton Gordon, was one of fourteen children and was born in Washington County, Pa., on Aug. 13, 1820. The family emigrated to Ripley County, Ind., where young Jonathan had a common school education. Later he studied law, following one term at Hanover College, and was admitted to the bar in 1844. His father had died in 1841.

He served in the Mexican War, and his health was so impaired that he was advised not to attempt public speaking, so he abandoned law as a career and began the study of medicine at Rush Medical College in Chicago; he later transferred and graduated in the Medical Department of Indiana Asbury (now De Pauw) University. For two years he practiced medicine at Moore's Hill, Indiana, then improvement in his health encouraged him to resume the practice of law, and he moved to Indianapolis in 1852 for this purpose.

To relieve his financial situation while he was starting his practice he became a reporter on the INDIANAPOLIS JOURNAL and also became editor of THE TEMPERANCE CHART, a weekly newspaper. In 1854 he was elected prosecuting attorney for Marion County, but his practice increased so much while he was in office that he resigned in order to take care of it. In 1856 he was elected to the Indiana General Assembly and was re-elected in 1858, serving as speaker of the House during his second term.

In the Civil War he served as major of the 11th Regiment of Indiana Volunteer Infantry. His only son, Joseph R. T. Gordon, was killed in action in 1861. In 1864, because of his inability to support his family on his officer's pay, he resigned his commission, returned to Indianapolis, and resumed the practice of law. In 1878 he was again elected to the Indiana General Assembly.

He was always active in political affairs, as a speaker, writer, and office-holder. According to Dunn—*Indiana and Indianans*, Vol. III, he was the foremost criminal lawyer of his day in Indiana. Despite his success in his field he was usually in debt because of his generosity to family and friends.

He was twice married: first to Catherine J. Overturf and, after her death, to Julia L. Dumont. He died in Indianapolis on Apr. 27, 1887.

Some of his early verse was printed in Coggeshall's *Poets and Poetry of the West*.

Information from *Representative Men of Indiana,* Vol. I, and Dunn—*Indiana and Indianans,* Vol. III.

* * *

An Argument Designed to Show the Origin of the Troubles in Kansas, and the Remedy Therefor. Delivered in Masonic Hall, Indianapolis, September 29, 1856. *Indianapolis,* 1856.

Speech Delivered at Milan, Indiana, in 1880.

GOUGAR, HELEN MAR JACKSON (MRS. JOHN D.): 1843–1907.

Helen Mar Jackson, daughter of William Jackson, was born in Hillsdale County, Mich., on July 18, 1843. Leaving the local elementary schools at the age of twelve, she attended Hillsdale College for three years and began teaching in the Lafayette, Ind., schools before her sixteenth birthday.

After teaching four years she was made principal of the Jenks School, Lafayette, where she continued until her marriage to John D. Gougar on Dec. 10, 1863. In 1870 she began her career as a reformer with a temperance address delivered at Delphi, Ind. Her work gained immediate attention and she acquired a national reputation as a speaker and writer in behalf of temperance and woman's rights. She died in 1907.

Information from de Hart—*Past and Present of Tippecanoe County,* 1909.

* * *

Matthew Peters, a Foreign Emigrant. 1899.
Forty Thousand Miles of World's Wandering. *Chicago,* 1905.

GRAVES, GORDON HARWOOD: 1884–

Born in Logansport, Ind., on July 10, 1884, Gordon Harwood Graves attended the public schools of Logansport, Phoenix, Ariz., Colorado Springs, and Richmond, Ind., and graduated from Earlham College in 1905. He also studied at Haverford College and received the A.M. (1909) and Ph.D. (1914) degrees from Columbia University. In 1916 he married Winifred Sibley.

Dr. Graves taught school in Pennsylvania and in 1915 joined the faculty of Purdue University.

Information from Gordon Harwood Graves.

* * *

Fantasies on Ancient Themes (with Hettie Elliott). *Richmond, Ind.,* 1914.

GRAVES, KERSEY: 1815–?

Kersey Graves, son of Enos and Elizabeth Jones Graves, was born in Brownsville, Pa., on Nov. 21, 1815.

He began teaching school at Richmond, Ind., when he was nineteen years old and continued for twenty years. He spent several years traveling and lecturing on phrenology, physiology, and physiognomy and was an active reformer, particularly in the causes of abolition and temperance. He married Lydia Michener.

Information from *Representative Men of Indiana,* Vol. I.

* * *

The Biography of Satan; or, an Historical Exposition of the Devil and His Fiery Dominions, Disclosing the Oriental Origin of the Belief in the Devil and Future Punishment. *Chicago, 1865.*

The World's Sixteen Crucified Saviours; or, Christianity Before Christ. *Boston, 1875.*

The Bible of Bibles. *Boston* [1878].

Robbing by Law. Forty Robberies of the People by the National Government. *San Francisco, 1888.*

GRAYDON, KATHARINE MERRILL: 1858–1934.

Katharine Merrill Graydon was the daughter of William M. and Mary Merrill Graydon. She was born in Indianapolis on Apr. 14, 1858.

Graduating from Butler University in 1878, she studied at Radcliffe College, Indiana University, the University of Chicago and the University of California.

She taught at Butler, 1877-78, and in private schools in Indianapolis, Hastings, Neb., Oakland, Calif., and Honolulu. She later returned to Butler to take the Katharine Merrill Chair of Literature. She received the Lit.D. degree from Butler in 1928.

Dr. Graydon died on Jan. 25, 1934.

Information from the Indiana State Library.

* * *

Thoughts on the Service of Homer to Humanity. n.p., 1889.

Butler College in the World War. *Indianapolis, 1922.*

Catharine Merrill, Life and Letters. *Greenfield, Ind.,* 1934.

GRAYDON, MARY MERRILL (MRS. WILLIAM M.): 1835–1917.

Mary Merrill, daughter of Samuel and Lydia Jane Anderson Merrill, was born in Indianapolis in 1835. The family had been distinguished in that place from its earliest days.

She married William M. Graydon in 1857 and resided in Indianapolis until her death on May 17, 1917.

Information from the Indiana State Library.

* * *

Early Indianapolis. *Indianapolis,* n.d.

GREEN, JONATHAN HARRINGTON: circa 1812–?

Jonathan H. Green was born in Marietta, O., probably about 1812. He does not mention his father's name in his various autobiographical notes, but he states that his mother died in his youth and that he was living with a Mr. John Bullock in Lawrenceburg, Ind., in 1828.

He married one of Bullock's granddaughters in 1846, and apparently he made that place his headquarters (he reports visiting his family there in 1847) until he moved to New Haven, Conn., in 1849.

Young Green became a gambler at an early age; by his own statement he was a gambler on Mississippi steamboats by 1833 and "followed gambling for twelve years." In 1842 he reformed. He entered Augustana (Ky.) College, where he studied (1843-44) and where he wrote his first book exposing gamblers' tricks and systems. Green says that the manuscript was corrected by the president of the college, for which service "he charged me *three hundred dollars.*"

Green traveled and lectured all over the U. S. but never quite established himself sufficiently in the eyes of the more critical of the public to put him above the counter-charges of gamblers and gambling interests. Although he apparently had endorsers in the distinguished persons of Horace Greeley and Edgar Allan Poe, he was in constant financial straits and was very frequently forced to answer charges (in the phrase of his original trade) of "double dealing."

Information from the author's own books.

* * *

An Exposure of the Arts and Miseries of Gambling; Designed Especially as a Warning to the Youthful and Inexperienced, Against the Evils of That Odious and Destructive Vice. *Philadelphia, 1843.*

The Gambler's Mirror. *Baltimore, 1844.* (A serial work issued in three parts.)

Gambling Unmasked. *New York, 1844.*

The Secret Band of Brothers. *Philadelphia, 1847.*

Twelve Days in the Tombs; or, a Sketch of the Last Eight Years of the Reformed Gambler's Life. *New York, 1851.*

The Reformed Gambler; or, the History of the Later Years of the Life of Jonathan H. Green (the "Reformed Gambler") . . . *Philadelphia,* n.d. [1858].

GREENE, GEORGE E.: 1861–1917.

"George E. Greene was born in Vincennes.

"He attended the public schools and also St. John's

College, Dayton, O., and Cecilian College in Elizabethtown, Ky.

"He entered the office of the VINCENNES SUN in 1873, where he learned the trade of compositor, varying it with reportorial and editorial work until 1882, when he accepted a position with the Louisville COURIER-JOURNAL, where he remained one year. When he returned to Vincennes he engaged in newspaper work until 1886, when he was elected city clerk. He was twice re-elected. In 1894 Mr. Greene was elected mayor and re-elected in 1898.

"He was never married and died Jan. 19, 1917, aged fifty-six."

From Hodge—*Vincennes in Picture and Story.*

* * *

History of Old Vincennes and Knox County. *Cleveland, 1911. 2 vols.*

GREENE, JOSEPH NELSON: 1868–

Joseph Nelson Greene was born in Valparaiso, Ind., in 1868. He received the A.B. and B.D. degrees from Indiana Asbury (now De Pauw) University and served as pastor of various Indiana Methodist churches.

Information from Federal Writers Project—*Indiana Authors, 1937.*

* * *

The Funeral, Its Conduct and Proprieties. *New York, 1905.*
The Gospel in Literature. *Cincinnati, 1910.*
The Exalted Fisherman: a Practical and Devotional Study in the Life and Experiences of the Apostle St. Peter. *New York, 1914.*
Portrait of the Prodigal; Life Studies in the Experiences of the Prodigal Son. *New York, 1921.*
Pastor's Personal Life Record. *New York, n.d.*

GREENWOOD, ALICE DAVIS ODEKIRK (MRS. ALBERT): 1850–1936.

Alice Davis, daughter of Oliver P. Davis, was born in Vermillion County, Ind., on Jan. 8, 1850. She was educated at St. Mary-of-the-Woods and at Colby College.

After her first husband's death she married Albert Greenwood, and they traveled a great deal, living in New Hampshire, Massachusetts, Illinois, Alabama, California, and Canada. She eventually returned to Indiana and lived at Rockville until her death in 1936.

Mrs. Greenwood contributed poems and prose to

papers and magazines. She sometimes wrote under the name of "Aunt Jemina."

Information from the Rockville Public Library.

* * *

Husks and Nubbins. *Concord, N. H., 1899.*
Songs of Home. *Oakland, Cal., 1907.*
Cawn Dodgahs. *Chicago, 1910.*

GRIGGS, NATHAN KIRK: 1844–1910.

Nathan Kirk Griggs, son of Lucien and Mary Townsend Kirk Griggs, was born at Frankfort, Ind., on Oct. 25, 1844.

Following a common school education he taught school for four years in Clinton County, Ind., then studied law at Indiana University, receiving the LL.B. degree in 1867. He began the practice of law at Beatrice, Neb., in the same year. On Dec. 21, 1869, he married Epsie E. Saunders.

In 1871 Mr. Griggs was a member of the Nebraska Constitutional Convention and from 1872 to 1876 was a member of the state senate. He was U. S. consul at Chemnitz, Saxony, from 1876 to 1882. After 1890 he served as attorney for the Northwestern division of the C.B. & Q. Railway. He removed to Lincoln, Neb., in 1893.

Mr. Griggs died in 1910.

Information from *Indiana University, 1820-1904,* and *Who Was Who in America.*

* * *

Lyrics of the Lariat: Poems with Notes. *New York, 1893.*
Hell's Canyon: a Poem of the Camps. *Chicago, 1899.*
Voices of the Winds Series. *Chicago, 1900. 6 vols.*
Five Addresses and Devotional Poems; with an Introductory Biography. In Memoriam. *Lincoln, Neb., 1911.*

GRISWOLD, BERT JOSEPH: 1873–1927.

Bert Joseph (originally Joseph Elbert) Griswold, son of James J. and Ruth Velerie Arnold Griswold, was born in Osage, Ia., on Oct. 13, 1873, and was educated in the public schools of Osage. He married Clara Louise Norton on Mar. 21, 1901.

He began newspaper work on the Osage WEEKLY NEWS, later working on papers in Waterloo and Cedar Rapids, Ia. Coming to Indiana, he was on the staffs of the TERRE HAUTE TRIBUNE and the INDIANAPOLIS STAR and in 1902 settled in Fort Wayne, where he was a cartoonist for the DAILY NEWS. In 1911 he joined the FORT WAYNE SENTINEL and in 1914 formed his own advertising agency, the Progressive Advertising Company. Mr. Griswold was also one of the founders of the Fort Wayne Engraving Co.

In addition to his newspaper and advertising work, he engaged in research and writing on the history of the Fort Wayne area. He died in Fort Wayne on Mar. 8, 1927.

> Information from The Public Library of Fort Wayne and Allen County, Indiana.

* * *

Some Fort Wayne Phizes. *Fort Wayne,* 1904.

Crayon and Character; Truth Made Clear Through Eye and Ear; or, Ten Minute Talks with Colored Chalks. *Indianapolis,* 1913.

Griswold-Phelps Handbook and Guide to Fort Wayne, Indiana, for 1913-14. *Fort Wayne,* 1913.

Pictorial History of Fort Wayne, Indiana. *Chicago,* 1917. 2 vols.

Builders of Greater Fort Wayne. *Fort Wayne,* 1926.

GROSVENOR, ABBIE JOHNSTON (MRS. ELMER B.): 1865–

Abbie Johnston was the daughter of Daniel Webster and Jane Bates Johnston. She was born in Richmond, Ind., on Sept. 21, 1865.

She attended the Richmond public schools, graduated from Richmond High School in 1884, and was a student in the Richmond Normal School in 1885. In 1886 she was privately tutored in English, French and German literature. She married Dr. Elmer Baer Grosvenor of Richmond on Sept. 13, 1888.

In 1900 Mrs. Grosvenor studied history and archaeology under Radice in France and Russell Forbes in Italy. After her return she made her home in Richmond, where she wrote her several children's books.

> Information from Morrisson-Reeves Library, Richmond, Indiana.

* * *

Merrie May Tyme. 1916.

Strange Stories of the Great Valley; the Adventures of a Boy Pioneer. *New York,* 1917. (Reissued in 1925 as Boy Pioneer.)

Strange Stories of the Great River; the Adventures of a Boy Explorer. *New York,* 1918. (Reissued in 1926 as Boy Explorer.)

Winged Moccasins; a Tale of the Adventurous Mound-Builders. *New York,* 1933.

GRUELLE, JOHN BARTON: 1880–1938.

John Barton Gruelle, son of Richard B. and Alice Benton Gruelle, was reared in a talented family. Following his birth in Arcola, Ill., in 1880, his parents moved to Indianapolis, where his father gained wide reputation as an artist and became a close friend of James Whitcomb Riley, from whose work John (or "Johnny" as he usually signed himself) drew many of his characters.

According to the notice of his death in the INDIANAPOLIS STAR:

"Adventuresome as a youth, Mr. Gruelle went to Cleveland on a 'bumming' trip when a boy and there met the McGinty who later was to play a prominent part in his books.

"He and a chum arrived in the city, broke and hungry, and Mr. Gruelle obtained a job as a piano player in a Cleveland saloon to earn money for food. McGinty—a Cleveland policeman—strolled in, and Mr. Gruelle, impressed by the character, drew the policeman's picture on the window of a back bar.

"McGinty called him to one side. 'Listen, bud,' he said, 'you've got the makings of a good cartoonist in you. Come to my house and you've got a home as long as you want it. I'll stake you until you can get a job on a newspaper.'

" 'I can't do that, McGinty,' Mr. Gruelle told the policeman. 'I've got some folks back in Indianapolis who are expecting me.' "

After working as a cartoonist on the staff of the INDIANAPOLIS STAR, he was employed by the CLEVELAND PRESS and later by a news association in Cleveland. There he looked up his friend, McGinty, and the two became close friends.

Staff artists reported at the office at seven o'clock in the morning and left when they had completed their work for the day. A rapid worker, Mr. Gruelle usually finished his cartoons early in the morning, but, seeing that his associates looked askance at his short hours, he decided to stay in the office. To pass the time he wrote the first draft, in verse, of *Raggedy Ann,* his first great children's book. Later, after he had removed to New York, as a cartoonist on the NEW YORK HERALD, he changed the text of *Raggedy Ann* from poetry to prose, and a publisher accepted it. The book had, by 1938, sold over 3,000,000 copies—said to exceed any children's book since *Alice in Wonderland.*

In New York, at a home he purchased in Silvermine, Conn., and, in his later years, in Florida, Gruelle turned out an enormous volume of writing and drawing. He produced Sunday supplement cartoons, cartoons for periodicals and text and illustrations for a large number of books—most successful of which continued to feature Raggedy Ann in various adventures and backgrounds.

Although a bit younger, John Barton Gruelle may well be classified with the crop of Indiana "greats" developed by various Indianapolis newspapers in the early decades of the Twentieth century.

He died at his home in Miami Springs, Fla., on Jan. 9, 1938, survived by his wife, the former Myrtle Swann, and his two sons.

Information from the INDIANAPOLIS STAR for Jan. 10, 1938.

* * *

Mr. Twee Deedle. *New York,* 1913.

Mr. Twee Deedle's Further Adventures. *New York,* 1914.

My Very Own Fairy Stories. *Chicago,* 1917.

Funny Little Book. *Chicago,* 1918.

Raggedy Ann Stories. *Chicago,* 1918.

Friendly Fairies. *Chicago,* 1919.

Little Sunny Stories; the Singing Thead; the Way to Fairyland; Mrs. Goodluck Cricket. *Chicago,* 1919.

Raggedy Andy Stories; Introducing the Little Rag Brother of Raggedy Ann. *Chicago,* 1920.

Orphant Annie Story Book, *Indianapolis,* 1921.

Eddie Elephant. *Chicago,* 1921.

Magical Land of Noom; with Sundry and Mondry. *Chicago,* 1922.

Johnny Mouse and the Wishing Stick. *Indianapolis,* 1922.

Beloved Belindy. (2nd ed.—*Chicago,* 1926.)

Paper Dragon; a Raggedy Ann Adventure. (2nd ed.—*Chicago,* 1926.)

Little Brown Bear. *Chicago.*

Raggedy Andy's Number Book. *Chicago.*

Raggedy Ann and Andy and the Camel with the Wrinkled Knees. *Chicago,* (Later dramatized as the Camel with the Wrinkled Knees.)

Raggedy Ann's Alphabet Book. *Chicago.*

Raggedy Ann's Wishing Pebble. *Chicago.*

Wooden Willie. *Chicago,* 1927.

Raggedy Ann's Magical Wishes. *Chicago,* 1928.

Cheery Scarecrow. *Chicago,* 1929.

Marcella Stories. *Chicago,* 1929.

All About Story Book (with others). *Chicago,* 1929.

Raggedy Ann in the Deep Woods. *Chicago,* 1930.

Raggedy Ann's Sunny Songs, Music by Will Woodin [William H. Woodin, Roosevelt's first secretary of the treasury]. *Chicago,* 1930.

Raggedy Ann in Cookie Land. *Chicago,* 1931.

Raggedy Ann's Lucky Pennies. *Chicago,* 1932.

Raggedy Ann and the Left Handed Safety Pin. *Racine, Wis.,* 1935.

Raggedy Ann in the Golden Meadow. *Racine, Wis.,* 1936. Golden Book. *Chicago.*

Raggedy Ann's Joyful Songs (with Charles Miller). *New York,* 1937.

Raggedy Ann in the Magic Book. *New York,* 1939.

Raggedy Ann and the Golden Butterfly. *New York,* 1940.

Raggedy Ann and the Happy Toad. *Springfield, Mass.,* 1940.

Raggedy Ann and the Laughing Brook. *Springfield, Mass.,* 1940.

Raggedy Ann Helps Grandpa Hoppergrass. *Springfield, Mass.,* 1940.

Raggedy Ann in the Garden. *Springfield, Mass.,* 1940.

Raggedy Ann and Andy and the Nice Fat Policeman. *New York,* 1942.

Raggedy Ann and Betsy Bonnet String. *New York,* 1943.

The Plaint of the Stick-at-Home Hoosier.

GRUELLE, RICHARD BUCKNER: 1851–1914.

Richard Buckner Gruelle, father of the well-known author and illustrator, John Barton Gruelle, and himself an outstanding Indiana artist, was born at Cynthiana, Ky., on Feb. 22, 1851.

He came to Indianapolis in 1879, after living in Illinois for a time, and opened a studio. Self-taught, he had hard going in his early years but eventually established himself and enjoyed a considerable contemporary reputation. He was a close friend of James Whitcomb Riley.

He moved to New York in 1905 but returned and died at his home in Indianapolis on Nov. 8, 1914. His wife, Alice Benton Gruelle, died in 1935.

Information from the Indiana State Library.

* * *

Notes: Critical and Biographical. *Indianapolis,* 1895.

GRUMMANN, PAUL HENRY: 1872–

Paul Henry Grummann, son of Albert U. and Augusta Storch Grummann, was born in Indianapolis, on Oct. 4, 1872, and was educated at Indiana University (A.B., 1896; A.M., 1900). After teaching in Manual Training High School in Indianapolis, he went to the University of Nebraska in 1900 as professor of modern German literature; from 1912 to 1931 he was professor of dramatic literature and director of the School of Fine Arts. In 1931 he became director of the Society of Liberal Arts, Joslyn Memorial, Omaha.

Besides the works listed, Mr. Grummann translated from the German, wrote textbooks and contributed verse and articles to various periodicals. He married Katherine Coleston on Aug. 26, 1891.

Information from *Who's Who in America*.

* * *

Ibsen's Symbolism in "The Master Builder" and "When the Dead Awake." *Lincoln, Neb.,* 1910.
Henrik Ibsen; an Introduction to His Life and Works. *Lincoln,* Neb., 1928.
Northern Mythology. *Lincoln, Neb.,* 1929.
Musical Dramas of Richard Wagner. *Lincoln, Neb.,* 1930.

H

HACK, ELIZABETH JANE MILLER (MRS. OREN S.): 1878–

Elizabeth Jane Miller, daughter of Timothy and Samantha West Miller, was born Aug. 17, 1878, on a farm near New Ross, Ind. Her parents farmed during the summer months and taught school in the winter. In 1883 the Millers moved to Indianapolis in order to give their children a better opportunity for higher education, and Elizabeth attended the public schools, Manual Training High School, and Butler University. While at Butler she began writing verse, contributing to the INDIANAPOLIS NEWS, and in 1904 published her first novel, *The Yoke*. On June 16, 1908, she married Oren S. Hack, Indianapolis attorney, who died in 1942.

Information from Dunn—*Indiana and Indianans,* Vol. III, and the Indianapolis Public Library.

* * *

The Yoke, a Romance of the Days When the Lord Redeemed the Children of Israel from the Bondage of Egypt. *Indianapolis,* 1904.
Saul of Tarsus. *Indianapolis,* 1906.
The City of Delight: a Love Drama of the Siege and Fall of Jerusalem. *Indianapolis,* 1907.
Daybreak, a Story of the Age of Discovery. *New York,* 1915.
The Science of Columbus. *Greenfield, Ind.,* 1921.

HADLEY, CHALMERS: 1872–

Chalmers Hadley, leader in the field of library science, was born in Indianapolis, Sept. 3, 1872, the son of Dr. Evan and Ella Quin Hadley. He received the B.L. degree from Earlham College in 1896 and from the New York State Library School, Albany, in 1906.

During the years from 1898 to 1905 he engaged in newspaper work at Philadelphia and at Indianapolis. After 1906 he devoted himself to library work, being successively secretary and state organizer for the Indiana Library Commission, director of the Indiana Summer Library School, secretary and executive officer of the American Library Association, and librarian at the Denver Public Library. He became librarian of the Public Library of Cincinnati and Hamilton County, Ohio, in 1924, retiring in 1946.

Information from *Who's Who in America*.

* * *

Notes on the Quaker Family of Hadley. *Denver,* 1916.
Library Buildings; Notes and Plans. *Chicago,* 1924.
John Cotton Dana, a Sketch. *Chicago,* 1943.

HADLEY, JOHN VESTAL: 1842–1915.

John Vestal Hadley, son of Jonathan and Ara Hadley, was born in Hendricks County, Ind., on Oct. 31, 1842, attended Northwestern Christian (now Butler) University from 1859 to 1861, and studied at Indiana Law School in 1886. He married Mary J. Hill on Mar. 15, 1865.

During the Civil War he served in the Union Army for three and one-half years. He was twice wounded in battle, was captured on May 5, 1864, and escaped from Columbia, S. C., to Knoxville, Tenn., on Dec. 10, 1864.

From 1869 to 1872 Mr. Hadley was a member of the Indiana Senate. He was a circuit judge in 1888-89 and a justice of the Supreme Court of Indiana from 1899 to 1911.

A resident of Danville, Ind., he died on Nov. 17, 1915.

Information from *Who Was Who in America*.

* * *

Seven Months a Prisoner. *New York,* 1898.
History of Hendricks County, Indiana. *Indianapolis,* 1914.

HAGERTY, JAMES EDWARD: ?–

James Edward Hagerty, son of John and Jane E. Crilly Hagerty, was born in LaPorte County, Ind., and graduated from Northern Indiana Normal School in 1888 and Indiana University in 1892. In 1900 he received the Ph.D. degree from the University of Pennsylvania. He also studied at the University of

Chicago, the University of Wisconsin, and in Germany. On Oct. 26, 1907, he married Lucille Joyce.

Following his graduation from college he taught mathematics for four years in LaPorte High School and in 1901 joined the faculty of Ohio State University as assistant professor of economics and sociology, later serving as professor, acting head of the department, director of the School of Social Administration, and professor of social administration. In 1916 he organized the College of Commerce and Journalism and was its dean from 1916 to 1926.

Information from *Who's Who in America.*

* * *

Mercantile Credit. *New York,* 1913.

The Training of Social Workers. *New York,* 1931.

Twentieth Century Crime—Eighteenth Century Methods of Control. *Boston,* 1934.

HALE, LOUISE CLOSSER (MRS. WALTER): 1872–1933.

Louise Closser, daughter of Joseph and Louise Paddock Closser, was born in Chicago on Oct. 13, 1872, and was educated in the public schools of Indianapolis. On Aug. 17, 1899, she married Walter Hale. Author and actress, she made her first stage appearance in Detroit in 1895. She died on July 26, 1933.

Information from *Who Was Who in America.*

* * *

A Motor Car Divorce. *New York,* 1906.

The Actress: Novel. *New York,* 1909.

The Married Miss Worth: a Novel. *New York,* 1911.

Her Soul and Her Body. *New York,* 1912.

Motor Journeys (with Walter Hale). *Chicago,* 1912.

We Discover New England. *New York,* 1915.

We Discover the Old Dominion. *New York,* 1916.

An American's London. *New York,* 1920.

Home Talent. *New York,* 1926.

The Canal Boat Fracas. *New York,* 1927.

HALE, WILLIAM BAYARD: 1869–1924.

William Bayard Hale, son of William Hadley and Anna Bunting Hale, was born in Richmond, Ind., on Apr. 6, 1869.

He was educated at Boston University, Harvard University and the Episcopal Theological Seminary at Cambridge, Mass., and received the honorary S.T.D.

from Hobart College in 1896 and the LL.D. from St. John's in the same year.

He was a clergyman until 1909, when he took up journalism. He married Olga Unger on Oct. 5, 1909.

Mr. Hale died in April, 1924.

Information from the Richmond Public Library.

* * *

An Address in Memory of Phillips Brooks. *Cambridge, Mass.,* 1893.

The Eternal Teacher. *New York,* 1895.

Making of the American Constitution. *New York,* 1896.

The New Obedience; a Plea for Social Submission to Christ. *New York,* 1897.

A Week in the White House with Theodore Roosevelt. *New York,* 1908.

Woodrow Wilson: The Story of His Life. *Garden City, N. Y.,* 1912.

American Rights and British Pretensions on the Seas; the Facts and the Documents, Official and Other, Bearing Upon the Present Attitude of Great Britain Toward the Commerce of the United States. *New York,* 1915.

The Story of a Style. *New York,* 1920.

HALL, ARNOLD BENNETT: 1881–1936.

Arnold Bennett Hall, son of Columbus Horatio and Theodosia Parks Hall, was born in Franklin, Ind., on July 22, 1881, and graduated from Franklin College in 1904, receiving the J.D. degree from the University of Chicago in 1907. He later received the honorary LL.D. degree from Franklin College, the University of California, and the College of Puget Sound. On June 15, 1911, he married Grace Stafford Carney.

Admitted to the Indiana bar in 1907, he taught at the University of Chicago (1907-09), Northwestern (1909-10), and the University of Wisconsin (1910-26). From 1926 to 1932 he served as president of the University of Oregon, and from 1933 until his death he was associated with the Brookings Institution, Washington, D. C.

He died on June 1, 1936.

Information from *Who Was Who in America.*

* * *

Outline of International Law. *Chicago,* 1915.

The Monroe Doctrine and the Great War. *Chicago,* 1920.

Dynamic Americanism. *Indianapolis,* 1920.

The Past, Present and Future of the Monroe Doctrine. *New York,* 1920.

Popular Government; an Inquiry Into the Nature and Methods of Representative Government. *New York,* 1921.

HALSTEAD, WILLIAM RILEY: 1848–1931.

William Riley Halstead, son of Reuben and Louisa Brown Halstead, was born in Vigo County, Ind., Mar. 19, 1848. After graduating from Indiana Asbury (now De Pauw) University in 1871, he was ordained to the Methodist ministry and held pastorates throughout his life in a number of Indiana towns and cities. For one year (1880-81) he was president of De Pauw College at New Albany, Ind. During the latter part of his life he lived in Terre Haute, Ind., where he died Dec. 19, 1931. He was married three times: first to Candace Kennedy, who died in 1873; then to Martha Taylor, who died in 1902; and in 1906 to Mrs. Ella B. Pegg.

> Information from *Who Was Who in America;* De Pauw University's *Alumnal Record, 1920;* and the Emmeline Fairbanks Memorial Library, Terre Haute, Ind.

* * *

Future Religious Policy of America. *Cincinnati,* 1877.
Civil and Religious Forces. *Cincinnati,* 1890.
Life on a Backwoods Farm; or, the Boyhood of Reuben Rodney Blannerhassett. *Cincinnati,* 1894.
Christ in the Industries. *Cincinnati,* 1898.
A Cosmic View of Religion. *Cincinnati,* 1913.
The Tragedy of Labor: a Monograph in Folk Philosophy. *New York,* 1919.
Some Social Aspects of Religion. 1919.
Creative Ideas in Religion. 1926.
Christ in the Universe. *New York,* 1929.

HAMILTON, JAMES HENRY: 1861–

James Henry Hamilton, son of Robert A. and Susan Saunders Hamilton, was born in Greensburg, Ind., on Oct. 31, 1861. He graduated from Hanover College in 1885, received the LL.B. degree from the University of Cincinnati in 1887, A.M. from Indiana University in 1894, and Ph.D. from the University of Wisconsin in 1896.

From 1896 to 1903 he was professor of sociology at Syracuse University, and from 1903 to 1909 he was connected with the University Settlement in New York. After 1909 he was mainly engaged in investigating social conditions in European countries. During the first World War he served with the American Red Cross in France. Mr. Hamilton wrote on economic and sociological subjects. He established post-graduate fellowships for students in Romance languages at Grenoble, Besançon, Florence, and Seville.

Information from *Who's Who in America.*

* * *

The Relation of Postal Savings Banks to Commercial Banks. *Philadelphia,* 1898.
Savings and Savings Institutions. *New York,* 1902.

HAMILTON, JOHN SHERMAN: 1870–

John Sherman Hamilton, son of Jonathan and Sarah Anderson Hamilton, was born in Ada, O., on Dec. 20, 1870. He received the A.M. degree from Ohio Northern University in 1895 and studied at Wooster University and the Princeton and McCormick Theological Seminaries.

He married Agnes Laughlin on July 27, 1898, and was ordained to the Presbyterian ministry in the same year. In 1904 he took up evangelistic work, in which he continued, with residence at Winona Lake, Ind.

Information from *Who's Who in America.*

* * *

Is Jesus Coming Again?
Home, How to Make It Happy.
The Christian and Amusements.

HAMMOND, MATTHEW BROWN: 1868–1933.

Matthew Brown Hammond, son of Seth and Sarah Longley Hammond, was born in South Bend, Ind., on June 13, 1868, and graduated from the University of Michigan in 1891, receiving the M.L. degree from the University of Wisconsin in 1893 and the Ph.D. from Columbia in 1898. He also studied in Germany. On July 2, 1902, he married Sunie Butler Denham.

He served as principal of Versailles (Mo.) Institute, acting assistant professor of economics at the University of Missouri, instructor and assistant professor of economics at the University of Illinois, and in 1904 joined the faculty of Ohio State University as assistant professor of economics, later becoming an associate professor and professor.

He died on Sept. 28, 1933.

Information from *Who Was Who in America.*

* * *

The Cotton Industry: an Essay in American Economic History. *New York,* 1897.
The Southern Farmer and Banking Reform. *New York,* 1898.
Railway Rate Theories of the Interstate Commerce Commission. *Cambridge, Mass.,* 1911.

Minimum Wage in Great Britain and Australia. *Philadelphia,* 1913.

British Labor Conditions and Legislation During the War. *New York,* 1919.

HANLY, JAMES FRANKLIN: 1863–1920.

Born in St. Joseph, Ill., on April 4, 1863, J. Frank Hanly (the style he used during his political career) son of Elijah and Anna E. Calton Hanly, had little formal education. In 1879 he went to Williamsport, Ind., where he worked on a farm, sawed wood, and had six months' schooling in a district school. From 1881 to 1889 he engaged in school teaching while reading law, and in 1889 he was admitted to the bar. He practiced in Williamsport and Lafayette, Ind., until 1905. His natural gift of oratory soon gave him a start in politics. He was a member of the state Senate in 1890, a member of the 54th Congress from 1895 to 1897, and a candidate for the U. S. Senate in 1899. In 1905 he was elected governor of Indiana.

Indiana and Indianans, Vol. II, reports that his career as governor was a stormy one because of his determination to govern with a strong hand. He did not believe in compromising or conciliating, and he attacked publicly abuses in his own party, forcing the resignations of several officeholders.

He became interested in the cause of temperance and served as president of The Flying Squadron, a temperance organization founded in 1915. In 1916 he was the nominee of the Prohibition Party for president. He practiced law in Indianapolis and for a time was editor of the NATIONAL ENQUIRER and the INDIANAPOLIS DAILY COMMERCIAL.

He married Eva A. Simmer in 1881 and died on Aug. 1, 1920.

Information from *Who Was Who in America* and Dunn—*Indiana and Indianans,* Vol. II.

* * *

Occasional Addresses. [*Lafayette, Ind.,* 1904.]

Patriotism of Peace; Public Addresses and State Papers of Governor J. Frank Hanly of Indiana; Compiled by George B. Lockwood. *Marion, Ind.,* 1906.

Dedicatory Address; Unveiling of Morton Monument, July 23, 1907. *Indianapolis,* 1907.

Indeterminate Sentence, an Address Delivered Before . . . the National Prison Association . . . September 16, 1907. n.p., n.d.

My Lord and Savior, Jesus Christ: an Address Delivered Before the Fifty-First Ohio State Sunday School Convention. *Indianapolis,* 1910.

County Option in Indiana. *Westerville, O.,* 1910.

Battle of Gettysburg from "The World Disarmed." *New York,* 1912.

Andersonville. *New York,* 1912.

Vicksburg. *New York,* 1912.

A Day in the Siskiyous; an Oregon Extravaganza. *Indianapolis,* 1916.

Address Accepting the Presidential Nomination. *Chicago,* 1916.

The Conqueror of the World. *Indianapolis,* 1918.

Robert G. Ingersoll; Richard W. Thompson; Abraham Lincoln. n.p., n.d.

HANNA, GUY CARLETON: 1879–

Guy Carleton Hanna, son of John Wilson and Mary Banta Chilcott Hanna, was born in White County, Ind., on Feb. 15, 1879, and graduated from Indiana State Teachers College in 1905. He also studied at the University of Chicago and the University of Minnesota, receiving his A.B. degree from the latter in 1922.

From 1907 to 1909 he was head of the teachers' training department at Marion College (Marion, Ind.), from 1909 to 1911 superintendent of training schools at Indiana State Teachers College, and from 1911 to 1917 superintendent of the Indiana Boys' School, a correctional institution. From 1917 to 1928 he was in Minnesota serving as superintendent of the Minnesota School for Feeble Minded and Colony for Epileptics, and later became an employee of the U. S. Treasury Department. On Aug. 12, 1899, Mr. Hanna married Clara Perry.

Information from *Who's Who in America.*

* * *

The Trouble with Agriculture.

Thomas Jefferson, Governor of Virginia.

Institution Service.

The Juvenile Criminal in a State Correctional Institution. *Plainfield, Ind.,* 1915.

The Menace of the Feeble Minded. n.p., n.d.

Occupational Efficiency of the Mentally Defective; a Survey of the Inmates of the Minnesota School for Feeble Minded and Colony for Epileptics, Faribault. *Minneapolis,* 1924.

HAPGOOD, NEITH BOYCE (MRS. HUTCHINS): 1872–

Neith Boyce Hapgood, whose writings were published under her maiden name of Neith Boyce, was born on Mar. 21, 1872, in Franklin, Ind., the daughter of

Henry H. and Mary E. Smith Boyce. She married Hutchins Hapgood, author, in June of 1899.

Information from *Who's Who in America*.

* * *

Songs by Neith Boyce; with Drawings by Ethelwyn Wells Conrey. *Boston, 1893.*

The Forerunner. *New York, 1903.*

The Folly of Others. *New York, 1904.*

The Eternal Spring. *New York, 1906.*

The Bond. *New York, 1908.*

Enemies (with Hutchins Hapgood). *New York, 1916.*

Proud Lady. *New York, 1923.*

Harry. *New York, 1923.*

HARBERT, ELIZABETH MORRISSON BOYNTON (MRS. WILLIAM S.): 1845–1925.

Born in Crawfordsville, Ind., on Apr. 15, 1845, Elizabeth Boynton Harbert, daughter of William and Abbey Upton Sweetser Boynton, graduated from Terre Haute Female College in 1862 and received the Ph.D. degree from Ohio Wesleyan University. She was married to William Soesby Harbert on Oct. 18, 1870.

For eight years she was editor of "Woman's Kingdom," a department of the CHICAGO INTER-OCEAN and for one year editor of THE NEW ERA. She also contributed to THE ARENA, THE COMING AGE, WOMAN'S JOURNAL, and other periodicals. She was a prominent clubwoman, lecturer, and worker for woman's suffrage. She died Jan. 19, 1925.

Information from *Who Was Who in America*.

* * *

The Golden Fleece. *Boston, 1867.*

Out of Her Sphere. *Des Moines, Ia., 1871.*

Social Economy of Illinois. *1879.*

Amore. *New York, 1892.*

HARDEN, SAMUEL: 1831–?

Born in Hamilton County, Ind., in 1831, Samuel Harden went to California in 1852 but returned in 1855 and settled at Markleville, Ind., where he was postmaster for a time. He served in the Civil War. In 1897 he was living in Anderson, Ind.

Information from the Barry Ms.

* * *

History of Madison County, Indiana, from 1820 to 1874. *Markleville, Ind., 1874.*

Early Life and Times in Boone County, Indiana, Giving an Account of the Early Settlement of Each Locality, Church Histories, County and Township Officers from the First Down to 1886; Histories of Some of the Pioneer Families of the County. Biographical Sketches of Some of the Prominent Men and Women. Communications from Well-Informed Citizens Throughout the County; List of Soldiers Who Went to the Late War of 1861-5 (with John Spahr). *Lebanon, Ind., 1887.*

Those I Have Met; or, Boys in Blue; in Which Is Remembered Those I Have Met Along the Road of Life . . . *Anderson, Ind., 1888.*

HARDING, CAROLINE HIRST BROWN (MRS. SAMUEL B.): ?–

Caroline Hirst Brown was born in Bloomington, Ind., and attended Indiana University, receiving the A.B. degree in 1890. In the same year she married Samuel B. Harding. She is listed, in 1904, as a resident of Bloomington. Her writing was apparently all in collaboration with her husband.

Information from The University Libraries, Indiana University, and the Indianapolis Public Library.

* * *

Stories of Greek Gods, Heroes, and Men: A Primer of the Mythology and History of the Greeks (with S. B. Harding). *Chicago, 1897.*

The City of the Seven Hills: a Book of Stories from the History of Ancient Rome. *Chicago, 1898.*

HARDING, GEORGE CANADY: 1829–1881.

Born near Knoxville, Tenn., on Aug. 26, 1829, George C. Harding was the son of Jacob Harding, a lawyer, and Love Nelson Harding. He was one of thirteen children. He spent his childhood and early youth in Tennessee and Illinois, and he supplemented a very limited formal education by extensive reading.

He began his newspaper career as a printer with Judge Conard of Terre Haute, publisher of the COURIER, and was soon writing for the paper. When his father started a newspaper, the PRAIRIE BEACON, in Paris, Ill., young George worked for him and also contributed articles to a literary weekly of Cincinnati, the GREAT WEST. During the Mexican War he enlisted but saw no action, since he spent most of the time in a hospital. His first editorial experience was on the Charleston, Ill., COURIER, which he made a Republican paper, despite the pro-slavery sentiments of the former Kentuckians who had settled the neighborhood. From this time until the Civil War he worked on various papers in Cincinnati and in Texas, and when the war broke out he enlisted in the 21st Indiana Regiment, from which he resigned in 1864 as a second lieutenant.

Six months after leaving the army he came to Indianapolis, where with one or two interruptions he spent the rest of his life in newspaper work, being connected at different times with the INDIANAPOLIS HERALD, (from which he retired as editor, after seven years' service, in 1880) the JOURNAL, the SENTINEL, and the MIRROR.

Mr. Harding was twice married, (first to Jennie Reeves and, in 1861, to Julia C. Bannister), and had seven children. While at the height of his success he met with an accident and died of blood poisoning on May 8, 1881.

Information from *Representative Men of Indiana*, Vol. I, and the Indianapolis Public Library.

* * *

The Miscellaneous Writings of George C. Harding (published posthumously by his wife). *Indianapolis,* 1882.

HARDING, LEWIS ALBERT: 1880–1944.

Lewis Albert Harding, son of James Lancaster and Eliza Hanking Harding, was born near New Point, Decatur County, Ind., on Feb. 1, 1880. Following his graduation from Indiana University in 1909, he spent two years (1909-11) as head of the English department of Wichita (Kan.) High School.

For two terms, beginning in 1912, he served as prosecuting attorney for the 9th Judicial Circuit Court of Indiana, and during this time he became known as a lecturer and historian. He later practiced law in Spokane, Wash., and taught elocution at the University of Louisiana.

Mr. Harding returned to Indiana and practiced law in Indianapolis, where he was active in Democratic politics. He died at Indianapolis on Sept. 9, 1944.

Information from Mrs. Clara Miller, Greensburg, Ind.

* * *

The Preliminary Diplomacy of the Spanish-American War, with an Introduction by Amos S. Hershey, Given at Greensburg, Indiana, November 21, 1912, Before the Athenaeum. *Indianapolis,* 1912.

The Call of the Hour. *Wichita, Kan.,* 1913.

The History of Decatur County, Indiana. *Indianapolis,* 1915.

A Few Spoken Words: the Consecration of the Sixties. *Indianapolis,* 1915.

HARDING, SAMUEL BANNISTER: 1866–1927.

Samuel Bannister Harding, son of George Canady and Julia Cora Bannister Harding, was born in Indianapolis on July 29, 1866. He graduated from Indiana University in 1890 and received the A.M. and Ph.D. degrees from Harvard University in 1894 and 1898, respectively. From 1895 to 1918 he was associate professor of history at Indiana University, from 1919 to 1921 managing editor of Compton's Encyclopedia, and from 1921 until his death was professor of history at the University of Minnesota.

He was twice married—first to Caroline Hirst in 1890, with whom he collaborated in many of his writings, then to Margaret Snodgrass in 1918. He died in Minneapolis Jan. 29, 1927.

Dr. Harding was author and co-author of many textbooks.

Information from *Who Was Who in America* and the Indianapolis Public Library.

* * *

American History, 1781-1829. *Albany, N. Y.,* 1892.

The "Minimum" Principle in the Tariff of 1828 and Its Recent Revival. *Philadelphia,* 1895.

Party Struggles Over the First Pennsylvania Constitution (with William Fletcher Harding). *Philadelphia,* 1895.

The Contest Over the Ratification of the Federal Constitution in the State of Massachusetts. *New York,* 1896.

Stories of Greek Gods, Heroes, and Men: a Primer of the Mythology and History of the Greeks (with Mrs. C. H. Harding). *Chicago,* 1897.

The City of the Seven Hills: a Book of Stories from the History of Ancient Rome (with Mrs. C. H. Harding). *Chicago,* 1898.

The Story of the Middle Ages. *Chicago,* 1901.

Essentials in Mediaeval and Modern History (with A. B. Hart). *New York,* 1904.

Life of George R. Smith, Founder of Sedalia, Missouri. *Sedalia, Mo.,* 1904.

Essentials in Mediaeval History (with A. B. Hart). *New York,* 1909.

Story of England (with William Fletcher Harding). *Chicago,* 1909.

Study of the Great War; a Topical Outline with Copious Quotations and Reading References. *Philadelphia,* 1918.

Geography of the War; Containing Thirteen Pages of Maps and Charts and Eight Outline Maps. *Philadelphia,* 1918.

HARLAN, JACOB WRIGHT: 1828–?

Jacob Wright Harlan, who was born and reared in Indiana and who became a California pioneer, was the son of Samuel Harlan. He was born on Oct. 14, 1828, in Wayne County, Ind.

Jacob Harlan's mother died when he was about two years old, and his father married a second wife. The stepmother did not get along well with the boy, and his father was persuaded to place him as a bound boy with an uncle. This uncle was reported to have worked his own son to death; he almost killed Jacob, also, before a severe illness rendered the boy unfit for farm work and he was transferred to the custody of another uncle, George Harlan of Niles, Mich.

On Oct. 14, 1845, George Harlan, his family and a party of relatives and neighbors started for California. They wintered on the frontier and on Apr. 6, 1846, started west as a part of a great emigrant train led by Judge Moran of Missouri. The ill-fated Donner party was a unit of this train.

Jacob Harlan was seventeen and his departure with his uncle for the West coincided very nearly with that of at least three other Hoosier young men who had, or who developed, literary talents and became historians of the westward movement—Overton Johnson, William H. Winter and Joel Palmer.

The Harlan party separated from the Donner party and successfully reached California in the late summer of 1846. Jacob joined Company F of Fremont's company, under Capt. L. W. Hastings, at San Jose and traveled to southern California. He was discharged in Los Angeles in April, 1847. Returning to San Jose, he found work scarce, so went into the redwoods on the present site of Oakland and cut out shingles, which he sold to William A. Leidesdorff at $5.00 per thousand. During the summer of 1847 he fenced some sixteen lots in Yerba Buena for Leidesdorff.

On Nov. 22, 1847, he married a daughter of William Fowler, Sr., of the Napa Valley, and shortly afterward moved to San Francisco, where he established a livery stable. It was while running the stable that he received a letter from his uncle, Peter Wimmer, about the gold discovery at Coloma, and he immediately set out with a stock of goods and set up a store at the site of the discovery. He sold out on Oct. 22, 1848, to L. W. Hastings and returned to San Francisco, but in March, 1849, he took a stock of goods to the southern mines and did some mining at Columbia, later returning to livery business in San Francisco.

Purchasing cows from his uncle, George Harlan, he went into the milk business. Selling milk at $4.00 per gallon, he soon gave up his livery business (June 15, 1850). In October he sold his milk business. Buying some land at San Jose mission he started farming, but it was a dry year and he lost so much money that he was obliged to sell his land. Joining with others, he formed a squatters' group which settled on an area of land claimed by both Castro and Estudillo, moving into his newly erected house Nov. 1, 1851. The next November he sold all his land, house and property for $9,300, and leaving his wife and family with relatives on the north side of the Bay, he left California on the *SS Golden Gate* for the eastern states via Panama.

Landing in New York, he paused long enough to buy himself a fine broadcloth suit, a stock, a silk hat and calf boots, entrained on what is now the New York Central Railroad and, after the necessary few days' ride, arrived in Goshen, Ind., a picture of far-western prosperity.

After visiting in Indiana and Michigan he started for California overland on Jan. 12, 1953, with over 200 head of cattle of a good milk-producing strain. Arriving on the San Joaquin River on Sept. 27, 1853, with 187 of his cattle, he bought land near the river and sent for his family. Buying more land adjoining, he thus acquired a half interest in Slocum's (later Johnson's) Ferry, the lowest on the San Joaquin River. Later he became sole owner of the ferry and was in a fair way to becoming wealthy, but for health reasons he was ordered by his doctor to leave the river. He traded his ferry for cattle, which he took to the Cholama Valley, San Luis Obispo County. He bought a squatter claim in Alameda County. On July 1, 1866, his wife died. His cattle had been lost in the great drought or had been run off by thieves from the Cholama Valley.

Depressed and anxious to begin a new type of life, he bought a hotel in Calistoga in January, 1872, but soon found that he was unsuited to hotel-keeping. Giving it up at the end of a year, he went to work for wages on a farm near San Leandro. He then took up 160 acres north of Livermore, where he remained until 1877. Selling out, he bought another small claim in the Tasajera Valley, while his eldest son bought the claim adjoining. They remained there until the fall of 1883, when both sold out. Jacob moved into Livermore and bought some rental property at auction.

Shortly afterward he became a policeman in Livermore, a job he held until his health failed in the fall of 1886. Much against his will and at a great sacrifice of pride he finally entered the County Infirmary. But Jacob Harlan's enterprise was not yet extinguished. In the Infirmary he began his memoirs—and those of

California—and when his manuscript was completed, it was published by The Bancroft Company, a highly reputable San Francisco publishing house. According to his cousin, Mary Harlan Smith, who survived at least until 1905, the proceeds of the sale of the book made his last years comfortable.

Information from the California State Library; Mr. C. W. Harlan, Lafayette, Ind.; and Peter Decker—*Catalog of the Collection of George W. Soliday,* Pt. I, No. 94; Pt. II, No. 499.

* * *

California, '46 to '88. *San Francisco, 1888.*

HARNEY, WILLIAM WALLACE: 1831–1912.

William Wallace Harney, son of John H. and Martha Wallace Harney, was born in Bloomington, Ind., on June 20, 1831, and moved with his family to Kentucky when he was a child. He received his preparatory education under private tutors.

Following his graduation from Louisville College in 1855 he became principal of the Louisville High School for one year, then from 1856 to 1858 he was professor of belles-lettres at Transylvania University in Lexington, Ky. From 1858 to 1869 he was associate editor of the LOUISVILLE DEMOCRAT. He spent the latter part of his life in Florida, where from 1883 to 1886 he edited a paper in Kissimmee and later contributed verse and prose to magazines and newspapers. Mr. Harney married Mary St. Mayer Randolph in 1868; she died in 1869, he in 1912.

Information from *Who's Who in America* and Parker and Heiney—*Poets and Poetry of Indiana.*

* * *

Spirit of the South. *Boston, 1909.*

HARPER, IDA HUSTED: 1851–1931.

"Ida Husted Harper (Feb. 18, 1851-Mar. 14, 1931), journalist and author, prominent in the woman's suffrage movement, was of New England ancestry, born in Fairfield, Franklin County, Ind., the daughter of John Arthur and Cassandra (Stoddard) Husted. When she was about ten years old her parents moved to Muncie, Ind., where she was graduated from the high school. She then entered Indiana University but spent only a year there, becoming at the age of eighteen principal of the high school in Peru, Ind. On Dec. 28, 1871, she was married to Thomas W. Harper, a young lawyer, and as long as they lived together

their home was in Terre Haute. Harper died in 1908, having married again in 1890 . . .

"During her residence in Terre Haute, Mrs. Harper began her career as a journalist, contributing to the papers of that city and of Indianapolis. For twelve years she conducted a department known as 'A Woman's Opinion' in the Terre Haute SATURDAY EVENING MAIL, and for a short time was managing editor of the Terre Haute DAILY NEWS. She also wrote political articles for the INDIANAPOLIS NEWS. In 1883 she became a contributor to the FIREMAN'S MAGAZINE, later called the LOCOMOTIVE FIREMAN'S MAGAZINE, under the editorship of Eugene V. Debs . . . , and in May 1884 was put in charge of its woman's department . . . For a considerable period her home was in New York, where she was for some time a department editor of the SUNDAY SUN and of HARPER'S BAZAAR, as well as a contributor to New York, Boston, Philadelphia, Washington, and Chicago papers.

"She was a sturdy champion of the woman's suffrage movement and closely associated with its leaders. In 1899 she went to London as a delegate to the International Council of Women, and thereafter attended practically all the European meetings of the Council and of the International Suffrage Alliance. Her ability as a writer and her journalistic experience enabled her to give much aid to the suffrage campaign through the press, and in the years immediately preceding the adoption of the Nineteenth Amendment to the Federal Constitution she had charge of publicity for the National American Woman Suffrage Association. She wrote *The Life and Work of Susan B. Anthony* at Miss Anthony's request, the first two volumes, published in 1899, being written in the reformer's home at Rochester, N. Y. The third volume appeared in 1908. She also assisted Miss Anthony in preparing the fourth volume (1902) of *The History of Woman Suffrage.* In 1922 she published two more volumes, bringing the history down to 1920. Her last days were spent in Washington, where she died from a cerebral hemorrhage at the Homeopathic Hospital. Her body was cremated and the ashes were sent to Muncie, Ind., for interment."

Condensed from H. E. S., *Dictionary of American Biography,* Vol. VIII.

* * *

The Associated Work of the Women of Indiana. *Indianapolis, 1893.*

Suffrage a Right. *New York, 1906.*

Woman Suffrage Throughout the World. *New York, 1907.*

History of the Movement for Woman Suffrage in the United States. *New York, 1907.*

The Life and Work of Susan B. Anthony, Including Public Addresses, Her Own Letters and Many from Her Contemporaries During Fifty Years. *Indianapolis, 1898-1908. 3 vols.*

Suffrage Snapshots. *Washington, D. C., 1915.*

A National Amendment for Woman Suffrage. *Washington, D. C., 1915.*

A Brief History of the Movement for Woman Suffrage in the United States. *New York, 1917.*

Woman Suffage; a Collection of Newspaper and Magazine Articles, Leaflets and Miscellaneous Matter (1896-1917) . . . Collected and Arranged by Her. 13 vols.

Story of the National Amendment for Woman Suffrage. *New York, 1919.*

The History of Woman Suffrage. (Vols. V and VI of the work begun by Susan B. Anthony.) *New York, 1922.* (Also co-author with Susan B. Anthony of Vol. IV, Rochester, N.Y., 1903.)

Life of Dr. Anna Howard Shaw. 1927.

HARRIS, BRANSON L.: 1817–1901.

Born Apr. 21, 1817, in Green township, Wayne County, Ind., Branson L. Harris arrived on the Indiana scene in time to experience all the hardships and pleasures of the first pioneers. His parents were James and Naomi L. Harris, farmers.

He married Martha Young in 1839 and survived her by less than a year, the couple having lived together sixty-one years.

Harris was elected to the Indiana State Legislature in 1853 and again in 1875 and 1877. He died in 1901.

> Information from the Indiana State Library and the Richmond Public Library.

* * *

Some Recollections of My Boyhood. *Indianapolis, 1907.*

HARRIS, LEE O.: 1839–1909.

Lee O. Harris, teacher, editor and poet, was the son of Samuel and Mary Harris. He was born in Chester County, Pa., on Jan. 30, 1839. His father was a minister of the Methodist Church. The family later lived in Washington County, Pa., until 1852, when they came to Indiana, and settled at Andersonville. Lee Harris was educated in schools and seminaries in that place. Extensive travel in the U. S. and Canada, including an overland trip to Oregon and Washington Territory in 1856-57, supplemented the young man's education.

For a time he studied medicine, but in 1858 he gave up the idea of becoming a doctor and went into the teaching profession, which he followed, working also as a newspaper editor, until 1880.

In 1860 he went to Greenfield, Ind., to publish the CONSTITUTION AND UNION, a Republican journal, and at the outbreak of the Civil War joined the Eighth Regiment, Indiana Volunteers. He later transferred to the Fifth Indiana Cavalry, but sickness compelled his resignation from the army. In 1864 he again entered the service and remained in the army until the close of the war, when he returned to Greenfield and resumed teaching.

He was one of James Whitcomb Riley's early teachers and is generally credited with stimulating young Riley's interest in verse in the latter's more mature years.

Mr. Harris began writing as a boy. Before he was fifteen years old he had written poetry, and at twenty he was a regular contributor to the New York MERCURY. After 1880 he devoted all of his time to writing.

On Mar. 14, 1861, he married America Foster. He died in 1909.

> Information from *Representative Men of Indiana,* Vol. I, and the Greenfield Public Library.

* * *

The Man Who Tramps: a Story of Today. *Indianapolis, 1878.*

Interludes. *Indianapolis, 1893.*

HARRIS, THOMAS LEGRAND: 1863–1941.

Thomas LeGrand Harris, son of Greene and Jane Wilson Harris, was born in Hamilton County, Ind., on Apr. 8, 1863. He was educated at Indiana University (A.B., 1892; A.M., 1895) and at Harvard (A.M., 1899). In 1922 he received his Ph.D. degree from Indiana University.

After teaching in country schools and high schools of Indiana, he became an instructor in history at Indiana University in 1905, and in 1912 went to Baker University as professor of history and head of the department. He also taught history during a number of summers at Denver University. On Aug. 14, 1913, he married Adah Shafer. After his retirement from teaching he lived at Greencastle, Ind., where he died on Aug. 23, 1941.

> Information from *Who Was Who in America.*

* * *

The Trent Affair; Including a Review of the English and American Relations at the Beginning of the Civil War. *Indianapolis,* 1896.

America and England in 1861. *Baldwin City, Kan.,* 1928.

HARRISON, BENJAMIN: 1833–1901.

"Benjamin Harrison . . . twenty-third president of the U. S., was descended from Benjamin Harrison . . . , signer of the Declaration of Independence and governor of Virginia. His son, William Henry Harrison, established his home in Ohio on an extensive estate on the Ohio River just below Cincinnati; here he was residing in 1840 when elected president. On an adjoining farm lived his eldest son, John Scott Harrison, congressman for two terms. His second wife, Elizabeth Irwin, was the mother of Benjamin.

"Private tutors and typical country school teachers prepared Benjamin Harrison for Farmer's College. He finished his college course with distinction in 1852 at Miami University. On Oct. 20, 1853, he married a college friend, Caroline Lavinia Scott, daughter of Dr. John Scott, president of the Oxford Female Institute; to them two children, Russell and Mary, were born. From 1852 to 1854 he read law in the offices of Storer and Gwynne, prominent attorneys in Cincinnati. In 1854, he settled in Indianapolis . . . His active interest in politics began during the first year of his law practice, when the struggle over slavery was at white heat . . . In 1858 he served as secretary to the Republican state central committee of Indiana; he was elected city attorney in 1857, and in 1860 and 1864 reporter of the Supreme Court of Indiana.

". . . In 1862, he helped raise the 70th Indiana Infantry and was appointed its colonel by Gov. Oliver P. Morton. The regiment was hurried to Bowling Green, Ky., to assist in stopping Bragg, even though its colonel knew practically nothing of war and its rank and file knew less. Fortunately it was given the prosaic duty of guarding the Louisville & Nashville Railroad. Two years of devotion to duty and study changed the untrained colonel into a seasoned brigade commander. Harrison soon became unpopular, however, because he insisted on turning raw recruits into disciplined soldiers. In 1864, his command was attached to Sherman's army and participated in the bloody battles of the Atlanta campaign, during much of which Harrison was in command of his brigade . . . After the capture of Atlanta, Harrison returned to Indiana at Governor Morton's request to help combat Copperhead influence in the political campaign of 1864. This service prevented his participation in the march through Georgia, but he rejoined his command in the Carolinas and led it in the grand review in Washington. On Mar. 22, 1865, he was brevetted brigadier-general 'for ability and manifest energy and gallantry.' Three years of war had fully matured him.

"Returning to the practice of his profession, Harrison was immediately recognized as one of the ablest lawyers in his state . . .

"His active interest in public affairs and local philanthropy continued after the war . . . In 1872, Morton, who had developed an antipathy for Harrison, prevented his receiving the Republican nomination for governor. In 1876, however, Orth, the Republican candidate, was forced off the ticket in the middle of the campaign by an effective Democratic attack on his previous financial transactions. In this predicament, the Republican state committee persuaded Harrison, with his unsullied reputation, that it was his duty to his party to accept the nomination which he had previously declined. A bitterly fought campaign followed. Harrison appealed strongly to the old soldiers and to the cities. The Democratic candidate, James Douglas Williams, called 'Blue Jeans,' was a well-to-do farmer who had some of Lincoln's rugged honesty, simplicity of manner, and homely appearance. The Democrats capitalized these points further by speaking of Harrison as 'Kid-glove' Harrison; and portraying him as being as 'cold as an iceberg.' From this charge he was to suffer as long as he was a candidate for or an occupant of public office. The Democrats carried the state by 5,139 majority. Harrison regretted the defeat of his party, but personally preferred to give his time to law . . . In 1879, Hayes appointed him a member of the newly created Mississippi River Commission. This office he held until 1881. During the national railroad strike in 1877, Governor Williams appointed him a member of the citizens' committee to settle the strike in Indianapolis and also placed him in command of the state troops there . . .

"While senator (1881-87), as chairman of the important committee on territories, Harrison successfully guided through the Senate a bill to grant civil government to Alaska and a bill to admit Dakota as a state, though the latter did not pass the House . . . He generally aligned himself with the moderate, progressive group of his party. Meantime, the Democrats had carried Indiana in 1884, gerrymandered the state, and defeated him for re-election in 1886 by a margin of one vote, after a dramatic campaign . . .

"As early as 1883, Wharton Barker, a wealthy Quaker banker of Philadelphia, had surmised that the bitter hostility between Blaine and Arthur would cause the defeat of either if nominated for the presidency and had suggested to independent Republican leaders in the East that Harrison would unite all elements of his party and carry the doubtful state of Indiana. Harrison attended the Republican National Convention at Chicago in 1884 and was seriously considered as a possible 'dark horse' candidate. That his name was not presented was due to his own unwillingness to launch a personal campaign . . . Beginning in 1887, Harrison's friends carried on a quiet but well-organized campaign to secure his nomination in 1888. Though he was fourth on the first ballot at Chicago, he was nominated on the eighth. A spectacular, spirited campaign followed with the tariff as the chief issue . . . Harrison set a precedent by conducting an effective 'front porch' campaign, making a large number of short speeches to visiting delegations. The archaic electoral college gave him 233 votes and Cleveland 169, in spite of the fact that the American people indorsed Cleveland's administration by a popular plurality of 100,000 . . .

"Harrison appreciated the new forces which were sweeping the U. S. onward into imperialism. He took great pride in the new navy of steel ships being built under Secretary Benjamin F. Tracy and saw his policy of developing a merchant marine auspiciously begun . . .

"By the second year of Harrison's term, Quay, Platt, Alger, 'Czar' Reed, and others had begun to form an anti-Harrison wing in the Republican party to prevent his renomination . . . The implacable hostility of the 'bosses' increased as 1892 approached until its virulence is hard to overestimate. Harrison's friends rallied under the leadership of L. T. Michener and renominated him over Blaine and McKinley, but in the election he was overwhelmingly defeated by Cleveland . . .

"Harrison returned to his home in Indianapolis to engage in writing and in the practice of law . . . During the campaign of 1894, Harrison spoke for his party; in 1896, he again took a leading part in the campaign, though he had little admiration for Mark Hanna and McKinley . . . No other ex-president resumed the bona-fide practice of law on such a large scale and so successfully as did Harrison . . .

"On Apr. 6, 1896, Harrison married Mrs. Mary Scott (Lord) Dimmick, a niece of his first wife; to them a daughter, Elizabeth, was born . . . He died of pneumonia on Mar. 13, 1901 . . ."

> Condensed from A. T. V., *Dictionary of American Biography*, Vol. VIII.

* * *

NOTE. During his candidacy for, and term as, President of the U. S., speeches and essays by Benjamin Harrison were printed and reprinted officially and unofficially to such an extent as to make their identification, verification and listing far beyond the limitations of this work. Here, therefore, are listed only those publications deemed by the editors to be most significant.

The Speeches of President Harrison on His Recent Trip from the Atlantic to the Pacific. *Kansas City, Kan.,* 1891.

Thirty Days with President Harrison; Containing All of His Speeches in Full on His Recent Vacation-Trip Through the Country; Also, a Full and Graphic Account of All the Receptions and Banquets Tendered Him. *New York,* 1891.

Speeches of Benjamin Harrison, Twenty-Third President of the United States. *New York,* 1892.

Public Papers and Addresses. *Washington, D. C.,* 1893.

Legal Aspects of the Controversy Between the American Colonies and Great Britain; a Lecture. *Indianapolis,* 1894.

"No Mean City"; a Response by . . . at a Dinner . . . Indianapolis April 21, 1897. *Indianapolis,* 1897.

This Country of Ours. *New York,* 1897. (Republished in England, 1897, as The Constitution and Administration of the United States of America.)

Views of an Ex-President: Addresses and Writings on Subjects of Public Interest Since the Close of His Administration. *Indianapolis,* 1901.

The Correspondence Between Benjamin Harrison and James G. Blaine, 1882-1893; Collected and Edited by Albert T. Volwiler. *Philadelphia,* 1940.

HARRISON, JOHN SMITH: 1877–

John Smith Harrison was born at Orange, N. J., Feb. 3, 1877, the son of William Ogden and Lottie Ann Smith Harrison. He was educated at Columbia University, where he received the degrees of A.B., A.M., and Ph.D. In 1907 he married Elisabeth Shepard Southworth.

During his career as an educator he taught English in the New York public schools and at Kenyon College, and in 1916 became a professor at Butler University, Indianapolis.

> Information from *Who's Who in America* and the Indianapolis Public Library.

* * *

Platonism in English Poetry of the Sixteenth and Seventeenth Centuries. *New York,* 1903.

The Teachers of Emerson. *New York,* 1910.

The Vital Interpretation of English Literature. *Indianapolis,* 1928.

Types of English Poetry; a Study of Literary Organisms. *Indianapolis,* 1941.

HARRISON, THOMAS: 1813–1903.

Thomas Harrison was born in Yorkshire, England, on Jan. 19, 1813. When he was fourteen years old he was apprenticed to a printer for seven years and, following his term of service, came to the United States, where he settled in Springfield, O., and became the publisher of a political newspaper.

From 1841 to 1848 he was an assistant editor of the WESTERN CHRISTIAN ADVOCATE and the LADIES REPOSITORY. He held a position in the Ohio Conference High School in Springfield and four years later established Linden Hill Academy in New Carlisle, O., which soon became known as a place of learning in the West.

Professor Harrison came to Indiana in 1864 as president of Moore's Hill (now Evansville) College, a position he held for six years. He was later president of a college in Brookville, Ind., and principal of Shelbyville High School.

About 1890 he retired from public life and settled in Shelbyville, where he conducted classes for private pupils until his last illness.

He was ninety years old when he died on Apr. 18, 1903.

> Information from the Carnegie Public Library, Shelbyville, Indiana.

* * *

A New Mode of Illustrating Elocution . . . *Shelbyville, Ind.,* 1874.

HARRISON, THOMAS G.: ?–

Thomas G. Harrison was a resident of Indianapolis, at least during the Seventies and Eighties when he was a national leader in the publication of "amateur" newspapers, a craze which swept the nation in that period.

Publication of these was the work of one person, or of a small group, and was usually carried on in the editor-publisher's attic or cellar through the medium of a hand press. The papers began by criticizing each other's products and ended by vilifying and condemning; their chief object soon became campaigning for their owners' election to office in the many associations which resulted from the highly individualistic behavior of the owners in convention.

Harrison's paper, THE REVEILLE, must have been one of the best, or worst, since Harrison served as president of the National Amateur Press Association and of the Western Amateur Press Association.

He advertised his book, in one issue of his paper, as "The Largest Amateur Book Ever Published. The Best Amateur Book Ever Published. Endorsed by Every Reader as a Triumph of Amateur Book Publishing . . . Largest Book Ever Issued by an Amateur Journalist . . ."

The address of Harrison in the Eighties was carried as 83 E. Market St., Indianapolis.

> Information from *The Reveille,* Indianapolis.

* * *

Career & Reminiscences of an Amateur Journalist and History of Amateur Journalism. n.p. [Indianapolis], n.d. [1883].

HART, JOSEPH KINMONT: 1876–

Joseph Kinmont Hart, son of David N. and Lucy Kinmont Hart, was born near Columbia City, Ind., on Feb. 16, 1876, graduated from Franklin College in 1900, and received the Ph.D. degree from the University of Chicago in 1909. He married Frances Stuyvesant Uhrig in 1929.

During his career as an educator he taught at Baker University, the University of Washington, Reed College, the University of Wisconsin, Vanderbilt University, and Columbia University. From 1920 to 1926 he acted as editor of the department of education for THE SURVEY.

> Information from Franklin College.

* * *

Critical Study of Current Theories of Moral Education. *Chicago,* 1910.

Democracy in Education. *New York,* 1918.

Community Organization. *New York,* 1920.

The Discovery of Intelligence. *New York,* 1924.

Social Life and Institutions; an Elementary Study of Society. *Yonkers-on-Hudson, N. Y.,* 1924.

Light from the North; the Danish Folk High-Schools, Their Meanings for America. *New York,* 1927.

Adult Education. *New York,* 1927.

Prophet of a Nameless God; a Poem Founded on Some Passages in the Books of the Kings and Rendering the Legend of Elijah into Its Modern Meanings. *New York,* 1927.

Inside Experience; a Naturalistic Philosophy of Life and the Modern World. *New York,* 1927.

A Social Interpretation of Education. *New York,* 1929.

Creative Moments in Education; a Documentary Interpretation of the History of Education. *New York,* 1931.

Education for an Age of Power. *New York,* 1935.

Education During Leisure—For What? *Nashville, Tenn.,* 1935.

Mind in Transition; Patterns, Conflicts and Changes in the Evolution of the Mind. *New York,* 1938.

HARTZLER, JOHN ELLSWORTH: 1879–

John Ellsworth Hartzler, son of Joseph Z. and Mary Byler Hartzler, was born at Ligonier, Ind., on Feb. 2, 1879, and graduated from Goshen College in 1909. He was a student at McCormick Theological Seminary and received the B.D. degree from Union Theological Seminary in 1910. In 1919 he received the A.M. degree from the University of Chicago, in 1923 the LL.B. from Hamilton College of Law (Chicago), and in 1924 the Ph.D. from Hartford Theological Seminary. He married Marie M. Yoder on Oct. 5, 1910.

In 1904 he was ordained to the Mennonite ministry and from 1904 to 1910 served as pastor at Garden City, Mo. From 1910 to 1913 he was pastor at Elkhart, Ind., and professor of Bible at Goshen College, serving as president of that institution from 1913 to 1918. He was president of Bethel College (Kan.) from 1918 to 1920 and of Witmarsum Theological Seminary (O.) from 1921 to 1931. In 1931-32 and again in 1934-35 he was visiting professor at American University, Beirut, Syria, and at the Near East School of Theology. After 1936 he was a lecturer at Hartford Theological Seminary (Conn.).

> Information from Goshen College and from *Who's Who in America.*

* * *

Jacob's Ladder in Ten Sermons. *Scottdale, Pa.,* 1908.

Paths to Perdition. *Scottdale, Pa.,* 1910.

The Heresy of Russell and Russellism . . . *Scottdale, Pa.,* 1911.

Education Among the Mennonites of America. *Danvers, Ill.,* 1925.

Voices from Bible Lands. 1935.

HARTZLER, JONAS SMUCKER: 1857–

Jonas S. Hartzler, eldest son of Samuel and Sarah Smucker Hartzler, was born on Aug. 8, 1857, in Noble County, Ind., and grew up on a large farm there. He was educated in the public schools and in a normal school. At the age of eighteen he began to teach in a school near his home and he married Fannie C. Stutzlan on Feb. 5, 1880.

Ordained to the ministry of the Mennonite Church when he was twenty-four years old, he served as pastor, evangelist, and teacher (at Elkhart Institute and Goshen College) for sixty-six years. From 1923 to 1940 he was pastor of the Prairie Street Mennonite Church in Elkhart, Ind. He was also secretary of the Mennonite General Conference from 1898 to 1924 and editor of the RURAL EVANGEL after 1930.

> Information from Jonas S. Hartzler and the Goshen College Library.

* * *

Mennonite Church History (with Daniel Kauffman). *Scottdale, Pa.,* 1905.

Among Missions in the Orient and Observations by the Way (with J. S. Shoemaker). *Scottdale, Pa.,* 1912.

Mennonites in the World War or Non-Resistance Under Test. *Scottdale, Pa.,* 1921.

HATFIELD, JOHN THOMAS: 1851–?

John Thomas Hatfield, born in 1851, was reared in Greenfield, Ind. It may be assumed, from the title of his autobiography, that he took up evangelistic preaching in about 1880. He is reported to have died in California.

> Information from the Greenfield Public Library.

* * *

Thirty-Three Years a Live Wire; Life of John T. Hatfield, the Hoosier Evangelist, by Himself. *Cincinnati,* 1913.

HAWKINS, JOHN ANDREW: 1855–

Born at Greencastle, Ind., on Mar. 16, 1855, John Andrew Hawkins graduated from Indiana Asbury (now De Pauw) University in 1874, received the A.M. degree in 1878, and received the Ph.D. degree from Illinois Wesleyan in 1896. He married Mary M. Moffett on Apr. 2, 1889.

After studying theology at Princeton and at Union Theological Seminary, he was admitted to the ministry in 1886. In 1889 he was a pastor in Illinois, and in 1901-02 he served as president of Westfield College (Ill.).

> Information from De Pauw University's *Alumnal Record, 1920.*

* * *

Sorrow; Its Worth, Its Cure.

Devotional Series.

HAWORTH, PAUL LELAND: 1876–1938.

Paul Leland Haworth, son of John D. and Fanny Hornor Haworth, was born in West Newton, Ind., Aug. 28, 1876. He was educated at Indiana University (A.B., 1899; A.M. 1901) and at Columbia University (Ph.D., 1906). On Sept. 1, 1903, he married Martha B. Ackermann.

He was an instructor in history at various colleges and universities, including Michigan Northern State Normal, Columbia, Bryn Mawr, and Indiana. From 1922 until his death he was professor of history at Butler University, Indianapolis. In 1916 and in 1919 he conducted explorations of the Canadian Rocky Mountains on assignments for SCRIBNER'S MAGAZINE.

He was an unsuccessful Progressive nominee for the Indiana Legislature in 1912 and was a member of the Legislature during the 1921-22 session. In addition to his books he wrote stories and historical articles for leading magazines. He died Mar. 24, 1938.

Information from *Who Was Who in America* and the Indianapolis Public Library.

* * *

The Hayes-Tilden Disputed Presidential Election of 1876. *Cleveland, 1906.*

The Path of Glory. *New York, 1911.*

Reconstruction and Union, 1865-1912. *New York, 1912.*

America in Ferment. *Indianapolis, 1915.*

George Washington: Farmer; Being an Account of His Home Life and Agricultural Activities. *Indianapolis, 1915.* (New edition in 1925 under title George Washington: Country Gentleman.)

On the Headwaters of Peace River; a Narrative of a Thousand-Mile Canoe Trip to a Little Known Range of the Canadian Rockies. *New York, 1917.*

The United States in Our Own Times, 1865-1920. *New York, 1920.*

Trailmakers of the Northwest. *New York, 1921.*

Our Country's History. *Indianapolis, 1926.*

Caverns of Sunset, Being the Story of Patricia Percy's Quest in the Pays en Haute. *Indianapolis, 1930.*

HAY, JOHN MILTON: 1838–1905.

Son of Charles and Helen Leonard Hay, John Milton Hay was born in Salem, Ind., on Oct. 8, 1838. The family soon moved to Warsaw, Ill., where Hay received his grammar school training. Later he attended Pittsfield Academy and took some work at college level in Springfield. He entered and was graduated from Brown University in 1858, studied law in Springfield—where he became acquainted with Abraham Lincoln—and was admitted to the Illinois bar in 1861.

In the same year he became one of the private secretaries of Lincoln and later was appointed his adjutant and aide-de-camp, being breveted colonel of the U. S. Volunteers. At the end of the Civil War he was appointed secretary of the Paris legation and later of the legation at Madrid. He became charge d'affaires at Vienna and, in 1870, returned to the United States.

Taking up newspaper work, he became an editorial writer and night editor for the NEW YORK TRIBUNE and, in his spare time, began his literary career. His first book (and one of his best) concerned the middle western scene, from which he was now so long removed. It was his *Pike County Ballads.*

In 1874 he married Clara Stone of Cleveland, and the next year he gave up newspaper work to devote all of his time to literature. Some of his contributions to periodicals were particularly successful—notably his dialect sketch, "Little Breeches," which continued a standby of professional and amateur elocutionists for fifty years.

In 1879 he was appointed first assistant Secretary of State and served until 1881, when he returned to journalism to take over Whitelaw Reid's desk as editor of the NEW YORK TRIBUNE for six months. Taking up literature again, he is supposed to have written a novel, *Breadwinners,* which was published anonymously in 1884, and he joined with John G. Nicolay in writing their *Abraham Lincoln, a History.* This work was published serially in the CENTURY MAGAZINE in 1886 and 1887 and appeared in book form in 1890. It was enormously successful, selling, judging from the frequence of its appearance in second-hand book stores, to every literate Union veteran.

In 1897 John Hay was appointed Ambassador to the Court of St. James but was recalled the next year to become Secretary of State. He died in 1905 at Newbury, N. H.

The cause of literature would have prospered had John Hay been in less demand as a statesman. His writing is, at times, so clean cut and so brilliant that it gives promise, had it been followed more consistently, of an even higher quality than it possessed: and this is in no way derogatory to the quality of writing he did achieve—a quality usually as good as, and frequently better than, that of his best contemporaries.

Information from *Who Was Who in America*; and Kunitz and Haycraft—*American Authors, 1600-1900.*

* * *

Castilian Days: Sketches of Travel in Spain. *Boston*, 1871.

Jim Bludso of the Prairie Belle, and Little Breeches. *Boston*, 1871.

Little Breeches; a Pike County View of Special Providence. *New York*, 1871.

Pike County Ballads and Other Pieces. *Boston*, 1871.

Poems. *Boston*, 1871.

The Pioneers of Ohio. An Address Delivered Before the Pioneers' Association of the Western Reserve . . . August 27, 1879. *Cleveland*, 1879.

Balance Sheet of the Two Parties. *Cleveland*, 1880.

Amasa Stone. *New York*, 1883.

The Breadwinners; a Social Study. *New York*, 1884.

The Enchanted Shirt. *Chicago*, 1889.

Abraham Lincoln, a History (with John G. Nicolay). *New York*, 1890.

Complete Poetical Works of John Hay. *Boston*, 1896.

In Praise of Omar: an Address Before the Omar Khayyam Club. *Portland, Me.*, 1898.

On Fitzgerald's Rubaiyat of Omar Khayyam. *New York*, 1898.

Memorial Address on the Life and Character of William McKinley. *Washington*, 1903.

Addresses. *New York*, 1906.

Letters of John Hay and Extracts from Diary. 3 vols. *New York*, 1908.

A Poet in Exile: Early Letters of John Hay (edited by Tickenor). *Boston*, 1910.

Lincoln and the Civil War in the Diaries and Letters of John Hay; Selected . . . by Tyler Dennett. *New York*, 1939.

HAYDEN, SARAH MARSHALL: ?–

No biographical material on Mrs. Sarah Marshall Hayden has been found, but she was recognized as an Indiana resident during the period in which she wrote. "D. S. A.," writing on the Indiana book collection of Daniel Hough in the CINCINNATI GAZETTE of Dec. 7, 1876, says: "If we except Eggleston's and Wallace's books, Hoosier novelists have done little for the entertainment of their readers or for the reputation of their State. A few personal friends may have 'waded' through . . . Sarah Marshall Hayden's *Early Engagements,* and *Florence,*—a sequel . . . But these books certainly never engaged the attention of any considerable number of readers."

Information from D. S. A. in the CINCINNATI GAZETTE, Dec. 7, 1876.

* * *

Early Engagements. *Cincinnati*, 1854.

Florence. (pub. with Early Engagements in 1854 ed.)

Mr. Langden's Mistake. *Washington*, 1901.

HAZZARD, GEORGE E.: 1845–1926.

Born in New Castle, Ind., on July 22, 1845, George E. Hazzard married Maria Eudora Tobey on June 30, 1870. He was the author of an excellent county history.

Information from the New Castle Public Library.

* * *

History of Henry County. *New Castle*, 1906. 2 vols.

HEATH, PERRY SANFORD: 1857–1927.

"Perry Sanford Heath (Aug. 31, 1857-Mar. 30, 1927), newspaper man and politician, was one of the six sons of Jacob W. and Rhoda A. Perdieu Heath, of Muncie, Ind. . . . Perry shifted for himself from an early age. At twenty-one he was editor and proprietor of Muncie's first daily newspaper, and three years later he was publishing the PIONEER at Aberdeen, Dakota Territory. For the next twelve years he worked as a newspaper correspondent at Washington . . . From 1894 to 1896 he was editor of the CINCINNATI COMMERCIAL-GAZETTE and . . . had a significant part in directing the publishing and printing for the Republican National Committee.

"When the McKinley administration took office Heath was made first assistant postmaster-general . . . He installed the rural free delivery system although some experimenting had been done during the Cleveland administration, and within three years the number of routes provided in this service was increased from 44 to 1,214 . . . When he resigned from the service in July, 1900, serious irregularities had come to light in the Cuban postal service, then administered by the United States . . . In 1903 came disclosures involving men in the department at Washington, several of whom owed their places to him . . . but when charges were made against him after his resignation, the District Attorney did not find sufficient evidence to indict him. In the meantime he had returned to newspaper work, having bought the SALT LAKE TRIBUNE in 1901, and established the TELEGRAM, an evening paper, in the following year. He had married Ella Conway, of Louisville, Ky., in 1890 . . ."

Condensed from W. B. S., *Dictionary of American Biography,* Vol. VIII.

* * *

A Hoosier in Russia. *New York, 1888.*

HEINEY, ENOS BOYD: 1868–

Enos Boyd Heiney (pen name, Ean Boyd Heiney) was born on a farm in Huntington County, Ind., on Feb. 26, 1868. He attended the country schools, Indiana State Normal School, and for twenty-two years taught in the country and town schools of Indiana. In 1910 he became traveling representative for a school book publishing company.

Mr. Heiney contributed verses and prose sketches to newspapers and poetry magazines, the first appearing in the INDIANAPOLIS JOURNAL in 1886.

Information from Enos Boyd Heiney.

* * *

Poets and Poetry of Indiana (compiler and editor with Benjamin S. Parker). *New York,* 1900.
Friends Ysame. 1903.
Salamonie and Other Rhymes. 1905.
In Jest or Earnest. 1907.
The Dreamer and Other Rhymes. *Greencastle, Ind.,* n.d. [1936].
Doleful Doggerel. 1937.
The Rubaiyat of a Four-Flusher. 1938.
Olla-Podrida. *Coatesville, Ind.,* 1939.
A Hindu Myth. *Coatesville, Ind.,* n.d. [1941].
Ballad of a Bookman. *Indianapolis,* 1942.
Kites in a Tree. *Coatesville, Ind.,* 1944.
The Road to Town. *Coatesville, Ind.,* 1945.
Through the Looking-Glass. *Coatesville, Ind.,* 1946.

HELLER, ISAAC: 1809–1836.

Isaac Heller (Young), son of John and Sarah Heller Young, was born in Dauphin County, Pa., on May 2, 1809. Tried for the murder of a young girl in his native state and acquitted on grounds of insanity, he was confined in chains at the poor house of the community.

After his release—apparently in 1831—he came West and settled outside the town of Liberty, Ind., changed his name from Young to Heller, married, joined a church and prospered moderately. Soon, however, he began to develop what appeared to be a religious mania, began to talk of his crime and to neglect work.

On Feb. 27, 1836, he killed his wife and their three small children with an axe. He fled but was captured, arrested and eventually hanged. The pamphlet giving his life story was written—or more probably dictated —by him while awaiting execution.

Information from Smith, O. H.—*Early Indiana Trials and Sketches* and the Indiana State Library.

* * *

The Life and Confession of Isaac Heller Alias Isaac Young Who Was Executed at Liberty, Union County, Ia. on the 29th Day of April, 1836, for the Murder of His Wife and Three Infant Children, to Which Is Appended a Brief History of the Trial, Together with the Sentence Pronounced Upon Him by Hon. Samuel Bigger, Presiding Judge. *Liberty, Ind.,* 1836.

HELM, THOMAS B.: 1822–1889.

"Thomas B. Helm . . . was born in Fayette County in 1822. In 1832 he moved to Logansport, Ind., and when he grew to manhood was a surveyor and civil engineer for several years. He was the first superintendent of schools in Cass County.

"Mr. Helm wrote most of the text for *Cass County Atlas* published in 1878 but his greatest contribution was *History of Cass County,* a work of 976 pages, published in 1886."

Powell—*History of Cass County,* 1913.

* * *

History of Cass County, Indiana. *Chicago,* 1878.
History of Hamilton County, Indiana. *Chicago,* 1880.
History of Allen County, Indiana. *Chicago,* 1880.
History of Delaware County, Indiana. *Chicago,* 1881.
History of Carroll County, Indiana. 1882.
History of Wabash County, Indiana. *Chicago,* 1884.
History of Cass County, Indiana. *Chicago,* 1886.

HENDERSON, CHARLES RICHMOND: 1848–1915.

"Charles Richmond Henderson (Dec. 17, 1848-Mar. 29, 1915), Baptist clergyman, sociologist, was born in Covington, Ind., the son of Albert and Loranna [probably Larainne] (Richmond) Henderson. His education was received at the old University of Chicago (A.B., 1870) and at the Baptist Union Theological Seminary (B.D., 1873). In 1901 he received the degree of Ph.D. from the University of Leipzig. He was ordained to the Baptist ministry and became pastor of the First Baptist Church of Terre Haute, Ind., in

1873, and was married the same year to Ella Levering of Lafayette, Ind. In 1882 he accepted a call to the pastorate of the Woodward Avenue Baptist Church, Detroit, where he remained until 1892 when he was invited to join the faculty of the new University of Chicago as university chaplain, assistant professor of sociology, and university recorder. From 1894 to 1897 he was associate professor of sociology, and from the latter date to his death, professor of sociology, becoming head of the department of practical sociology in 1904. Throughout these years he remained the chaplain of the University.

"As a student he served a small church back of the stockyards in Chicago, and from this experience dates his interest in social problems. At Terre Haute he was the first president of the local charity organization, and on going to Detroit he at once allied himself with the charitable organizations of that city. While still a pastor he made a study of prisons and prison management and became a recognized authority in that field. He took an active interest in labor problems, and when a strike on the Detroit street car lines was imminent he was largely responsible for settling the differences between the contending parties. At the University of Chicago he found opportunity to give himself more freely to social studies and during his service there he published sixteen books and more than one hundred articles. Many of these publications are of pioneer importance in the field of penology, industrial insurance, and industrial legislation . . . Besides contributing frequently to sociological and religious journals, he served for many years as associate editor of the AMERICAN JOURNAL OF THEOLOGY; THE AMERICAN JOURNAL OF SOCIOLOGY, and the JOURNAL OF THE AMERICAN INSTITUTE OF CRIMINAL LAW AND CRIMINOLOGY. He was president of the National Conference of Charities, 1898-99 . . . president of the United Charities of Chicago, 1913 . . . president of the National Prison Association, 1901-02.

"As a teacher and investigator he was a pioneer in a new field . . . He was characterized, by those who knew him and his work, as both academic and practical, respected both by scientists and men of practical affairs. Overwork was responsible for his sudden death, which occurred at Charleston, S. C., to which place he had gone with Mrs. Henderson in March 1915, expecting to recover his health . . ."

> Condensed from W. W. S., *Dictionary of American Biography*, Vol. VIII.

* * *

Introduction to the Study of the Dependent, Defective and Delinquent Classes. *Boston*, 1893.

Catechism for Social Observation. *Boston, 1894.*

The Development of the Doctrine in the Epistles. *Philadelphia, 1896.*

The Social Spirit in America. *Meadville, Pa., 1897.*

Social Elements, Institutions, Character, Progress. *New York, 1898.*

Social Settlements. *New York, 1899.*

Practical Sociology in the Service of Social Ethics. *Chicago, 1903.*

Modern Prison Systems. *Washington, D. C., 1903.*

World Currents in Charity Theory and Practice. *Philadelphia, 1903.*

Die Arbeiter-Versicherung in den Vereinigten Staaten von Nord-Amerika. *Berlin,* 1907. (Published in the United States, Chicago, 1909, as *Industrial Insurance in the United States.*)

Social Duties from the Christian Point of View. *Chicago,* 1909.

Education with Reference to Sex. *Chicago,* 1909.

Reasonable Social Policy for Christian People. *Philadelphia,* 1909.

Preventive Agencies and Methods. *New York,* 1910.

Working-Men's Insurance. *Philadelphia,* 1912.

Social Programmes in the West: Lectures Delivered in the Far East. *Chicago,* 1913.

The Cause and Cure of Crime. *Chicago,* 1914.

Citizens in Industry. *New York,* 1915.

HENDRICKS, ELDO LEWIS: 1866–1938.

Eldo Lewis Hendricks, son of Samuel and Henrietta Stinehouse Hendricks, was born in Rossville, Ind., on Oct. 2, 1866, graduated from Franklin College in 1894, and received the A.M. degree from Indiana University in 1899. He also studied at Harvard, the University of Chicago, and Columbia.

In 1894 he was county superintendent of schools in Johnson County, Ind. He was superintendent of schools in Delphi, Ind., from 1901 to 1906, when he became supervisor in the Indianapolis schools. After 1915 he was president of Central Missouri State Teachers College. In 1930-31 Mr. Hendricks was a member of the Fact Finding Commission to India.

He married Viola Murphy in 1910 and died on Nov. 22, 1938.

> Information from *Who Was Who in America.*

* * *

After Ten Years. 1904.

History and Civil Government of Indiana. *New York,* 1908.

A Study in Reading. *Chicago,* 1911.

The Teacher in Politics. *Warrensburg, Mo.,* 1920.

Missouri's Opportunities . . . n.p., n.d. [1921].

The Scope of the Work to Be Done by the Teachers College . . . n.p., 1923.

Our Colleges and the Church . . . *Warrensburg, Mo.*, 1926.

In-Service Training for Rural School Teachers . . . n.p., 1928.

Rimming the Mediterranean. *Kansas City, Mo.*, 1935.

HENNINGER, JOSEPH BURNS: 1847–1943.

Born in Clinton County, Ind., in 1847, Joseph Burns Henninger was an orphan at nine years of age. During the Civil War, when he was thirteen years old, he enlisted in the Union forces, was sent home, and re-enlisted when he was sixteen. He graduated from Barnes Medical University in St. Louis in 1900 and practiced in the U. S. and Great Britain. He was forced to resign from the presidency of Riley Ophthalmology College in St. Louis because of ill health. In 1938, at the age of ninety-one, he was still active and had served eight years as Assistant Adjutant General and Assistant Quartermaster General of the Grand Army of the Republic, with offices in the State House in Indianapolis.

Information from the Barry Ms.

* * *

Crumbs. n.d.

HENRY, DAVID W.: 1852–

Born in Columbus, O., in 1852, David W. Henry was a long-time resident of Terre Haute, Ind.

Information from the Emmeline Fairbanks Memorial Library, Terre Haute, Indiana.

* * *

Richard W. Thompson Memorial. *St. Joseph, Mich.*, n.d. [1906].

Abraham Lincoln: an Address Delivered by Hon. David W. Henry . . . Terre Haute, Ind., Feb. 12, 1925. *Terre Haute, Ind.*, 1925.

HENRY, WILLIAM ELMER: 1857–1936.

William Elmer Henry, son of John and Elizabeth Chapman Henry, was born near Connersville, Ind., on Nov. 7, 1857. He was graduated from the Indiana State Normal School in 1885, received the A.B. degree, 1891, and the A.M. degree, 1892, from Indiana University, and carried on graduate study at the University of Chicago.

He was an instructor in English at Indiana University, 1891-93, professor of English at Franklin College, 1895-97, Indiana State Librarian, 1897-1906, and librarian of the University of Washington from 1906 until his retirement in 1929.

Mr. Henry married Margaret Atkinson Roberts on July 30, 1895, and, after her death in 1900, married Sylvia M. Allen on Mar. 26, 1903. He died on Mar. 20, 1936.

Information from *Who Was Who in America.*

* * *

Literature as a Subject for College Study. *Franklin, Ind.*, 1895.

Librarianship; What It Implies. *Indianapolis*, 1902.

Municipal and Institutional Libraries of Indiana. History, Condition and Management. *Indianapolis*, 1904.

Some Elements of Indiana's Population; or, Roads West and Their Early Travelers. *Indianapolis*, 1908.

My Own Opinions Upon Libraries and Librarianship. *Seattle, Wash.*, 1931.

The Indiana State Library, the Historical Library of the State, Established 1825. *Indianapolis*, n.d.

HEPBURN, CHARLES McGUFFEY: 1859–1929.

Charles McGuffey Hepburn, son of Andrew Dousa and Henrietta McGuffey Hepburn, was born in Rockbridge County, Va., in 1859 and graduated from Davidson College in 1878. In 1880 he received the LL.B. degree from the University of Virginia and in 1908 the LL.D. from Miami University. He married Julia Benedict on Oct. 10, 1891.

After teaching at Davidson College for a year, he was admitted to the Ohio bar in 1881 and practiced at Cincinnati until 1903. From 1897 to 1903 he was also a lecturer at the Cincinnati Law School. In 1903 he moved to Bloomington, Ind., where he taught in the law school of Indiana University. From 1918 to 1925 he served as dean of the law school and after 1925 as research professor of law. He wrote at least five technical law books besides the title listed here.

He died in 1929.

Information from *Indiana University, 1820-1904*, and *Who Was Who in America.*

* * *

The Historical Development of Code Pleading in America and England . . . *Cincinnati*, 1897.

HERRON, GEORGE DAVIS: 1862–1925.

"George Davis Herron (Jan. 21, 1862-Oct. 9, 1925), clergyman, lecturer, and writer, was born at Montezuma, Ind., of devoutly religious parents of Scotch origin, William and Isabella (Davis) Herron. His childhood he describes as obsessed with premonitions of a religious world mission, out of which, perhaps, grew the vivid and passionate conviction of messiahship and of an imminent kingdom of heaven on earth which in changing forms dominated his mature life. He attended the preparatory department of Ripon College, Ripon, Wis., from 1879 to 1882, working at the printer's trade to secure funds. In 1883 he married Mary Everhard and entered the ministry. His further education consisted of reading and independent reflection.

"Herron first attracted public notice in 1891 when as pastor of the First Congregational Church of Lake City, Minn., he addressed the state Association of Congregational Ministers, meeting at Minneapolis, upon the theme: 'The Message of Jesus to Men of Wealth.' This address, published that same year, was an earnest and moving appeal for the application of Christian ethics to business, and resulted in Herron's being called to the pastorate of the First Congregational Church of Burlington, Ia. Seventeen months later a professorship of applied Christianity was founded for his occupancy in Iowa College (later Grinnell) by Mrs. E. D. Rand of Burlington. During the six years of his service Iowa College became the center of nation-wide interest because of his attempt to translate Christianity into social, political, and economic terms. He brought to this work a fervor and eloquence which attracted students and impressed many men and women of insight and influence. His scathing criticism of existing institutions aroused bitter antagonism, however, and ultimately alienated many of his most loyal supporters.

"As a consequence, he resigned his professorship in 1899. Joining the Socialist party, he tried to organize within it a 'social crusade,' which should give religious character to the movement. Mrs. E. D. Rand and her daughter, Carrie Rand, cooperated with him in various undertakings to this end in Chicago and in New York. Partly through his influence the Rand School of Social Sciences was founded in New York City in 1906 by Mrs. Rand. In March 1901 his wife divorced him for 'cruelty culminating in desertion,' and was given for the support of herself and the five children the personal fortune of Carrie Rand, amounting to sixty thousand dollars. On May 25, 1901, he and Carrie Rand were married in New York City by a ceremony, wherein

'each chose the other as companion,' thus dramatizing his avowed opposition to 'all coercive institutions.' He was at once deposed from the ministry and shortly afterward took up permanent residence with his wife and her mother upon an estate near Fiesole, Italy. . . .

"Like many Socialists, he viewed the World War at its outbreak as the capitalist catastrophe prophesied by Karl Marx. Later, however, he became violently anti-German, abandoned his pre-war platform, and broke with the Socialist party for its tolerance of Germany and of Bolshevism, trying even to divert from the Rand School the funds of the Rand estate. America's entrance into the war he envisioned as a 'sacred crusade' wherein 'for the first time in the earth's annals, a great and powerful people has gone to war for humanity' . . . Of Woodrow Wilson he wrote an extravagant eulogy, *Woodrow Wilson and the World's Peace* (1917). During the negotiations for peace he appears to have had a large place in the confidence of the German emissaries and of President Wilson. He influenced the German representatives to trust Wilson's power to enforce upon the Allies conditions favorable to Germany . . . Early in the Russian Revolution he seems to have been favorable to the Bolshevists but he soon became alienated from their program. President Wilson's appointment of Herron and William Allen White as America's representatives to the abortive Prinkipo Conference aroused a storm of protest in the American press, based chiefly upon Herron's views regarding marriage. When the terms of peace became known he was inevitably discredited with both radicals and conservatives and was bitterly hated in Prussia. He turned to Italy as a final Utopian hope and in 1920 published in periodicals of Europe and America his 'ecstatic confidence' that Italy would become a 'more Christly society than the world has yet known.' On the death of his second wife in 1914, he married Friede B. Schoeberle. His books are for the most part collections of sermons and lectures, or reprints of articles in American and European periodicals . . . His war papers, two volumes of which were sealed for twenty-five years, were deposited in the Hoover Library of Stanford University. He died at Munich, Bavaria, in his sixty-fourth year . . ."

Condensed from C. M. S., *Dictionary of American Biography*, Vol. VIII.

* * *

The Larger Christ. *Chicago,* 1891.

The Message of Jesus to Men of Wealth. *New York,* 1891.

The Call of the Cross; Four College Sermons. *New York,* 1892.

A Plea for the Gospel. *New York, 1892.*

The New Redemption: a Call to the Church to Reconstruct Society According to the Gospel of Christ. *New York, 1893.*

The Christian Society. *Chicago, 1894.*

The Christian State: a Political Vision of Christ: a Course of Six Lectures Delivered in Churches in Various American Cities. *New York, 1895.*

Social Meanings of Religious Experiences. *New York, 1896.*

Between Caesar and Jesus. *New York, 1899.*

Why I Am a Socialist. *Chicago, 1900.*

Wagner and Parsifal. *1903.*

The Day of Judgment. *Chicago, 1904.*

From Revolution to Revolution: Address in Memory of Paris Commune, 1871. *Chicago, 1907.*

Woodrow Wilson and the World's Peace. *New York, 1917.*

The Menace of Peace. *New York, 1917.*

Germanism and the American Crusade. *New York, 1918.*

Greater War. *New York, 1919.*

The Defeat in the Victory. *London, 1921.*

The Revival of Italy. *London, 1922.*

War and Peace Under Socialism.

HERSCHELL, WILLIAM: 1873–1939.

William Herschell, Hoosier journalist and poet, was born in Spencer, Ind., on Nov. 17, 1873. As a youth he lived in Huntingburg, Ind., and began his newspaper career there as a reporter for the INDEPENDENT. For three years he worked on the PRINCETON NEWS, then came to Indianapolis, where he spent the remainder of his life. He was associated with the INDIANAPOLIS NEWS for thirty-seven years.

Herschell started as a feature writer for the NEWS and eventually added poetry as a medium of expression. His poems about everyday life and simple people were widely read throughout Indiana, and his patriotic songs during the first World War were familiar to the nation. The most popular of his war songs was "Long Boy," known to most people as "Good-bye, Ma! Good-bye, Pa!" the opening lines of the refrain. In recognition of his war poetry he was awarded an honorary A.M. degree by Wabash College in 1917.

He was married to Josephine Pugh in 1908 and died in Indianapolis on Dec. 2, 1939.

Information from *Who's Who in America* and the Indianapolis Public Library.

* * *

Songs of the Streets and Byways. *Indianapolis, 1915.*

The Kid Has Gone to the Colors; and Other Verse. *Indianapolis, 1917.*

The Smile-Bringer, and Other Bits of Cheer. *Indianapolis, 1919.*

Howdy All, and Other Care-Free Rhymes. *Indianapolis, 1922.*

Meet the Folks. *Indianapolis, 1924.*

Hitch and Come In. *Indianapolis, 1928.*

HERSHEY, AMOS SHARTLE: 1867–1933.

Amos Shartle Hershey, son of Martin and Mary Ann Shartle Hershey, was born in Hershey, Pa., on July 11, 1867, and graduated from Harvard University in 1892. In 1894 he received the Ph.D. degree from the University of Heidelberg. He was a student in Harvard Law School in 1891-92 and studied in Paris in 1894-95. He married Lillian Wilcox on Sept. 6, 1892.

In 1895 he moved to Bloomington, Ind., where he was a member of the faculty of Indiana University from 1895 to 1933, serving as assistant professor of political science until 1900, associate professor of European history and politics until 1905, and professor of political science and international law after 1905. After 1914 he was head of the department of political science. In 1918-19 he was a member of the staff of the American Commission to Negotiate Peace, Paris.

He died on June 12, 1933.

Information from *Indiana University, 1820-1904,* and *Who Was Who in America.*

* * *

Die Kontrolle Über Die Gesetzgebung in den Vereinigten Staaten von Nord Amerika. *Heidelberg, 1894.*

The International Law and Diplomacy of the Russo-Japanese War. *New York, 1906.*

The Essentials of International Public Law. *New York, 1912.* (Reissued in 1927 as The Essentials of International Public Law and Organization.)

Modern Japan; Social, Industrial, Political (with Susanne W. Hershey). *Indianapolis, 1919.*

Les Doctrines de Calvo et de Drago.

HERVEY, JAMES WALTER: 1819–1905.

Dr. James Walter Hervey, first Indiana writer to attempt "horror stories," was born near Brookville, Ind., in 1819. He studied medicine in Ohio and practiced in Indianapolis and Oakland City, Ind.

He was a member of the State Legislature in 1854 and served as a surgeon in the Civil War. He was later active in the beginnings of public health work in the state.

Information from Briscoe, Orah Cole—unpublished Ms. *The Hoosier School of Fiction.*

* * *

The Scroll and Locket; or the Maniac of the Mound. *Indianapolis,* 1858.

HESSLER, ROBERT: 1861–1942.

"Robert Hessler, A.M., M.D., was a physician of Logansport, Ind. and a thorough student of science and medicine. He contributed to many scientific and medical journals and in 1912 he published a popular medical work . . . which contained many original ideas."

From Powell—*History of Cass County,* 1913.

* * *

The Evolution of Medicine in Indiana. *Indianapolis,* 1906.
Dusty Air and Ill Health: a Study of Prevalent Ill Health and Causes. *Indianapolis,* 1912.
Mineral Waters of Indiana with Indications for Their Therapeutic Application. *Logansport, Ind.,* n.d.

HIATT, JAMES M.: ?–?

Except for the fact that he was a resident of Indianapolis, at least between 1864-78, and that he was a newspaper man and reformer, no information has come to light on the life of James M. Hiatt. On his last known book he collaborated with Luther Benson, Indiana temperance worker.

Information from the Indiana State Library and books by Hiatt.

* * *

The Political Manual, Comprising Numerous Important Documents Connected with the Political History of America. *Indianapolis,* 1864. (Republished in German, 1865.)
The Test of Loyalty. *Indianapolis,* 1864.
The War for Democratic Succession. n.p., 1866.
The Voter's Text Book. *Indianapolis,* 1868.
Murder and Mob Law in Indiana. *Indianapolis,* 1872.
The Ribbon Workers (with Luther Benson). *Chicago,* 1878.

HIBBARD, MRS. J. R.: ?–?

D. S. A., writing in the CINCINNATI DAILY GAZETTE for Dec. 7, 1876, of Daniel Hough's collection of books by Indiana authors, states that *"Flossy*

Lee, and *Flossy Lee at the Mountains,* are a couple of books for children that have been very popular. Their author, 'Faith Wynne,' is Mrs. Dr. J. R. Hibbard, of Richmond."

No further biographical data upon Mrs. Hibbard has been located, but the Flossy Lee books were, and long continued to be, reading matter which could be unanimously endorsed for righteous tone and moral content.

Information from D. S. A. in the CINCINNATI GAZETTE, Dec. 7, 1876.

* * *

Flossy Lee at the Mountains. *Philadelphia,* 1870.
Flossy Lee. *Philadelphia,* 1871.

HIBBEN, WILLIAM W.: ?–?

William W. Hibben, prominent Indiana minister from 1835 to 1865, was born in Uniontown, Pa., and removed with his parents to Ohio at an early age.

He was licensed as a Methodist minister at Hillsborough, O., in 1832 and came to Indiana in March, 1835. He held pastorates at Lafayette, Indianapolis and elsewhere in the state, retiring from the ministry after a term as presiding elder of the Jeffersonville district.

Throughout his career he wrote for newspapers and the religious press and acted as associate editor of a periodical, THE MASONIC ADVOCATE, for several years after 1871.

Information from Nowland—*Sketches of Prominent Citizens of 1876.*

* * *

Rev. James Havens, One of the Heroes of Indiana Methodism. *Indianapolis,* 1872.

HIGGINS, WILLIAM R.: 1838–1895.

William R. Higgins was born in Logansport, Ind., in 1838. He was educated in the Logansport schools and was graduated from Wabash College in 1861, receiving his M.A. in 1865. He also was graduated from Lane Theological Seminary and entered the Presbyterian ministry. He married Mary E. Condon on Dec. 29, 1861. The Rev. Mr. Higgins died in Terre Haute, Ind., on July 4, 1895.

Information from Powell—*History of Cass County* and the Wabash College Archives.

* * *

Cardinal Points. *Cleona, Pa.,* n.d.

HIGHT, JOHN J.: 1834–1886.

Born at Bloomington, Ind., on Dec. 4, 1834, John J. Hight graduated from Indiana University in 1854. For eleven years he was an associate editor of the WESTERN CHRISTIAN ADVOCATE, a Methodist publication. He died at Cincinnati, O., on Dec. 18, 1886.

Information from the Princeton Public Library.

* * *

Hight's History of the Fifty-Eighth Indiana Regiment (with Gilbert R. Stormont). *Princeton, Ind.,* 1895.

HILLES, HOWARD: 1877–

Howard Hilles was born near Alliance, O., on Sept. 12, 1877. After attending grade and high schools at Mt. Union and Alliance, O., he studied at Mt. Union College for two years.

He married Miss Sadie Croad, and the couple purchased a farm west of Bourbon, Ind., in 1906. He regularly contributed verse to newspapers in the neighborhood.

Information from a newspaper sketch by Mrs. S. E. Boys.

* * *

Rhymes at Random. 1910.
Untraveled Trails. *Boston,* 1916.

HITT, ROSE BIRCH (MRS. ISAAC R., JR.): 1863–

Rose Birch Hitt, daughter of the Rev. William J. Birch was born in Elkhart, Ind., April 25, 1863. She graduated from the Fort Wayne High School and attended Northwestern University. In 1887 she came to Logansport with her parents and resided there until 1890. She was married in Logansport Nov. 13, 1889, to Isaac R. Hitt, Jr. of Chicago, and later resided in Washington, D. C.

Information supplied by the Logansport Public Library.

* * *

Hitt Instrument Tuned. *New York,* 1904.

HOAGLAND, MERICA EVANS: 1858–1933.

Born at Fort Wayne, Ind., in 1858, Merica Evans Hoagland contributed articles to the INDIANAPOLIS NEWS in 1915 and 1916. She died in Indianapolis in 1933. She was interested in the advancement of women in professional and business fields, in clubs, and in library work.

Information from the Barry Ms.

* * *

Bits of Indiana History. *Indianapolis,* 1915.

HOBBS, BARNABAS COFFIN: 1815–1892.

Born at Salem, Ind., on Oct. 4, 1815, Barnabas Coffin Hobbs began teaching at the age of eighteen and continued in that profession throughout his life.

In 1839 he took charge of a boarding school at Mt. Pleasant, O., and in 1843 he married Rebecca Tatum and moved to Richmond, Ind., where he became superintendent of what is now Earlham College. From 1851 to 1866 he served as president of Friends' Bloomingdale Academy. He became first president of Earlham College in 1866 and professor of English literature. In 1870 he served a term as state Superintendent of Public Instruction, in 1871 became president of Bloomingdale Academy again, and in 1879 was sent on a peace mission to Europe, remaining abroad for two years.

Mr. Hobbs was awarded an honorary A.M. by Wabash College in 1858 and an LL.D. by Indiana University in 1870.

He died at Bloomingdale, Ind., on June 22, 1892.

Information from the Rockville Public Library.

* * *

Earlham Lectures. *Richmond, Ind.,* 1885.

HODELL, CHARLES WESLEY: 1872–

Charles Wesley Hodell, son of George and Mary E. Shoemaker Hodell, was born in Lawrenceburg, Ind., on Apr. 16, 1872. After graduating from De Pauw University in 1892 and receiving the Ph.D. degree from Cornell in 1894, he was an instructor in English and history at Shady Side Academy in Pittsburgh from 1894 to 1897 and professor of English at Woman's (now Goucher) College in Baltimore from 1897 to 1912. Before his death he was treasurer and director of the Finance and Guaranty Company in Baltimore. He married Willa M. Ricketts on Apr. 5, 1899.

He edited, criticized and traced the sources of some Browningiana in works not listed here.

Information from *Who Was Who in America.*

* * *

The Ring and the Book; Its Moral Spirit and Motive. *Shelbyville, Ind.,* 1894.

HODGIN, CYRUS WILBURN: 1842–1908.

Cyrus Wilburn Hodgin, son of Tilnias and Rachel Hinshaw Hodgin, was born near Farmland, Ind., on Feb. 12, 1842, and graduated from Illinois State Normal University in 1867. He received his A.M. degree from Earlham College in 1888 and in 1892-93 was a graduate student in history and political science at the University of Chicago. He married Emily Caroline Chandler on Aug. 22, 1867.

In 1868-69 he served as principal of the Richmond High School, from 1872 to 1881 as professor of history in Indiana State Normal School, in 1882-83 as superintendent of the Rushville, Ind., schools, and from 1883 to 1887 as principal of the Richmond Normal School. He became connected with Earlham College in 1887 as professor of history and political economy. From 1896 to 1898 he acted as conductor of the Chautauqua College of History. A lecturer on peace, education, temperance, and arbitration, he died in 1908.

Information from *Who Was Who in America*.

* * *

Indiana and the Nation. *Boston*, 1893.

A Study of the American Commonwealth (as Reflected by Orations of Burke and Webster) (with James Albert Woodburn). *Boston*, 1893.

A Short Sketch of the History of Indiana. *New York*, 1906.

HOLCOMBE, JOHN WALKER: 1853–1940.

John Walker Holcombe was born in LaPorte, Ind., in 1853. He graduated from Harvard University and became a teacher, serving two terms as Indiana State Superintendent of Public Instruction in the early Eighties. He married Effie Burford McOuat of Indianapolis.

In 1887 he went to Washington, where he was employed first by the Bureau of Education and later by the Department of the Interior. He died Feb. 10, 1940, in Washington, D. C.

Information from the INDIANAPOLIS STAR for Feb. 13, 1940.

* * *

The School Law of Indiana. *Indianapolis*, 1884.

The Life and Public Services of Thomas A. Hendricks (with Hubert M. Skinner). *Indianapolis*, 1886.

The Electoral College. *Washington, D. C.,* 1913.

HOLLAND, ERNEST OTTO: 1874–

Ernest Otto Holland, son of Philip C. and Ann A. Chittenden Holland, was born at Bennington, Ind., on Feb. 4, 1874, and graduated from Indiana University in 1895. He studied in Europe in 1905, 1909, and 1923-24, received the Ph.D. degree from Columbia University in 1912, and was awarded LL.D. degrees by Indiana University (1937) and Whitman College (1942).

After teaching in the high schools of Indiana for five years, in 1900 he became head of the English department of Boys' High School in Louisville, remaining in this position until 1905, when he joined the faculty of Indiana University. From 1911 to 1916 he was superintendent of schools in Louisville, and after 1916 he was president of Washington State College.

Information from *Who's Who in America*.

* * *

The Pennsylvania State Normal Schools and Public School System. *New York*, 1912.

College and University Administration (with E. E. Lindsay). *New York*, 1930.

HOLLIDAY, FERDINAND C.: 1814–?

Born near Mt. Auburn, N. Y., in 1814, Ferdinand C. Holliday came to Indiana with his family in 1817. His youth was spent in Dearborn County, and he came to Indianapolis in 1847, where he was pastor of Wesley Chapel for two years. He was one of the founders of Moore's Hill College.

Information from the Indianapolis Public Library.

* * *

Anniversary Book for Sunday Schools. 1837.

Life and Times of Rev. Allen Wiley, A.M., Containing Sketches of Early Methodist Preachers in Indiana, and Notices of the Introduction and Progress of Methodism in the State; Also, Including His Original Letters, Entitled; "A Help to the Performance of Ministerial Duties." By Rev. F. C. Holliday, A.M. Edited by Rev. D. W. Clark, D.D. *Cincinnati*, 1853.

A Bible Handbook, Theologically Arranged; Designed to Facilitate the Finding of Proof-Texts on the Leading Doctrines of the Bible. *Cincinnati*, 1870.

Indiana Methodism. *Cincinnati*, 1873.

HOLLIDAY, JOHN HAMPDEN: 1846–1921.

John Hampden Holliday, son of the Rev. William A. and Lucia S. Cruft Holliday, was born in Indianapolis, on May 31, 1846. He was educated at Hanover College (A.B., 1864; A.M., 1867). During the Civil War he served in the 137th Indiana Volunteers.

In 1869 he founded the INDIANAPOLIS NEWS and in 1899, with William J. Richards, founded the INDIANAPOLIS PRESS, which consolidated with the NEWS in 1901. From 1869 to 1892 he was editor of the NEWS. He was a banker—founder of the Union Trust Company in 1893—and a civic leader in the community.

He married Evaline M. Rieman Nov. 4, 1875, and died in Indianapolis on Oct. 20, 1921.

> Information from *Who Was Who in America* and the Indianapolis Public Library.

* * *

The Pew to the Pulpit: an Address Delivered to the Graduating Class of McCormick Theological Seminary of Chicago, Apr. 7, 1892. n.p., 1892.

The Hospital as a Public Charity: an Address to the Indianapolis Medical Society . . . January Nineteenth, 1904. *Indianapolis,* 1904.

War and Precedents; Address. *Indianapolis,* 1919.

Third of a Century. *Indianapolis,* n.d.

HOLLIS, IRA NELSON: 1856–1930.

"Ira Nelson Hollis (Mar. 7, 1856-Aug. 14, 1930), naval engineer, educator, was born . . . in Floyd County, Ind., the son of Ephraim Joseph Hollis (1825-1910) and Mary (Kerns) Hollis. During the Civil War his father became captain in the 59th Indiana Regiment . . . later [he] became owner and operator of a quarry at Louisville, Ky. His wife was the daughter of a farmer in Steubenville, O. Ira's youth was spent at Louisville in straitened circumstances. He attended the local high school and then became an apprentice in a machine shop. He later secured a clerical position with a railroad, and then with a cotton commission house in Memphis. At the age of eighteen he took the examination for admission to the United States Naval Academy at Annapolis and came out at the head of the list, a position which he retained throughout the course. After graduating as cadet-engineer in 1878, he spent three years on the cruiser *Quinnebaug* . . . at the conclusion of the cruise [he] was detailed as professor of marine engineering at Union College, Schenectady, N. Y. In 1884 he served with the advisory board for the construction of the ships of the White Squadron. Ordered to the Pacific coast in January 1887, he spent three years at the Union Iron Works, supervising the construction of the *Charleston,* and

three years on board that vessel . . . In 1892 he was designated to lecture on naval engineering at the Naval War College at Newport, his lectures being subsequently published as a textbook for the navy. He then became assistant to the chief of the Bureau of Steam Engineering, but resigned from the navy in 1893 to take charge of the development of instruction in engineering at Harvard University.

"During his twenty years as professor of mechanical engineering at Harvard, Hollis built up a reputation as an educator and an administrator . . . He was active also in improving intercollegiate athletic relations, in establishing the Harvard Union . . . in founding the Engineers Club of Boston . . . In 1913 Hollis was called to the presidency of the Worcester Polytechnic Institute . . . he was elected president of the American Society of Mechanical Engineers and in that position did valuable work for national preparedness. He resigned the presidency of the Institute in 1925 on account of ill health, returned to Cambridge, Mass., and devoted himself to writing until his death some five years later . . . On Aug. 22, 1894, he was married to Caroline (Lorman) Hollis, the daughter of Charles Lorman of Detroit. He was survived by four children . . ."

> Condensed from L. S. M—s., *Dictionary of American Biography.* Vol. IX.

* * *

War College Lectures on Naval Ships. 1892.

The Frigate Constitution: the Central Figure of the Navy Under Sail. *Boston,* 1900.

HOLLOWAY, JOHN NELSON: 1839–1887.

John Nelson Holloway was born near Lafayette, Ind., on Mar. 9, 1839. He entered De Pauw University but, since he is known to have married Henrietta Hall on July 1, 1861, probably taught school or did other work from time to time at intervals in his college work. He received the A.B. degree in 1862 and the A.M. in 1865.

He acted as principal of Wesley Academy for a short time and moved to Kansas in 1866. He eventually returned East (probably, from the date of publication of his book, by 1868), acted as superintendent of schools in Pana and Centralia, Ill., and began the practice of law in Chester, Ill., in 1874, continuing in Danville after 1876.

In 1881 he settled on a farm near Lafayette, Ind., where he died on Apr. 19, 1887.

Information from De Pauw University's *Alumnal Record, 1920*.

* * *

History of Kansas: From the First Exploration of the Mississippi Valley, to Its Admission into the Union: Embracing a Concise Sketch of Louisiana; American Slavery, and Its Onward March; the Conflict of Free and Slave Labor in the Settlement of Kansas, and the Overthrow of the Latter, with All Other Items of General Interest. *Lafayette, Ind., 1868.*

HOLLOWAY, WILLIAM ROBESON: 1836–1911.

William Robeson Holloway, consul and Indianapolis journalist, was born on Dec. 6, 1836, in Richmond, Ind., the son of David P. and Jane Ann Paulson Holloway. He learned the printing business on his father's paper, the Richmond PALLADIUM, and from 1852 to 1857 worked on the CINCINNATI TIMES. In 1858 he returned to Richmond and married Miss Eliza Burbank of Centerville, Ind. He was admitted to the bar in 1860.

During the Civil War he was private secretary to Indiana's governor, Oliver P. Morton. Following a year in business in New York City, he purchased the INDIANAPOLIS JOURNAL in 1864 and was its editor for several years. From 1869 to 1881 he was postmaster of Indianapolis. He then started the INDIANAPOLIS TIMES and edited it until 1886. In 1897 he was appointed U. S. Consul-General at St. Petersburg, Russia.

Information from *Representative Men of Indiana*, Vol. II, and the Indianapolis Public Library.

* * *

History of Richmond and Wayne County. 1858.

Indianapolis: a Historical and Statistical Sketch of the Railroad City, a Chronicle of Its Social, Municipal, Commercial and Manufacturing Progress, with Full Statistical Tables. *Indianapolis, 1870.*

A Bad Record, Hendricks as a Public Man. Speech at Greencastle, Indiana, 1884. *Boston, 1884.*

HOLMAN, JESSE LYNCH: 1784–1842.

Jesse Lynch Holman, Indiana Territorial Legislator, Territorial, State and Federal judge, Baptist elder and public-spirited citizen, apparently holds another, unpublicized, distinction:

He must have been Indiana's first resident novelist.

He was the son of Henry Holeman (the son, Jesse

Lynch, omitted the "e" from the name), a Virginian who had come to Kentucky in 1776 and who had been in the thick of the Indian warfare which plagued the settlers of the Bluegrass and the Kentucky River valley for twenty years. The Holeman name appears in connection with many of the engagements in the stockades of the Kentuckians and Henry Holeman is said to have been killed by the Indians in 1789 while attempting to run supplies to a blockhouse in which his wife, the former Jane Gordon, and their children were besieged.

There were fourteen children in the Holeman family (Jane Gordon Holeman being Henry Holeman's third wife) and Jesse Lynch Holman was one of the younger. He was born near Danville, Ky., in 1784.

Times were hard for all westerners in the period and the Holemans, though some of the family were men and women at the time of the father's death, had great difficulty in making ends meet. However, Jesse Lynch Holman managed to get an education of sorts and began to teach subscription schools while still only a boy. He began to preach occasionally, also—a practice he continued throughout his life.

He is supposed to have read law under the guidance of Henry Clay in Lexington shortly after 1800: whether or not this was the case, he was admitted to the Kentucky bar on Sept. 2, 1805.

He practiced at New Castle, Henry County, Ky. (a town laid out by his famous cousin, George Holman, whose captivity by the Indians is described by Sandford Cox in his *Recollections of the Early Settlement of the Wabash Valley*), in Port William (now Carrollton) and later at Frankfort. At Port William he met Elizabeth Masterson and they were married in 1810, after he had settled in Frankfort.

It was in this same year that Holman's novel was published. The title page reads *The Prisoners of Niagara, or Errors of Education. A New Novel, Founded on Fact. By Jessee* [sic] *L. Holman, a Native of Kentucky* . . . and it is a duodecimo of 357 pages, very poorly printed by William Gerard, in Frankfort, Ky.

Holman must, at first, have had a considerable regard for the work, for he named one of his daughters "Emerine" after the heroine. Later in his life he is reputed to have become convinced, according to Blake —*The Holmans of Veraestau*, ". . . that the morals of the book were not suitable for the minds of young people and he attempted to buy up and destroy the entire edition." More likely, it would appear, Holman's desire to destroy the work may have been the result of the understandable horror with which a middle-aged judge, of position and dignity, would look upon a piece of over-florid dramatic writing indiscreetly committed to print by him in his youth: such feelings have prompted similar actions before and since.

In his address "To the Reader" Holman says: "When this 'airy trifle' was presented to the public, the author was conscious it contained a sufficiency of errors to amuse the attention of the critic; but when he examined the printed copy, owing to his absence while the work was at press, the difficulty of the manuscript, and various other causes, there are more errors in the impression than he expected. This circumstance, together with the consideration, that the paper is inferior to what he intended, induces him in justice to release from their obligations, all those friends who have been so polite as to subscribe for the work. The binding will now be different from the first propositions, and every person is at liberty to purchase the book *as it is*." And there appear to have been, indeed, errors enough, including the misspelling of the author's first name on the title page!

Of the story itself Blake reports ". . . The book deals much with Virginia and the western country during the time of the American Revolution, with Indians, hairbreadth escapes and other dramatic incidents. 'The Errors of Education' portion of the title is accounted for by the training of the hero in Richmond, Va.; 'The Prisoners of Niagara' is explained by the fact that Fort Niagara plays an important part in the story. The entire novel is told by the hero in the first person and undoubtedly represents much that Holman heard from the lips of his father. Perhaps the actual episodes are from his father's life, as he was a Virginian who migrated to Kentucky. The style of the novel is somewhat Byronic—very intense, passionate, often extremely sentimental. The spirit is that of adventure, love of freedom, hatred of slavery, and opposition to drunkenness and all forms of immorality."

These conclusions may very well be questioned: the assumption that Holman's father, who came to Kentucky in 1776, could have had Revolutionary War service, least of all in the remotest connection with Fort Niagara, seems doubtful indeed. It is also difficult to imagine Jesse Holman gathering in his first four years any great body of reminiscence from a father who died before Jesse's fifth year began.

Whatever the merits of the work, it is a novel; and it unquestionably made Jesse Lynch Holman a novelist: when, the year after its publication, he came to Indiana to reside for the rest of his life, he apparently became Indiana's first novelist.

In the course of his later life Jesse Lynch Holman wrote much verse. Some of it was published in the ephemeral newspapers which were blooming and wilt-

ing week by week in the Southern Indiana river towns but little can be accurately identified. He also wrote two long narrative poems relating to Indians and Indian legends which are preserved in manuscript in the Holman family papers.

To resume Holman's biography: in 1811 he left Frankfort for Indiana. Chances are that he had had many a long look at the bluffs on the Indiana side of the Ohio while he was practicing law—and courting—in Port William, at the point where the Kentucky River joins the Ohio. While Port William—Carrollton of today—is as beautifully situated as a town might be, the Indiana hills still present an interesting prospect across the Ohio, and in 1810, very nearly uninhabited, they attracted many another ambitious young Kentuckian.

In 1811 the Holmans went upstream to a place near the present site of the town of Aurora where Holman —possibly with the assistance of Judge Richard M. Masterson, his father-in-law and a man of considerable property—had bought a piece of land. They took Elizabeth's slaves with them but when they arrived at the new home site the slaves were freed in accordance with Holman's conviction that the somewhat ambiguous phraseology of the Ordinance of 1787 did actually prohibit slavery already in existence: a conviction on which, as judge, Holman later helped to pass conclusive judgment from the bench, in the case of Col. Hyacinth Lasselle's mulatto wench, Polly.

The Holmans followed the customary practice of the comfortably well-off emigrant—providing themselves with a log cabin to live in during the construction of a brick house, for which they had selected a beautiful site, high on a hill over the Ohio. After the Virginia-Kentucky custom, they named it in the classical manner—VER for spring; AEST for AESTUS, summer; AU for AUTUMNUS, autumn—there was to be no winter in that home, they decided.

From the very year of his arrival, Holman was engaged in public service: had he not been a man of strong character who was unwilling to vary in the slightest part of a degree from what he believed to be the proper course, he might have enjoyed a career in the executive branch of government as well as the judicial. As it was he had, at one time or another, ambition toward elective offices but he could not make the necessary concessions: his career was almost entirely by appointment, and he left a reputation behind him, when he died in 1842, which seldom accrues to governors, senators and the like.

In 1811 Governor William Henry Harrison appointed · him Prosecuting Attorney for Dearborn

County (fact of the matter is that in Dearborn's small share of Indiana Territory's 25,000 people there was not much accredited competition for the post) and he acquitted himself well.

In 1814 he was a member of the Territorial Legislature and, in the same year, was appointed Presiding Judge of the Second Judicial District. ("President" these presiding judges were called by their fellow citizens, and their importance being what it was, and the ashes of the recently-burned Washington being so far away, they carried honor enough almost to warrant the title).

In 1816 Holman was appointed judge of the Third Circuit and served as a presidential elector for the new State of Indiana. The same year he was appointed judge of the Indiana State Supreme Court for a seven-year term and, at the end of that, was reappointed for another seven years.

After the second term came the election of Governor James Brown Ray—a megalomaniac whose like was not to be seen again in North America until the rise of Huey Long—and the axe fell on all appointed officers. (It was Governor Ray who rode to the Falls of Fall Creek where the "Indian Murderers" were in process of being hung and—according to William Wesley Woollen's *Biographical and Historical Sketches of Early Indiana*—waited until the youngest, and most obviously feeble-minded of the trio was on the gallows to dash up on a charger, rein in before the culprit and declaim, "There are but two powers known to the law that can save you from hanging by the neck until you are dead; one is the Great God of the Universe, the other is J. Brown Ray, Governor of the State of Indiana . . .")

Holman retired to Veraestau, more respected than ever because of his fall at the hands of Ray. He renewed his license to practice law, devoted even more time to the Baptist Church and the Sunday School movement in which he was a national leader, served as county superintendent of schools and bided his time.

In 1834 he was ordained to the ministry; he aided and encouraged that truly great man of God, Isaac McCoy, in his mission to the Indiana and Michigan Indians. He had already helped to guide the organization of Indiana College (now University) and he was now one of the founders of Franklin College and a founder of the Historical Society of Indiana.

But his judicial career was not yet ended; in fact, his greatest honor came when, on March 29, 1836, his appointment as Federal District Judge of Indiana was confirmed by a Senate which, politically, should have

been hostile to him. He continued in office until his death.

Jesse Holman's life ended, as he would have wished, at his beloved Veraestau on March 28, 1842, in his fifty-eighth year. Oliver H. Smith, a writer not too easily moved to sentiment, says of him, in his *Early Indiana Trials and Sketches*: ". . . Jesse Lynch Holman . . . a good lawyer and one of the most just and conscientious men I ever knew."

Information from Blake—*The Holmans of Veraestau*; Cox—*Recollections of the Early Settlement of the Wabash Valley*; Smith—*Early Indiana Trials and Sketches*; and Woollen—*Biographical and Historical Sketches of Early Indiana*.

* * *

The Prisoners of Niagara, or, Errors of Education. A New Novel, Founded on Fact. By Jessee [sic] L. Holman, a Native of Kentucky. *Frankfort, Ky.,* 1810.

HOOPER, CYRUS LAURON: 1863–

Cyrus Lauron Hooper was born at Rockport, Ind., in 1863. He graduated from Indiana University, receiving the Ph.B. degree in 1887 and the A.M. in 1888, and attended Northwestern University and the University of Chicago. He became a member of the administrative staff of the Chicago city school system.

Mr. Hooper is editor, author and co-author of many text books, most notable being the American Language Series, not listed here.

Information from the Barry Ms.

* * *

A Cloverdale Skeleton. *New York,* 1889.

Gee-Boy. *Chicago,* 1903.

Lamb's Literary Motive. *Chicago,* 1904.

Banking and Business Ethics (with W. E. Borden). *Chicago,* 1921.

Johnny Goes A-Hunting. *Chicago,* 1925.

HOOVER, DAVID: 1781–1866.

David Hoover was born in Randolph County, N. C., on Apr. 14, 1781, the son of Andrew Hoover. He migrated to Ohio in 1802 and thence to what is now Wayne County, Ind., in 1807. While his formal education had been very limited, he was widely read and well informed.

Hoover married Catherine Yount the same year he came to the Indiana Territory, and the couple settled on a farm near the present Fountain City; here they became the parents of seven children. David Hoover was active in Indiana politics in the Forties and Fifties, and the fact that he, a Democrat, was elected to the Indiana Legislature from a strong Whig county is a testimonial to the regard in which he was held. It may be assumed that he served his constituency well, although he is chiefly remembered politically as the man whose vote, with that of Daniel Kelso, sent Edward Allen Hannegan to the United States Senate.

David Hoover died on Sept. 12, 1866.

Information from the Richmond Public Library; Woollen—*Biographical and Historical Sketches of Early Indiana* and Smith—*Early Indiana Trials and Sketches.*

* * *

Some Recollections of My Boyhood Days. *Indianapolis,* n.d.

Memoirs of David Hoover. *Richmond, Ind.,* 1857.

HOPKINS, THOMAS M.:?–?

Little is known of the Rev. T. M. Hopkins except that he was pastor of the First Presbyterian Church of Bloomington, Ind., from 1857 or 1858 to 1869 and that, apparently, he was still residing in Indiana in 1874.

His writing, in the last two titles listed below, seems to indicate a long acquaintance with the Rev. James Chute and Col. John Ketcham.

Information from the University Libraries, Indiana University.

* * *

A Discourse on the Death of Abraham Lincoln, Delivered in the First Presbyterian Church in Bloomington, Indiana, April 19th, 1865. n.p., n.d. [1865]

Reminiscences of Col. John Ketcham, of Monroe County, Indiana, by His Pastor, Rev. T. M. Hopkins, of Bloomington, Indiana. *Bloomington, Ind.,* 1866.

In Memoriam. Rev. James Chute, First Pastor of the First Presbyterian Church of Fort Wayne, Indiana. Printed for Family Use. 1874.

HORNADAY, WILLIAM TEMPLE: 1854–1937.

William Temple Hornaday, son of William and Martha Varner Hornaday, was born near Plainfield, Ind., on Dec. 1, 1854. He studied at Iowa State College and was a student of zoology and museology in the U. S. and Europe. He received his D.Sc. degree from the University of Pittsburgh in 1906, A.M. from Yale in 1917, and Ph.M. from Iowa State College in 1923.

In 1874 he was employed by Henry A. Ward at his natural science establishment in Rochester and during the course of this employment was sent on expeditions to collect rare specimens in natural history. He visited Cuba, Florida, the West Indies, South America, India, Ceylon, the Malay peninsula, and Borneo from 1875 to 1879. In 1880 he founded the National Society of American Taxidermists. He served as chief taxidermist of the U. S. National Museum from 1882 to 1890 and in 1886 went to Montana in charge of a Smithsonian expedition for buffalo. He was in the real estate business from 1890 to 1896, then became director of the New York Zoological Park, a position he held until his retirement in 1926. A member of various zoological societies and the recipient of honors from foreign countries, he was active in promoting game preserves and new legislation for the protection of wild life.

He married Josephine Chamberlain in 1879 and died on March 6, 1937.

Information from *Appletons' Cyclopaedia of American Biography,* Vol. III and *Who Was Who in America.*

* * *

Two Years in the Jungle. The Experiences of a Hunter and Naturalist in India, Ceylon, the Malay Peninsula and Borneo. *New York,* 1885.

Canoe and Rifle on the Orinoco. 1885.

The Extermination of the American Bison; with Sketch of Discovery and Life History. *Washington, D. C.,* 1887.

Free Rum on the Congo, and What It Is Doing There. *Chicago,* 1887.

The Last Buffalo Hunt. *Washington, D. C.,* 1887.

Taxidermy and Zoological Collecting. A Complete Handbook for the Amateur Taxidermist, Collector, Osteologist, Museum-Builder, Sportsman, and Traveler (with chapters by W. J. Holland). *New York,* 1891.

The Man Who Became a Savage: a Story of Our Own Times. *Buffalo,* 1896.

Popular Official Guide to the New York Zoological Park, as Far as Completed. *New York,* 1900.

The Destruction of Our Birds and Mammals. *New York,* 1901.

Notes on the Mountain Sheep of North America. *New York,* 1901.

The American Natural History. A Foundation of Useful Knowledge of the Higher Animals of North America. *New York,* 1904.

Camp-Fires in the Canadian Rockies. *New York,* 1906.

Camp-Fires on Desert and Lava. *New York,* 1908.

Our Vanishing Wild Life; Its Extermination and Preservation. *New York,* 1913.

Wild Life Conservation in Theory and Practice. *New Haven, Conn.,* 1914.

Mammals, Birds, Reptiles and Fishes. 1914. 4 vols.

A Searchlight on Germany; Germany's Blunders, Crimes and Punishment. *New York,* 1917.

Awake! America; Object Lessons and Warnings. *New York,* 1918.

Old-Fashioned Verses. *New York,* 1919.

Minds and Manners of Wild Animals. *New York,* 1922.

Tales From Nature's Wonderlands. *New York,* 1924.

A Wild-Animal Round-Up; Stories and Pictures from the Passing Show. *New York,* 1925.

Wild Animal Interviews and Wild Opinions of Us. *New York,* 1928.

The French War Debt and America's Duty. *Stamford, Conn.,* 1928.

Thirty Years' War for Wild Life; Gains and Losses in the Thankless Task. *New York,* 1931.

HORNER, FRANCIS ASBURY: 1849–1920.

Born at Fredericksburg, Ind., on Apr. 18, 1849, Francis Asbury Horner graduated from De Pauw University in 1870 and received the M.S. degree in 1873. On Apr. 22, 1873, he married Sylvia I. Reed.

In 1870-71 he studied law at New Albany and at Bowling Green, Ind., in 1872 he began the practice of law, and in 1918 he retired. He served as prosecuting attorney for Clay and Putnam counties, state senator for Clay and Owen counties, and city attorney of Brazil, Ind.

Mr. Horner died at Brazil on Feb. 21, 1920. He edited and published technical law books besides those listed.

> Information from De Pauw University's *Alumnal Record, 1920.*

* * *

Criminal Forms for the State of Indiana Complete Under All the Criminal Statutes of the State. *Chicago,* 1896.

Horner's Treatise on the Liquor Laws of Indiana . . . *Indianapolis,* 1900.

HOSHOUR, SAMUEL KLINEFELTER: 1803–1883.

"Samuel Klinefelter Hoshour (Dec. 9, 1803-Nov. 29, 1883), clergyman, pioneer educator in eastern Indiana, was born in Heidelburg township, York County, Pa., his great-great-grandfather having immigrated to the state from Alsace early in the Eighteenth Century. Left fatherless at fourteen, the eldest of six children, Samuel was hired out to neighboring farmers as a helper. He received about three months' schooling each year, however, and at the age of sixteen was appointed teacher of the local school. Aspiring to become a German Lutheran minister, in 1822 he entered the academy at York where he remained until 1824, and then studied for two years more at Newmarket, Shenandoah County, Va., under Dr. Samuel S. Schmucker. On Feb. 7, 1826 he married Lucinda, daughter of Jacob Savage. After serving as principal of Newmarket Academy for a year, in the spring of 1828 he became pastor of the newly formed Lutheran parish in Smithsburg, Washington County, Md., having been ordained Oct. 23, 1827. In 1831 he removed to Hagerstown where he taught in a private school for a time but soon accepted a call to St. John's Lutheran Church of that place. While here he embraced the views of the Disciples of Christ, and in 1835 his name was expunged from the rolls of the (Lutheran) Synod.

"Having sacrificed his professional prospects and lost many of his friends by being true to his convictions, he decided to make a new start in the West. Accordingly, in Sept. 1835, he and a brother-in-law, putting their families into two covered wagons and a carriage, slowly made their way through the mountains and across Ohio to Indiana, where they settled at Centerville, Wayne County. Although he preached almost every Sunday for years, the remainder of his long life was devoted chiefly to education. His first work was in connection with private schools, and in the annals of the state he is numbered among a little group of pioneer teachers who brought these schools to such a degree of efficiency as to set a standard for the whole educational system. In the spring of 1836 he became principal of the Wayne County Seminary. This school was then the center of learning for much of eastern Indiana. Among his pupils were Oliver P. Morton and Lew Wallace. In 1839 he was asked to establish a similar institution in Cambridge City, and in November of that year he opened Cambridge Seminary, which he conducted successfully until 1846, when ill health caused him to seek less exacting duties. For the next five or six years he was principally engaged in giving special German courses in the colleges and cities of the West. Partly for the benefit of his health, in 1851 he bought a farm in Wayne County, which he superintended until 1858 when he was elected president of North Western Christian (now Butler) University, . . . Indianapolis, the institution, although opened in 1855, having had no head previously. In 1861 he resigned, but remained as professor of languages for fourteen years more. From May 15 to Nov. 25, 1862, he was also state Superintendent of Public Instruction.

In 1875, to use his own figure, the faculty tree was shaken, and having attained a ripe age, he fell off. The closing years of his life were spent in Indianapolis, where he gave private lessons in German . . ."

Condensed from H. E. S., *Dictionary of American Biography*, Vol. IX.

* * *

Letters to Esq. Pedant, in the East, by Lorenzo Altisonant, an Emigrant to the West. Published for the Benefit of Youth: By a Lover of the Studious. "Tolle et Lege." *Cambridge City, Ind.,* 1844.

Address on Education Delivered in the Hall of Representatives, at Indianapolis . . . 17th of February, 1852. *Indianapolis,* 1852.

Observations and Notes by the Way on Things East of the Mountains. *Indianapolis,* 1867.

Autobiography of Samuel K. Hoshour (with introduction by Isaac Errett). *St. Louis,* 1884.

HOUGHTON, WALTER RALEIGH: 1845–1929.

Born near Mt. Pleasant, Ia., on Oct. 3, 1845, Walter Raleigh Houghton was educated in the schools of Mt. Pleasant and of Washington, Ind., and graduated from Indiana University in 1871, receiving an honorary A.M. in 1872. In 1910 he received the Ph.D. degree from Oskaloosa College. He was a veteran of the Civil War.

From 1872 to 1884 he served as principal of the preparatory department of Indiana University and he was later principal of the high school at Connersville, Ind. He died on Jan. 24, 1929, and was buried at Connersville.

Information from The University Libraries, Indiana University.

* * *

Conspectus of the History of Political Parties and the Federal Government. *Indianapolis,* 1880.

Address on the Union of the Public School Systems of Indiana . . . *Indianapolis,* 1882.

A History of American Politics (Non-Partisan), Embracing a History of the Federal Government and of Political Parties in the Colonies and United States from 1607 to 1882. *Indianapolis,* 1883.

Rules of Etiquette and Home Culture. *Chicago,* 1884.

The Lives of Blaine and Logan. *Chicago,* 1884.

Early Life and Public Career of Hon. James G. Blaine, Patriot, Statesman, and Historian . . . *Lincoln, Neb.,* 1884.

True Life: or, Lessons on the Virtues for Individuals, Home, Schools, and Societies. *Connersville, Ind.,* 1898.

Stories and Exercises for Opening School; or, Lessons on the Virtues. *Chicago.*

HOUSE, BENJAMIN DAVENPORT: 1844–1887.

Benjamin Davenport House, son of a Congregational minister of St. Johnsbury, Vt., was born at sea in 1844. His mother died during his infancy. During the Civil War he ran away from home to enlist in the Union Army and was severely wounded. Transferred to the Veteran Reserve Corps, he was eventually mustered out of the army at Indianapolis, where he spent the remainder of his life.

Mr. House was associated at various times with a number of Indianapolis newspapers. He died in 1887, survived by his wife, and in 1892 his book of poems was privately printed by friends.

Information from Parker and Heiney—*Poets and Poetry of Indiana*; Nicholson—*The Hoosiers*; and the Indianapolis Public Library.

* * *

Poems, Edited by Meredith Nicholson, with Biographical Sketch. *Indianapolis,* 1892.

HOVEY, ALVIN PETERSON: 1821–1891.

"Alvin Peterson Hovey (Sept. 6, 1821-Nov. 23, 1891), jurist, Union soldier, governor of Indiana, was the youngest of the eight children of Abiel and Frances (Peterson) Hovey . . . The Hoveys moved to Indiana in 1818, and Alvin was born in that state, near Mount Vernon, Posey County. Two years later his father died, and when he was fifteen, his mother also died. He was apprenticed to his brother, a brick-layer, but at nineteen years of age had so improved his meager opportunities for study that he began teaching school, and two years later, having read law in the office of Judge John Pitcher, was admitted to the bar. He became at once a successful lawyer, winning considerable local fame by ousting the executors of the estate of the eccentric philanthropist, William McClure of New Harmony, and himself becoming the administrator. On the outbreak of the war with Mexico he became first lieutenant of a company of volunteers but never saw actual service. He was elected a member of the Indiana constitutional convention of 1850, and from 1851 to 1854 served as circuit judge under the appointment of Gov. Wright. In the latter year he was chosen a member of the Indiana Supreme Court, to fill a vacancy, being the youngest man, up to that time, to serve on the Indiana supreme bench . . . In 1856 he was appointed U. S. district attorney by President Pierce, but was removed in 1858 by President Buchanan for his support of Stephen A. Douglas. In that year he ran for Congress as a Republican, but was defeated.

"At the opening of the Civil War he was made colonel of the 1st Regiment of the Indiana Legion, and later colonel of the 24th Indiana Infantry. He was advanced to the rank of brigadier-general, Apr. 28, 1862, for gallantry at the battle of Shiloh . . . In July 1864 he was brevetted major-general of volunteers and directed to raise 10,000 recruits . . . In 1864-65 he was placed in command of the district of Indiana, then considered a difficult post because of the supposed danger from the 'Sons of Liberty' and 'Knights of the Golden Circle' who were thought at the time to be numerous in Indiana.

"After the war he was appointed (December 1865) minister to Peru, and held that post until 1870, when he returned to his law practice at Mount Vernon, Ind. . . . in 1886 was elected to Congress and two years later was chosen to the governorship. In this campaign he was accused of being exclusive, aristocratic, and unpopular. It was said that he claimed to be the reincarnation of Napoleon, and it was his custom to retire to solitary contemplation on the anniversary of Napoleon's death . . . He died in office.

"Hovey was a man of distinguished appearance and soldierly bearing, and maintained a reputation throughout his life for integrity and public spirit. He was married on Nov. 24, 1844, to Mary Ann James, a native of Baton Rouge, La., the daughter of Col. E. R. James. She was the mother of five children of whom only two lived to maturity. After her death, which occurred in 1863, he married Rosa Alice, daughter of Caleb Smith and widow of Maj. William F. Carey . . ."

Condensed from W. W. S., *Dictionary of American Biography*, Vol. IX.

* * *

Centennial History, Sketch of Posey County, Indiana. n.p., n.d.

Soldiers' Rights. An Appeal to the Loyal People of the United States and Their Representatives in Congress . . . November 1889. *Indianapolis, 1889.*

HOVEY, HORACE CARTER: 1833–1914.

Horace Carter Hovey, son of Prof. Edmund Otis and Mary Carter Hovey, was born at Rob Roy, Ind., on Jan. 28, 1833, and graduated from Wabash College in 1853. He received the A.M. degree from Wabash in 1856 and the D.D. degree in 1883. In 1857 he graduated from Lane Theological Seminary in Cincinnati. He married Helen Lavinia Blatchley on Nov. 18, 1857.

Ordained to the Presbyterian ministry in 1858, he served as home missionary until 1862, pastor at Florence, Mass., from 1863 to 1866, and pastor at New Albany, Ind., from 1866 to 1869. He then held pastorates in Illinois, Missouri, Connecticut, Minnesota, and Massachusetts until 1909, after which he engaged in occasional preaching and in literary and scientific work.

He died on July 27, 1914.

Information from *Who Was Who in America.*

* * *

The National Fast. A Sermon Preached at Coldwater, Mich., January 4, 1861. *Coldwater, Mich., 1861.*

Celebrated American Caverns, Especially Mammoth, Wyandot and Luray; Together with Historical, Scientific, and Descriptive Notices of Caves and Grottoes in Other Lands. *Cincinnati, 1882.*

Guide Book to the Mammoth Cave of Kentucky. *Cincinnati, 1882.*

The Mammoth Cave of Kentucky, an Illustrated Manual (with R. E. Call). *Louisville, 1897.*

A Memoir of Daniel Hovey. [*Newburyport, Mass., 1900*]

House of God: Historical Discourse on Sesquicentennial of Old South Meeting House of Newburyport, Mass., Dec. 16, 1906. *Newburyport, Mass., 1906.*

Hand Book of the Mammoth Cave of Kentucky: a Practical Guide to the Regulation Routes. *Louisville, 1909.*

Bibliography of Mammoth Cave, Ky. (with R. E. Call).

HOWARD, TIMOTHY EDWARD: 1837–1916.

"Timothy Edward Howard (Jan. 27, 1837-July 9, 1916) . . . was born of Irish parentage on a farm near Ann Arbor, Mich. His parents, Martin and Julia (Beahan) Howard, came to America in 1832, settling first in Vermont, but soon removing to Michigan Territory where the father entered some government land in the midst of the forest. He died in 1851, leaving large responsibilities upon his widow and eldest son. Young Howard attended a rural school near his home and later an academy at Ypsilanti for two terms, then entered the University of Michigan, but left in 1856, before completing his sophomore year. After teaching a rural school two years, he secured the opportunity of teaching and attending classes in the University of Notre Dame, at South Bend, Ind. In February 1862, he enlisted in the 12th Michigan Infantry and a few weeks later took part in the battle of Shiloh, where he received wounds in the neck and shoulder. After two months in a hospital at Evansville, Ind., he returned home on a furlough, but was finally discharged as unfit for further service. He resumed his teaching and received his degree in 1862, graduating in a class of five. At the age of forty-six he took up the study of law, receiving the law degree in due course, though he did not begin to practise until 1883.

"Becoming interested in local politics, though never a politician in the ordinary sense, he was elected county clerk in 1878, and in the same year was chosen a member of the city council. He later served as city and county attorney. Elected to the state Senate in 1886 and again in 1890, he was recognized as a most useful and influential member of that body . . . He became the Democratic nominee from the 5th district for justice of the state Supreme Court in 1892; was elected, and served from 1893 to 1899, being three times chosen chief justice. His decisions as chief justice . . . have been widely quoted and have been reprinted in collections of decisions.

"After retiring from the bench in 1899, Howard resumed the practice of law in South Bend, and in 1906 became professor of law at the University of Notre Dame, which position he was holding at the time of his death . . . he took an active part in beautifying South Bend and was instrumental in securing the city's first park, which was named in his honor . . . He was president of the Northern Indiana Historical Society at the time of his death.

"Howard was married on July 14, 1864, to Julia A. Redmond of Detroit, and to them were born ten children of whom four sons and three daughters grew to maturity . . ."

> Condensed from **W. W. S.**, *Dictionary of American Biography*, Vol. IX.

* * *

Excelsior: Essays on Politeness, Education and Means of Obtaining Success in Life: Pt. 1 for Young Gentlemen, by T. E. Howard; Pt. 2 for Young Ladies, by a Lady. *Baltimore,* 1868.
Christian Politeness (with others). *New York,* n.d.
Musings and Memories. *Chicago,* 1905.
A History of St. Joseph County, Indiana. *Chicago,* 1907.
Uncle Edward Stories. n.d.

HOWBERT, IRVING: 1846–1934.

Irving Howbert, son of William and Martha Marshall Howbert, was born in Columbus, Ind., on Apr. 11, 1846, and was educated in the high schools of Iowa and Colorado. Beginning in 1878 as cashier of the First National Bank in Colorado Springs, from 1880 to 1889 he served as president, and for many years continued as vice-president and chairman of the board. He was a member of the Colorado Senate from 1882 to 1886 and chairman of the Republican State Central Committee in Colorado in 1894-95. From 1880 to 1921 he was a trustee of Colorado College, receiving the honorary degrees of LL.D. and Litt.D. from that institution. He died on Dec. 21, 1934.

> Information from *Who Was Who in America.*

* * *

The Indians of the Pike's Peak Region, Including an Account of the Battle of Sand Creek, and of Occurrences in El Paso County, Colorado, During the War with the Cheyennes and Arapahoes, in 1864 and 1868. *Colorado Springs,* 1914.
Memories of a Lifetime in the Pike's Peak Region. *New York,* 1925.

HOWE, DANIEL WAIT: 1839–1921.

A descendant of John Howe, first settler of Marlborough, Mass., Daniel Wait Howe was born on Oct. 24, 1839, in Patriot, Ind. He was the son of Daniel H. and Lucy Hicks Howe. He was educated at Franklin College, where he received the A.B. degree in 1857.

During the Civil War he was a private in the 7th Indiana Volunteers and a captain in the 79th Volunteers. He took part in the battles of Carrick's Ford, Stone River, Chickamauga, and Missionary Ridge, and because of wounds received in the battle of Kenesaw Mountain he was discharged from the army in 1864. Following his discharge he entered Albany Law School, received his degree in 1867, and in that year began the practice of law in Franklin, Ind., where he acted as city attorney. In 1871 he married Inez Hamilton of Decatur County, Ind.

He moved to Indianapolis in 1873, where he was a judge of the Superior Court from 1876 to 1890, then engaged in the practice of law until his retirement. He was once president of the Indiana Historical Society and, in addition to his books, wrote articles for legal periodicals. He died on Oct. 28, 1921.

> Information from Dunn—*Indiana and Indianans,* Vol. IV; *Who's Who in America*; and the Indianapolis Public Library.

* * *

The Laws and Courts of Northwest and Indiana Territories. *Indianapolis,* 1886.
The Puritan Republic of the Massachusetts Bay in New England. *Indianapolis,* 1899.
Civil War Times, 1861-1865. *Indianapolis,* 1902.
Making a Capital in the Wilderness. *Indianapolis,* 1908.

The Mississippi Valley in the Movement for Fifty-Four Forty or Fight. *Cedar Rapids, Ia.,* 1912.

Political History of Secession, to the Beginning of the American Civil War. *New York,* 1914.

Howe Genealogies. (Revised and enlarged by Gilman Bigelow Howe.) *Boston,* 1929.

HOWE, EDGAR WATSON: 1853–1937.

Edgar Watson Howe, son of Henry and Elizabeth Irwin Howe, was born at Treaty, Ind., on May 3, 1853. Except for brief attendance at common schools he was self-educated, and at the age of twelve he started to work in a printing office. For two years he worked on the HERALD at Falls City, Neb. At nineteen he was publisher of the GOLDEN GLOBE in Golden, Col., and in 1877 he started the ATCHISON DAILY GLOBE in Atchison, Kan., which he published for thirty-four years.

Other newspapers over the U. S. reprinted material from the GLOBE, which became known as the most extensively quoted paper in the country. In 1911 Howe retired from his paper, gave it to his two sons, and devoted himself to travel and the publication of E. W. HOWE'S MONTHLY. Accounts of his travels were printed in the GLOBE and later published in book form. The MONTHLY, except for occasional reprints, was written entirely by Howe, who took this means of expressing his views on a variety of subjects. The paper attained a wide circulation and was published until 1933.

His first novel, *The Story of a Country Town,* was rejected by New York publishers, but Howe printed it himself, and it received such favorable reviews that it was published by six publishers within the next fifty years. H. L. Mencken, in his introduction to *Ventures in Common Sense,* describes Howe as unusually candid and honest in the expression of his opinions and his books as being very readable.

Mr. Howe married Clara L. Frank in 1873. He died on Oct. 3, 1937. He was known as the "Sage of Potato Hill."

Information from *Who Was Who in America;* *Appletons' Cyclopaedia of American Biography,* Vol. III; the Barry Ms.; Burke and Howe—*American Authors and Books, 1640-1940;* and the Introduction to *Ventures in Common Sense.*

* * *

The History of the Class of 'Seventy-Eight at the U. S. Military Academy. *New York,* 1881.

The Story of a Country Town. *Atchison, Kan.,* 1883.

The Mystery of the Locks. *Boston,* 1885.

A Moonlight Boy. *Boston,* 1886.

A Man Story. *Boston,* 1888.

An Ante-Mortem Statement. *Atchison, Kan.,* 1891.

The Confession of John Whitlock, Late Preacher of the Gospel. *Atchison, Kan.,* 1891.

Daily Notes of a Trip Around the World. 1907. 2 vols.

The Trip to the West Indies. *Topeka, Kan.,* 1910.

Country Town Sayings: A Collection of Paragraphs from the Atchison Globe. *Topeka, Kan.,* 1911.

Travel Letters from New Zealand, Australia and Africa. *Topeka, Kan.,* 1913.

Success Easier than Failure. *Topeka, Kan.,* 1917.

The Blessing of Business. *Topeka, Kan.,* 1918.

Ventures in Common Sense. *New York,* 1919.

The Anthology of Another Town. *New York,* 1920.

Plain People, an Autobiography. *New York,* 1929.

The Indignations of E. W. Howe. *Girard, Kan.,* 1933.

HOWE, JOHN BADLAM: 1813–1882.

Born in Boston, Mass., on Mar. 3, 1813, John Badlam Howe graduated from Trinity College in 1832. He moved to Indiana, where he was a member of the state Legislature in 1840 and of the state constitutional convention in 1850. He died in Lima, Ind., on Jan. 22, 1882.

Information from *Appletons' Cyclopaedia of American Biography,* Vol. III.

* * *

The Political Economy of Great Britain, the United States and France in the Use of Money. A New Science of Production and Exchange. *Boston,* 1878.

Monetary and Industrial Fallacies. A Dialogue. *Boston,* 1878.

Production and Exchange: a Definition of Money and Deposits. *New York,* 1878.

Mono-Metalism and Bi-Metalism; or, the Science of Monetary Values. *Boston,* 1879.

The Common Sense, the Mathematics, and the Metaphysics of Money. *Boston,* 1881.

A Reply to Criticisms on Same, n.p. [*Boston*], 1882.

HOWERTH, IRA WOODS: 1860–1938.

Ira Woods Howerth, son of John and Elizabeth Amelia Bright Howerth, was born in Brown County, Ind., on June 18, 1860, and graduated from Northern Indiana Normal (now Valparaiso University) in 1885. He received an A.B. degree from Harvard in 1893 and the A.M. and Ph.D. degrees from the University of Chicago in 1894 and 1898. Until 1891 he was a teacher and principal in the public schools. He was admitted to the Illinois bar in 1889.

From 1896 to 1912 he taught sociology at the University of Chicago, from 1912 to 1918 he was connected with the University of California as professor of education and director of university extension, and after 1921 he was professor of sociology and economics at Colorado State Teachers College. In 1919 he was a member of the educational corps in Europe with the A. E. F. He married Cora Olive Cissna in 1881 and died on July 4, 1938.

He was the author of several textbooks besides the work listed here.

Information from *Who Was Who in America.*

* * *

The Art of Education. *New York,* 1912.

Work and Life: a Study of the Social Problems of To-day. *New York,* 1913.

State Boards of Education. *Berkeley, Calif.,* 1913.

War and the Survival of the Fittest. *Berkeley, Calif.,* 1916.

The Theory of Education; the Philosophy of Education as Derived from the Process of Organic, Psychic, and Social Evolution. *New York,* 1926.

Bible Stories and Modern Science; a Series of Lectures Before the College Sunday School Class of Park Congregation Church, Greeley Colorado. *Greeley, Colo.,* 1932.

HOWLAND, LOUIS: 1857–1934.

Born in Indianapolis on June 13, 1857, Louis Howland was educated in a private school in his native city and at Yale University, from which he graduated in 1879. He spent some time in the East, where he was on the staff of FORUM magazine, but returned to Indianapolis in 1892 and was associated with the INDIANAPOLIS NEWS for the remainder of his life. He was editor of the paper from 1911 to 1934. Mr. Howland was one of the organizers of the Indianapolis Literary Club. His death occurred in Indianapolis on Mar. 26, 1934.

Information from the Indianapolis Public Library.

* * *

Day Unto Day. *Indianapolis,* 1911.

Stephen A. Douglas. *New York,* 1920.

The Mind of Jesus. *Indianapolis,* 1926.

Case and Comment; Meditations of a Layman on the Christian Year. *Indianapolis,* 1927.

Autobiography of a Cathedral. *New York,* 1927.

HUBBARD, FRANK McKINNEY: 1868–1930.

No one else ever succeeded in catching the exact flavor of the humor and philosophy native to Indiana—and perhaps to a large portion of the American Midwest besides—as did Kin Hubbard.

He labeled his locale "Brown County," because Brown County, Ind., had always been a little on the backward side—haven of hill-billies, gully-runners, artists and other non-conforming folk—but his readers could recognize representation of almost any county in almost any midwestern or midsouthern state in the remarks of his characters.

Frank McKinney Hubbard (he was always "Kin") was born in Bellefontaine, O., on Sept. 1, 1868. His parents were Thomas and Sarah Jane Miller Hubbard, Thomas being editor and publisher of the BELLEFONTAINE EXAMINER, a newspaper of some importance in west-central Ohio.

A man never given to seeking personal publicity, Hubbard left behind him no great amount of biographical material. Only a short sketch, given to another distinguished Ohio writer, Fred C. Kelly, who stayed in that state, exists to give any extensive view of Kin Hubbard as he saw himself at the peak of his career. Mr. Kelly has graciously offered this manuscript for inclusion here. In it Hubbard reports of himself.

"Have two children—a girl at the age to talk too long to peddlers and letter carriers, and a boy who is just beginning to press his trousers ever' day and use 600-W on his hair. Born at Bellefontaine, Ohio, entered school at usual age carrying volumes of Mark Twain's *Roughing It* and *Behind the Scenes at Washington.* Retired from school in one of the early grades and went to work in a paint shop where I learned to cast raised letters and gild the big watches that stand in front of jewelry stores. Later returned to school and was going big when Cleveland was elected and my father was appointed postmaster. Went into post office where I remained five years off and on. During this period I made a tour of the South as a silhouette artist and closed in Louisville and walked home. Also on this tour I hired out in Chattanooga to drive a bread wagon, two white mules hitched tandem. Held this job two weeks and was required to take the mules down to the Cumberland river an' scrub the red mud off once per week. Returning to Bellefontaine, Ohio, I decided to attend the Detroit Museum of Art. Attended the better part of one week, and then hung around Miner's theater and the DETROIT JOURNAL office till Spring opened up. At this time I was wearin' a loud plaid cape overcoat, a close-reefed brown derby, long, narrow shoes, a cane and long matty hair! I was loafing, knowing I could go back in the post office any old time.

"The following winter I organized Bellefontaine's Grand Operatic Minstrels and Prof. Tom Wright's Solo Orchestra, local talent, and gave a grand benefit performance for the cemetery receiving vault fund. I played one extreme end (tambo) and made a hit which disqualified me for any real usefulness for some years.

"In a letter to an Indianapolis friend describing this show I made a lot of thumb nail sketches. This letter was shown to the late John H. Holiday, founder of the INDIANAPOLIS NEWS, and he suggested that I come on to Indianapolis and go on the NEWS as an artist. I remained on the NEWS three years. I soon endeared myself to the whole staff by making two imaginative one column portraits of the Dalton Boys, bandits, who were killed in attempting to rob a bank at Coffeyville, Kansas.

"The NEWS put on a new managing editor at the end of my three years and, like all new managing editors, he raised hell with everything and everybody. I was the pioneer newspaper artist of Indianapolis. I used the chalk plate process of making pictures and had to wear a linen duster and a sponge on my nose on account of the dust. I illustrated everything that happened in town, together with Frank Carpenter's weekly letter and only got $12 per week. I was what's called a natural artist, one with no knowledge of drawing, no idea of perspective or color or anything, but I got along fine until the new managing editor dropped in one day and told me that all of the local banks had installed new and modern fixtures. He wanted a two-column sectional view of each bank, showing various new styles in bank fixtures, etc. I told him I could not undertake it, but that I would hire it done and pay for it. He said that would do, but that he would have to have the stuff in two days. I got a jewelry engraver to make the sketches and they cost me three weeks' salary. Then Decoration Day was just in the offing. The managing editor wanted a long graceful angel swooping across a whole page scattering lilies in her wake. Something "allegorical for the occasion" he said. I got Fertig and Keevers, housepainters, to plan and execute the angel at a princely outlay. Then the vacation period arrived and I was the first out. I went to Bellefontaine to spend vacation. The second day at home I received a letter from the managing editor. He told me that the NEWS had grown to be such a great and powerful paper that from then on it would require an artist that could draw anything, layouts, caricatures, cartoons, decorations, etc., and that I might return and stay

till I found something else. I stayed while I earned enough for a new blue serge suit and extra brown derby.

"Returning to Bellefontaine that summer I organized a local minstrel show and gave a grand complimentary benefit for the K. of P. lodge, holding out only enough to get some new shirts.

"Later I went to the Atlanta Exposition. Failing to get a newspaper job I signed up with the manager of a mummified Aztec mother and child, who were exhibited in a covered wagon. I sold tickets with one hand and took them with the other while the manager lectured. Later coming to Cincinnati, I hit it just in time to get in on the Pearl Bryan murder mystery, and went to work for the TRIBUNE, anti-Cox organ, and made pictures of white horses and cabs and attorneys and jurymen till Spring, when I bought a new blue serge suit and brown derby an' had my hair evened up and joined out with Lagoon Park, where I turned the stile at $9 per, roomin' at Covington, eating at Bromley and getting my other shirt and collar done up in Cincinnati.

"In the fall I returned to Bellefontaine and gave a 'Ladies Minstrels' for the benefit of the Kings Daughters, holding out only enough for some shoes. Then to Mansfield, O., where I worked on the NEWS, cut my own kindling, puddled my own metal, cast my own cuts and routed them and did everything but make up the paper. Got $11 per. Used chalk plate process. It took fourteen hours to finally get a one column cut in the paper. Col. Wm. Capeller, well known Ohio politician, owned the paper. One day he came to me and said. 'Hubbard, I know you're a damned Democrat, but I want you to help clean up Mansfield and vote for Huntington Brown for mayor tomorrow. I'll let you off all day if you will.' I studied a while and decided that inasmuch as there were no great national issues involved I would condescend to vote for a reform mayor. Was at the polls when they opened and voted for Brown and a Democratic council. The Fort Wayne baseball club was stopping at the same wooden shoe hotel where I lived and the club was managed by a former schoolmate and we soon got to talking about old times, and by noon I was on the swinging rings. The next morning I woke up sitting by a fountain soaking wet in the heart of Cleveland. By my side was all my scenery, cape overcoat, two canes, and telescope. Here I was the guest of an old Bellefontaine boy who was employed in Cleveland by a large department store. He did nothing from morning till evening but knock crates off new bicycles, but he was mighty liberal. Thence to Bellefontaine where I organized Frank K. Hubbard's High Class Vaudevilles and toured the star route towns, coming to grief at Roundhead, where the advance sale did not justify the moving of an organ up two flights of stairs to the opery hall. The fellow who drove my wagon stood up and looked all over town, and said, 'Hubbard, the money haint here.'

"Back to Bellefontaine. Then a letter from the INDIANAPOLIS SUN saying a newspaper, THE PRESS, was soon to be launched and that the SUN would be in the fight and to come on and go to work for $15 per.

"Returned to Indianapolis, worked year on the SUN and then back to the NEWS again where I've always remained. Until 'Abe Martin' started I was employed solely as a caricaturist, attending all conventions, local, state and national, and supplying the NEWS with single columns and splatters, touring Indiana with political celebrities, etc. The next day after the Parker-Roosevelt election I launched Abe Martin. Abe has appeared daily in the NEWS ever since. Have made a new drawing for each appearance. Abe Martin is probably the oldest continuous newspaper feature. Has been syndicated twelve years. 'Short Furrows,' a weekly essay, has been syndicated eight years. I located Abe in Brown county, Ind., on account of the topography and the primitive condition of things, no telephones, railroads, or telegraph and few roads.

"I also learned the printer's trade in the office of the BELLEFONTAINE EXAMINER, a paper established in 1830 and owned by my father, who at his death, was the oldest editor in Ohio.

"I bought a tambourine with the first money I ever earned. Worked around the opera house at Bellefontaine and was well on in years before I quit trying to look like a showman, and no mother ever hated to cut her boy's curls off any worse than I hated to cut my hair short and get down to work. I always owned a cluster diamond pin, even when walking from one town to another. I also owned seven different cape overcoats all loud plaid an' richly lined. I married rather late, or after I got three or four hundred dollars together. I date all of my good luck from that hour. And while my wife does not write my stuff, she has all the peculiarities of the genius and is a good manager.

"I have published 18 volumes of Abe Martin material and the greatest fun I have is during the month of December when I market them and open the mail each day. I rarely have any material ahead or know when I'm going to have any. But somehow something allus shows up at the eleventh hour, not always good stuff, but about as fair as most of the stuff that's getting over. One really good paragraph in six days is a fine week's work. I make my own illustrations, and not infrequently they supply any humor that's lacking in the text. I do not make public appearances and talk and draw. I tried it once and it knocked $60 off my book sales. I rather prefer the background and keep away from banquets. Also I've had a couple of chances to go to New York and make something of myself, but like a friend I used to have, whose uncle wanted him to go to Denver and take charge of a big drug store said, I'd rather stay here where I can get in the ban Have two hobbies—mowing my lawn and circuses. A taking up golf although I feel as good as I ever did, in fact better. It's the only game where you can chew tobacco with impunity. And most of them do. I often meet acquaintances on the Indianapolis streets who ask me what I'm doing now, and I'm often introduced to people who never heard of me, but I don't care. The world is full of people who don't know who Tony Pastor was. Indianapolis is a great literary center, and we have men and boys in the stereotyping and press rooms of the NEWS that contribute regularly to magazines as a side line. Everyone in the State is either a politician or writer. Of course there's a fair sprinkling of tradesmen an' farmers, but only enough t' supply the wants of the writers and politicians.

"The only thing any teacher ever said to me, that I now recall, was, 'Well, Kin, be that as it may, Mr. Hayes took his seat.' Some boy had just named the presidents of the United States and included Rutherford B. Hayes and I got up and said he was not elected fair and that Tilden was counted out.

"The first year at school I raised my hand one day and teacher said, 'What is it, McKinney?' and I said, 'I've got a sister that's half Indian.' She was very dark.

"Never was on a bicycle or roller skates. I went about for years covered with perfume and wearing a fuchsia in my lapel, but I let the girls alone till I was 17 or 18.

"My one big night was Friday night, when I traded a copy of father's WEEKLY EXAMINER for a couple of twofers at Carter Brothers grocery and sat on the court house fence and watched the passing show.

"First tobacco chewed was Jackson's Best. I soaked it in molasses to make it palatable.

"I never dreamed of doing anything else but owning a good, well painted, comprehensive one-ring circus, and even today I feel rather miffed at losing out on the proposition.

"I leaned a little toward minstrelsy and bought a tambourine with my first money. At nine years of age I also owned a pair of real plantation song and dance shoes—sending to New York for them.

"First hall show I ever saw was Annie Ward Tiffany in 'The Child Stealer,' then the Wallace Sisters, Minnie Palmer, 'Under the Gas Light,' Jane Coombs, Joe

Cawthorn in 'The Little Nugget,' and 'Lights O'-London' followed in rapid succession.

"Greatest aversions—office holders, banquet speakers and 1000 Island dressing.

"Books—*East Lynne, Roughin' It, Beyond the Mississippi, Called Back* (Hugh Conway) and Wash. Irving's *Sketch Book*.

"Cannon acts were all the vogue when I was a kid—catching cannon balls and firing women out of cannons, etc.—in circuses. I made a cannon out of a wooden pump and mounted it on wheels and used a black rubber ball. Devoted one whole summer trying to stop the ball. Still have a squatty blue (circus color) chair and lettered across the back is, 'Great Cannon Ball Act.' "

There is Kin Hubbard as he saw himself—his lack of success in following in the theatrical footsteps of his wagon-show owning maternal grandfather, Capt. John B. Miller, far overshadowing his achievements as a cartoonist, humorist, satirist and philosopher.

The feature for which he first became famous, the sayings of "Abe Martin," first appeared on Dec. 31, 1904. The feature was an immediate hit: Abe's comments were current, critical and unfailingly telling, and Hubbard was soon a state and, very little later, when they began to be syndicated, a national figure.

He married Josephine Jackson, of Indianapolis, on Oct. 12, 1905. Hubbard enjoyed his home, and particularly his garden—throughout his career he avoided lecturing, radio appearances and other proffered engagements which would interfere with his home life.

His books enjoyed a wide annual sale, some of the earlier ones now being collector's items, and his syndicated "Abe Martin's Sayings" have been reprinted continuously since his death. They are now (1948) appearing regularly in a list of papers extensive enough to gladden the hearts of any current paragraphers, and most of the quips are as pointed and as appropriate to the modern scene as they were to that of thirty or forty years ago.

Kin Hubbard died on Dec. 26, 1930, having influenced the thinking of the American people along the lines of plain, homely horse sense far more widely than any serious philosopher of his day.

> Information by Fred C. Kelly and from *Who Was Who in America*.

* * *

Collection of Indiana Lawmakers and Lobbyists. *Indianapolis*, 1903.

Caricatures of Law Makers, Clerks and Doorkeepers of the Sixty-Fourth General Assembly of Indiana. *Indianapolis*, 1905.

Abe Martin of Brown County, Indiana, by Kin Hubbard. Compiled from *The Indianapolis News*. *Indianapolis*, 1907.

Abe Martin's Almanack, by Kin Hubbard . . . with Illustrations by the Author. *Indianapolis*, 1907.

Abe Martin's Almanack, by Kin Hubbard . . . Illustrated by the Author. *Indianapolis*, 1908.

Abe Martin Scrapbook. n.p., n.d. [1908].

Abe Martin's Brown County Almanack, by Kin Hubbard; a Volume of Philosophy, Incidents and Scenes Direct from the Paw Paw Belt of Indiana. Illustrated by the Author. *Indianapolis*, 1909.

Brown County Folks, by Kin Hubbard; Being a Full Year's Review of the Sayings and Doings of Abe Martin and His Brown County, Indiana, Neighbors, Including a Stirring Tale by Miss Fawn Lippincut Entitled the Lost Heiress of Red Stone Hall. Illustrated by the Author. *Indianapolis*, 1910.

Abe Martin's Almanack, by Kin Hubbard . . . Illustrated by the Author . . . *Garden City, N. Y., 1911*.

Short Furrows, by Kin Hubbard . . . Illustrated by the Author. *Indianapolis*, 1912.

Back Country Folks, by Kin Hubbard. A New Full Year's Accumulation of the Philosophy and Sketches of Abe Martin . . . Illustrations by Francis Gallup. *Indianapolis*, 1913.

Abe Martin's Primer; the Collected Writings of Abe Martin and His Brown County, Indiana, Neighbors, by Kin Hubbard. Illustrations by Francis Gallup. *Indianapolis*, 1914.

Abe Martin's Sayings and Sketches, by Kin Hubbard. *Indianapolis*, 1915.

New Sayings, by Abe Martin and Velma's Vow, a Gripping Love Tale by Miss Fawn Lippincut . . . *Indianapolis*, 1916.

Abe Martin's Back Country Sayings, Compiled from *The Indianapolis News* and Revised and Edited by the Author. *Indianapolis*, 1917.

Abe Martin on the War and Other Things—Being a Full Year's Review of the Sayings and Doings of Abe Martin and His Brown County, Indiana, Neighbors, Including Several Articles of Some Length Compiled from *The Indianapolis News* and Revised, Edited and Illustrated by the Author. *Indianapolis*, 1918.

Abe Martin's Home Cured Philosophy; the Writings of Abe Martin and His Brown County, Indiana, Neighbors . . . *Indianapolis*, 1919.

Abe Martin, the Joker on Facts, by Kin Hubbard . . . Illustrated by the Author. *Indianapolis*, 1920.

Abe Martin's Almanack, by Kin Hubbard. The Comments, Philosophy an' Essays of Abe Martin an' His Neighbors . . . Illustrations by th' Author . . . *Indianapolis*, 1921.

These Days; a Sort of Paragraphic Review of the Fads and Foibles and Waves and Trends of the Present Age, by Abe Martin (Kin Hubbard). Pictures by the Author. *Indianapolis*, 1922.

Comments of Abe Martin and His Neighbors, and Several More or Less Helpful Essays Bearing Directly on a Variety of Important Matters, by Kin Hubbard. Pictures by the Author. *Indianapolis, 1923.*

Fifty Two Weeks of Abe Martin; a Full Twelve Months' Output of Abe Martin's Writings, Revised and Brushed Up by the Author. Also a Few Articles on Life Sentences, Dance Orchestras and Other Menaces, by Kin Hubbard. *Indianapolis, 1924.*

Abe Martin on Things in General; Quiet Observations and Conclusions About Everything That Has Happened During the Past Twelve Months, Intermingled with a Few Friendly Jibes at Bare Knees, Prohibition, Florida, Spinach, an' Bandits, Together with a Dozen or More Extended Articles Dealing with Things That Need Dealing With, by Kin Hubbard. *Indianapolis, 1925.*

Abe Martin, Hoss Sense and Nonsense, by Kin Hubbard. *Indianapolis, 1926.*

Abe Martin's Wise Cracks and Skunk Ridge Papers, by Kin Hubbard. Pictures by the Author. *Indianapolis, 1927.*

Abe Martin's Barbed Wire, by Kin Hubbard . . . *Indianapolis, 1928.*

Abe Martin's Town Pump, by Kin Hubbard . . . *Indianapolis, 1929.*

Book of Indiana; the Story of What Has Been Described as the Most Typically American State in the American Democracy Told in Terms of Biography, Compiled Under the Direction of the James O. Jones Co. *Indianapolis, 1929.*

Abe Martin's Broadcast, Kin Hubbard Announcing . . . Illustrations by the Author. *Indianapolis, 1930.*

Abe Martin's Wisecracks, by 'Kin' Hubbard, Selected by E. V. Lucas. *London, 1930.*

HUFFINGTON, AGNES MARIA (MRS. JOHN B.): 1859–1935.

Agnes Maria Huffington was, according to a brief obituary in the INDIANAPOLIS NEWS, a resident of Indianapolis and the widow of John B. Huffington.

Information from the Barry Ms.

* * *

God's Truth; Twentieth Century Revelation to the Spirit of Truth. *Indianapolis, 1902.*

HUFFMAN, JASPER ABRAHAM: 1880–

Jasper Abraham Huffman, son of John W. and Martha Howenstine Huffman, was born in Elkhart County, Ind., on Feb. 28, 1880, and was ordained in the ministry of the Mennonite Brethren in Christ in 1904. He graduated from Bonebrake Theological Seminary in 1909, received his A.B. degree from Bluff-

ton (O.) College in 1915 and his B.D. degree from McCormick Theological Seminary in 1919, and was awarded the D.D. degree by Taylor University in 1920.

From 1911 to 1914 he served as pastor in Dayton, O. In 1914-15 he was an instructor at Bluffton College, from 1915 to 1922 professor at Witmarsum Theological Seminary, from 1922 to 1936 dean of the Marion College School of Theology, and after 1936 dean of the School of Religion at Taylor University in Upland, Ind. In 1930 he was a member of the staff of a joint expedition for Palestinian excavation of Xenia Theological Seminary and the American School for Oriental Research. He edited the GOSPEL BANNER from 1913 to 1925 and the Bethel Series of Sunday School literature since 1914. On May 5, 1901, he married Elizabeth D. Lambert.

Information from Who's Who in America.

* * *

Redemption Completed. *New Carlisle, O., 1904.*

Old Testament Messages of the Christ. *Dayton, O., 1909.*

Job, a World Example. *Bluffton, O., 1913.*

Upper Room Messages. *New Carlisle, O., 1915.*

The Progressive Unfolding of the Messianic Hope. *New York, 1924.*

Young People and the Christ Life. *Chicago, 1925.*

A Guide to the Study of the Old and New Testaments For Use in the High Schools of Indiana. *Dayton, O., 1926.*

Voices from Rocks and Dust Heaps of Bible Lands. *Marion, Ind., 1928.*

With Christ in the Deeper Lessons. *1929.*

Biblical Confirmations from Archaeology. *Upland, Ind., 1930.*

Youth and the Christ Way. *Marion, Ind., 1932.*

Building the Home Christian. *Marion, Ind., 1935.*

With Christ During Passion Week. *Marion, Ind., n.d.*

The Holy Spirit. *Upland, Ind., 1938.*

The Messianic Hope in Both Testaments. *Upland, Ind., 1939.*

Introduction to Archaeology.

HUFFORD, MRS. LOIS GROSVENOR (MRS. GEORGE W.): 1845–1937.

Born in Paxton, Mass., in 1845, Lois Grosvenor attended school in Worcester, Mass., and was graduated from Antioch College in 1868. She was married to George W. Hufford on the day after her graduation. Her teaching career began in the East and continued in Indiana, where she was a teacher for fifty-one years. Coming to Indianapolis in 1878, she was head of the

English department at Shortridge High School for sixteen years. She was one of the originators of the Free Kindergarten Movement and founded the first daily high school paper—the SHORTRIDGE ECHO. She died in Indianapolis on Nov. 17, 1937. She annotated and edited several works besides those listed.

Information from the Indianapolis Public Library.

* * *

Plans for the Study of Some English Poems. *Indianapolis,* 1891.
Shakespeare in Tale and Verse. *New York,* 1902.

HUME, JOEL: 1807–1891.

Joel Hume, son of Jarred Hume, was born in Campbell (now Kenton) County, Ky., on June 13, 1807. His father died when Joel was an infant and left the family in straitened circumstances.

With only a limited formal education, young Joel came to Indiana when he was about fifteen years of age and located in Switzerland County. At seventeen he married Malinda Dusky. About two years later they moved to Parke County, where they lived for six or seven years.

In 1831 Joel Hume was baptized in the Primitive Baptist Church and in 1837 was ordained. In 1840 he moved to Posey County. Two years later he became pastor of the Bethlehem Church, near Poseyville, a pulpit he held for nearly twenty-eight years. He was also pastor of Bethany Church from 1845 until his death, which occurred on Mar. 29, 1891.

Information from the Alexandrian Free Public Library, Mount Vernon, Ind.

* * *

A Debate on Total Hereditary Depravity . . . *Mount Vernon, Ind.,* 1854.

HUNTER, HIRAM A.: 1800–1883.

Born in Kentucky on Aug. 10, 1800, the Rev. Hiram A. Hunter, minister in the Cumberland Presbyterian Church, was a resident of southern Indiana. He is known to have been a teacher in the "Old Seminary" in Gibson County in 1832, and, since his son was born and resided in the state, it seems safe to assume that a significant portion of the Rev. Mr. Hunter's life was spent in Indiana. He also held pastorates in Kentucky and Pennsylvania.

In 1830 he married Susannah Robb of Princeton, Ind. She died in 1835, and he was subsequently married twice. The last wife, Emmeline Griffith, survived him.

He died in Louisville, Ky., on Nov. 4, 1883.

His one recorded book is a rare and important narrative of an Indian captivity.

Information from Stormont—*History of Gibson County Indiana* and Josephine Hunter, granddaughter of Hiram A. Hunter.

* * *

A Narrative of the Captivity and Sufferings of Isaac Knight from Indian Barbarity. Giving an Account of the Cruel Treatment He Received from the Savages While Afflicted with the Small Pox: His Escape and Joyful Return After Enduring the Hardships of an Indian Prisoner, During Two Years and Six Months. Communicated by Himself, and at His Request Written by Hiram A. Hunter. *Evansville, Ind.,* 1839.

HUNTER, WILES ROBERT: 1874–

Robert Hunter (he did not use the name Wiles) was born in Terre Haute, Ind., on Apr. 10, 1874. A student of sociology, he held numerous important offices in charitable organizations in Chicago, New York and Berkeley, Calif. He was a candidate for the governorship of Connecticut in 1910. Besides his activities in the U. S., he was connected with settlement work in London.

Information from the Emmeline Fairbanks Memorial Library, Terre Haute, Ind.

* * *

Tenement House Conditions in Chicago. *Chicago,* 1901.
Poverty. *New York,* 1904.
Socialists at Work. *New York,* 1908.
Crisis: the Unions and the Courts, the Tyranny of Injunctions, the Power of Unity. *Chicago,* 1909.
Violence and the Labor Movement. *New York,* 1914.
Labor in Politics. *Chicago,* 1915.
Why We Fail as Christians. *New York,* 1919.
Bolshevism and the Labour Movement. *New York,* 1919.
The Links. *New York,* 1926.
Revolution; Why, How, When? *New York,* 1940.

HYMAN, MAX ROBINSON: 1859–1927.

Max Robinson Hyman was born in Edinburg, Ind., on Mar. 16, 1859. Coming to Indianapolis as a youth, he and his brother, Benjamin R., were employed on various Indianapolis newspapers and founded and edited for a time a humorous weekly, THE SCISSORS. Mr. Hyman died in Indianapolis on Apr. 28, 1927.

Information from the Indiana State Library.

* * *

A Centennial History and Handbook of Indiana; the Story of the State from Its Beginning to the Close of the Civil War and a General Survey of Progress to the Present Time (with George S. Cottman). *Indianapolis,* 1915.

Indianapolis; an Outline History and Description of the Hoosier Capital. *Indianapolis,* 1916.

I

IGLEHART, FERDINAND COWLE: 1845–1922.

Born in Warrick County, Ind., on Dec. 8, 1845, Ferdinand Cowle Iglehart, son of Asa and Ann Cowle Iglehart, was educated at De Pauw University, receiving the A.B. degree in 1867, A.M. in 1869, and D.D. in 1892.

In 1870 he was ordained in the Methodist Episcopal ministry, and from 1870 until 1882 he served as pastor of churches in Indiana. He was a pastor in Illinois and New York from 1882 to 1905. Until 1916 he was district superintendent of the New York Anti-Saloon League. He also served on the editorial staff of the CHRISTIAN HERALD. He married Nannie Dorsey Stewart in 1869 and died on July 21, 1922.

Information from *Who Was Who in America.*

* * *

The Speaking Oak and 300 Other Tales of Life, Love and Achievement. *New York,* 1902.

King Alcohol Dethroned. *Westerville, O.,* 1917.

Theodore Roosevelt: the Man as I Knew Him. *New York,* 1918.

INGRAHAM, ELLEN M.: 1832–1919.

Mrs. Ellen M. Ingraham, who wrote under the pen name of Grace Lintner, was born in New Haven, Conn., in 1832 and came to Indianapolis in April, 1865. She was a painter and art teacher. She died in 1919.

Information from the Barry Ms.

* * *

Bond and Free, a Tale of the South. *Indianapolis,* 1882.

J

JACOBS, SAMUEL: 1821–1891.

Samuel Jacobs was born in Pennsylvania in 1821 and moved to Logansport, Ind., in 1871. For a time

he was editor of the LOGANSPORT SUN and was mayor of the city from 1877 to 1881. He died in 1891 and was buried at Goodland, Ind. Before coming to Indiana he had been a Presbyterian minister but left the church.

Information from Powell—*History of Cass County,* 1913.

* * *

The Seventh Angel. 1856.

JEFFRIES, C.: ?–

The Indiana residence of "C. Jeffries" must be assumed from the general implications, in the title of his book, that it was written by a citizen of Lafayette for the entertainment and instruction of fellow citizens. The author is included here because of the great Indiana interest of his book.

The book is described as No. 35973 in Sabin—*Dictionary of Books Relating to America; from Its Discovery to the Present Time*—and is extremely rare.

Information from Walker—*The Beginnings of Printing in the State of Indiana.*

* * *

Wabash Captives; or the Awful Sentence: Thrilling Narrative of Crime and Death, and Wonderful Adventures of James Brady and Others, among the Indians on the Wabash, 60 Years Ago, Near the Spot Where Lafayette Now Stands; Founded on Facts. *Lafayette, Ind.,* 1846.

JELLEY, SYMMES M.: ?–

According to the Rising Sun, Ind., Public Library, Symmes M. Jelley was a resident of that place. No definite biographical data has been located.

As will be seen, Jelley's pen name is a loosely constructed anagram of his full name.

Information from the Rising Sun (Ind.) Public Library.

* * *

Shadowed to Europe, by Le Jemlys. *Chicago,* 1885.

Successful Writing, a Literary Compendium . . . *Chicago,* 1887.

The Voice of Labor. *Philadelphia,* 1888.

The Scarlet Handkerchief, by Le Jemlys. *Chicago,* 1889.

JENKINS, CHARLES FRANCIS: 1867–1934.

Son of Amasa Milton and Mary Ann Thomas Jenkins, Charles Francis Jenkins was born on Aug. 22, 1867.

He was educated in the Fountain City, Ind., schools, the Spiceland (Ind.) Academy and was a student at Earlham College, which in 1928 granted him the honorary Sc.D. degree in recognition of his achievements as an inventor.

He married Grace Love of Darlington, Md., on Jan. 30, 1902, and spent most of his adult life in the East, working mostly in the fields of motion pictures, radio and television.

Information from the Richmond Public Library.

* * *

Picture Ribbons, Exposition of the Methods and Apparatus Employed in the Manufacture of the Picture Ribbons Used in the Projecting Lanterns to Give the Appearance of Objects in Motion. *Washington, D. C.,* 1897.

Animated Pictures; an Exposition of the Historical Development of Chronophotography, Its Present Scientific Applications and Future Possibilities. *Washington, D. C.,* 1898.

Handbook for Motion Picture and Stereoptican Operators (with Oscar B. Depue). *Washington, D. C.,* 1908.

Motion Pictures in Teaching. *Washington, D. C.,* 1916.

Vision by Radio, Radio Photographs, Radio Photograms. *Washington, D.C.,* 1925.

Radio Movies, Radiovision, Television. *Washington, D. C.,* 1929.

The Boyhood of an Inventor. *Washington, D. C.,* 1931.

JENKINSON, ISAAC: 1825–1911.

Isaac Jenkinson was the son of John Jenkinson of Piqua, O. He was born on Apr. 29, 1825. Little information on his youth is available, but in his early manhood he lived on a farm in Randolph County, Ind., and in the early Fifties he married Narcissa Lewis and settled in Fort Wayne, Ind.

In partnership with David W. Jones he founded the FORT WAYNE GAZETTE in 1863 and acted as its editor through the Civil War years.

He was appointed U. S. consul at Glasgow in 1869 and served until 1874, when he returned to Indiana and purchased the RICHMOND PALLADIUM, then a weekly newspaper. He began its daily issue and managed it for twenty-five years. He was interested in state and national affairs, wrote for the press and spoke considerably. He served as a trustee of Indiana University for more than thirty years.

Isaac Jenkinson died on Oct. 25, 1911.

Information from the Richmond Public Library.

* * *

The Peace Party and Its Policy. Speech of Isaac Jenkinson, at Fort Wayne, Indiana, March 16, 1863. *Fort Wayne, Ind.,* 1863.

Aaron Burr; His Personal and Political Relations with Thomas Jefferson and Alexander Hamilton. *Richmond, Ind.,* 1902.

JEWETT, CHARLES L.: 1848–1931.

Charles L. (Reid) Jewett, son of Jonathan and Mary Wells Reid, was born in Hanover, Ind., on Oct. 6, 1848. His father died soon after his birth, and his mother married Judge P. H. Jewett, who adopted the boy.

Jewett attended Indiana University and Hanover College. He went to Montana Territory as a young man and engaged in prospecting, mining and as a government surveyor. Returning to Indiana in 1869, he was admitted to the bar at New Albany, where in the following years he held numerous county offices, including justice of the peace, prosecuting attorney, and district attorney.

Information from *Representative Men of Indiana,* Vol. I.

* * *

Memorial Address to Indianapolis Lodge, No. 13, B.P. O.E., . . . Dec. 1, 1895. *Indianapolis,* 1895.

Selected Addresses, Arranged and Published by Charles W. Cottom. *Indianapolis,* 1901.

JOHN, JOHN PRICE DURBIN: 1843–1916.

John Price Durbin John, son of Robert and Martha Wiles John, was born in Brookville, Ind., on Nov. 25, 1843. Until he was sixteen years old he attended Brookville College, then taught in the public schools of Franklin County from 1860 to 1863. He received the A.M. degree from McKendree College in 1867. He was professor of mathematics and president of three schools—Brookville College, Moore's Hill College, and DePauw University. After 1895 he was a platform lecturer. He married Orra Poundstone in 1869 and died on Aug. 7, 1916.

Information from *Who Was Who in America.*

* * *

Did Man Make God or Did God Make Man. *Indianapolis,* 1898.

Signs of God in the World. *New York,* 1907.

The Worth of a Man. *New York,* 1907.

JOHNSON, ALEXANDER: 1847–1941.

Alexander Johnson, son of John and Amelia Hill Johnson, was born at Ashton-under-Lynn, Lancashire, England, on Jan. 2, 1847. Following an education in private schools and in Mechanics' Institute and Owens College (now Victoria University) in Manchester, he came to the U. S. in 1869 and engaged in the clothing business until 1884.

He was secretary of charitable organizations in Cincinnati and Chicago until 1889, when he came to Indiana as secretary for the State Board of Charities. From 1893 to 1903 he was superintendent of the Indiana School for Feeble Minded Youth, and from 1904 to 1913 he served as general secretary for the National Conference of Charities and Corrections in Fort Wayne, Ind. After 1921 he was staff representative of the Southern Division of the American Red Cross. He married Eliza Ann Johnston in 1872 and died on May 17, 1941.

Information from *Who Was Who in America*.

* * *

The Ethical Basis of Charity. An Essay Read before the Fortnightly Club, Fort Wayne, Ind., January 6, 1896. n.p., 1896.

The Almshouse, Construction and Management. *New York,* 1911.

Menace of the Mentally Defective (with Margaret Johnson Lane). *Boston,* 1916.

Adventures in Social Welfare; Being Reminiscences of Things, Thoughts and Folks During Forty Years of Social Work. *Fort Wayne, Ind.,* 1923.

JOHNSON, FRANCIS: 1837–1908.

Francis Johnson was born in Rostock, Germany, in 1837, the son of Lewis Johnson, then professor of modern literature and history at the local university. The family came to Lafayette, Ind., in 1855.

Francis Johnson traveled in Europe in 1868-69 and returned to the U. S. to take an editorial position on THE LAKESIDE MONTHLY, Chicago, in May, 1870. After the Chicago fire he went to New York and did free-lance writing and editorial work until 1873, when he returned to Lafayette, Ind.

In 1874 he established a German language newspaper, DER DEUTSCH-AMERIKANER, and continued to edit and publish it in Lafayette until 1904, when failing health made its abandonment necessary. He died on Mar. 5, 1908.

de Hart—*Past and Present of Tippecanoe County,* 1909.

* * *

Famous Assassinations of History. *Chicago,* 1903.

JOHNSON, OVERTON: ?–1849.

Overton Johnson, with William H. Winter, wrote what is probably the most consistently high in value of all collected books by Indiana authors—*Route Across the Rocky Mountains, with a Description of Oregon and California . . . Lafayette,* 1846.

The book was reprinted in 1932 in the Princeton University Press series *Narratives of the Trans-Mississippi Frontier.* The reprint carries a foreword by Carl L. Cannon who, unfortunately, had very little authentic information about the authors. However, Mrs. Louis B. Hopkins, acting as Wabash College archivist in 1940-41 gathered a considerable amount of data on the two authors, especially during their college years, and it is partly from her notes that the following sketch of the life of Overton Johnson is compiled:

Overton Johnson, son of James B. Johnson, was probably born in Ohio sometime around 1820. His parents moved to the Crawfordsville, Ind., neighborhood before 1834 and young Overton was enrolled in the Wabash College preparatory department for the years 1834-35 and 1835-36, with his home address given as Crawfordsville: the address shows, however, for the years 1836-37 and 1837-38 as Tippecanoe County. The Johnson family was reasonably prosperous and the elder Johnson was able to send his son on to college. He was enrolled as a freshman at Wabash College in 1838-39, and as a sophomore in 1839-40. In these two college years he gives his residence as his father's home in Crawfordsville—apparently indicating that the family had returned from Tippecanoe County.

He continued as a student in 1840-41 but in that academic year he gave his home address as Concord, Ind. It is known that his father was postmaster of this town and that he owned a considerable tract of land in the neighborhood so it may be presumed that it had become the family's permanent residence.

It is apparent from the college records that Overton Johnson did not complete this third year and it seems possible that he may have gone to Missouri, during the previous summer vacation, to visit William Henry Winter, whom he had known as a student at Wabash and who had already gone as far west as Missouri.

F. S. McCabe, of the Wabash College class of 1846, writing an article containing college reminiscences for the Wabash College yearbook of 1896, says: "In 1841 Mr. Overton Johnson, a student belonging to a family residing a little north of town, returned from an overland trip to the Pacific Coast. [Mr. McCabe is obviously in error in this, as Johnson definitely did not go to the Pacific Coast before 1843; he probably has confused the date and refers to this visit which it is supposed Johnson made to Winter in Missouri, probably during the summer vacation of 1841.] Though Johnson wore his brown hair falling over his shoulders, after the manner of plainsmen, he was a very quiet and amiable gentleman. He was the author of a book containing an account of his journey, and he published the MORION which I think was the first [news]paper published by a student of Wabash College."

It seems very likely that the trip to Oregon may have been planned by the two young men during this visit and that Johnson may have returned to school but found his unrest too acute to allow him to finish the college year.

Besides being "a very quiet and amiable gentleman" Overton Johnson seems to have been a slightly absent-minded and a rather affluent one, for Judge John M. Cowan, of the class of 1842, relates that, at the time the college dormitory burned in 1838, "There were some amusing incidents occurred during the fire, showing the utter lack of coolness on the part of some of the students. One I remember was that of Overton Johnson, who occupied a room on the second floor. In his excitement he threw out of his window his looking glass, basin, pitcher, and gold watch, and afterwards came down the stairs carrying some of his clothes and bedding. Incidentally, I might say, that same gold watch was the only one owned by anyone in college, not even excepting the members of the faculty."

There is an apparently unfounded tradition that Johnson went west because of an unhappy love affair: no such motive was needed in those days of excitement over the Northwest and it is much more likely that he was simply afflicted with that restlessness which has been common to college juniors of all times.

Be the reasons what they may, Johnson went west, returned, and in 1846, published the book which he and Winter had written.

Among the papers of the Rev. E. O. Hovey, first member of the Wabash College faculty, is a manuscript copy of the Wabash College catalogue for Nov. 12, 1845, which contains the name of Overton Johnson. While his name was not printed in the college catalogue for that year he very evidently re-enrolled in college upon his return from the West, made a brief attempt to continue college work but soon gave it up.

In subsequent college directories he is listed as an "ex" member of the class of 1847. This probably represents the estimate of the registrar as to the date at which Johnson could complete his work for a degree at the time he re-enrolled in 1845.

Few details of his last years are available. He is said to have taught school at Dayton, Ind., in 1847-48, and a letter exists, written by Mrs. Joanna Elston Lane (wife of Henry S. Lane) which mentions the fact that her half-uncle, William Henry Winter, planned to return to California in 1849 and that she had agreed to outfit "another young man" to accompany him, she to receive a fourth of whatever he should make in the mines. This young man was, presumably, Overton Johnson. Whatever hopes of gain Mrs. Lane may have had she was to be disappointed, for Overton Johnson died on Feb. 15, 1849, while still residing in Indiana.

Information from the Wabash College Archives.

* * *

Route Across the Rocky Mountains, with a Description of Oregon and California; Geographical Features. Their Resources, Soil, Climate, Productions, Etc., Etc. (with William H. Winter). *Lafayette,* 1846.

JOHNSON, RICHARD OTTO: 1859–1928.

Born at Lewisville, Ind., in 1859, Richard Otto Johnson was educated in Indianapolis and at Wittenberg College, Earlham College, and the Virginia Military Institute. He was connected with the Indiana State School for the Deaf as bookkeeper and as superintendent and was at one time business manager of the Indianapolis schools. He died in Indianapolis in 1928.

Information from Indianapolis Public Library.

* * *

Flashlights of Literature. *Indianapolis,* 1891.

Standardization, Efficiency, and Heredity in Schools, with Special Reference to the Deaf. *Indianapolis,* 1920.

JOHNSON, ROBERT UNDERWOOD: 1853–1937.

Born in Washington, D. C., on Jan. 12, 1853, Robert Underwood Johnson was reared in Centerville, Ind., educated in the Wayne County schools, and received the B.S. degree from Earlham College in 1871. He later received an honorary Ph.D. from Earlham in 1889, A.M. from Yale in 1891, and L.H.D. from New York University in 1911. He entered the employ of the publishing firm of Charles Scribner's Sons in 1873.

Three years later he married Katherine McMahon of Washington and they made their home in New York.

Johnson became an associate editor of the CENTURY MAGAZINE in 1881 and editor-in-chief in 1909, continuing until 1913. With Clarence Clough Buel he edited the monumental *Battles and Leaders of the Civil War*, and it was he who persuaded General Grant that his memoirs might bring in enough financial return to help liquidate the debts which the honesty and guilelessness of the doughty old general had enabled his associates to leave him.

He took an active part in the movement to set aside land in the Yosemite Valley as a national park and in the correction of abuses in the current international copyright laws: for his work in the latter field he was decorated by the French and Italian governments.

He died in 1937.

> Information from Parker and Heiney—*Poets and Poetry of Indiana* and supplied by the Richmond Public Library.

* * *

The Winter Hour, and Other Poems. *New York,* 1892.

Songs of Liberty and Other Poems; Including Paraphrases from the Servian after Translations by Nikola Tesla: with a Prefatory Note by Him on Servian Poetry. *New York,* 1897.

Poems. *New York,* 1902. (Followed by an enlarged collection in 1908.)

Saint Gaudens, an Ode and Other Verse; being the Third Edition of His "Poems." *New York,* 1910.

The "Coastwise Exemption," the Nation Against It: an Appeal on Behalf of the National Honor and a Sound Business Policy. *New York,* 1913.

Poems of War and Peace. *Indianapolis,* 1916.

Italian Rhapsody and Other Poems of Italy. *New York,* 1917.

Collected Poems, 1881-1919. *New Haven, Conn.,* 1920.

Remembered Yesterdays. *Boston,* 1923.

Poems of the Longer Flight. *New York,* 1928.

The Pact of Honor and Other Poems. *New York,* 1929.

Poems of the Lighter Touch. 1930.

Poems of Fifty Years. *New York,* 1931.

Aftermath. *New York,* 1933.

Heroes, Children and Fun. *New York,* 1934.

Your Hall of Fame. *New York,* 1935.

JOHNSTON, ANNIE FELLOWS: 1863–1931.

(See also sketch of Albion Fellows Bacon.)

"Annie Fellows Johnston . . . author of books for children, was born in Evansville, Ind., of pioneer stock. . . . One of the grandparents of her mother, Mary Erskine . . . was a Scotch Covenanter who emigrated from Ireland to join the New Harmony Colony and eventually settled in the frontier hamlet of Evansville. Her father, Albion Fellows, a Methodist minister whose parents were early Illinois settlers from New Hampshire, died when Annie was two years old. She and her two sisters grew up in rural MacCutchanville, not far from Evansville. Here she lived a wholesome country life, listened to stories of pioneer endeavor and accomplishment, learned to work with a conscientious regard for duty, attended the district school, read the entire Sunday school library, the sentimental GODEY'S LADY'S BOOK, ST. NICHOLAS, and the YOUTH'S COMPANION, and wrote stories and poems in imitation of those she read.

"When she was seventeen she taught for one term in the district school which she had been attending. After a year of study at the University of Iowa, 1881-82, she taught in the public school of Evansville for three years and then when teaching threatened her health, she worked in an office. She traveled for a few months in New England and in Europe. But whether in the school room or the office, in college or traveling she lived in the midst of cousins whose number was legion and whose social environment and religious beliefs were similar to her own. It is therefore not surprising that she married a cousin, William L. Johnston, a widower with three young children (1888). He encouraged her to write, and during the three years of their married life she contributed occasional stories to the YOUTH'S COMPANION. Her husband's death in 1892 and the necessity of supporting his children gave a forced impetus to her writing. Her first book, *Big Brother,* was published in 1893. After the completion of *Joel: a Boy of Galilee,* in 1895, Mrs. Johnston visited in the Pewee Valley, near Louisville, Ky., where her stepchildren had lived with relatives. A spirited little girl who resembled a colonel of the old school and the atmosphere of leisure and of aristocratic living which still lingered in the valley from the days of slavery so caught her fancy that when she returned to Evansville she depicted them in *The Little Colonel* (1895), the first of a series of twelve books.

"Pewee Valley became the setting not only of many of her most popular books but of her own life. She moved there in 1898 and it remained home to her until her death more than thirty years later. From 1901 until her stepson died in 1910 she made a temporary home for him where the climate would benefit his health, first in Arizona, then in California, and, for eight years, in Texas. Her sojourn in the Southwest gave her the setting for several of her stories . . . Without superior gifts of imagination, keen and balanced observation, or psychological acuteness, Mrs. Johnston entertained thousands of children and inspired many of them to emulate the integrity of her characters, who lived in a world where good intentions prevail and where simple virtues are glorified. By drawing upon her own idealized childhood and the scenes and people she loved, she created a glamour about her characters which charmed her youthful readers . . ."

Condensed from V. L. S., *Dictionary of American Biography*, Vol. X.

* * *

Big Brother. *Boston, 1894.*

Joel: a Boy of Galilee. *Boston, 1895.*

The Little Colonel. *Boston, 1896.*

In League with Israel: A Tale. *New York, 1896.*

Songs Ysame (with Albion Fellows Bacon). *Boston, 1897.*

Ole Mammy's Torment. *Boston, 1897.*

The Gate of the Giant Scissors. *Boston, 1898.* (Reissued in 1906 under title, Giant Scissors.)

Two Little Knights of Kentucky, Who Were the Little Colonel's Neighbors. *Boston, 1899.*

The Story of Dago. *Boston, 1900.*

The Little Colonel's House Party. *Boston, 1901.*

The Little Colonel's Holidays. *Boston, 1901.*

Asa Holmes; or, at the Cross-Roads. *Boston, 1902.*

Cicely and Other Stories. *Boston, 1903.*

The Little Colonel's Hero: Music by Albion Fellows Bacon. *Boston, 1903.*

Aunt Liza's Hero, and Other Stories. *Boston, 1903.*

Little Colonel Stories. *Boston, 1904*

Flip's "Islands of Providence." *Boston, 1904.*

Little Colonel at Boarding-School. *Boston, 1904.*

The Quilt That Jack Built. *Boston, 1904.*

The Little Colonel in Arizona. *Boston, 1905.*

In the Desert of Waiting: the Legend of Camelback Mountain. *Boston, 1905.*

Three Weavers: a Fairy Tale for Fathers and Mothers as well as for their Daughters. *Boston, 1905.*

Keeping Tryst. *Boston, 1906.*

Little Colonel: Maid of Honor. *Boston, 1906.*

Mildred's Inheritance; Just Her Way; Ann's Own Way. *Boston, 1906.*

Little Colonel's Christmas Vacation. *Boston, 1906.*

Legend of the Bleeding Heart. *Boston, 1907.*

Little Colonel's Knight Comes Riding. *Boston, 1907.*

Mary Ware, the Little Colonel's Chum. *Boston, 1908.*

Rescue of the Princess Winsome: a Fairy Play for Old and Young. *Boston, 1908.*

The Jester's Sword. *Boston, 1909.*

Little Colonel's Good Times Book. *Boston, 1909.*

The Little Colonel Doll Book, Representing Characters and Costumes from the Books of the Little Colonel Series. *Boston, 1910.*

Mary Ware in Texas. *Boston, 1910.*

Travelers Five Along Life's Highway: Jimmy, Gideon Wiggan, the Clown, Wexley Snathers, Bap Sloan. *Boston, 1911.*

Mary Ware's Promised Land. *Boston, 1912.*

Miss Santa Claus of the Pullman. *New York, 1913.*

Mary Ware Doll Book: a Companion Volume to the Little Colonel Doll Book; Representing Characters and Costumes from the Books of the Little Colonel Series. *Boston, 1914.*

Georgina of the Rainbows. *New York, 1916.*

Little Colonel Story Hour Books. *Boston, 1917.*

Georgina's Service Stars. *New York, 1918.*

Little Man in Motley. *Boston, 1918.*

Story of the Red Cross as told to the Little Colonel. *Boston, 1918.*

It was the Road to Jericho. *New York, 1919.*

The Road of the Loving Heart. *Boston, 1922.*

The Land of the Little Colonel; Reminiscence and Autobiography. *Boston, 1929.*

Little Colonel Stories; Second Series. *Boston, 1930.*

For Pierre's Sake, and Other Stories. *Boston, 1934.*

JOHNSTON, REMINGTON ALLEN: 1875–1946.

Remington Allen Johnston was born in Ossian, Ind., on Sept. 18, 1875, the youngest son of James and Mary Ann Glass Johnston, who were pioneers from Ohio. He graduated from Ossian High School and attended Wabash College for two years, a member of the class of 1901.

While in college he was a roommate of Edwin Meade Robinson, famous among Wabash men for having written the words to the college song and known nationally as a newspaperman, author, and critic of long service on the CLEVELAND PLAIN DEALER; and the friendship begun then between the two men lasted throughout their lifetimes. Both died in 1946.

On Nov. 24, 1903, Mr. Johnston married May Hamilton of Beaver, Pa., and in 1905 he went to Chicago to become associate editor of RED BOOK under Trumbull White. When ill health forced his retirement from this work, he returned to Indiana.

He was best known for his short stories, many of them published in RED BOOK and GREEN BOOK magazines. From May, 1917, to September, 1922, he conducted a humorous column, "The Transfer Corner," in a Fort Wayne newspaper. In addition to his literary and editorial work Mr. Johnston spent many years as an instructor in short story writing.

He died on Mar. 24, 1946.

Information from Mrs. Remington Johnston.

* * *

Starshine and Dew, and Other Poems. *Ossian, Ind.,* 1900.
Whispers from the Vast. 1907.
Practical Points on Short Story Writing and Selling. *Ossian, Ind.,* 1924.

JOHNSTONE, WILLIAM JACKSON: 1867–1939.

William Jackson Johnstone, son of Brison Blair and Lydia Overton Johnstone, was born in Daviess County, Ind., on Aug. 7, 1867, and graduated from the normal school in Bloomfield, Ind., in 1884. He was also a student at DePauw University, and Johns Hopkins University, which in 1935 awarded him the A.B. degree as of 1892.

After teaching in the country schools and serving as principal at Odon, Ind., he became a minister in the United Brethren Church in 1887 and was pastor at Odon for one year. In 1888 he became principal of the normal department of Otterbein University, and from 1891 to 1893 he was a pastor in Baltimore, Md. In 1895 he was ordained to the Presbyterian ministry. The remainder of his life was spent principally in Minnesota, where he was pastor of churches in Minneapolis and St. Paul and field secretary for Macalester College. He married Jeannette C. Walls in 1888 and died on Apr. 18, 1939.

Information from *Who Was Who in America.*

* * *

Abraham Lincoln, the Christian. *New York,* 1913.
George Washington, the Christian. *New York,* 1919.
Manual of Moral Welfare. 1920.
Prohibition Addresses. 1921.
How Lincoln Prayed. *New York,* 1931.
How Washington Prayed. *New York,* 1932.
Robert E. Lee, the Christian. *New York,* 1933.

JONES, AMOS: 1821–1903.

"Amos Jones was born in Massachusetts in 1821. He was graduated from Dartmouth College in 1843 and from Lane Theological Seminary in 1846. He moved to Cass County, Ind., in 1881 where he lived until 1896. He became a disciple of Alexander Dowie and moved to Zion City, Ill., where he died in 1903. He was married twice, the last time to Mary H. Martin of Logansport, in 1882.

From Powell—*History of Cass County,* 1913.

* * *

The Great Builder. (Poems.)

JONES, EPAPHRAS: ?–?

The only evidence of Indiana residence of this author is the dating of the title page—which also serves as a sort of dedication, apology and *raison d'etre* in general —as "Providence, Ind., May 2d, 1831."

His work is a contribution to the discussion then flourishing as to whether or not the American Indians were descended from one of the "Lost Tribes of Israel."

It is possible that Mr. Jones was an itinerant minister.

Information from Walker—*Beginnings of Printing in the State of Indiana.*

* * *

On the Ten Tribes of Israel, and the Aborigines of America, Etc. Etc. By a Bible Professor. This Publication is not made to Gratify Man, but to Aid the Cause of God; Therefore, Anyone is at Liberty to Approve, or Disapprove of the Work. It Is, However, to be Hoped that the Right Object will be Kept in View. The Arrangement Might Have Been Better, but that is of Little Consequence. Nett Sales of the Publication will be Appropriated to the Canada Mission—to the Indians. Providence, Indiana, May 2d, 1831. *New Albany, Ind.,* 1831.

JORDAN, DULCINA MASON (MRS. JAMES J.): 1833–1895.

Dulcina Mason was born at Marathon, N. Y., on July 21, 1833. She came to Indiana, presumably with her parents, when she was ten years old and is said to have secured an education entirely by her own efforts.

When quite young she married James J. Jordan, a business man of Richmond, Ind. She became the mother of five children and during almost all of her adult years she managed to keep up newspaper work in Indiana and, for three years, in Ohio as associate editor of the CINCINNATI SATURDAY NIGHT. She is described as a woman of boundless energy.

Mrs. Jordan died in Richmond, Ind., on Apr. 25, 1895. Her one book is a volume of verse.

Information from Parker and Heiney—*Poets and Poetry of Indiana* and the Richmond Public Library.

* * *

Rosemary Leaves. *Cincinnati,* 1873.

JUDAH, MARY JAMESON (MRS. ?): 1851–1930.

Mrs. Mary Jameson Judah was born in Indianapolis in 1851 and lived there all of her life, except for a few years in Memphis, Tenn. She is referred to as the "friend and adviser of James Whitcomb Riley and Booth Tarkington." She contributed many stories to SCRIBNER'S and HARPER'S. She died in 1930.

Information from the Indianapolis Public Library.

* * *

The Outcomings of Addisonville: a Story (with May Louise Shipp). *Indianapolis,* 1892.
Down Our Way; Stories of Southern and Western Character. *Chicago,* 1897.

JUDSON, CLARA INGRAM (MRS. JAMES MCINTOSH): 1879–

Born in Logansport, Ind., on May 4, 1879, Clara Ingram, daughter of John Carl and Mary Colby Ingram, moved with her family to Indianapolis when she was six and graduated from the Indianapolis Girls' Classical School in 1898. She married James McIntosh Judson on June 26, 1901. They lived in Richmond, Ind., for ten years, then moved to Chicago, and later to Evanston, Ill.

A writer principally of juvenile fiction, Mrs. Judson is also well known as a lecturer, a contributor to magazines, and the originator of several newspaper features. She was at one time treasurer of the Society of Midland Authors.

Information from *Who's Who in America*; Burke and Howe—*American Authors and Books, 1640-1940*; and Mrs. Judson.

* * *

Flower Fairies. *Chicago,* 1915.
Good-Night Stories. *Chicago,* 1916.
Billy Robin and His Neighbors. *Chicago,* 1917.
Foxy Squirrel. 1917.
Cooking Without Mother's Help; a Story Cook Book for Beginners. *New York,* 1918.
Sewing Without Mother's Help; a Story Sewing Book for Beginners. *New York,* 1918.
Mary Jane—Her Book. *New York,* 1918.
Mary Jane—Her Visit. *New York,* 1918.
Mary Jane's Kindergarten. *New York,* 1918.
Tommy Tittlemouse. *Chicago,* 1918.
Mary Jane Down South. *New York,* 1919.

Mary Jane's City Home. *New York,* 1920.
Junior Cook Book. *New York,* 1920.
The Camp at Gravel Point. *Boston,* 1921.
Foxy Squirrel in the Garden. *Chicago,* 1921.
Business Girls Budget Book. *Chicago,* 1921.
Mary Jane in New England. *New York,* 1921.
Garden Adventures of Tommy Tittlemouse. *Chicago,* 1922.
Mary Jane's Country Home. *New York,* 1922.
Household Budget Book. *Chicago,* 1922.
Jerry and Jean, Detectors. *Chicago,* 1923.
Business Man's Budget Book. *Chicago,* 1923.
My Household Day Book. *Chicago,* 1923.
Garden Adventures in Winter. *Chicago,* 1923.
Mary Jane at School. *New York,* 1923.
Mary Jane in Canada. *New York,* 1924.
Mary Jane's Summer Fun. *New York,* 1925.
Mary Jane's Winter Sports. *New York,* 1926.
Virginia Lee. *New York,* 1926. (Reissued in 1939 as Virginia Lee's Bicycle Club.)
The Child Life Cook Book. *Chicago,* 1926.
Mary Jane's Vacation. *New York,* 1927.
Alice Ann. *New York,* 1928.
Mary Jane in England. *New York,* 1928.
Mary Jane in Scotland. *New York,* 1929.
Mary Jane in France. *New York,* 1930.
Mary Jane in Switzerland. *New York,* 1931.
Mary Jane in Italy. *New York,* 1933.
Mary Jane in Spain. *New York,* 1937.
Play Days. *New York,* 1937.
Mary Jane's Friends in Holland. *New York,* 1939.
Pioneer Girl: the Early Life of Frances Willard. *Chicago,* 1939.
People Who Come to Our House. *Chicago,* 1940.
Boat Builder: the Story of Robert Fulton. *New York,* 1940.
Railway Engineer: the Story of George Stephenson. *New York,* 1941.
They Came From Sweden. *Boston,* 1942.
People Who Work Near Our House. *Chicago,* 1942.
Soldier Doctor, the Story of William Gorgas. *New York,* 1942.
Donald McKay, Designer of Clipper Ships. *New York,* 1943.
People Who Work in the Country and in the City. *Chicago,* 1943.
They Came From France. *Boston,* 1943.
They Came From Scotland. *Boston,* 1944.
Petar's Treasure. *Boston,* 1945.
Michael's Victory. *Boston,* 1946.
Summer Time. *Nashville,* 1947.
The Lost Violin. *Boston,* 1947.

JULIAN, GEORGE WASHINGTON: 1817–1899.

"George Washington Julian (May 5, 1817-July 7, 1899), abolitionist leader, son of Isaac and Rebecca (Hoover) Julian, was born in a log cabin a mile and a half south of Centerville, Wayne County, Ind. His father . . . was a soldier in the War of 1812 and at one time a member of the Indiana Legislature. His mother, of German descent, was a Quaker . . . Isaac Julian died when George was only six years old, but by hard work and frugality the widowed mother managed to bring up the family of children. George attended the common schools, at eighteen taught a district school, presently studied law, and in 1840 was admitted to the bar, practicing successively in New Castle, Greenfield, and Centerville. In 1845 he was elected to the state Legislature as a Whig . . . About the same time he began to write newspaper articles attacking slavery. Defeated in 1847 in an attempt to secure the Whig nomination for state senator, he presently joined the Free-Soil Party and the next year attended the Buffalo convention that nominated Van Buren. His activities as an abolitionist had caused him to be ostracized by many former friends and associates and had even brought about the dissolution of a law partnership with his brother, but the political tide presently turned in his favor and in 1848, having been nominated for Congress by the Free-Soilers, he was elected, with the assistance of many Democratic votes. As a member of the little group of anti-slavery men in Congress he vigorously opposed the compromise measures of 1850. Beaten for re-election in that year, he resumed the practice of law but continued his advocacy of abolition both in speeches and in the press. In 1852 he was nominated for the vice-presidency by the Free-Soil party and took an active part in the campaign.

"Julian's real opportunity came with the rise of the Republican party, of which the Free-Soil party had been a forerunner. In 1856 he participated in the Pittsburgh convention that formally organized the new party, and was chosen one of the vice-presidents and chairman of the committee on organization. His earnest fight for human freedom brought reward at last when in 1860 he was elected to Congress. Four times re-elected, he speedily won a prominent place in legislative deliberations, and among the committees on which he served was the very important committee on the conduct of the war. He early began to urge the emancipation of slaves as a war measure, advancing the argument of John Quincy Adams that such a step would be within the war powers of the president and Congress. As chairman of the committee on public lands

he had an important part in the passage of the celebrated Homestead Act, a measure he had urged in 1851. Though he thought Lincoln too slow in some respects and opposed his reconstruction plan, Julian refused to join in the attempt in 1864 to nominate Chase in Lincoln's stead . . . He stood . . . with the Radicals in their battles with President Johnson, and in 1867 was one of the committee of seven appointed by the House to prepare the articles of impeachment against the President. In 1868 he proposed an amendment to the Constitution conferring the right of suffrage upon women, a reform he continued to champion to the end of his life.

"Failing of renomination in 1870, he devoted much of his time to recuperating his broken health . . . He had come to be out of sympathy with the influences that dominated the Republican party nationally and in Indiana, and joined the Liberal Republican movement, presiding during parts of two days over the Cincinnati convention (1872) that nominated Horace Greeley. The next year he removed to Irvington, a suburb of Indianapolis, and for some years was occupied with writing and championing reform measures. He supported Tilden in the campaign of 1876, and two million copies of his speech, 'The Gospel of Reform,' were distributed by the Democratic National Committee. In the years that followed he contributed notable articles on politics, the public lands, and other subjects to the NORTH AMERICAN REVIEW and other periodicals . . . After the election of Cleveland in that year he was appointed surveyor general of New Mexico, a post for which he was particularly fitted. During his administration (July 1885-September 1889) he brought to light many flagrant frauds in connection with public land grants . . . He died at his home in Irvington in the summer of 1899.

"Julian was twice married. His first wife was Anne Elizabeth Finch of Centerville, who died in November, 1860, a few days after his election to Congress. His second wife, whom he married Dec. 31, 1863, was Laura Giddings, daughter of Joshua R. Giddings. She died in 1884."

Condensed from P. L. H., *Dictionary of American Biography*, Vol. X.

* * *

Speech on the Slavery Question May 14, 1850. n.p., n.d.

Speech Delivered . . . Indianapolis, Ind., on Friday Evening, November 17, 1865. [*Indianapolis*, 1865.]

Dangers and Duties. Reconstruction and Suffrage. *Cincinnati*, 1865.

Select Speeches . . . Delivered in the House of Representatives of the United States Since the Beginning of the Rebellion. *Cincinnati,* 1867.

Speeches on Political Questions. *New York,* 1872.

Political Recollections. 1840 to 1872. *Chicago,* 1884.

Later Speeches on Political Questions with Select Controversial Papers (Edited by Grace Julian Clarke). *Indianapolis,* 1889.

The Rank of Charles Osborn as an Anti-Slavery Pioneer. *Indianapolis,* 1891.

The Life of Joshua R. Giddings. *Chicago,* 1892.

President Harrison and Civil Service Reform. [*Indianapolis,* 1892.]

JULIAN, ISAAC HOOVER: 1823–?

Isaac Hoover Julian, son of Isaac and Rebecca Hoover Julian and younger brother of George Washington Julian, was born near Centerville, Ind., on June 19, 1823. He was chiefly self-educated. In 1846 he moved to Iowa, but he returned to Indiana in 1850, settled in Centerville, and was admitted to the bar in 1851.

From 1858 to 1872 he edited THE TRUE REPUBLICAN, first published in Centerville and later in Richmond, Ind. He moved to San Marcos, Tex., in 1873, where he edited the FREE PRESS for seventeen years and the PEOPLE'S ERA until June of 1900. Mr. Julian was a leader in anti-slavery and temperance movements and was an early contributor to periodicals. He was married first to Virginia M. Spillard, who died in 1873, and in 1893 he married Isabel McCoy Harvey.

Information from *Who Was Who in America* and *Appletons' Cyclopaedia of American Biography,* Vol. III.

* * *

Memoir of David Hoover. *Richmond, Ind.,* 1857.

Sketches of the Early History of the Whitewater Valley. n.p., 1857.

Late-Gathered Leaves in Verse and Prose.

Outline History of the Julian and Hoover Families.

Eustace and Caroline; a Pastoral Tale. *San Marcos, Tex.,* 1901.

Samples of the Briefer Poems of . . . *San Marcos, Tex.,* 1903.

JUSTICE, MAIBELLE HEICKS MONROE (MRS. ?): 1871–

Maibelle Heicks Monroe Justice, daughter of James and Grace E. Heicks Monroe, was born in Logansport, Ind., in 1871. She was educated in Logansport and in

New York City. In 1899 she moved to Chicago and later to New York. She contributed a considerable number of short stories to popular periodicals between 1898 and 1910 and was a member of the Gotham Club, Authors Guild and other literary societies.

Information from Powell—*History of Cass County,* 1913.

* * *

Love Affairs of A Worldly Man. *Chicago,* 1894.

K

KARN, ESTHER NELSON (MRS. ?): 1880–

Born near New Philadelphia, O., in 1880, Esther Nelson Karn grew up in De Kalb County, Ind., was educated at Hicksville Union High School, where she taught for one year, and attended the Detroit School of Journalism and the De Silva School of Oratory in Fort Wayne, Ind. Following her marriage she moved to Fort Wayne.

Information from Parker and Heiney—*Poets and Poetry of Indiana* and the Barry Ms.

* * *

Snow Flakes. *Philadelphia,* 1900.

Violets. 1908.

Wild Roses. *Fort Wayne, Ind.,* 1915.

Lure of the Wilds. *Boston,* 1925.

The First Easter Dawn (Illus. by the author).

KATTERJOHN, MONTE MELCHIOR: 1891–

Monte M. Katterjohn, second son of Quincy F. and Cornelia Mae Aust Katterjohn, was born in Warrick County, Ind., on Oct. 20, 1891. He resided in Boonville until twenty-two years of age, developing as news correspondent, magazine contributor and author of motion picture stories when that industry was in its infancy.

In 1908 he prepared a small volume entitled *A History of Warrick County and Its Prominent People,* which was issued in 1909.

Before 1912 he launched THE MONTHLY WARRICK MAGAZINE, MOTOR TOPICS (subsequently published by others as AUTOMOBILE TOPICS), and MOTION PICTURE ALBUM.

In 1914 he was placed in charge of the scenario department of the Universal Film Manufacturing Company (now Universal Pictures). For about two years he was associated with the late Thomas H. Ince as a staff writer for Triangle Plays.

During the first World War Mr. Katterjohn continued writing for the motion picture industry but also worked in the Film Division of the Bureau of Public Information, providing propaganda films.

Much of his work since the advent of talking pictures has been as editor of story material and picture production details for Warner Brothers, Paramount, and independent releases. More recently he has been associated with films and current publications as consultant, contributor, special assignment writer, and critic and is currently completing two historical novels.

Information from Mr. Katterjohn.

* * *

A History of Warrick County and Its Prominent People. *Boonville, Ind.*, 1909.

How To Write and Market Moving Picture Plays; Being a Complete Mail Course in Picture Play Writing Prepared in the Form of a Book and Containing Twenty Complete Articles. *Boonville, Ind.* [1912].

KEITH, ARTHUR LESLIE: 1874–1942.

Arthur Leslie Keith, son of John Lawson and Mary Ann Robertson Keith, was born in Worthington, Ind., on Apr. 25, 1874, and graduated from the University of Nebraska in 1898, receiving the A.M. degree in 1908 and the Ph.D. (from the University of Chicago) in 1910. On June 13, 1900, he married Mabelle Harding Homerick.

After spending eight years as an instructor in St. John's Military School in Kansas and one year as professor of Greek at the University of South Dakota, from 1910 to 1922 he was assistant professor and professor of Latin at Carleton College, returning to the University of South Dakota in 1922 as professor of Greek. After 1933 he was professor of Latin.

Information from *Who's Who in America.*

* * *

Simile and Metaphor in Greek Poetry from Homer to Aeschylus. *Menasha, Wis.,* 1914.

KEITH, BENJAMIN F.: 1825–?

Benjamin F. Keith, son of John and Delilah Keith, was born in Knox County, Ind., on May 15, 1825. His parents had moved from Kentucky to Indiana in 1814. Following a youth spent on his father's farm, in 1849 young Benjamin went to Edwardsport, Ind., where

he studied medicine for two years under Dr. J. T. Freeland.

He then began the practice of medicine at Jonesboro, Ind., remaining there until 1854, when he went to Robinson, Ill., and practiced for three years. In 1857 he entered Rush Medical College, graduating the following year and locating permanently in Edwardsport, Ind.

Dr. Keith married Emily Culbertson on Nov. 6, 1849. After her death he married a Mrs. Koons on Aug. 23, 1860.

Information from *Representative Men of Indiana,* Vol. I.

* * *

History of the Maria Creek Church. *Vincennes,* 1889.

KELSO, ISAAC: ?–?

Little is known of Isaac Kelso except that he was certainly a citizen of Indiana (perhaps a member of the Switzerland County family of that name) and that his first novel was not highly regarded. D. S. A., writing in the CINCINNATI DAILY GAZETTE of Dec. 7, 1876, says, "A few personal friends may have 'waded' through . . . Isaac Kelso's *Light, More Light; or Danger in the Dark* . . . But it never engaged the attention of any considerable number of readers . . . Kelso 'aimed a decisive blow at intolerant Romanism.'"

Information from D. S. A. in the CINCINNATI DAILY GAZETTE, Dec. 7, 1876.

* * *

Light, More Light; or, Danger in the Dark. *Cincinnati,* 1855.

The Stars and Bars; or, the Reign of Terror in Missouri. *Boston,* 1864.

KEMPER, GENERAL WILLIAM HARRISON: 1839–1927.

General (not a title but a first name) William Harrison Kemper, son of Arthur Smith and Patience Bryant Kemper, was born in Rush County, Ind., on Dec. 16, 1839. He was educated in the common schools, attended medical lectures at the University of Michigan (1864-65), and received the M.D. degree from Long Island College Hospital in 1865. In 1886 he was a post-graduate student at New York Polyclinic. He married Harriet Kemper, of Oskaloosa, Ia., on Aug. 15, 1865.

In 1861 he enlisted as a private in the Seventh Indiana Volunteers, but after three months he was transferred to the 17th Indiana Volunteers, in which regiment he served as hospital steward until 1863 and after that as assistant surgeon. Following his graduation from medical school he practiced in Muncie, Ind.

In addition to his books, Dr. Kemper contributed articles to medical journals.

He died on Sept. 26, 1927.

Information from *Representative Men of Indiana,* Vol. I, and *Who Was Who in America.*

* * *

The Uses of Suffering. *Cincinnati,* 1896.

The World's Anatomists: Concise Biographies of Anatomic Masters from 300 B.C. to the Present Time. *Philadelphia,* 1905.

A Twentieth Century History of Delaware County, Indiana. *Chicago,* 1908. 2 vols.

Medical History of the State of Indiana. *Chicago,* 1911.

KENDALL, ENION: ?–1856.

The only biographical information on Enion Kendall, pioneer poet of Cass County, is found in J. Z. Powell's *History of Cass County,* which says:

"Enion Kendall, who died in 1856, was Logansport's pioneer poet, although he could not read nor write. He dictated 'History of Kansas and March of the Western Army to Santa Fe and San Diego' which was published in the DELPHI TIMES in 1854 and was preserved in the Biddle Miscellany in the Logansport Library, volume 14."

From Powell—*History of Cass County,* 1913.

* * *

A New Edition to the Narrative of Eliza Allen. [*Logansport, Ind.*], 1853.

The History of Kansas and March of the Western Army to Santa Fe and New Mexico, Thence to San Diego in California. *Delphi, Ind.,* 1854.

KETCHAM, JOHN: 1782–1865.

John Ketcham, Indiana pioneer, Indian fighter and leader in settlement and development, was born in Maryland on Sept. 10, 1782. The family moved to Shelby County, Ky., in 1784, and young John was reared and received some education there. Life was precarious: there was the constant threat of Indians from the north, and Samuel Ketcham, father of the family, was himself a captive for some months.

In 1802 John married Elizabeth Pearcy, and they set up housekeeping in the same locality. In 1811 the couple moved with their six children (there were to be as many more) to what was then Jackson County, Indiana Territory; but almost immediately Indian hostilities in the neighborhood (which preceded the War of 1812 in the West) began, and Ketcham soon took his family back to Kentucky.

Ketcham came back across the Ohio and assisted in driving the Indians from the lands recently purchased in southern Indiana. His chief activities were in the defense of the central Indiana settlements against raids —of which the Pigeon Roost Massacre is a notable example. In 1813 he enlisted in Capt. James Bigger's company of Mounted Rangers, raised in the Territory by the government: service in this campaign was largely limited to skirmishes in the upper Wabash Valley, but the troops performed an important service.

After the war Ketcham was appointed an Associate Judge of the Territory—soon to become a state—and in April, 1818, he brought his family to the land in Monroe County (near present Elletsville) which he had bought. Here he immediately became, and continued until his death, a leading and vastly popular citizen. Perhaps his popularity was due to the qualities which enabled him to summarize humorously his later life and achievements—"I was solicited to build the Court House, which I did, thirty or forty years ago. It still stands firm. Because I had built a good Court House, and had a sword and several pistols, the people thought I ought to be a Colonel. I was so elected . . . But my honors did not stop here. The people knew I had killed an Indian, and had decided three law suits in about forty minutes,—they said I must go to the Legislature. I agreed to it. My popularity not high enough yet,—my old friend Dr. Foster . . . knew I had been wounded by the Indians, and had killed and scalped an Indian, went to the Democratic Convention at Indianapolis, and told them what Ketcham had done, and said he must be appointed one of Genl. Jackson's Electors . . . and here I am yet, one of Genl. Jackson's Electors!"

When John Ketcham died on Feb. 7, 1865, the regard of his friends and neighbors was by no means limited to that extended to a man whose only claim to fame was as "one of Genl. Jackson's Electors."

Information from Hopkins, Rev. T. M.—*Reminiscences of Col. John Ketcham.*

* * *

The Devil's Dream Interpreted and Corruptions Adversary: or Ketcham's Exposition of Whitcomb's Circular, and Conduct on the Eve of the August Election of

1830, with General Remarks, to Which Is Added a Few Biographical Sketches of the Aforesaid Whitcomb. *Bloomington, Ind.,* 1832.

KETTLEBOROUGH, CHARLES: 1878–1938.

Charles Kettleborough, born in Lincolnshire, England, on Mar. 22, 1878, came to Indiana with his parents when he was an infant and, after his mother's death, became the ward of a family in Topeka, Ind. He was educated in the local schools, taught for a time, and graduated from Indiana University in 1907, receiving the Ph.D. degree in 1911.

From 1911 until his death he served the Legislative Bureau of Indiana, acting as its head after 1918. He died in Indianapolis on Mar. 28, 1938, as a result of injuries received when he was struck by an automobile two weeks earlier.

> Information from the Indianapolis Public Library and the INDIANA HISTORY BULLETIN, Feb., 1939.

* * *

Inheritance Taxation. *Indianapolis,* 1912.

Drainage and Reclamation of Swamp and Over-flowed Lands. *Indianapolis,* 1914.

Constitution Making in Indiana; a Source Book of Constitutional Documents, with Historical Introduction and Critical Notes (Editor). *Indianapolis,* 1916-30. 3 vols.

The State Constitutions and the Federal Constitution and Organic Laws of the Territories and Other Colonial Dependencies of the United States of America. *Indianapolis,* 1918.

Analysis of the Finances of the State of Indiana, 1913-1923 (with F. H. Guild). *Bloomington, Ind.,* 1924.

Public Indebtedness in Indiana. *Bloomington, Ind.*

Legislative Procedure in the General Assembly of the State of Indiana. *Indianapolis,* 1928.

Indiana Voters' Handbook (also subsequent editions). *Indianapolis,* 1930.

KILLIKELLY, SARAH HUTCHINS: 1840–1912.

Sarah Hutchins Killikelly, daughter of the Rev. B. B. and Mary Meech Killikelly, was born in Vincennes, Ind., on Jan. 1, 1840, and graduated from Eden Hall Seminary in Pennsylvania. She also studied piano and organ.

Moving with her family to Pittsburgh, she there conducted classes, chiefly of women, in literature, history, foreign travel, and Bible study. Out of these classes she developed her book, *Curious Questions.*

Miss Killikelly was made a Foundation Fellow of the Society of Science, Letters and Art in London and received from that society the gold crown prize for papers on the Victorian era. She also contributed to magazines.

> Information from *Who Was Who in America* and Dunn—*Indiana and Indianans,* Vol. III.

* * *

Curious Questions in History, Literature, Art, and Social Life; Designed as a Manual of General Information. *Philadelphia,* 1886-1900. 3 vols.

The History of Pittsburgh, Its Rise and Progress. *Pittsburgh,* 1906.

KIMBERLING, HADLEY SIEGEL: 1862–1920.

Hadley Siegel Kimberling, son of James Wesley and Hannah Johnson Kimberling, early settlers in Shelby County, was born at Shelbyville, Ind., on Mar. 20, 1862. He attended school at Norristown, Shelby County. He was a tailor by trade.

He contributed poems to newspapers and magazines and left several unpublished manuscripts.

He was married to Anna M. Farrell and died on Nov. 21, 1920.

> Information from the Carnegie Public Library, Shelbyville, Ind.

* * *

Llewellyn (pseudonym, Franz Sigel). *Indianapolis,* 1903.

KING, HOYT: 1870–

Born in Danville, Ind., in 1870, Hoyt King graduated from high school in 1888 and from the law school at Indiana University in 1892. In 1892 he removed to Chicago, where he engaged in business and the practice of law. He married Maude Lemon of Springfield, Ill., in 1898.

> Information from the Barry Ms.

* * *

Reform Movement in Chicago. *Philadelphia,* 1905.
Citizen Cole of Chicago. *Chicago,* 1931.

KING, IRVING: 1874–

Irving King, son of Edward and Mary Buffington Evans King, was born in Richmond, Ind., on July 17, 1874, and graduated from Earlham College in 1896, receiving the Ph.D. degree from the University of Chicago in 1904. On Sept. 7, 1898, he married Alta F. Burke.

He served as principal of Tonganoxie Academy in Kansas and Bloomingdale Academy in Indiana, professor of psychology at Oshkosh State Normal School, professor of psychology and the history of education at Pratt Institute, and assistant professor of education at the University of Michigan. From 1909 to 1920 he was professor of education at the State University of Iowa.

Information from *Who's Who in America*.

* * *

Psychology of Child Development. *Chicago, 1903.*

Differentiation of the Religious Consciousness. *Lancaster, Pa., 1905.*

The Development of Religion: a Study in Anthropology and Social Psychology. *New York, 1910.*

Social Aspects of Education, a Book of Sources and Original Discussions . . . *New York, 1912.*

Education for Social Efficiency: a Study in the Social Relations of Education. *New York, 1913.*

The High-School Age. *Indianapolis, 1914.*

KINGSBURY, SARA R.: 1876–

Born in Ohio in 1876, Sara R. Kingsbury attended the Indianapolis public schools, graduated from Butler University in 1899, and was a resident of Indianapolis.

Information from the Barry Ms.

* * *

The Atonement (A Story). *Boston, 1905.*

The Rich Young Man, a Play in Three Acts. *New York, 1924.*

The Crowning of Spring. *New York.*

Our Christ Liveth: an Easter Play in Three Acts. *New York, 1930.*

The Christmas Guest (Play).

KIRKWOOD, DANIEL: 1814–1895.

"Daniel Kirkwood (Sept. 27, 1814-June 11, 1895), astronomer, teacher, . . . was born in Harford County, Md. His grandfather was an emigrant from Ireland who settled in Delaware; his parents were John and Agnes (Hope) Kirkwood. Daniel spent his early life on a farm and attended school in his native county. He began his career as a teacher in 1833, at Hopewell, York County, Pa. Since one of his pupils wished to study algebra, the two of them worked through Bonny-

castle's Algebra together. The following year Kirkwood entered the York County Academy, and in 1838 was appointed mathematical instructor. In 1843 he accepted the principalship of the Lancaster High School and later became principal of the Pottsville Academy. In 1845 he married Sarah A. McNair of Newton, Bucks County, Pa.

"His first college position was in Delaware College, Newark, Del., where he was professor of mathematics from 1851 to 1856, during the last two years serving also as president of the college . . . In 1856 he was called to Indiana University as professor of mathematics, and served there for thirty years, with the exception of a two-year interval (Aug. 2, 1865-Dec. 18, 1867) as professor of mathematics and astronomy at Jefferson College, Canonsburg, Pa. In 1891 he was appointed lecturer in Leland Stanford, Jr., University. He died at Riverside, Calif., in his eighty-first year."

Condensed from R. S. D., *Dictionary of American Biography*, Vol. X.

* * *

Meteoric Astronomy: a Treatise on Shooting-Stars, Fireballs and Aerolites. *Philadelphia, 1867.*

Comets and Meteors: Their Phenomena in All Ages, Their Mutual Relations, and the Theory of Their Origin. *Philadelphia, 1873.*

The Asteroids: or, Minor Planets Between Mars and Jupiter. *Philadelphia, 1888.*

KITCH, JOHN WALTER: 1866–1946.

John Walter Kitch (who wrote under the pseudonym of Aleck Davis) was born in Bremen, Ind., on June 8, 1866, the son of Martin V. and Amanda Lehr Kitch. He attended the Marshall County schools and entered Valparaiso University, where he began to study law. Withdrawing, he went to Adair, and later to Coon Rapids, Ia., where he read law. During this period he taught school in Marshall County, Ind., Holland, Mich., and Coon Rapids, Ia., where he was superintendent of schools, 1892-95. He also published the weekly ADAIR NEWS.

In 1898 he returned to Bremen, Ind., and opened a law office, later removing to South Bend and, in 1916, to Plymouth, Ind. He represented Marshall County in the Indiana Legislature and served as a trustee of the Indiana School for the Feeble Minded. From June 1, 1938, to Jan. 1, 1945, he served as judge of the Marshall County Circuit Court. He was married three times: first to Oma Simpson, on Sept. 12, 1890; second to Mae Southworth; and third to Anna Eliza Richards. He died on May 30, 1946.

Information from the Indiana State Library; the Plymouth Public Library; and Roll—*History of Indiana*, Vol. 5.

* * *

Centennial History of Indiana, by Aleck Davis. *Plymouth, Ind., 1916.*

KITSELMAN, LESLIE CURTIS (MRS. ALVA L.): 1892–

Born in Denver, Colo., in 1892, Leslie Curtis was educated in Denver and at the American Academy of Dramatic Art in New York City. She was a post-graduate student at Ball State Teachers College in Muncie, Ind.

In 1911 she was married to Alva L. Kitselman of Muncie and became a resident of that city. In addition to her books she is known as the author of numerous newspaper stories, moving picture scenarios, and radio scripts.

Information from the Barry Ms.

* * *

Reno Reveries. *Reno, Nev.,* [1912].
Jackstraws. *Greenfield, Ind.,* [1932].
The Sins of Sally. *Chicago,* 1935.

KITSON, HARRY DEXTER: 1886–

Harry Dexter Kitson, son of Clarence and Nellie Hamblin Kitson, was born in Mishawaka, Ind., on Aug. 11, 1886. He received the A.B. degree from Hiram College in 1909, the A.M. from the University of Minnesota in 1913, and the Ph.D. from the University of Chicago in 1915.

In 1912-13 he was an assistant in psychology at the University of Minnesota. From 1915 to 1919 he was an instructor at the University of Chicago, and from 1919 to 1925 he was professor of psychology at Indiana University. In 1925 he became professor of education at Teachers College, Columbia. During the first World War he was an officer in the A.E.F. He married Angeline S. Freeman, now deceased, on June 14, 1922.

Dr. Kitson edited many works on applied psychology in addition to the works of which he is author.

Information from *Who's Who in America.*

* * *

How To Use Your Mind: a Psychology of Study; Being a Manual for the Use of Students and Teachers in the Administration of Supervised Study. *Philadelphia,* 1916.

Scientific Study of the College Student. *Princeton, N. J.,* 1917.
The Mind of the Buyer: a Psychology of Selling. *New York,* 1921.
Extra Incentive Wage Plans from a Psychological Point of View. *New York,* 1925.
The Psychology of Vocational Adjustment. *Philadelphia,* 1925.
Scientific Advertising. *New York,* 1926.
Job Analysis (with Sterling B. Cramer). *New York,* 1927.
How to Find the Right Vocation. *New York,* 1929.
Vocational Guidance Through the Library; a Guide Showing How the Librarian Can Serve People Who Are Trying to Choose a Vocation. *Chicago,* 1931.
I Find My Vocation. *New York,* 1931.
Finding a Job During the Depression. *New York,* 1933.
Vocations for Girls (with M. R. Lingenfelter). *New York,* 1939.
Vocations for Boys (with M. R. Lingenfelter). *New York,* 1942.
Vocational Guidance for Victory. *New York,* 1942.

KNOX, WALTER: 1863–1892.

Walter Knox, son of George P. and Mary Spotswood Knox, was born in Vevay, Ind., on Mar. 29, 1863. Before completing high school he became a "printer's devil" in the office of the VEVAY REVEILLE, and at eighteen years of age he founded and edited the VEVAY TIMES, a weekly. On Nov. 6, 1884, he married Mary Louise Simmons. Mr. Knox wrote poetry from an early age, and after his death, which occurred on Sept. 3, 1892, his wife had published a small volume of his poems.

Information from Mrs. Eloise Knox Niemeyer.

* * *

Living Leaves. n.p., n.d.

KONKLE, BURTON ALVA: 1861–1944

Burton Alva Konkle, son of Simon Kenton and Cornelia Gale Konkle, was born in Albion, Ind., on Apr. 25, 1861, and was educated at Lake Forest College, McCormick Theological Seminary, the University of Chicago, and Huron College, receiving the A.M. from the last-named institution in 1906.

From 1876 to 1882 he was connected with the public schools of Evilla and Wawaka, Ind., and from 1882 to 1886 he was engaged in historical work in various parts of the country. Ordained to the Presbyterian ministry in 1894, he served as pastor of churches in Illinois and Colorado for a time. After 1897 he devoted all of his time to historical writing. He married Susie Montague Ferry in 1900 and died in 1944. Mr. Konkle was a founder of the Pennsylvania History Club.

Information from *Who's Who in America*.

* * *

The Life and Times of Thomas Smith, 1745-1809. *Philadelphia, 1904.*

The Life and Speeches of Thomas Williams, Orator, Statesman and Jurist, 1806-1872. *Philadelphia, 1905.*

The Life of Chief Justice Ellis Lewis, 1798-1871. *Philadelphia, 1907.*

James Wilson and the Constitution. *Philadelphia, 1907.*

George Bryan and the Constitution of Pennsylvania, 1731-1791. *Philadelphia, 1922.*

John Motley Morehead and the Development of North Carolina, 1796-1866. *Philadelphia, 1922.*

Delaware: A Grant Yet Not A Grant. *Wilmington, Del., 1930.*

Joseph Hopkinson, 1770-1842: Jurist, Scholar, Inspirer of the Arts, Author of Hail Columbia. *Philadelphia, 1931.*

Benjamin Chew, 1722-1810; Head of the Pennsylvania Judiciary System Under Colony and Commonwealth. *Philadelphia, 1932.*

Thomas Willing and the First American Financial System. *Philadelphia, 1937.*

David Lloyd and the First Half Century of Pennsylvania, 1656-1731.

The Life and Writings of James Wilson. 6 vols.

The Life of Nicholas Biddle.

Land O' Lakes, a Hoosier Tale of North, South, West and East.

The Life of Andrew Hamilton, 1676-1741; the Day-Star of the American Revolution. *Philadelphia, 1941.*

KOPELKE, JOHANNES: 1854–

Johannes Kopelke was born in Germany on June 14, 1854. Coming to the U. S. as a young man, he studied law at the University of Michigan and practiced in Crown Point, Ind. He served as a judge in Lake County, Ind., and in the state senate.

Information from the Indiana State Library.

* * *

Sommerausflug Nach Europa, Hauptsaechlich Deutschland.

The Bench and Bar of Lake County, Indiana, 1918. *Crown Point, Ind., 1919.*

KRAMER, HAROLD MORTON: 1873–1930.

Harold Morton Kramer was born in Frankfort, Ind., Apr. 28, 1873. The youngest of ten children born to Philip Edward and Mary Choate Kramer, he was educated in the Frankfort public schools.

On Sept. 6, 1897, he married Miss Nora Caroline Lee, a teacher.

In April, 1898, he enlisted in Company C, 158th Infantry in the Spanish-American War and was commissioned first lieutenant. In 1917 Mr. Kramer entered service for the first World War. Being over age for armed service, he became a Y.M.C.A. secretary and was sent to the front in France, where he served both American and English soldiers and did some lecturing for the Y.M.C.A.

Mr. Kramer's first trade was that of printer, from which he advanced to editorial work, becoming night editor of the DAILY MORNING TIMES of Frankfort. In 1910 he retired from newspaper work to enter the lecture field. In 1925 he was elected executive secretary of the International Lyceum Association with headquarters in Chicago. He filled this office until his sudden death Mar. 20, 1930, in Chicago.

Information from Mrs. Harold Morton Kramer.

* * *

Hearts and the Cross. *Boston, 1906.*

Gayle Langford; Being the Romance of a Tory Belle and a Patriot Captain. *Boston, 1907.*

The Castle of Dawn. *Boston, [1908].*

The Chrysalis. *Boston, 1909.*

The Rugged Way. *Boston, 1911.*

With Seeing Eyes; the Unusual Story of an Observant Thinker at the Front. *Boston, 1919.*

KRETZMANN, PAUL EDWARD: 1883–

Paul Edward Kretzmann, son of Carl H. E. and Elizabeth Polack Kretzmann, was born in Dearborn County, Ind., on Aug. 24, 1883, and graduated in 1902 from Concordia College, Fort Wayne, Ind. He received the A.M. degree from the University of Minnesota in 1913 and the Ph.D. degree in 1915. In 1920 he received the B.D. degree from Chicago Lutheran Seminary, and the same institution awarded him the D.D. in 1922. He was also a student at Concordia Seminary in St. Louis and Washington University.

Before his ordination to the Lutheran ministry in 1906 he taught in Colorado and Kansas. He served as pastor in churches in Kansas, Colorado, and Missouri, and from 1912 to 1919 he was professor of sciences and mathematics at Concordia College in St. Paul, Minn. In 1923 he became professor of theology at Concordia Seminary, St. Louis. He married Louise Schroeder in 1907.

Information from *Who's Who in America.*

* * *

A Short Introduction to Church Architecture and Ecclesiastical Art, Especially from the Standpoint of the Lutheran Church. *St. Louis, 1912.*

Keuschheit und Zucht. *St. Louis, 1915.*

Education Among the Jews from the Earliest Times to the End of the Talmudic Period. *Boston, 1916.*

The Liturgical Element in the Earliest Forms of Medieval Drama with Special Reference to the English and German Plays. *Minneapolis, 1916.*

Die Pastoralbriefe. *St. Louis, 1918.*

Unto Us; Text by Paul Kretzmann; Music by J. C. Albert Kaeppel. *St. Louis, 1919.*

A Brief History of Education. *St. Louis, 1920.*

Psychology and the Christian Day-School. *St. Louis, 1920.*

Agnus Dei; the Lamb of God (with J. C. Albert Kaeppel). *St. Louis, 1920.*

Christian Art in the Place and in the Form of Lutheran Worship. *St. Louis, 1921.*

Der 46 Psalm. *St. Louis, 1921.*

Popular Commentary of the Bible. *St. Louis, 1921-24.* 4 vols.

The Teaching of Arithmetic (with E. H. Engelbrecht). *St. Louis, 1923.*

Knowing and Doing. 1923.

Our King Victorious: an Easter Cantata (with B. Schumacher). *St. Louis, 1924.*

Cantate! A Song Service. *St. Louis, 1924.*

Establishment and the Propagation of the Christian Church. *St. Louis, 1925.*

Life of Jesus the Savior. *St. Louis, 1925.* 2 vols.

Vacation Bible Schools for Lutheran Churches. *St. Louis, 1925.*

The Problems of Adolescence and Youth and Their Treatment in Educational and Pastoral Work. *Burlington, Ia., 1925.*

The Mysterious Ways of God. 1925.

While It Is Day! *St. Louis, 1926.*

Teaching of Religion. *St. Louis, 1926.*

The Good Shepherd (with J. F. Ohl). *St. Louis, 1927.*

Missionary Stories for Young People. *Columbus, O., 1927.*

A Few Pages from the Life of Luther. *St. Louis, 1927.*

Liturgical Service for Rally Day. *St. Louis, 1927.*

Prayers for Lutheran Sunday-Schools. *St. Louis, 1927.*

Of Judah's Tribe and David's House (with Walter Wismar). *St. Louis, 1927.*

John Ludwig Krapf, the Explorer-Missionary of Northeastern Africa. *Columbus, O., 1928.*

Heroes of Missions and Their Work. *St. Louis, 1928.*

The Mountain School. 1928.

Lutheran Principle of Indoctrination vs. the Pedagogy of Modernism. *St. Louis, 1928.*

Search the Scriptures. *St. Louis, 1928.* Vols. 4-8.

What Lutheran Sunday-School Teachers Should Know; a Short Summary for Instructors and Pupils in Sunday-School Teachers' Meetings and Institutes. *St. Louis, 1928.*

The Christian Woman as a Social Worker. *Berne, Ind., 1929.*

The Religion of the Child, and Other Essays; an Inquiry into the Fundamental Errors of Modern Religious Pedagogy and Their Correction. *St. Louis, 1929.*

The Pot of Gold, and Other Missionary Stories. *Columbus, O., 1929.*

He Lives! A Children's Vesper Service for Easter Day. *St. Louis, 1929.*

Glimpses of the Lives of Great Missionary Women. *St. Louis, 1930.*

From Heaven Above; a Vesper Song Service for Christmas. *St. Louis, 1932.*

A Believer's View of the New Testament. 1933.

Preaching Christ Crucified. 1934.

The Doctrine of the Call. 1934.

New Testament in the Light of a Believer's Research. *Grand Rapids, Mich., 1934.*

Story of the German Bible; a Contribution to the Quadricentennial of Luther's Translation. *St. Louis, 1934.*

Foundations Must Stand! The Inspiration of the Bible and Related Questions. *St. Louis, 1936.*

Up to Jerusalem. *Minneapolis, 1936.*

It Is The King, Up to Jerusalem, The Foundations Must Stand. 1936.

Guiding the Junior. 1937.

Finding Our Way into the Bible, Knowing the Truth. 1938.

That Vexing Problem. 1940.

My Job as Youth Counselor. 1942.

The God of the Bible and Other Gods. *St. Louis, 1943.*

Toward Lutheran Union; a Scriptural and Historical Approach. *St. Louis, 1943.*

In Dulci Jubilo. *St. Louis, n.d.*

Soli Deo Gloria; a Jubilee Cantata. *St. Louis, n.d.*

The Teaching of English. *St. Louis, n.d.*

KROUT, CAROLINE VIRGINIA: 1852–1931.

Caroline Virginia Krout was one of the daughters of Robert Kennedy and Caroline Brown Krout.

In order to get a clear picture of her life, and of that of her more famous sister, Mary Hannah Krout, it is necessary to give considerably more than the usual attention to the parents—more especially to the father,

Robert Krout, a sort of Hoosier Bronson Alcott, who seems to have had a rather profound influence upon the careers of his brilliant daughters.

*

Robert Krout spent his early years in Covington, Ky., where his maternal grandfather held a lucrative franchise for a ferry running between that place and Cincinnati, O., and where his family owned considerable property. Young Krout was eleven when an employee of his grandfather—for reasons now unknown—brought him to a farm in still wild and hilly southwestern Montgomery County, Ind., in the section known as "Balhinch."

At the school in Alamo (capital-by-consent of the vaguely defined Balhinch district) young Krout was tutored in Greek and Latin by a local schoolmaster, James Gilkey, who would eventually leave his mark on half a dozen Indiana writers.

After six years of tutoring in the classics—plus less esoteric subjects in the local schools—the young man was admitted to Wabash College. He was then seventeen. Robert Krout received the A.B. degree in 1848 and, while still an undergraduate, began to read law in the office of Lane and Wilson.

At the time of his baccalaureate Robert K. Krout was considered by his professors and by himself to be a young man of extraordinary promise: it was, however, a promise never to be fulfilled, and as the years passed this unfortunate circumstance came to have a profound effect both upon his own attitude toward the world and upon the lives of the members of his family.

As a senior undergraduate he was a youth in rebellion—his last appearance before his college literary society in March, 1848, being an oratorical complaint against the manner in which the Mexican War was being waged and a plea for universal military training (except for young men in their senior year in college), for justice for all and for attention to the voice of youth. Young college seniors in rebellion are, of course, no phenomena, but it was Robert Krout's misfortune to remain quietly in that state until his last day.

Within a year of his graduation he married Miss Caroline Van Cleve Brown, daughter of a Crawfordsville physician. The Browns lived across the street from the cottage in which young Krout roomed as a student. Caroline's brother was a firm friend of Robert, and Caroline—as her wedding picture attests—was a beautiful girl of seventeen at the time of the wedding.

Robert Krout's interest in the law waned (as did many another interest in his later life) as soon as he

had mastered its rudiments. Some time in 1849 he and his bride went to New Orleans and, later, to Arkansas, where they set up a private school. Two years of school-keeping sufficed for Robert, and the young couple returned to the Brown home in Crawfordsville in time for Robert to go through the rather perfunctory motions of qualifying for an A.M. degree at Wabash and in time for Caroline to bear the first of her nine babies in her father's home in the fall of 1851.

The sanctuary of the Brown home for the young mother was convenient, but the usefulness of an advanced degree for Robert was questionable. His classical learning was to be employed, as time went on, in assisting him as a chemist in the drug store which his brother-in-law had opened. There were interludes of lightning-rod and buggy selling, some ventures into the then questionable realms of insurance and a constant correspondence with the newspapers. Community service took the form of long-time and contentious membership on the city school board.

Robert Krout's scrap-book, covering the last thirty years of his life, is filled with clippings of newspaper yarns of strange adventures, weird discoveries and exposés of the foibles and frailties of the great, interleaved with woodcut GODEY'S LADIES' BOOK plans for Italian villas and be-jigsawed country houses —all this while the cottage which he had inherited through his wife from her father progressed from, in 1879, "a queer, dark, dull little house" in which "the weather boards begin to warp and get frayed and dingy . . . the fence needs paint . . ." to, in 1900, "a low, long structure . . . the weatherboarding looks as though it had never made the acquaintance of paint in all its history . . . the roof is old and weatherbeaten. The trees and shrubs are thick around the cottage . . . But when you think of the occupants . . . the mind goes back to the home of the Brontes . . . the father, for whose sake the cottage is left unrepaired . . . dislikes to have the old cottage changed in the least, it is said, and with sweet patience the sisters live on in it leaving it undisturbed . . ." according to contemporary newspaper accounts.

Perhaps recalling Robert Krout's failure appears somewhat less than the handsome thing to do: it would certainly be so, except that this very failure had a most profound bearing upon the ultimate literary successes of his daughters. His criticism of their early efforts at writing (his own contribution to letters was almost wholly confined to temperature readings and weather observations to the local newspaper) and his constitutional inability to be satisfied with less than perfection on their parts drove them to success. Probably also (although she never mentioned it and may never have realized it) Robert Krout must have been the tyrannical male who first convinced his eldest daughter that a campaign for equal rights for women was a project well in order. Robert Krout was demanding, exacting and critical, and by these very qualities he became important to Indiana literature.

*

Robert and Caroline Krout's first daughter, Mary Hannah, was born in the grandparents' home in Crawfordsville on Nov. 3, 1851. The subject of this sketch, Caroline Virginia, was born a bit more than eleven months later, on Oct. 13, 1852.

Caroline Krout—Cary to her sisters and her very few friends—attended a Crawfordsville subscription, and later a public, school. When she was sixteen her mother died and, her older sister (an educated woman of seventeen) having already begun to teach at the Bunker Hill School, it fell upon Caroline's shoulders to take over the keeping of her father's house and the care of the four younger children who had survived babyhood, until, three years later, her next younger sister, Jane, graduated from high school and took over the housekeeping—an assignment at which she continued for almost seventy years.

Caroline V. Krout began teaching in Crawfordsville schools in her nineteenth year—money was, as always in those days, a scarce article in the Krout household—and she continued for five years, when, as she is quoted in an interview in the INDIANAPOLIS NEWS for April 19, 1900, "my health gave way and I became a nervous invalid for several years." During her illness she wrote her first story and presently became an occasional contributor of short stories and feature articles to the INTER-OCEAN, INTERIOR, CHICAGO DAILY NEWS, CHICAGO JOURNAL and other papers.

Recovering somewhat, Caroline took employment as assistant court reporter in Crawfordsville and, after a time and through the offices of her sister, Mary Hannah, already a newspaper woman of importance in Chicago, she went to that city and secured a place on the staff of the Newberry Library.

Poor health made her resignation necessary, and about 1896 she returned to Crawfordsville. Unable to take regular employment and encouraged by her older sister's long-time patron and advisor, Susan Elston Wallace (wife of General Lew Wallace, and herself a successful writer), Caroline V. Krout first tried writing for the periodical market.

Her first sales were to ST. NICHOLAS and the COSMOPOLITAN, and her subject—in her first

three stories—was Robin Hood and his followers, a result perhaps of Crawfordsville's preoccupation with the archery which Maurice and Will Thompson had popularized, first in Crawfordsville, then in the nation.

There were twenty or so short stories, and then, in 1900, her first novel, *Knights in Fustian*, under the name "Caroline Brown." It was a story of the Copperhead movement in Indiana—and particularly in the "Balhinch" district of Montgomery County which she and her family knew so well. The book was an immediate success. Although many reviewers bruised Caroline's always sensitive spirit, sales were good, and even such a student of history as Gov. Theodore Roosevelt of New York wrote to the author to say: ". . . you have given me far and away the best and most vivid idea I ever had of the Indiana Copper-heads and also an exceptionally good picture of life in the western farming communities."

Caroline Krout's shyness kept her from capitalizing upon her first success, and the fact that another of her novels, *On the We-a Trail,* employed the same locale and period as *Alice of Old Vincennes* by her fellow citizen, Maurice Thompson, almost caused her to give up writing altogether. Neither she nor Thompson had the slightest idea of the other's interest and Thompson, when he learned of her embarrassment, exerted all of his native kindliness to put her at ease.

There were two more novels, the last in 1911, then Caroline Krout gave up writing almost altogether. She was sensitive both to criticism and to the defects in her own writing, and the combination was an impossible one for a career in writing. She became, in effect, a happy, home-loving recluse during the last thirty or forty years of her life.

She died, in the home which she and her sisters had modernized and rebuilt after a decent interval of mourning for their father, on Oct. 9, 1931.

Information from Miss Roberta Krout, Krout family papers, and contemporary newspaper articles.

* * *

Knights In Fustian, a War-Time Story of Indiana. *Boston,* 1900.
On the We-a Trail; a Story of the Great Wilderness. *New York,* 1903.
Bold Robin and His Forest Rangers. *New York,* 1905.
Dionis of the White Veil. *Boston,* 1911.

KROUT, MARY HANNAH: 1851–1927.

Indiana was the home of two of America's leading feminists—Frances Wright, for the brief period of

Robert Owen's New Harmony Community experiment in the 1820's, and Mary Hannah Krout, during her childhood, girlhood and declining years. Frances Wright was beautiful, erratic and ineffectual; Mary Hannah Krout was plain, blunt and, by her years of writing and speaking in its favor, a great contributor toward the success of the movement which won equal rights for women.

To understand the forces which shaped the career of Mary Hannah Krout it is necessary to know of her parentage, particularly of her father (his life and his character are outlined in the biography of his second, but alphabetically first, daughter, Caroline Virginia Krout). Into the peculiar home life there described Mary Hannah, eldest daughter, was born on Nov. 3, 1851.

Mary Hannah Krout was sent to a subscription school in Crawfordsville. She continued at a public school after the efforts of Prof. Caleb Mills, a neighbor of the Krouts across the Wabash College campus, had made such a radical departure possible in Indiana, and her progress was rapid.

It was so rapid, indeed, that she had a poem published in a newspaper—and reprinted in others, at that—before her twelfth birthday; and in her fifteenth year she contributed another, "Little Brown Hands," which was not only bought and paid for by a juvenile periodical but which also swept the country and was to be incorporated into most grade school readers during the next half century. It created an immediate demand for her work (an order of things not at all common among budding poets).

So great was the impression made by "Little Brown Hands" that the young author was invited, the next year, to address an audience at Lafayette, Ind., twenty-six miles north. She appeared and spoke well, her subject being a very daring appeal for the vote for women. Her welcome was so enthusiastic that she decided to stay a while, but her mind was changed by her father who, as soon as the time of her expected return had passed with no Mary Hannah in evidence, went to Lafayette and, to the great chagrin of the young advocate of the emancipation of women, brought her back to Crawfordsville.

Next year she taught at Bunker Hill School and after that year's experience, began to teach in Crawfordsville, where she continued for eleven years.

Meanwhile she wrote for various newspapers, and about 1879, deciding that she could make a living in that field, she applied for, and got, a job on the CRAWFORDSVILLE JOURNAL, padding her income by contributions to Indianapolis and Cincinnati papers. Be-

sides regular reporting she conducted what would now be a gossip column, under the name of "Heinreich Karl," and her reports of Crawfordsville affairs to Indianapolis papers were lively—and frequently libelous. So much did she add to the JOURNAL that in 1881 she was made associate editor and, in the following year, was hired by the TERRE HAUTE EXPRESS as editor. This was a radical departure for the day, but Mary Hannah Krout was apparently waging her campaign for emancipating women by first emancipating herself.

She says, however: "During this time I worked almost incessantly from 9 A.M. to 11 P.M. and, as you may suppose, my health gave way." Susan Elston Wallace, her sponsor for several years before, came to her rescue: Mrs. Wallace sent some money—enough to make work unnecessary for a while—with instructions to the effect that her protegée was to rest, and to pay back the loan as convenient.

Writing continued, but there was no steady employment for some time. Then, says Miss Krout: "In 1888 I came to Chicago. I was willing to do anything in the line of newspaper work only to gain a foothold. I was confident of my ability to work my way up to the tip-top of my desires. Finally I obtained a position as society reporter on the CHICAGO INTER-OCEAN."

She spent ten years on the staff—until the paper was sold to the CHICAGO TRIBUNE—and in its service she made her reputation.

The INTER-OCEAN sent her to Hawaii to report the installation of the provisional government, and the trip resulted in her first book, *Hawaii and a Revolution,* and eventually in two biographies of prominent women of Hawaii.

From then on Mary Hannah Krout specialized in the world-shaking events of her day; Nelly Bly, her contemporary but in no way her equal, had adventures not comparable to hers. She called upon the Boxers in China, alone except for a single missionary; she covered Queen Victoria's Diamond Jubilee; and she visited any out-of-the-way spot to which her current employer could be persuaded to send her. There was never the appearance of the daring woman traveler: Miss Krout favored alpaca jackets with braid, boned collars on her shirt-waists and plenty of petticoats.

Always, when the opportunity offered, she lectured on women's suffrage—in the States, in England, in New Zealand, in China, in Hawaii. Far from a beautiful woman, she was still a handsome one and she had suitors enough—one distinguished colonel spent twenty-five years in hopeless courtship—but she never quite had time for marriage. There were too many other things to be done first.

In 1906, after a trip to Australia, she tired of travel and retired to the family home in Crawfordsville, kept meanwhile by three of her unmarried sisters and her bachelor brother, and devoted the remainder of her life to writing and study. She completed General Lew Wallace's *Autobiography*—with the assistance of his widow and her friend, Susan Elston Wallace—and it is possibly true that the work of these two ladies (both facile with the pen) helped to make this the most readable of Wallace's books. Miss Krout also wrote some of the best of her essays during this period. Gradually, however, she withdrew from public contact (as one of her sisters had done upon finishing high school and as her sister Caroline did as soon as her writing brought in a little income) and her literary production ceased after 1910. After an extended illness she died on May 31, 1927.

> Information from the scrap books and ms. of Mary Hannah Krout and from her youngest sister, Miss Roberta Krout.

* * *

Hawaii and a Revolution. *New York*, 1898.
A Looker-On in London. *New York*, 1899.
Alice's Visit to the Hawaiian Islands. *New York*, 1900.
Two Girls in China. *New York*, 1903.
Memoirs of General Lew Wallace. (Completed by Mary Hannah Krout and Susan Elston Wallace.) 1906.
Memoirs of Hon. Bernice Pauahi Bishop. *New York*, 1908.
Reminiscences of Mrs. Mary S. Rice. *Honolulu*, 1908.
Platters and Pipkins. *Chicago*, 1910.

L

LAMB, MARY ELIZABETH JORDAN: 1839–?

Aside from the entry "Mary E. Lamb, widow of George W. Lamb" in a Crawfordsville, Ind., city directory for 1903, the existence of presentation copies of her two novels to her fellow-citizen, Mary Hannah Krout, and vague recollections of contemporary residents of Crawfordsville, no information on Mrs. Lamb's life has been located.

Local tradition establishes her residence in Crawfordsville at least between the approximate dates, 1894-1908, and her two romantic novels (one laid in the South and the other, with a Southern girl as heroine, in a European scene) appear to have been rather widely circulated.

Information from sources listed above.

* * *

The Mystery of Walderstein, a Story from the Life of Two Prussian Officers. *Chicago* [1894].
Irene Liscomb, a Story of the Old South. *New York* [1908].

LAMBERT, GEORGE: 1853–1928.

George Lambert, son of David C. and Catherine Unangst Lambert, was born in Northampton County, Pa., on May 11, 1853. He was reared on his father's farm and attended the common school. In 1872 he married Amanda Gehman.

Entering the ministry in 1878, in 1881 he was ordained by the Indiana and Ohio Conference of the Mennonite Brethren in Christ Church. During the famine in India (1896-97) he was instrumental in calling a conference of leaders representing the different branches of the Mennonite Church. The Home and Foreign Relief Commission was organized, with offices located in Elkhart, Ind., and the Rev. Lambert was sent to India to supervise the distribution of provisions donated by the Mennonite people of America.

He died July 3, 1928.

> Information from Mrs. Oscar J. Sommer, daughter.

* * *

Around the Globe and Through Bible Lands. *Elkhart, Ind.*, 1896.
India, the Horror-Stricken Empire . . . *Elkhart, Ind.*, 1898.

LANDIS, FREDERICK: 1872–1934.

Frederick Landis, one of seven children of Abraham H. and Mary A. Kumler Landis, was born at Seven Mile, O., on Aug. 18, 1872, and received his early education in the public schools of Logansport, Ind. In 1895 he graduated from the University of Michigan law department and began the practice of law in Logansport. From 1903 to 1907 he was a member of the 58th and 59th Congresses. Following his retirement from Congress, he turned to literature, writing several successful books. For three years he was on the editorial staff of the NEW YORK AMERICAN.

In 1912 he joined the Progressive Party and was its candidate for lieutenant governor of Indiana. He later became editor of the Logansport PHAROS-TRIBUNE and also spoke over the radio as "The Hoosier

Editor." In 1933-34 he published a monthly magazine, THE HOOSIER EDITOR, made up entirely of his own writings. Mr. Landis was elected again to Congress in 1934 but died on Nov. 16 of that year of pneumonia contracted during the strenuous political campaign. He married Bessie A. Baker in 1909.

> Information from *Who Was Who in America* and the INDIANAPOLIS STAR, Nov. 16, 1934.

* * *

The Glory of His Country. (Dramatized as The Copperhead, with John Barrymore in the leading role.) *New York,* 1910.

The Angel of the Lonesome Hill: a Story of a President. *New York,* 1910.

Lonesome Hill. *New York,* 1914.

Days Gone Dry; Cartoons in Color by Gaar Williams. *Indianapolis,* 1919.

Just Dog. *East Aurora, N. Y.,* 1940.

LARD, MRS. –?–

Mrs. Lard, although apparently an Indiana writer, must be taken largely on faith. A copy of her little volume of verse—there are only five numbered pages—is preserved in the collection of the Historical & Philosophical Society of Ohio, Cincinnati, and an undated clipping from an early issue of the CINCINNATI GAZETTE pasted on the inner wrapper states that it is the work of Mrs. Lard, "a lady of Indiana."

> Information from Prof. R. Carlyle Buley, Indiana University; the Historical and Philosophical Society of Ohio.

* * *

The Banks of the Ohio. *Windsor, Vt.,* 1823.

LARRABEE, WILLIAM CLARK: 1802–1859.

"William Clark Larrabee (Dec. 23, 1802-May 5, 1859), Methodist Episcopal clergyman, educator . . . was born at Cape Elizabeth, Me., his father, a sea captain, dying soon after the boy's birth. From his seventh year, he lived with his grandparents, and with his uncle Jonathan, at Durham, Me., working on the farm and attending school. Frequenting Methodist meetings, then just being introduced into that locality, he soon professed conversion, and in June 1821 was licensed to preach . . . After being licensed, he attended New Market Academy in New Hampshire, and later, Farmingham Academy, Maine, where he was prepared to enter the sophomore class at Bowdoin College, from

which he graduated in 1828. From 1828 to 1830 he was principal of Alfred Academy, Maine, and in 1830 he was appointed tutor of a preparatory school at Middletown, Conn., which was the forerunner of Wesleyan University. The next year he was made the principal of Oneida Conference Seminary, Cazenovia, N.Y., and in 1832 was admitted to membership in the Oneida Conference of the Methodist Episcopal Church. After four successful years at Cazenovia, he became the principal of Maine Wesleyan Seminary, Kents Hill, where he enlarged his reputation as an educator. In 1837-38 he also assisted in the first geological survey of the state.

"He was the delegate to the General Conference of the Methodist Episcopal Church at Baltimore in 1840, and there met Matthew Simpson . . . the young president of a new Methodist institution, Indiana Asbury University (De Pauw University), just established at Greencastle. Simpson persuaded Larrabee to accept the professorship of mathematics and natural science, and from 1841 to 1852 he was not only a leading member of the faculty, but from 1848 to 1849, was the acting president, introducing numerous reforms in the course of study and doing much to raise educational standards. In 1848 he was one of the board of visitors at the United States Military Academy, West Point, and later was offered, but declined, several important educational positions, among them the presidency of Indiana and of Iowa universities. Elected in 1852 editor of the LADIES' REPOSITORY, a Methodist magazine published in Cincinnati, he soon resigned to accept nomination, on the Democratic ticket, for the superintendency of public instruction in the state of Indiana, to which he was elected. The new state constitution (1851) made provision for a uniform system of public schools, and Larrabee, the first state superintendent, was in a sense the founder of the Indiana public school system. In 1854 he was defeated for re-election, but in 1856 was again chosen to that office and devoted his second term to a reconstruction of the school system, the former school laws having been declared unconstitutional. He retired from office in January, 1859 and died the following May.

"He was married, Sept. 28, 1828, to Harriet, daughter of Col. William Dunn, and was the father of four children . . ."

> Condensed from W. W. S., *Dictionary of American Biography,* Vol. XI.

* * *

Lectures on the Scientific Evidence of Natural and Revealed Religion. *Cincinnati,* 1850.

Wesley and His Coadjutors. *Cincinnati, 1851. 2 vols.*

Asbury and His Coadjutors. (Edited by D. W. Clark.) *Cincinnati, 1853. 2 vols.*

Rosabower: a Collection of Essays and Miscellanies. *Cincinnati, 1855.*

LARRABEE, WILLIAM HENRY: 1829–1913.

William Henry Larrabee, son of William Clark and Harriet Dunn Larrabee, was born in Alfred, Me., on Sept. 20, 1829, and came with his family to Greencastle, Ind. in 1841. He graduated from Indiana Asbury (now De Pauw) University in 1845, receiving his A.M. in 1848, and studied law, was admitted to the bar, but never practiced.

From 1846 to 1850 he engaged in teaching and farming. From 1853 to 1859 he was a clerk in the office of the superintendent of public instruction of Indiana. Mr. Larrabee left Indiana in 1860 and spent the remainder of his life in New York. He was on the editorial staffs of THE METHODIST, the BROOKLYN DAILY UNION, POPULAR SCIENCE MONTHLY, and the CHRISTIAN ADVOCATE. On June 25, 1856, he married Letitia B. Frazier, who died in 1909. He died on May 13, 1913.

> Information from *Who Was Who in America* and the DePauw University Archives.

* * *

History of the War in the East (with A. J. Schem). *New York, 1878.*

Education Through the Agency of the Several Religious Organizations. *Albany, N. Y., 1904.*

Earthquakes and Volcanoes. *Plainfield, N. J., 1905.*

How The World Was Made. *Plainfield, N. J., 1905.*

LASSELLE, NANCY POLK (MRS. HYACINTH): ?–1866.

According to J. Z. Powell's *History of Cass County* "Mrs. Nancy Polk Lasselle, wife of Hyacinth Lasselle, came to Logansport in the early 1830's. In 1849 they went to Washington, D.C., where she edited a society magazine THE METROPOLITAN . . . She died in 1866."

It may be added that Hyacinth Lasselle, her husband, was of the French-Canadian family which had come to the middle west as traders and voyageurs long before American, or, for that matter, even British encroachments, and had remained in prominent civil and business capacities along the Wabash through the Revolution and the War of 1812.

Nancy Polk had been a member of a prominent Eastern family before her marriage and she found her husband entirely in sympathy with her aristocratic ideas, in spite of his backwoods background.

> Information from Powell—*History of Cass County.*

* * *

Anna Grayson.
Hope Marshall.

LAW, JOHN: 1796–1873.

John Law deserves special consideration in this work, since he was one of the two first Indiana historians who appear to have been gathering notes at about the same time. (John B. Dillon first published in 1843, Law in 1839.) He is, by comparison with Dillon, a minor scholar indeed but his contribution was important and related to Vincennes, first white town of the state.

The following excerpts from an article in the MAGAZINE OF AMERICAN HISTORY for May, 1891, by Frank A. Myers, of Vincennes, give an outline of his busy life:

"New London, Connecticut, was the birthplace of Judge Law, and he first saw the light October 2, 1796. His early life was in nowise distinguished from the ordinary youth of his day. When eighteen years old he was graduated from Yale, afterward studied law, and in 1817 was admitted to the bar of the supreme court of his native state. The same year, which was that after Indiana was admitted into the Union, he started for the 'great far west,' as Post Vincennes was considered when there were no railroads or telegraph lines in the country. In that pioneer French town he opened a law-office and practiced his profession. He soon gained prominence, and in the course of a long and useful life held many responsible official positions. His talents and eloquence advanced him in public estimation, and for nearly a century he was a leading citizen of the southern part of Indiana.

"Not long after the alliance of his interests with those of Vincennes he was elected prosecuting attorney of that circuit, then embracing nearly one-half of the settled portion of the state . . . He was elected to the Legislature in 1823 and served in that body actively and well, yet his tastes did not run in political directions and when his term expired he returned to the practice of his profession. In 1830 the Indiana legislature elected him judge of the Seventh Judicial Circuit, a position he held for one year, retiring March 30, 1831. He presided, however, as judge upon the same bench from March, 1844, to March, 1850. President Van Buren in 1838 appointed him receiver of public moneys for the district of Vincennes, a post he filled faithfully four years. His commission included the power to adjust land titles.

"Associated with James B. McCall, Lucius H. Scott, and his brother William H. Law, Judge Law purchased a tract consisting of seven hundred acres of land on the Ohio river, adjoining Evansville, and laid it out in lots, giving it the name of Lamasco, now a part of Evansville . . . After the completion of the Wabash & Erie canal to Evansville he moved there with his family in 1851. In 1855 President Pierce appointed him judge of the Court of Claims for Indiana and Illinois, the court to be held at Vincennes. Being a man of large intellectual calibre his decisions were rarely called in question. His patriotic friends induced him to run for Congress from the first district of Indiana in 1860, and he was elected, serving on the library committee and on the committee on Revolutionary pensions . . . Law was re-elected to Congress in 1862, and his congressional career was eminently useful. He impressed his fellow-members with his broad and liberal intellect, and gained their respect, and received the regrets of his constituents when he retired once more to private life. On several occasions he was a prominent candidate for the United States Senate. He died in Evansville Oct. 7, 1873 . . .

"Judge Law married Sarah Ewing, a daughter of Nat[haniel] Ewing, the first receiver of public moneys at the Vincennes land office. He reared a large family of sons and daughters . . .

"Colonel Francois Vigo presented a claim against the United States for provisions and war materials furnished General George Rogers Clark in 1779, when Clark captured Vincennes from the British, and Judge John Law was his attorney in this celebrated case against the government. More than forty years after the goods were furnished Congress agreed to pay the principal of the draft drawn by General Clark. The claim was for nearly eight thousand dollars, but Colonel Vigo refused the proposed payment unless the interest was also paid. Both principal and interest were paid in 1877, but prior to the settlement both Colonel Vigo and Judge Law had passed away. Justice was never done them by the government they served. The payment of the claim to the heirs was the sorriest sort of justice . . .

"His greatest work, that which will do him the most honor in after generations, is *The History of Vincennes,* at first an address before the Vincennes Historical and Antiquarian Society when he was its president. Two thousand copies of it were soon exhausted, and in 1858 he published a new edition with

additions and illustrations, which was also soon exhausted, so that now it is extremely difficult to secure a copy."

Condensed from the MAGAZINE OF AMERICAN HISTORY, May, 1891.

* * *

Address Delivered Before the Vincennes Historical and Antiquarian Society, Feb. 22, 1839. *Louisville,* 1839.
Later published in extended form as:
The Colonial History of Vincennes, Under the French, British, and American Governments, from Its First Settlement Down to the Territorial Administration of General William Henry Harrison . . . *Vincennes,* 1858.
Early History of Masonry in Indiana. An Address Delivered Before the Masonic Fraternity of Evansville, Ind., on St. John's Day, 1867. *Evansville, Ind.,* 1868.

LAWTON, CHARLES BRACEY: 1867–1899.

Charles Bracey Lawton, son of Chauncey N. and Augusta Corbett Lawton, was born June 27, 1867, near Fort Wayne, Ind. In 1871 he moved with his family to South Bend, Ind., where he graduated from high school. The family later moved to Scotland, S.D., and in 1894 Charles Lawton married Miss Marie Wenzloff. He was killed in a farm accident in 1899 and was buried in Scotland, S.D. His book of poems was published shortly after his death.

Information from the South Bend Public Library.

* * *

Lest You Forget: Some Thoughts of One Called Home, Gathered Together for Those He Loved. *South Bend, Ind.,* 1899.

LEEPER, DAVID ROHRER: 1832–1900.

David Rohrer Leeper, son of Samuel and Elizabeth Rohrer Leeper, was born Jan. 12, 1832, in a log cabin near South Bend, Ind. His boyhood was spent on the family farm on Sumption Prairie near South Bend.

When the California gold rush began, young Leeper, who was seventeen years old, was attending the Seminary in South Bend. He persuaded his father to fit him out for a pilgrimage west. With several young friends and two ox teams he started for the West and arrived in the coveted gold fields after seven months and sixteen days of hardship and adventure.

In 1854, at the age of twenty-two, Mr. Leeper returned to South Bend and again attended school. He took an active interest in politics and served as state senator for several terms. In 1892 he was elected mayor of South Bend.

Mr. Leeper was a public-spirited man and possessed considerable literary ability. He wrote valuable articles on local history for the local papers. His brother, Samuel Leeper, kept the manuscript of *The American Idea* for many years, finally consenting to its publication in 1917.

David Leeper died on Nov. 27, 1900.

Information from the South Bend Public Library.

* * *

The Argonauts of '49. *South Bend,* 1894.

The American Idea, Being a Short Study of the Tendency of Political History, with Special Reference to the Origin, Development, and Destiny of the Federal-Republican Polity of the United States. *South Bend,* 1917.

Early Inns and Taverns of South Bend, Ind. *South Bend, Ind.,* n.d.

LEMCKE, JULIUS AUGUSTUS: 1832–1911.

Born in Hamburg, Germany, on Sept. 11, 1832, Julius Augustus Lemcke emigrated to the U.S. in 1846 and lived with his uncle, William L. Dubler, on a farm ten miles from Evansville, Ind., for four years. He then went to work in an Evansville store, studied bookkeeping at night, and after a year went to New Orleans as receiving clerk on a passenger steamer. When he returned, he took charge of a country store in Kentucky. In 1852 he was in charge of a railroad station which was the northern terminus of the Evansville and Terre Haute line.

Mr. Lemcke later returned to Evansville, engaged in a variety of occupations, and began to take an interest in politics. He campaigned for Fremont and the Republican party in 1856. In 1858 he was elected city clerk of Evansville.

He lost money in a wholesale grocery venture but built a good hotel and became a steamboat owner and operator. During the Civil War he patrolled the lower Ohio River to prevent transportation of supplies to the Confederacy.

In 1876 he was elected city treasurer of Evansville, in 1880 became county sheriff, and in 1886 was elected state treasurer. At this time he moved to Indianapolis, where he was in business until his death. He later declined the post of U.S. treasurer offered him by President Harrison.

Mr. Lemcke married Emma O'Riley on Jan. 1, 1874, and died in Indianapolis in 1911.

Information from Dunn—*Indiana and Indianans,* Vol. III.

* * *

Reminiscences of an Indianian,—from the Sassafras Log Behind the Barn in Posey County to Broader Fields. *Indianapolis,* 1905.

LEMON, ALEXANDER DOWNING: 1834–?

Born in Lawrence County, Ind., on Aug. 17, 1834, Alexander Downing Lemon was educated in the district schools of Monroe County and graduated from Indiana University in 1858, receiving the LL.B. degree in 1859. Engaging in the practice of law, he served as a district attorney, member of the state Legislature, and presidential elector. He was also a superintendent of schools.

Information from The University Libraries, Indiana University.

* * *

The Union of the States Must Be Maintained. *Bedford, Ind.,* 1861.

Reconstruction of the States. *Bedford, Ind.,* 1868.

Political Questions of the Day. 1868.

Facts for the People. 1872.

Influence of Popular Education. 1874.

An Address in Support of the Election of Samuel J. Tilden for President of the United States. *San Francisco,* 1876.

Centennial Oration, Published by the Citizens of San Diego County, California, July 4, 1876. *San Diego,* 1876.

Funeral Oration on the Death of Garfield, Delivered September 4, 1881, in Phoenix, Arizona.

Prison Reforms, and Libraries for Penal Institutions. *Phoenix, Ariz.,* 1883.

An Address on the Silver Question and Bi-Metallism. *San Francisco,* 1895.

LEMON, WILLIAM HERSCHEL: 1832–?

Born in Lawrence County, Ind., on Oct. 14, 1832, William Herschel Lemon was educated at home and graduated from Indiana University in 1854, receiving the A.B. and A.M. degrees. From 1854 to 1858 he was president of the Sugar Grove Institute, Tippecanoe County, Ind. During the Civil War he served as surgeon with the 54th Indiana Volunteers and the 83rd Indiana Volunteers.

Information from The University Libraries, Indiana University.

* * *

Evidence of Pre-Glacial Man, in Greene County, Indiana. 1856.

The Valley of the Ghor, and the Noachian Deluge. 1859.

Olam Haba, or the World Arrested at the Theism of the Jews. 1882.

Gisdubar, the Pre-Adamite Man. 1886.

Bichloride of Gold, or the Skeleton in the Closet. 1890.

Ithuriel, or the Legend of Eros; a Romance of Eschatology (also listed under the title Ithuriel, the Days of the Demiurge). 1903.

LESH, ULYSSES SAMUEL: 1868–

Ulysses Samuel Lesh, son of Joseph and Sarah Lesh, was born in Wells County, Ind., on Aug. 9, 1868, and graduated from the law school of the University of Michigan in 1891. He began the practice of law in Huntington, Ind., first as a partner in Kenner & Lesh and later in partnership with his younger brother. From 1902 to 1904 he was Huntington city attorney, from 1907 to 1909 county attorney, from 1917 to 1921 assistant attorney general of Indiana, and from 1921 to 1924 attorney general. He married Minnie Fulton in 1894.

Information from *Who's Who in America.*

* * *

A Knight of the Golden Circle. *Boston,* 1911.
Three Profiteers. *Boston,* 1934.

LEVERING, JOHN: 1826–?

John Levering was born in Philadelphia on Apr. 19, 1826. Reared in the East, he married and in 1849 brought his wife and child to Cincinnati, O., moving on to Lafayette, Ind., the next year. There Henderson farmed for several years and eventually established a real estate and loan business.

At the outbreak of the Civil War Gov. Morton requested him to undertake the task of making contracts in Philadelphia for equipment of Indiana troops; this work successfully completed, he was commissioned captain in the Quartermaster Department and served throughout the war, being mustered out with the rank of colonel.

Information from Levering—*The Levering Family.*

* * *

The Levering Family; History and Genealogy. *Indianapolis,* 1897.

LEVERING, JULIA HENDERSON (MRS. MORTIMER): 1851–

Julia Henderson was born in Covington, Ind., in 1851. Her parents, Albert and Larainne [variously spelled "Lorana" and "Loranna"] Richmond Henderson, removed to Lafayette near the end of the Civil War, and Julia Henderson received her education in the schools of the two towns, graduating from Lafayette High School.

She married Mortimer Levering in Lafayette in 1872, and the couple resided there. After her husband's death, in 1909, Mrs. Levering lived in New York. In addition to her book Mrs. Levering had articles on educational, philanthropical, and sociological subjects published by various magazines.

Information from de Hart—*Past and Present of Tippecanoe County,* 1909, and Dunn—*Indiana and Indianans,* Vol. III.

* * *

Historic Indiana: Being Chapters in the Story of the Hoosier State. *New York,* 1909.

LEWIS, HENRY HARRISON: 1863–1923.

Henry Harrison Lewis, son of William H. H. and Amelia E. Lewis, was born in Anderson, Ind., on Mar. 29, 1863, and was educated in Indianapolis. From 1890 to 1893 he was a writer of juvenile stories, from 1893 to 1898 he was on the editorial staff of the Street and Smith publishing house and after 1898 he was a feature writer for magazines, contributing to MCCLURE'S, MUNSEY'S, AINSLEE'S, WORLD'S WORK, EVERYBODY'S MAGAZINE, and others. In June of 1900 he established Lewis' Literary Syndicate. He married Helena M. Smith in 1897 and died in 1923.

Information from *Who's Who in America.*

* * *

A Gunner Aboard the Yankee. 1898.

Centreboard Jim; or, the Secret of the Sargasso Sea: a Yachting Story. *New York,* 1901.

Ensign Merrill. *New York,* 1901.

Midshipman Merrill. *New York,* 1901.

The King of the Island; or, the Strange Fortunes of Ellis Kirk. *New York,* 1902.

Sword and Pen; or, a Young War Correspondent's Adventures. *New York,* 1902.

The Valley of Mystery; or, the Search for the Flower of Gold: a Story of Venezuela. *New York,* 1903.

Yankee Boys in Japan; or, the Young Merchants of Yokohama. *New York,* 1903.

At the Mikado's Court; the Adventures of Three American Boys in Modern Japan. *New York,* 1907.
How Fortunes Are Made in Advertising. *Chicago,* 1908.

LIDDELL, MARK HARVEY: 1866–1936.

Mark Harvey Liddell, son of Thomas and Sophronia Swan Liddell, was born in Clearfield, Pa., on Apr. 1, 1866, and graduated from Princeton University in 1887, later studying at Oxford University and the University of Berlin. On Dec. 30, 1890, he married Mary Stanley Field.

After teaching English at the universities of Texas and Louisville and at Butler University in Indianapolis, in 1913 he joined the faculty of Purdue University, where he was successively instructor, assistant professor, associate professor, and professor of English until his retirement in 1932. He died on July 28, 1936. He edited and annotated many English classics besides the works listed here, and contributed to learned journals.

Information from *Who Was Who in America.*

* * *

An Introduction to the Scientific Study of English Poetry: Being the Prolegomena to a Science of English Prosody. *Garden City, N. Y.,* 1902.
A Brief Abstract of a New English Prosody, Based Upon the Laws of English Rhythm. *Lafayette, Ind.,* 1914.
The Typography of Shakespeare's Midsomer Nightes Dreame. *Indianapolis,* 1918.
Relation of Energy to Frequency as a Determinant of Sound Quality. 1925.
Energy Frequency Ratios of Diphthongs. 1927.
A New Theory of Sound. *New York,* 1935.

LINCOLN, FREDERICK S.: 1874–

Frederick S. Lincoln was born in Ottumwa, Ia., in 1874 and moved with his family, when he was two or three years old, to Logansport, Ind., the birthplace of his mother and older brother and sister. He also lived for a time in Columbus, Ind.

Information from the Barry Ms.

* * *

An Indiana Girl. *Washington, D. C.,* 1901.

LINDLEY, ERNEST HIRAM: 1869–1940.

Ernest Hiram Lindley, son of Hiram and Laura White Lindley, was born in Paoli, Ind., on Oct. 2, 1869, and graduated from Indiana University in 1893,

receiving the A.M. degree in 1894 and the Ph.D. from Clark University in 1897. He also studied in Germany and at Harvard and received honorary degrees from various institutions. On Sept. 18, 1895, he married Elisabeth Kidder.

From 1893 to 1917 he was a member of the faculty of Indiana University, from 1917 to 1920 president of the University of Idaho, and from 1920 to 1939 chancellor of the University of Kansas. He died on Aug. 21, 1940.

Information from *Who Was Who in America.*

* * *

Arthur Griffith, Arithmetical Prodigy (with W. L. Bryan).

LINDLEY, HARLOW: 1875–

The Quaker historian, Harlow Lindley, son of Mahlon and Martha Newlin Lindley, was born in Sylvania, Parke County, Ind., on May 31, 1875. He attended the Bloomingdale Academy and received the B.Litt. degree in 1898 and the A.M. degree in 1899 from Earlham College. He married Olive S. Rogers on June 24, 1908.

Dr. Lindley served on the Earlham College and various other college faculties between 1899 and 1928, was director of the Department of History and Archives, Indiana State Library, from 1907 to 1923; secretary from 1915 to 1923 and director in 1923-24 of the Indiana Historical Commission; librarian of the Hayes Memorial Historical Library and Museum in 1928; curator of history, Ohio State Archaeological and Historical Society, from 1929 to 1934, and secretary, editor and librarian from 1934 to 1946.

Information from *Who's Who in America.*

* * *

The Government of Indiana. *Boston,* 1909.
Possibilities in State Historical Celebrations. *Lincoln, Neb.,* 1918.
A Century of Quakerism in Indiana. 1922.
History of a Century of Medicine in Ohio. 1932.
John Lewis Roth, the First White Child Born in the Moravian Mission at Gnadenhutten. *Columbus, O.,* 1935.
The Ordinance of 1787 and the Old Northwest Territory. 1937.
The Quaker Contribution to the Old Northwest. 1938.
Children of Light (co-author). *New York,* 1938.
Ohio in the Twentieth Century. *Columbus, O.,* 1942.

LINDLEY, WALTER: 1852–1922.

Walter Lindley, son of Milton and Mary E. Banta Lindley, was born in Monrovia, Ind., on Jan. 13, 1852. He was educated at Minneapolis High School, Long Island College Hospital, and King's School of Anatomy in Philadelphia. After 1875 he engaged in the practice of medicine.

Dr. Lindley was health officer of Los Angeles in 1879, superintendent of the Los Angeles County Hospital in 1885, and dean of the Medical Department of the University of Southern California from 1902 to 1904. In 1889-90 he was president of the California State Medical Society. He was also editor and publisher of the SOUTHERN CALIFORNIA PRACTITIONER. He died on Jan. 24, 1922.

Information from *Who Was Who in America.*

* * *

California of the South (with J. P. Widney). *New York,* 1888.
The Delinquent Child in Great Britain and France. 1908.
The Traducers of Shakespeare. 1908.
Nation's Outlook for Health. *Fort Wayne, Ind.,* 1908.
Delinquent Child in England. *Fort Wayne, Ind.*
Irish Dramatists and the Irish Drama. 1914.

LINTON, LULU GARSHWILER (MRS. I. W.): 1870–1936.

At the time of her death there on Nov. 18, 1936, the NORTHVILLE (Mich.) RECORD published a sketch of Mrs. Linton's life of which the following is an extract:

"Lulu Garshwiler, the daughter of John R. and Elizabeth (Luyster) Garshwiler, was born on a farm near Franklin, Ind., April 13, 1870. Here she spent her girlhood and later attended Franklin College. Early feeling the urge to write she tried her hand at a story at the age of eight years, beginning a career which lasted on throughout her life.

"On Aug. 13, 1890 she was married to I. W. Linton who taught school in Franklin for a number of years . . .

"It was during their life in Indiana that Mrs. Linton began writing for publication. Besides contributing to magazines she wrote half-column articles and 'Little Stories of Daily Life' for the INDIANAPOLIS NEWS . . .

"In May, 1918, the Lintons left their Indiana home for frontier life in Oklahoma and it was here among the sand and high winds of that raw country that Mrs. Linton enlarged her fund of human interest stories.

Before long she was writing regularly for the OKLAHOMAN a serial called 'Letters from a Blue Sky Rancher.'

"During these twelve years while her husband kept the village post office at Jones, Mrs. Linton, as his assistant, watched the life stories of the community pass through the office and sensed the 'lives and loves and sorrows of her people.'

"During her literary career Mrs. Linton has had published more than 300 stories in leading magazines, among them the LADIES' HOME JOURNAL and WOMAN'S HOME COMPANION . . ."

From the NORTHVILLE (Mich.) RECORD, Nov. 18, 1936.

* * *

More Than Coronets. *Cincinnati,* 1903.
Half Columns. *Tuttle, Okla.,* n.d.
Across The Sea. *Cincinnati,* n.d.

LIPPINCOTT, CHARLES AUGUSTUS: 1865–1929.

Charles Augustus Lippincott, son of Ebenezer Wood and Annabelle Weir Lippincott, was born in Piedmont, W. Va., on July 30, 1865, and graduated from Washington and Jefferson College in 1887, receiving the D.D. degree in 1912. He also studied at Princeton University, Princeton Theological Seminary, Union Theological Seminary, and McCormick Theological Seminary, graduating from the last named institution in 1890. In 1922 he received the LL.D. degree from the University of Notre Dame. He married Anna M. Irwin on Oct. 8, 1890.

Ordained to the Presbyterian ministry in 1890, he served as pastor in Joliet, Ill., Chicago, and Flint, Mich., and in 1913 came to South Bend, Ind., where he was a pastor until 1919, when he became manager of the cooperative department of the Studebaker Corporation. He died on Mar. 14, 1929.

Information from *Who Was Who in America.*

* * *

History of Flint, Michigan.

LIPPS, OSCAR HIRAM: 1872–

Born at Fayette, Ind., on July 8, 1872, Oscar Hiram Lipps was educated in the public schools of Tennessee and at Powel's Valley Seminary and American University. He married Maude Etta Rader on Dec. 19, 1897.

After serving as a teacher and principal in the public schools of Tennessee and Louisiana, in 1898 he entered the U. S. Indian Service as a teacher, serving in an administrative capacity after 1900. He was Superintendent of Indian Affairs from 1926 to 1931, superintendent of Sacramento Indian Agency from 1931 to 1935, and field representative from 1935 to 1937. In 1936 he made a survey and report of the Indians and Eskimos of Alaska. He retired in 1937.

Information from Who's Who in America.

* * *

A Little History of the Navajos. *Cedar Rapids, Ia.,* 1909.
Daily Lesson Plan Book for Academic or Vocational Instructors. *Milwaukee, Wis.,* 1919. (2nd ed.)
The Case of the California Indians. *Chemawa, Ore.,* 1932.
Our National Indian Problem and the Chief Factors in Its Solution. 1933.

LITTLE, GEORGE OBADIAH: 1839–?

George Obadiah Little, son of the Rev. Henry and Susan N. Smith Little, was born in Madison, Ind., on May 2, 1839, and was graduated from Amherst College in 1860 and from Lane Theological Seminary in 1863. In 1862 he was ordained to the Presbyterian ministry.

From 1864 to 1870 he was a Presbyterian pastor in Fort Wayne, Ind., and from 1870 to 1873 in Connersville, Ind. In 1873 he went to Washington, D.C., as pastor of Assembly's Church, which he served until 1898. After 1894 he was connected with Howard University as professor in the theological department and as professor of ethics and Greek. He married Martha H. Mitchell of Cincinnati in 1863.

Information from Who's Who in America.

* * *

Mission of Our Government . . . A Sermon. *Fort Wayne, Ind.,* 1864.
The Royal Houses of Israel and Judah—An Interwoven History, with a Harmony of Parallel Passages. *New York,* 1900.

LOCKWOOD, GEORGE BROWNING: 1872–1932.

George Browning Lockwood, son of W. W. and Mary Waite Lockwood, was born in Forest, Ill., on Nov. 7, 1872, and moved with his family to Peru, Ind., where be graduated from high school. In 1894 he graduated from De Pauw University and became the first editor of the TERRE HAUTE EVENING TRIBUNE.

From 1896 to 1902 he was in Washington as private secretary to Col. George W. Steele, congressman, and as Washington correspondent for the American Press Association. He returned to Indiana to serve from 1902 to 1908 as superintendent of the press bureau of the Republican State Committee of Indiana, and during this time he was on the staff of the governor of Indiana. From 1906 to 1912 he was editor and publisher of the EVENING CHRONICLE, Marion, Ind. Until his death, on Feb. 12, 1932, he was editor and publisher of the MUNCIE EVENING PRESS. He married Anne Lloyd Carlisle in 1897.

Mr. Lockwood began his study of the New Harmony community while attending De Pauw University, and his books contain the first scholarly research on the community and movements.

Information from Dunn—Indiana and Indianans, Vol. II, *and Who Was Who in America.*

* * *

The New Harmony Communities. *Marion, Ind.,* 1902.
The New Harmony Movement (with Charles A. Prosser). *New York,* 1905.
Americanism; with a Compilation, by John T. Adams, of Utterances on Americanism by Great Americans. *Washington, D. C.,* 1921.
Thoughts on Americanism. *Washington, D. C.* [1927].

LODGE, HARRIET NEWELL (MRS. ?): 1848–1904.

Harriet Newell was born in Madison, Ind., in 1848. Her husband's first name has not been learned. She died in January, 1904.

Information from the Indiana State Library and the INDIANAPOLIS JOURNAL for Jan. 18, 1904.

* * *

Consider The Lilies. *Cliftondale, Mass.,* n.d. [1888].
Blaisemann, An Allegory. *Indianapolis,* 1891.
A Bit of Finesse; a Story of Fifty Years Ago. *Indianapolis,* 1894.

LOEB, ISAAC ANDERSON: 1868–

Born in Anderson, Ind., in 1868, Isaac Anderson Loeb graduated from Indiana University in 1890, after having previously attended Wabash College. He later resided in Chicago.

>Information from The University Libraries, Indiana University.

* * *

The Jewess of the Apocrypha. *Chicago, 1901.*

LONG, MASON: 1842–1903.

Mason Long was born in Luray, Licking County, O., on Sept. 10, 1842. He was left an orphan at ten and was brought up by a German farmer in Medina County, O. He enlisted in the Union Army in 1862 and served until the end of the Civil War.

In 1865 he moved to Fort Wayne, Ind. For fifteen years he was a professional gambler and a drunkard. Becoming repentant, he joined the Baptist Church, tried to lead a model life and became a professional reformer. One of his books describes his gambling and drinking career and his subsequent reform.

Long was married in 1880 to Kitty Sarah Henderson of Fort Wayne. He died in Fort Wayne in Nov., 1903.

>Information from The Public Library of Fort Wayne and Allen County, Indiana.

* * *

The Life of Mason Long, the Converted Gambler. *Chicago,* 1878.
Fallen Women. *Fort Wayne,* 1880.
Save The Girls. *Fort Wayne,* 1883.

LOUTTIT, GEORGE WILLIAM: 1868–

Born in Dayton, O., in 1868, George William Louttit moved with his family to Fort Wayne, Ind., where he was educated in the public schools. After taking a law course at the University of Michigan, in 1890 he began the practice of law in Allen County. He was elected first judge of the municipal court of Fort Wayne and served as an Allen County representative in the Indiana General Assembly.

>Information from the Barry Ms.

* * *

A Maid of the Wildwood: a Romance of the Middle West in Early Days. *Fort Wayne, Ind.,* 1901.
The Gentleman from Jay. *New York,* 1903.
King Fez. *Fort Wayne, Ind.,* 1907.
The Eddyite, a Christian Science Tale. *Fort Wayne, Ind.,* 1908.
A Prince of the Church.
Bits and Hits in the Devil's Verse. *Boston,* 1928.

LUECKE, MARTIN: 1859–1926.

Martin Luecke, son of Christian and Emily Von Henning Luecke, was born in Sheboygan County, Wis., on June 22, 1859. He graduated from the preparatory school of Concordia College in Fort Wayne, Ind., in 1878 and from Concordia Theological Seminary in St. Louis in 1881, being ordained to the Evangelical Lutheran ministry in the latter year. From 1881 to 1903 he served as a pastor in Illinois, and after 1903 he was president of Concordia College. He married Sina Mansholt in 1882 and died on April 13, 1926.

>Information from *Who Was Who in America* and Dunn—*Indiana and Indianans,* Vol. III.

* * *

History of the Civil War of the United States. *St. Louis, Mo.,* 1892.
Der Buergerkrieg der Vereinigten Staaten, 1861-65. *St. Louis, Mo.,* 1892.
History of Concordia Seminary at Springfield, Illinois. *St. Louis, Mo.,* 1896.
Synopsis of the Holy History of the Old and New Testaments. *St. Louis, Mo.,* 1906.
Short Life of Christ. *St. Louis, Mo.,* 1911.

LYBYER, ALBERT HOWE: 1876–

Albert Howe Lybyer, son of Salem Henry and Jane Estella Layman Lybyer, was born near Putnamville, Ind., on July 29, 1876. He received the A.B. degree from Princeton University in 1896, the A.M. in 1899, and graduated from Princeton Theological Seminary in 1900, being ordained a Presbyterian minister the same year. From 1900 to 1907 he was professor of mathematics at Robert College in Constantinople, from 1907 to 1909 he was an assistant in history at Harvard (he received the Ph.D. from Harvard in 1909), and from 1909 to 1913 he taught history at Oberlin College. He was associate professor of history at the University of Illinois until 1916, when he became professor of history at Ohio State University.

In 1918 Dr. Lybyer was a member of Col. House's commission of inquiry into terms of peace, at the close of the first World War, and in 1919 he served as an assistant in the Balkan division of the American Commission to Negotiate Peace and also as technical adviser to the American Commission on Mandates in Turkey.

He married Clara Sidney Andrews on July 25, 1901.

>Information from *Who's Who in America.*

* * *

The Government of the Ottoman Empire in the Time of Suleiman, the Magnificent. *Cambridge, Mass.,* 1913.

Question of the Near East. *New York,* 1921.

Question of the Far East.

LYNCH, MARTHA C. MARTIN (MRS. ALLON T.): 1854–?

Martha C. Martin, daughter of John G. and Margaret Fitzpatrick Martin, was born on Apr. 5, 1854. Her father served in Company F, 140th Indiana Infantry, during the Civil War.

She married Allon T. Lynch on Jan. 22, 1873, and they lived in various places in Jay and Randolph counties, Ind. When her book was published, they were living in Decatur, Ind.

> Information from Melvin B. Stratton of Indianapolis.

* * *

Reminiscences of Adams, Jay and Randolph Counties. *Fort Wayne, Ind.*

LYON, RICHARD HILL: 1846–1907.

Richard Hill Lyon, son of Capt. Eli and Louisa Augusta Winton Lyon, was born in 1846 near Bridgeport, Conn. The family moved to Ypsilanti, Mich., in 1860. In 1876 Mr. Lyon married Miss Frances A. Kurtz of Buffalo, N.Y.

In 1874 Mr. Lyon became identified with newspaper work in South Bend, Ind., when he accepted a position with the SOUTH BEND TRIBUNE. At the time of his death, April 4, 1907, he was chief editorial writer for the paper. Mr. Lyon was a talented musician and sang in a Presbyterian quartet for many years. He wrote many historical articles and several sacred songs and anthems.

> Information from the South Bend Public Library.

* * *

Lasalle in the Valley of the St. Joseph: An Historical Fragment (with Charles H. Bartlett). *South Bend, Ind.,* 1899.

LYONS, ROBERT EDWARD: 1869–1946.

Robert Edward Lyons, son of Mathew J. and Alice Eveleigh Lyons, was born at Bloomfield, Ind., on Oct. 24, 1869, and graduated from Indiana University in 1889, receiving the A.M. degree in 1890. He studied in Germany and Denmark from 1892 to 1895 and

was awarded the Ph.D. degree by Heidelberg in 1894. On Mar. 23, 1898, he married Eleanor Joslyn.

In 1889 he was an instructor in chemistry at Indiana University, from 1890 to 1895 was on the faculty of Heidelberg University, and from 1895 to 1938 served as professor of chemistry and head of the department at Indiana University. During these years he was also on the staff of Central College of Physicians and Surgeons, the Medical College of Indiana, and the Indiana University School of Medicine, Indianapolis.

Dr. Lyons was the author of many scientific articles. He died on Nov. 25, 1946.

> Information from *Indiana University, 1820-1904,* and *Who's Who in America.*

* * *

Die Phenylverbindungen von Schwefel, Selen und Tellur. *Heidelberg,* 1894.

The Qualitative Analysis of Inorganic Bodies (with L. S. Davis). *Anderson, Ind.,* 1897.

A Manual of Toxicological Analysis (with L. S. Davis). *Anderson, Ind.,* 1899.

M

McBRIDE, JOHN RANDOLPH: 1842–?

John Randolph McBride was born in Morgan County, Ind., in 1842.

He enlisted in the 33rd Indiana Volunteer Infantry on Sept. 16, 1861, with the rank of quartermaster sergeant. He served throughout the war, being promoted to adjutant on Oct. 1, 1864, and mustered out on July 21, 1865.

> Information from the Indianapolis Public Library and the Indiana State Library.

* * *

History of the Thirty-Third Indiana Volunteer Infantry, During the Four Years of Civil War . . . *Indianapolis,* 1900.

McBRIDE, ROBERT WESLEY: 1842–1926.

Robert Wesley McBride, son of Augustus and Martha Ann Barnes McBride, was born on Jan. 25, 1842, in Richland County, O. He attended Ohio public schools and, after the removal of his family to that state, schools of Iowa and the Kirkwood Academy. He served in the Civil War as a member of the Union Light Guard of Ohio (President Lincoln's bodyguard).

He was admitted to the Iowa bar in 1867. The next year he married Ida S. Chamberlain and they made their home in Waterloo, Ia., where McBride practiced law and served as circuit judge until 1890, when they removed to Indianapolis.

At Indianapolis McBride served as a justice of the Indiana Supreme Court from 1890 to 1893 and practiced law in that city from 1893 until his death in 1926.

Information from *Who Was Who in America.*

* * *

Lincoln's Body Guard, the Union Light Guard of Ohio; with Some Personal Recollections of Abraham Lincoln. *Indianapolis*, 1911.

Personal Recollections of Abraham Lincoln; with Introduction by Albert J. Beveridge. *Indianapolis*, 1926.

McCAIN, THOMAS HART BENTON: 1839–1898.

T. H. B. McCain, son of the Rev. Hugh B. McCain, was born on a farm near Frankfort, Ind., on Jan. 24, 1839. He attended local schools, with an additional year or two at the Thorntown (Ind.) Academy.

He began work in a Frankfort printing office in his twelfth year, while attending school, and, except for four years in the Union Army during the Civil War, spent his entire life in the printing and publishing business.

After the war he married Miss Salome Snow, came to Crawfordsville, Ind., and purchased an interest in the CRAWFORDSVILLE JOURNAL on Apr. 16, 1868. Within the next few years he acquired full possession of the paper. He died on May 1, 1898.

Information supplied by the McCain family.

* * *

The Eighty-Sixth Regiment Indiana Volunteer Infantry ... (with Barnes and Carnahan). *Crawfordsville, Ind.,* 1895.

McCARTER, MARGARET HILL (MRS. WILLIAM A.): 1860–1938.

Margaret Hill, daughter of Thomas Thornburg and Nancy Davis Hill, was born in Charlottesville, Ind., on May 2, 1860, and graduated from the State Normal School at Terre Haute. She also received honorary degrees from Baker and Washburn universities and from the College of Emporia. She married William Arthur McCarter.

Mrs. McCarter taught in the Indiana schools and was later head of the English department of Topeka (Kan.) High School. In addition to her books she con-

tributed short stories to magazines and was a lecturer on literary and educational subjects.

She died on Aug. 31, 1938.

Information from *Who Was Who in America.*

* * *

The Cottonwood's Story. *Topeka, Kan.,* 1903.
Cuddy's Baby, Story of Kansas Folks. *Topeka, Kan.,* 1907.
Cuddy, and Other Stories. *Topeka, Kan.,* 1908. (4th ed.).
In Old Quivira. *Topeka, Kan.,* 1908.
The Price of the Prairie: a Story of Kansas. *Chicago,* 1910.
The Peace of the Solomon Valley. *Chicago,* 1911.
A Wall of Men. *Chicago,* 1912.
A Master's Degree. *Chicago,* 1913.
Winning the Wilderness. *Chicago,* 1914.
The Corner Stone. *Chicago,* 1915.
Vanguards of the Plains, a Romance of the Old Santa Fé Trail. *New York,* 1917.
The Reclaimers. *New York,* 1918.
Paying Mother; the Tribute Beautiful. *New York,* 1920.
Homeland. *New York,* 1922.
Widening Waters. *New York,* 1924.
The Candle in the Window. *Chicago,* 1925.

McCARTY, IDA HELEN DOUTHETT (MRS. MARSHALL B.): 1876–

Ida Helen Douthett, eldest of the four children of William and Alice Ida Howard Douthett, was born on a farm in Hocking County, O., on June 19, 1876. Her mother died in 1882.

Receiving her early schooling in a log school house, she later attended the public schools of Nelsonville, O., and graduated from the Athens (O.) High School. She taught school at the age of sixteen. After completing a course at Manns' Business College in Columbus, O., she entered Ohio State University as a special student in journalism. She then returned to Athens, taught school, and at the same time pursued studies at Ohio University.

All during her years in high school and while teaching and doing college work, she was writing for publication—verses, stories, sketches for newspapers, magazines, and church periodicals.

She married Marshall B. McCarty and after January, 1900, was a resident of Pennville, Jay County, Ind., where she continued to write short stories, historical sketches, and features.

Information from the Portland, Ind., Public Library.

* * *

Mariam'ne of the Cedars. *New York,* 1911.

McCAUGHEY, MARETTA ROBISON (MRS. GEORGE B.): 1852–1907.

Maretta Robison, daughter of John A. Robison, was born at Findlay, O., on Aug. 13, 1852, was educated in the public schools, and taught in the Findlay schools for eight years. On June 4, 1878, she was married to George Bruce McCaughey.

In 1887 they moved to Frankfort, Ind., and the following year moved to a farm west of Frankfort. Mrs. McCaughey was active in church work and in a literary club until her health failed. For several years before her death, on Jan. 7, 1907, she suffered from tuberculosis.

She began writing verse when she was a young girl, and her poems were published in various periodicals. After her death these poems were collected by her family and published.

Information from the Frankfort Public Library.

* * *

When Lilacs Bloom and Other Poems. *Cincinnati,* n.d. [1909].

McCLAIN, WILLIAM THOMAS: 1845–1937.

Born in Scott County, Ind., on May 31, 1845, William Thomas McClain was the son of the Rev. Matthew and Emily A. Swincher McClain. He was educated in Scott County schools, in an academy at Madison, Ind., and took a commercial course in an Indianapolis business college.

The McClain family moved to Marion County, Ind., about 1865 and settled on a farm in Pike township. William married Frances A. Case on Feb. 6, 1867. She died in 1920.

McClain was organizer and for many years secretary-treasurer of the Farmers Mutual Insurance Company of Marion County. He died at the home of a son in Indianapolis on Apr. 28, 1937.

Information from *Memoirs of Indianapolis and Marion County* and the INDIANAPOLIS STAR for May 1, 1937.

* * *

Life and Labors of the Rev. Matthew McClain, with Recollections and Events Through a Life of Seventy Years. *Indianapolis,* 1876.

McCOY, ISAAC: 1784–1846.

Isaac McCoy, friend of the Indian, crusader for his rights and gentleman of God, was born in Fayette County, Pa., on June 13, 1784. Six years later the McCoy family moved to Shelby County, Ky.

In Kentucky young McCoy acquired an adequate education. (There were probably more educated men, capable and willing to teach their own and their neighbors' children on the seventy-five miles of the lower Kentucky River in the 1790-1810 period than in all the rest of the Ohio River country combined.) Before his twentieth birthday he married Christina, one of the daughters of Capt. Polls, and the young people began forty-two years of the most gruelling hardships ever suffered by a frontier couple.

Isaac had become interested in the Baptist ministry and he had been preparing himself for the pulpit: unlike his fellows of the day he took no interest in sectarian squabbles. In 1804, shortly after their marriage, Isaac and Christina set out for Vincennes, in the Indiana Territory, where Isaac hoped to be assigned to a church.

Naturally they expected to serve among the whites: at that time they probably despised the Indians, as most frontier couples did, and especially since Christina and her mother had been captives of the Ottawas for some time in her childhood.

In 1805 Isaac was called to Clark County, Ind., where he was licensed to preach in the Silver Creek Baptist Church, and in 1810 he was called to the famous Maria Creek Baptist Church in Vigo County—probably the best pastorate in the state at the time.

He visited St. Louis on a preaching tour and, impressed by the depravity of the remnants of the French and Indians and the dissolute trappers and adventurers who made it their home, decided to take up missionary work. He made this decision known to the Baptist Board of Missions, and the Board agreed, asking him to report as to the places in Indiana and Illinois "most destitute of preaching."

Isaac replied, naming those un-Godly spots as requested but adding what was then a new note for a Baptist—especially a Kentucky or Indiana Baptist. He asked, he says, ". . . that I might extend my labors to the Indians." On Oct. 17, 1817, he received a commission which permitted him to labor among the Indians *for one year*: one way or another, with or without salary, Isaac McCoy extended his one year to thirty-nine—until his death.

The following June he introduced himself to the Miamis, Weas and Kickapoos at their annual meeting to receive treaty goods. They were mostly drunk—as they always were when white traders came among them at treaty payment—but McCoy thought he saw encouraging signs. He wrote and distributed a circular in Indiana, Kentucky and Illinois and toured these states soliciting funds for his projected mission school and church.

On his return from one of these trips he found that his eldest daughter, thirteen, had died: "We afterwards believed the event was sanctified," says McCoy, "in inducing us to let go the hold . . . upon . . . civilized society . . . We had felt great anxiety on account of this daughter; our other children were small, but she was of an age to make it particularly desirable that she enjoy the benefit of a good school in the midst of good society." The death of this daughter was not to be their last sacrifice: the McCoys were to bury ten of their children during their joint missionary labors.

In November, 1818, they began construction of their first mission on the Wabash, near the mouth of Raccoon Creek on land only recently taken from the Indians by the "New Purchase."

They began cabins, secured a teacher (he was an infidel but McCoy later converted him—and he was an enthusiastic aid, even in his Godless state) and McCoy began making the rounds of the Indian villages in search of pupils. Difficulties were great: the interpreters were mostly French-Canadians and Catholics, some traders were not particularly interested in the preaching of temperance to their customers and the Indian agents were, as a rule, uninterested in either missions or Indians. Finally, however, school was opened on Jan. 6, 1819, with six white pupils and one Indian boy.

Isaac McCoy began to study the Miami language—no small task since most interpreters were French-Canadians, speaking neither good Miami, good English nor good French—and he finally gave it up and learned Delaware from Christmas Dashney (properly Dagnett), a Delaware who had been educated at a Catholic mission.

Pressure from the white squatters very soon became intolerable, and in 1820 the school was removed to Fort Wayne.

Here it prospered moderately, and some conversions were made among the Indians and part-Indians, but now a new trial came to plague the McCoys: members of the Baptist Mission Board, many of whom had been reared on the frontier, began to harass their Indian missionary over money matters—expenditures were too high, it was senseless to operate a school, it was better, in short, to shoot Indians than to minister to them.

In this emergency McCoy turned to Lewis Cass, governor of the Michigan Territory and a friend of the Indians. Cass helped and, better still, he secured federal aid. At his advice the McCoy mission was removed to the St. Joseph River, in Michigan, among the Potawatomis.

It was these people whom McCoy thereafter considered his own. When in 1830 it became obvious that they must move west of the Mississippi, he got himself appointed surveyor and agent to help them locate their new homes; he did what he could to aid them on their death-march to the west. Later, with his sons, Dr. Rice McCoy and John McCoy, he performed similar service for other tribes, surveying or directing the surveys of most of the reservations in Kansas and in the Cherokee Outlet.

He hoped for an Indian state; he was constantly in touch with Washington, trying in every way to ameliorate the condition of the Indians and to protect their interests. Between times he preached, prayed, taught and counseled.

By 1842 the white Christians were twenty-five years further from the bloodshed of the frontier than they had been at the beginning of McCoy's labors, and even the most narrow of them had been forced to acknowledge his zeal, his spirit and his ability: they appointed him first corresponding secretary of the Indian Mission Association at Louisville, Ky.

It must have cheered his last years to head such an organization, but he had but few of these years ahead: constant hardships and killing labor had made him an old man at fifty-eight, and at sixty-two, on June 21, 1846, he died.

* * *

(Circular Requesting Funds for a Mission; Published July, 1818.) No copy located.

Remarks on the Practicability of Indian Reform, Embracing Their Colonization; with an Appendix. *Boston, 1827.*

Address to Philanthropists in the United States, Generally and to Christians in Particular, on the Condition and Prospects of the American Indians. n.p., 1831.

Annual Register of Indian Affairs within the Indian Territory. 1835-1838. (Published serially)

History of Baptist Indian Missions: Embracing Remarks on the Former and Present Condition of the Aboriginal Tribes; Their Settlement within the Indian Territory, and Their Future Prospects. *Washington, D. C.,* 1840.

McCOY, WILLIAM HENRY HARRISON: 1837–1918.

William Henry Harrison McCoy, son of Spencer Collins McCoy and his first wife, Nancy Delilah McDaneld, was born in Clark County, Ind., on Apr. 26, 1837.

He graduated from Franklin College in 1861 with the degrees of A.B. and A.M. and in 1863 married Elizabeth Amanda Potter. In the ten years following Mr. McCoy's graduation from Franklin he served as principal of the public schools at Seymour, then as professor of mathematics at Moore's Hill College and Eleutherian College, and later as principal of schools at Dupont and Vernon. The next eighteen years he alternated between farming and merchandising. In 1889 he was appointed industrial teacher and clerk at the government school for Indians at Fort Lapwai, Id. Returning to Indiana in 1893, he became superintendent of buildings and grounds at Franklin College, a position he held until his retirement from active life in 1915. He died in the state of Washington, at the home of a son, on Christmas Day, 1918.

From 1871 to 1873 and again from 1877 to 1884 Mr. McCoy was a member of the board of directors of Franklin. In addition to his books, he was the author of articles on the college which appeared in newspapers and Baptist periodicals.

Information from Elizabeth Hayward, granddaughter of Mr. McCoy.

* * *

History of the Oldest Baptist Church in Indiana by One of Its Members. *Louisville, Ky.,* 1880.

Notes on the McCoy Family, 1915. (Edited by Elizabeth Hayward.) *Rutland, Vt.,* 1939.

McCULLOCH, HUGH: 1808–1895.

Hugh McCulloch was born at Kennebunk, Me., on Dec. 7, 1808, the son of Hugh and Abigail Perkins McCulloch. Hugh, senior, was a ship-owner in the West Indies trade.

Young McCulloch attended Bowdoin College for two years, with the class of 1829, but left school to study law. He was admitted to the bar in Boston, Mass., in 1832.

The next year he came to Fort Wayne, Ind., where he opened a law office but devoted most of his attention to the Fort Wayne branch of the State Bank of Indiana, which he served as cashier and manager from 1835 to 1856. In the latter year he became president of the bank and next year saw it through a panic in which only one or two other state banks of any size survived in the entire country.

The old state banking system being abandoned in 1863 in favor of the national system, McCulloch was, properly, put in charge of the organization of the new system as U.S. Comptroller of the Currency. At the end of the Civil War he was appointed Secretary of the Treasury by President Lincoln. He served through the first of the difficult reconstruction years but retired in 1869 to enter private banking. Once more, during the last months of President Arthur's administration, he served as Secretary of the Treasury, filling out the term of Walter Q. Gresham.

Hugh McCulloch spent his last years in Prince George's County, Md. He had married Susan Mann at Fort Wayne in 1838, and their four children survived him. He died on May 24, 1895.

Information from the *Dictionary of American Biography* and *Who Was Who in America.*

* * *

Our National and Financial Future. Address of . . . Secretary of the Treasury, at Fort Wayne, Indiana, October 11, 1865. *Fort Wayne, Ind.,* 1865.

Bi-Metallism: a Lecture Delivered at Harvard University, May 8, 1879. *New York,* 1879.

Men and Measures of Half a Century: Sketches and Comments. *New York,* 1888.

Addresses, Speeches, Lectures and Letters Upon Various Subjects. *Washington, D. C.,* 1891.

McCULLOCH, HUGH, JR.: 1869–1902.

Hugh McCulloch, Jr., son of Fred H. and Carrie Riddle McCulloch, was born in Fort Wayne, Ind., on March 9, 1869. He was the grandson of Hugh McCulloch, secretary of the treasury under Lincoln and other presidents.

Mr. McCulloch was educated at Harvard University, where he was class poet of his graduating class. After graduation he left for Italy and spent the remainder of his life in that country, in reading and study and in the writing of poetry.

He died in Italy of typhoid fever on Mar. 27, 1902.

Information from The Public Library of Fort Wayne and Allen County, Indiana.

* * *

The Quest of Heracles, and Other Poems. *Cambridge, Mass.,* 1894.

Written in Florence: the Last Verses of Hugh McCulloch. *London,* n.d. [1902].

McCULLY, CHARLES HARVY: 1868–1941.

Charles Harvy McCully was born in Idaville, Ind., in 1868. He attended Cincinnati Eclectic Medical School and Indiana Medical College. In 1901 he went to Logansport, Ind., where he became a practicing physician. He married Florence M. Vernon of Huntington, Ind., in 1909. His death occurred in Logansport in 1941.

From Powell—*History of Cass County,* 1913.

* * *

Chemistry of Embalming. 1899.
Shadows of Futurity. 1899.
Sanitation and Disinfection. *Chicago,* 1906.

McCUTCHEON, BEN FREDERICK: 1875–1934.

Ben Frederick McCutcheon, son of John Barr and Clara Glick McCutcheon and brother of John T. and George Barr McCutcheon, was born in Lafayette, Ind., on May 31, 1875. He was educated at Purdue University, where his father was director of the university farms, and after leaving college entered newspaper work in Chicago.

For many years he conducted a daily column in the CHICAGO TRIBUNE, of which he was commercial editor after 1905, and he was later head of a publishing company.

He married Anna Barnes on June 5, 1900, and died in Chicago on Aug. 27, 1934. He wrote under the pen name of "Benjamin Brace."

Information from *Who Was Who in America* and the INDIANAPOLIS STAR, Aug. 28, 1934.

* * *

Sunrise Acres. *New York,* 1905.
The Seventh Person. *New York,* 1906.

McCUTCHEON, GEORGE BARR: 1866–1928.

George Barr McCutcheon, eldest of the three distinguished McCutcheon brothers (see sketches of Ben Frederick and John Tinney McCutcheon), was born in Tippecanoe County, Ind., on July 26, 1866. His parents were John Barr and Clara Glick McCutcheon. John Barr McCutcheon was a farmer and stock raiser. He had literary tastes (he is said to have written a play which he cast from among his neighbors and produced locally), but he was primarily a follower of agriculture,

and a follower good enough to be selected, from among all those eligible on the good black earth of Tippecanoe County, to take charge of the first farm owned by Purdue University after it was opened as Indiana's "agricultural and mechanical" educational institution.

George Barr McCutcheon attended rural schools and, after the family had moved to town, those of Lafayette, Ind. He and his brothers all wrote and drew for amusement—probably not discouraged by their father—and the first remembered literary effort of George Barr is an unfinished narrative entitled "Panther Jim": it is to be feared that dime novels had somehow been introduced into the McCutcheon household.

George Barr—and in due time his brothers—entered Purdue University, that institution harboring in that period, besides the McCutcheons, George Ade and Booth Tarkington—strange worshippers at the shrine of agriculture and mechanics.

During his brief enrollment (1882-83) George Barr reported student activities for the LAFAYETTE JOURNAL and, soon finding more glamour in the newspaper world, left education to take full-time employment. In 1893 he left the JOURNAL for the LAFAYETTE DAILY COURIER, where he acted as city editor until 1901.

After his establishment as a novelist, McCutcheon moved to New York. He married Mrs. Marie Van Antwerp Fay on Sept. 26, 1904. He died on Oct. 23, 1928.

Summarizing McCutcheon's literary career, S. G. B., writing in the *Dictionary of American Biography,* says:

"McCutcheon's first published story was 'The Ante-Mortem Condition of George Ramor,' which appeared in the NATIONAL MAGAZINE, October 1896. His letters in dialect, 'Waddleton Mail,' had previously had newspaper publication. In spare moments at the editorial office he wrote a romance, *Pootoo's Gods,* which at first sold poorly, but later, under the new title, *Nedra* (1905), became a season's success. *Graustark* (1901), written in the same way and sold for $500, brought McCutcheon his first fame and is said to have cleared over $250,000 for publishers and theatrical producers. The publishers later voluntarily paid him royalties. This tale of a mythical Balkan country, whose name was a combination of the German words Grau and Stark, with its capital Edelweiss and its princess Yetive, actually deceived many readers who wrote to ask McCutcheon for the best route to Graustark. His next romances were *Castle Craneycrow* (1902), *Brewster's Millions* (1902), and *The Sherrods* (1903). To test the sales value of his name he published *Brewster's Millions* under the pseudonym Richard Greaves. It became a best seller when *The Sherrods* had only moderate sales . . .

"McCutcheon wrote with zest and lived for the time in his own romances. For *Graustark* he prepared a complete geographical and genealogical plan. He wrote only one draft, with pencil, from an elaborate outline, and produced about a thousand words a day. He worked best in the afternoon, but he frequently wrote in the evenings. Though his success was in the realm of romance, he much preferred realism. With an output of almost two books a year, he published much that was hasty and slight. Even at his best, he can hardly be called a great romanticist, but he furnished wholesome, not too extravagant, romances to a public weary of extreme realism and materialism. One editorial at the time of his death said that he supplied innocent happiness for 'many college boys, kitchen maids, and daughters of millionaires' (NEW YORK TIMES, Oct. 24, 1928) . . ."

> Condensed from S. G. B., *Dictionary of American Biography*, Vol. XII.

* * *

Pootoo's Gods. (Reissued in 1905 as Nedra.)

Graustark: the Story of a Love Behind a Throne. *Chicago*, 1901.

Castle Craneycrow. *Chicago*, 1902.

Brewster's Millions. (Richard Greaves, pseudonym.) *Chicago*, 1903.

The Sherrods. *New York*, 1903.

The Day of the Dog. *New York*, 1904.

Beverly of Graustark. *New York*, 1904.

Nedra. (A reissue of Pootoo's Gods.) *New York*, 1905.

The Purple Parasol. *New York*, 1905.

Cowardice Court. *New York*, 1906.

Jane Cable. *New York*, 1906.

The Flyers. *New York*, 1907.

The Daughter of Anderson Crow. *New York*, 1907.

The Husbands of Edith. *New York*, 1908.

The Man from Brodney's. *New York*, 1908.

The Alternative. *New York*, 1909.

Truxton King. *New York*, 1909.

The Rose in the Ring. *New York*, 1910.

The Butterfly Man. *New York*, 1910.

Brood House: a Play in Four Acts. *Chicago*, 1910.

Mary Midthorne. *New York*, 1911.

What's-His Name. *New York*, 1911.

The Hollow of Her Hand. *New York*, 1912.

Her Weight in Gold. *New York*, 1912.

A Fool and His Money. *New York*, 1913.

Black Is White. *New York*, 1914.

The Prince of Graustark. *New York*, 1914.

Mr. Bingle. *New York*, 1915.

From The Housetops. *New York*, 1916.

The Light That Lies. *New York*, 1916.

Green Fancy. *New York*, 1917.

The City of Masks. *New York*, 1918.

Shot with Crimson. *New York*, 1918.

One Score and Ten; a Comedy in Four Acts. *New York*, 1919.

Sherry. *New York*, 1919.

Anderson Crow, Detective. *New York*, 1920.

West Wind Drift. *New York*, 1920.

Quill's Window. *New York*, 1921.

Viola Gwyn. *New York*, 1922.

Yollop. *New York*, 1922.

Oliver October. *New York*, 1923.

East of the Setting Sun. *New York*, 1924.

Romeo in Moon Village. *New York*, 1925.

Kindling and Ashes. *New York*, 1926.

The Inn of the Hawk and the Raven. *New York*, 1927.

Blades. *New York*, 1928.

The Merivales. *New York*, 1929.

Books Once Were Men: an Essay for Booklovers. *New York*, 1931.

McCUTCHEON, JOHN TINNEY: 1870–

John Tinney McCutcheon, son of John Barr and Clara Glick McCutcheon, was born near South Raub, Tippecanoe County, Ind., on May 6, 1870. (See sketches of Ben Frederick and George Barr McCutcheon.) He lived on a farm until 1876, when the family moved to Lafayette, Ind., where the elder McCutcheon became first director of the Purdue University farms.

John T. McCutcheon was educated at Purdue University, graduating with the B.S. degree in 1889, and he went to Chicago, where for the next two years he worked for the CHICAGO RECORD. From 1901 to 1903 he was associated with the CHICAGO RECORD-HERALD and after 1903 with the CHICAGO TRIBUNE.

He is best known for his political cartoon work, which he began in the campaign of 1896. During his newspaper career he was sent to Asiatic countries and the Philippines following the Spanish-American War and to South Africa during the Boer War. He made another trip to Africa in 1909-10, to Mexico in 1914, and to Europe in 1914-16. He won the Pulitzer prize for his cartoons.

He married Evelyn Shaw on Jan. 20, 1917.

> Information from *Who's Who in America*.

* * *

Stories of Filipino Warfare. 1900.

Boy Calendar. *Chicago, 1903.*

Cartoons: a Selection of One Hundred Drawings; Including the famous "Boy in Spring Time Series," Etc.; with an Introduction by George Ade. *Chicago, 1903.*

Bird Center Cartoons: Chronicle of Social Happenings at Bird Center. *Chicago, 1904.*

The Mysterious Stranger and Other Cartoons. *New York, 1905.*

Congressman Pumphrey, the People's Friend. *Indianapolis, 1907.*

What Does Christmas Really Mean? (with J. L. Jones). *Chicago, 1908.*

Doing the Grand Canyon. [*New York, 1909*].

In Africa: Hunting Adventures in the Big Game Country. *Indianapolis, 1910.*

T. R. in Cartoons. *Chicago, 1910.*

History of Indiana. *Indianapolis, 1911.*

Dawson '11, Fortune Hunter. *New York, 1912.*

The Restless Age. *Indianapolis, 1921.*

An Heir At Large. *Indianapolis, 1923.*

The Island Song Book, Being a Small Collection of Our Favorite Ballads, Anthems, Lullabies and Dirges of this Particular Section of the Bahama Islands ... *Chicago, 1927.*

McDONALD, DANIEL: 1833–1916.

Daniel McDonald, newspaper editor and writer on Indiana history, was born near Connersville, Ind., on May 6, 1833. His parents moved to Marshall County, Ind., in 1836, and there Daniel McDonald spent most of his life.

He was editor of the PLYMOUTH DEMOCRAT for thirty years and was elected to the Indiana Legislature in 1889 and 1905. He retired from business in 1902 and died on Jan. 10, 1916.

Information from the INDIANA MAGAZINE OF HISTORY, Vol. 12.

* * *

History of Marshall County, Indiana, 1836 to 1880. *Chicago, 1881.*

The Big 4 Wonders of America. *Plymouth, Ind., 1893.*

Indiana Newspaper Reminiscences; a Paper Prepared for ... the Democratic State Editorial Association, June 11, 1897. n.p., 1897.

A History of Freemasonry in Indiana from 1806-1898. *Indianapolis, 1898.*

Removal of the Pottawattomie Indians from Northern Indiana. *Plymouth, Ind., 1899.*

History of Lake Maxinkuckee. *Indianapolis, 1905.*

A Twentieth Century History of Marshall County, Indiana. *Chicago, 1908.* 2 vols.

MacDOUGAL, DANIEL TREMBLY: 1865–

Born at Liberty, Ind., on Mar. 16, 1865, Daniel Trembly MacDougal graduated from De Pauw University in 1890. He received the A.M. degree from De Pauw in 1894 and the M.S. and Ph.D. degrees from Purdue in 1893 and 1897, respectively. On Jan. 24, 1893, he married Louise Fisher.

From 1890 to 1892 he was an instructor in biology at Purdue University, in 1892-93 a special agent of the U. S. Department of Agriculture, and from 1893 to 1895 he taught at the University of Minnesota. In 1899 he was appointed director of the laboratories of the New York Botanical Garden, and in 1904 was made assistant director of the New York Botanical Garden.

After 1906 he was connected with the department of botanical research, Carnegie Institution of Washington, D. C. He published a great many textbooks and scientific articles in learned journals and serials which are not listed here.

Information from De Pauw University's *Alumnal Record, 1920.*

* * *

Experimental Plant Physiology. *New York, 1895.*

Living Plants and Their Properties: a Collection of Essays. *Little Rock, Ark., 1898.*

A Practical Text-book of Plant Physiology. *New York, 1901.*

Elementary Plant Physiology. *New York, 1902.*

Green Leaf: the Major Activities of Plants in Sunlight. *New York, 1930.*

Tree Growth. *Waltham, Mass., 1938.*

MACE, WILLIAM HARRISON: 1852–1938.

William Harrison Mace, son of Ira and Nancy Johnson Mace, was born near Lexington, Ind., on Nov. 27, 1852, and graduated from the State Normal School at Terre Haute in 1876. He also received degrees from the Universities of Michigan, Indiana, Syracuse, and Jena and was a graduate student at Cornell. He married Ida Dodson on Sept. 10, 1878.

He held administrative positions in the public schools of Logansport and Winamac, Ind., and of McGregor, Ia. From 1885 to 1890 he was professor of history at De Pauw University Normal School, and from 1891 to 1916 he was professor of history and political science at Syracuse University.

In addition to the books listed below, Dr. Mace was the author of several textbooks.

He died on Aug. 10, 1938.

Information from *Who Was Who in America.*

* * *

American Revolution: Outlines and References. *Albany, N. Y., 1891.*

American Constitution: Outlines and References. *Albany, N. Y., 1892.*

Development of the Nation: Outlines and References. *Albany, N. Y., 1893.*

American Colonial Institutions: Outlines and References. *Albany, N. Y., 1898.*

History of the United States. *Chicago, 1903.*

Civil War and Some of Its Problems: Outlines and References. *Albany, N. Y., 1905.*

American Revolution: Syllabus. *Philadelphia,* n.d.

Stories of Heroism. *Chicago, 1911.*

Lincoln, the Man of the People. *Chicago, 1912.*

Story of Old Europe and Young America (with Edwin P. Tanner). *Chicago, 1915.*

Washington, a Virginia Cavalier. *Chicago, 1916.*

History of the United States (with Frank S. Bogardus). *Chicago, 1921.*

Notebook by Cloyce B. Ulery. *Chicago, 1929.*

My Country, the Men Who Made It (with W. A. Hannig). *Chicago, 1930-31.*

Lincoln and Douglas. *Syracuse, N. Y., 1933.*

Stories of Great American Explorers and Pioneers. *Chicago, 1941.*

Stories of Great American Heroes. *Chicago, 1941.*

Stories of Great American Leaders. *Chicago, 1941.*

McGOVERN, JOHN: 1850–1917.

"John McGovern (Feb. 18, 1850-Dec. 17, 1917), journalist and author, was born in Troy, N. Y., the eldest of three children of James and Marion (Carter) McGovern. In 1854, when his father and sister died of cholera, his mother took him to Ligonier, Ind., where she died four years later. The boy then lived with Judson Palmiter, a printer, in Ligonier, where he attended school and worked during the summer months on the farm of his uncle, Henry Carter, at Lima, Ind. In 1862 when Palmiter moved to Kendallville, Ind., to publish the NOBLE COUNTY JOURNAL, McGovern began his journalistic career by working in the printing office . . . He worked as a printer in Sturgis, Mich., in 1866, returning the following year to Kendallville, and thence going to Kalamazoo to join the staff of the MICHIGAN TELEGRAPH. In 1868 he moved to Chicago, became a typesetter on the CHICAGO TRIBUNE, and gradually advanced to proof-reader, telegraph editor, and night editor. In these years he began to write poetry, some of which

was published in the TRIBUNE. In 1877 he was married to Kate C. Van Arsdale of Philadelphia, who bore him two sons and a daughter. For two years (July 1884-July 1886) he was associate editor and for a few weeks (July-October 1886) sole editor of the CURRENT, a literary magazine, which printed poems, essays, and editorials by him, and from 1887 to 1889 he was chief editorial writer for the CHICAGO HERALD.

"Encouraged by his growing literary experience, he gave up newspaper work to devote his time to literature. . . . His novel, *David Lockwin; The People's Idol* (1892), is of interest because McGovern accused the British novelist, Gilbert Parker, of taking its plot for his novel, *The Right of Way* . . . In 1899 McGovern served as literary expert for Samuel Eberley Gross in his plagiarism case against Edmund Rostand, and studied texts of *Cyrano De Bergerac* and the *Merchant Prince of Cornville* for similarities. His testimony and evidence won the case for Gross (May 21, 1902). After 1902 he became an occasional lecturer on literary and biographical subjects. He was a genial person, was referred to as the 'grand old man' of the Chicago Press Club, where he gave many lectures, and was the leading spirit of the Old Printers Club. The last two years of his life were dark with sickness. He died in Chicago . . ."

Condensed from R. W. B.—*Dictionary of American Biography,* Vol. XII.

* * *

The Golden Censer; or, the Duties of To-day and the Hopes of the Future. *Chicago, 1881.*

A Pastoral Poem and Other Pieces. *Chicago, 1882.*

Memories for Decoration Day. *Chicago, 1886.*

Daniel Trentworthy; Tale of the Great Fire of Chicago. *Chicago, 1889.*

Jason Hortner. 1889.

Burritt Durand. *Chicago, 1890.*

David Lockwin, the People's Idol. 1891.

Golden Legacy.

Dream City. 1894.

American Statesmen. 1898.

Famous Women of the World. 1898.

The Toiler's Diadem; for Thinkers, Workers and Believers. *Chicago, 1898.*

The Fireside University of Modern Invention, Discovery, Industry, and Art; with Complete Indexes. *Chicago, 1898.*

John McGovern's Poems. *Evanston, Ill., 1902.*

The Right of Way. 1903.

Shakespeariana (Trees, Woman's Hair, My Lord Hamlet) (with Jessie Edson Hall). 1907-09.

Hospitality; Mine Host, from the Time of Babylon to the Age of the Aeroplane. *Chicago, 1910.*

Empire of Information. *Chicago, n.d.*

Lord of Como.

Joan of Arc.

Patrick Henry.

King Darwin.

Goeffrey.

The New Fireside University for Home Circle Study; or, Familiar Talks About Common Things. *Chicago, 1917.*

McGOVNEY, DUDLEY ODELL: 1877–

Dudley Odell McGovney, son of Samuel Taylor and Florence Louisa Wright McGovney, was born at Huntington, Ind., on June 23, 1877, and graduated from Indiana University in 1901. He received the A.M. degree from Harvard in 1904 and the LL.B. from Columbia University in 1907. On Apr. 22, 1902, he married Laura Woodburn.

From 1901 to 1903 he was an instructor in government at the Insular Normal School, Manila, and in the summer of 1907 he was an instructor in political science at Indiana University. He then taught law at the University of Illinois, Tulane, the University of Missouri, and the State University of Iowa. In 1925 he became professor of law at the School of Jurisprudence of California.

During the Spanish-American War Mr. McGovney served as a corporal in the 159th Indiana Volunteers.

Information from *Indiana University, 1820-1904,* and *Who's Who in America.*

* * *

Civil Government in the Philippines. *Chicago, 1903.*

Stories of Long Ago in the Philippines. *New York, 1906.*

McGUIRE, ULYSSES MELVILLE: 1856–1939.

Ulysses Melville McGuire, son of William Edward and Nancy Violetta Deputy McGuire, was born in Jennings County, Ind., on Apr. 7, 1856, and was educated at Hanover College and Southern Baptist Theological Seminary. He received the D.D. degree from Franklin College in 1921. On Mar. 7, 1880, he married Elba Graham, who died in 1914.

He was ordained to the Baptist ministry in 1881 and was pastor of various village churches until 1892, after which time he held pastorates in Anderson, Sullivan, Washington, Lawrenceburg, Princeton, and Greencastle, Ind. For five years he served as editor of

THE BAPTIST OBSERVER and was editor of THE BAPTIST until 1931. In 1931-32 he engaged in organization and relief work among the unemployed in Chicago.

He died on July 5, 1939.

Information from *Who Was Who in America.*

* * *

The Church as an Educational Institution. *Philadelphia, 1897.*

McKAIG, ROBERT NEWTON: 1842–?

Aside from the facts that he was born in Logansport, Ind., in 1842 and that he received the A.B., A.M., and D.D. degrees from De Pauw University, no information on the Rev. Robert Newton McKaig has been located.

Information from Federal Writers Project—*Indiana Authors, 1937.*

* * *

The Life and Times of the Holy Spirit. *Chicago, 1908.* 2 vols.

McKAY, MARTHA NICHOLSON (MRS. HORACE): 1843–1934.

Martha Nicholson was born in Warren County, O., in 1843. She married Horace McKay and came to Indianapolis in 1866. She and her husband were among the founders of the Unity Church in Indianapolis in 1868—the church formed at that time later became the All Souls Unitarian Church. Mrs. McKay was also one of the founders of the Indianapolis Woman's Club and was active in work of the Indianapolis Public Library and in campaigns for women's suffrage.

Mrs. McKay's history of literary clubs of Indiana is still considered a reliable source of reference for the period prior to its publication in 1894. In 1929 she published a book, *When the Tide Turned in the Civil War.* The original manuscript for this book was written in 1897. It dealt with the attack of Col. Robert Gould Shaw and his regiment of Negroes, the 54th Massachusetts, on Fort Wagner.

She died at her home in Indianapolis on Mar. 4, 1934.

Information from the INDIANAPOLIS STAR for Mar. 5, 1934.

* * *

Literary Clubs of Indiana. *Indianapolis, 1894.*

When the Tide Turned in the Civil War. *Indiaanpolis, 1929.*

McKEE, THOMAS HUDSON: ?–?

"Thomas H. McKee, son of Robert McKee, was born in Washington County, Pa. He served in a West Virginia regiment in the Civil War and moved to Cass County, Ind., in 1868. He married Nancy M. Funk of Cass County in 1869. For many years he was Clerk of the House of the U. S. Senate and edited and compiled many books, mostly of political nature."

From Powell—*History of Cass County*, 1913.

* * *

Forty Thousand Questions Answered. 1875.

McKee's Hand Book of U. S. Government. *Washington, D. C.*, 1885.

A Manual of Congressional Practice. *Washington, D. C.*, 1892.

Text Book of the National Republican Committee. 1896.

Views and Reviews of the Civil War. *Washington, D. C.*, 1906.

Edwin MacMasters Stanton, the Great War Secretary. *Washington, D. C.*, 1908.

The Test of Loyalty in the State of Virginia in 1861. *Washington, D. C.*, 1912.

McKNIGHT, LEVI ADOLPHUS: 1846–?

Born in 1846 and a long-time resident of Benton County, Ind., L. A. McKnight is believed to have been a teacher and school executive during most of his life, serving as superintendent of Benton County schools from 1907 to 1916. During this time he was active in preparing school exhibits, showing the progress and development of the Benton County Schools, and in starting oratorical work in high schools. He was at one time editor of the FOWLER ERA.

Information from the Indiana State Library.

* * *

Progress of Education in Benton County, Indiana. *Indianapolis*, 1906.

Indiana, a Drama of Progress: History in a Play. *Fowler, Ind.*, 1908.

McLEAN, WILLIAM E.: 1832–1906.

William E. McLean was born in 1832, resided in Terre Haute, Ind., served in the Civil War as a member of the 43rd Regiment, Indiana Volunteer Infantry, and died in 1906.

Information from the Emmeline Fairbanks Memorial Library, Terre Haute, Indiana.

* * *

Forty-Third Regiment of Indiana Volunteers. *Terre Haute, Ind.*, 1903.

McMANUS, SILAS BETTES: 1845–1917.

Silas Bettes McManus was born in Rootstown, O., Sept. 17, 1845. Coming to Indiana as a young man, he was graduated from the Medical College of Fort Wayne and had one year of post graduate work at the University of Michigan. He married Mary Hillegass of Huntertown, Ind., in 1880.

During most of his adult life he contributed to leading magazines, and from 1876 to 1882 he was connected with the Fort Wayne JOURNAL GAZETTE. Beginning in 1892 he served a term as state senator. Dr. McManus died suddenly on Apr. 15, 1917, at his home near Howe, Ind.

Information from the LaGrange Public Library.

* * *

'Lijah, Delivered August 5th, 1896, at Island Park, Rome City, Indiana, at the Tri-State Meeting—Ohio, Michigan and Indiana—of the Knights of Pythias, and with Hale and Fraternal Regards, Dedicated to the K. of P's, Their Mothers, Wives, Sisters and Sweethearts. *Toledo*, n.d.

Fot Would You Take for Me; and Nine or Ten Other Rhymes. *LaGrange, Ind.*, n.d. [1894].

Rural Rhymes. *Cincinnati*, n.d. [1898].

McMASTER, ERASMUS DARWIN: 1806–1866.

Erasmus Darwin McMaster, son of the Rev. Gilbert McMaster, was born in Mercer, Pa., on Feb. 4, 1806, and graduated from Union Theological Seminary in 1827, receiving the D.D. degree in 1841. He then studied theology under his father and in 1831 was ordained pastor of the Presbyterian Church in Ballston, N. Y.

In 1838 he came to Indiana as president of Hanover College, a position he held until 1845 when he became president of Miami University. In 1849 he returned to Indiana and was professor of systematic theology in New Albany Theological Seminary until 1866. For a few months before his death, on Sept. 11, 1866, he taught in the Theological Seminary of the Northwest at Chicago.

Information from *Appletons' Cyclopaedia of American Biography*, Vol. IV.

* * *

A Discourse Delivered November 7th, 1839, on the Occasion of the Author's Inauguration as President of Hanover College, Indiana. *Hanover, Ind.*, 1838.

Address Delivered to the Candidates for Degree of Bachelor of Arts, in Hanover College, Indiana . . . September 25, 1839. *Cincinnati, 1839.*

Speech in the Synod of Indiana, October 4, 1844, in Relation to Madison University. *Madison, Ind., 1844.*

The Relations Between Religion and Academic Education: an Address at the Author's Inauguration as President of Miami University. *Oxford, O., 1845.*

An Address on the Occasion of the Author's Resigning the Office of President of Miami University, August 9, 1849. *Cincinnati, 1849.*

Address at Laying the Corner Stone of the Third Presbyterian Church in Indianapolis, September 7, 1853. *Indianapolis, 1853.*

The True Life of a Nation; an Address Delivered . . . July 2, 1856. *New Albany, Ind., 1856.*

The Nation Blessed of the Lord: a Sermon Preached in the First Presbyterian Church, New Albany, 6 July, 1856. *New Albany, Ind., 1856.*

McNUTT, CYRUS F.: 1837–1912.

Born in Johnson County, Ind., in 1837, Cyrus F. McNutt studied law at North Western Christian (now Butler) University and practiced in Franklin and Martinsville, Ind. From 1874 to 1877 he was professor of law at Indiana University but resigned in 1877, moved to Terre Haute, and resumed his practice there. He died in 1912.

> Information from the Barry Ms. and the Emmeline Fairbanks Memorial Library, Terre Haute, Ind.

* * *

Broken Lives. *Chicago,* 1888.
The Trial of Jesus.
The Daughter of a Drab.

MacNUTT, FRANCIS AUGUSTUS: 1863–1928.

Francis Augustus MacNutt was born in Richmond, Ind., on Feb. 15, 1863. He was educated in the Richmond public schools and in the Friends' Academy at that place. Later he spent two years in Phillips Exeter Academy and one in the Harvard Law School, followed by travel and study in Europe.

In 1887 he entered the Accademia Ecclesiastica at Rome, an institution of the Catholic Church for training in the diplomatic administrative function of the church. Eventually he became a diplomat of the church and from 1898 to 1906 he occupied the post of High

Chamberlain at the Pontifical Court in Rome. He married Margaret Van Cortland Ogden in Jan., 1898, and died in 1928.

> Information from the Richmond Public Library.

* * *

Bartholomew de Las Casas, His Life, His Apostolate and His Writings. *New York,* 1909.
Fernando Cortes and the Conquest of Mexico, 1485-1547. *New York,* 1909.
Three Plays. *New York,* 1916.
Six Decades of My Life. *Brixen [Austria],* 1927. 2 vols.
Papal Chamberlain, the Personal Chronicle of F. A. MacNutt. *London,* 1936.

McSHEEHY, HENRY JAMES: 1852–1911.

H. J. McSheehy was born in Ireland and brought to New York and later to Lafayette, Ind., in which places he attended the local schools. He returned to New York, worked on the NEW YORK HERALD and came to Logansport in 1875, while accompanying Robert Ingersoll on a lecture tour. Seeing an opening for another newspaper, he stayed there and founded the LOGANSPORT CHRONICLE, which he edited and published until his death in 1911. He married Minnie Maurer and they were the parents of three sons. His one book describes his experiences while on a hunting trip in Colorado.

> Information supplied by the Logansport Public Library.

* * *

A Hunt in the Rockies . . . n.p., 1893.

McTURNAN, LAWRENCE: 1874–1945.

Born in Rigdon, Madison County, Ind., Nov., 1874, Lawrence McTurnan was graduated from Indiana State Teacher's College in 1897. He was Madison County school superintendent from 1897 to 1902, acting superintendent of city schools in Alexandria from 1902 to 1903, and assistant state superintendent of schools from 1903 to 1909. He engaged in educational publication work for Laidlaw Brothers, Inc., of Chicago from 1909 to 1935, acting as corporate secretary of the firm, and as joint author and editor of some of its textbooks. From 1937 until his death he held an executive position on the board of the National Rock Wool Corporation, Indianapolis. He died Sept. 26, 1945.

Information from the Indianapolis Public Library.

* * *

The Personal Equation; with an Introduction by James L. Hughes. *New York,* 1910.

Guide Books to Literature (with J. O. Engleman). *Chicago,* 1925-1926.

MACY, ALBERT WILLIAM: 1853–

Born in Randolph County, Ind., in 1853, Albert William Macy was educated in the Mooresville, Ind., schools and at Earlham College, from which he graduated in 1877 with the A.B. degree. For several years he held the position of literary reader with the publishing firm of S. C. Griggs & Co. of Chicago, and later became western manager of the Macmillan Publishing Company, with residence at Western Springs, Ill.

Information from Parker and Heiney—*Poets and Poetry of Indiana.*

* * *

Short-Cut Philosophy, Home-Made and Hand-Turned. *New York,* 1909.

Curious Bits of History. *New York,* 1912.

MACY, JESSE: 1842–1919.

Jesse Macy was born near Knightstown, Ind., on June 21, 1842. His parents were William and Phoebe Hiatt Macy.

Quakers, the Macys were active in the Underground Railroad work which assisted slaves to escape from Kentucky to Canada.

In 1856 the family moved to Lynnville, Ia., and young Macy attended school at Grinnell and at the Friends' Institute near Oscaloosa. He joined the Union forces as a non-combatant hospital orderly and served throughout the Civil War. He graduated from Grinnell College in 1870 and joined the faculty of the school, acting as professor of political economy until 1912. After 1912 he traveled and lectured in England and the eastern states, finding himself, perhaps to his surprise, a man of wide reputation in his field.

On July 25, 1872, he married Mary Maude Little. He died on Nov. 3, 1919.

Information from *Who Was Who in America* and the *Dictionary of American Biography.*

* * *

Civil Government in Iowa. *Grinnell, Ia.,* 1881.

Institutional Beginnings in a Western State. *Baltimore,* 1883.

Our Government; How It Grew, What It Does, and How It Does It. *Boston,* 1886.

The English Constitution, a Commentary on Its Nature and Growth. *New York,* 1897.

Political Parties in the United States, 1846-61. *New York,* 1900.

Party Organization and Machinery. *New York,* 1904.

Government of Iowa (with Karl Frederick Geiser). *Boston,* 1905.

Comparative Free Government (with J. W. Gannaway). *New York,* 1915.

Jesse Macy: An Autobiography. (Edited by Katherine Macy Noyes.) *Springfield, Ill.,* 1933.

MAGEE, B. F.: ?–?

B. F. Magee was a resident of Lafayette, Ind., who served in the Civil War as a sergeant in the 40th Regiment, Indiana Volunteer Infantry.

de Hart—*Past and Present of Tippecanoe County,* 1909.

* * *

History of the Fortieth Regiment (with Rev. W. R. Jewell).

MAJOR, CHARLES: 1856–1913.

Charles Major was one of the Indiana novelists who dominated the field of American best sellers from 1900 to 1905.

And *dominated* is the word, for there were Major's *Dorothy Vernon of Haddon Hall* and *A Forest Hearth* (his first and greatest success, *When Knighthood Was in Flower,* had been published in 1898). There were also Thompson's *Alice of Old Vincennes,* McCutcheon's *Graustark* and *Brewster's Millions,* Tarkington's *Monsieur Beaucaire* and *The Two Van Revels* (his *Gentleman from Indiana,* published in 1899, was still going strong). Dreiser's *Sister Carrie* and *Jennie Gerhardt* came out to shock the prudish. David Graham Phillips was represented by *The Great God Success,* *The Deluge* and eight less successful novels. It was a great period for royalties paid to Hoosiers—a source of revenue then, apparently, second only to corn and hogs to the citizens of the state of Indiana.

Charles Major was born to Stephen and Phoebe Gaskill Major in Indianapolis on July 25, 1856. When he was thirteen the family removed to Shelbyville, Ind., where Charles spent his entire life. He attended local schools, read law in his father's office, attended the University of Michigan law school, and was admitted to the bar in 1877. His chief interest, even above his profession, was the Tudor period in English history, and by constant reading he became, with no advanced academic guidance in the field, a fairly competent authority on the period. Later he became interested in local Indiana history, and this also furnished subject matter for some of his books.

On Sept. 27, 1885, he married Alice Shaw of Shelbyville, Ind. According to a contemporary, he accepted only enough law business in the years before the success of his first novel, *When Knighthood Was in Flower,* to make a respectable living; after the remarkable success of that work he maintained an office only in order to have a quiet place to work.

Mr. Major died on Feb. 13, 1913.

> Information from Esarey—*A History of Indiana* and the *Dictionary of American Biography.*

* * *

When Knighthood Was in Flower; or, the Love Story of Charles Brandon and Mary Tudor, the King's Sister, and Happening in the Reign of King Henry VIII (pseudonym, Edwin Caskoden). *Indianapolis,* 1898.

The Bears of Blue River. *New York,* 1901.

Dorothy Vernon of Haddon Hall. *New York,* 1902.

A Forest Hearth, a Romance of Indiana in the Thirties. *New York,* 1903.

Yolanda, Maid of Burgundy. *New York,* 1905.

Uncle Tom Andy Bill. *New York,* 1908.

A Gentle Knight of Old Brandenburg. *New York,* 1909.

The Little King: a Story of the Childhood of Louis XIV, King of France. *New York,* 1910.

The Touchstone of Fortune; Being the Memoir of Baron Clyde, Who Lived, Thrived, and Fell in the Doleful Reign of the So-Called Merry Monarch, Charles II. *New York,* 1912.

Rosalie. (Revised and published posthumously by Mrs. Major, assisted by Test Dalton.) *New York,* 1925.

MAJOR, DAVID R.: 1866–1936.

David R. Major, son of Thomas and Almeda Allen Major, was born at Frankfort, Ind., on Mar. 26, 1866, and graduated from Wabash College in 1890, receiving the Ph.D. degree from Cornell University in 1896 and the LL.B. from Indiana University Law School in 1916. On Jan. 8, 1901, he married Mary Randolph Campbell.

From 1890 to 1898 he served as a superintendent and principal of various public schools, in 1899-1900 was professor of pedagogy at the University of Ne-

braska, in 1900-01 was professor of pedagogy at Columbia University, and from 1901 to 1914 was professor of the psychology of education at Ohio State University. Following his graduation from law school, he practiced law at Columbus, O., until his death.

> Information from *Who Was Who in America.*

* * *

Teleology in the Critical Philosophy of Kant. *Ithaca, N. Y.,* 1897.

First Steps in Mental Growth. *New York,* 1906.

The Elements of Psychology. *Columbus, O.,* 1913.

Introduction to Philosophy. *Garden City, N. Y.,* 1933.

MAKEEVER, IDAEL CHILDERS (MRS. ?): ?–

Idael Childers, daughter of Mr. and Mrs. George W. Childers of Kouts, Porter County, Ind., as a young woman contributed verse to newspapers, and after her marriage and removal to Stormsburg, Neb., she published two volumes of selections from her works.

> Information from Cutler—*History of Porter County,* Vol. 1.

* * *

Goldenrod.

Prairie Flowers.

MAKER, HUGH ANTHONY: 1864–1946.

Hugh Anthony Maker, son of Seth R. and Nancy J. Hamble Maker, was born on July 21, 1864. He grew up on his father's farm, attended Noblesville (Ind.) High School and Central Normal (now Canterbury) College, and taught school for a time. Later he returned to the farm.

He served as justice of the peace for a number of years and was a member of the Western Association of Writers.

He died on Aug. 23, 1946.

> Information from the Noblesville Public Library.

* * *

Odd Odes. *Indianapolis,* n.d. [1901].

MANN, CHARLES WESLEY: 1862–1909.

Charles Wesley Mann was born in Huntertown, Ind., in 1862. He attended De Pauw University, receiving the A.B. and A.M. degrees, and died in Chicago in 1909.

> Information from Federal Writers Project—*Indiana Authors, 1937.*

* * *

Fort Dearborn, Its Place in the History of the Frontier. School Recreations and Amusements. *New York, 1896.*

MANN, MARY L. RIDPATH (MRS. CHARLES WESLEY): 1867–

Mary L. Ridpath Mann, daughter of John Clark and Hannah R. Smythe Ridpath, was born in Lawrenceburg, Ind., on Sept. 19, 1867, graduated from De Pauw University in 1887, and received the A.M. degree from that institution in 1891. On Sept. 12, 1888, she married Charles Wesley Mann of Chicago, who died in 1909.

In addition to her books, she was a contributor to magazines and newspapers and, after 1909, a lecturer for the Chicago Historical Society.

> Information from *Who's Who in America* and De Pauw University's *Alumnal Record, 1920.*

* * *

The Building of a Nation (with May E. Hoss). *Chicago,* n.d. [1911].
The Unofficial Secretary. *Chicago, 1912.*
Royal Women, Their History and Romance. *Chicago,* 1913.

MARINE, SARAH CATHERINE KING (MRS. WILLIAM ALBINES): 1855–1940.

Sarah Catherine King, daughter of Robert F. and Eliza T. King, was born in Boone County, Ind., on Oct. 19, 1855. She received her schooling in the country schools near her home north of Pittsboro, Ind., and later taught school in the same vicinity. Four years after the death of her father in 1878, the family moved to Mooresville, Ind. In 1887 she married William Albines Marine, of Mooresville, a first cousin of James Whitcomb Riley, who was a carpenter by trade and also a writer.

The Marines lived in Mooresville until 1923, when they moved to Indianapolis to live with one of their sons. Here Mr. Marine died in 1934. In 1940 Mrs. Marine went to Chattanooga, Tenn., where she died a few weeks after her arrival.

Mrs. Marine was a Bible student, taught for many

years in the Methodist Church, and wrote mainly on religious subjects. Several of her poems were published in books of sacred music.

> Information from Clarence M. Marine, of Indianapolis.

* * *

The Garland (with Elvira Nelson). *Indianapolis, 1883.*
Who Was It? *Plainfield, Ind.,* n.d. [1910].
The Virgin Mary; a Careful and Authentic Study of the Life and Character of Mary, the Mother of Christ. *Louisville, Ky., 1912.*
A Story of Two Soldier Boys. *Franklin, Ind., 1923.*

MARTIN, MARTHA EVANS (MRS. ?): ?–1925.

Martha Evans was born in Terre Haute, Ind.

She graduated from De Pauw University, taught school for a year and served as court reporter for Wayne County, Ind., for three years before she took up writing as a profession. Having married (her husband's given name is unknown) she became associated with her husband in editing the RICHMOND (Ind.) DAILY TELEGRAM. She eventually left newspaper work to become editor of DEMOREST'S MAGAZINE.

Her chief interest was nature study and her books deal with popular astronomy. She died Jan. 6, 1925.

> Information from Emmeline Fairbanks Memorial Library, Terre Haute, Ind.

* * *

The Friendly Stars. *New York, 1907.*
The Ways of the Planets. *New York, 1912.*

MARTIN, WILLIAM ALEXANDER PARSONS: 1827–1916.

"William Alexander Parsons Martin (Apr. 10, 1827-Dec. 17, 1916), missionary, educator, and author, was born in Livonia, Ind., the son of William Wilson Martin and Susan Depew, both of frontier Scotch-Irish stock. His father was a Presbyterian minister . . . He was graduated from Indiana University in 1846 and for three years thereafter studied theology in the Presbyterian seminary at New Albany, Ind. In 1849, the year of his graduation, he married Jane Vansant (who died in 1893) and was ordained to the ministry by the Presbytery of Salem, Ind. . . . In the spring of 1850 he and his brother Samuel Newall and their wives arrived in China. He was assigned to

Ningpo and early proved himself both energetic and able. Before he had been six years in China he had worked out, through public lectures and discussions before Chinese audiences, a series of studies on evidences of Christianity which sought to present the Christian gospel convincingly to Chinese. These he put into the literary language and had published. They became very popular, and went into many editions in both China and Japan.

"Martin learned not only the local dialect and the literary language, but Mandarin, and it was his knowledge of the latter colloquial which helped to open to him the opportunity which led him away from Ningpo and into the region where the major part of his life was to be spent. During the second war between Great Britain and China, he was appointed, on his own application, as an interpreter to William B. Reed . . . , who obtained for the United States the treaty of 1858 with China. Martin had a share in the negotiations . . . For a short time [he] was connected with the Presbyterian Mission Press in Shanghai. While there he translated into Chinese Wheaton's *Elements of International Law*. The following year he removed to Peking, founding in that city a mission of his denomination which later grew to large proportions.

"In Peking his contact with officials, begun during the negotiation of the Treaty of Tientsin, continued, and his interest increased in the diplomatic relations with Western powers into which China was so reluctantly and awkwardly entering. In 1868, accordingly, he accepted a position as teacher of international law in the T'ungwên Kuan, a school which had recently been formed by the government to train in Western languages and learning Chinese youths who were to serve in intercourse with foreign countries . . . in 1869 he assumed his duties, not only as teacher, but as head of this institution. In these positions he continued until 1894, and through his translations and original works in Chinese, his contacts with officials, and his teaching, he had a significant part in introducing Western learning to China. In 1898 he was made president of the imperial university which the reform movement of that year had brought into existence. The Boxer outbreak (1900) caught him in Peking, and, although then past seventy years of age, he was active in the defense of the legations. After the raising of the siege he was in the United States for a time, lecturing on China, and then, at the invitation of the Viceroy Chang Chih-tung, he once more returned and lectured on international law in an institution which that dignitary was attempting to establish

in Wuchang. With the transfer of Chang Chih-tung to Nanking, Martin deemed it advisable to withdraw. Most of the remainder of his life was spent in Peking. Here he taught individual Chinese students, wrote, and, about 1911, rejoined the staff of the Presbyterian mission, serving on it until his death.

"Martin's literary output was voluminous. It included many works in Chinese on international law, natural science, and Christianity, and a number of works on China in English . . . He received many honors, both in China and in the United States . . ."

Condensed from K. S. L.—*Dictionary of American Biography*, Vol. XII.

* * *

Evidences of Christianity. 1855.

The Three Principles. 1856.

Religious Allegories. 1857.

Natural Philosophy. 1866.

Hanlin Papers. *Shanghai*, 1880. (Republished as The Chinese. Their Education, Philosophy, and Letters. *New York*, 1881.)

Mathematical Physics. 1885.

Hanlin Papers: Second Series. *Shanghai*, 1894.

A Cycle of Cathay; or, China, South and North, with Personal Reminiscences. *New York*, 1896.

The Siege in Peking: China Against the World, by an Eyewitness. *New York*, 1900.

The Lore of Cathay, or the Intellect of China. *New York*, 1901.

The Awakening of China. *Garden City, N. Y.*, 1907.

Chinese Legends, and Other Poems.

Understand the Chinese. *New York*, 1934.

MARTINDALE, ELIJAH: 1793–

Elijah Martindale was born in South Carolina on Nov. 10, 1793, and moved with his parents to Ohio when he was a child. In 1811 they emigrated to Indiana and settled in Wayne County.

In 1815 he married Elizabeth Boyd—they became the parents of fifteen children, fourteen of whom lived to adulthood—and in 1818 he became a minister. He moved to Henry County, four miles southeast of New Castle, Ind., in 1832, where he helped build the first schoolhouse and the first church in the county.

Information from the New Castle Public Library.

* * *

Autobiography of Elder Elijah Martindale . . . also Pioneer History of the Boyd Family, by Belle Sanford. *Indianapolis*, 1892.

MARTINDALE, JAMES BOYD: 1836–1904.

James Boyd Martindale was the son of Elijah and Elizabeth Boyd Martindale, residents of Indiana since territorial days. Born on a farm in Henry County, Ind., in 1836, he was educated in the public schools and the New Castle Seminary, studied law, and was admitted to the bar. He then established, in Chicago, the Martindale Law and Collection Agency. In addition to his legal writings, he wrote poetry. He died in 1904.

Information from Parker and Heiney—*Poets and Poetry of Indiana.*

* * *

Indiana Executor's Guide. *New Castle, Ind.,* 1871.
Unclaimed Money, Lands, and Estates. *Chicago,* 1884.

MARTLING, JAMES ABRAHAM: 1825–1880.

James Abraham Martling, born in 1825, lived in Mishawaka, Ind., for many years. He was educated at Oberlin College and taught there for a time. He was also superintendent of schools in St. Louis, Mo.

Information from South Bend Public Library.

* * *

London Bridge; or, Capital and Labor: a Poem for the Times. *Boston,* 1881.
Poems of Home and Country. *Boston,* 1885.

MASON, AUGUSTUS LYNCH: 1859–1939.

Augustus Lynch Mason was born on Feb. 10, 1859, at Bloomington, Ind. He was the son of William Fisher and Amanda D. Lynch Mason. From 1873 to 1875 he was a student in Northwestern Christian (now Butler) University in Indianapolis, and in 1879 he received the Ph.B. degree from De Pauw University. He married Annie D. Porter on June 25, 1893.

After studying law from 1879 to 1882, he became a member of the firm of McDonald, Butler and Mason, then for three years acted as dean of the De Pauw University Law School. He served as president of the Citizen's Street Railroad Company of Indianapolis from 1893 to 1897, and from 1899 to 1905 he was a lecturer for the Indiana Law School, University of Indianapolis. In 1910 he retired from law practice and died Feb. 13, 1939.

Information from *Who Was Who in America;* De Pauw University's *Alumnal Record, 1920;* and the Indianapolis Public Library.

* * *

The Romance and Tragedy of Pioneer Life. A Popular Account of the Heroes and Adventurers Who, by Their Valor and War-Craft, Beat Back the Savages from the Borders of Civilization and Gave the American Forests to the Plow and Sickle. Embracing the Legend of Powhatan; the Trials of LaSalle; the Fate of Philip, Etc. With an Introduction by John Clark Ridpath. *Cincinnati,* 1883. (Reissued in 1904 as Indian Wars and Famous Frontiersmen.)
Pioneer History of America. 1884.
Trusts and Public Welfare. *Indianapolis,* 1901.
Duties of Citizenship. *Indianapolis,* 1902.
Our Pioneers. *Springfield, Mass.,* 1904.
Corporations and Social Changes. *Indianapolis,* 1908.
Government of Indianapolis. *Indianapolis,* 1910.
Guiding Principles for American Voters. An Introduction to the Study of Elementary Americanism. *Indianapolis,* 1920.
True Stories of Our Pioneers; with Introduction and Special Contributions by J. C. Ridpath; with Additional Chapters by T. White. *Chicago,* n.d.

MATHEWS, FRANCES AYMAR: ?–

Frances Aymar Mathews, daughter of Daniel A. and Sara Webb Mathews, was born in New York City and was educated at home by private tutors. She was a granddaughter of Mathew Livingston Davis, Aaron Burr's biographer. A novelist and playwright, she resided in Indianapolis.

Information from *Who's Who in America.*

* * *

His Way and Her Will. *Chicago,* 1888.
To-night at Eight: Comedies and Comediettas. *Chicago,* 1889.
A Married Man. *Chicago,* 1899.
The New Yorkers and Other People. *New York,* 1900.
My Lady Peggy Goes to Town. *Indianapolis,* 1901.
A Little Tragedy at Tien-tsin. *New York,* 1904.
Pamela Congreve. *New York,* 1904.
The Marquise's Millions. *New York,* 1905.
Billy Duane: Novel. *New York,* 1905.
Staircase of Surprise. *New York,* 1905.
Undefiled: a Novel. *New York,* 1906.
Allee Same. *New York,* 1907.
If David Knew: a Novel. *New York,* 1910.
Flame Dancer. *New York,* 1910.
All For Sweet Charity: Comedy. *New York,* n.d.

American Hearts: Drawing Room Scene. *New York.*
Apartment: Flat-apartment Scene. *New York.*
Stronger Spell.
Under The Mistletoe.
Barbara.
The Prima Donna.
Knight of the Quill: Play. *New York.*
New Professor: Comedy. *Chicago.*
On the Staircase: Hall-stair-case Scene. *New York.*
Paying the Piper: Play. *New York.*
Proposal: Play. *New York.*
Scapegrace: Newport Drawing-room Scene. *New York.*
Six To One: Comedietta. *Boston.*
Snow-bound: Country Hotel Parlor Scene. *New York,*
Teacups: Theosophic Farce. *New York.*
Title and Money: Play. *New York.*
War to the Knife: Play. *New York.*
Wedding Tour: Play. *New York.*
Woman's Forever: Hotel Private Parlor Scene. *New York.*
Wooing A Widow: Sketch. *Boston.*
At the Grand Central: Railroad-station Scene. *New York.*
Both Sides of the Counter: Store Scene. *New York.*
Charming Conversationalist: Ball-room Scene. *New York.*
Courier: Hotel Private-parlor Scene. *New York.*
Cousin Frank: Farce. *Boston.*
En Voyage: Ship-deck Scene. *New York.*
Finished Coquette: Country-house Reception-room Scene. *New York.*
Honeymoon: Fourth Quarter: Apartment Drawing-room Scene. *New York.*
Christmas Honeymoon. *New York, 1912.*
My Lady Peggy Leaves Town. *New York, 1913.*
Fanny of the Forty Frocks. *Philadelphia, 1916.*
Joan D'Arc.
Pretty Peggy.
Mamzelle.
The Red Swan.
Stranger Passing By.
Up To Him.
Miss Carliney.

MÄTTER, JOHN: 1883–

John Mätter, son of Philip and Lile Harter Mätter, was born in Marion, Ind., on June 19, 1883, and graduated from Princeton University in 1905, receiving the A.M. degree in 1914. In addition to engaging in manufacturing, advertising, and farming, he published various articles and verse in magazines, was the author of numerous short stories, and contrib-

uted newspaper features to the CHICAGO DAILY NEWS, CHICAGO TIMES, and CHICAGO JOURNAL OF COMMERCE.

Information from the Marion Public Library.

* * *

Once. *New York, 1910.*
Three Farms. *New York, 1913.*
The Amateur Vagabond (with Robert Mätter). *New York, 1918.*
The Country Banker. *Chicago, 1932.*

MATTHEWS, JAMES NEWTON: 1852–1910.

Born in New Castle, Ind., in 1852, James Newton Matthews left the state while young but returned to attend and graduate from De Pauw University. He then practiced medicine in Mason, Ill. He has been called "The Poet of the Prairies."

Information from Parker and Heiney—*Poets and Poetry of Indiana.*

* * *

Temple Vale and Other Poems. *Chicago, 1888.*
Lute of Life. *Cincinnati, 1911.*

MAYNARD, JACOB BECKWITH: 1819–1902.

Jacob Beckwith Maynard, son of Andrew and Athalinda Beckwith Maynard, was born in New York City on Feb. 19, 1819, and was educated in a private school in Brooklyn and at Essex Academy in Connecticut.

In 1835 he came west to Illinois, where he worked on an uncle's farm and in a country store for four years before moving on to St. Louis. In 1842 he became connected with the American Cannel Coal Company at Honesville, Ky. The company was moved to Cannelton, Ind., in 1843, and Mr. Maynard then became a resident of Indiana.

In 1847 he married Elizabeth Archer, who died in 1874. He went into the mercantile business at Cannelton in 1848 but in 1852 returned to the American Cannel Coal Company, remaining with that firm until 1857, when he purchased the Cannelton REPORTER.

In 1862 he removed to Louisville and spent the next twelve years working for various newspapers—the LOUISVILLE DEMOCRAT, the COURIER, the COURIER-JOURNAL, and the LEDGER. In 1874 he purchased an interest in the St. Joseph, Mo., GAZETTE, becoming its editor-in-chief. Two years later he sold his interest in this paper and returned to Indiana, where he was commercial editor of the Indianapolis SENTINEL and later chief editorial writer.

Information from *Representative Men of Indiana*, Vol. II.

* * *

Men of Progress (with Will Cumback). *Indianapolis*, 1899.

MEACHAM, ALFRED B.: 1826–1882.

Born in Orange County, Ind., on Apr. 29, 1826, Alfred B. Meacham emigrated with his family to Iowa in 1841, settling near Iowa City.

In 1845 the young man aided in the work of moving the Sac and Fox Indians to the reservations assigned them after the Black Hawk War. In 1850 he and his brother went to California in search of gold. They engaged in mining for several years, then finally founded Meacham's Station on the trail from Idaho to Oregon. They built a tavern and a toll road.

In 1852 Meacham had returned to Iowa to marry Orpha Ferree.

From 1869 to 1873 he served as superintendent of Indian affairs for Oregon, and in 1873 he was seriously wounded by the Modoc Indians, who left him for dead. He represented Oregon in the Electoral College in 1872.

He was a leader in the temperance movement, but his principal interest was the Indian cause. Besides his books written in defense of that race, he published the COUNCIL FIRE, a paper devoted to their interests.

He died in Washington, D. C., in 1882.

Information from *Representative Men of Indiana*, Vol. I, and the Barry Ms.

* * *

Wigwam and Warpath. *Boston*, 1875. (2nd. ed.)

Wi-Ne-Ma (The Woman Chief) and Her People. *Hartford, Conn.*, 1876.

Tragedy of the Lava Beds. n.p., 1877.

MEAD, ELWOOD: 1858–1936.

Elwood Mead, son of Daniel and Lucinda Mead, was born in Patriot, Ind., on Jan. 16, 1858, and graduated from Purdue University in 1882, receiving the M.S. degree in 1884 and the E.D. in 1904. He also received degrees from Iowa State University and the University of Michigan. He was twice married— first to Florence Chase, then to Mary Lewis.

Mr. Mead was an engineer for the U. S. government and for the state of Wyoming and taught at Colorado Agricultural College and the University of California. After 1924 he was U.S. Commissioner of Reclamation. In addition to the titles listed below, he was the author of many government publications.

He died on Jan. 26, 1936.

Information from *Who Was Who in America*.

* * *

Irrigation Institutions: a Discussion of the Economic and Legal Questions Created by the Growth of Irrigated Agriculture in the West. *New York*, 1903.

Government Aid and Direction in Land Settlement: an Address. *Denver, Colo.*, 1916.

Progress Report on the Production and Distribution of Milk. *Berkeley, Calif.*, 1917.

Helping Men Own Farms. *New York*, 1920.

MEEKER, EZRA: 1830–1928.

While Ezra Meeker was latest to publish and least significant as a writer among the Indianians who wrote books promoting the settlement of the West Coastal country, he alone is linked with the Twentieth century and he took far more than a casual part in the development of the West. As late as 1910 or 1915 he was still campaigning, at his own expense, through the Middle West and East for trans-continental highways, for historical markings for the old Oregon Trail and for the greater glory of the Pacific Northwest. Since he lived until Dec. 3, 1928, he saw the highways, the historical markings and the consciousness of the importance of the great Northwest for which he had campaigned as accomplished facts—a boon seldom granted to crusaders.

Ezra Meeker was born in Butler County, O., on Dec. 29, 1830. His father, Jacob Redding Meeker, was a farmer and miller by trade; his mother was the former Phoebe Baker. In 1837 the family moved to Covington, Ind., stayed there for a few years, spent some time in Waveland and finally settled on a farm they had purchased near Plainfield, on the National Road.

By this time Ezra was twelve or fourteen years old, had had the conventional amount of schooling (he is known to have attended subscription schools in both Covington and Waveland) and he now took over the operation of the farm while his father followed his trade nearby.

According to his own account in *The Ox-Team; or the Old Oregon Trail,* he had contracted the prevailing western fever early but his inclination was toward the Northwest, rather than the gold regions, and, besides, he had another project on his mind— the courting of Eliza Jane Sumner, a neighbor. Eliza finally accepted him, agreed to go to Oregon and they were married in May, 1851. In October they set out in Ezra's wagon (he was extremely proud of it, and of the quality of his oxen) loaded with Eliza's dowry, for Iowa.

They wintered in Iowa, Eliza had her first baby in due time, and in the spring they joined an emigrant train forming at Council Bluffs. The Meekers' preparations were most careful—Meeker stresses the plans they made, and the comfortable traveling as compared with that of some of the less provident of the party— and on Oct. 1 they arrived at Portland.

According to W. J. G. in the *Dictionary of American Biography,* Vol. XII:

". . . Early the following year, in company with his brother Oliver, he journeyed to the north of the Columbia in search of a site for a home. He settled on McNeil's Island, in Puget Sound, later removing to the site of Puyallup, where he built the first cabin. For the greater part of fifty-three years he remained in this region as a farmer and hop-grower, though he spent four winters in London and made several prospecting trips to the Yukon.

"Well versed in the history of the Pacific Northwest and deeply impressed with the significance of the emigration movement, he resolved, in his seventy-fifth year, to devote the rest of his life to the commemorative marking of the Oregon Trail. On Jan. 29, 1906, with an ox-team drawing a covered wagon, he started from Puyallup, following such parts of the Trail as were still open, painting inscriptions on various landmarks and urging the citizens of the various settlements to set up inscribed stones and monuments. From the end of the Trail he continued on a tour of the East, everywhere attracting great attention. In 1910 he repeated this performance; in 1915 he traveled over a considerable part of the Trail in an automobile, and in 1924, at the age of ninety-three, he followed its course for 1300 miles in an airplane. Two years later he founded the Oregon Trail Memorial Association, Inc., with headquarters in New York City. From the Atlantic Coast, in the summer of 1928, he started in an automobile to follow the Trail again; but on the way he was taken ill, and after remaining for a time in a Detroit hospital, was conveyed to Seattle, where, two months later, he died.

"Below medium height, of somewhat slender build, his head and face framed in a luxuriant shock of hair and bushy beard, Meeker became, in his later years, a familiar figure throughout a great part of the country. He also became widely known as an author . . . During his last years he was engaged on a revision of his autobiographical writings, but the work was not finished. Despite his loose and disconnected style and his carelessness with dates and incidents, his work will remain valuable as a picture of the migration and settlement period . . ."

From **W. J. G.**, *Dictionary of American Biography,* Vol. XII; Meeker—*The Ox-Team; or the Old Oregon Trail*; and from Ms. Notes of Elizabeth May Banta.

* * *

Washington Territory West of the Cascade Mountains. *Olympia, Wash.,* 1870.

Pioneer Reminiscences of Puget Sound. *Seattle, Wash.,* 1905.

The Ox-Team; or the Old Oregon Trail, 1852-1896. *Indianapolis,* 1906. (Reprinted at other places and on other dates.)

Ventures and Adventures of Ezra Meeker, or Sixty Years of Frontier Life. *Seattle, Wash.,* 1909.

Personal Experiences on the Oregon Trail Sixty Years Ago. *St. Louis,* 1912. (Reissue of the Ox-Team.)

Story of the Lost Trail to Oregon. *Seattle, Wash.,* 1915.

The Busy Life of Eighty-Five Years of Ezra Meeker; Ventures and Adventures, Sixty-Three Years of Pioneer Life in the Old Oregon Country; an Account of the Author's Trip Across the Plains with an Ox-Team, 1852; Return Trip, 1906-7; His Cruise on Puget Sound, 1853; Trip Through the Natchess Pass, 1854; Over the Chilcoot Pass, Flat-Boating on the Yukon, 1898. *Seattle,* 1916. (A revision of Ventures and Adventures.)

Seventy Years of Progress in Washington. *Seattle,* 1921.

Ox-Team Days on the Oregon Trail. *Yonkers-on-Hudson, N. Y.,* 1922. (A revision of The Ox-Team.)

Kate Mulhall, a Romance of the Oregon Trail; Drawings by Margaret Landers Sanford, Rudolf A. Kausch and Oscar W. Lyons, Map of the Oregon Trail and Photographs. *New York,* 1926.

MERCER, HAMILTON: ?–?

Hamilton Mercer, one-time editor of the Greensburg, Ind., EVENING TIMES, was a student of sociology, a writer of scholarly editorials, and a physical culture enthusiast. He left Greensburg in 1916 and died in California a few years later.

Information from the Barry Ms.

* * *

The Reproach of Capital Punishment, a Brief. *Greensburg, Ind.,* 1915.

MERRILL, CATHARINE: 1824–1900.

Catharine Merrill, teacher and author, was born Jan. 24, 1824, at Corydon, Ind., then the capital of the state. Her father, Samuel Merrill, at that time State Treasurer, had been educated at Dartmouth College. When Mr. Merrill moved the treasury to the new capital of Indianapolis, his family accompanied him to the pioneer community, and there he added teaching to his other duties by opening a school.

Catharine studied under her father, then opened a primary school of her own. For a time she taught at the Female Seminary in Cleveland, O. From 1859 to 1861 she studied in Germany but returned to the U. S. to go into service as a nurse during the Civil War. Until 1885 she was professor of English literature at Northwestern Christian (now Butler) University in Indianapolis, and from 1885 until her death she taught privately. She died May 30, 1900.

> Information from Dunn—*Indiana and Indianans,* Vol. III; *The Man Shakespeare and Other Essays;* and the Indianapolis Public Library.

* * *

The Soldier of Indiana in the War for the Union. *Indianapolis,* 1866-69. 2 vols.

The Man Shakespeare and Other Essays (by Catharine Merrill with Impressions and Reminiscences of the Author by Melville B. Anderson, and with Some Words of Appreciation from John Muir. (Published posthumously through the agency of friends and admirers.) *Indianapolis,* 1902.

Catharine Merrill, Life and Letters, Collected and Arranged by Katharine Merrill Graydon. *Greenfield, Ind.,* 1934.

MERRILL, SAMUEL: 1792–1855.

"Samuel Merrill (Oct. 29, 1792—Aug. 24, 1855), Indiana official, was the second of nine sons of Jesse and Priscilla (Kimball) Merrill of Peacham, Vt. . . . Samuel Merrill attended an academy at Peacham and studied for a year, 1812-13, as a sophomore at Dartmouth College. He then taught school and studied law for three years at York, Pa. In 1816 he settled at Vevay, Switzerland County, Ind., in the next year was admitted to the bar, and soon took his place as an active member of the community . . . he was a representative of the county in the General Assemblies of 1819-20, 1820-21, and 1821-22. The General Assem-

bly elected him State Treasurer on Dec. 14, 1822, and he held the office for four terms, till 1834. In 1824 he moved the state offices from Corydon to Indianapolis, one wagon sufficing for all the records and money. It took eleven or twelve days to cover the distance (125 miles by present highways); the road through the wilderness was impassable in some places, and a new way had to be cut through the woods.

"He lived henceforth at the capital . . . he personally conducted a school; he acted for a time as captain of the first military company, served as a commissioner for the erection of the state capitol building, which was finished in 1835, was an early president of the Temperance Society, a manager of the State Colonization Society, a trustee of Wabash College, and the second president of the Indiana Historical Society, 1835-48. He was active in the organization of the Second Presbyterian Church (New School) and an intimate friend of Henry Ward Beecher during his pastorate. On Jan. 30, 1834, the General Assembly elected him president of the State Bank of Indiana. In this capacity he personally examined each of the thirteen branches twice a year. An excellent law and the efficient service of officers such as Merrill, Hugh McCulloch, and J. F. D. Lanier combined to develop one of the best of all the state banks. After two terms in the office, Merrill was replaced by the choice of a Democratic Legislature. From 1844 to 1848 he was president of the Madison & Indianapolis Railroad, during which time it was completed to Indianapolis. He spent the next two years compiling a third edition of the *Indiana Gazetteer* and in 1850 he bought Hood and Noble's bookstore, which later, under the name of the Merrill Company, undertook some publishing and eventually entered into the Bowen-Merrill (now the Bobbs-Merrill) publishing company. He also, with others, constructed a mill on Fall Creek.

"On Apr. 12, 1818, Merrill married Lydia Jane Anderson of Vevay, daughter of Capt. Robert and Catherine (Dumont) Anderson. Ten children were born to them. After his wife's death in 1847, he was married, second, to Elizabeth Douglas Young, of Madison, Ind. Throughout his life he was the personification of traditional New England Puritanism; conscientious, industrious, and devout . . . A bitter, twenty-four-page pamphlet which he published in 1827 attacking Gov. James Brown Ray illustrates the thoroughness with which he performed 'an unpleasant task.' During the existence of the Whig party, he adhered to it—with a strong anti-slavery leaning—and was an active party worker. He died in Indianapolis.

Condensed from C. B. C., *Dictionary of American Biography*, Vol. XII.

* * *

To the Public. Defense Against Accusations Supposedly Made by James B. Ray. *Indianapolis*, 1827.

The Indiana Gazeteer. *Indianapolis*, 1850. (3rd. ed.)

MERRILL, SAMUEL: 1831–1924.

Samuel Merrill, son of Samuel and Lydia Jane Anderson Merrill, was born in Indianapolis, May 30, 1831. He was educated at Wabash College, receiving his A.B. degree in 1851 and A.M. in 1854. He started his career as a publisher and bookseller in Indianapolis in 1852, entering the business his father had purchased in 1850. During the Civil War he was an officer in the 70th Indiana Volunteer Infantry and from 1889 to 1893 he served as consul-general at Calcutta, India. His death occurred in Indianapolis on Sept. 3, 1924.

Information from *Who Was Who in America* and the Indianapolis Public Library.

* * *

The Seventieth Indiana Volunteer Infantry in the War of the Rebellion. *Indianapolis*, 1900.

MILLER, ANNE ARCHBOLD (MRS. EUGENE HARPER): ?–

Anne Archbold, daughter of William Dana Archbold, was born in Fredonia, N. Y. On Aug. 10, 1896, she married Eugene Harper Miller, prominent banker, who died in 1940. She is now (1946) a resident of South Bend, Ind.

Information from the South Bend Public Library.

* * *

Little Old Outlaws. *Chicago*, 1910.
Huldy's Whistle. *Chicago*, 1919.
Little Bigs. *New York*, 1925.
Square Dog and Other Stories. *New York*, 1926.

MILLER, CINCINNATUS HINER (JOAQUIN): 1838–1913.

Although his residence in the state was brief, and his fame was gained as a Far Westerner, Cincinnatus Hiner Miller was an Indianian by birth and must be considered here, whether or not he was, as critic Van Wyck Brooks has said, "the greatest liar living . . . half a mountebank and all the time a showman."

Cincinnatus Hiner Miller was born, son of Hulings and Margaret Witt Miller, in Liberty, Ind., on Mar. 10, 1839. Hulings Miller was a Quaker; a schoolmaster by profession and a wanderer by preference. The family had lived in Ohio before Cincinnatus was born and they moved on to the west as he grew up, stopping in various states and territories while the elder Miller taught a term or two of school. Finally, in 1852 the Millers reached their destination, the Oregon country. According to the *Dictionary of American Biography,* in Oregon, "At about the age of seventeen, his son 'Nat' as he was called, ran away from home in company with another boy. They found their way to one of the mining camps in Northern California where Miller obtained employment as a cook. Being a rather delicate lad, he fell seriously ill with the scurvy as the result of the bad food and his own cooking. He was nursed back to health by a Dr. Ream in Yreka, Cal., and was subsequently befriended by a gambler named James Thompson, who figures attractively in his writings as 'The Prince.' Despite Miller's lifelong assertion that he was wounded in the battle of Castle Rocks against the Modocs, on June 15, 1855, residents of that vicinity scouted the claim that he had taken part in the skirmish. Probably in 1856 Miller made the acquaintance of Joseph De Bloney, known as 'Mountain Joe.' According to Miller's story, the mountaineer proposed to establish an Indian republic at the base of Mount Shasta. If so grandiose a scheme was planned, it went no further than the building of a road-house in which Miller did the cooking. In the spring of 1857 he went to live with an Indian tribe, the Diggers, and married one of their women, who bore him a daughter, Cali-Shasta. His native associates were noted horse-thieves, and Miller, as a preliminary to establishing the republic, fell in with their ways. He was captured, after an exciting chase, on July 8, 1859, but was rescued the same night by a friend who sawed through the bars of the jail window. Although he had no share in the Pit River massacre of this year, the Shasta region became very unsafe for any Indian sympathizer, and Miller, soon after it, wisely returned to Oregon.

"He then for a time attended an academy named 'Columbia College' in Eugene, taught school for a while in Clarke, Washington Territory, studied law on the side, and was admitted to the bar in Portland, Ore., in 1861. Instead of practising, he established in 1862, in company with one Isaac Mossman, a pony express between Washington Territory and Idaho. With its proceeds, he purchased in 1863 the DEMO-CRATIC REGISTER in Eugene and became an editor. His first appearance in print had been a letter in defense of the Mexican bandit, Joaquin Murietta, which had resulted in his friends nick-naming him 'Joaquin;' the name pleased him better than his own more burdensome one and in time he adopted it as his pen name. Some verses of his attracted the attention of a poetically minded girl in Port Orford, Ore., named Minnie Theresa Dyer, who wrote to him enthusiastically about them. After some correspondence, Miller rode over to Port Orford and returned the same week with Minnie Myrtle, as he called her, as his bride. His newspaper being suppressed by the government because of its support of the Confederacy, the editor moved to Canyon City, Ore., where he soon won the favor of his fellow-townsmen by successfully leading a party of them against a band of hostile Indians. He was rewarded by being elected judge of the Grant County court in 1866. A little later his wife, now the mother of two children, separated from him. Miller solaced his loneliness by bringing out two volumes of poetry, *Specimens* (1868) and *Joaquin et Al* (1869). Those attracted some attention, and in 1870 he went down to San Francisco to enjoy his reclame and was there admitted to the circle which included Bret Harte, Charles Warren Stoddard, and Ina Coolbrith.

"Thence he started on a literary pilgrimage to England. After visiting the Burns and Byron shrines, he attempted to find a London publisher for a compilation of his own verse, some of which had already appeared in newspapers, under the title, *Pacific Poems.* Failing in this, he printed the book privately and succeeded in gaining the attention of the critics. William Michael Rossetti took him up and introduced him to London literary circles, where his striking appearance in chaps and sombrero, which he wore indoors and out, soon made him the sensation of the season. In 1871 Longmans published his *Songs of the Sierras,* which in spite of its cheap rhythms and Byronic imitations was loudly acclaimed by the British. Its reception in America was less favorable, critics refusing to accept its romanticism as a genuine expression of the Far West. Attention was also unkindly called to the author's lack of learning which had led him into sundry errors in his poems, such as riming 'Goethe' with 'teeth.' A brief visit to America convincing the poet of his unpopularity, he sought consolation in foreign travel. During the next few years he visited South America, Europe, and possibly the Near East. In 1873

he published *Songs of the Sun-Lands,* and, in prose, *Life Amongst the Modocs* (republished with variations under other titles), regarded by Stuart Sherman as 'his most interesting book.' These were followed by *The Ship in the Desert* (1875), *The Baroness of New York* (1877), *Songs of Italy* (1878), showing the influence of Browning, and a prose Indian romance, *Shadows of Shasta* (1881). He also published several dramas, of which *The Danites in the Sierras* (1881), a Mormon play, was the most successful. In 1884 appeared *Memorie and Rime,* an autobiographical miscellany, and in 1886 *The Destruction of Gotham,* an unsuccessful novel. His last prose works were *An Illustrated History of Montana* (1894), a typical subscription history, and *The Building of the City Beautiful* (1897), showing Miller as a Utopist. In 1897, also, he published the *Complete Poetical Works of Joaquin Miller.* His narrative poem, *Light,* which was published in 1907, was his last bid for fame and represents his closest approach to full maturity as a poet.

"Meanwhile, Miller had returned to America and tried living in New York, Boston, and Washington, all of which were too crowded for his taste. In 1883 he married Abbie Leland, and in 1886 he settled permanently in Oakland, Cal. There on the hills above the town he purchased an estate, known as 'The Heights' (in Miller's spelling usually 'The Hights'), which he adorned with trees and stone monuments to Fremont, Browning, and Moses, and with a funeral pyre to be used at his own death. For many years he was one of the landmarks of California. As a bearded sage and advocate of the simple life he was looked upon with a respect which was mingled with amusement at his eccentricities and horror at his theories of free love. In 1897-98 he found renewed adventures as correspondent of the NEW YORK JOURNAL in the Klondike. By the time of his death in 1913 the West that he loved had vanished. The best of his work remains of significance as an attempt, never wholly successful, to celebrate on a heroic scale its freedom and its beauty . . ."

E. S. B., *The Dictionary of American Biography,* Vol. XII.

* * *

Specimens. 1868.
Joaquin Et Al. *Portland, Ore.,* 1869.
Pacific Poems [privately printed in England]. 1871.
Songs of the Sierras. *Boston,* 1871.
Songs of the Sun-Lands. *Boston,* 1873.
Life Amongst the Modocs. *London, Eng.,* 1873. (Published in America in 1874 under the title Unwritten

History and later reissued with slight variations under several titles.

Arizonian. *Baltimore, 1874.*

The Ship in the Desert. *Boston, 1875.*

First Fam'lies in the Sierras. *Chicago, 1876.*

The One Fair Woman. *New York, 1876.*

The Baroness of New York. *New York, 1877.*

The Danites in the Sierras, and Other Choice Selections; Edited by A. V. D. Honeyman. *New York, 1877.*

Songs of Italy. *Boston, 1878.*

Songs of Far-Away Lands. *London, 1878.*

Shadows of Shasta. *Chicago, 1881.*

Paquita, the Indian Heroine. *Hartford, Conn., 1881.*

The Poetical Works of Joaquin Miller. *Boston, 1882.*

The Silent Man: a Comedy-Drama, in Four Acts. *New York, 1883.*

Memorie and Rime. *New York, 1884.*

'49, the Gold-Seeker of the Sierras. *New York, 1884.*

The Destruction of Gotham. *New York, 1886.*

The Little Gold Miners of the Sierras. *Boston, 1886.*

Songs of the Mexican Seas. *Boston, 1887.*

Tennyson's Fairies and Other Stories (with others). *Boston, 1889.*

In Classic Shades, and Other Poems. *Chicago, 1890.*

My Own Story. *Chicago, 1890.*

Songs of Summer Lands. *Chicago, 1892.*

The Building of the City Beautiful. A Poetic Romance. *Cambridge, 1893.*

An Illustrated History of the State of Montana. *Chicago, 1894.*

The Battle of Castle Crags. *San Francisco, 1894.*

Songs of the Soul. *San Francisco, 1896.*

The Complete Poetical Works of Joaquin Miller. *San Francisco, 1897.*

Chants for the Boer: a Series of Stirring War Poems. *San Francisco, 1900.*

True Bear Stories; with Introductory Notes by David Starr Jordan; Together with a Thrilling Account of the Capture of the Celebrated Grizzly "Monarch." *Chicago, 1900.*

As It Was in the Beginning: Poem: Dedicated to the Mother of Men. *San Francisco, 1903.* (Reissued as Light in 1907 and later as A Song of Creation.)

Happy Days: Stories and Poems (with others). *Akron, O., 1906.*

Columbus; a Short Cantata for Mixed Voices; Music by E. S. Hosmer. *Boston, 1917.*

Columbus, a Study of Joaquin Miller's Great Poem. *Lansing, Mich., 1919.*

Autobiography and Favorite Poems. *San Francisco, 1919.*

Trelawny with Shelley and Byron. *Pompton Lakes, N. J., 1922.*

Overland in a Covered Wagon; an Autobiography; Edited by Sidney G. Firman. *New York, 1930.*

A Royal Highway of the World. *Portland, Ore., 1932.*

Joaquin Miller: His California Diary Beginning in 1855 and Ending in 1857; with an Introduction by John S. Richards. *Seattle, 1936.*

The Great Discoverer.

The Life of Christ.

An Oregon Idyl.

The Whitewater Canal.

Exodus for Oregon.

Cuba Libre, with Other Selections. *New York.*

Tally-Ho.

Songs of the American Seas.

MILLER, FREEMAN EDWIN: 1864–

Born in Fountain County, Ind., in 1864, Freeman Edwin Miller graduated from De Pauw University in 1887 and received his A.M. degree in 1890. He was admitted to the bar in 1886, went to Texas the following year, where he was attorney for Hemphill County in 1888 and district attorney in 1889, and in 1890 moved to Oklahoma.

From 1894 to 1898 Miller was professor of English at Oklahoma Agricultural and Mechanical College.

Information from the Barry Ms.

* * *

Oklahoma and Other Poems. *Buffalo, N. Y., 1895.*

Songs from the Southwest Country. *New York, 1898.*

Oklahoma Sunshine. *Stillwater, Okla., 1905.*

MILLER, GEORGE MOREY: 1868–?

George Morey Miller was born in Hope, Ind., in 1868 and graduated from the Franklin, Ind., high school. He received the A.B. degree from Indiana University in 1892; A.M. from Harvard in 1898 and the Ph.D. from Heidelberg in 1911.

Miller taught in the Peru and Noblesville, Ind., high schools from 1892 to 1897; was an instructor in English at the University of Cincinnati in 1898-99; at Radcliffe, 1899-1900; Washington State College, 1900-1901; University of Wisconsin, 1901-02; University of Cincinnati, 1902-13; Wabash College, 1913-17; and became head of the English department at the University of Idaho in 1917.

Besides his other writing, Miller is the author of several successful textbooks.

Information from *Who's Who in America.*

* * *

The Dramatic Element in the Popular Ballad. *Cincinnati, 1905.*

Suggestions for Teachers of English in Elementary and
  Secondary Schools. *Cincinnati, 1905.*

Alt Heidelberg. 1911.

The Historical Point of View in English Literary Criticism from 1570-1770. *Heidelberg, 1913.*

An Exaltation of Education in Indiana. 1916.

State Course of Study in English for the High Schools
  of Idaho. 1920.

South African Harvest, and Other Poems. *Oxford, Eng.,*
  1939.

Thudding Drums; an Anthology of English and South
  African Poetry. *London, 1942.*

MILLER, SADIE LOUISE: 1870–

Born in Honesdale, Pa., in 1870, Sadie Louise
Miller was educated in the local schools and at Taylor
University, in Indiana, where she graduated, majoring
in music. A resident of Upland, Ind., she was a contributor of poetry to several anthologies, magazines,
and newspapers.

Information from the Barry Ms.

* * *

Poems. [1908 ?]

MILLER-JENNINGS, EULORA (MRS. RUFUS JENNINGS): ?–

Eulora Miller was born in Lafayette, Ind., probably
in the late Fifties or early Sixties, since she was a
younger sister of Melville W. Miller, who is known
to have been born in 1856.

She attended the Lafayette schools and studied, for
a time at least, at Purdue University. She served as
librarian of the Lafayette Public Library in 1887-88
and married Rufus Jennings in 1890. Her later years
were spent in California. Her recorded literary production consists entirely of plays.

de Hart—*Past and Present of Tippecanoe County,*
  1909.

* * *

Mrs. Oakley's Telephone. *New York,* n.d.

Tom's Fiancée. *New York,* n.d.

Dinner at the Club. *New York,* n.d.

Die Prinzessin Barnhof. *New York,* n.d.

MILLIS, HARRY ALVIN: 1873–

Harry Alvin Millis, son of John and Maria Bruner
Millis, was born in Paoli, Ind., on May 14, 1873,
and graduated from Indiana University in 1895, receiving the A.M. degree in 1896. In 1899 he received
the Ph.D. from the University of Chicago. He married Alice M. Schoff in 1901.

After teaching at the University of Arkansas, Stanford University, and the University of Kansas, in 1916
he became professor of economics at the University of
Chicago, serving as chairman of the department from
1928 to 1938. Later he served on the National Labor
Relations Board, being appointed chairman in 1940.

Information from *Who's Who in America.*

* * *

The Japanese Problem in the United States; an Investi-
  gation for the Commission on Relations with Japan
  Appointed by the Federal Council of the Churches of
  Christ in America. *New York,* 1915.

Sickness and Insurance; a Study of the Sickness Problem
  and Health Insurance. *Chicago,* 1937.

Economics of Labor (with R. E. Montgomery). *New
  York,* 1938-45. 3 vols.

How Collective Bargaining Works; a Survey of Experience in Leading American Industries (with others).
  New York, 1942.

MILLIS, WILLIAM ALFRED: 1868–1942.

William Alfred Millis, son of John and Maria
Bruner Millis, was born at Paoli, Ind., on June 17,
1868, and graduated from Indiana University in 1889,
receiving the A.M. degree in 1890. He was awarded
the LL.D. degree by Franklin College in 1908 and the
D.D. by Hanover College in 1927. He was first married to Laura Clark of Bloomington, Ind., on Aug.
27, 1889, and after her death to Harriett Harding of
Crawfordsville, on June 9, 1921.

He served as superintendent of the public schools
of Paoli, (1889-94), Attica, (1894-1900), and Crawfordsville, Ind. (1900-1908). After 1908 he was president of Hanover College. From 1895 to 1902 he was
dean of the Winona summer school and in 1904-05
was a lecturer on education at Indiana University.
He was on the faculty of Wabash College in 1900-01
and 1907-08. Dr. Millis was a Presbyterian minister, a
director of McCormick Theological Seminary, and a
lecturer on educational and social problems.

He died in Crawfordsville.

Information from *Who's Who in America* and
Mrs. William Alfred Millis.

* * *

God or Mammon; Hanover College Baccalaureate Sermon. *Hanover, Ind.,* 1910.

The Teaching of High School Subjects (with Harriett Millis.) *New York,* 1925.

Half Hours with College Students. *Boston,* 1926.

The History of Hanover College from 1827-1927. *Hanover, Ind.,* 1927.

Talks to College Students.

MILLS, CALEB: 1806–1879.

Caleb Mills, "father of the public school system of Indiana," first, and longtime (1833-1879) member of the Wabash College faculty, was born in Dunbarton, New Hampshire, in 1806. He and his twin sister, Tamar, were the last of the eight children of Caleb Mills, described as a "wealthy farmer."

Reared on the family farm, he entered Dartmouth College in 1824 and graduated in 1828. After a year in Andover Theological Seminary he became a traveling agent for one of the Sunday School Union organizations and traveled through the Middle West and South, visiting, and apparently becoming interested in, the Indiana scene.

He returned to Andover, and was graduated in 1833. Shortly after his graduation he saw an advertisement in the HOME MISSIONARY JOURNAL for a qualified young man who could preach on Sundays in Crawfordsville, Ind., and could teach in the new college and teachers training school being organized there. Having already decided upon the new West as a home, he answered the advertisement, found immediate support from his Dartmouth classmate, Edmund O. Hovey, who was one of the founders of the new institution, and was accepted.

With a profession, a paying position and a home in view, he married Miss Sarah Marshall, a Dunbarton young lady educated far beyond the custom of her day, and the young couple (accompanied by three young women whose avowed aim was to "go west to teach") arrived in Crawfordsville in Nov., 1833.

In December Professor Caleb Mills welcomed the first preparatory class of twelve hopeful young Hoosiers to what would, as soon as they were prepared for admission, become Wabash College. Mills was the entire faculty during the first year.

Two years later, when enough students had been prepared for study at the college level, the Wabash College faculty was organized with Mills as professor of languages; eventually he confined himself to the teaching of Greek, serving until 1876.

There was plenty of work for all connected with the struggling institution, but Caleb Mills had been first impressed with the need of common school educa-

tion for all in the Middle West and, according to C. W. Moores' *Caleb Mills and the Public School System of Indiana,* "he agitated and argued, in season and out . . . in the public press and from the pulpit, upon the street corner and in the classroom until his system was adopted and established."

Most effective weapon in his campaign against the reactionary Indiana legislators (and their even more reactionary constituents) was his series of six pamphlets, caption-titled *Read, Circulate and Discuss* and signed "One of the People." Every General Assembly for six years, beginning in 1846, found a fresh blast on its hands at the opening of each annual session, and the pamphlets were widely circulated throughout the state. Finally, as legislators are wont to do under the lash of persistent lobbying, the necessary acts were passed, and the first State Superintendent of Public Instruction was appointed in 1852.

Caleb Mills was the second to hold this office, and under his administration his system became effective. He helped to found the Indiana State Teachers' Association in 1854, and his campaigning eventually resulted in the establishment of many county "seminaries" and, eventually, in the state-operated teacher training colleges. He was interested in higher education for women and campaigned for an Indiana women's college throughout his public life.

In 1876 Caleb Mills (whose orchard and whose sound investments in Crawfordsville real estate had made him financially independent), resigned his professorship and devoted his remaining years to building up the Wabash College library collections.

He died in 1879.

> Information supplied by Moores—*Caleb Mills and the Public School System of Indiana* and by Hopkins, Mrs. Louis B.—*Caleb Mills* (Ms. in the Wabash College Archives).

* * *

Read, Circulate, Discuss. An Address to the Legislature of Indiana at the Commencement of Its Session, Dec. 7, 1846. By "One of the People." *Indianapolis,* 1846.

(Read, Circulate and Discuss.) An Address to the Legislature of Indiana, at the Commencement of Its Session, December 6th, 1847. Upon Popular Education. By One of the People. *Indianapolis,* 1847.

Read, Discuss and Circulate. An Address to the Legislature of Indiana, on Common Schools, Showing the Advantages of a System of General Education. By One of the People. *Terre Haute,* 1849.

Read, Circulate and Discuss. An Address to the Legislature of Indiana at the Commencement of the Session . . . By "One of the People." *Indianapolis,* 1850.

Fifth Annual Message. By One of the People. Four Letters to the Members of the Constitutional Convention, in 1852 . . . *Indianapolis, 1852.*

Sixth Annual Address on Popular Education, to the Legislature of Indiana. By One of the People. *Indianapolis, 1852.*

Suggestions on the Formation of Character. An Address to Youth, Delivered During Tours of County Visitation in 1856, by Caleb Mills, Superintendent of Public Instruction for the State of Indiana. *Indianapolis, 1857.*

Suggestions on the Revision of the Common School Law of Indiana. *Indianapolis, 1859.*

A Plea for a Female College for Indiana. *Crawfordsville, Ind., 1871.*

A Plea for Wabash College Library, and a Description of the New Building. *Crawfordsville, Ind., 1871.*

Read, Discuss, and Circulate! Educational Suggestions, Prepared for the Consideration of the House Committee on Education, in the Indiana Legislature, During the Session of 1873. *Indianapolis, 1873.*

New Departures in Collegiate Control and Culture. *New York, 1880.*

MILLS, FRANK MOODY: 1831–?

Frank Moody Mills was born in Ladoga, Ind., in 1831. He was educated in the local schools and attended the Wabash College preparatory department before entering for his first work in the collegiate department in 1843.

At fourteen he had begun to learn the printing trade, and, when he left college in 1845, he took up the business seriously, being, variously, a newspaper, law book and periodical publisher in Springfield, Ill., and Des Moines, Ia. He also engaged in farming, merchandising and in the promotion and operation of traction and bus lines.

Mr. Mills was active throughout his life, serving as acting president of the Sioux Falls, Ia., traction system in his mid-nineties.

> Information from *Who's Who in America*; Mills —*Early Days in a College Town*; and the Wabash College Archives.

* * *

Something About the Mills Family and Its Collateral Branches . . . *Sioux Falls, S. D., 1911.*

Home-Made Jinglets Cast in the Rough at Odd Times. *Sioux Falls, S. D., 1914.*

Early Days in a College Town and Wabash College in Early Days and Now with Autobiographical Reminiscences. *Sioux Falls, S. D., 1924.*

The Notings of a Nonogenarian; a Study in Longevity. *Boston, n.d. [1926].*

Life and Services of Capt. Jacob Westfall.

MINTURN, JOSEPH ALLEN: 1861–1943.

Joseph Allen Minturn, widely known patent attorney, was born in Athens County, O., on June 20, 1861. He came to Indianapolis at the age of fifteen.

He was educated at Pennsylvania Military College, majoring in civil engineering and chemistry and graduating with honors in 1880. After graduation he began to study law, was admitted to the Indiana bar and began practice as a patent attorney in the early Nineties. He served in the Indiana Legislature in 1901.

He enlisted for service in the first World War, was discharged because of his age (he was fifty-five) but appealed, was reinstated and served overseas in the Quartermaster Corps, being discharged with the rank of captain.

Joseph Allen Minturn was an amateur painter, engraver and illustrator, illustrating some of his books. He died on Apr. 3, 1943.

> Information from the INDIANAPOLIS STAR for Apr. 4, 1943.

* * *

Inventor's Friend; or, Success with Patents . . . *Indianapolis, 1893.*

Price-Regulation Under Patents. *Indianapolis, 1916.*

The American Spirit. *Indianapolis, 1921.*

Frances Slocum of Miami Lodge; the Dramatic Story of the White Girl that Became an Indian Princess and Her Relation to the Stirring Events Through which the Northwest Territory was wrested from the British and Indians. *Indianapolis, 1928.*

Brown County Ballads. *Indianapolis, 1928.*

Historical and Other Poems. *Indianapolis, 1939.*

MITCHELL, JOHN FOWLER, JR.: 1883–

John Fowler Mitchell, Jr., son of John F. and Minnie Belle Mitchell, was born in 1883. He studied at Butler and Yale Universities and returned to Greenfield, Ind., to operate the William Mitchell Printing Company which his grandfather had founded there.

> Information from the Greenfield Public Library.

* * *

The Rooster—Its Origin as a Democratic Emblem. *Greenfield, Ind., 1913.*

The Way There: a Morality Play in Four Acts (with Minnie Belle Mitchell). n.p. [Greenfield], n.d. [1914].

Heroes of War, Past and Present. *Greenfield, Ind., 1918.*

MITCHELL, MINNIE BELLE ALEXANDER (MRS. JOHN F.): 1863–

Minne Belle Alexander was born in Victoria, Tex., on July 24, 1863. Reared in Greenfield, Ind., she married John F. Mitchell, newspaper publisher of that place who was a schoolmate and childhood friend of James Whitcomb Riley. Mrs. Mitchell was long active in Indiana women's literary club work.

> Information supplied by the Greenfield, Ind., Public Library.

* * *

The Way There: a Morality Play in Four Acts (with John F. Mitchell, Jr.). n.p., n.d.

Greenfield, the Historic Birthplace of the Nation's Poet, James Whitcomb Riley. *Greenfield, Ind.,* 1925.

Gray Moon Tale and Others. *Indianapolis,* 1926.

Hoosier Boy. *Indianapolis,* 1942.

MOFFETT, THOMAS CLINTON: 1869–1945.

Thomas Clinton Moffett, son of Samuel Schuman and Maria J. McKee Moffett, was born in Madison, Ind., on July 29, 1869. He received the B.S., A.M. and D.D. degrees from Hanover College in 1890, 1894 and 1910, respectively, and studied theology at Union Theological Seminary and at Free Church College, Edinburgh, Scotland.

He was ordained to the Presbyterian ministry in 1893 and held pastorates at Flagstaff, Ariz., Raton, N. Mex. and Portland, Ore., from 1893 to 1901. He served as a missionary in Arizona from 1901 to 1906 and as Superintendent of Indian Work for the Presbyterian Board of National Missions, New York, from 1906 to 1928.

He died in 1945.

> Information from *Who's Who in America.*

* * *

The American Indian on the New Trail; the Red Man of the United States and the Christian Gospel. *New York,* 1914.

The Bible in the Life of the Indians.

MONCRIEF, JOHN WILDMAN: 1850–1936.

John Wildman Moncrief, son of Jeptha and Grace Moncrief, was born in Wirt, Ind., on Sept. 10, 1850, and graduated from Denison University in 1873. He married Lucy L. Wood in 1878.

From 1873 to 1875 he was a tutor in history and

Greek at Franklin College. He studied at the University of Leipzig in 1875-76 and received the A.M. degree from Franklin College in 1876. He taught at Franklin College and Denison University until 1897, when he became an associate professor at the University of Chicago.

He died in 1936.

> Information from *Who Was Who in America.*

* * *

Short History of the Christian Church for Students and General Readers. *New York,* 1902.

MONFORT, FRANCIS CASSATTE: 1844–?

Francis Cassatte Monfort, son of Joseph Glass and Hannah Congar Riggs Monfort, was born in Greensburg, Ind., on Sept. 1, 1844, and graduated from Wabash College in 1864, receiving the A.M. degree in 1867. He studied theology at McCormick Theological Seminary and Lane Theological Seminary and in Europe. In 1883 he received the D.D. degree from the University of Wooster. He married Anna Louisa Hubbard on May 17, 1871.

Ordained to the Presbyterian ministry in 1870, he served as pastor of a church in Cincinnati but resigned in 1873 to become editor of his father's journal, THE HERALD AND PRESBYTER. In 1879 he resumed his ministerial work in Cincinnati, at the same time continuing his editorship.

> Information from *Who's Who in America* and *Appletons' Cyclopaedia of American Biography,* Vol. IV.

* * *

Sermons for Silent Sabbaths: an Offering to Christian Families and Vacant Churches. *Cincinnati,* 1884.

Socialism and City Evangelization. 1887.

The Law of Appeals. 1893.

Ecclesiastical Discipline. 1900.

Applied Theology. *Cincinnati,* 1904.

MONROE, PAUL: 1869–

Born at North Madison, Ind., June 7, 1869, Paul Monroe, son of the Rev. William Y. and Juliet Williams Monroe, received the B.S. degree from Franklin College in 1890. From 1895 to 1897 he was a Fellow in Sociology at the University of Chicago and received the Ph.D. degree from that institution in 1897. In 1901 he was a student at the University of Heidelberg.

His other degrees include the LL.D., University of Peking (1913), Franklin College (1918), University of Brazil (1939), and the Litt. D., Columbia (1929) and University of Dublin (1933).

After two years as instructor in history at Teachers College, Columbia University, he became professor of the history of education there in 1899. He became professor emeritus in 1938.

During his long career as an educator Dr. Monroe served as President of the Educational Section of the American Social Science Association, and under appointment of the Bureau of Insular Affairs of the War Department he served as commissioner to report on the Philippine school system. His contributions to the study of the history of education gave him an international reputation and his written works have done much to establish the subject as important in the training of teachers in the U. S.

Besides his text books (omitted from the following list), his greatest contribution to the whole field of education, however, was his work as editor-in-chief of the five volume *Encyclopedia of Education*.

Information from the Madison, Ind., Public Library and *Who's Who in America*.

* * *

A Source Book of the History of Education for the Greek and Roman Period. *New York,* 1901.

Thomas Platter and the Educational Renaissance of the Sixteenth Century. *New York,* 1904.

The American Spirit; a Basis for World Democracy (with Irving E. Miller). *Yonkers-on-Hudson, N. Y.,* 1918.

A Report on Education in China. *New York,* 1922.

China: a Nation in Evolution. *Chautauqua, N. Y.,* 1927.

Essays in Comparative Education. *New York,* 1927 and 1932. 2 vols.

Founding of the American Public School System; a History of Education in the United States from the Early Settlements to the Close of the Civil War Period. *New York,* 1940.

MONTGOMERY, DAVID B.: 1845–?

David B. Montgomery was born in Owensville, Ind., on Oct. 20, 1845, and spent nearly all of his life in that place. He attended local schools and probably continued his education elsewhere, for he eventually became a minister in the Baptist Church and the scholarly research involved in the preparation of his three books is not of a sort likely to result from only an attendance in the Indiana elementary schools of the

Fifties. His genealogical work is something of a collector's item.

Information supplied by the Owensville, Ind., Carnegie Library.

* * *

General Baptist History. *Evansville,* 1882.

A Genealogical History of the Montgomerys and Their Descendants. *Owensville,* Ind., 1903.

Life and Labors of A. D. Williams. *Owensville, Ind.,* 1905.

MONTGOMERY, JAMES SHERA: 1864–

James Shera Montgomery, son of the Rev. William M. and Anna Newlove Montgomery, was born at Mt. Carmel, Ind., in 1864 and graduated from the Muncie, Ind., Academy in 1881. He then studied at De Pauw and Northwestern universities and at Oxford in England and in 1892 received the B.D. degree from Garrett Bible Institute. He was ordained to the Methodist Episcopal ministry in 1893.

The Rev. Mr. Montgomery was pastor of churches in Toledo, O., and in Minneapolis before becoming, in 1916, pastor of the Metropolitan Methodist Episcopal Church in Washington, D. C. After 1921 he served as chaplain of the House of Representatives.

He was twice married: first to Emma Shortie in 1885, then to Elsie May Farnham on Apr. 21, 1924.

He was a contributor to religious papers and reviews and a lecturer on sociologic and literary subjects.

Information from *Who's Who in America*.

* * *

John Ruskin, the Voice of a New Age. *Cincinnati,* 1902.

Memorial Day Oration, May 30, 1913, Delivered . . . at Arlington Cemetery, Va., *Washington, D. C.,* 1913.

MONTGOMERY, MARCUS WHITMAN: 1839–1894.

Marcus Whitman Montgomery, son of Mathew Peter and Mary Sherwood Bull Montgomery, was born in Prattsburg, N. Y., on June 21, 1839. He was named for Dr. Marcus Whitman, of Oregon fame, who was an intimate friend of his father.

When he was less than a year old, he was brought to Jay County, Ind., by his parents. His father died when he was a boy in his teens he became stenographer for the Missouri Legislature. Returning to Indiana, now twenty years of age he founded a newspaper, THE JAY TORCHLIGHT, and edited it for three years, publishing in it much Jay County history and starting at this time to collect material for his *History of Jay County, Indiana.*

He attended Liber College, where he met and married Mary Votaw, in 1859, and he graduated from Amherst College in 1869. After spending six years in business in Cleveland, O., he entered Yale Theological Seminary, from which he graduated in 1878. While a student at the seminary he wrote a history of the English Bible which was never published.

His first and only pastorate was with the Congregational Church in Fort Scott, Kan. In 1881 he became superintendent of Minnesota and North Dakota for the churches of the American Home Missionary Society and in 1884 superintendent of church work among U.S. Scandinavians. He twice visited Sweden and Norway and investigated the free-church movement there.

In 1887 he traveled to Utah to study the Scandinavian-Mormon population and, in consequence of this trip, wrote a widely published article which was an attempt to stem the tide of Scandinavian converts to Mormonism. He also wrote a book in this cause and made addresses.

At the time of his death, on Feb. 6, 1894, he was an instructor at Chicago Theological Seminary.

Information from the Portland Public Library.

* * *

History of Jay County, Indiana. Chicago, n.d. [1864].
A Wind from the Holy Spirit in Sweden and Norway.
The Whole Story about the Mormons.
Mormon Delusion: Its History, Doctrine, and the Outlook in Utah. Boston, n.d. [1890].

MONTGOMERY, RICHMOND AMES: 1870–

Richmond Ames Montgomery, who wrote under the pen name of Timothy Kilbourn, was born in Hendricks County, Ind., on July 16, 1870, the son of John Martin and Frances Caroline Wright Montgomery. After studying at De Pauw University and at Hanover College, he graduated from Miami University in 1893, and from McCormick Theological Seminary in 1896 and was ordained to the Presbyterian ministry. He married Mary Frances Allhands in 1897.

From 1896 to 1917 he held pastorates in several midwestern states, and from 1917 until 1932 he served as president, successively, of Parsons College in Iowa, Centre College in Kentucky, Kentucky College for Women, and Lane Theological Seminary. From 1932

to 1940 he was on the faculty of Presbyterian Theological Seminary in Chicago.

Information from *Who's Who in America.*

* * *

The Secret Place; Studies of Prayer. *Chicago,* 1901.
The Triumphant Ministry, Letters from Timothy Kilbourn to Fred Gaynor. *Philadelphia,* 1914.
The Winning Team of Centre College. *Danville, Ky.,* 1923.
Thomas Dove Foster, 1847-1915. A Biography. *Cedar Rapids, Ia.,* 1929.
Timeless Elements in Preaching. Inaugural Address as Professor of Homiletics at the Opening of the 106th Year of the Seminary, 1935-1936, September 10, 1935. *Chicago,* 1936.
Preparing Preachers to Preach. *Grand Rapids, Mich.,* 1939.
Expository Preaching. *New York,* 1939.
Reality in Religion; Studies of the Atonement of Jesus. *New York,* 1941.
Work-a-Day Religion.
Lyman Beecher, a Study in Personality.
The Masterful Man.
The Open Door.
The Challenge of the New Learning to the Church.
The Function of the Christian Colleges.

MOODY, WILLIAM VAUGHN: 1869–1910.

"William Vaughn Moody, American poet and playwright, was born in Spencer, Ind., on July 8, 1869, the sixth of seven children. His father, Francis Burdette Moody, was a retired riverboat captain who had plied between Pittsburgh and New Orleans until his steamer was seized by the Southern troops at the beginning of the Civil War. His mother was Henrietta Emily Stoy, daughter of a pioneer Indiana family.

"When Moody was one year old the family moved to New Albany, on the Ohio River, and there he spent his boyhood. He began writing poems at fifteen, usually tearing them up as soon as they were written. After leaving high school, where he was editor of two newspapers, he studied drawing and painting for a year at the Pritchett Institute of Design in Louisville, Ky.

"The death of Moody's mother in 1884 and his father in 1886 broke up the family home, and he taught country school for a year near New Albany. During the next two years he prepared for college at the Riverview Academy, New York, earning his way by teaching.

"In 1889, at the age of twenty, Moody entered Harvard, his entire capital consisting of twenty-five dollars. He supported himself by working at typewriting, tutoring, and proctoring, and in his senior year, having acquired enough points for graduation, he traveled in Europe as tutor to the son of a wealthy family. The trip was notable for a walking tour of the Black Forest and Switzerland, a winter spent in Florence, and a visit to Greece. Returning in time to read the class day poem, 'The Song of the Elder Brothers,' he was graduated in 1893.

"The next year he did graduate work at Harvard in medieval philology, earning his living by doing editorial work on Bulfinch's *Mythology* with his intimate friend, Robert Morss Lovett. The following year he was an assistant in the English department at Harvard and at Radcliffe College. The poems of this period were mostly in imitation of Keats, Browning, and Walt Whitman, and there were few of them that he did not later reject.

"After a summer of travel in Europe with Daniel Gregory Mason, Moody went to the University of Chicago in 1895 as instructor in English and rhetoric and he remained there seven years, attaining the rank of assistant professor in 1901. During those years his heart was never in his work, he longed for the vacations and leisure to write, and took frequent leaves of absence.

"In the spring of 1898 and the winter of 1899 he was in New York editing the Cambridge edition of Milton. The year 1900 he lived in New England, dividing his time between creative work and a textbook he was writing with Lovett. That year he made his debut in print with the publication of *The Masque of Judgment*, a lyrical drama in five acts. It had been begun three years before on a walking trip thru the Dolomite country of the Italian Tyrol. The summer of 1901 he went camping in the Rocky Mountains with Hamlin Garland. A collection of his *Poems* appeared in 1901.

"The publication of Moody's and Lovett's *History of English Literature* in 1902 liberated Moody from the drudgery of the classroom and permitted him to devote all his time to writing. John M. Manly, head of the English department at the University of Chicago, repeatedly scheduled courses for him, and he was offered full salary to lecture a single quarter a year, but he declined and taught no more classes after 1902, maintaining, however, a nominal connection with the university until 1907. He took a trip to Greece in 1902, spending much of his time reading Greek tragedy. The next few years he divided his time between Boston,

New York, and Chicago. His New York home was in Waverly Place in Greenwich Village.

"In 1904 Moody published *The Fire-Bringer*, another lyrical drama intended as the first member of a trilogy on the Promethean theme, of which *The Masque of Judgment* was the second member. After this his work was sought by magazines. . . .

"He went on a trip to Arizona with Ferdinand Schevill in 1905. He lived for a week at Oraibi among the Hopi Indians and saw the spring dance at Walpi, and definitely planned his prose play, *The Great Divide*, which was based on a story from real life related to him by Mrs. Harriet Converse Brainerd of Chicago, who later became his wife. The play was written on his return from the trip. It is the story of the marriage by capture of a New England girl with an Arizona outlaw, providing a contrast between Eastern puritanism and the paganism of the West.

"*The Great Divide* made Moody's name known to the general public. He showed the play to Margaret Anglin, the actress, who gave it a trial performance in Chicago at the close of her season in the spring of 1906 under the title of *A Sabine Woman*. After the triumphant first act, she declined to go on with the play until Moody had affixed his name to a contract, while the audience waited tensely. He spent the summer at Cornish, N. H., revising the play, working with fierce concentration, and it was produced in New York by Henry Miller in the fall of 1906.

"Moody wrote with facility and thought it easier to write blank verse than prose. Poetry was his one ambition; all other undertakings were for the purpose of financial remuneration. He declined offers of assistance from friends, preferring to live poorly and have his independence. He helped support his sisters.

" 'Physically he was slightly above medium height,' recalls Lovett, 'graceful and well proportioned, in young manhood with a strength beyond his stature, and with great endurance. In college he wore a moustache; later in life, a Van Dyke beard. His hands were unusually deft and sensitive. His voice was clear and resonant.' He had blue eyes and a ruddy complexion. 'He was always a good companion, walking, swimming, riding, at a concert or art gallery, spending the night smoking before the fire or under the stars. I think he was at his best with one other person, or at least a small group . . .' In large groups he was inclined to be self-conscious and silent. He had a varied store of songs which he would render to the accompaniment of a guitar. He was very fond of tobacco. In literature he liked particularly the medieval French romances.

Returning to his early love, painting, he did, among other things, his own portrait.

"Moody was in perfect health until 1906 when he had an operation for the removal of a growth from his leg which had been injured in a severe fall while climbing Mount Parnassus four years earlier. (He was passionately fond of mountain-climbing.) The pain returned while he was on a trip to Italy in 1907, and in the spring of 1908, while living in New York, he had a serious attack of typhoid fever from which he never completely recovered. He spent that summer with Ridgely Torrence, the poet, on an island off the coast of Maine, and was nursed by Mrs. Brainerd, who became his wife in Quebec on May 7, 1909. There was a falling off in Moody's high spirits and his work after this, but he completed his second prose play, *The Faith Healer*, which had been forming in his mind since 1896 when he read newspaper accounts of Schlatter, a Western faith-healer. He called the play 'a queerish thing, at the antipodes from *The Great Divide* in method and feeling . . .' *The Faith Healer* was produced in St. Louis in the autumn of 1909, and in New York in Dec. 1909. Dramatically, it was less successful than its predecessor.

"After the play opened, he visited London and broke down badly. He wrote to a friend at home: 'The work which I did on *The Faith Healer*, together with the excitement of attending its production, came too soon after my typhoid convalescence.' Thereafter he was extremely ill.

"He died in Colorado Springs on Oct. 17, 1910, at the age of forty-one. He left unfinished *The Death of Eve*, intended to complete the trilogy of dramatic poems. His works were collected in 1912 in two volumes under the title *Poems and Poetic Plays*. Daniel Gregory Mason edited *Some Letters of William Vaughn Moody* and Robert Morss Lovett edited his *Selected Poems* in 1931 . . ."

Condensed from *Authors Today and Yesterday*.

* * *

The Masque of Judgment: a Masque-Drama in Five Acts, and a Prelude. *Boston, 1900.*

Poems. *Boston, 1901.*

History of English Literature (with Robert Morss Lovett). *New York, 1902.*

The Fire-Bringer. *Boston, 1904.*

The Great Divide: a Play. *New York, 1909.*

Gloucester Moors, and Other Poems. *Boston, 1910.*

The Faith Healer: a Play in Three Acts. *New York, 1910.*

Poems and Plays. *Boston, 1912. 2 vols.*

Some Letters of William Vaughn Moody. (Edited by Daniel Gregory Mason.) *Boston, 1913.*

Selected Poems. (Edited by Robert Morss Lovett.) *Boston, 1931.*

Letters to Harriet; (edited by Percy Mackaye). *Boston, 1935.*

MOONEY, JAMES: 1861–1921.

Although little of his writing appears except in learned publications, serials, etc., James Mooney is worthy of far more than casual attention. The *Dictionary of American Biography* says of him, in part:

". . . [James Mooney], son of James and Ellin (Devlin) Mooney, was born at Richmond, Ind. He began his education in the common schools and later taught two terms. He was strongly interested in Indians, reading everything available on the subject, but his interest did not lead to any apparent avenue of support, and he entered the office of the RICHMOND PALLADIUM, where he worked both as a compositor and in an editorial capacity. After he had saved a little money he journeyed to Washington with a secret intent of going to Brazil to study the Indians of that country. In Washington he met Maj. J. W. Powell in 1885, and through him Mooney found an outlet for his enthusiasm in the Bureau of American Ethnology, where he remained for the rest of his life. His early Indian studies had taken the form of a list of tribes amounting to 3,000 entries and this came into use as material for the *Handbook of American Indians* . . . in the preparation of which he took an active part. In North Carolina he studied the language, folk lore, mythology, and material culture of the Cherokees (*Myths of the Cherokees,* Nineteenth Annual Report of the Bureau of American Ethnology . . . 1895-96, 1900). At a fortunate juncture he discovered an ancient Cherokee ritual written in the Cherokee script (*The Sacred Formulas of the Cherokees,* Seventh Annual Report . . . 1885-86, 1891). About 1890 the last ebullition of Indian race-consciousness took place with the outbreak of the Ghost Dance—an endeavor to rehabilitate the Indian to his former status—and this phase of Indian life Mooney studied exhaustively (*The Ghost-Dance Religion and the Sioux Outbreak of 1890,* Fourteenth Annual Report . . . 1892-93, 1896). Some of his best years were spent in the investigation of the Kiowa (*Calendar History of the Kiowa Indians,* Seventeenth Annual Report . . . 1895-96, 1898), and at the time of his death he was engrossed with a large work on Kiowa heraldry. He also investigated the seemingly anomalous presence of Siouan language tribes on the borders of the Virginia Algonquians and his research went far to clear up the history of the migrations of this great stock (*The Siouan Tribes of the East*, Bulletin 22 of the Smithsonian Institute, Bureau of Ethnology, 1894).

"Mooney's parents had come from Meath, Ireland, and he was deeply ingrained with Irish lore. One of his first papers was *The Funeral Customs of Ireland* (Proceedings of the American Philosophical Society, 1888, vol. XXV, 1888, pp. 1-56). His scientific writing was mostly confined to large, thoroughly prepared monographs. A particularly lucid style characterized his writing . . ."

In 1897 he married Ione Lee Gaut of Tennessee. He died in 1921.

> W. H., *Dictionary of American Biography*, Vol. XIII.

* * *

Funeral Customs of Ireland. *Philadelphia*, 1882.
Myths of the Cherokees. *Cambridge, Mass.*, 1888.
Cherokee Ball Play. *New York*, 1890.
Cheyenne Indians, n.p. [*Lancaster, Pa.*], 1907.

MOORE, ADDISON WEBSTER: 1866–1930.

Addison Webster Moore was born in Plainfield, Ind., on July 30, 1866. His parents were John Sheldon and Adaline Hockett Moore.

Moore was educated in local schools and received the A.B. (1890) and A.M. (1893) degrees from De Pauw University. He received the Ph.D. from the University of Chicago in 1898. He married Ella E. Adams in 1891 and was an instructor and professor of philosophy at the University of Chicago from 1895 to shortly before his death, which occurred on Aug. 25, 1930.

> Information from *Who Was Who in America*.

* * *

Functional Versus Representational Theories of Knowledge in Locke's Essay. *Chicago*, 1902.
Studies in Logical Theory (with John Dewey and others). *Chicago*, 1903.
Existence, Meaning, and Reality in Locke's Essay and in Present Epistemology. *Chicago*, 1903.
Pragmatism and Its Critics. *Chicago*, 1910.
Creative Intelligence; Essays in the Pragmatic Attitude (with John Dewey and others). *New York*, 1917.

MOORE, AMBROSE YOEMANS: 1822–1904.

A. Y. Moore came to South Bend, Ind., in 1849 as minister of the Presbyterian Church. As a resident of that city he was intimately acquainted with Schuyler Colfax, who was to become vice-president of the U. S., and whose biographer he later became.

Dr. Moore left South Bend in 1854 and served as an instructor in Valparaiso College and later as treasurer of Hanover College.

> Information from the South Bend Public Library; the Valparaiso Public Library; and the Northern Indiana Historical Society.

* * *

The Life of Schuyler Colfax. *Philadelphia*, 1868.
History of the Presbytery of Indianapolis. *Indianapolis*, 1876.
Memorial Sermon, Sabbath, May 25, 1890. *Madison, Ind.*, 1890.
History of Hanover College. *Indianapolis*, 1900.

MOORE, EDWARD E.: 1866–1940.

Edward E. Moore, author, editor and newspaper publisher, son of Isaac and Josephine Snyder Moore, was born Mar. 12, 1866, on his father's farm near the Ohio River in Lawrence County, O. Edward was the seventh of a family of twelve children—six boys and six girls. Two of his elder brothers and one sister being school teachers, Edward early in life determined to acquire an education and qualify himself for the profession of teaching school. He made good use of his time, studied diligently in the short country school terms, and worked out his problems by the light of coal oil lamps at night. Graduating from the common school, he attended Holbrook Normal School in Lebanon, O., and realized his ambition to teach in the public schools at the age of twenty.

In the year 1890, after five years of successful work in the public schools of his native state, Edward and his younger brother, Elbert, purchased a small newspaper and printing office in College Corner, O., where for eight years they edited and published the COLLEGE CORNER CHRONICLE, an independent weekly newspaper. A large subscription list was built up for their paper in the populous adjoining counties of Preble and Butler, in Ohio, and Union, in Indiana. In 1898, having greatly increased their plant facilities and outgrown their territory, the brothers disposed of a part of their holdings and moved the newspaper equipment to Connersville, Ind., twenty miles away, where they enlarged their outfit and began the publication of the CONNERSVILLE COURIER, which they sold to new management five years later.

Edward Moore studied law and was admitted to the bar but never engaged in the practice of law. He was elected Indiana state senator in 1908 and served two terms in the upper branch of the Legislature during the administration of Gov. J. Frank Hanly. Much of his effort as a member of the Legislature was devoted to the enactment of legislation favorable to higher educational advantages in the public school system of the state.

About the year 1911 or 1912 he took employment with the Osborne Calendar Company, New York, and was sent to Los Angeles, Calif., as the company's state representative. Concluding his contract with this company, he embarked in the real estate brokerage business in Los Angeles, then "booming," where marked success rewarded his efforts. He virtually grew up with the city and became a part of it the rest of his life.

He died in his Los Angeles home on Oct. 23, 1940.

Supplied by Elbert Moore (brother).

* * *

A Century of Indiana. *New York*, n.d. [1910].
Words Fitly Spoken. *Indianapolis*, n.d. [1912].
Guiding Stars, *Indianapolis*, n.d. [1913].

MOORE, ROBERT WEBBER: 1862–

Robert Webber Moore, son of Cameron and Mary Jane Webber Moore, was born in Delphi, Ind., on Dec. 14, 1862, and graduated from the University of Michigan in 1887. He also studied in Europe and at the University of Chicago and in 1915 received the L.H.D. degree from Hamilton College. In 1887 he married Alice Booth Wheeler, who died in 1938.

For two years, 1887-1889, he taught Latin and French at Georgetown College, Ky., and after 1890 he was on the faculty of Colgate University as professor of German and French.

He lectured extensively on Germany and German literature, and on China and was a reviewer of German books for the NATION. He was also a frequent commencement speaker.

Information from *Who's Who in America.*

* * *

History of German Literature. *Hamilton, N. Y.*, 1900. (8th ed.)
Weimar, the Athens of Germany. *Hamilton, N. Y.*, 1908.

MOORES, CHARLES WASHINGTON, JR.: 1862–1923.

Charles Washington Moores, Jr., was born in Indianapolis Feb. 15, 1862. He was the son of Charles Washington and Julia Dumont Merrill Moores and the grandson of Samuel Merrill. After graduation from Wabash College in 1882 he studied law at Central Law School, Indianapolis, and began the practice of law in 1883. He was a lecturer at the Indiana Law School and at the Indiana University School of Law, a U. S. commissioner, and a member of the law firm of Pickens, Moores, Davidson and Pickens. In 1896 he married Elizabeth Nichols of Philadelphia. In addition to his books he was also the author of articles which were published in various law journals and magazines. He died in 1923.

Information from Dunn—*Indiana and Indianans, Who Was Who in America*; and the Indianapolis Public Library.

* * *

Caleb Mills and the Indiana School System. *Indianapolis,* 1905.
The Life of Abraham Lincoln for Boys and Girls. *Boston,* 1909.
The History of Indiana for Boys and Girls. *Boston,* 1909.
The Life of Christopher Columbus for Boys and Girls. *Boston,* 1912. (Also published under the title, The Story of Christopher Columbus.)
Lincoln Selections. 1913.
President Lincoln At Home.
Abraham Lincoln, Lawyer. *Greenfield, Ind.,* 1922.

MORAN, THOMAS FRANCIS: 1866–1928.

Thomas Francis Moran, son of John and Mary Moran, was born in Columbia, Mich., on Jan. 9, 1866. He received his early education in the public schools and graduated from the University of Michigan in 1887, being admitted to the Michigan bar in the same year. In 1895 he received the Ph.D. degree from Johns Hopkins University. He married Louise R. Upham on Aug. 5, 1896.

From 1887 to 1892 he was superintendent of schools at Elk River, Minn., and after 1895 was associated with Purdue University as professor of history and head of the department of history and economics. For many years he was the university's representative on the Western Intercollegiate Conference. He was also active in campus affairs, especially the establishment of the Purdue Memorial Union and the organization of the semi-centennial in 1924. Dr. Moran was a recognized authority on English and American constitutional history, had a nation-wide reputation as a scholar, speaker, and writer, and, in addition to the books listed below, was the author of many textbooks (in collaboration with Dr. James A. Woodburn of Indiana University) and contributed to reviews and educational publications on political and historical topics.

He died on Oct. 21, 1928.

Information from the Purdue University Libraries; *Who Was Who in America* and *Thomas Francis Moran. A Memorial.*

* * *

The Rise and Development of the Bicameral System in America. *Baltimore, 1895.*

The Theory and Practice of the English Government. *New York, 1903.*

The Formation and Development of the Constitution. *Philadelphia,* n.d. [1904].

American Presidents; Their Individualities and Their Contributions to American Progress. *New York,* n.d. [1917].

The History and Government of Indiana (with James A. Woodburn). *New York, 1920.*

Constitution of Indiana, with Questions and Notes (with James A. Woodburn). *New York, 1926.*

The Ethics of Politics; an Address Delivered . . . Before the Phi Beta Kappa Club of Purdue University, March 21, 1927, n.p., n.d. [1927].

The Character and Ideals of Abraham Lincoln . . . n.p. [Indianapolis], n.d. [1927].

Active Citizenship (with James A. Woodburn). *New York, 1928.*

Our United States (with James A. Woodburn and H. C. Hill). *New York, 1930.*

MORGAN, DICK THOMPSON: 1854–1920.

Dick Thompson Morgan, son of Valentine and Frances Thompson Morgan, was born in Prairie Creek, Ind., on Dec. 6, 1854, and graduated from Union Christian College in 1876, receiving the M.S. degree in 1882. He graduated from Central Law School in Indianapolis in 1880. On May 30, 1878, he married Ora Heath.

Following his graduation from law school he practiced law in Terre Haute, Ind., and in 1880-81 was a member of the Indiana Legislature. From 1882 to 1886 he was editor and publisher of the TERRE HAUTE COURIER.

He was an attorney for the Atchison, Topeka and Santa Fe Railroad for three years, then in 1889 settled in Guthrie, Okla. From 1909 to 1921 he was a member of Congress from that state.

He died on July 4, 1920.

He published and annotated several law books not listed here.

Information from *Who Was Who in America.*

* * *

Land Credits—a Plea for the American Farmer. *New York, 1915.*

MORGAN, THOMAS JEFFERSON: 1839–1902.

"Thomas Jefferson Morgan (Aug. 17, 1839-July 13, 1902), soldier, Baptist clergyman, educator, and denominational leader, . . . [was] the son of Rev. Lewis Morgan and his third wife, Mary C. Causey (or Cansey), he was born in Franklin, Ind. His grandfather had been a slaveholder, but his father was an anti-slavery advocate and a leader in religious, political, and educational matters. Thomas was fitted for college in the preparatory school of Franklin College and received the degree of A.B. from that institution in 1861, though he left in his senior year to enlist in the Union army. After three months' service, he took charge of public education at Atlanta, Ill., but on Aug. 1, 1862, was appointed first lieutenant in the 70th Indiana Volunteer Infantry. His period of military service continued for over three years. Prominent in the enlistment of negro troops and eloquent in their defense, he became lieutenant-colonel of the 14th United States Colored Infantry on Nov. 1, 1863, and colonel on Jan. 1, 1864. He commanded a division at the battle of Nashville and was brevetted brigadier-general, Mar. 13, 1865 . . .

"After leaving the army he entered Rochester Theological Seminary, graduating in 1868. He was ordained a Baptist minister, at Rochester, N. Y., in 1869, but held only one brief pastorate—at Brownville, Nebr., 1871-72. From 1872 to 1874 he was president of the Nebraska Normal School at Peru; from 1874 to 1881, he taught homiletics and ecclesiastical history in the Baptist Union Theological Seminary, Chicago, spending several months in Germany in 1879; from 1881 to 1883 he served as principal of the New York State Normal School at Potsdam, and from 1884 to 1889, as principal of the State Normal School at Providence, R. I. In the latter year, he was appointed commissioner of Indian Affairs by President Harrison . . .

"In 1893 he renewed his denominational activity, accepting the position of corresponding secretary of the American Baptist Home Missionary Society, in which position he served until his death almost a decade later . . . Under his skillful promotion, schools for thousands of negro men and women were established and equipped. He was editor of the BAPTIST HOME MISSION MONTHLY, 1893-1902 . . . In 1870 he married Caroline Starr . . ."

> Condensed from C. H. M., *Dictionary of American Biography*, Vol. XIII.

* * *

Reminiscences of Service with Colored Troops in the Army of the Cumberland, 1863-65. *Providence, R. I.,* 1885.

What Is the True Function of a Normal School? *Boston,* 1886.

Educational Mosaics: Collected from Many Writers of Thoughts Bearing on Educational Questions of the Day. *Boston,* 1887.

Studies in Pedagogy. *Boston,* 1889.

The Present Phase of the Indian Question. *Boston,* 1891.

A Plea for the Papoose, n.p., n.d. [1892].

Man or Baboon? *New York,* n.d. [1895].

Patriotic Citizenship. *New York,* 1895.

The Negro in America and the Ideal American Republic. *Philadelphia,* 1898.

MORRIS, BENJAMIN FRANKLIN: 1810–1867.

B. F. Morris, born in 1810, was a resident of Indiana for most of his active life. W. R. Holloway reports him as having been a resident of Indianapolis in 1830, where he was one of the founders of the Indiana Historical Society and was elected its first secretary. The title of one of his books indicates his occupation of the Presbyterian pastorate in Rising Sun, Ind., in 1846. He died in 1867.

> Information from Holloway, W. R.—*Indianapolis. A Historical and Statistical Sketch of the Railroad City* and Walker—*Beginnings of Printing in the State of Indiana.*

* * *

Addresses, Delivered at the Sunday School Celebration of the Fifty-Fourth Anniversary of American Independence, in Indianapolis, on Saturday, the 3d of July, 1830 (with Gov. James Brown Ray). *Indianapolis,* 1830.

A Discourse on the Christian Character and Influence on Washington, Delivered in Rising Sun, Indiana, on Sabbath, Feb. 22, 1846. *Rising Sun, Ind.,* 1846.

Our Country. Three Discourses, on National Subjects. By Rev. B. F. Morris, A.M., Pastor of the Presbyterian Church of Rising Sun, Ind. *Lawrenceburg, Ind.,* 1848.

Address on Agriculture . . . Delivered Before Agricultural Society . . . *Rising Sun, Ind.,* Oct. 1852.

The Life of Thomas Morris; Pioneer and Long a Legis-

lator of Ohio, and U. S. Senator from 1833 to 1839. Edited by His Son. *Cincinnati,* 1856.

Historical Sketch of Rising Sun, Indiana, and the Presbyterian Church. A Fortieth Anniversary Discourse, Delivered September 15, 1856. *Cincinnati,* 1858.

Christian Life and Character of the Civil Institutions of the United States, Developed in the Official and Historical Annals of the Republic. *Philadelphia,* 1864.

MORRIS, GEORGE DAVIS: 1864–

George Davis Morris, son of William Frampton and Mary Ellen Swain Morris, was born in Elwood, Ind., on May 25, 1864, and graduated from Indiana University in 1890. In 1895 he received the A.M. degree from the same institution. He also studied in France, at the University of Paris and the University of Grenoble. He married Emma Zeiss of Oxford, Ind., on Dec. 27, 1899.

After teaching in Kansas for a year and Colorado for two years, in 1893 he came to Indiana University as instructor in French and from 1919 to 1938 was professor of French there. He translated and edited several books of French and English literature not listed here.

> Information from *Who's Who in America.*

* * *

Fenimore Cooper et Edgar Poe D'Après La Critique Française du Dix-Neuvième Siecle. *Paris, 1912.*

MORRISON, HENRIETTA ATHON (MRS. JAMES): ?–

Henrietta Athon Morrison, who wrote under the pen name of Hetty Athon Morris, lived in Indianapolis and was the wife of James Morrison and mother of Dr. Frank A. Morrison. Her father, Dr. James S. Athon, was once prominent in Indiana politics. A writer of sketches and poems for newspapers and periodicals, she published one book.

> Information from the Indianapolis Public Library and from Parker and Heiney—*Poets and Poetry of Indiana.*

* * *

My Summer in the Kitchen. *Indianapolis, 1878.*

MORRISON, SARAH ELIZABETH: ?–?

Born in Indiana, Sarah Elizabeth Morrison was educated privately. She was a resident of Philadelphia in the early 1900's.

Information from *Who's Who in America.*

* * *

Chilhowee Boys. *New York, 1893.*
Chilhowee Boys in War Time. *New York, 1895.*
Chilhowee Boys at College. *New York, 1896.*
Chilhowee Boys in Harness. *New York, 1898.*

MORRISON, SARAH PARKE: 1833–1916.

Sarah Parke Morrison, daughter of John I. Morrison, was born at Salem, Ind., in 1833 and was educated at Mount Holyoke Seminary and Indiana University, graduating from the latter institution in 1869 and receiving the A.M. degree in 1871. She was the first woman graduate of the university.

She taught English literature at Indiana University from 1873 to 1875 and was later a resident of Knightstown, Ind.

She died in 1916.

Information from *Indiana University, 1820-1904,* and Dunn—*Indiana and Indianans,* Vol. II.

* * *

A Monody to a Father's Memory. *Cambridge, Mass.,* 1891.
Among Ourselves: to a Mother's Memory; Being a Life Story of Principally Seven Generations. *Plainfield, Ind.,* 1901, 1902, 1904. 3 vols.
Sicily; a Poem Dedicated to the Memory of Dante Alighieri. *Richmond, Ind.,* 1910.

MORROW, JACKSON: 1849–1930.

Jackson Morrow, son of Charles and Sarah Lamb Morrow, who moved to Howard County in 1845, was born on a farm south of Kokomo, Ind., on Mar. 3, 1849.

When he was eight years old, he attended a two months' term of winter school in a log cabin, and when he was fifteen, he attended Kokomo Normal School for the fall term. At sixteen he was licensed to teach. For two years he taught a country school near Alto during the winter and attended Kokomo Normal during the fall terms. He entered the University of Michigan when he was nineteen and graduated four years later. In 1873 he married Mary E. Henderson. They lived on his farm in Harrison Township, Howard County, and he taught school when he was not farming.

Mr. Morrow held several public offices, including those of trustee, county surveyor, civil engineer of Kokomo, and police commissioner. His first wife died in 1891, and in 1905 he married Mrs. Myra Bird. They moved to Kokomo in 1898.

Mr. Morrow died at his farm on Aug. 5, 1930.

Information from the Carnegie Public Library of Kokomo.

* * *

History of Howard County, Indiana. *Indianapolis,* 1909. 2 vols.

MORTON, OLIVER THROCK: 1860–1898.

Oliver Throck Morton was born at Centerville, Ind., on May 23, 1860, the son of Oliver P. Morton, the Civil War governor of Indiana, and Lucinda M. Burbank Morton. He was educated at Yale and Oxford universities.

In 1886 he was admitted to the Indiana bar and in 1891 was appointed clerk of the U. S. Circuit Court of Appeals. He was editor and owner of the old INDIANAPOLIS DAILY TIMES.

He died in 1898.

Information from Houghton Mifflin—*A Catalogue of Authors,* 1899.

* * *

The Southern Empire. With Other Papers. *Boston, 1892.*

MOTE, CARL HENRY: 1884–1946.

Carl Henry Mote, son of Oliver P. and Emma Alice Thomas Mote, was born in Randolph County, Ind., on June 25, 1884. He attended Indiana University for two years, graduated from De Pauw University in 1907, and spent two years, 1910-12, at the Indiana University Law School.

After engaging in school administrative work for two years, in 1909 he became city editor of the MUNCIE STAR and in 1910 a reporter for the INDIANAPOLIS STAR. From 1911 to 1913 he was editor of the INDIANAPOLIS SUN. In 1913 he was appointed to the state legislative bureau, leaving it in 1917 to become secretary of the public service commission. He was admitted to the Indiana bar in 1921 and began his practice as a utility attorney in Indianapolis.

In 1942 he testified before a federal grand jury in Washington that was investigating seditious activity. Mr. Mote had attacked both President Roosevelt and Wendell Willkie during the 1940 campaign.

In 1944 he was chairman and principal speaker of the

America First Party national convention. Elected president of the National Farmers Guild in 1944, he headed the faction which broke off in 1945 and became the United Farmers of America, after Mote was ousted from the guild presidency by the board of directors. He edited a monthly magazine, AMERICA PREFERRED, which was pro-isolationist, anti-New Deal, and anti-foreign.

Mr. Mote was twice married: first to Mary Hook in 1914, from whom he was divorced in 1932, then to Blanche Shaw on Apr. 2, 1936, from whom he was divorced in 1941. He died on Apr. 29, 1946.

Information from *Who's Who in America* and the *Indianapolis Times.*

* * *

Learning to Earn; a Plea and a Plan for Vocational Education (with John A. Lapp). *Indianapolis,* 1915.

Industrial Arbitration; a World-Wide Survey of Natural and Political Agencies for Social Justice and Industrial Peace. *Indianapolis,* 1916.

The New Deal Goose Step. *New York,* 1939.

Christmas Message. 1940 Model. *Indianapolis,* 1940.

"Revolution and the Triple A"; An Address . . . Before Corn Belt Liberty League, Claypool Hotel, Indianapolis, Oct. 3, 1940. n.p., 1940.

Christian Morality and Our "New Social Order." n.p., 1941.

G.O.P. "Fifth Column" Finds the Fleshpots; Autopsy on Antics and "Loyal Opposition" of Comrade Wendell L. Willkie. n.p., 1942.

MURRAY, CHARLES THEODORE: 1843–1924.

Charles Theodore Murray was born in Goshen, Ind., Mar. 30, 1843. His parents were Charles Lefferts and Ann Maria Spriggs Murray.

Murray served three years in the Union forces during the Civil War. He attended Indiana University as a member of the class of 1869 and received the LL.B. degree from Columbian (now George Washington) University in 1870. On May 25, 1871, he married Ada M. Nealy.

He established the SOUTH BEND HERALD in 1874 and took an active, and apparently ultra-partisan, part in politics; he was shot through the right lung during a political altercation over the Hayes-Tilden campaign, and his obituary appeared next morning in his own paper. Murray survived both the wound and possible embarrassment over his staff's editorial error, however, to become Washington correspondent for the ST. LOUIS GLOBE-DEMOCRAT, PITTSBURGH DISPATCH, PHILADELPHIA TIMES and NEW YORK HERALD and a writer

for MCCLURE'S MAGAZINE, the INDIANAPOLIS NEWS and other papers and periodicals. He was a founder of the Gridiron Club.

In his later years Murray resided in Wardensville, W. Va.

Information from *Who's Who in America.*

* * *

Sub-Rosa: a Novel. *New York,* 1880.

Summer Girls. 1885.

Autobiography of a Pair of Pistols.

The Cashier.

A Modern Gypsy. *New York,* 1897.

Mlle. Fouchette; or, the Monkey and the Tiger. *Philadelphia,* 1902.

MURRAY, LOIS LORINA ABBOTT (MRS. SAMUEL): 1826–?

The ancestors of the subject of this sketch left New England in 1807 in company with about thirty families and came west to establish a home in central Ohio. I. F. Abbott, one of the young emigrants, married a daughter of Samuel Everiett, who had bought for the colony the land where Granville, O., is now located. Lois Lorina Abbott was the first child of this marriage, being born Mar. 3, 1826.

One of her poems states she taught school when she was fifteen years old. When she was about twenty-one, her parents moved to Rochester, Ind., and after two years, in 1850, moved to Goshen, Ind.

She married Samuel Murray in 1851, and in 1860 the couple left Indiana to settle in Kansas. Hardships and affliction were their lot there, but with the aid of her deep religious faith Mrs. Murray survived her troubles.

In 1878, after death and marriages had taken her own family from home, she returned to Goshen, Ind., where her mother resided.

Information from Murray—*Incidents of Frontier Life.*

* * *

Incidents of Frontier Life. *Goshen, Ind.,* 1880.

N

NASH, WILLARD GLOVER: 1833–1893.

"Willard G. Nash was born in Maine in July, 1833, and died at Addison, Me., Oct. 11, 1893. He came with his father, Addison Nash, to Logansport in

1843 and was educated in the Logansport schools. On Nov. 17, 1855, he married Mary J. Aldrich of Logansport. They had six children. Mr. Nash was sheriff of Cass County from 1862 to 1866, County Auditor from 1866 to 1870 and editor of the LOGANSPORT PHAROS from 1871 to 1875. He was a fluent and caustic writer and . . . published *A Century of Gossip* which portrays the characters in a New England village of which a miserly parson is the main character."

From Powell—*History of Cass County,* 1913.

* * *

A Century of Gossip; or, the Real and the Seeming of New England Life. *Chicago,* 1876.

NATHAN, GEORGE JEAN: 1882–

George Jean Nathan, a plant rather more exotic than might have been expected to spring from the Indiana corn-lands, was a considerable force in guiding the renaissance of the American essay, of verse and of criticism during the first World War and in the Twenties.

H. L. Mencken and Nathan, first in the SMART SET, then in the AMERICAN MERCURY, set the pace and the style and pruned back the ebullience of young American literary hopefuls from 1914 to 1930. That was a period which saw the American taste desert the total allegiance which it had given to the novel during the two or three preceding decades, and this dissatisfaction was unquestionably for the good.

Nathan's production became only occasional after the end of the Twenties, but he had crowded into the first forty-two years of his life a career of sufficient importance, and marked by activity enough, to have served to memorialize half a dozen names.

Unlike the majority of western writers transferred to the metropolitan scene, Nathan gave no evidence of his midwestern beginnings. He divorced himself completely from the back-country and became highly sophisticated. In speaking of himself he is, in fact, a bit too detached, too elegantly above the world, for plausibility—for his writing, his criticism and his editing displayed a warmth certainly not capable of having sprung from such a source as Nathan makes himself appear to have been.

Nathan is best described by a contemporary, writing for *Living Authors*:

" 'What interests me most in life,' confesses George Jean Nathan, the American dramatic critic, 'is the surface of life: life's music and color, its charm and ease, its humor and its loveliness. The great problems of the world—social, political, economic and theological—do not concern me in the slightest . . . If all the Armenians were to be killed tomorrow and if half of Russia were to starve to death the day after, it would not matter to me in the least. What concerns me alone is myself and the interests of a few close friends.'

"His life has been called a comedy of manners. A bachelor by choice, he has lived for the past twenty years in a theatrically luxurious, if somewhat fusty, apartment on the top floor of a venerable apartment hotel on West Forty-fourth Street, New York. The apartment is noted for its 'divans, cushions, shaded lights, and various elegant devices for the holding, passing around, and consumption of alcoholic liquors.' He is a handsome, dapper man of medium height, with dark eyes widely set and a slightly smiling mouth. He eats well and smokes incessantly. Long ivory cigarette holders are among his favorite accessories. His wardrobe included thirty-eight overcoats at the last published inventory, ranging from 'heavy Russian fur to the flimsiest homespun . . . and one with an alpine hood attachment.'

"George Jean Nathan was born in Fort Wayne, Ind., on Feb. 14, 1882, but it seems doubtful whether he will ever look more than thirty-five. He received his A.B. degree in 1904 from Cornell University, where he edited one of the college papers, and spent the following year in Italy at the University of Bologna. On his return to the United States he worked on the editorial staff of the NEW YORK HERALD (1905-06); and from 1906 to 1908 he was dramatic critic and associate editor of the BOHEMIAN MAGAZINE and OUTING. In 1908 began his famous association with the SMART SET, of which he was dramatic critic until 1923 and co-editor with Mencken from 1914 to 1923. THE AMERICAN MERCURY was founded by Nathan and Mencken in 1924; Nathan was co-editor until 1925, and from 1925 to 1930 he was contributing editor. Although he has given up active editorial connection with ·the MERCURY, Nathan can hardly be said to be idling: he is dramatic editor of JUDGE (since 1922) and THE NEW FREEMAN (since 1930), consulting editor of ARTS AND DECORATION (since 1924), and editorial contributor to the LONDON DAILY EXPRESS and the LONDON SUNDAY CHRONICLE. He is the one living American dramatic critic with an international reputation. In prestige he is the successor of Huneker, at whose feet he sat in his early newspaper days in New York, when it was a great privilege to drink Pilsener with that prodigious conversationalist at the round table sanctum in Scheffel Hall off Union Square. Nathan likes to hark back to those days.

"No criticism can be crueler than Nathan's . . . when he wants to be cruel. He has no patience with bad plays. His exits from the theatre are watched with grave concern. If he gathers up his stick and high hat and strides up the aisle at the end of the first act, the producers weep; if he stays through the second act, they become animated with hope; if he remains till the final curtain—which is Nathan's great silent compliment—there is no limit to their exuberance. That is not to imply that Nathan himself is incapable of enthusiasm. 'He brings to the theatre,' writes Ernest Boyd, 'an endless delight and interest in all its manifestations, and he is as happy to praise the beautiful body of a Ziegfeld Follies girl as the first manuscript of a Eugene O'Neill, to applaud a W. C. Fields as a Dunsany, to do propaganda for native organizations like the Washington Square Players, the Neighborhood Playhouse, and the Provincetown Theatre, as for foreign dramatists as dissimilar as Lennox Robinson, Schnitzler, Sean O'Casey, Molnar, Shaw, and Sacha Guitry. And he will deride all these with equal gusto when pretentiousness causes them to deteriorate . . .'

"Nathan denies that he is an iconoclast or cynic (except regarding marriage, politics, and bad plays). He cites his early editorship with Mencken of the SMART SET as proof of his constructive attitude. This magazine was the first to recognize Eugene O'Neill and F. Scott Fitzgerald. Nathan also points to his espousal of the cause of Dreiser, 'the most important American author'; of Sinclair Lewis, 'the most significant'; and of Willa Cather, 'the best of our stylists.'

"Nathan's deliberately insolent attitudes and confessions might persuade us to regard him as a quite inhuman and unbearable person, 'but the truth is,' we are told, 'he is a highly entertaining and pleasant fellow, whose very hypochondria is not distressing, even when it takes the strange form of perpetually plugging his nostrils with pink cotton over which some medicinal incantation has been pronounced, or of unceasingly inhaling a tube of menthol—these being apparently his chief winter sports.'"

> From *Living Authors*, edited by Dilly Tante, published by the H. W. Wilson Company, 1932.

* * *

The Eternal Mystery. *New York,* 1913.
Europe After 8:15 (with H. L. Mencken and W. H. Wright). *New York,* 1914.

Another Book on the Theatre. *New York,* 1915.
Mr. George Jean Nathan Presents. *New York,* 1917.
Bottoms Up, an Application of the Slapstick to Satire. *New York,* 1917.
The Popular Theatre. *New York,* 1918.
A Book Without a Title. *New York,* 1918.
Comedians All. *New York,* 1919.
Heliogabalus, a Buffoonery in Three Acts (with H. L. Mencken). *New York,* 1920.
The American Credo; a Contribution Toward the Interpretation of the National Mind (with H. L. Mencken). *New York,* 1921.
The Theatre, the Drama, the Girls. *New York,* 1921.
The Critic and the Drama. *New York,* 1922.
The World in Falseface. *New York,* 1923.
Materia Critica. *New York,* 1924.
The Autobiography of an Attitude. *New York,* 1925.
The House of Satan. *New York,* 1926.
The New American Credo. *New York,* 1927.
Land of the Pilgrim's Pride. *New York,* 1927.
Art of the Night. *New York,* 1928.
Monks Are Monks; a Diagnostic Scherzo. *New York,* 1929.
Testament of a Critic. *New York,* 1931.
Friends of Mine. 1931.
Intimate Notebooks. *New York,* 1932.
Since Ibsen; a Statistical Historical Outline of the Popular Theatre Since 1900. *New York,* 1933.
Passing Judgments. *New York,* 1935.
The Morning After the Night Before.
The Theatre of the Moment; a Journalistic Commentary. *New York,* 1936.
The Avon Flows. *New York,* 1937.
The Morning After the First Night. *New York,* 1938.
Encyclopaedia of the Theatre. *New York,* 1940.
The Bachelor Life. *New York,* 1941.
The Entertainment of a Nation; or, Three-Sheets in the Wind. *New York,* 1942.
Beware of Parents; a Bachelor's Book for Children. *New York,* 1943.

NEEDHAM, WILLIAM P.: 1853–1899.

Born in Fountain City, Ind., on Dec. 11, 1853, William P. Needham attended the public schools of northern Wayne County until he was twelve years old. He then entered the office of the WINCHESTER (Ind.) JOURNAL to learn printing and eventually became the successful editor and publisher of the WINCHESTER PHANTASMAGORIAN. He was town clerk of Winchester for twenty years. Mr. Needham died in 1899.

Information from Parker and Heiney—*Poets and Poetry of Indiana.*

* * *

Phantasmagorian Philosophy and Other Things. *Indianapolis,* 1887.

The House of Graydon: a Novel. *Richmond, Ind.,* 1888.

NEFF, FLORA TRUEBLOOD BENNETT (MRS. J. N.): ?–

"Flora Trueblood was graduated from Kokomo high school in 1878. In 1895 she married Dr. J. N. Neff and moved with him to Logansport, Ind. In 1911 she published a book of poems . . . She was an active temperance worker."

From Powell—*History of Cass County,* 1913.

* * *

Along Life's Pathway: a Poem in Four Cantos with Recreations. *Logansport, Ind.,* 1911.

NEFF, THEODORE LEE: 1858–1936.

Theodore Lee Neff was born in Hartford City, Ind., in 1858. He attended De Pauw University, receiving the Ph.B. and A.M. degrees, and received the Ph.D. degree from the University of Chicago in 1896, where he served as a faculty member for several years. He died in Kansas City on Nov. 11, 1936, and was buried at Greencastle, Ind.

Information from the Indiana State Library.

* * *

La Satire des Femmes dans la Poesie Lyrique Française du Moyen Age. *Paris,* 1900.

NELSON, N. ELVIRA KING (MRS. GEORGE): ?–?

Elvira King, daughter of Robert F. and Eliza T. King, was born and reared in Boone County, Ind. Four years after the death of her father in 1878, the family moved to Mooresville, Ind. She married a Civil War veteran, George Nelson of Mooresville, and died while still a young woman. Her husband died in 1941.

Information from Clarence M. Marine, of Indianapolis.

* * *

The Garland (with Sarah King Marine). *Indianapolis,* 1883.

NESBIT, WILBUR DICK: 1871–1927.

Wilbur Dick Nesbit, son of John Harvey and Isabel Fichthorne Nesbit, was born in Xenia, O., on Sept. 16, 1871, and was educated in the public schools of Cedarville, O.

He became a printer and in 1889 located in Anderson, Ind., where he became editor of the ANDERSON TIMES. He subsequently moved to Muncie, Ind., then to Indianapolis and, while in the latter city, engaged in advertising work. His contributions also appeared in many issues of the INDIANAPOLIS JOURNAL. After a period in the East as a feature writer for the BALTIMORE AMERICAN, he went to Chicago as a member of the staff of the CHICAGO TRIBUNE—for which he conducted the column "A Line o' Type or Two" for many years—and later the CHICAGO EVENING POST. Before his death, on Aug. 20, 1927, he was vice-president and director of the copy staff of the William H. Rankin advertising agency of Chicago.

Mr. Nesbit was nationally known as a toastmaster and after-dinner speaker and was in great demand as such. He wrote, in addition to his published books, the book of "The Girl of My Dreams," a successful musical comedy, and other theatrical features. He sometimes worked in collaboration with C. A. Briggs, well-known cartoonist.

In 1899 he married Mary Lou Jenkins, daughter of Dr. J. H. Jenkins of Shelbyville.

Information from Dunn—*Indiana and Indianans, Who Was Who in America;* and the INDIANAPOLIS STAR, Aug. 21, 1927.

* * *

Little Henry's Slate. *Evanston,* 1903.

The Trail to Boyland and Other Poems. *Indianapolis,* 1904.

An Alphabet of History. *San Francisco,* 1905.

The Gentleman Ragman. *New York,* 1906.

A Book of Poems. *Chicago,* 1906.

The Land of Make-Believe and Other Christmas Poems. *New York,* 1907.

Baby: a Little Book of Big Thoughts About Little Ones. *Chicago,* 1910.

A Friend or Two. *Chicago* [1910].

Masklets. *Chicago,* n.d.

If the Heart Be Young. *Chicago,* 1911.

My Company of Friends. *Chicago,* 1911.

Old, Old Wish Christmas Book. *Chicago,* 1911.

Who's Hoosier. *Indianapolis,* 1912. 2 vols.

Always Christmas. *Chicago,* 1912.

Friend O' Mine. *Chicago,* 1912.

Jolly Kid Book. *Chicago,* 1912.

Your Best Friend. *Chicago,* 1912.

God Bless You. *Chicago,* 1913.

Oh Skin-Nay! The Days of Real Sport, by Briggs; Verses by W. D. Nesbit. *Chicago,* 1913.

Our Good Old World. *Chicago,* 1913.

To All Good Fellows Like You. *Chicago,* 1913.

Value of a Smile. *Chicago,* 1913.

All to Myself. *Chicago,* n.d.

Sayin' Goodbye. *Chicago,* n.d.

When a Feller Needs a Friend; Cartoons by C. A. Briggs. *Chicago,* 1914.

I Sat in Lodge with You. *Chicago,* 1916.

First Principles of Advertising. *New York,* 1922.

In Tumbledown Town. *Chicago,* 1926. (9th ed.)

The Paths of Long Ago; with a Foreword by George Ade. *Chicago,* 1926.

After-Dinner Speeches and How to Make Them. *Chicago,* 1927.

Sermons in Song; Poems of Homely Philosophy. *Chicago,* 1929.

As Children Do; Poems of Childhood. *Chicago,* 1929.

Just Because of You. *Chicago,* n.d.

Yesterdays with You. *Chicago,* n.d.

NEW, CATHERINE McLAEN: 1870–

Catherine McLaen New was born in Toronto, Ont., Canada, in 1870. In 1891 she married Harry Stewart New of Indianapolis, postmaster-general, 1923-29, from whom she was later divorced. She lived in Indianapolis for a number of years.

Information from the Indianapolis Public Library.

* * *

A Woman Reigns. *Indianapolis,* 1896.

NICHOLAS, ANNA: 1849–1929.

Anna Nicholas, daughter of Dr. John and Rachel Gardiner Nicholas, was born in 1849 in Meadville, Pa., where she attended public and private schools. For fifty-three years she was on the staff of the INDIANAPOLIS STAR and its predecessor, the JOURNAL, as an editorial writer, book reviewer, and contributor of miscellaneous writings. She also contributed to other newspapers and periodicals. She died Jan. 29, 1929.

Information from *Who's Who in America* and the Indianapolis Public Library.

* * *

An Idyl of the Wabash, and Other Stories. *Indianapolis,* 1898.

The Making of Thomas Barton. *Indianapolis,* 1913.

A History of Crown Hill. *Indianapolis,* 1926.

The Story of Crown Hill. *Indianapolis,* 1928.

NICHOLS, REBECCA REED (MRS. WILLARD): 1819–1903.

Rebecca Reed, daughter of Dr. E. B. Reed, was born in New Jersey in 1819, resided in Philadelphia for a time and came west with her father when quite young, spending some time in Louisville before coming to Indiana. In 1838 she married Willard Nichols, a printer who was interested in literature.

For more than twenty-five years she was a resident of Indianapolis. She contributed verse to newspapers and periodicals, her most productive period being between 1840 and 1855.

Information from Parker and Heiney—*Poets and Poetry of Indiana.*

* * *

Bernice: or, the Curse of Minna, and Other Poems. *Cincinnati,* 1844.

Songs of the Heart and the Hearthstone. *Philadelphia,* 1851.

NICHOLSON, MEREDITH: 1866–1947.

Meredith Nicholson was born in Crawfordsville, Ind., on Dec. 9, 1866, the son of Edward Willis and Emily Meredith Nicholson. The father was born in Kentucky, of a long line extending back to colonial days. Coming to Montgomery County, Ind., as a young man, Edward Nicholson soon became one of the substantial farmers of that county, a member of the Montgomery Guards, a Zouave company which became in the Civil War the nucleus of the Eleventh Indiana Infantry, commanded by Gen. Lew Wallace. At the end of three months' service Nicholson enlisted in the artillery, becoming captain of the Twenty-second Indiana Battery. He continued with his command until the close of the war, having been with Sherman on the march to the sea and having sighted and fired the first gun at the Battle of Shiloh.

The mother of Meredith Nicholson was born at Centerville, Ind., the daughter of an early settler there, Samuel Caldwell Meredith, one of the pioneer editors and publishers of that district. As a young woman during the Civil War, she gave effective services as a nurse in the South. Shortly after the close of the war, she and Capt. Nicholson were married and took up their residence in Crawfordsville, where their son (and his younger sister) were born. For a time during the war Capt. Nicholson had been assigned to detail duty in Indianapolis in the drilling of new batteries, so, in 1872, when young Meredith was about five years old, the family moved to the capital city, where they continued to reside until 1888, when Capt. Nicholson moved to Washington, D. C. His son, however, remained in Indianapolis, where he lived afterward, with the exception of the years spent in South and Central America with the State Department (1932-1942) and three years in Denver, Colo., in the late Nineties.

The background of the youthful Nicholson was thus set: the intense interest in the Civil War, due to the services and experiences of both of his parents, and the deep feeling for all that is characteristic of Hoosierdom and its inhabitants, their "folksy" qualities, sociable and companionable, the feeling for newspaper work, editorial and reportorial, which came down from his maternal grandfather, Samuel Meredith, and an appreciation of and respect for the pioneer spirit which went into the making of his native state of Indiana.

Of formal education he had no more than nine years in the Indianapolis public schools, leaving, when about fifteen, during his first year in high school. Then came a succession of jobs, always leading him nearer and nearer to his chosen work of writing. A brief spell as a clerk in a drug store and work in a printer's shop, where he learned the rudiments of the printer's trade plus a smattering of shorthand, a position as court reporter, then employment by a law firm followed. At the age of nineteen he commenced the study of law in the office of Dye and Fishback. Later he continued his studies under one of Indianapolis's outstanding lawyers of that day, William Wallace, brother of Gen. Lew Wallace.

It was during his days as a law student that Meredith Nicholson began to manifest his natural taste, using what spare time he could muster from his law books to begin his first serious efforts at writing. He had the usual success of the talented amateur: the local newspapers printed his efforts, but without pay. Before long, however, he became identified with newspaper work in Indianapolis. After a year on the INDIANAPOLIS SENTINEL, in 1884, he became a valued and versatile member of the editorial staff of the INDIANAPOLIS NEWS, where he remained from 1885 to 1897. After a year in stock brokerage, a three-year residence in Denver, Colo., followed, during which period he was auditor and treasurer of a coal-mining corporation.

Returning to Indianapolis at the turn of the century,

he began to devote his entire time to literary work. Outside of his various newspaper writings during the 1890's, only one published volume stood to his credit —a book of poems entitled *Short Flights*, published in 1891. But from 1900 on his published writings were issued with increasing frequency. In that year he published *The Hoosiers*, a volume of brief historical essays, about which he once remarked that it was his personal favorite of all of his writings and the one by which he expected to be longest remembered. In particular, his essay on the variously attributed origins of the term Hoosier remains the best account of the beginning of that much-disputed word.

Progress had been slow up to the point where Nicholson received his first real pay for any of his writings, the earliest being the very modest sum—even for those days—of three dollars given him by an Eastern newspaper for a poem. A bit later he won a prize of ten dollars offered by a Chicago newspaper for a short story. The story was "The Tale of a Postage Stamp." These small returns were a far cry from the returns of a quarter of a century later when his books numbered among the best sellers of their day. With *The Main Chance* and *Zelda Dameron*, he became one of the best known of American writers, even abroad, where his *House of a Thousand Candles* was published in Paris in a French translation and drew the enthusiastic approval of French critics. His success, as shown by the accompanying bibliography, was consistent up to the time that he retired as a writer in the 1930's, but it was as an essayist rather than as a novelist that he preferred to be known—perhaps because at heart he was an editorialist. With a profound belief in democracy, he spoke for self-government and tolerance: because he believed in people he was fundamentally an optimist.

Always in his writing—especially in his essays—Nicholson remained a Hoosier, a midlander, varying from the majority viewpoint only in his political attachment, and even in that he remained, although a Democrat, a Jeffersonian Democrat, which is an understandable faith, even to the most dyed-in-the-wool midwestern Republicans.

He kept up a constant and lively interest in politics. President Wilson offered him the post of minister to Portugal in 1913 but he refused. Later he served as envoy extraordinary and minister plenipotentiary from the U. S. to Paraguay (1933-34), Venezuela (1935-38), and Nicaragua (1938-41), when he retired to private life in Indianapolis. In his last years he contributed many articles—mainly essays and editorials on his favorite subject, the Hoosier scene with its people, its custom, its way of life—to the Indianapolis papers.

His lack of formal education after the first year of high school was more than compensated for by his own efforts. Filled with sincere regret that he had rejected the advice of his mother and had left school, he undertook, during his newspaper days, to make up for this deficiency by self-instruction in Latin and Greek as well as French and Italian, a knowledge of languages being considered in the 1880's as the mark of an educated man. Newspaper training showed in his handwriting, and even his personal notes and letters displayed the neat, small but legible handwriting, without indentation for paragraphs, which are merely indicated by the printer's sign, and they possess the same delightful style that endeared him to all reading Americans. His self-acquired knowledge of foreign languages contributed much to his writings in his mother tongue.

Both his literary attainments and his contributions to statesmanship were recognized with honorary degrees: from Wabash College, Butler University and Indiana University. He was also an honorary member of Phi Beta Kappa and a member of the National Institute of Arts and Letters.

On June 16, 1896, he married Eugenie Kountze, by whom he had three children, Elizabeth (Mrs. Austin H. Brown), Meredith, Jr., and Charles Lionel. Her death occurred in 1931, and he married Mrs. Dorothy Wolfe Lannon in 1933. They were divorced ten years later.

After his return from Nicaragua Mr. Nicholson resumed residence in Indianapolis, heart of the Hoosierland which he had done so much to publicize. The dean of Indiana litterateurs, he died in his eighty-first year on Dec. 22, 1947—still as ardent a Hoosier as might be found.

> Information from the children of Meredith Nicholson.

* * *

Short Flights. *Indianapolis, 1891.*
The Hoosiers. *New York, 1900.*
The Main Chance. *Indianapolis, 1903.*
Zelda Dameron. *Indianapolis, 1904.*
The House of a Thousand Candles. *Indianapolis, 1905.*
Poems. *Indianapolis, 1906.*
The Port of Missing Men. *Indianapolis, 1907.*
Rosalind at Red Gate. *Indianapolis, 1907.*
The Little Brown Jug at Kildare. *Indianapolis, 1908.*
The Lords of High Decision. *Garden City, N. Y., 1909.*
The Siege of the Seven Suitors. *Boston, 1910.*
A Hoosier Chronicle. *Boston, 1912.*

The Provincial American and Other Papers. *Boston, 1912.*
Otherwise Phyllis. *Boston, 1913.*
The Poet. *Boston, 1914.*
The Proof of the Pudding. *Boston, 1916.*
The Madness of May. *New York, 1917.*
A Reversible Santa Claus. *Boston, 1917.*
The Valley of Democracy. *New York, 1918.*
Lady Larkspur. *New York, 1919.*
Blacksheep! Blacksheep! *New York, 1920.*
The Man in the Street; Papers on American Topics. *New York, 1921.*
Honor Bright (with Kenyon Nicholson). *New York, 1921.*
Best Laid Schemes. *New York, 1922.*
Broken Barriers. *New York, 1922.*
The Hope of Happiness. *New York, 1923.*
And They Lived Happily Ever After. *New York, 1925.*
The Cavalier of Tennessee. *Indianapolis, 1928.*
Tell Me Your Troubles. (Play by Kenyon Nicholson, based on a short story of the same name by Meredith Nicholson.) *New York, 1928.*
Old Familiar Faces. *Indianapolis, 1929.*

NICHOLSON, WATSON: 1866–

Watson Nicholson, son of Abraham and Maria Davis Nicholson, was born in Pendleton, Ind., on Sept. 23, 1866. He was a student for three years at Indiana University and graduated from Stanford University in 1892, receiving the A.M. degree from Harvard in 1895 and the Ph.D. from Yale in 1903. From 1884 to 1887 he was a teacher in the schools of Indiana, and from 1892 to 1901—with the exception of two years spent at Harvard—he taught in California. He married Florence Emily Beaver in 1897.

He engaged in university extension teaching from 1903 until 1905, when he became an instructor in English literature in the Sheffield Scientific School at Yale. From 1910 to 1915 he was employed by the British Museum.

> Information from *Who's Who in America.*

* * *

A Syllabus of Six Lectures on American Literature, with Bibliography. *Philadelphia, 1903.*
The Struggle for a Free Stage in London. *Boston, 1906.*
The Historical Sources of DeFoe's "Journal of the Plague Year." *Boston, 1919.*
Anthony Aston, Stroller and Adventurer; to Which Is Appended Aston's Brief Supplement to Colley Cibber's Lives; and a Sketch of the Life of Anthony Aston, Written by Himself. *South Haven, Mich., 1920.*

NOBLE, HARRIETT: 1851–?

Born in Centerville, Ind., in 1851, Harriett Noble is believed to have been a resident of Indiana throughout most of her life.

> Information from the Emmeline Fairbanks Memorial Library, Terre Haute, Ind., and from book-dealers' catalogs.

* * *

Literary Art. *Terre Haute, Ind.,* 1897.

NOLL, JOHN FRANCIS: 1875–

John Francis Noll, son of John G. and Anna Ford Noll, was born in Fort Wayne, Ind., on Jan. 25, 1875. He attended St. Lawrence College and graduated from Mt. St. Mary's Seminary in Cincinnati in 1898, receiving the LL.D. degree from Notre Dame in 1917.

In 1898 he was ordained a priest in the Roman Catholic Church and occupied pulpits in various Indiana towns until 1925, when he was consecrated Bishop of Fort Wayne. He was highly successful in church and institutional building and fund raising and in 1904 founded the periodical, OUR SUNDAY VISITOR.

> Information from *Who's Who in America.*

* * *

Freundes-Worte von Deinem Seelsorger. (Kind Words from Your Pastor.) *St. Louis,* 1904.
For Our Non-Catholic Friends. *New York,* 1912.
Father Smith Instructs Jackson. *Huntington, Ind.*
The Fairest Argument. 1914.
Vest Pocket Book of Catholic Facts. *Huntington, Ind.,* 1927.
It Is Happening Here. 1936.
Civilization's Builder and Protector. *Huntington, Ind.*
The Decline of Nations; Its Causes and Cure. *Huntington, Ind.,* 1940.
Our National Enemy Number One; Education without Religion. *Huntington, Ind.,* 1942.
Religion and Life. *Huntington, Ind.,* 1943.
Christ Losing His World.
Books of Meditation.
The A.B.C.'s of Religion.

NORRIS, ALLEN ANSON: ?–

Little is known of Allen Anson Norris except that he received the A.B. degree from Indiana University in 1902 and was serving as superintendent of the Syracuse, Ind., schools in 1904.

Since his one book was published in Bloomington in 1898, either before he began college work or during an interim in study, it may be assumed that he was a resident of the state for a considerable period of time.

> Information from *Indiana University, 1820-1904.*

* * *

Studies in the Life of St. Paul (with Charles O. Davis). *Bloomington, Ind.,* 1898.

NOWLAND, JOHN HENRY BYRNE: 1813–1899.

Born in Frankfort, Ky., in 1813, John H. B. Nowland, son of Matthias R. Nowland, came with his family to Indianapolis when he was seven years old. The site of what was to become Indianapolis had just been chosen for the new state capital, and the Nowland family first lived in a log cabin which had not been completed as to chimney, windows, or door, so, according to John H. B. Nowland, the occupants made their exits and entrances through a space made by removing one of the logs. When town lots were auctioned off in 1821, the family purchased lots and built a cabin in which they lived for forty-five years.

In 1840 John Nowland married Amelia T. Smith, in the first church wedding to take place in the community. Mr. Nowland evinced a deep interest in local history and had a wealth of first-hand information on such matters. He died Aug. 1, 1899.

> Information from the INDIANAPOLIS STAR, Nov. 9, 1930, and the Indianapolis Public Library.

* * *

Early Reminiscences of Indianapolis, with Short Biographical Sketches of Its Early Citizens, and a Few of the Prominent Business Men of the Present Day. *Indianapolis,* 1870.
Sketches of Prominent Citizens of 1876, with a Few of the Pioneers of the City and County Who Have Passed Away. *Indianapolis,* 1877.
Early Reminiscences of Indianapolis, 1820-'76. *Indianapolis,* 1879.

O

OAKEY, CHARLES COCHRAN: 1845–1908.

Charles Cochran Oakey was born in Knox County, Ill., in 1845. Most of his life was spent as a newspaper writer in Terre Haute. He died on Mar. 17, 1908.

> Information from the Emmeline Fairbanks Memorial Library, Terre Haute, Ind.

* * *

Greater Terre Haute and Vigo County. *Chicago, 1908.* 2 vols.

ODELL, FRANK IGLEHART: 1886–

Born at Evansville, Ind., on July 22, 1886, Frank Iglehart Odell graduated from Evansville High School in 1905 and attended Northwestern University and the University of Illinois. In 1914 he married Helen Heilman of Evansville.

He served as a reporter and copy-reader on the EVANSVILLE COURIER, the EVANSVILLE PRESS and the EVANSVILLE JOURNAL NEWS; he was a reporter for the City Press Association of Chicago, the CHICAGO TRIBUNE, and the INDIANAPOLIS STAR; and from 1907 to 1912 he was telegraph editor and city editor of the INDIANAPOLIS SUN. From 1912 to 1946 Mr. Odell was a commercial fruit grower and served for a time as president of the Indiana Horticultural Society and the Indiana Fruit-Growers Association.

Information from the Evansville Public Library.

* * *

Larry Burke, Freshman. *Boston,* 1910.
Larry Burke, Sophomore. *Boston,* 1911.

O'DONNELL, CHARLES LEO: 1884–1934.

Charles Leo O'Donnell, son of Neil and Mary O'Donnell, was born in Greenfield, Ind., the birthplace of another Indiana poet, James Whitcomb Riley, on Nov. 15, 1884. Following his graduation from the University of Notre Dame in 1906, he took graduate work at Holy Cross College, Harvard, and the Catholic University of America, receiving his Ph.D. from the last-named institution in 1910. In the same year he was ordained to the Congregation of the Holy Cross and became professor of English literature at Notre Dame. From 1928 until his death in 1934 he was president of the university. The Rev. Fr. O'Donnell was named provincial of his congregation in the U. S. in 1920 and in 1926 was made assistant superior general. During the first World War he served as a chaplain in the American Expeditionary Forces.

Information from the University of Notre Dame Library.

* * *

Francis Thompson: a Critical Essay. *Notre Dame, Ind.,* 1906.
A Study of the Prose Writings of Francis Thompson. 1913.

Ode: for Indiana Day, Panama-Pacific International Exposition. n.p., 1915.
The Dead Musician and Other Poems. *New York,* 1916.
Cloister and Other Poems. *New York,* 1922.
A Rime of the Rood and Other Poems. *New York,* 1928.
Collected Poems. (Compiled and edited by Charles M. Carey.) *Notre Dame, Ind.,* 1942.

OGG, FREDERIC AUSTIN: 1878–

Frederic Austin Ogg, son of William R. and Sarah S. Ogg, was born in Solsberry, Ind., on Feb. 8, 1878, and graduated from De Pauw University in 1899. He received the A.M. degree from Indiana University in 1900, from Harvard in 1904, and the Ph.D. from Harvard in 1908. He married Emma Virginia Perry on Sept. 9, 1903.

After teaching history for two years at Indianapolis Manual Training High School and for one year at Indiana University, he went to Harvard in 1903 as a fellow and assistant in history. From 1905 to 1914 he was in the history department at Simmons College, and after 1914 he served on the faculty of the University of Wisconsin, as professor of political science and, after 1925, as chairman of the graduate division of social studies.

He served as associate editor and later as managing editor of the AMERICAN POLITICAL SCIENCE REVIEW and contributed numerous articles to current periodicals.

Information from *Who's Who in America* and De Pauw University's *Alumnal Record, 1920.*

* * *

The Opening of the Mississippi—a Struggle for Supremacy in the American Interior. *New York,* 1904.
Social Progress in Contemporary Europe. *New York,* 1912.
The Governments of Europe. *New York,* 1913.
Daniel Webster. *Philadelphia,* 1914.
Economic Development of Modern Europe. *New York,* 1917.
National Governments and the World War (with Charles A. Beard). *New York,* 1917.
National Progress, 1907-17. *New York,* 1918.
The Old Northwest; a Chronicle of the Ohio Valley and Beyond. *New Haven, Conn.,* 1919.
The Reign of Andrew Jackson; a Chronicle of the Frontier in Politics. *New Haven, Conn.,* 1919.
Introduction to American Government (with P. O. Ray). *New York,* 1922.
Builders of the Republic. *New Haven, Conn.,* 1927.
Research in the Humanistic and Social Sciences. *New York,* 1928.

English Government and Politics. *New York, 1929.*

Essentials of American Government (with P. O. Ray). *New York, 1932.*

European Governments and Politics. *New York, 1934.*

Rise of Dictatorship in France. *New York, 1941.*

OLCOTT, CHARLES SUMNER: 1864–1935.

Charles Sumner Olcott, son of John Milton and Miriam J. Brown Olcott, was born in Terre Haute, Ind., on Feb. 20, 1864, and graduated from De Pauw University in 1883, receiving the A.M. degree in 1886. He married Allie M. Gage in 1886.

From 1891 to 1933 he acted as general manager of the subscription department of Houghton Mifflin Publishing Company. He was also known as a lecturer on literary subjects.

He died on May 3, 1935.

> Information from *Who Was Who in America* and De Pauw University's *Alumnal Record, 1920.*

* * *

George Eliot—Scenes and People in Her Novels. *New York, 1910.*

The Country of Sir Walter Scott. *Boston, 1913.*

The Lure of the Camera. *Boston, 1914.*

The Life of William McKinley. *Boston, 1916.* 2 vols.

Literary Landmarks of New England.

At the Home of Rafael Sabatini. *Boston, 1927.*

O'NEAL, JAMES: 1875–

James O'Neal, son of John and Clara Miller O'Neal, was born in Indianapolis on Mar. 13, 1875, and was educated in the public schools.

In 1900 he became active in organizing the Socialist Party. He lectured in the U. S. and Canada on socialism, was assistant to the national secretary of the Socialist Party for two years, acted as associate editor of THE WORKER (1906-08), and was state secretary of the party for Indiana (1911-13) and Massachusetts (after 1915).

He married Ella Oswald of Arlington, N. J., on Apr. 24, 1915.

> Information from *Who's Who in America.*

* * *

The Workers in American History. *Terre Haute, Ind., 1910.*

Sabotage; or, Socialism vs. Syndicalism, a Critical Study of Theories and Methods. *St. Louis, 1913.*

Labor and the Next War. *Chicago, 1923.*

History of the Amalgamated Ladies' Garment Cutters' Union, Local 10, Affiliated with the International Ladies Garment Workers' Union. *New York, 1927.*

American Communism: a Critical Analysis of Its Origin, Development and Programs. *New York, 1927.*

Militant Socialism. *St. Louis.*

Labor in England and America. *Chicago,* n.d.

OSBORN, CHARLES: 1775–1850.

"Charles Osborn (Aug. 21, 1775-Dec. 29, 1850), abolitionist . . . the son of David and Margaret (Stout) Osborn, was born in Guilford County, N. C. About 1794 he removed to Knox County, Tenn., where he became a Quaker preacher. He lived in Jefferson County, Tenn., Mount Pleasant, O., and from 1819 to 1842 in Wayne County, Ind., excepting the years from 1827 to 1830 that he spent in Warren and Clinton counties, O. In 1842 he removed to Cass County, Mich., and in 1848 to Porter County, Ind., where he died. On Jan. 11, 1798, he married Sarah Newman, who died on Aug. 10, 1812, leaving seven children, and on Sept. 26, 1813, he married Hannah Swain, who bore him nine children. . . .

"In December 1814, at the house of his father-in-law, Elihu Swain, he began his career as an anti-slavery leader by laying the foundations for the Tennessee Manumission Society, whose organization he did not, however, complete until the next February at Lostcreek Meeting House. In 1816 he founded similar societies in Guilford County, N. C. While at Mount Pleasant, O., he published the PHILANTHROPIST, from Aug. 29, 1817, to Oct. 8, 1818, a paper partially devoted to anti-slavery agitation. It has been asserted that he himself and, through him, the manumission societies and PHILANTHROPIST were the earliest advocates of immediate emancipation. This assertion cannot be substantiated. The societies definitely advocated gradual emancipation . . . Following Quaker tradition he long opposed the use of products of slave labor, considering them stolen goods because slaves' labor was stolen by their masters. His exhortations resulted in the formation on Jan. 22, 1842, of the Free Produce Association of Wayne County, Ind., and the establishment of a propagandist newspaper, the FREE LABOR ADVOCATE AND ANTI-SLAVERY CHRONICLE. When the conservatives, who, only mildly abolitionist, believed in confining anti-slavery activity to their own religious organizations, gained control over the Indiana Yearly Meeting, which before 1842 was dominated by the active abolitionist radicals, they removed him and others from the Meeting for Sufferings, a governing committee of the Church, on which he had served for years. This was a severe and unexpected blow to him. Bitterly lamenting the conservatives' position, he participated prominently in the session of 2,000 radicals who formed the Indiana Yearly Meeting of Anti-Slavery Friends in February, 1843. He continued his interest in the later activities of the seceders and died condemning the Fugitive-slave Law. After his death, in 1854 the Church published *The Journal of That Faithful Servant of Christ, Charles Osborn.*

> Condensed from R. A. K., *Dictionary of American Biography*, Vol. XIV.

* * *

A Testimony Concerning the Separation Which Occurred in the Indiana Yearly Meeting of Friends, in the Winter of 1842 and '43; Together with Sundry Remarks and Observations, Particularly on the Subjects of War, Slavery, and Colonization. *Centerville,* 1849.

Journal of That Faithful Servant of Christ, Charles Osborn, Containing an Account of Many of His Travels and Labors in the Work of the Ministry, and His Trials and Exercises in the Service of the Lord, and in Defense of the Truth, as It Is in Jesus. *Cincinnati,* 1854.

OSBORN, CHASE SALMON: 1860–

Chase Salmon Osborn, son of George A. and Margaret Fannon Osborn, was born in Huntington County, Ind., on Jan. 22, 1860. His parents were both physicians.

Following his graduation from Purdue University in 1880, Osborn started in newspaper work on the LAFAYETTE (Ind.) HOME JOURNAL and continued that career in Chicago, Wisconsin, and Michigan. He married Lillian G. Jones on May 7, 1881.

Mr. Osborn finally settled in Michigan, where he graduated from the Detroit College of Medicine in 1909 and where he played a prominent part in state affairs, holding various offices and, in 1911-12, serving as governor of the state. Oct. 4, 1939, was proclaimed Chase S. Osborn Day by the governor of Michigan in honor of this newspaperman, author, world traveler, orator, and statesman.

> Information from *Who's Who in America* and the INDIANAPOLIS STAR, Feb. 9, 1941.

* * *

The Andean Land. *Chicago,* 1909. 2 vols.

The Iron Hunter. *New York,* 1919.

The Law of Divine Concord. 1921.

Madagascar, the Land of the Man-Eating Tree. *New York,* 1924.

Short History of Michigan. 1926.

The Earth Upsets. *Baltimore,* 1927.

Following the Ancient Gold Trail of Hiram of Tyre and Solomon. 1932.

Northwoods Sketches. 1934.

The Conquest of a Continent (with Stella Brunt Osborn). [*Lancaster, Pa.*] 1939.

Schoolcraft—Longfellow—Hiawatha (with Stella Brunt Osborn). *Lancaster, Pa.,* 1942.

Hiawatha with Its Original Indian Legends (with Stella Brunt Osborn). *Lancaster, Pa.,* 1944.

Errors in Official U. S. Area Figures (with Stella Brunt Osborn). *Lancaster, Pa.,* 1945.

OVERMAN, NATHAN R.: 1827–1883.

Born in Randolph County, Ind., on April 11, 1827, Nathan R. Overman had few opportunities for formal education but overcame this handicap by study at home. At eighteen years of age he began teaching.

In 1849, while engaged with his father in a brick-making business, he began the study of law and for the next eleven years he alternated teaching, farming, brick-making, and the study of his chosen profession. He married Mary J. Cox on May 27, 1854. In 1861 he began the practice of law in Tipton, Ind., and in 1878 he was elected judge of the Thirty-sixth Judicial Circuit.

He died in 1883.

> Information from *Representative Men of Indiana*, Vol. II.

* * *

Pre-Historic and Indian History of Howard and Tipton Counties, Indiana. n.p., 1883.

OWEN, DAVID DALE: 1807–1860.

David Dale Owen, third son of Robert [see, also, sketches of Richard and Robert Dale Owen] and Ann Caroline Dale Owen and brother of Robert Dale and Richard Owen, was born near New Lanark, Scotland, on June 24, 1807. He was educated by private tutors and at Lanark Academy, and then, like his brothers, went to Emanuel von Fellenberg's school in Hofwyl, Switzerland.

In 1827 he accompanied his brother Richard to the U. S. and to Indiana, where his father had started his socialistic experiment at New Harmony. It had already failed, insofar as his father's plan was concerned, and he subsequently returned to Europe and spent two years studying geology and chemistry. He also studied drawing and painting—later putting this talent to use in illustrating his geological surveys.

In 1832 he returned to the U. S., entered Ohio Medical College, and in 1836 received the M.D. degree from that institution. He became state geologist for Indiana in 1837, U. S. geologist in 1847, and state geologist for Kentucky in 1854. In 1857 he also accepted an appointment as state geologist for Arkansas, but he died before he had completed his work in this connection.

In addition to the surveys he made for the federal and various state governments, he also conducted examinations for private individuals and corporations. Before he died he was regarded as the pre-eminent geologist in America. In his large private museum and laboratory at his home in New Harmony he had one of the most complete geological and natural history collections in the country at that time. After his death this collection was purchased by the state of Indiana for Indiana University.

On March 23, 1837, David Dale Owen married Caroline C. Neef, daughter of Joseph Neef—one of the Pestalozzian teachers brought to the New Harmony Community by William Maclure. David Dale Owen died at New Harmony on Nov. 13, 1860. Most of Owen's works, being state or federal government publications, are not listed here.

> Information from *Representative Men of Indiana*, Vol. I, and the *Dictionary of American Biography*, Vol. XIV.

* * *

Report of a Geological Reconnaissance in 1837. *Indianapolis, 1839.*

Geological Report on the Marble Hill Quarry. *Louisville, 1853.*

Report of a Geological Reconnaissance of Indiana Made During the Years 1859 and 1860 Under the Direction of the Late D. D. Owen. (Completed and published by Richard Owen.) *Indianapolis, 1862.*

OWEN, RICHARD: 1810–1890.

Richard Owen, youngest son of the Nineteenth century reformer Robert Owen [see, also, sketches of David Dale and Robert Dale Owen] and his wife, Caroline Dale Owen, was born near New Lanark, Scotland, on Jan. 6, 1810.

At the time of Richard's birth his father was at the peak of his career as a cotton processor employing a humane and enlightened labor policy to the profit of himself, his partners and his employees. The family fortune, later to be wrecked by dreams of world reform, was being made, and to be a son of Robert Owen was to have access to all that was new and hopeful in education.

Robert Owen was an avowed deist, while his wife, Caroline, was an uncompromising Presbyterian: Richard and the other children listened to the arguments of both sides. Their education began at home, at the hands of their mother and of the tutors she selected, and continued in the model school which their father had organized in New Lanark for the children of his employees. Like his brothers, Richard was eventually enrolled in Emanuel von Fellenberg's Pestalozzian school at Hofwyl, Switzerland, but unlike his elder brother, Robert Dale, he continued in more conventional work at the Andersonian Institute in Glasgow. His chief interest was in science.

Robert Owen's dreaming of social reform rendered his partners sufficiently hostile to make his withdrawal from the mills advisable. This state of affairs coincided with Richard Flower's opportune arrival from the U. S. with a commission to sell George Rapp's religio-communistic Harmony Community on the Wabash, and the Owens, full of plans for a modern Utopia, purchased the village and land and came to America.

The history of the difficulties which beset Robert Owen's New Harmony community for the few brief months of its survival is too complicated to be reported here. It should be noted, however, that Richard seems to have taken no very active part in its activities. He taught in the school for a while, went about the country on geological collecting trips, and cut an attractive figure at the community dances. That, it appears, was about the total of his participation.

With the dissolution of the community as such Richard Owens farmed for a while in Pennsylvania, spent three years in Cincinnati, where he employed his Glasgow chemical training in a brewery, and returned to New Harmony about 1840, to farm the land which had been his share of the settlement of his father's American property. In 1837 he had married Anna Eliza Neef.

Owen enlisted in the 16th U. S. Infantry for the Mexican War, was commissioned captain and served until August, 1848, most of the time in the service of supply.

Following the war he assisted his brother, David Dale, in the geological survey of Wisconsin, Iowa, Minnesota, and part of Nebraska Territory, joined the faculty of the Western Military Institute at Drennen Springs, Ky., and remained there for nine years. The institute was eventually moved to Nashville, Tenn., and Owen occupied his spare time—he was teaching natural sciences, French, German, Spanish, military science and fencing—by studying medicine at Nashville University, receiving the M.D. degree in 1858.

Shortly before the outbreak of the Civil War he had returned to Indiana and had undertaken a geological survey of the state. When hostilities began he was commissioned lieutenant-colonel of the 15th Indiana Volunteers. His most distinguished service was as commandant in charge of Confederate prisoners at Camp Morton, Indianapolis, where he inaugurated a humanitarian policy which brought considerable criticism from the North but under which he was most popular with his prisoners. This policy became, moreover, more or less the model for prisoner-of-war regulation in this and other civilized countries until the second World War.

Col. Owen's regiment was sent to the front in May, 1862. He and his two sons were captured at Mumfordville, Ky., but, due to his popularity with the prisoners he had entertained at Indianapolis and his acquaintance with former students from the Western Military Institute in the Confederate ranks, they received gracious treatment.

Richard Owen joined the faculty of Indiana University on Jan. 1, 1864, as an instructor in geology, chemistry and natural philosophy. There he remained, as a distinguished member of the faculty, until 1879.

In 1871 first ground was broken for construction on the future campus of Purdue University, and in 1872 —during the long organization process which that institution underwent—Richard Owen was appointed president. He did not serve, for his recommendation for organization, submitted the following year to the trustees, appeared to them and to the public generally as if, in its advanced ideas as to the importance of sanitary conveniences, beautification of the grounds and elaborate living arrangements, it might have been formulated by "Old Bob" Owen himself. "No farm college," said the people of Indiana, "should aspire to such fol-de-rols," and that was that. President Owen of Purdue resigned and continued as Professor Owen of Indiana University.

Upon his retirement from active duty Richard Owen returned to the home in New Harmony where for years he had spent his summers and where his interest in things scientific, religious, medical, and literary continued unflagging until his death in 1890.

Material taken from Albjerg—*Richard Owen.*

* * *

Key to the Geology of the Globe. *Nashville, Tenn.,* 1857.
"Honor to the Illustrious Dead." A Lecture Delivered in Behalf of the Mount Vernon Association; Delivered in . . . Nashville, Dec. 4, 1857. *Nashville,* 1857.

Report of a Geological Reconnaissance of Indiana, Made During the Years 1859 and 1860, Under the Direction of the Late David Dale Owen. (Begun by David Dale Owen.) *Indianapolis,* 1862.

Industrial Colleges. Added, a Communication on the General Plan of the College Building, by R. Owen (with Lewis Bollman). *Washington, D. C.,* 1864.

Report on the Mines of New Mexico. *Washington, D. C.,* 1865.

Report of a Geological Examination Made on the Lands of the Wabash Petroleum and Coal Mining Company in Warren, Fountain and Parke Counties. *Indianapolis,* 1866.

Report of a Geological Examination, Made on Certain Lands and Mines, in the Counties of Haywood, Madison, Buncombe, Jackson, and Macon, N. C., and in Cocke County, Tennessee. *Indianapolis,* 1869.

Happiness and Home, Temporal and Eternal; Farewell Address Delivered at . . . Indiana State University, May 11, 1879. *Bloomington, Ind.,* 1879.

The Rappites: Interesting Notes About Early New Harmony (with J. Schnack). *Evansville, Ind.,* 1890.

OWEN, ROBERT DALE: 1801–1877.

Robert Dale Owen, a son of the notable but erratic Robert Owen, was born on Nov. 9, 1801.

His father was a man of vast talent, deep human sympathy, great executive ability, unlimited faith in mankind and an almost complete lack of balance. His mother was Ann Caroline Dale Owen, aristocratic, well educated, proper daughter of a wealthy Scotch industrialist. It is not difficult to see how these two happened to marry, even though Ann Caroline's father had his doubts at the time, for their match was made at a time when Robert Owen's abilities were concentrated on an unorthodox but highly successful effort to demonstrate that mill-hands produced more goods when they were well fed, clothed and housed than they did when they were starved: his ideas succeeded most profitably and it was some years later, after he and Ann Caroline had long been married, when he began to believe that workers at all levels need not only be well fed but should preferably also not work. Then it became evident that Ann Caroline's father was right—that Robert Owen had little, if any, judgment.

By that time Ann Caroline had borne Robert Dale, David Dale, William and Richard Owen and divorce was unthinkable for a strict Scot Presbyterian woman, no matter if the woman's husband had adopted a retinue of pensioners who preached freedom for women and even free love for both sexes—so she remained Robert Owen's wife until her death. The two were, separated, however, most of the time after 1825 and she was almost entirely out of touch with her sons, who had followed their father, even though William and David Dale, the more stable of the four, had followed him not necessarily in spirit.

To this ill-matched couple Robert Dale Owen was born. He was reared and educated, after his very earliest years, according to his father's dictates. He attended the very good model schools set up by his father for the mill-workers' children at New Lanark and he had private tutors who prepared him for higher education. When he reached his eighteenth year he was sent to the progressive school at Hofwyl, Switzerland, which Emanuel von Fellenberg had recently opened and which had attracted the attention of Robert Owen.

Robert Dale Owen spent four years at Hofwyl and his conscientious approach to his studies is evidenced by the meticulous notebooks which he kept there. Von Fellenberg's system—tutorial, but with no restraint on progress—was good for a serious minded student and Robert Dale Owen certainly gained an excellent liberal education there. He kept meticulous note books and occasional journals while touring England and Scotland to visit public institutions and industrial communities with his father during and immediately after his school days.

This touring of institutions was carried on with a purpose: Robert Owen had already begun to plan a model community, where arts and manufactures came from the same hands; where writers grew crops and where field workers gained culture; where cooking, dish-washing and house-keeping were community problems and required only a small part of anyone's time; where all were well dressed, well-fed, well educated and well bred—and where all contributed and all shared alike. He hoped he and his son would find some ideas in practice in orphan asylums, schools, and homes for the indigent and unfortunate which would be useful.

The plans went on. An Englishman who owned land on the west side of the Wabash (which, incidentally, was for sale) told Robert Owen that he had secured an option giving him a commission to sell Father George Rapp's community, Harmony, on the Wabash. Robert Owen had his choice between trying continued improvement in a Scotland still dubious of the propriety of allowing mill-hands' children to learn to read, or of buying this ready-made town in a country where there were still few neighbors to dis-

approve of whatever reforms he might wish to try. He put the question to his son and, to quote Robert Dale Owen himself when his father asked, "Which shall it be, New Lanark or New Harmony?", the twenty-four year old Robert Dale replied, "Oh, Father! Let it be New Harmony!"

The two came to the U. S. in November, 1825. The Harmony property had been bought and partially paid for. The aims of the new community had been widely published and welcomed by a vast number of serious people who hoped for a final solution to the social problems which they saw all about them, by reformers who saw here an opportunity to get their own pet theories adopted, by people who had always had an aversion to the sight of wealth in the hands of their neighbors, by those who had a desire to express talents previously unappreciated, and by people who had never believed that any considerable amount of work was either necessary or desirable. Some hundreds of these were already in New Harmony before the Owens even sailed, and hundreds more were on the long and arduous way.

William Owen had gone ahead and was on the ground, but Robert and Robert Dale Owen felt this was not a particularly fortunate circumstance because William was a practical young man with a talent for milling and other realistic pursuits: they felt he did not comprehend the Utopian aims of the community.

Robert Owen went to Washington to outline his plan to Congress and to any other gatherings which might be expected to listen. Robert Dale accompanied him for a while, then went to Philadelphia to join the party of educators, artists and scientists, protegées of the hard-headed but scholarly old William Maclure. That wealthy old gentleman had agreed to furnish and to feed the party while they set up the school systems in Robert Owen's new town. They were an inspired and an inspiring group: Thomas Say, naturalist; Madame Fretageot, former Hofwyl teacher and mistress of Maclure's interests, if not of Maclure himself; the two charming wards of Charles Alexandre Lesueur, Lucy Virginia du Palais, and Lucy Sistaire, whom Madame Fretageot chaperoned; Lesueur himself; Joseph Neef, another ex-Hofwyl teacher, and his daughter Caroline; Gerard Troost, naturalist; Capt. Donald Macdonald, young adventurer, who traveled to America with the Owens; and others of like charm and distinction.

They started down the Ohio by flatboat, in winter. As might have been anticipated by a more practical party they were soon frozen in and made quite a long journey of it, but the "Boat Load of Knowledge" (as some romantic chronicler of the New Harmony movement nominated it) eventually reached a spot on the Ohio from which it could get transportation to the community on the Wabash.

Robert Dale Owen had arrived in the Hoosier Utopia.

He was completely charmed. He could see none of the reasons for doubting success which the prosaic William hinted at. He plunged immediately into community life.

He began to teach in old Neef's school and he began to edit the newspaper, THE NEW HARMONY GAZETTE. Robert Dale Owen also immediately volunteered for manual labor but soon found his constitution unfit for it.

As the result of circumstances too long for consideration here there was quite shortly no New Harmony Community. There was also only enough left of the Dale and the Owen fortunes to keep Ann Caroline quietly established in Scotland and to pay the modest expenses of Robert Owen as he traveled and lectured in Europe and the British Isles. The Owen sons—Robert Dale, David Dale, William and Richard—were pretty much on their own, except for some partially developed Indiana farm land.

Robert Dale Owen had become acquainted with the beautiful and talented but odd Frances Wright when she, like many other reformers, had paid an investigating visit to the New Harmony Community during its brief existence. Now, New Harmony as a community being at an end, he became her abject follower. For six or seven years he followed her about, trying to resuscitate her Nashoba Community for freed slaves, as her fellow editor of the New York FREE ENQUIRER, as her fellow-lecturer, as her fellow-lobbyist. But soon enough this happy association was terminated: Frances married Phiquepal d'Arusmont, one of those who had been at New Harmony, and that gentleman, taking over his wife's estate in conformity with the European custom but in direct opposition to the tenets of women's rights which that lady had long preached, soon put publishing, philanthropy, and lecturing beyond her reach. She no longer required the assistance of Robert Dale Owen.

And so in 1832 he went to England where for six months he assisted his father in the editing of a short-lived organ of reform, THE CRISIS. At the end of this six months Robert Dale Owen may have begun to see the world about him more realistically; perhaps he thought it wise to see if some part of the family investment could be salvaged from New Harmony equities. He returned to the Wabash and began that

memorable part of his career which, in spite of occasional digressions and dreams of Utopia, is his monument.

In 1836 he was elected to the Indiana State Legislature. His advanced ideas, balanced by the reactionary instincts of the Indiana farmers with whom he served, resulted in worth-while legislation which gave the state a future income with which to set up a public school system.

He was elected to Congress and served from 1843 to 1847. His measure began the activity which resulted in the peaceful settlement of the Oregon Question; he introduced the bill which set up the Smithsonian Institution and included publication of reports of research as one of its functions, and he served as chairman of its building committee.

Back in Indiana he became interested in the construction of year-round roads and, after careful study, published a book explaining the construction of plank roads. He sat as a delegate to the state Constitutional Convention of 1850 and succeeded in writing in reasonably liberal laws concerning divorce and women's property rights.

In 1853 he was appointed United States charge d'affaires at Naples and in 1855 he was appointed minister. He served with distinction until 1858. But it was during this period that he began another of those digressions which had led him in a hopeless chase for so many of his younger years: the study of spiritualism, which he now took up, within seven or eight years cost him his usefulness and in a few more years his reason.

Fortunately he was not so quickly enthralled by this new interest as he had been, for instance, by community living, dress reform, women's rights and the others: he was able to forget spiritualism enough to give excellent service as purchasing agent for Indiana in preparation for equipping state troops for the Civil War, to serve as chairman of the committee to investigate the condition of freedmen and to battle the Copperheads and adroit fellow-travelers in Indiana.

After the War he devoted himself mainly to writing and to further investigation of the spirit world which was now rapidly becoming his ruling interest.

As a young man he had been infatuated with two women of as widely divergent background as can well be imagined: the first was a daughter of a mill-hand in New Lanark, whom he gave up for New Harmony and whom he long remembered, and the second was, of course, the dynamic Frances Wright. He was afterward twice married. His first wife, Mary Jane Robinson, he married on Apr. 12, 1832. She died in 1871 and on June 23, 1876, he married Lottie Walton Kellogg.

He suffered a complete mental breakdown about the time of his second marriage and died at his summer home on Lake George, N. Y., on June 24, 1877.

* * *

An Outline of the System of Education at New Lanark. *Glasgow, Scotland, 1824.*

Moral Physiology; or, a Brief and Plain Treatise on the Population Question. *London,* [1830].

Popular Tracts (with others). *New York, 1830.*

Address on the Hopes and Destinies of the Human Species. *London, 1836.*

Pocahontas: a Historical Drama, in Five Acts; with an Introductory Essay and Notes. By a Citizen of the West. *New York, 1837.*

A Lecture on Consistency. *London, 1842.*

Address on Free Inquiry. *London, n.d.*

Address on Free Inquiry. On Fear as a Motive of Action. *London, 1843.*

Hints on Public Architecture. *New York, 1849.*

A Brief Practical Treatise on the Construction and Management of Plank Roads. *New Albany, 1850.*

Discussion on the Authenticity of the Bible (with Origen Bacheller). *Philadelphia, 1854.*

Divorce: Being a Correspondence Between Horace Greeley and Robert Dale Owen. *New York, 1860.*

Footfalls on the Boundary of Another World. *Philadelphia, 1860.*

The Future of the Northwest. *Philadelphia, 1863.*

The Policy of Emancipation (with S. P. Chase and E. M. Stanton). *Philadelphia, 1863.*

Emancipation Is Peace. [*New York, 1863.*]

The Conditions of Reconstruction; in a Letter . . . to the Secretary of State. Letter from Hon. S. P. Chase. *New York, 1863.*

The Wrong of Slavery, the Right of Emancipation, and the Future of the African Race in the United States. *Philadelphia, 1864.*

Beyond the Breakers: Story of the Present Day. *Philadelphia, 1870.*

The Debatable Land Between This World and the Next. *New York, 1872.*

Threading My Way: Twenty-Seven Years of Autobiography. *New York, 1874.*

Address on the Influence of the Clerical Profession. *New York, n.d.*

OWEN, WILLIAM DUNN: 1846–?

"William D. Owen was born Sept. 6, 1846, at Bloomington, Ind. He attended Indiana University and studied law in Lafayette. He became a Christian

minister and in 1881 settled in Logansport and engaged in the practice of law with D. C. Justice. He was a Congressman from the Tenth Indiana district from 1884 until 1890. He was Secretary of State from 1894 to 1896 and commissioner of immigration during the McKinley administration . . ."

From Powell—*History of Cass County, 1913.*

* * *

Success in Life, and How to Secure It; or, Elements of Manhood and Their Culture. *Chicago, 1878.*

The Genius of Industry. *Chicago, 1883.*

P

PACKARD, EDGAR: 1869–

"Edgar Packard taught in the Logansport schools for a number of years, later moving to Berlin, Wis. In 1895, while living in Logansport, he published *A Study of the Song of Solomon.*"

From Powell—*History of Cass County, 1913.*

* * *

A Study of the Song of Solomon. 1895.

Picture Readings; a Study of Paintings by the Great Masters. *Bloomington, Ill., 1918.*

Outlines for the Study of Shakespeare's Plays. *Kent, O.* [1927].

PACKARD, JASPER: 1832–1899.

Jasper Packard, son of Thomas and Nancy Ann Berry Packard, was born in Mahoning County, O., on Feb. 1, 1832, and moved with his family to Indiana in 1835, where they settled in Marshall County. He received his early education in the common schools, later attended Michigan Central College and Oberlin College, and graduated from the University of Michigan in 1855. On Oct. 4, 1855, he married Harriet S. Tibbits.

In 1855-56 Packard taught school at Hillsdale, Mich., and from 1856 to 1858 at La Porte, Ind. During these two years he also studied law and edited THE UNION. From 1857 to 1861 he served as school examiner for La Porte County and as justice of the peace. In 1861 he was admitted to the bar.

In 1861 he enlisted in the 48th Indiana Volunteers and during the war rose through the ranks until, in April, 1865, he was brevetted brigadier general. He served in a number of campaigns, including the siege of Vicksburg, where he was severely wounded, and the campaign against Atlanta, where he was in command of the 128th Indiana Regiment.

Following his discharge from the army in 1866 he became auditor of La Porte County for a two-year term. From 1869 to 1875 he was a member of Congress and from 1876 to 1884 an internal revenue agent. In 1874 he established and published the LAPORTE CHRONICLE, which he sold in 1878, and in 1886 he became owner and editor of the LAPORTE DAILY PUBLIC SPIRIT. He was also owner and editor of the NEW ALBANY EVENING TRIBUNE.

For two years before his death, which occurred in 1899, he served as a member of the Indiana Legislature.

> Information from *Who Was Who in America*; *Representative Men of Indiana*, Vol. II; and *Appletons' Cyclopaedia of American Biography*, Vol. IV.

* * *

History of Laporte County, Indiana, and Its Townships, Towns and Cities. *LaPorte, Ind.,* 1876.

PAINE, DANIEL L.: 1830–1895.

Born in Richmond, Me., on October 30, 1830, Daniel L. Paine started in newspaper work in Bangor, Me., published a temperance paper for a time, and when he was twenty years of age moved to St. Anthony (Minneapolis), Minn., where he started a weekly newspaper. He has been credited with the naming of Minneapolis.

About 1860 he came to Indianapolis, where he was associated with newspapers for more than thirty years. His principal connection was with the INDIANAPOLIS NEWS as an editorial writer.

Mr. Paine died at Indianapolis on May 6, 1895.

> Information from Parker and Heiney—*Poets and Poetry of Indiana.*

* * *

Club Moss. [*Grand Rapids*], 1890.

PAINTER, GEORGE ALEXANDER STEPHEN: 1864–

George A. S. Painter, son of George Washington Alexander and Elvessa Louise Norris Painter, was born at Summitville, Ind., on Dec. 25, 1864. After attending Greencastle Academy he entered Harvard University, from which he was graduated with the A.B. degree in 1892. He also studied at Boston University and the University of Jena, receiving the Ph.D. degree from the latter institution in 1896.

He began teaching philosophy at Tufts College in 1897 and later was a member of the faculties of Bryn Mawr, George Washington University, Mt. Union College, and Clark University. After 1912 he was professor of philosophy at New York State College for Teachers.

> Information from *Who's Who in America.*

* * *

Herbert Spencer's Evolutions—theorie Dargestellt, Beurteilt und mit Einer Übersicht über die Geschichte des Entwicklungsbegriffes Versehen . . . *Jena,* 1896.

Philosophy of Christ's Temptation, a Study in Interpretation. *Boston,* 1914.

Fundamental Psychology. *New York,* 1938.

Science and Evolutionary Theory. *Takoma Park, Md.,* 1940.

PALMER, FRANCIS LESEURE: 1863–

Francis Leseure Palmer, son of William R. and Clara Skeele Palmer, was born at Fort Wayne, Ind., on Aug. 28, 1863, and graduated from Amherst College in 1885, receiving the A.M. degree in 1902. In 1892 he graduated from Cambridge Episcopal Theological School. Seabury Divinity School awarded him a D.D. degree in 1923. On Oct. 1, 1895, he married Elizabeth E. Paine.

Ordained to the Protestant Episcopal ministry in 1893, he occupied pulpits in Gardner, Mass., Walla Walla, Wash., and Stillwater, Minn. From 1910 to 1913 he was an instructor at Seabury Divinity School, serving as professor of divinity in 1922-23. He was registrar and historiographer for the Diocese of Minnesota, and acted as canon of the Cathedral of Our Merciful Saviour, Fairbault, Minn. From 1886 to 1890 and again from 1898 to 1900 he was an assistant editor of Webster's International Dictionary. He was also a book reviewer for church publications.

> Information from *Who's Who in America.*

* * *

Mahlon Norris Gilbert, Bishop Coadjutor of Minnesota. *Milwaukee,* 1912.

The Class of 1885 of Amherst College; a Retrospect After Fifty-Five Years. n.p., 1940.

PALMER, FRANK NELSON: 1859–

Frank Nelson Palmer, son of Eben Hawkins and Frances Boyd Nelson Palmer, was born in Danville, Ill., on Oct. 12, 1859.

He received the A.B. degree from Wabash College in 1881, the A.M. in 1884 and the D.D. in 1903. He was a student in Union Theological Seminary in 1883-84 and McCormick Theological Seminary, 1884-85. He married Sarah Cynthia Hawkins, of Kankakee, Ill., on Dec. 8, 1892.

Palmer was ordained a Presbyterian minister in 1887 and held various pastorates in Colorado from that date until 1891. He became pastor of the Dayton, Ind., Presbyterian Church in 1897 and served until 1903, when he became an instructor in the Winona, Ind., schools. He was director of the Winona Bible Summer School from 1908 until 1911 and in 1918 became pastor of the First Church of Warsaw, Ind.

Information from *Who's Who in America.*

* * *

A Bird's Eye View of the Bible. *Winona Lake, Ind.,* 1906.
Old Testament Characters. *Winona Lake, Ind.,* 1912.
David and the Psalms. *Winona Lake, Ind.,* 1913.
The Mastery of Genesis. *Winona Lake, Ind.,* 1914.
Comparative Study of the Four Gospel Records. *Winona Lake, Ind.,* 1915.
The Life of Christ. 1915.

PALMER, JOEL: 1810–1881.

Joel Palmer, son of Ephraim and Hannah Phelps Palmer, was born in Ontario, Canada, on Oct. 4, 1810. His parents were Quakers who returned to New York state at the beginning of the War of 1812. When he was sixteen years old, young Joel went to Bucks County, Pa., and worked as a laborer on canals and other public improvement projects. He learned canal construction and, since canals were being dug along most every likely waterway in the Midwest, found plenty of employment. By 1836 he was a resident of Laurel, Ind., with a contract for the construction of a part of the Whitewater Canal. He prospered, at least moderately, and was elected a representative (1843-45) of Franklin County in the Indiana General Assembly.

Public honors and private prosperity were not enough to hold even a successful young business man when the Western fever struck, and in the middle Forties Joel Palmer made a trip to the West and wrote an account of his adventures.

It is a very small book, bound sometimes in printed wrappers and sometimes (evidently for the more affluent book buyers of the day) in cloth: in either case its modern selling price is well up in three figures. According to *American Authors, 1600-1900,* it is

"the only complete written record of pioneering along the old Oregon trail" (p. 592). This would appear to be a rather broad statement, but it is certainly an informative, a fairly well written and a very rare book.

Palmer returned to Indiana in 1847 for a brief time, then went back to Oregon, where he laid out the town of Dayton and built a grist mill. In 1853 he was Superintendent of Indian Affairs for the Oregon Territory, and he was active in state politics throughout the remainder of his life.

He died in Dayton, Ore., on June 9, 1881. Palmer was first married to Catherine Caffee. After her death he married Sarah Ann Derbyshire in 1836.

Information from Kunitz and Haycraft—*American Authors, 1600-1900.*

* * *

Journal of Travels Over the Rocky Mountains to the Mouth of the Columbia River. *Cincinnati,* 1847.

PARKER, BENJAMIN STRATTAN: 1833–1911.

Born in a pioneer's cabin in Henry County, Ind., on Feb. 10, 1833, Benjamin Strattan Parker was educated at home by his parents. In 1869 he married Huldah Wickersham. During his life he was a teacher, editor, office-holder, and businessman and, in addition to his books, contributed poetry and prose to periodicals of his day. He was a resident of New Castle, Ind. He died in 1911.

Information from Parker and Heiney—*Poets and Poetry of Indiana.*

* * *

The Lesson: and Other Poems. *New Castle, Ind.,* 1871.
The Cabin in the Clearing, and Other Poems. *Chicago,* 1887.
Hoosier Bards with Sundry Wildwood and Other Rhymes. *Chicago,* 1891.
Rhymes of Our Neighborhood. *New Castle, Ind.,* 1895.
Poets and Poetry of Indiana. (Compiler and editor with Enos B. Heiney.) *New York,* 1900.
After Noontide. *Richmond, Ind.,* 1905.
Pioneer Life in Henry County.

PARKER, GEORGE FREDERICK: 1847–1928.

George Frederick Parker, son of Thomas W. and Eliza Ann Kirk Parker, was born in Lafayette, Ind., Dec. 30, 1847.

The family removed to Iowa and young Parker was

educated in the public schools and attended the University of Iowa for two years. He later received LL.D. degrees from Simpson College and Washington and Lee and Iowa State universities. He married Eloise Florence Dibble on Apr. 27, 1890.

Parker began his career in journalism in October, 1873. He edited newspapers in Iowa, Indiana, Washington, D. C., New Hampshire, Pennsylvania and New York City. He contributed to the LONDON TIMES from 1895 to 1905, and to many American and foreign periodicals. He served as U. S. consul at Birmingham, England, from 1893 to 1898 and served occasionally on the Democratic National Committee.

He died on May 31, 1928.

Information from *Who Was Who in America.*

* * *

A Life of Grover Cleveland with a Sketch of Adlai E. Stevenson. *New York,* 1892.

Recollections of Grover Cleveland. *New York,* 1909.

John Pierpont Morgan: a Memorial Address. *New York,* 1913.

PARRY, DAVID MACLEAN: 1852–1915.

Born on a farm near Pittsburgh, Pa., on Mar. 26, 1852, David MacLean Parry, son of Thomas J. and Lydia MacLean Parry, worked on the home farm until he was seventeen years old, attending school during the winter months.

Following a varied business career in Iowa, New York, and Indiana, he established a manufacturing business in Rushville, Ind., in 1882, a business which he moved to Indianapolis four years later. Mr. Parry was also a railway official and president of the National Association of Manufacturers. He retired from the manufacturing business in 1911. He was twice married: first to Cora Harbottle, who died in 1882, then to Hessie Maxwell. Mr. Parry died on May 12, 1915.

Information from *Who Was Who in America* and the Indianapolis Public Library.

* * *

The Scarlet Empire. *Indianapolis,* 1906.

Tariff Revision (with others). *Philadelphia,* 1908.

PATTERSON, ANNE VIRGINIA SHARPE (MRS. ROBERT E.): 1841–1913.

Anne Virginia Sharpe, daughter of George Washington and Caroline Rebecca Snider Sharpe, was born in Delaware, O., in 1841 and was educated in private schools and at Delaware Female College. On Jan. 4, 1866, she married Robert E. Patterson.

In 1892 Mrs. Patterson moved to Indiana, where she was a resident of Kokomo. She was editor of what was said to be the first newspaper children's page in America. Active in the conservation movement, she was a leader in the widespread bird-house campaign among school children.

She died on May 30, 1913.

Information from *Who Was Who in America.*

* * *

The American Girl of the Period: Her Ways and Views. By Garry Gaines. *Philadelphia,* 1878.

Speeches, Prose, Rhyme and Jingle for the Trades' Carnival. *Springfield, O.,* 1889.

Supplement to Business Men's Jubilee, or Trades' Carnival. *Urbana, O.,* 1889.

Dickey Downy: the Autobiography of a Bird. *Philadelphia,* 1899.

Lady of the Green Scarf: an Entertainment Exercise for Schools Embodying the Need for Conserving Our Country's Natural Resources, Suitable for Weekly Rhetoricals, Class Exercises and Arbor Day. *Chicago,* 1910.

PERKINS, LUCY FITCH (MRS. DWIGHT HEALD): 1865–1937.

Lucy Fitch, prolific author and illustrator of juvenile fiction, was born in Maples, Ind., on July 12, 1865, the daughter of Appleton Howe and Elizabeth Bennett Fitch. She graduated from the Museum of Fine Arts School in Boston in 1886, and from 1887 to 1891 she taught in the Pratt Institute in Brooklyn. On Aug. 18, 1891, she married Dwight Heald Perkins.

Mrs. Perkins' "Twins" series of books sold—and still sell—in astonishing numbers, furnishing pleasant and mildly instructive reading matter for at least two generations of American children. Probably no series of juveniles—except possibly the "Brownie" books by another Indiana author—has run through so many individual titles.

The chronology of the bibliography reveals two occasions (1919 and 1926) when the author made an effort to abandon twins—only to be forced by her publisher and her juvenile admirers to resume writing about them.

She died on Mar. 18, 1937.

Information from *Who Was Who in America* and Burke and Howe—*American Authors and Books, 1640-1940.*

* * *

The Goose Girl: Children's Rhymes. *Chicago*, 1906.
A Book of Joys: Story of a New England Summer. *Chicago*, 1907.
The Dutch Twins. *Boston*, 1911.
The Japanese Twins. *Boston*, 1912.
The Irish Twins. *Boston*, 1913.
The Eskimo Twins. *Boston*, 1914.
The Mexican Twins. *Boston*, 1915.
The Cave Twins. *Boston*, 1916.
The Belgian Twins. *Boston*, 1917.
The Dutch Twins Primer. *Boston*, 1917.
The French Twins. *Boston*, 1918.
The Spartan Twins. *Boston*, 1918.
The Scotch Twins. *Boston*, 1919.
Cornelia: the Story of a Benevolent Despot. *Boston*, 1919.
The Italian Twins. *Boston*, 1920.
The Puritan Twins. *Boston*, 1921.
The Swiss Twins. *Boston*, 1922.
The Filipino Twins. *Boston*, 1923.
The Colonial Twins of Virginia. *Boston*, 1924.
The American Twins of 1812. *Boston*, 1925.
The American Twins of the Revolution. *Boston*, 1926.
Mr. Chick, His Travels and Adventures. *Boston*, 1926.
The Pioneer Twins. *Boston*, 1927.
The Farm Twins. *Boston*, 1928.
Kit and Kat: More Adventures of the Dutch Twins. *Boston*, 1929.
The Indian Twins. *Boston*, 1930.
The Pickaninny Twins. *Boston*, 1931.
The Norwegian Twins. *Boston*, 1933.
The Spanish Twins. *Boston*, 1934.
The Chinese Twins. *Boston*, 1935.
The Dutch Twins and Little Brother. *Boston*, 1938.

PETTIJOHN, GRACE SMITH (MRS. FRED L.): 1876–

Grace Smith, daughter of Samuel M. and Aletha White Smith, was born on a farm in Hamilton County, Ind., in 1876, and graduated from Friend's Academy, in Westfield, Ind., and from De Pauw University. On Sept. 12, 1901, she married Dr. Fred L. Pettijohn. A resident of Indianapolis, Mrs. Pettijohn was active as a member and officer in numerous national and civic organizations.

Information from Mrs. Grace Smith Pettijohn.

* * *

Memorial Tribute to John Smith and Martha Pickens. *Indianapolis,* 1912.
Handbook of Drama. *Indianapolis,* 1940.

PFRIMMER, WILL WOOD: 1856–1935.

Will Wood Pfrimmer was born on Jan. 27, 1856, in Massac County, Ill., the son of Daniel A. and Melinda Conrad Pfrimmer, both natives of Indiana. His mother died when he was four years old, and his grandfather, Samuel Pfrimmer, took him to the old home in Harrison County, Ind., where he lived for nine years. Upon the death of his grandfather, he went to his father's home in Newton County, Ind.

He was educated for the law but from natural inclination drifted into school work. From 1889 to 1899 he was superintendent of schools of Newton County. In May of 1878 he was married to Mary Ellen Webster, and after Mr. Pfrimmer's retirement in 1910, they lived for a few years in Arkansas and later in Missouri, where Mrs. Pfrimmer died in 1926.

Mr. Pfrimmer died at the home of a daughter in Washington, D. C., on Dec. 24, 1935.

Information from Mabel Pfrimmer Hollister, daughter of Mr. Pfrimmer.

* * *

Driftwood. *Buffalo,* 1890.
The Legend of Grape Island and Other Poems. *Watseka, Ill.,* 1907.

PHILIPSON, DAVID: 1862–

David Philipson, son of Joseph and Louisa Freudenthal Philipson, was born in Wabash, Ind., on Aug. 9, 1862, and graduated from the University of Cincinnati in 1883. Also in 1883 he graduated from Hebrew Union College in Cincinnati as rabbi, receiving the D.D. degree in 1886. He married Ella Hollander on Sept. 9, 1886.

From 1884 to 1888 he served as rabbi of the Har Sinai Congregation in Baltimore, and from 1888 to 1938 he was rabbi of the B'ne Israel Congregation in Cincinnati. After 1891 he was also connected with Hebrew Union College, first as professor of homiletics and later as lecturer. He served as consulting editor of the *Jewish Encyclopedia* and contributed to magazines.

Information from *Who's Who in America.*

* * *

The Jew in English Fiction. *Cincinnati,* 1889.
The Oldest Jewish Congregation in the West. 1894.

Old European Jewries. *Philadelphia,* 1894.

A Holiday Sheaf. *Cincinnati,* 1898.

Lectures. *New York,* n.d.

The Reform Movement in Judaism. *New York,* 1907.

The Jew in America. *Cincinnati,* 1909.

Children's Harvest Service. *New York,* n.d.

Max Lilienthal—American Rabbi. *New York,* 1915.

Centenary Papers and Others. *New York,* 1919.

History of the Hebrew Union College. 1925.

My Life as an American Jew; an Autobiography. *Cincinnati,* 1941.

The Reform Movement in America. *New York,* n.d.

PHILLIPS, DAVID GRAHAM: 1867–1911.

"David Graham Phillips, American novelist, journalist, and reformer, was born in Madison, Ind., on Oct. 31, 1867, the fourth child and the first son of David Graham Phillips, a banker, and his wife, Margaret Lee Phillips, who came from the family made famous by 'Light-Horse' Harry Lee.

"After attending the Madison public schools, and studying foreign languages under a tutor at home, he attended Asbury College (now De Pauw University) in Greencastle, Ind., for two years, and then transferred to Princeton University, graduating with a Bachelor of Arts degree in June 1887, the youngest member in a class of eighty-six.

"Phillips had already begun to write while in college, and in the summer following his graduation, he visited the office of James A. Green, city editor of the CINCINNATI TIMES-STAR, to ask whether there was an opening for which he might be considered. His statement that he had 'just graduated from Princeton' had no startling effect on Green, who looked at the 'conspicuously patterned suit, the eighteen-inch trousers, the dangling cigarette, and shuddered,' before answering in the negative. The city editor's reply, however, had no more effect on Phillips than Phillips' qualifications had on Green. With no trace of disappointment, Phillips made a very innocent request: he asked—and readily received—permission to come to the office to read the daily papers. The next morning, when Green arrived at the office at seven-thirty, he found Phillips ahead of him, calmly reading the exchanges. This performance continued for several weeks, and Green, and all the members of his staff, conceived a hearty dislike for the over-dressed Princetonian who refused to believe that a newspaper could exist without his services.

"The endurance contest that followed, in which Green's problem was to keep his temper, finally ended with Princeton as the winner, when the opportunity that Phillips was waiting for arrived. Some one committed a murder at the time best calculated to aid Phillips: when all the reporters were out on assignments, and the city editor was alone in his office. Unable to leave his desk, Green asked Phillips, who was busily engaged in reading a paper, to find out the facts and to return with them by twelve-thirty, so that he (Green) could write the story. At twelve twenty-five, Phillips stood in front of Green's desk, not with the facts, but with the complete story of the murder written in the approved TIMES-STAR manner. Green, who was above professional jealousy, printed it without changing a word, and, after another look at his trousers, offered Phillips a position.

"Phillips worked on the TIMES-STAR staff for less than a year, not because he was not good enough, but because he was too good. He soon became the 'talk of the town,' and Murat Halstead, editor of the CINCINNATI COMMERCIAL GAZETTE, and the father of a classmate of Phillips, offered him double the salary that Green could afford to pay. In speaking of the affair, Green said, 'Halstead told me that I had done remarkably well in training the young man, but he did not need any training: he was a born reporter.'

"Phillips remained with the COMMERCIAL GAZETTE for three years, constantly duplicating the successful performances that had induced Halstead to send for him. Only a few years before, the reporting staff had been honored by no less a writer than Lafcadio Hearn, and Halstead and his associates held him up as an example to be followed by young reporters. To Phillips, who paid attention to style, it was enjoyable to work for a paper that definitely encouraged literary merit, as well as mere form.

"His relations with Halstead were so pleasant that Phillips might have remained with him for a considerably longer period, had it not been for the continual urging of his married sister, Mrs. Carolyn Frevert, who was always telling him that New York was the 'only place' for a man anxious to make a name for himself as a writer. Finally, in the summer of 1890, he decided to accept her advice and to come to New York, to widen his experience and to avail himself of the better opportunities offered by a large city. After a very short time on the TRIBUNE, he joined the staff of the SUN, at a salary of fifteen dollars a week, his assignment being to cover the 'human interest' stories of the Jefferson Market Police Court. His first real chance came when the city editor, Daniel F. Kellogg, sent him to investigate the story of a child lost in the Catskill Mountains. Phillips' highly dramatic account

—'the kind of story that makes editors cheer and women weep'—attracted attention throughout the country, gave him a national reputation as a reporter, and brought him an increase in salary. It was not long before his superiors began to give him dull ordinary assignments that seemed to promise nothing, as a tradition arose in the SUN office that 'D. G. could see a story where no other reporter would believe one existed.' An illustration of this is offered by a statement in an after-dinner speech by Joseph Choate: 'it would be a good thing for this country if all the Irishmen, instead of trying to control politics here, would go back to Ireland and govern their own sorely misgoverned land.' Phillips made a feature story out of it, while other reporters struggled for half a column.

"Early in 1893, he left the SUN for the WORLD, where he came under the notice of Joseph Pulitzer. Besides his genius for news, Phillips, according to all accounts, was an exceedingly likeable personality, and Pulitzer's respect for his talent soon deepened into affection for his character. He sent him to London as a special correspondent, and in June 1893, Phillips 'achieved one of the historic beats of the decade' in his exclusive report of the sinking of *H. M. S. Camperdown*, in collision with the *H. M. S. Victoria* off the coast of Asia Minor. Upon his return to New York, he was rewarded by promotion to the WORLD's editorial staff, and he frequently took charge of the editorial page in the absence of William H. Merrill when he was ill or away on vacation.

"In 1901, as 'John Graham,' he published his first novel, *The Great God Success*, an appropriate title in view of the enthusiastic reception it gained from readers and critics. The general verdict that it was one of the best 'newspaper novels' ever written, and the urging of his sister encouraged him, early in 1902, to give up daily journalism for freelance magazine writing. An interesting feature of the novel is that Pulitzer figures in it prominently as one of the characters. He was not especially pleased with the fictional presentation of his personality, and he was wounded when he found out that Phillips was the author, not only because of the way in which he was portrayed, but because he felt that employees of the WORLD should devote their talents exclusively to his organization.

"Phillips began his magazine experience with a series of articles on some unpleasant aspects of journalism, for the SATURDAY EVENING POST. He also contributed to MCCLURE's, MUNSEY's, EVERYBODY's, SUCCESS, HARPER's WEEKLY, the DELINEATOR, and many others. It was as a magazine writer that he aroused the anger of Theodore Roosevelt, earning from him the title of 'muck-raker' for his sensational articles, *The Treason of the Senate,* in which he exposed the political corruption of that body. The title is still remembered, and it is to be feared that it does him, today, more harm than it did when it was first applied. Phillips is, and always was, much more than a 'muck-raker' and the name has done its share in unjustly lowering his reputation.

"From 1901 to 1911, Phillips wrote twenty-three novels and a four-act play. His drama, *The Worth of a Woman*, was produced, with only moderate success, at the Madison Square Theatre in February, 1908, with Katherine Grey as Diana Merivale, the heroine. Historically it is of interest as being one of the first plays to exploit what is now one of the staples of American entertainment: sex appeal. He also wrote a one-act play, *A Point of Law*, that was popular with amateur dramatic societies.

"On Jan. 23, 1911, Phillips was shot in the street without warning, by a paranoiac, Fitzhugh Coyle Goldsborough, of a well-known Washington, Boston, and Maryland family, and the son of Dr. Edmund K. Goldsborough, a prominent Washington physician. Goldsborough, who had a quixotic strain in him, resented the novelist's portrayal of American women in general, and was under the ridiculous impression that Margaret Severence, in *The Fashionable Adventures of Joshua Craig*, was intended as a portrait of his sister. Although he had no radical interests, Goldsborough lived in a small room on the top floor of the Rand School of Social Science—opposite 119 East 19th Street, where Phillips lived with his sister Carolyn— and it appeared that he had been watching his intended victim for several weeks. As for Phillips, who was walking in the direction of the Princeton Club to keep a luncheon engagement, he was entirely unaware of the existence of his assassin, or of the latter's sister. He was almost at the entrance of the club, when Goldsborough emerged from his hiding-place and fired six shots into Phillips' body, crying 'Now, I have you.' The assassin then shot himself in the temple. Phillips died in Bellevue Hospital on Jan. 24 . . .

"Phillips' place in American fiction is still to be determined. He has been called America's greatest novelist by Frank Harris and H. L. Mencken, an 'American Balzac' by J. C. Underwood, and an 'American Zola' by his friend and biographer, I. F. Marcosson. Granville Hicks, on the other hand, holds that Phillips was a journalist from beginning to end, a journalist and nothing more."

Condensed from H. S. R., *Authors Today and Yesterday*.

* * *

The Great God Success. (John Graham, pseud.) *New York*, 1901.

A Woman Ventures. *New York*, 1902.

Her Serene Highness. *New York*, 1902.

The Golden Fleece. *New York*, 1903.

The Master-Rogue. *New York*, 1903.

The Cost. *Indianapolis*, 1904.

The Reign of Gilt. *New York*, 1905.

The Plum Tree. *Indianapolis*, 1905.

The Social Secretary. *Indianapolis*, 1905.

The Deluge. *Indianapolis*, 1905.

The Fortune Hunter. *Indianapolis*, 1906.

The Treason of the Senate. 1906.

Light-Fingered Gentry. *New York*, 1907.

The Second Generation. *New York*, 1907.

The Worth of a Woman. *New York*, 1908.

A Point of Law. *New York*, 1908.

Old Wives for New. *New York*, 1908.

The Fashionable Adventures of Joshua Craig. *New York*, 1909.

The Hungry Heart: a Novel. *New York*, 1909.

Husband's Story: a Novel. *New York*, 1910.

White Magic: a Novel. *New York*, 1910.

Grain of Dust: a Novel. *New York*, 1911.

The Conflict: a Novel. *New York*, 1911.

The Price She Paid: a Novel. *New York*, 1912.

George Helm. *New York*, 1912.

Degarmo's Wife, and Other Stories. *New York*, 1913.

Susan Lenox: Her Fall and Rise. *New York*, (Feb.) 1917. 2 vols. (On demand of John S. Sumner and the Society for the Suppression of Vice the second edition, Sept. 1917, was cut to 474 and 490 pp.)

PIATT, JOHN JAMES: 1835–1917.

"John James Piatt . . . poet, journalist, was born at James' Mills (later Milton), Ind., the son of John Bear and Emily (Scott) Piatt . . . When John James was six years old his parents moved to Ohio, establishing themselves near Columbus. The boy attended the high school in that place, and later, Capital University and Kenyon College. Apprenticed to the publisher of the OHIO STATE JOURNAL to learn the printer's trade, he became acquainted with William Dean Howells, who was then associated with that paper, and the two formed a lasting friendship. Some of Piatt's verses appeared in the LOUISVILLE JOURNAL in 1857, and soon afterward he accepted an editorial position on it. In 1859 he began contributing to the ATLANTIC MONTHLY. His poem 'The Morning Street' evoked Howells' praise and the statement that he himself wished he could write something worthy of inclusion in the ATLANTIC. The following year (1860) the two published in collaboration *Poems of Two Friends*.

"On June 18, 1861, he married Sarah Morgan Bryan, poet and contributor to the LOUISVILLE JOURNAL. They went to live in Washington where Piatt was a clerk in the U. S. Treasury Department from 1861 to 1867. During this period he became acquainted with Walt Whitman, who frequently referred to Piatt's writings. In 1867 Piatt joined the staff of the CINCINNATI CHRONICLE, and removed to North Bend, just below Cincinnati, on the Ohio River. From 1869 to 1878 he was literary editor and correspondent of the CINCINNATI COMMERCIAL, but also served as assistant clerk (1870) and as librarian (1871-75) to the U. S. House of Representatives. From 1882 to 1893 he was U. S. consul at Cork, Ireland, and for a few months in the latter year at Dublin.

"During all these years he was writing and publishing poetry and some prose . . . Piatt's poetry shows the regular meters of his time but is original and varied in subject matter and appreciative of natural beauty, literary associations, and human feelings . . . When political changes caused Piatt's recall from the consulate of Ireland, he settled at North Bend, O. He continued his literary work, contributing to the CINCINNATI INQUIRER as editor of book reviews and to various periodicals, until a few years before his death, when he became an invalid through injuries received in a carriage accident. He died at Cincinnati, his wife, three sons, and one daughter surviving him."

He edited and compiled *The Hesperian Tree: an annual of the Ohio Valley* for 1900 (reissued in 1901) and for 1900-03.

Condensed from S. G. B., *Dictionary of American Biography*, Vol. XIV.

* * *

Poems of Two Friends (with William Dean Howells). *Columbus, O.*, 1860.

The Nests at Washington and Other Poems (with Sarah Morgan Bryan Piatt). *New York*, 1864.

Poems in Sunshine and Firelight. *Cincinnati*, 1866.

Western Windows, and Other Poems. *New York*, 1869.

Landmarks, and Other Poems. *New York*, 1872.

The Lost Farm, and Other Poems. *Boston*, 1877.

May Festival, 1878. Ode for the Opening of the Cincinnati Music Hall. [*Cincinnati*, 1878.]

Poems of House and Home. *Boston*, 1879. (Reissued in 1888 as Dream of Church Windows, Etc.: Poems of House and Home.)

Pencilled Fly-Leaves: a Book of Essays in Town and Country. *Cincinnati, 1880.*

Idyls and Lyrics of the Ohio Valley. *Cincinnati, 1881.*

Children Out-of-Doors: Verses (with Sarah Morgan Bryan Piatt). *Cincinnati, 1885.*

At the Holy Well; with a Handful of New Verses. *Cincinnati, 1887.*

A Book of Gold and Other Sonnets. *London, Eng., 1889.*

Lost Hunting Ground, Etc.; Little New-World Idyls and Other Poems. *New York, 1893.*

The Ghost's Entry, and Other Poems. 1895.

Odes in Ohio, and Other Poems. *Cincinnati, 1897.*

How the Bishop Built His College in the Woods. *Cincinnati, 1906.*

PIERCE, GILBERT ASHVILLE: 1839–1901.

Gilbert Ashville Pierce was born in East Otto, Cattaraugus County, N. Y., on Jan. 11, 1839. His parents were Sylvester and Mary Olive Treat Pierce.

He was educated in the common schools, accompanied his parents to Porter County, Ind., and was employed as a clerk in the general store which his father opened ten miles south of Valparaiso.

He married Anne Marie Bartholomew in 1858 and the couple settled in Valparaiso, where he began to read law. He studied in the old University of Chicago for two years and was admitted to the Indiana bar.

At the beginning of the Civil War he enlisted in the 9th Indiana Volunteers and was elected second lieutenant and was discharged with the rank of colonel at the close of hostilities. He returned to Valparaiso, practiced law and began to contribute to newspapers. In 1869 he served in the state Legislature and was later appointed secretary to Gov. Oliver P. Morton.

In 1872 he joined the staff of the CHICAGO INTER-OCEAN, serving later as managing editor. After twelve years he joined the CHICAGO DAILY NEWS staff. His first book had been published in 1872 and most of his literary production occurred during his residence in Chicago.

Pierce had been an active Republican and was appointed governor of Dakota Territory, removing his family there in 1884 and serving until 1886. Upon the division of the Territory he was chosen a senator from North Dakota.

In 1891 he moved to Minneapolis, worked first on the staff of the DAILY PIONEER PRESS and shortly bought a half interest in the MINNEAPOLIS TRIBUNE. He was appointed Minister to Portugal in January, 1893, but was forced to resign because of ill health the following April. He died in Chicago in 1901.

Information from the *Dictionary of American Biography,* Vol. XIV, and the Valparaiso Public Library.

* * *

The Dickens Dictionary. A Key to the Characters and Principal Incidents in the Tales of Charles Dickens (with W. A. Wheeler). *Boston, 1872.*

Zachariah, the Congressman. *Chicago, 1880.*

One Hundred Wives. (Play) 1880.

A Dangerous Woman: Experiences of the Hon. John Billings, M.C. *Chicago, 1883.*

Peggy, a Country Heroine. *Chicago, 1883.*

PIPER, DAVID ROY: 1887–

David Roy Piper was born in Hartsville, Ind., in February, 1887. No other information, except that he entered the Christian ministry, is available.

Information from the Indiana State Library.

* * *

The Yoke. *Minneapolis, 1914.*

Saving Rural Religion. *Elgin, Ill., 1926.*

Community Churches; the Community Church Movement. *Chicago, 1928.*

How Would Jesus Teach? *Elgin, Ill., 1931.*

Youth Explores the Bible. *Boston, 1941.*

PLANTZ, MYRA GOODWIN (MRS. SAMUEL): 1856–1914.

Myra Goodwin, daughter of the Rev. Thomas A. and Content L. Craft Goodwin, was born in Brookville, Ind., on July 22, 1856. She was educated at Indianapolis High School, Mt. Vernon Seminary in Washington, and under private teachers. She also spent one year abroad. For two years she taught in De Pauw University. She married Samuel Plantz, Methodist minister, author, and president of Lawrence University, on Sept. 16, 1885. She died in 1914.

Information from *Who Was Who in America.*

* * *

Corner Work; or, Look Up and Lift Up. *Cincinnati, 1892.*

A Great Appointment. *New York, 1895.*

Why Not? *Cincinnati, 1900.*

Songs for Quiet Hours. *New York, 1915.*

PLEAS, ELWOOD: 1831–1897.

Elwood Pleas was born in Richmond, Ind., in 1831. He became a resident of Henry County during his early years, and his small history of that county is one of the early interesting works of its kind—produced before the introduction of paid biographical sketches robbed this type of historical writing of its interest and usually of its truth.

Pleas died near Spiceland, Ind., in 1897.

Information from the Indianapolis Public Library.

* * *

Henry County, Past and Present, 1821-71. *New Castle, Ind.,* 1871.

PLUMMER, MARY WRIGHT: 1856–1916.

"Mary Wright Plummer (Mar. 8, 1856-Sept. 21, 1916), librarian, teacher, poet, was a native of Richmond, Ind., the daughter of Jonathan Wright and Hannah (Ballard) Plummer, and a descendant of Thomas Plummer born in Prince Georges County, Md., in 1723 . . . She received her education in local, private and public schools, and in her early days was described as a 'book hungry' girl. After special study at Wellesley in 1881-82, she spent the following four years with her family in Chicago, reading widely, and teaching. On Jan. 5, 1887, she entered the recently opened library school at Columbia College . . . In the following October she entered as student in the senior course and as a teacher for the incoming junior class. The next two years she served as cataloguer in the St. Louis Public Library under Frederick M. Crunden.

"Resigning in 1890, she spent the summer in Europe, and in the autumn went to the library of Pratt Institute established in Brooklyn in 1887. In 1894 she was made librarian and put in charge of the library school, being given a year's leave of absence, which she spent in Europe. In September 1895 she returned to finish the planning of the new library building, which was opened in 1896 . . . In 1900 she served as one of the United States delegates to the International Congress of Libraries in Paris. In 1904 she resigned as librarian of the Institute to give her whole time to the school. She left Pratt Institute in 1911 and became head of the new library school opened in connection with the dedication of the central building of the New York Public Library, and there she spent the rest of her life . . . In June, 1915, [she] was chosen president of the American Library Association. Her fatal illness pre-

vented her presiding at the next meeting in 1916 . . . She died at the home of her brother in Dixon, Ill.

Condensed from H. M. L., *Dictionary of American Biography,* Vol. XV.

* * *

Hints to Small Libraries. (Anonymous.) *Brooklyn, N. Y.,* 1894.

Verses. *New York,* 1896.

Contemporary Spain as Shown by Her Novelists. *New York,* 1899.

The Pros and Cons of Training for Librarianship. [Chicago], 1903.

Roy and Ray in Mexico. *New York,* 1907.

Roy and Ray in Canada. *New York,* 1908.

Stories from the Chronicle of the Cid. *New York,* 1910.

Training for Librarianship. *Chicago,* 1913.

The Seven Joys of Reading. *New York,* 1915.

POKAGON, SIMON: 1830–1899.

Whether Simon Pokagon, last chief of the Pottawattamie Tribe in the midwest, was born in Indiana or Michigan is a matter of only a few rods, one way or the other. His tribe claimed the territory for many miles along the southern shores of Lake Michigan, without regard to territorial lines imposed by the whites, and the village of his father, Chief Leopold Pokagon, as reported by Daniel McDonald in his *History of the Removal of the Pottawattamie Indians from Northern Indiana,* "was located on the line between Indiana and Michigan, north of South Bend and about one mile west of the St. Joseph River."

The tribe was forced to sell its lands—including the sites of Chicago, Hammond, Gary, Elkhart, South Bend and many other cities—by treaty, payment being made sixty years later. The Pottawattamies were expected to take lands in the West, but those offered were barren and they resisted. Finally they were taken by force, and their removal west of the Mississippi was one of the major scandals of Indian management.

The Pottawattamies in this locality had been educated and instructed in religion for decades by the Catholic fathers and by the Rev. Isaac McCoy's Carey Mission near Niles, Mich. Some of those less amenable to culture were willing to make the western move had decent lands been offered, but many preferred to keep their Illinois, Indiana, and Michigan lands and to continue their farming. In the late Thirties Gen. John Tipton, then Indian agent, enlisted the northern militia companies, herded together all the Pottawattamies that could be caught, and drove them to the Indian territory, a large percent of the victims dying on the way, due to a total lack of preparation or arrangement for their care or comfort.

Pokagon's and a few other small bands then residing in Michigan escaped removal and managed to retain a little swamp and dune land upon which they eked out an existence until time brought about either their oblivion or their assimilation.

Simon Pokagon was born at his father's town in 1830, shortly before the general removal. Chief Leopold, his father, a wise leader and a Christian, died in 1840 or 1841. Leopold's wife, Elizabeth, encouraged their son to gain an education.

At fourteen, when he entered the preparatory department of Notre Dame University, he spoke only his native language. He remained at Notre Dame three years, attended Oberlin College for one year, and studied at Twinsburg, O., for two years more.

By 1860 he was back with his people, recognized as chief of the eastern Pottawattamies and a leader in race betterment. He had a knowledge of Greek and Latin, translated at least a thousand sermons into his language, learned to play the organ in order to accompany church services, wrote verse and prose for publication, and, year in and year out, devoted his efforts to securing the payment for his people's lands, which the government, characteristically in such matters, withheld. Finally, in 1897, when the value of the lands involved had risen to perhaps two or three thousand times the price promised the Pottawattamies, the original $150,000 was paid.

During his later years Pokagon lectured widely and contributed to such currently leading periodicals as HARPER'S, THE ARENA, THE CHAUTAUQUAN, REVIEW OF REVIEWS, and THE FORUM. He appeared at the Columbian Exposition in Chicago, representing his people as original owners of Chicago lands (then still not paid for) and was enthusiastically received.

Simon Pokagon died at his home in Lee Township, Allegan County, Mich., on Jan. 27, 1899.

Information from Pokagon—*O-Gi-Maw-Kwe Mit-I-Gwa-Ki*; McDonald—*Removal of the Pottawattamies from Northern Indiana*; Indiana Historical Society—*The Tipton Papers*, etc.

* * *

The Red Man's Greeting. (Printed on birchbark.) *Hartford, Mich.*, 1893.

O-Gi-Maw-Kwe Mit-I-Gwa-Ki (Queen of the Woods). Also Brief Sketch of the Algaic Language. *Hartford, Mich.*, 1899.

PORTER, GENE STRATTON (MRS. CHARLES DARWIN): 1868–1924.

Gene Stratton, popular novelist of the first quarter of the Twentieth century, whose books are still widely read, was born on a farm in Wabash County, Ind., in 1868. She was the youngest of twelve children of Mark and Mary Shellenbarger Stratton and developed an interest in nature during her early life on the farm.

In 1886 she married Charles Darwin Porter. The couple lived in a cabin adjoining the Limberlost swamp —later made famous by Mrs. Porter in her books—and she continued her studies of wild life. For two years she edited the camera department of RECREATION, for another two years was on the natural history staff of OUTING, and for four years served as a specialist in natural history photography on PHOTOGRAPHIC TIMES ANNUAL ALMANAC.

While criticism can be made of her literary skill and her sugary sentiment, no one can deny her thoroughgoing knowledge of nature and wild life, particularly of birds.

She died in Los Angeles, Calif., in 1924.

Information from *Who Was Who in America* and *Twentieth Century Authors*.

* * *

The Song of the Cardinal: a Love Story; the Illustrations Being Camera Studies from Life by the Author. *Indianapolis*, 1903.

Freckles. *Garden City, N. Y.*, 1904.

What I Have Done with Birds. *Indianapolis*, 1907. (Reissued in 1917 as Friends in Feathers.)

At the Foot of the Rainbow. *New York*, 1907.

Birds of the Bible. *New York*, 1909.

A Girl of the Limberlost. *Garden City, N. Y.*, 1909.

Music of the Wild; with Reproductions of the Performers, Their Instruments and Festival Halls. *New York*, 1910.

The Harvester. *Garden City, N. Y.*, 1911.

Moths of the Limberlost; with Water Color and Photographic Illustrations from Life. *Garden City, N. Y.*, 1912.

After the Flood. *Indianapolis*, 1912.

Laddie; a True Blue Story. *Garden City, N. Y.*, 1913.

Birds of the Limberlost. *Garden City, N. Y.*, 1914.

Michael O'Halloran. *Garden City, N. Y.*, 1915.

Morning Face. *Garden City, N. Y.*, 1916.

Friends in Feathers; Character Studies of Native American Birds Which, Through Friendly Advances, I Induced to Pose for Me, or Succeeded in Photographing by Good Fortune, with the Story of My Experiences in Obtaining Their Pictures. *Garden City, N. Y.*, 1917. (Reissue of What I Have Done with Birds.)

A Daughter of the Land. *Garden City, N. Y.,* 1918.
Homing with the Birds. *Garden City, N. Y.,* 1919.
Her Father's Daughter. *Garden City, N. Y.,* 1921.
The Fire Bird. *Garden City, N. Y.,* 1922.
The White Flag. *Garden City, N. Y.,* 1923.
Jesus of the Emerald. *Garden City, N. Y.,* 1923.
Wings. *Garden City, N. Y.,* 1923.
The Keeper of the Bees. *Garden City, N. Y.,* 1925.
Tales You Won't Believe. *Garden City, N. Y.,* 1925.
Magic Garden. *New York,* 1927.
Let Us Highly Resolve. *Garden City, N. Y.,* 1927.
Freckles Finds Himself.

POST, MARTIN MERCILLIAN: 1805–1876.

"Martin M. Post was born in Vermont in 1805. He was educated at Middlebury College and Andover Theological Seminary. On Christmas Day, 1829, he arrived at Logansport, Ind., to be the first minister of the gospel to locate there. He served the community faithfully in his profession until he died in 1876.

"Under his guidance the first church in Cass County was erected . . . President Tuttle of Wabash College assisted Rev. Post in dedicating the second church in December, 1862.

"The Reverend Post had five sons all of whom became Presbyterian ministers. His one daughter married Stanley Coulter, well known educator of Indiana.

"Rev. Post wrote many articles and addresses which were published by the religious and secular press."

From Powell—*History of Cass County,* 1913.

* * *

Retrospect of Thirty Years of Ministerial Work. *Logansport, Ind.,* 1860.

POST, MARTIN, JR.: ?–

Reared in Logansport, Ind., if not born there, Martin Post was the son of the Rev. Martin Mercillian Post, long-time (1829-1876) Presbyterian minister of that place. He attended Logansport schools and received the A.B. degree from Wabash College in 1858. Entering the Presbyterian ministry, he was occupying a pulpit in Georgia at the time he published his one recorded book—reminiscences of his father's life in Logansport.

Information from the Wabash College Archives.

* * *

The Riverton Minister; a Story of the Early Days in Logansport, *Atlanta, Ga.,* 1897.

POTTER, LEMUEL: 1841–1897.

Lemuel Potter, son of Jesse and Margaret Sams Potter, was born in Edwards County, Ill., on Oct. 28, 1841, and received a limited education in the district schools. His mother died when he was ten years old, and, until he was a young man, he helped his father on the farm. In March of 1863 he married Lydia Jane Humphreys.

He began teaching in 1862 but joined the Baptist Church in the fall of 1863 and following his conversion felt himself drawn to the ministry, which he formally entered in January of 1865. For about twelve years, beginning in 1868, he preached at Grayville, Ill., and had charge of four other churches in Posey County, Ind., traveling to them on horseback or by carriage. He was not paid for his preaching at this time and had to farm to support his family.

In December of 1880 he moved to Posey County, Ind. In 1885 he became pastor of the church at Owensville, Ind., while continuing to serve his former churches.

Information from *Labors and Travels of Elder Lemuel Potter* . . .

* * *

Joint Discussion of Foreign Missions Between the Rev. H. Clay Yates, Pastor of the Owensville Cumberland Presbyterian Church and Elder Lemuel Potter, Pastor of the Owensville Regular Baptist Church, Held in Owensville, Indiana, December 14-19, 1885. *Nashville, Tenn.,* 1886.

A Two Days' Debate on the Atonement, Between Elder Lemuel Potter . . . and Elder Thomas W. Dickey . . . Held at the Lilly Meeting House in Wayne County, Ill., on . . . April 19-20, 1887. *Evansville, Ind.,* 1887.

Labors and Travels of Elder Lemuel Potter, as an Old School Baptist Minister, for Thirty Years, with a Brief Sketch of His Earlier Life, Christian Experience, and Call to the Ministry, Together with His Doctrinal Sentiments on Some Vital Points. *Evansville, Ind.,* 1894.

POWELL, JEHU Z.: 1848–1918.

Jehu Z. Powell, son of Jacob and Martha A. Troutman Powell, was born in Cass County, Ind., on Aug. 13, 1848. He attended the Logansport schools and the Presbyterian Academy and was graduated from the literary department of the University of Michigan in 1871 and from the medical department in 1874. He opened an office in Logansport in the same year.

Dr. Powell was a member of the city council for four years, a presidential elector in 1896 and postmaster of Logansport from 1892 to 1902. He was chairman of the Cass County Republican Committee from 1892 to 1896.

Dr. Powell was married three times. His first wife, Mary J. Leffel, died in 1877. His second marriage was to Mrs. Louisa F. Ewing (nee Harris) who died in 1899, and Catherine A. Market was his third wife.

Dr. Powell served as secretary of the Cass County Medical Society for 25 years, and in 1903 he was a delegate to the International Medical Congress at Madrid, Spain.

He edited the *History of Cass County* which was published in 1913. It was a distinctive piece of work. Unlike most compilers of county histories, Dr. Powell took a keen and scholarly interest in the subjects of his biographical sketches. He took a particular interest in those citizens who had written for publication and the information he gives is accurate and complete. His work is the source of most of the Cass County entries in this compilation.

He died on Jan. 8, 1918.

Information from the Logansport Public Library.

* * *

History of Cass County. *Chicago,* 1913. 2 vols.

PRAIGG, DAVID TODD: 1850–1937.

David Todd Praigg was born in Louisville, Ky., on Feb. 16, 1850, and came to Franklin, Ind., as a young teacher.

He became city editor of the INDIANAPOLIS SENTINEL in 1881, soon after his marriage to Agnes Noble of Greenwood, Ind. He also acted as Indiana representative for metropolitan dailies throughout the country and wrote occasional fiction and verse for periodicals.

In 1908 he bought the Portland (Ind.) COMMERCIAL-MAIL and operated it until 1916, when he established the INDIANA INSTRUCTOR, a periodical for teachers, which he published for a year or two.

He died on June 9, 1937.

Information from the Indiana State Library.

* * *

Almetta. *Indianapolis,* 1894.
Marriage Made Easy. *Lebanon, O.,* 1922.

PRATT, SARAH SMITH (MRS. W. D.): 1853–1942.

Few facts are available on the life of Mrs. Sarah Smith Pratt. She was born in 1853 and in 1883-86 was a resident of Logansport, Ind., where she was editing a weekly newspaper called the SUNDAY CRITIC which belonged to her husband, W. D. Pratt, and to which she contributed a column, "Flotsam and Jetsam."

She was founder and for six years editor of ON MERIDIAN, a publication of the Indianapolis Y.W.C.A. In 1917 she was contributing to the LIVING CHURCH, the CHURCHMAN and to other periodicals.

Information from the Barry Ms., quoting Indianapolis newspapers.

* * *

Blue Cashmere Gown: a Story of a Missionary Box. *Milwaukee,* 1914.
The Old Crop in Indiana. *Indianapolis,* 1928.
Episcopal Bishops in Indiana; a Churchwoman's Retrospect. *Indianapolis,* 1934.
Guess This Word. *Indianapolis,* 1938.

PRESTON, ELLEN LASSELLE (MRS. ROBERT EMMETT): 1839–1909.

"Mrs. Ellen Lasselle Preston, daughter of Hyacinth and Nancy (Polk) Lasselle, was born in Logansport in 1839 and moved with her parents to Washington, D. C., in 1849. In 1863 she married Robert Emmett Preston; they had five children. She died May 1, 1909."

From Powell—*History of Cass County,* 1913.

* * *

Magdalene the Enchantress.

PRICE, WILLIAM HENRY: 1855–?

William Henry Price, clergyman, was born in Kokomo, Ind., on July 10, 1855. His parents were John and Anna D. Wentz Price.

Price graduated from Capital University (O.) and the German Lutheran Theological Seminary at Columbus, O., in 1883. On Sept. 25, 1884, he married Charlotte C. Schmalz at Patricksburg, Ind.

He served Evangelical Lutheran churches as pastor and synod officer in Indiana and Ohio.

Information from *Who's Who in America.*

* * *

Life and Labor of Rev. Christian Frederick Schwartz. *Columbus, O.,* n.d.

PROSSER, CHARLES ALLEN: 1871–

Charles Allen Prosser, son of Reese William and Sarah Emma Prosser, was born at New Albany, Ind., on Sept. 20, 1871, and graduated from De Pauw University in 1897, receiving the A.M. degree in 1906 and the Ph.D. in 1919. In 1898 he graduated from the law school of the University of Louisville. In 1915 he received a Ph.D. degree from Columbia University and he also received honorary degrees from various institutions. He married Zerelda A. Huckeby on Dec. 30, 1896.

After teaching in the New Albany public schools, he served as superintendent from 1900 to 1908. In 1909-10 he was superintendent of the Children's Aid Society in New York, from 1910 to 1912 assistant commissioner of education for Massachusetts, and after 1915 director of William Hood Dunwoody Institute in Minneapolis. He lectured at various colleges and universities.

Information from Who's Who in America.

* * *

The New Harmony Movement (with George B. Lockwood). 1905.

Training of the Factory Worker Through Industrial Education: Address Delivered before 5th Annual Convention of National Society for Promotion of Industrial Education. Cincinnati, November, 1911. *New York,* 1912.

Why Federal Aid for Vocational Education? *New York,* 1912.

Teacher and Old Age (with W. I. Hamilton). *Boston,* 1913.

Study of the Boston Mechanic Arts High School, being a Report to the Boston School Committee. *New York,* 1915.

Vocational Retraining; a National Conservation. *New York,* 1918.

Vocational Education in a Democracy (with C. R. Allen). *New York,* 1925.

Have We Kept the Faith? America at the Cross-Roads in Education (with C. R. Allen). *New York,* 1929.

The Evening Industrial School. 1929.

Adult Education; the Evening Industrial School (with M. R. Bass). *New York,* 1930.

Information Book on Selecting an Occupation; Helpful Information, Suggestions, and Directions for Finding the Demands and Opportunities of Occupations; for Checking Individual Assets against Such Demands; and for Selecting a Suitable Occupation (with R. H. Palmer). *Bloomington, Ill.,* 1936.

Information Book on Getting a Job (with W. A. Anderson). *Bloomington, Ill.,* 1936.

Information Book on Keeping Physically Fit (with W. A. Anderson). *Bloomington, Ill.,* 1936.

Information Book on a Health Program; Information, Suggestions, Directions, and Practice in Doing the Things that Promote Good Health, Safeguard Against Disease, and Lengthen Life, through All Such Things as: Fighting Disease Germs; Fresh Pure Air, Etc. (with W. A. Anderson). *Bloomington, Ill.,* 1936.

Information Book on Taking a Look at Yourself; Information Regarding the Principal Personal Qualities that Make for Success, Usefulness, and Happiness in Life; Regarding the Ways by which One's Personality Can be Checked and Improved. *Bloomington, Ill.,* 1937.

Secondary Education and Life. *Cambridge, Mass.,* 1939.

Q

QUINN, ALICE MAY: ?–

According to D. S. A., writing in the CINCINNATI GAZETTE for Dec. 7, 1876, regarding Daniel Hough's collection of books by Indiana authors, Alice May Quinn had formerly lived in Connersville, Ind., and was then (1876) living in Indianapolis and contributing to the INDIANAPOLIS PEOPLE.

Information from the CINCINNATI GAZETTE, Dec. 7, 1876.

* * *

Sweet Astreanere and Other Poems. *Cincinnati,* 1872.

R

RABB, FRANCES MORRISON (MRS. ALBERT L.): ?–

Born in Indianapolis into a family which played an important part in the history of Indiana, Frances Morrison was just out of college at the time of World War I. Judge Morrison, her grandfather, was the first attorney general of the state of Indiana, and her father was an important physician of Indianapolis.

She was married to Albert L. Rabb, son of Albert and Kate Milner Rabb. She contributed to many poetry magazines and published a collection of poetry. After her husband's death in 1940 she managed her five hundred and fifty-five acre farm.

Information from the Indianapolis Public Library.

* * *

Poems: Frannie's First Book. *Indianapolis,* 1914.

RABB, KATE MILNER (MRS. ALBERT): 1866–1937.

Born on Aug. 9, 1866, in Rockport, Ind., Kate Milner was the daughter of the town's leading physician (Dr. I. Livingston Milner) and a descendant of pioneers who had moved to Indiana from Kentucky prior to the Civil War. After graduation from the Rockport High School she entered Indiana University, where she became engaged to Albert Rabb. She received the A.M. degree at Indiana, then taught school in Jeffersonville and Rockport before her marriage to Albert Rabb in 1891. They made their home in Indianapolis, where Mr. Rabb was a prominent attorney. He died in 1918.

Although she had shown an early interest in writing and had had poems and stories published in the local papers, it was only after her marriage that she began to take her writing seriously. In addition to her books, she wrote stories for various magazines—the DELINEATOR, ST. NICHOLAS, and the YOUTH'S COMPANION—and she conducted a weekly column in the INDIANAPOLIS STAR known as the "Hoosier Listening Post." Mrs. Rabb died in Indianapolis on July 3, 1937.

Mrs. Rabb translated a juvenile from the German, compiled a collection of essays and edited a ten-volume collection of humor, besides the works listed here.

Information from the Indianapolis Public Library and the INDIANA HISTORY BULLETIN, Feb., 1938.

* * *

The Pageant of Spencer County, Presented July 4, 1916 at Rockport, Indiana. n.p., 1916.

A Tour Through Indiana in 1840; the Diary of John Parsons of Petersburg, Virginia. (Editor [actually author].) *New York,* 1920.

No Mean City. *Indianapolis,* 1922.

RANDALL, JAMES GARFIELD: 1881–

James Garfield Randall, son of Horace and Ellen Amanda Kregelo Randall, was born in Indianapolis on June 24, 1881. After graduating from Shortridge High School and Butler University and taking advanced degrees at the University of Chicago, he was a teacher of history and political science at various universities and colleges—Illinois, Michigan, Syracuse, Chicago, Roanoke, and Richmond. He was acting professor at Butler University and became professor of American history at the University of Illinois in 1920. He was married first to Edith Laura Abbott, who died in 1913, then to Ruth Elaine Painter.

Besides his books he wrote many articles on Lincoln and his period and contributed to various historical and political science reviews.

Information from *Who's Who in America* and the Indianapolis Public Library.

* * *

Confiscation of Property during the Civil War. *Indianapolis,* 1913.

Constitutional Problems under Lincoln. *New York,* 1926.

The Civil War and Reconstruction. *New York,* 1937.

Lincoln, the President; Springfield to Gettysburg. *New York,* 1945.

Lincoln and the South. *Baton Rouge, La.,* 1946.

RATH, EMIL: 1873–1943.

Born in Barmen, Germany, in 1873, Emil Rath came to the U. S. as a young man and graduated from a Pittsburgh, Pa., high school. In 1909 he moved to Indianapolis as a member of the North American Gymnastic Union faculty, remaining with that institution until 1934 and serving as president for twenty-five years. After 1934 he was director of physical education and health in the Indianapolis public schools. He was a nationally known authority in the field of physical education. He died in Indianapolis on Oct. 21, 1943. He wrote several textbooks on gymnastics not listed here.

Information from Indianapolis Public Library.

* * *

Aesthetic Dancing. *New York,* 1914.

Theory and Practice of Physical Education. *Indianapolis,* 1915-16. 3 vols.

Folk and School Dances. *Indianapolis,* 1919.

Frolic of the Brownies. *Indianapolis,* 1920.

Outlines of Some Physical Education Activities. *Indianapolis,* 1926.

Folk Dance in Education. *Minneapolis,* 1939.

RATLIFF, WALTER STEVENS: 1860–1941.

Walter Stevens Ratliff, son of James Cornelius and Mary Crawford Ratliff, was born in Richmond, Ind., on Apr. 24, 1860. His ancestors were among the earliest settlers of eastern Indiana. After attending the district schools he entered Purdue University in 1879 and graduated with honors, although he had largely supported himself while in school. He also received a degree from Earlham College and did post graduate work in forestry, entomology and botany at the University of California, as well as studying for one year in Paris.

For many years Mr. Ratliff was an outstanding authority as a horticulturist, entomologist, and biologist, contributing to magazines and agricultural periodicals. He was a member of the Indiana Legislature and of the State Board of Agriculture.

He died in Richmond, Ind., on May 10, 1941.

> Information from Roll—*Indiana*, Vol. IV, and the INDIANAPOLIS STAR, May 11, 1941.

* * *

Wayne County Centennial History.
Memoirs of Wayne County and the City of Richmond.

RAVE, HERMAN CHARLES FREDERICK: circa 1849–1929.

Born in Kiel, Germany, Herman Rave came to New York at the age of sixteen and later made his home in Jeffersonville, Ind. He was a reporter for both the NEW ALBANY TRIBUNE and the NEW ALBANY LEDGER, and his column, "Country Jottings," was well known throughout southeastern Indiana. He died in New Albany on Dec. 13, 1929.

> Information from Parker and Heiney—*Poets and Poetry of Indiana* and the New Albany Public Library.

* * *

Songs and Ballads. *Indianapolis*, 1893.

RAWLES, WILLIAM A.: 1863–1936.

William A. Rawles was born in Remington, Ind., in 1863, son of Lycurgus and Catherine Baker Oilar Rawles.

He received the A.B. and A.M. degrees from Indiana University in 1884 and 1899 and the Ph.D. from Columbia University in 1903. He married Harriet McClure Post on June 26, 1895.

After serving as teacher and high school principal in Indiana and Missouri, he joined the Indiana University faculty in 1894 as instructor and professor, variously, of history, economics and political economy. He became dean of the university's school of commerce and finance in 1920.

Dr. Rawles died May 17, 1936.

> Information from *Who Was Who in America*.

* * *

The Government of the People of the State of Indiana (with Francis N. Thorpe). *Philadelphia*, 1897.
Tax Facts about Indiana. *Indianapolis*, 1924.

RAY, CHARLES WAYNE: 1872–1928.

Charles Wayne Ray, son of William Riley and Hester Ann Lee Ray, was born in Riley, Ind., on Apr. 2, 1872, and graduated from De Pauw University in 1900. He was ordained to the Methodist Episcopal ministry in 1894. In 1902 he received the A.M. degree from Taylor University and in 1905 the D.D. degree from Nebraska Wesleyan. He was pastor of various churches in Nebraska for many years. In 1907 he toured Europe and Asia Minor, and he revisited Europe in 1910 and 1913. For his two poems, "No Man's Land" and "The Dead In Flanders," he was decorated by King Albert of Belgium.

The Rev. Mr. Ray married Arethusa S. Ervin in 1907 and died in April, 1928.

He wrote a number of essays and poems published in leaflet form besides the titles listed here.

> Information from *Who Was Who in America*.

* * *

Bible Questions Answered. *Cincinnati*, 1903.
The Radiant Life. *Cincinnati*, 1907.
Heart Echoes. 1913.
The Bright Side of Living. *Lyons, Neb.*, 1916.
Ray-Poems, the Tides of Fortune. *Norfolk, Neb.*, 1923.

REAM, LAURA: 1828–1913.

Born in Lebanon, O., in 1828, Laura Ream came to Indianapolis with her parents when she was quite young and attended the Episcopal Female School of Indianapolis and the Catholic Female Seminary near Bardstown, Ky. Her parents died soon after she returned from the seminary, and she lived with a widowed sister and younger brother until the sister's death in 1855. Afterwards she lived with a friend and, having only a small income left by her father, she determined to use her ability as a writer and became a newspaper correspondent, writing for the CINCINNATI DAILY COMMERCIAL. She died in Indianapolis in 1913.

> Information from the Indianapolis Public Library.

* * *

History of a Trip to the Great Saginaw Valley, June 1871. *Indianapolis*, 1871.

RECORD, SAMUEL JAMES: 1881–1945.

Samuel James Record was born in Crawfordsville, Ind., on Mar. 10, 1881, the son of James K. P. and Mary M. Hutton Record. He graduated from Crawfordsville High School in 1899. Entering Wabash College, he received the A.B. degree in 1903, the A.M. in 1906 and the M.F. from Yale University in 1905. Wabash College awarded the Sc.D. in 1930. Samuel James Record and Mary E. Strauss were married on Apr. 1, 1906.

In 1904 he had become identified with the U. S. Forestry Service, where he continued until he joined the Yale University faculty in 1910. At Yale he was successively instructor, professor and, after 1939, dean of the school of forestry. His special interests were forest products and their uses and tropical forestry. He was editor and manager of the quarterly TROPICAL WOODS after 1925.

He contributed largely to learned journals and serials in his field.

Dean Record died Feb. 3, 1945.

Information from *Who's Who in America* and the Wabash College Archives.

* * *

Identification of the Economic Woods of the United States, Including a Discussion of the Structural and Physical Properties of Wood. *New York*, 1912.

Mechanical Properties of Wood, Including a Discussion of the Factors Affecting the Mechanical Properties, and Methods of Timber Testing. *New York*, 1914.

Timbers of Tropical America (with C. D. Mell). *New Haven, Conn.*, 1924.

Identification of the Timbers of Temperate North America, Including Anatomy and Certain Physical Properties of Wood. *New York*, 1934.

North American Trees; a Guide to the Charles F. Millspaugh Hall of Field Museum. *Chicago*, 1934.

Forests of British Honduras. 1936.

Timbers of the New World. *New Haven, Conn.*, 1943.

REDDING, JACOB: ?–?

Dr. Jacob Redding was the son of Iredell Redding of Henry County, Ind. He was born sometime in the Thirties and, after studying medicine, practiced in New Castle and Knightstown, Henry County, at least through the Nineties, when he is recorded as practicing in the former city. He is said to have invented a bicycle coaster brake.

Information from the Indiana State Library.

* * *

The Molecular Theory of Physics. [No copy located but listed as Redding's work on the title page of his physiology.]

Physiology: Its Science and Philosophy, a Treatise Comprising the Substance of a Course of Lectures . . . *New Castle, Ind.*, 1891.

REED, CHARLES ALFRED LEE: 1856–1928.

Charles Alfred Lee Reed, son of Dr. Richard Cumming Stockton and Nancy Clark Reed, was born at Wolf Lake, Ind., on July 9, 1856, and graduated from the Cincinnati College of Medicine and Surgery in 1874. In 1894 he received an honorary A.M. degree from Miami University. He married Irene E. Dougherty on May 27, 1880.

From 1882 to 1896 he taught at the Cincinnati College of Medicine and Surgery, from 1902 to 1909 at the Medical College of Ohio (now the University of Cincinnati), and from 1909 to 1917 at the University of Cincinnati. After 1898 he held the post of gynecologist at Cincinnati Hospital. During the first World War Dr. Reed was a major in the U. S. Army Medical Corps. He served as president of the American Medical Association in 1900-01.

In addition to his books Dr. Reed wrote articles for newspapers and magazines on medico-sociological subjects.

He died in Cincinnati on Aug. 28, 1928.

Information from *Who Was Who in America.*

* * *

Christian Science: a Sociological Study. *Cincinnati*, 1898.

Diseases of Women; Medical and Surgical Gynecology. *New York*, 1913.

Marriage and Genetics: Laws of Human Breeding and Applied Genetics. *Cincinnati*, 1913.

Stomach and Intestines. 1913.

Chronic Convulsive Toxemia. 1919.

The First Estate. *Boston*, 1927. (Novel.)

REED, HUGH T.: 1850–1934.

Son of Irvin and Mary Mifflin Reed, Hugh T. Reed was born on Aug. 17, 1850, on a farm in Wayne County, near Richmond, Ind.

He was educated at the University of Michigan and at West Point. He entered the regular army upon his graduation in 1873, married Sallie E. Ferguson in 1882 and held the rank of colonel when he reached retirement age. He died in 1934.

Information from the Richmond Public Library.

* * *

Signal Tactics. *Baltimore, 1880.* (Later issued as Standard Signal Tactics.)

Cadet Regulations, Prepared for Cadets of the Military Department at the Southern Illinois Normal University. *Richmond, Ind., 1881.*

Elements of Military Science and Tactics. *Baltimore, 1882.*

Broom Tactics; or, Calisthenics in a New Form for Young Ladies. *Baltimore, 1883.*

Standard Infantry Tactics. *Baltimore, 1883.*

Cadet Life at West Point. *Chicago, 1896.*

REED, ISAAC: 1787–?

Isaac Reed, pioneer Presbyterian minister in Indiana, was born in Granville, N. Y., on Aug. 27, 1787. Following his graduation from Middlebury College in Vermont in 1812, he tried teaching for a while, studied law, but eventually turned to the ministry as his field.

Because he thought that a different climate might benefit his health, he decided upon missionary work in the West, and in 1816 he was sent to Kentucky by the Presbyterian Societies of New England. For a short time he preached on a circuit in Kentucky, and in July, 1818, made a visit to Indiana, where in October of the same year he became pastor of a church in New Albany. While serving in this capacity he made frequent preaching excursions through the southern part of the state and founded the first Sunday School in Indiana.

He resigned his pastorate at the end of the year and began traveling through Kentucky and Indiana for the Missionary Society of Connecticut. On Sept. 26, 1819, he organized the Presbyterian Church in Bloomington. While attending a synod at Danville, Ky., he met Elinor Young, a sister of Mrs. Baynard Rush Hall (wife of the first president of what is now Indiana University), and they were married. In 1822 he became pastor of the Bethany Church in Owen County, where he built a home.

He led in the organization of the Salem Presbytery in 1823 and helped organize churches at Crawfordsville, Greencastle, Bethlehem, and Terre Haute. In the fall of 1823 he took charge of churches at Indianapolis and Bloomington—traveling the distance of more than fifty miles on horseback.

Reed returned East and settled, temporarily, at least, in Moriah, N. Y., some time in 1827.

His book, *The Christian Traveler,* published immediately after his return to the East, describes his travels and adventures in Indiana and Kentucky. It is

a narrative of considerable charm and historical importance, and is now quite rare.

Information from the INDIANA MAGAZINE OF HISTORY, Vols. 21 and 22.

* * *

The Christian's Duty, Stated, Proved, and Applied. *Indianapolis, 1824.*

The Christian Traveler. *New York, 1828.*

The Youth's Book, in Four Parts. *Indianapolis, 1840.*

REED, JOSEPH SAMUEL: 1852–circa 1920.

Born in Sullivan County, Ind., in 1852, Joseph Samuel Reed attended the public schools of Sullivan until 1862, when he moved with his father to a farm in Fairbanks Township. He then attended the district schools and in 1870 entered Franklin College, where he remained one year. In 1875 he married Emma Davis.

Following his year at college, he returned to Sullivan and became a drug clerk and in 1875 engaged in the drug business for himself. He was a member of the Western Association of Writers, serving as treasurer of that organization for three years.

Mr. Reed died about 1920.

Information from *Art Souvenir of Leading Citizens and Farmers' Directory of Sullivan County, Indiana,* 1896 and THE INDIANIAN, Vol. III, No. 2.

* * *

Winnowed Grasses. *Indianapolis, 1892.*

From Nature's Nooks. *Indianapolis, 1905.*

REED, PETER FISHE: 1819–?

Born in Boston, Mass., on May 5, 1819, Peter Fishe Reed was a resident of Vernon, Ind., around 1850 and of Indianapolis for many years. He later removed to Lockland, O., and he died at the home of a son in Iowa.

While a resident of Indiana he was at various times a farmer, shoemaker, house and sign painter, editor, doctor, photographer, music teacher, artist, and writer.

Information from Parker and Heiney—*Poets and Poetry of Indiana* and D. S. A. in the CINCINNATI DAILY GAZETTE, Dec. 7, 1876.

* * *

Incidents of the War; or, the Romance and Realities of Soldier Life. *Indianapolis, 1862.*

Voices of the Wind and Other Poems. *Chicago, 1868.*

Beyond the Snow: History of Trim's Adventures in Nordlichtschein. *Chicago, 1873.*

REEVES, ARTHUR MIDDLETON: 1856–1891.

Arthur Middleton Reeves was the son of Mark Evan and Caroline Middleton Reeves. Born in Cincinnati, O., on Oct. 7, 1856, he learned the printer's trade as a boy.

Mr. Reeves was graduated from Cornell in 1878, having taken a prominent part in undergraduate activities, especially in student publications.

He established a successful printing business in Richmond, Ind., which later became the job department of THE RICHMOND PALLADIUM. Having acquired an interest in languages, history, mythology and folkways, he devoted much time to travel and study and wrote extensively on Norse history and mythology. Several of his translations are still standard.

Mr. Reeves was killed in a railroad accident near Hagerstown, Ind., on Feb. 25, 1891.

He translated several important works from the Norse and Icelandic which are not listed here.

> Information from the Richmond Public Library and the *Dictionary of American Biography.*

* * *

The Finding of Wineland the Good; the History of the Icelandic Discovery of America. (Editor.) *London,* 1890.

Jan, a Short Story. *Chicago,* 1892.

REEVES, JESSE SIDDALL: 1872–

Jesse Siddall Reeves was born in Richmond, Ind., on July 27, 1872. He attended Kenyon College but transferred to Amherst and received the B.S. degree there in 1891. He received the Ph.D. degree from Johns Hopkins University in 1894 and was awarded the L.H.D. degree by Amherst in 1926.

He was instructor in American history at the Woman's College of Baltimore in 1893-1894, a lecturer on diplomatic history at Johns Hopkins University from 1904 to 1906. In 1897 he returned to Richmond, Ind., was admitted to the Wayne County bar and practiced law there from 1897 to 1907. In the latter year he gave up the practice of law and became assistant professor of political science at Dartmouth College, remaining there until 1910, when he became professor of political science at the University of Michigan.

Dr. Reeves served as associate editor of THE AMERICAN JOURNAL OF INTERNATIONAL LAW and lectured in America and abroad.

> Information from *Who's Who in America* and the Richmond Public Library.

* * *

The International Beginnings of the Congo Free State. *Baltimore,* 1894.

The Napoleonic Exiles in America, 1815-1819. *Baltimore,* 1905.

Jeremy Bentham and American Jurisprudence, n.p., 1906.

American Diplomacy under Tyler and Polk. *Baltimore,* 1907.

La Communauté Internationale. *Paris,* 1925.

REID, JOHN S.: ?–?

John S. Reid is one of those characters who appear and disappear, making considerable impression by their presence but failing to elicit enough interest during their lives to make it worthwhile for any contemporary to record biographical facts.

He is thought to have been born in Ireland and he was living in Connersville, Ind., in 1845 when his narrative poem *Gulzar, Or The Rose Bower,* was published in Indianapolis.

The breadth of Reid's education must have been singular in its day. He is said to have translated from the Persian, and the inspiration for the poem mentioned above was believed at the time to have come from Persian literature. It is more reasonable, however, to credit the inspiration to Tom Moore's "Lalla Rookh." No matter what the source of its inspiration, the book must have sold rather widely in its time because D. S. A., writing in the CINCINNATI GAZETTE for Dec. 7, 1876, reported that Judge Reid disowned authorship of the poem after lawyers had quoted from it, to his annoyance; and he was believed to have bought up and burned all available copies of the edition. If he hoped to eliminate all traces of the poem, he was unsuccessful, for copies occasionally come to light to this day.

Judge Reid died at Indianapolis.

> Information from Parker and Heiney—*Poets and Poetry of Indiana,* and D. S. A. in the CINCINNATI GAZETTE, Dec. 7, 1876.

* * *

Gulzar, or the Rose Bower. A Tale of Persia. *Indianapolis,* 1845.

REISNER, GEORGE ANDREW: 1867–1942.

George Andrew Reisner, archaeologist and Egyptologist, was born in Indianapolis on Nov. 5, 1867, the son of George Andrew and Mary Elizabeth Mason

Reisner. He was educated at Harvard University, where he received the A.B., A.M., and Ph.D. degrees. Following a year spent in Berlin as assistant in the Egyptian department of the Royal Museum and a year of teaching at Harvard, he was in Cairo, Egypt, for two years. From 1899 to 1905 he was at the University of California, and after 1905 he was connected with Harvard. He directed many Egyptian expeditions and excavations. He died in Cairo on June 7, 1942.

> Information from *Who's Who in America* and the Indianapolis Public Library.

* * *

Sumerisch-Babylonische Hymenn, nach Thontafeln Griechischer Zeit. *Berlin, 1896.*

Tempelurkunden aus Telloh. *Berlin, 1901.*

Hearst Medical Papyrus. *Berkeley, 1906.*

The Early Dynastic Cemeteries of Naga-ed-der. *Berkeley, 1908.* Part 1.

First Annual Report, Nubian Archaeological Survey. 1910.

Egyptian Conception of Immortality: the Ingersoll Lecture, 1911. *Boston,* [1912].

Models of Ships and Boats. 1913.

Excavations at Kerma. *Cambridge, Mass.,* 1923. 2 vols.

Harvard Excavations at Samaria, 1908-1910 (with C. S. Fisher and D. Lyon). *Cambridge,* 1924. 2 vols.

Mycerinus; the Temples of the Third Pyramid at Giza. *Cambridge, Mass.,* 1931.

A Provincial Cemetery of the Pyramid Age: Naga-ed-der. *Berkeley,* 1932. Part 3.

Development of the Egyptian Tomb down to the Accession of Cheops. *Cambridge, Mass.,* 1936.

RERICK, JOHN H.: 1830–?

John H. Rerick, son of Henry and Elizabeth Lamb Rerick, was born on Feb. 4, 1830, near Dayton, Tippecanoe County, Ind. His father was a farmer. After being educated in the common schools and at the academy at South Bend, he taught school for a time, and in 1851 he entered the medical department of the University of Michigan, from which he graduated in 1853. On Dec. 2, 1853, he married Elizabeth Green, who died in 1855, and on May 1, 1856, he married Marianette Devor.

Dr. Rerick practiced at Sumption Prairie (St. Joseph County), Fort Wayne, South Bend, and Elkhart before settling in Lagrange, Ind., in 1859. During the Civil War he served as assistant surgeon, and later as surgeon, of the 44th Indiana Infantry for a period of four years. At the close of the war he returned to La-

grange and resumed his practice, but in 1867 he purchased the LAGRANGE STANDARD, discontinued medicine, and became its editor. He also served for a time as clerk of the Circuit Court.

> Information from *Representative Men of Indiana,* Vol. II.

* * *

The Forty-Fourth Indiana Volunteer Infantry. *Lagrange, Ind.,* 1880.

RICE, ALONZO LEORA: 1867–

Alonzo Leora Rice, son of James C. and Elizabeth Rice, was born at Little Blue River, Ind., on June 12, 1867, and graduated from Central Normal (now Canterbury) College in Danville, Ind., in 1896.

A teacher by profession, he was a contributor to many newspapers and magazines and acted as literary editor of the SUNNY SOUTH, published at Atlanta, Ga. Among other newspapers to which he contributed were the ATLANTA CONSTITUTION and the BOSTON TRANSCRIPT.

> Information from *Who's Who in America* and Parker and Heiney—*Poets and Poetry of Indiana.*

* * *

Prize Poems from Judge, Boston Transcript. *Indianapolis,* 1892.

Sunways of Song. (Introduction by Charles Major.) *Boston,* 1910.

RICE, ELIHU S.: 1827–?

Elihu S. Rice was born in Genesee County, N. Y., on Feb. 28, 1827. He came to Logansport, Ind., in 1838 and became a leading merchant in the town. He married Jeanette Malon in 1854.

Active in the Baptist Church, he wrote several songs, one of which, "Shall We Meet Beyond the River," still appears in many collections. His first book is a collection of rhymes which had appeared in the LOGANSPORT PHAROS in 1865.

> Information supplied by the Logansport Public Library.

* * *

Hardware. *Logansport, Ind.,* 1907.

Book of Commemoration of the 75th Anniversary of the Logansport Baptist Church, n.p. [Logansport], 1922.

RICE, LOUISE GUEST: 1884–

Louise Guest, daughter of James Harvey and Harriet Noel Davis Guest, was born in New Albany, Ind., on Apr. 24, 1884. After graduating from high school, she entered St. Mary's Academy at St. Louis, Mo., from which she graduated in 1898.

In 1901 she began as a reporter with the ST. LOUIS STAR and from 1901 to 1904 worked for various newspapers of the southern states and New York City. After 1905 she was a practicing graphologist. In 1925 she founded the Louise Rice Graphological Institute in New York and served as its president. She was a consulting psychologist and contributor to magazines.

Information from *Who's Who in America.*

* * *

Character Shown in Handwriting. 1908.

Dainty Dishes from Foreign Lands. *Chicago,* 1909.

Girl Who Walked Without Fear; a Comment on Christian America. *New York,* 1915.

New Blood; a Story of the Folks That Make America. *New York,* 1922.

Character Reading from Handwriting; with Numerous Line Drawings. *New York,* 1927.

By Whose Hand? *New York,* 1930.

Who Is Your Mate? What the Handwriting Reveals. *New York,* 1930.

RICHARDS, LOUISE PARKS (MRS. SAMUEL): 1852–1931.

Born in Bedford, Ind., in 1852, Louise Parks, daughter of R. M. Parks, a Baptist minister, attended Baptist Female Seminary in Indianapolis. After her marriage to Samuel Richards, she lived in Anderson, Ind., for fifty-five years, with intervals abroad. She died in Muncie, Ind., in 1931.

Information from the Barry Ms.

* * *

Oberammergau; Its Passion Play and Players. *Munich,* 1910.

RICHMAN, GEORGE J.: 1876–

George J. Richman was born in Greenfield, Ind., on Mar. 1, 1876. He graduated from Indiana State Normal School in 1899 and from the Indiana Law School, Indianapolis, in 1908.

After teaching at New Palestine, Ind., for three years he became superintendent of schools for Hancock County and served for twelve years. He then practiced law for three years, served as postmaster of Greenfield (1919-1923) and entered the banking business at Kempton, Ind., in 1924. Moving to Tipton, Ind., he became cashier of the Farmers Loan and Trust Co. in 1935 and executive vice-president in 1944.

Information from George J. Richman.

* * *

History of Hancock County, Indiana; Its People, Industries and Institutions; with Biographical Sketches of Representative Citizens and Genealogical Records of Many of the Old Families. *Indianapolis,* 1916.

History of Hancock County during the World War (joint author). [1919?].

RIDPATH, GILLUM: 1842–1881.

Gillum Ridpath was born in Putnam County, Ind., on Aug. 7, 1842, and graduated from De Pauw University in 1867, receiving the A.M. degree in 1870. He married Elizabeth Lupher on Nov. 11, 1877.

He was associated with public school administration in various Indiana communities—Greencastle, Anderson, Martinsville, Zionsville, and Scottsburg. For one year, 1877-78, he was professor of mathematics at Tullahoma Collegiate Institute in Tennessee, and prior to his death, which occurred on Nov. 4, 1881, in Aurora, Ill., he was professor of science at Jennings Seminary in Aurora.

Information from De Pauw University's *Alumnal Record, 1920.*

* * *

A History of Putnam County, Indiana. 1879.

RIDPATH, JOHN CLARK: 1841–1900.

Despite the fact that his amazingly voluminous output occasionally included hack work of the most obvious sort, the contribution which John Clark Ridpath made to the diffusion of knowledge in the U. S. in the Nineteenth century was of great importance.

Born on a farm in Putnam County, Ind., on Apr. 26, 1841 (some sources give 1840), he attended local schools and graduated from Indiana Asbury (now De Pauw) University in 1863. He received the A.M. from the same institution in 1866 and, in 1880, an honorary LL.D. from Syracuse University.

On Dec. 22, 1862, he married Hannah R. Smythe and, after receiving his degree the following spring, took up teaching. He taught in the Boone County

(Ind.) Academy, was superintendent of the Lawrenceburg schools for three years and, in 1869, returned to
Greencastle as a member of the Asbury Institute faculty,
which he continued to serve variously as professor of
English literature, belles lettres, history and political
science, and as vice-president, until 1885.

It was Ridpath who secured for Asbury the De
Pauw endowment which put the institution on a firm
financial basis and which resulted in the changing of its
name.

Besides his work as an educator, administrator and
writer, Ridpath spent a year (1897-98) as editor of
The Arena, a Boston periodical, contributed largely
to the press and was for some time literary director of
the Jones Brothers Publishing Company. He died on
July 31, 1900.

Textbooks are omitted from the list of his works.

> Information from the Greencastle Public Library;
> *Who's Who in America*; De Pauw University's
> *Alumnal Record, 1920; American Authors, 1600-
> 1900*; and Parker and Heiney—*Poets and Poetry
> of Indiana*.

* * *

History of the U. S. Prepared Especially for Children.
Philadelphia, 1874.

A Popular History of the United States of America. *Cincinnati*, 1876.

United States: a History of the United States of America
from the Aboriginal Times to the Present Day. *Cincinnati*, 1878.

The Life and Work of James A. Garfield. *Cincinnati*,
1881.

Alexander Hamilton: a Study of the Revolution and the
Union. *Cincinnati*, [1881].

Epoch of Integration. 1883.

History and Historical Study. 1885.

Beyond the Sierras. 1888.

The True Evolution. 1889.

The Suppression of the Intellectual Life. 1892.

Columbus and Columbia: a Pictorial History of the Man
and the Nation (with J. G. Blaine, J. W. Buel, and
B. Butterworth). 1892.

The Citizen Soldier; His Part in War and Peace. *Cincinnati*, 1892.

The Man in History: an Oration for the Columbian
Year, Delivered under the Auspices of the Indiana
Historical Society, at Indianapolis, Indiana, October
20, 1892. *Indianapolis*, 1893.

The Life and Work of James G. Blaine (with S. Connor and others). 1893.

Epic of Life. *New York*, 1893.

Ridpath's Universal History. *Cincinnati*, 1894-99.

Life and Memoirs of Bishop William Taylor. 1894-95.

Napoleon Bonaparte. 1895.

People's History of the United States. *Philadelphia*,
[1895]. (Reissued as Chronology of Events . . . *Washington, D. C.*, 1904.)

Notable Events of the Nineteenth Century. *New York*,
1896.

The Bond and the Dollar . . . *Boston*, [1896].

A Brief Chronological History of All Nations.

The Cry of the Poor . . . *Boston*, 1897.

Democracy: Its Origins and Aspects . . . *Boston*, 1897.

Prosperity; the Sham and the Reality. *Boston*, 1897.

Spurious Bimetallism. An Argument in Refutation of
Double Coinage . . . *Boston*, 1897.

The True Inwardness of Wall Street. *Boston*, 1897.

History of the World; being an Account of the Principal
Events in the Career of the Human Race from the
Beginnings of Civilization to the Present Time; Com-
prising the Development of Social Institutions and the
Story of All Nations from Recent and Authentic
Resources. *Indianapolis*, 1898. 4 vols. (Reissued in 9
vols. in 1909 and as With the World's People in 1911.)

James Otis: the Pre-Revolutionist; a Brief Interpretation
of the Life and Work of a Patriot. *Chicago*, 1898.

Life and Times of William E. Gladstone. *Cincinnati*,
1898.

A Working University in the Home Reference Library.
New York, 1898.

Gov. Will Cumback. [Greensburg, Ind.]

The Standard Encyclopedia of Arts, Sciences, History,
Geography, Statistics, and General Knowledge. 1900.
10 vols.

History of the United States. *Washington, D. C.*, 1900.

History of the United States. Academic Edition. *New
York*, 1902.

New Complete History of the United States of America.
New York, 1904. 15 vols.

Battles and Commanders of the Civil War (with Rossiter
Johnson and others). *Washington, D. C.*, [1907].

The Story of South Africa (with E. S. Ellis). *New York*,
[1909].

History of the United States from Aboriginal Times to
Taft's Administration. *New York*, 1911. 4 vols.

With the World's People. *Cincinnati*, 1911. 8 vols. (New
edition of History of the World.)

History of Texas.

RIGDON, JONATHAN: 1858–1933.

Jonathan Rigdon, son of Pryor and Mary A. Fleener
Rigdon, was born at Rigdon, Ind., on Dec. 22, 1858,
and graduated from Central Normal (now Canterbury) College, in Danville, Ind., in 1886. He received
the A.B. degree in 1891 and the Ph.D. in 1905 from
Boston University. From 1904 to 1906 he studied at
Clark University. He married Alberta Smith in 1907.

From 1887 to 1900 he served as a professor of philosophy at Central Normal (now Canterbury) College, holding the position of president of the college from 1897 to 1900, and in 1908 he founded Winona College, at Winona Lake, Ind., of which he was president until 1916. From 1918 to 1929 he was again president of Central Normal College.

He died on Dec. 30, 1933.

Dr. Rigdon was the author of about a dozen textbooks, 1887-1932, which are not listed here.

Information from *Who Was Who in America*.

* * *

Methods in Arithmetic. *Danville, Ind., 1893.*

Infinitives and Participles. *Danville, Ind., 1895.*

College Ideals. *Danville, Ind., 1915.*

The English Sentence. *New York, 1925.*

Science and Religion as They Look to a Layman. *Danville, Ind., 1928.*

RILEY, JAMES WHITCOMB: 1849–1916.

To some hundreds of thousands who still read and enjoy his verse, James Whitcomb Riley *is* Indiana. No American poet—those patriarchs of New England included—has thus far caught the popular fancy, has thus far enjoyed the voluntary following, that was and is his.

The beginnings of James Whitcomb Riley were auspicious enough, although he showed very little of what biographers of his day liked to call "early promise." He was born in Greenfield, Ind., on Oct. 7, 1849, (probably, although biographers differ as to the year), the son of Reubin A. and Elizabeth Riley. His father was a reasonably prosperous small town lawyer. He was named for an Indiana governor and he attended the local schools, where he fortunately had a teacher who was interested in both the reading and writing of poetry. The teacher was Lee O. Harris, who, although his own efforts at verse brought him no fame, was credited by Riley with having been a strong influence. Riley apparently had his first poem published in the GREENFIELD COMMERCIAL in the fall of 1870. Once out of the school, however, he began a rather aimless existence.

For a short time he read law in his father's office, without hope, interest or success—and his father, probably noting his very apparent incapacity, seems to have given at least tacit consent to his defection. Thereupon, James Whitcomb took up sign-painting, which ranked as a profession only slightly above that of minstrel man or medicine show spieler in that day. Perfecting himself in that trade he engaged as advance agent and display advertising specialist (in the barn-side and back fence media) for a wagon-show.

Shortly, however, he found an outlet for his talent for versifying, partially discovered in his school days. The wagon-show had a musical department, topical songs were in vogue, and Riley began to write their lyrics. In 1872 he sent several poems to the Indianapolis SATURDAY MIRROR, a literary weekly. These were published through March, April and May over the signature "Jay Whit." In 1873, only twenty-four years old but a widely traveled man of the world, he returned to Greenfield.

His literary experience and his travels gave him a good background for journalism, and he became an employee of one of the local papers.

He continued his contributions to Indianapolis papers and presently, beginning to make use of his experience in publicity, he wrote some advertising jingles for the GREENFIELD NEWS. He still accepted a sign-painting order occasionally, and one of the jingles advertised this service.

Next move was to the ANDERSON DEMOCRAT in April, 1877. While working on that paper he wrote a poem, "Leonainie," in the style of, and signed with the initials of, Edgar Allan Poe. He sent it to the KOKOMO DISPATCH with a note to the effect that it had been discovered on the flyleaf of an old dictionary. Many critics accepted it as an unknown Poe production, and quite a few of them maintained their pronouncements correct even after Riley had admitted his authorship. The ANDERSON DEMOCRAT, horrified (according to tradition) at its employee's lapse of literary integrity, cast him out; but the INDIANAPOLIS JOURNAL, which knew a good newspaperman when it saw one, hired him, and there he stayed from 1877 to 1885.

There were routine assignments on the JOURNAL, but there was also a space to be filled with poetry and Riley soon began to take far more than his share of these columns. He had contributed rather widely during the preceding two or three years, but in 1878, encouraged by a welcome in Indianapolis, his greatest period of production began. His first appearance in a periodical of national circulation is thought to have been with the poem "A Destiny" in the April, 1875, issue of HEARTH AND HOME. Possibly because all of his energies were now devoted to filling the JOURNAL and other papers in Indianapolis and elsewhere with poems, letters and sketches over a variety of pseudonyms, there was little further contribution to periodicals until the middle Eighties.

His first book of collected poems, *The Ole Swimmin'*

Hole, and 'Leven More Poems, by Benj. F. Johnson, of Boone [James Whitcomb Riley], did not inspire any publisher with enthusiasm, but George C. Hitt, business manager of the INDIANAPOLIS JOURNAL and Riley together financed its publication. The book was an immediate success, and by his venturesome spirit Mr. Hitt earned the eternal gratitude of all Hoosiers and a good slice of other North Americans as well.

As a craftsman Riley was indefatigable, polishing and repolishing until his verse was near technical perfection. In his great talent for the accurate hearing and the true recording of dialect he was unsurpassed in his time. His Hoosier was perfection itself—most of us who were reared in Indiana, unless we are constantly alert, find ourselves lapsing into recognizable, if modified, Rileyesque—but much of his dialect is also recognizable as careless Americana of almost any state. Perhaps it was this infallible ear for everyday speech which is most accountable for Riley's enormous popularity: the Raggedy Man was obviously everyone's odd-job man; the little boy who reported upon the arrival of his grandmother lived down the street from almost any reader.

There were many sides to James Whitcomb Riley. To the children to whom he read he was a benevolent old gentleman (he was always old to them, even though he died at sixty-seven, because children naturally believed that anyone who spoke so nearly their own language must of necessity be very old or very young and no one very young could possibly support that vast expanse of white waistcoat, that magnificent watch chain). To those elders who attended his evening programs he was Art, but an Art singularly understandable. To his contemporaries in letters he was a gay and wonderful companion. Many an Eastern audience, attending his recitals to see what sort of rustic character wrote that backwoods verse, was astonished to find that Riley was urbanity itself, with a polished good taste which met even the rigid standards of Boston. Riley was also given an honorary A.M. degree by Yale University.

James Whitcomb Riley progressed rapidly, and apparently easily, from an object of regard to an object of something very like worship. No Indiana schoolchild of 1900-1910 (the period in which he read his works most widely in Indiana schools) is likely ever to forget the hushed awe with which his teacher introduced Riley when he stopped in to deliver "The Raggedy Man" and "Little Orphant Annie" to the deeply impressed, if not always fully understanding, young audience.

Long before his sixtieth birthday Riley's Lockerbie Street residence in Indianapolis had become a mecca where small, starched Indianapolis boys and girls were taken to be photographed on the poet's knee as he recited to them. Before his birthdate was four score years past, both the Lockerbie Street house and his birthplace were memorials, visited by more admirers than are the shrines of most ex-presidents.

Riley never married. He enjoyed the company of women, but his verse, his correspondence, his reading and conversation with his friends filled his life completely. His (perhaps abstract) liking for children, rather than having been concentrated on a few of his own, was showered upon a nation of them.

Riley died, one of America's most widely known literary figures, on July 22, 1916, at the age of sixty-six.

Information from Burke and Howe—*American Authors and Books, 1640-1940;* Russo—*A Bibliography of James Whitcomb Riley;* and Dickey—*Youth of James Whitcomb Riley.*

* * *

"The Old Swimmin'-Hole," and 'Leven More Poems, by Benj. F. Johnson, of Boone. *Indianapolis,* 1883.

Character Sketches the Boss Girl a Christmas Story and other Sketches. *Indianapolis,* 1886.

Afterwhiles. *Indianapolis,* 1888.

Old-Fashioned Roses. *London,* 1888.

Nye and Riley's Railway Guide (with Edgar W. Nye). *Chicago,* 1888.

Pipes O' Pan at Zekesbury. *Indianapolis,* 1889.

Rhymes of Childhood. *Indianapolis,* 1891.

"The Old Swimin'-Hole" and 'Leven More Poems Neighborly Poems on Friendship Grief and Farm-Life by Benj. F. Johnson, of Boone. *Indianapolis,* 1891.

The Flying Islands of the Night. *Indianapolis,* 1892.

Green Fields and Running Brooks. *Indianapolis,* 1893.

Poems Here At Home. *New York,* 1893.

Armazindy. *Indianapolis,* 1894.

The Days Gone by and Other Poems. *Chicago,* n.d. [1895].

A Tinkle of Bells and Other Poems. *Chicago,* n.d. [1895].

A Child-World. *Indianapolis,* 1897.

Rubaiyat of Doc Sifers. *New York,* 1897.

The Golden Year from the Verse and Prose of James Whitcomb Riley. *London,* 1898.

Riley Love-Lyrics. *Indianapolis,* n.d. [1899].

Home-Folks. *Indianapolis,* n.d. [1900].

The Book of Joyous Children. *New York,* 1902.

An Old Sweetheart of Mine. *Indianapolis,* n.d. [1902].

His Pa's Romance. *Indianapolis,* n.d. [1903].

Out to Old Aunt Mary's. *Indianapolis,* n.d. [1904].

A Defective Santa Claus. *Indianapolis,* n.d. [1904].

Riley Songs O' Cheer. *Indianapolis,* n.d. [1905].

While the Heart Beats Young. *Indianapolis,* n.d. [1906].

Morning. *Indianapolis,* n.d. [1907].

The Raggedy Man. *Indianapolis,* n.d. [1907].

The Boys of the Old Glee Club. *Indianapolis,* n.d. [1907].

The Orphant Annie Book. *Indianapolis,* n.d. [1908].

Riley Songs of Summer. *Indianapolis,* n.d. [1908].

The Lockerbie Book. *Indianapolis,* n.d. [1911].

The Riley Baby Book. *Indianapolis,* n.d. [1913].

Riley Songs of Friendship. *Indianapolis,* n.d. [1915].

The Old Soldier's Story. *Indianapolis,* n.d. [1915].

The Hoosier Book. *Indianapolis,* n.d. [1916].

The Homestead Edition. The Poems and Prose Sketches of James Whitcomb Riley. *New York,* 1897-1914. 16 vols.

The Complete Works of James Whitcomb Riley. *Indianapolis,* n.d. [1913]. 6 vols.

Memorial Edition James Whitcomb Riley's Complete Works. *Indianapolis,* 1916. 10 vols.

[The three editions of collected works above contain material not previously published. Other editions of collected works include little or no significant matter which had not previously appeared.]

RILEY, WILLIAM BELL: 1861–

William Bell Riley was born in Greene County, Ind., on Mar. 22, 1861. His parents were Branson Radish and Ruth Anna Jackson Riley.

Riley attended Valparaiso Normal and Hanover College, receiving the A.B. degree in 1885 and the A.M. in 1888. In the latter year he also graduated from the Southern Baptist Theological Seminary. He later received the LL.D. from John Brown University (1938) and the D.D. from Union University (1911).

He married Lillian Howard on Dec. 31, 1890. She died in 1931, and on Sept. 1, 1933, he married Marie R. Acomb.

The Rev. Mr. Riley had been ordained to the Baptist ministry in Kentucky in 1883, and he occupied pulpits in Warsaw and Carrollton, Ky., New Albany and Lafayette, Ind., and Bloomington and Chicago, Ill., between 1884 and 1897. In the latter year he became pastor of the First Church, Minneapolis, where he occupied the pulpit until 1942, when he retired. In 1902 he founded the Northwestern Bible Training School at Minneapolis and continued as its president. He founded and became president of the Northwestern Evangelical Seminary in 1935. One of the most voluminous of modern writers on religion, he was also executive secretary of The World's Christian Fundamentals Association and editor of THE NORTHWESTERN PILOT.

Information from *Who's Who in America.*

* * *

Baptist Fundamentals. (Co-author.)

The Greater Doctrines of Scripture. 1893.

The Seven Churches of Asia. *New York,* 1895.

Fads and Fanaticisms. 1895.

The Gospel in Jonah. *New York,* 1895.

Vagaries and Verities. *Minneapolis,* 1903.

The Finality of the Higher Criticism; or the Theory of Evolution and False Theology. *Minneapolis,* 1909.

The Evolution of the Kingdom. *New York,* 1913.

Messages for the Metropolis. *Minneapolis,* 1913.

The Perennial Revival; a Plea for Evangelism. *Minneapolis,* 1913.

The Coming and Kingdom of Christ. 1914.

Crisis of the Church. *New York,* 1914.

The Menace of Modernism. *New York,* 1917.

Daniel vs. Darwinism. *Minneapolis,* 1918.

Light on Prophecy. 1918.

Ephesians; the Three-Fold Epistle; Seven Studies. *Chicago,* 1919.

God Hath Spoken. *Minneapolis,* 1919.

Inspiration or Evolution? *Minneapolis,* 1923.

The Bible of the Expositor and the Evangelist. *Cleveland, O.,* 1924-38. 40 vols.

Christ the Incomparable. *Chicago,* 1924.

Sermons for the Times. 1924.

The Blight of Unitarianism. 1926.

Revival Sermons; Essentials in Effective Evangelism. *Chicago,* 1929.

The Minneapolis Pulpit. 1929.

Ten Burning Questions. *Chicago,* 1932.

The Goal of Religion. 1935.

The Philosophies of Father Coughlin; Four Sermons. *Grand Rapids, Mich.,* 1935.

Pastoral Problems. *Chicago,* 1936.

Youth's Victory Lies This Way. *Grand Rapids, Mich.,* 1936.

The Only Hope of Church or World; What Is It? *Glasgow,* 1936.

The Victorious Life. *Grand Rapids, Mich.,* 1937.

Is Jesus Coming Again? *Grand Rapids, Mich.,* 1937.

My Bible; an Apologetic. *Grand Rapids, Mich.,* 1937.

Saved or Lost? *Grand Rapids, Mich.,* 1938.

Wives of the Bible; a Cross-Section of Femininity. *Grand Rapids, Mich.,* 1938.

Seven New Testament Soul-Winners. *Grand Rapids, Mich.,* 1939.

Wanted—a World Leader. 1939.

The Conflict of Christianity with Its Counterfeits. *Minneapolis,* 1940.

Re-Thinking the Church. *Chicago,* 1940.

Seven New Testament Converts. *Grand Rapids, Mich.,* 1940.

Problems of Youth. *Grand Rapids, Mich.,* 1941.

At Sunset; or, After 80. *Butler, Ind.,* 1944.

Fundamentalism vs. Liberalism.

Christian Science; Its Opposition to the Word of God. *New York.*

Will Christ Come Again? *Minneapolis.*

Divine Healing; or, Does God Answer Prayer for the Sick? *New York.*

Spiritualism; a Subject That Should Be Studied in the Light of God's Word. *New York.*

Theosophy. *New York.*

Arguments Against; McCabe-Riley Debates. *Minneapolis.*

Bible; Is It an Evolution or an Inspiration. *Minneapolis.*

The Challenge of Orthodoxy. *Minneapolis.*

Christian Confederacy. *Chicago.*

The Eclipse of Faith. *Minneapolis.*

Evolution; Does It Tend to Atheism? *Minneapolis.*

Great Question, Who Was Christ?

Interchurch; or, the Kingdom by Violence. *Minneapolis.*

Jerusalem and the Jew. *Minneapolis.*

Liberty of Faith vs. License of Infidelity. *Minneapolis.*

Mistakes of Millennial Dawn. *Los Angeles.*

Modern Amusements. *Minneapolis.*

Old Testament Types. *Los Angeles.*

The Redemption of the Downtown. *Minneapolis.*

Riley vs. Fosdick. *Minneapolis.*

Seven Churches of Asia. *New York.*

The Challenge of Youth.

The Christian Fundamentalist.

God Hath Chosen.

Unveiling the Future.

RISTINE, FRANK HUMPHREY: 1884–

Born in Crawfordsville, Ind., on Apr. 11, 1884, Frank Humphrey Ristine graduated from Wabash College in 1905 and received the A.M. (1907) and Ph.D. (1910) degrees from Columbia University. In 1933 he was awarded the L.H.D. degree by Wabash College.

He served as acting professor of English at Wabash in 1909-10 and as an instructor at Columbia in 1911-12. After 1912 he was associated with Hamilton College as professor of English literature and, after 1932, as dean.

Information from *Directory of American Scholars.*

* * *

English Tragicomedy; Its Origin and History. *New York,* 1910.

RITTER, ELI F.: 1838–1913.

Eli F. Ritter was born in Hendricks County, Ind., June 18, 1838. Of Quaker stock, he was the son of James and Rachel Jessup Ritter, who had emigrated from the South to Hendricks County because of their anti-slavery sentiments. Eli was educated in the public schools, graduated from De Pauw University in 1863, and received the A.M. degree in 1866, being admitted to the bar in that year. His college studies had been interrupted by the Civil War, during which he served in the 79th Indiana Infantry. He married Narcie L. Lockwood on July 13, 1865. Col. Ritter died Dec. 11, 1913, in Indianapolis.

Information from Dunn—*Indiana and Indianans,* Vol. II; De Pauw University's *Alumnal Record, 1920;* and the Indianapolis Public Library.

* * *

Is License Constitutional? A Brief Before the Supreme Court of Indiana; in the Case of Mary E. Haggart and Sarah C. Rathwell vs. J. H. Stehlin and G. Heidt. *New York,* 1891.

Moral Law and Civil Law, Parts of the Same Thing. *New York,* 1896.

ROBBINS, WILLIAM EDWIN: 1845–1919.

Born near Paoli, Ind., on Mar. 8, 1845, William Edwin Robbins graduated from De Pauw University in 1868, receiving the A.M. degree in 1871.

After teaching in Iowa and California for two years and serving as a Methodist Episcopal pastor in Indiana for two more years, in 1872 he went as a missionary to India, where he spent most of the remainder of his life. He married Alice Ellen Miles in Bombay, India, on Mar. 1, 1876. He served for a time as acting editor of THE BANNER OF ASIA.

The Rev. Mr. Robbins died in Los Angeles on Sept. 15, 1919.

Information from De Pauw University's *Alumnal Record, 1920.*

* * *

Hand-Book of India and British Burmah. *Cincinnati,* 1883.

Outlines of Christian Evidences.

To Sunrise and Back.

ROBERTS, ELMER: 1863–1937.

Elmer Roberts, son of the Rev. Lewis and Mary McKim Roberts, was born in Lagro, Ind., on Apr. 7,

1863, and attended De Pauw University, leaving college in his senior year. On May 12, 1896, he married Claire Livingston, who died in 1929.

From 1885 to 1896 he worked on various newspapers—the TERRE HAUTE EXPRESS, PERU REPUBLICAN, FORT WAYNE GAZETTE, CHICAGO DAILY NEWS, CHICAGO TIMES, NEW YORK HERALD, and JACKSONVILLE CITIZEN (he assisted in founding the last-named paper)—and in 1897 he became connected with the Associated Press, continuing this connection until 1929. He served as a correspondent in London (1899-1901), Berlin (1902-10), and Paris (1911-29).

Mr. Roberts died on Nov. 17, 1937.

Information from *Who Was Who in America.*

* * *

Monarchical Socialism in Germany. *New York,* 1913.

ROBINSON, CHARLES ASBURY: ?–

Aside from the fact that he was a resident of Greenfield, Ind., at least during the period 1902 to 1909, and that one of his titles indicates he was an active member of the Order of Red Men, a fraternal association, no information regarding Charles Asbury Robinson has been located.

Information from the Greenfield Public Library.

* * *

Roving Red Rangers; or, Laura Lamar of the Susquehanna: A Thrilling Romance of the Old Colonial Days. *Greenfield, Ind.,* 1902.

Uncle Robie's Baby Book. *Greenfield, Ind.,* 1902.

The Trail of the White Wolf; or the Doom of the Delawares. *Greenfield, Ind.,* 1903.

This Book Contains One Hundred Reasons Why I Am a Red Man and Some Nuggets of Gold. *Greenfield, Ind.,* 1909.

ROBINSON, EDWIN MEADE: 1878–1946.

Edwin Meade Robinson was born in Lima (now Howe), Ind., on Nov. 1, 1878. His parents were William Edwin and Alice Maude Drake Robinson. After graduating from Howe School, in his home town, he enrolled in Wabash College.

There, as "Ted" Robinson, a name he always preferred to those by which he was christened, he became a popular student, developed a facility for graceful writing and best of all, in the opinion of Wabash men, he wrote the words to the college song. Its writing came at a time when Wabash College was about to enjoy a period of rapid development; it was first publicly sung at the inauguration of President William Patterson Kane in 1899, and it made an immediate hit. According to Osborne and Gronert—*Wabash College: The First Hundred Years:*

"Music, perhaps, had as much to do with the great uprising of college spirit under the Kane administration as athletics: in the beginning at least it had more to do with it. It was a great thing to have so completely successful a college song. Ragan [composer of the music] and Robinson might well have said, after old Fletcher of Saltoun, that they cared not who taught the classes or even who made the touchdowns for the college since it had been given to them to write its song."

Of this performance Ted Robinson remarked, a few years before his death, "There was a period, after I had been out of college for a time and had begun to take my writing seriously, that I was not too proud of those lyrics. But I find, as I grow older, and seem to be regarded as a sort of vestal virgin who tended the eternal fire of Wabash spirit in the past century, I am becoming quite proud of myself."

Robinson received his A.B. from Wabash and spent a year as teacher of English in the Attica, Ind., High School and joined the staff of THE INDIANAPOLIS SENTINEL, remaining with this paper and THE INDIANAPOLIS JOURNAL until 1904, when he went to THE CLEVELAND (O.) LEADER. In 1909 he married Martha Coon.

He joined THE PLAIN DEALER in 1910 as a column conductor and associate editor. His column, "Philosopher of Folly," achieved almost immediate popularity. Under his direction as literary editor after 1922, the book section of THE PLAIN DEALER became one of the country's best, with a strong influence on northern Ohio book buyers.

Robinson lectured at Cleveland College on philology between 1926 and 1942. He received the Litt.D. from Wabash College in 1927. He died at his summer home in Provincetown, Mass., on Sept. 20, 1946.

Information from *Who's Who in America;* Osborne and Gronert—*Wabash College: The First Hundred Years;* and from conversation with Mr. Robinson.

* * *

The First Born. 1899.

Mere Melodies. *Philadelphia,* 1918.

Piping and Panning. *New York,* 1920.

Enter Jerry. *New York,* 1921.

Life, Love and the Weather. 1945.

ROBINSON, SOLON: 1803–1880.

"Solon Robinson (Oct. 21, 1803-Nov. 3, 1880), pioneer, agriculturist, author, was born at Tolland, Conn., the fourth child of Jacob and Salinda (Ladd) Robinson and a descendant of the Rev. John Robinson, pastor of the Pilgrims at Leyden. An orphan at the age of ten, a carpenter's apprentice at fourteen, and a Yankee peddler at eighteen, he made his way alone in the world. In 1828 he had become a cashier for a theatre in Cincinnati, and in October of that year married Mariah Evans of Bucks County, Pa.

"Two years later, at Madison, Ind., the young man was writing for the local press and interested in the promotion of an urban land site near North Vernon. In the fall of 1834, because of a dearth of buyers, he disposed of most of his land and traveled to northern Indiana. Here, in the wilderness, he opened a general store and soon built up a large trade with the Potawatomi Indians and incoming settlers. The Indians gave him the name of 'Wyonett Tshmokeman' sometimes translated 'Chief Big Knife.' To preserve his own holdings and those of others, in the area then known as Robinson's Prairie, he formed a Squatter's Union in 1836 for protection against speculators and made it possible for some five hundred members to secure their land at government prices. Henceforth, by popular acclaim, he was known as the 'King of the Squatters.' After Lake County was organized in 1837, he served at various times as county clerk, justice of the peace, register of claims, and postmaster. At the county seat, Crown Point, on the first printing press in the region he published intermittently a small news sheet. Active in politics, he took a prominent part in the Log Cabin Convention at Lafayette in 1840 . . .

"As early as 1837 Robinson began to contribute articles on various aspects of the frontier to the Albany CULTIVATOR and other agricultural periodicals. The simple, homely, and often humorous style of these essays, signed 'Solon Robinson of Indiana,' reflected the personality of the author, and they soon won a large following. His enthusiasm and spirit carried conviction. Before 1840, in company with James Mercer Garnett, Henry L. Ellsworth, and others, he advocated the formation of a national agricultural society . . . The society had hoped to establish a national agricultural school and journal, but failure to receive an anticipated bequest made by James Smithson to the United States defeated this plan and was largely responsible for the premature dissolution of the organization. However, these activities paved the way for the formation of the United States Agricultural Society in 1852 by Robinson and others. This in turn played an influential role in the establishment of the Department of Agriculture ten years later.

"Robinson's descriptions of rural life observed on his journey to and from Washington in 1841 were the first of his discerning travel sketches. During the next decade he made a number of tours, covering practically every state in the Union, and regularly reported his observations in the CULTIVATOR, PRAIRIE FARMER, and AMERICAN AGRICULTURIST, from which they were reprinted in the SOUTHERN CULTIVATOR and other periodicals. These travel sketches today form an invaluable historical record of rural society of that period . . . In 1852 at New York City he published a periodical called THE PLOW, and the following year became agricultural editor of the NEW YORK TRIBUNE. His editorial work, combined with visits to various parts of the country, was largely responsible for the widespread circulation of the weekly edition of the TRIBUNE and the subsequent national influence of that publication. At Westchester, N. Y., Robinson conducted an experimental farm which provided the basis for many of his articles.

"Illness in 1868—he suffered nearly all his life with tubercular tendencies—forced him to retire to Florida. Residing at Jacksonville, he published the FLORIDA REPUBLICAN, wrote for the NEW YORK TRIBUNE, and carried on other literary work. He was the author of novels, short stories, and poetry, in addition to his travel sketches and agricultural articles . . . After the death of his first wife, by whom he had five children, he married, June 30, 1872, Mary Johnson of Barton, Vt. He died at Jacksonville in November, 1880."

> Condensed from H. A. K., *Dictionary of American Biography,* Vol. XVI.

* * *

The Will: a Tale of the Lake of the Red Cedars and Shabbona. 1841.

Guano: a Treatise of Practical Information for Farmers. *New York,* 1853.

Hot Corn: Life Scenes in New York, Tales of Slum Life. *New York,* 1854.

Facts for Farmers: Also for the Family Circle. *New York,* 1864. 2 vols.

Me-Won-I-Toc. A Tale of Frontier Life and Indian Character; Exhibiting Traditions, Superstitions and Character of a Race That Is Passing Away. A Romance of the Frontier. *New York,* 1866.

How to Live: Saving and Wasting; or Domestic Economy Illustrated by the Life of Two Families of Opposite Character, Including the Story of a Dime a Day. *New York,* 1873.

Hot-Corn Katy; or, Life in New York. *New York,* 1882.
History of Lake County.
Solon Robinson, Pioneer and Agriculturist; Selected Writings. (Edited by H. A. Kellar.) *Indianapolis,* 1936. (Indiana Historical Collections, vol. 21-22) 2 vols.

ROHRER, FRED: 1867–1936.

Born at Boligen, near Bern, Switzerland, Dec. 9, 1867, Fred Rohrer came to this country at the age of sixteen. He was married to Miss Emma Reusser on Nov. 16, 1893.

As editor of the BERNE WITNESS, a tri-weekly newspaper which he established in 1896, and author of *The Saloon Fight at Berne, Indiana,* Fred Rohrer received wide attention when, with courage undiminished by bombings and other violence, he waged a series of valiant battles against the liquor traffic in his town. The campaign furnishes subject matter for his book, first published in 1913. Newspapers throughout the country took notice of the occurrence described in the book, which went through four editions, three English and one German.

As editor, publisher and author, he expressed his views and voiced his opinions. He was thoroughly sincere and deeply religious and a practical and useful citizen.

Mr. Rohrer died Dec. 1, 1936, at his home in Berne, Ind.

Information from the Berne, Ind., Public Library.

* * *

The Saloon Fight at Berne, Indiana. Not a Novel, but a Real History. *Berne, Ind.,* 1913.

ROSE, HENRIETTA (MRS. HAMILTON): ?–

Henrietta Rose, whose birth date is unknown, was born in Ohio. She was a teacher before her marriage, and before and after her marriage took an active part in the women's rights and temperance movements.

The article on Indiana authors by D. S. A. in the CINCINNATI GAZETTE of Dec. 7, 1876, describes her as an Indiana writer and remarks of the one title for which she is known, "*Nora Wilmot* is a tale of temperance and women's rights. The style is rigid, and the plot as transparent as the characters are commonplace and rigid."

Information from the Barry Ms. and D. S. A. in the *Cincinnati Gazette,* Dec. 7, 1876.

* * *

Nora Wilmot: a Tale of Temperance and Woman's Rights. *Columbus, Ind.,* 1858.

ROSS, MORRIS M.: 1850–1915.

Born in Indianapolis on Aug. 21, 1850, Morris M. Ross attended a private school in Indianapolis and was graduated from Cornell University in 1870. He began work in 1872 on the INDIANAPOLIS SENTINEL, was copy editor on the NEW YORK TRIBUNE in 1875, and returned to Indianapolis in 1876 as editorial writer and dramatic critic for the INDIANAPOLIS NEWS, of which he became managing editor in 1892. In 1900 he retired to editorial writing, which he continued until his death in September, 1915.

Information from Indianapolis Public Library.

* * *

The Portfolio, an Address. *Indianapolis,* 1890.
Labor, Society and the Church. *Indianapolis,* 1891.

ROTHERT, OTTO ARTHUR: 1871–

Otto Arthur Rothert was born in Huntingburg, Ind., the son of Herman, a native of Hanover, Germany, and Franziska Weber Rothert, who had been born in Baden. The Rotherts were prosperous citizens of the southern Indiana German community and young Otto had every advantage.

After attending local schools he was entered in the preparatory department and later the University of Notre Dame, receiving the A.B. degree in 1892.

The Rotherts moved to Louisville, Ky., in 1889, and young Otto joined them there after graduation. He helped in his father's tobacco exporting business and clerked at that ancient Louisville hostlery, The Galt House, when his talents for the tobacco business became obvious by their almost total absence.

After his father's death in 1904 Otto Rothert toured Mexico and the West and on his return began to visit historic sites in Kentucky and the Middle West. The family had purchased 2600 acres in Muhlenberg County, Ky., and he became greatly interested in the locality. This interest resulted in his first book, the *History of Muhlenberg County,* a remarkably fine piece of local history recording.

In 1908 he had become a member of The Filson Club of Louisville, an organization devoted to the preservation of Kentucky and midwestern history, which then had among its members Col. Reuben T. Durrett, Basil W. Duke, James S. Pirtle, Thomas W. Bullitt, C. Ballard Thruston, Alfred Pirtle and others of the most justly celebrated of America's amateur historians. Rothert's interest in the club grew with his interest in historical writing: he was elected secretary in 1917.

Under the guidance and financial support of the president, C. Ballard Thruston, and the new secretary the club grew and prospered, acquiring a beautiful club house in 1929 and, over the years, a remarkable collection of historical material. Both officers continued until Otto Rothert resigned, due to ill health, on Apr. 1, 1945.

From Tapp—*Otto A. Rothert, 1871—*

* * *

History of Muhlenberg County. *Louisville, 1913.*

A History of Unity Baptist Church, Muhlenberg County, Kentucky. *Louisville, 1914.*

The Story of a Poet: Madison Cawein; His Intimate Life as Revealed by His Letters and Other Hitherto Unpublished Material, Including Reminiscences by His Closest Associates; Also Articles from Newspapers and Magazines, and a List of His Poems. *Louisville, 1921.*

Picturography of Madison Cawein; a Reprint of the First Chapter of the Story of a Poet: Madison Cawein. *Louisville, 1921.*

The Filson Club and Its Activities, 1884-1922; a History of the Filson Club, Including Lists of Filson Club Publications and Papers on Kentucky History Prepared for the Club, Also Names of Members. *Louisville, 1922.*

The Outlaws of Cave-in-Rock; Historical Accounts of the Famous Highwaymen and River Pirates Who Operated in Pioneer Days Upon the Ohio and Mississippi Rivers and Over the Old Natchez Trace. *Cleveland, O., 1924.*

Forest Retreat and Its Garden, in Muhlenberg County, Kentucky, Near Greenville. *Louisville, 1938.*

List of Shrubs and Trees in the Garden at Forest Retreat. *Louisville, 1942.*

RUMELY, EDWARD ALOYSIUS: 1882–

Edward Aloysius Rumely, son of Joseph J. and Margaret Zimmerman Rumely, was born in LaPorte, Ind., on Feb. 28, 1882, and was educated at the University of Notre Dame, Heidelberg, and Freiburg, receiving an M.D. degree from the last-named institution in 1906. He was married on Apr. 2, 1910.

In 1907 he founded and organized The Interlaken School, of which he was president, and he served as secretary and treasurer of the M. Rumely Company. Mr. Rumely developed the mechanical tractor.

Information from *Who's Who in America.*

* * *

Power and the Plow (with L. W. Ellis). *Garden City, N. Y., 1911.*

Some Thoughts on Agricultural Education. *New York, 1912.*

Interlaken School: to Teach Boys to Live. *LaPorte, Ind., 1915.*

RUNCIE, CONSTANCE OWEN FAUNTLEROY (MRS. JAMES): 1836–1911.

Constance Owen Fauntleroy was born in Indianapolis on Jan. 15, 1836, the daughter of Robert Henry and Jean Dale Owen Fauntleroy. She was a granddaughter of Robert Owen of New Harmony fame and spent her girlhood in New Harmony. Following a period of five years of study in Germany, she returned to the U. S., married the Rev. James Runcie, and lived in Madison, Ind., from 1861 to 1871, later moving to St. Joseph, Mo. While in New Harmony she organized the Minerva Club, said to be the first woman's club organized in America. She edited a church paper for six years and was an officer in various woman's clubs and organizations. She composed an opera, a cantata and several offertories.

Information from *Who Was Who in America* and the Indianapolis Public Library.

* * *

Divinely Led. *New York, 1881.*
Poems, Dramatic and Lyric. *New York, 1888.*
Essay on Woman. 1904.
Fables.

RUSSELL, JOSEPH P.: 1815–1893.

Joseph P. Russell was born in Bourbon County, Ky., on July 23, 1815, the son of Joseph and Elizabeth Penn Russell.

He completed his medical education in Kentucky and, after his marriage to Mary Ellen Penn, came to Waveland, Ind., and practiced medicine there for almost fifty years before his death on Feb. 11, 1893.

Information from Russell—*Writings With Biography.*

* * *

Writings With Biography. *Indianapolis. 1901.*

RYAN, OSWALD: 1888–

Oswald Ryan, son of William Antony and Agnes Fitzgerald Ryan, was born at Anderson, Ind., on Apr.

11, 1888, and was educated at Butler University, Harvard (A.B., 1911), and Harvard Law School. On July 1, 1918, he married Rebecca B. Noland.

He began the practice of law at Anderson, Ind., in 1913. In 1916 he was elected state's attorney for the 50th Indiana Judicial District but resigned in 1918 to enlist for service in the first World War. He was city attorney of Anderson from 1925 to 1929 and state's attorney for the 50th Judicial District from 1929 to 1931. From 1932 to 1938 he acted as general counsel for the Federal Power Commission. After 1938 he was a member of the Civil Aeronautics Board. In addition to his books, he contributed to HARPER'S, AMERICAN POLITICAL SCIENCE REVIEW, PUBLIC UTILITIES FORTNIGHTLY, JOURNAL OF AIR LAW AND COMMERCE, POPULAR SCIENCE MONTHLY, etc.

Information from *Who's Who in America.*

* * *

Municipal Freedom: a Study of the Commission Government. *Garden City, N. Y.,* 1915.
The Challenge of the Prophets. *Anderson, Ind.,* 1929.

S

SADLER, WILLIAM SAMUEL: 1875–

William Samuel Sadler, son of Samuel Cavins and Sarah Isabele Wilson Sadler, was born at Spencer, Ind., on June 24, 1875, and was educated at Battle Creek College, Cooper Medical College, the University of Chicago, and American Medical Missionary College of the University of Illinois, receiving an M.D. from the last-named institution in 1906. He also studied in Europe. On Dec. 3, 1897, he married Lena C. Kellogg.

After 1906 he practiced medicine in Chicago, serving as director and chief psychiatrist of the Chicago Institute of Research and Diagnosis.

Information from *Who's Who in America.*

* * *

The Cause and Cure of Colds. *Chicago,* 1910.
The Science of Living; or, the Art of Keeping Well. *Chicago,* 1910.
The Physiology of Faith and Fear; or, the Mind in Health and Disease. *Chicago,* 1912.
Worry and Nervousness; or, the Science of Self-Mastery. *Chicago,* 1914.
Mother and Her Child (with Lena K. Sadler). *Chicago,* 1916.

Long Heads and Round Heads; or, What's the Matter with Germany. *Chicago,* 1918.
How to Reduce and How to Gain (with Lena K. Sadler). *Chicago,* 1920. (Reissued in 1930 as Diets and Food Values; How to Reduce and How to Gain.)
Race Decadence; an Examination of the Causes of Racial Degeneracy in the United States. *Chicago,* 1922.
What a Salesman Should Know About His Health; a Straight Talk to Salesmen on Keeping Physically Fit. *Chicago,* 1923.
The Truth About Spiritualism. *Chicago,* 1923.
Personality and Health; a Talk to Business Women on Efficiency. *Chicago,* 1924. (Reissued in 1930 as The Business Woman: Her Personality and Health.)
Americanitis—Blood Pressure and Nerves. *New York,* 1925.
Constipation, How to Cure Yourself. *Chicago,* 1925.
Elements of Pep; a Talk on Health and Efficiency. *Chicago,* 1925. (Reissued in 1930 as Road to Attainment; the Elements of Pep.)
Essentials of Healthful Living. *New York,* 1925.
How You Can Keep Happy. *Chicago,* 1926. (Reissued in 1930 as The Quest for Happiness; How You Can Keep Happy.)
The Truth About Heredity; a Concise Explanation of Heredity Written for the Layman. *Chicago,* 1927.
The Truth About Mind Cure. *Chicago,* 1928.
The Mind at Mischief; Tricks and Deceptions of the Subconscious and How to Cope with Them. *New York,* 1929.
Woman and the Home (with Lena K. Sadler). *Chicago,* 1930.
The Boy and His Body. *Chicago,* 1930.
Piloting Modern Youth; a Guide for Parents, Teachers, and Others Dealing with Adolescents (with Lena K. Sadler). *New York,* 1931.
Theory and Practice of Psychiatry; a Psychiatric Textbook for Neuropsychiatric Specialists and General Practitioners of Medicine. *St. Louis,* 1936.
Psychiatric Educational Work.
Psychiatric Nursing (with Lena K. Sadler and Anna B. Kellogg). *St. Louis,* 1937.
Living a Sane Sex Life (with Lena K. Sadler). *Chicago,* 1938.
The Truth About Mental Healing (with Lena K. Sadler). *Chicago,* 1938.
The Cause and Cure of Headaches, Backaches and Constipation (with Lena K. Sadler). *Chicago,* 1938.
The Mastery of Worry and Nervousness (with Lena K. Sadler). *Chicago,* 1938.
Sex Life, Before and After Marriage (with Lena K. Sadler). *Chicago,* 1938.
Growing Out of Babyhood; Problems of the Preschool Child (with Lena K. Sadler). *New York,* 1940.
Prescription for Permanent Peace. *Chicago,* 1944.

SAGE, ELIZABETH: 1868–

Born in Buffalo, N. Y., on Feb. 8, 1868, Elizabeth Sage graduated from St. Margaret's in Buffalo in 1887 and received the B.S. degree from Columbia University in 1917. From 1913 to 1937 she was professor of economics at Indiana University.

Information from The University Libraries, Indiana University.

* * *

Occupations for Little Fingers (with Anna M. Cooley). *New York,* 1905.
A Study of Costume; from the Days of the Egyptians to Modern Times. *New York,* 1926.
Textiles and Clothing. *New York,* 1930.

SANCHEZ, NELLIE VAN DE GRIFT (MRS. ADULFO): 1856–1935.

Nellie Van de Grift, daughter of Jacob and Esther Keen Van de Grift and youngest sister of Mrs. Robert Louis Stevenson, was born in Indianapolis on Nov. 24, 1856. She graduated from Indianapolis High School in 1875 and studied at the University of California from 1905 to 1910. On Sept. 12, 1880, she married Adulfo Sanchez, who died in 1890.

Mrs. Sanchez engaged in historical research and the translation of original Spanish documents. She died on Jan. 4, 1935.

Information from *Who Was Who in America.*

* * *

Spanish and Indian Place Names of California, Their Meaning and Their Romance. *San Francisco,* 1914.
Life of Mrs. Robert Louis Stevenson. *New York,* 1920.
A Short History of California (with Dr. Rockwell D. Hunt). *New York,* 1929.
Stories of the States; Tales of Early Exploration and Settlement. *New York,* 1931.
Stories of the Latin American States. *New York,* 1934.

SANDERS, NEWELL: 1850–1939.

Newell Sanders, son of John and Miriam Coffey Sanders, was born in Owen County, Ind., on July 12, 1850, and graduated from Indiana University in 1873, receiving the LL.D. degree in 1931. He married Corinne Dodds in 1873.

From 1873 to 1877 he was a merchant at Bloomington, Ind., and in 1878 moved to Chattanooga, Tenn., where he was engaged in the manufacture of plows.

He was president and general manager of the Chattanooga Plow Company from 1882 to 1901 and again from 1915 to 1919. In 1919 the Chattanooga Plow Company was sold to International Harvester. He established the Newell Sanders Plow Company in 1901, of which he was sole owner, and served as an officer and director of other organizations.

Mr. Sanders was active in politics. He was a leader of the prohibition movement in Tennessee and from Apr. 8, 1912, to Feb. 2, 1913, served as U. S. senator from that state—the only Republican senator from Tennessee in sixty years.

He died at Chattanooga on Jan. 26, 1939.

Information from *Indiana University, 1820-1904,* and *Who Was Who in America.*

* * *

Wendell Sanders. *Chattanooga, Tenn.,* 1893.

SAY, THOMAS: 1787–1834.

Thomas Say, son of Dr. Benjamin Say, a leading citizen of Philadelphia, and his first wife, Ann Bonsall, was born on June 27, 1787. His father was an enlightened doctor of medicine and apparently a patron of the arts and sciences in general and his mother was a granddaughter of the American botanist, John Bartram; consequently it is not strange that Thomas Say's interest turned to the biological sciences at an early age.

Nothing is known of Thomas Say's childhood. His was a Quaker family, and he was enrolled in the Westtown Boarding School at the time of its opening. He was then twelve years old. It appears that his education did not prosper greatly, and he was soon removed and put to work in the apothecary shop which his father operated in connection with his medical practice. Before long young Say became interested in natural history—a subject which was certainly not taught at Westtown School or any other in that day. He began to collect beetles and butterflies and was encouraged in his studies by his great-uncle, William Bartram, then still living. He found some other young men who were interested in the same studies and he was soon thinking of nothing else: Thomas Say had found his field.

He was one of the founders of the Philadelphia Academy of Natural Sciences. His father had set him up in the drug business—unfortunately with John Speakman, another budding naturalist—and the firm failed dismally in a very short time. After the failure young Say took up residence in the Academy's rooms, sleeping, it was said, under one of the displays, the skeleton of a horse, and eating, when it occurred to him, bread and milk. Such was to be Thomas Say's mode of life, except when someone took him in hand for a period now and then, until his death in 1834.

Say served briefly in the War of 1812, his total pay during the campaign amounting to $7.06. He then returned to haunt the Academy, now occupying new and commodious quarters.

In 1817 he published his first book on entomology; it consisted of ten pages, including six plates. In that same year the Academy elected a new president. He was William Maclure, a Scotch merchant who had come to Philadelphia after having amassed a fortune in London and who was now intent upon making a complete geological survey of North America. Maclure became, and continued until his death, the patron not only of the Academy but also of Thomas Say.

In 1819 Say was appointed zoologist to accompany the expedition on which the War Department had ordered Maj. Stephen H. Long and Col. Henry Atkinson to the Yellowstone, Long to make a scientific survey and Atkinson to intimidate the British fur traders who were encroaching on the upper Louisiana Territory. Through the report of this expedition Thomas Say gained his first national recognition as a scientist and, probably as a result, was appointed curator of the American Philosophical Society in 1821 and professor of natural history at the University of Pennsylvania in the following year.

In 1823 another government expedition was dispatched to the West with the same declared and undeclared purposes. Maj. Long commanded and Say was "Zoologist and Antiquary." This expedition visited the source of St. Peter's River, Lake of the Woods, etc. To the report of this expedition (Keating, William H.—*Narrative of An Expedition to the Source of the St. Peter's River* . . . Philadelphia, 1824) Say made considerable contribution.

He had now had opportunity to collect over a broader territory than any other American entomologist; and the result, in 1824, was his second book, *American Entomology* . . . Philadelphia, 1824. It received immediate, although not financially profitable, recognition.

The year 1824 was a significant period in Say's life. In December Robert Owen bought the Harmony Community on the Wabash River from the Rappites with the intention of setting up a communistic society, a "New Moral World" as he called it. His plans were grandiose, but the details had failed to interest him

sufficiently, and when hundreds of hopeful thinkers began to flock to the new settlement he found that he had neither sufficient funds to care for them nor any concrete plan for carrying on the educational activities which were to be a main feature of the movement.

In this dilemma Owen sought out William Maclure in Philadelphia. Maclure's understanding of Owen's social plans seems to have been hazy, but his fanatical interest in education made him an eager investor, and he agreed to put $150,000 into the venture and to supply, from the Philadelphia teachers and scientists to whose support he was contributing, a faculty which he hoped would make New Harmony the educational center of America. The contingent of learned men and women who set out for New Harmony under Maclure's patronage in November, 1825, included Thomas Say, Charles Alexandre Lesueur, French artist and naturalist; Gerard Troost, geologist; John Chappelsmith, English artist and engraver; Madame Marie Louise Duclos Fretageot, who had operated a school for young ladies under Maclure's sponsorship and who acted as his representative in financial matters, and one of her teachers, Phiquepal d'Arusmont.

The party did not reach New Harmony until late in January, 1826, and by the following summer the community, as such, was in a state of complete anarchy. Early 1827 saw the departure of the last of the more visionary and irresponsible of the hundreds of members. A few more months, during which a bitter dispute raged between Owen and Maclure over financial responsibility, left New Harmony an ordinary capitalistic town, but a town with such a collection of learned citizens as existed nowhere else west of the Alleghenies.

Most of Maclure's people were still there and they continued, with him, their interest in education: Maclure's Seminary, The Orphan's Manual Training School, and the School of Industry opened their doors in 1827, with Thomas Say as superintendent of literature, science and education.

On Jan. 4, 1827, Professor Say married Lucy Way Sistare, a young lady who had come to New Harmony as a former pupil and an assistant to Madame Fretageot. Connubial bliss, however, could not compete with the charms of collecting entomological specimens, and the next fall Say seized the opportunity of Maclure's departure for Mexico to accompany him. Apparently Say did not return to New Harmony until the late summer or early autumn of 1828. His health, never good, was now distinctly poor.

The Says set up housekeeping in one of the Rappite houses but, both suffering from frequent illnesses, spent much time with Madame Fretageot. That lady suspected Lucy Say of prolonging her illnesses to avoid housekeeping. Meanwhile Say taught, had charge of Maclure's school garden, the school press, the school paper, and, of course, found time to collect. Lucy Say, though she may not have fancied housekeeping, was certainly not idle, for she taught, spun and knit wool stockings, and made clothing for the students. In addition, she drew many of the plates for Say's later books and assisted Caroline Tiebout in coloring them.

Most of these works, published between 1830 and 1840 (the last book appearing after Say's death), represented a new field in writing, that of conchology. The year 1831 was Say's most productive.

So things went with the Says. Thomas's responsibilities increased even more when, after Madame Fretageot's death, he took over the entire management of Maclure's New Harmony property. His health was growing steadily worse, largely due to his extremely irregular habits, for he still ate only when someone suggested it and slept only when entirely exhausted.

Recurrent attacks of fever and dysentery finally accomplished their expected results upon his weakened constitution, and he died in New Harmony on Oct. 10, 1834. He left his wife, Lucy, who survived until Nov. 15, 1886, and who disposed of his collections in such an intelligent way as to preserve as great contributors to the natural sciences in America not only the name of Thomas Say but also her own.

> Information from Weiss, Harry B., and Ziegler, Grace M.—*Thomas Say*; Walker, Mary Alden—*Beginnings of Printing in Indiana*; Lockwood, George—*The New Harmony Communities*.

* * *

American Entomology, or Descriptions of the Insects of North America. Illustrated by Coloured Figures from Drawings Executed from Nature . . . *Philadelphia, 1817.*

American Entomology, or, Descriptions of the Insects of North America. Illustrated by Coloured Figures from Original Drawings Executed from Nature . . . *Philadelphia, 1824-1828.* 3 vols.

American Conchology; or, Descriptions of the Shells of North America. Illustrated by Coloured Figures from Original Drawings Executed from Nature . . . *New Harmony, Ind., 1830-1834.* (Issued in six parts, with a seventh part, completed by T. A. Conrad, issued after Say's death.)

Descriptions of New Species of Curculionites of North America, with Observations on some of the Species Already Known. *New Harmony, Ind., July, 1831.*

Descriptions of New Species of Heteropterous Hemiptera of North America . . . *New Harmony, Ind., 1831.*

Descriptions of New Species of North American Insects, Found in Louisiana by Joseph Barabino . . . *New Harmony, Ind., 1831.*

A Glossary to Say's Conchology. *New Harmony, Ind., 1832.*

Descriptions of Some New Terrestrial and Fluviatile Shells of North America, 1829, 1830, 1831 . . . *New Harmony, Ind., 1840.*

SAYLER, HARRY LINCOLN: 1863-1913.

Born in Little York, O., on Feb. 13, 1863, Harry Lincoln Sayler was brought to Shelbyville, Ind., in 1868. He graduated from De Pauw University in 1885, in 1887 was temporary editor of the WABASH TIMES, and moved to Chicago in 1888. In 1890 he became one of the managers of the City Press Association of Chicago.

Mr. Sayler married Nora H. Elliott in 1899. In addition to his books he was the author of many magazine articles and pamphlets. He wrote under several pseudonyms—"Ashton Lamar," "Elliott Whitney," and "Gordon Stuart"—all of these names being used by other writers after his death. He died on May 31, 1913.

> Information from De Pauw University's *Alumnal Record, 1920,* and Burke and Howe—*American Authors and Books, 1640-1940.*

* * *

Terrible Teddy and Peaceful Bill; or, the Quest of the Treasure Box. *Chicago, 1908.*

Johnny Hep, the Soldier Boy. *Chicago, 1908.*

The Air Ship Boys. *Chicago, 1909.*

The Air Ship Boys Adrift; or, Saved by an Aeroplane. *Chicago, 1909.* (2nd ed.)

The Air Ship Boys Due North; or, by Balloon to the Pole. *Chicago, 1910.*

Aeroplane Express; or, the Boy Aeronaut's Grit. *Chicago, 1910.*

The Air Ship Boys in Barren Lands; or, the Secret of the White Eskimos. *Chicago, 1910.*

Boy Aeronaut's Club; or, Flying for Fun. *Chicago, 1910.*

Stolen Aeroplane; or, How Bud Wilson Made Good. *Chicago, 1910.*

The Air Ship Boys in Finance; or, the Flight of the Flying Cow. *Chicago, 1911.*

Battling the Bighorn; or, the Aeroplane in the Rockies. *Chicago, 1911.*

The Air Ship Boys' Ocean Flyer; or, New York to London in Twelve Hours. *Chicago, 1911.*

Cruise in the Sky; or, the Legend of the Great Pink Pearl. *Chicago, 1911.*

In the Clouds for Uncle Sam; or, Morey Marshall of the Signal Corps. *Chicago, 1911.*

White Tiger of Nepal. *Chicago, 1912.*

Giant Moose. *Chicago, 1912.*

The Blind Lion of the Congo. *Chicago, 1912.*

Boy Scouts of the Air at Eagle Camp. *Chicago, 1912.*

Boy Scouts of the Air at Greenwood School. *Chicago, 1912.*

Boy Scouts of the Air in Indian Land. *Chicago, 1912.*

Boy Scouts of the Air in Northern Wilds. *Chicago, 1912.*

King Bear of Kodiak Island. *Chicago, 1912.*

When Scout Meets Scout; or, the Aeroplane Spy. *Chicago, 1912.*

The Air Ship Boys as Detectives. *Chicago, 1913.*

On the Edge of the Arctic; or, an Aeroplane in Snowland. *Chicago, 1913.*

Rogue Elephant. *Chicago, 1913.*

Boy Scouts of the Air on the Great Lakes. *Chicago, 1914.*

Pirate Shark. *Chicago, 1914.*

SCHELLING, FELIX EMANUEL: 1858–1945.

Felix Emanuel Schelling, son of Felix and Rose White Schelling, was born in New Albany, Ind., on Sept. 3, 1858. He graduated from the University of Pennsylvania in 1881, received the LL.B. degree in 1883, and the A.M. degree in 1884. He was later awarded honorary degrees by the University of Pennsylvania and other institutions. From 1893 until his death he was professor of English literature at the University of Pennsylvania.

Dr. Schelling was twice married: first to Caroline Derbyshire, who died in 1935, and second to Gertrude Bueb. He was an elder brother of Ernest Henry Schelling, noted composer and conductor. He died on Dec. 15, 1945.

His contributions to learned journals and serials are not listed here.

Information from *Who's Who in America.*

* * *

Humanities Gone and to Come; an Address.

The English Chronicle Play: a Study in Popular Historical Literature Environing Shakespeare. *New York, 1902.*

The Queen's Progress and Other Elizabethan Sketches. *Boston, 1904.*

Elizabethan Drama, 1558-1642, a History of the Drama in England . . . *Boston, 1908.* 2 vols.

English Literature During the Lifetime of Shakespeare. *New York, 1910.*

The Restoration Drama. *1912.*

The English Lyric. *Boston, 1913.*

English Drama. *New York, 1914.*

Thor and Some Other War Rhymes. *Philadelphia, 1918.*

Appraisements and Asperities as to Some Contemporary Writers. *Philadelphia, 1922.*

Foreign Influences in Elizabethan Plays. *New York, 1923.*

Summer Ghosts and Winter Topics. *Philadelphia, 1924.*

Elizabethan Playwrights; a Short History of the English Drama from Medieval Times to the Closing of the Theaters in 1642. *New York, 1925.*

Shakespeare and Demi-Science; Papers on Elizabethan Topics. *Philadelphia, 1927.*

Pedagogically Speaking; Essays and Addresses on Topics More or Less Educational. *Philadelphia, 1929.*

Shakespeare. *Chicago, 1930.*

Shakespeare Biography, and Other Papers, Chiefly Elizabethan. *Philadelphia, 1937.*

SCHERGER, GEORGE LAWRENCE: 1874–1941.

George Lawrence Scherger, son of Christian and Marguerite Rush Scherger, was born at Lawrenceburg, Ind., on Oct. 21, 1874, and graduated from Indiana University in 1894. From 1895 to 1898 he studied in Germany at the University of Leipzig and the University of Berlin and in 1899 received the Ph.D. degree from Cornell University. He married Bertha Mittelstaedt on Jan. 18, 1898.

From 1899 until his death Dr. Scherger was associated with Armour Institute of Technology in Chicago, as instructor, assistant professor, and, after 1903, as professor of history. He served as pastor and superintendent of the Armour Mission from 1905 to 1931 and as pastor of St. Paul's Evangelical Lutheran Church after 1929. He was the author of numerous papers and reviews.

He died on Mar. 31, 1941.

Information from *Indiana University, 1820-1904,* and *Who Was Who in America.*

* * *

The Evolution of Modern Liberty. *New York, 1904.*

The Evolution of the German Empire. *Chicago, 1914.*

Men of the Hour. *Chicago, 1932.*

SCHLEPPEY, BLANCHE BLOOR (MRS. JOHN H.): 1861–1927.

Born near Edinburg, Ind., in 1861, Blanche Bloor was educated there and at Oldenburg Academy. In 1893 she moved to Indianapolis with her husband, John H. Schleppey. She contributed stories and illustrated feature articles to Indianapolis papers and was among the first in the U. S. to write such articles for newspapers. She died in 1927.

Supplied by the Indianapolis Public Library.

* * *

Oriental Symbology of Art. *Indianapolis*, 1907.
Soul of a Mummy, and Other Stories. *Indianapolis, 1908.*

SCHNEIDER, FREDERICK WILLIAM: 1862–1941.

Frederick William Schneider, son of Charles and Philippine Hepp Schneider, was born in Boonville, Ind., on Dec. 28, 1862, and graduated from German Wallace College in Ohio in 1886, receiving the A.M. degree in 1888. In 1899 he graduated from Drew Theological Seminary. Baldwin University conferred the D.D. degree on him in 1906. He was twice married; first to Mary Anna Severinghaus in 1890, then to Emma Josephine Freyhofer on Aug. 15, 1899.

From 1886 to 1894 he taught at German Wallace College, in 1894-95 was pastor of the Methodist Episcopal Church in Delaware, O., in 1895-96 was pastor of a church in Pittsburgh, and from 1897 to 1909 was again on the faculty of German Wallace College. He then occupied the pulpit of a church in Brooklyn for five years. From 1914 to 1918 he was with the Sunday School Board of the Methodist Episcopal Church, from 1918 to 1920 was engaged in editorial work in Cincinnati, and after 1920 was vice-president and professor of Bible and religion at Morningside College, Ia.

He died on Dec. 18, 1941.

Information from *Who's Who in America.*

* * *

System der Christlichen Lehre. *Cincinnati,* 1908.

SCHURMANN, HELEN: 1829–1896.

Helen Schurmann was a resident of Indianapolis. She was born on Apr. 16, 1829, and died on Apr. 28, 1896.

Information from Hilton U. Brown, Indianapolis.

* * *

The Solitary Survivor, and Other Stories. *Indianapolis,* 1896.

SCOTT, ALVA ROY: 1863–

Born at Leavenworth, Ind., on Apr. 20, 1863, Alva Roy Scott graduated from De Pauw University in

1886, receiving the A.M. degree in 1889, and graduated from McCormick Theological Seminary in 1891. He received the Ph.D. degree from the University of Worcester in 1896 and the A.M. from Harvard in 1899.

In 1891 he was ordained to the Presbyterian ministry but in 1900 entered the Unitarian fellowship and after 1904 served as minister of the Unitarian Church at Bangor, Me. He was also a lecturer at the University of Maine. He married Alberta Garber on Aug. 21, 1901.

Information from De Pauw University's *Alumnal Record, 1920.*

* * *

A Study of Human Progress.
The Principle and Aims of the Unitarian Fellowship.
A Historic and the Ideal Christ.
Jesus and Salvation in the Evolution of Man.

SCOTT, CARRIE EMMA: 1874–1943.

Carrie Emma Scott, daughter of Robert R. and Lavicy Harvey Scott, was born at Mooresville, Ind., on Aug. 22, 1874, and graduated from Indiana University in 1898. For several years she taught in the high schools of Rockville and Mooresville, Ind., and in 1903-04 was with the Indiana State Library. She then studied at the New York State Library School and at the Carnegie Library School in Pittsburgh, Pa.

From 1907 to 1917 Miss Scott served as assistant state organizer for the Public Library Commission of Indiana and, after 1917, as supervisor of children's work at the Indianapolis Public Library. She was also an instructor at summer sessions of the library schools of the University of Iowa and the University of Minnesota. She compiled several collections of stories for juveniles.

She died on July 27, 1943.

Information from *Who's Who in America.*

* * *

A Manual for Institution Libraries. *Chicago,* 1916.

SCOTT, FRED NEWTON: 1860–1931.

"Fred Newton Scott (Aug. 20, 1860-May 29, 1931), rhetorician, was born in Terre Haute, Ind., the son of Mary (Bannister) and Harvey D. Scott, a lawyer who was a congressman from Indiana in 1855 and for some years a county judge. After taking the degrees of A.B., 1884, A.M., 1888, and Ph.D., 1889, at the University of Michigan, meanwhile serving as library assistant and later as assistant librarian, Scott became an instructor in English and for almost forty years was a member of the university faculty. As head of the department of rhetoric, 1903-21, and of rhetoric and journalism, 1921-27, he exerted a wide influence. He encouraged the establishment of schools of journalism in state colleges, modified the teaching of English composition in colleges . . . and was a stimulating teacher of graduate students . . . He was president of the Modern Language Association of America, 1907; one of the founders and the first president of the National Council of Teachers of English, 1911-13; president of the North Central Association of Colleges and Secondary Schools, 1913, and of the American Association of Teachers of Journalism, 1917. A member of several British learned societies as well, he had a wide acquaintance and a high reputation among foreign scholars. In 1887 he married Isadore Thompson, daughter of Prof. Bradley M. Thompson of the law school of the University of Michigan, by whom he had a daughter and two sons. A year after her death in 1922, he married Georgia Jackson of New York City, who with his three children survived him. Upon his retirement in 1927 as professor emeritus, he and his wife lived in Tucson, Ariz.; he died in San Diego, Calif.

"Although Scott's distinction rests particularly upon his influence as a teacher, his list of more than a hundred publications contains convincing evidence of his scholarly interests and attainments. . . . he wrote numerous essays and technical articles that appeared in magazines ranging from the CLASSICAL JOURNAL to the ATLANTIC MONTHLY on subjects that varied from the prosody of Walt Whitman to the psychology of speech. His chief concern was always with matters of style and with the fundamentals of literary effect and appreciation . . . His writing was smooth, polished, urbane, packed with implication . . . Modest and extremely reticent, with a grave courtesy, he was to many of his students an enigmatic figure, whose preference was always for questioning rather than for arriving at fixed conclusions. He was keenly sensitive and easily wounded, but he had a delicate wit and took great pleasure in good talk. He had some reputation as an after-dinner speaker. He was perhaps half the scholar, half the old-style journalist who could write excellent editorials in a style not so far from Addison and sometimes much better for the purpose in hand . . ."

His textbooks, compilations and works upon which he served as editor are not listed here.

Condensed from D. G—d., *Dictionary of American Biography,* Vol. XVI.

* * *

The Principles of Style. *Ann Arbor, Mich.,* 1890.

Guide to the Literature of Aesthetics (with C. M. Gayley). *Berkeley, Calif.,* 1890.

Aesthetics, Its Problems and Literature. *Ann Arbor, Mich.,* 1890.

An Introduction to the Methods and Materials of Literary Criticism (with C. M. Gayley). *Boston,* 1899.

The Teaching of English in the Elementary and the Secondary School (with George R. Carpenter and F. T. Baker). *New York,* 1903.

Congress of Letters. *Columbia, Mo.,* 1917.

The Standard of American Speech, and Other Papers. *New York,* 1926.

American Slang (with O. Jesperson). *New York,* 1926.

Genesis of Speech. *Ann Arbor, Mich.*

SCOTT, J. WALTER: ?—

"J. Walter Scott came to Lafayette [Ind.] from Oxford, Ind. Mr. Scott was a business man and his time and energies were given to his business affairs. Nevertheless he found time to write a novel . . ."

de Hart—*Past and Present of Tippecanoe County,* 1909.

* * *

Anita, or the Specter of a Snow Storm. *New York,* 1891.

SCOTT, JOHN: ?—

Although no biographical material on John Scott has been located, he was an early Indiana printer and a writer of considerable local importance. His little book, *The Indiana Gazetteer,* earliest scholarly description of the state, its people, its products, and its resources, had become scarce in the original edition by 1876, as witness the description of Dan Hough's collection of Indiana authors in an article by D. S. A. which appeared in the CINCINNATI DAILY GAZETTE of Dec. 7, 1876:

"Earliest and most valuable work in the collection . . . Scott wrote and published the book, acting as his own compositor and binder. He was a careful, painstaking author . . . Previous to publication he had prepared a map of the state . . . Mr. Hough experienced much trouble in tracing out a copy of this little work, and, when at last one was found he had to pay dearly for the privilege of owning it. He regards it as the gem of the collection and very properly . . ."

Information from D. S. A. in the CINCINNATI GA-ZETTE, Dec. 7, 1876, and Walker—*The Beginnings of Printing in the State of Indiana.*

* * *

The Indiana Gazetteer; or Topographical Dictionary, Containing a Description of the Several Counties, Towns, Villages, Settlements, Roads, Lakes, Rivers, Creeks, Springs, Etc. in the State of Indiana, Alphabetically Arranged by John Scott. *Centerville, Ind.,* 1826.

SCOTT, LEROY: 1875–1929.

"Leroy Scott . . . author, was born in Fairmount, Ind., the son of Eli J. and Eleanor (Reader) Scott. After graduating from Indiana University in 1897, he worked for a few months on a Louisiana newspaper owned by his brother and then went to Chicago, where he was a reporter for the CHICAGO JOURNAL. In 1900 and 1901 he was assistant editor of the WOMAN'S HOME COMPANION. He had developed an interest in settlement work as a result of living at Hull House in Chicago, and in 1902 he became assistant headworker of the University Settlement, New York City. Here he met Miriam Finn, whom he married on June 24, 1904; they had two daughters and a son.

"When in 1904 he gave up settlement work to devote himself to writing, he did not give up his interest in social reform. His first novel, *The Walking Delegate* (1905), showed not merely his confidence in organized labor but also his hope for far-reaching social reorganization. In *To Him That Hath* (1907) he revealed the difficulties of a man who has been in prison, and in *Counsel for the Defense* (1912) he described a woman's struggle for economic independence. *The Shears of Destiny* (1910) was concerned with the Russian revolutionary movement and was based on Scott's observations, made during a visit to Russia with his wife in 1905-06. From 1904 to 1912 he wrote frequently for the magazines on such topics as unemployment, life insurance, and strike-breaking. After his return from Russia he contributed several articles to the OUTLOOK and to EVERYBODY'S on conditions in that country, and especially on the activities of the revolutionaries. In short, he is to be numbered among the muck-rakers. He was always moderate in his methods, but a strong social purpose informed what he wrote and is to be observed in his novels as well as his articles. It also found expression in other activities, for he was interested in organizing the Woman's Trade Union League, an active worker for child-labor laws, and one of the founders and an executive of the Intercollegiate Social-

ist Society. When the muck-raking movement declined, he took advantage of another form of popular fiction. In *Partners of the Night* (1916) he dealt with crime and its detection, and the success of the book encouraged him to write a series of stories about the activities of criminals and policemen. These novels were based on an exact knowledge of criminal methods, derived from careful investigation, and all of them indicated the need for changes in the social structure and in the handling of offenders against the law; although the moral may not have been plain to most of Scott's readers, it was constantly in his mind. His last novel, *The Trail of Glory* (1926), dealt with some of the problems of an amateur tennis champion. He was drowned at Chateaugay Lake, N. Y. At his best he was a skillful story-teller, but he commonly employed romantic and improbable plots, showed no great insight into character, and had no stylistic distinction. He frankly and successfully competed with writers whose sole aim was to divert their readers; his work is on a higher level than theirs only because of the sincerity and firmness of his social purpose . . ."

Condensed from G. H., *Dictionary of American Biography,* Vol. XVI.

* * *

The Walking Delegate. *New York,* 1905.
To Him That Hath. *New York,* 1907.
The Shears of Destiny. *New York,* 1910.
Counsel for the Defense. *New York,* 1912.
No. 13 Washington Square. *Boston,* 1914.
Partners of the Night. *New York,* 1916.
Mary Regan. *Boston,* 1918.
A Daughter of Two Worlds; a Novel of New York Life. *Boston,* 1919.
Children of the Whirlwind. *Boston,* 1921.
Cordelia the Magnificent. *New York,* 1923.
The Heart of Katie O'Doone. *Boston,* 1925.
Folly's Gold. *Boston,* 1926.
The Trail of Glory. *Boston,* 1926.
The Living Dead Man. *New York,* 1929.

SCOTT, NANCY ELNORA: 1879–

Nancy Elnora Scott was born in Fort Wayne, Ind., in 1879. It is believed that she was educated at the University of Pennsylvania.

Information from Federal Writers Project—*Indiana Authors,* 1937.

* * *

The Limits of Toleration Within the Church of England from 1632 to 1642. *Philadelphia,* 1912.

Historical Method in the Seventeenth Century.

SCOTT, SAMUEL W.: ?–

Born and reared in Elizabethton, Tenn., Samuel W. Scott served in the Civil War with the Thirteenth Regiment, Tennessee Volunteer Cavalry. In 1867, he settled in Owensville, Ind., where he resided until 1895, when he returned to Tennessee, making his home in Carter County.

> Supplied by Owensville Carnegie Library.

* * *

History of the Thirteenth Regiment of Tennessee Volunteer Cavalry. *Knoxville, Tenn.,* 1903.

SCOVELL, JOSIAH THOMAS: 1841–1915.

Dr. Josiah Thomas Scovell (he held an M.D. degree although, apparently, his interests lay chiefly in the fields of natural history) was a long-time member of the faculty of Indiana State Teachers' College at Terre Haute. His death occurred in 1915. In addition to his other books, he was the author of several textbooks not listed here.

> Information from the Emmeline Fairbanks Memorial Library, Terre Haute, Indiana.

* * *

Roads and Road Materials of a Portion of Western Indiana. 1906.

Fort Harrison on the Wabash.

An Old Channel of the Niagara River.

SCRIBNER, BENJAMIN FRANKLIN: 1825–1900.

Benjamin Franklin Scribner, son of Abner Scribner (who, in 1813, with his brothers helped lay out the town of New Albany, Ind.), was born in that place on Sept. 20, 1825.

He served in the Mexican War in the Second Indiana Volunteers and during the Civil War was colonel of the 38th Indiana Volunteers, taking part in numerous campaigns, in one of which he was wounded in the leg. He was brevetted brigadier-general in 1864. He retired from service in that year because of ill health.

In 1865 he was appointed collector of internal revenue for the Second Collecting District of Indiana, a position he held for six years. He was half-owner of a large drug house in New Albany but sold his interest to his partner in 1878 and established a drug brokerage office in New York City, which he gave up several months later to become U. S. treasury agent in Alaska.

He married Anna Martha Maginness on Dec. 20, 1849, and died in Louisville, Ky., in 1900.

> Information from *Representative Men of Indiana,* Vol. I, and the New Albany Public Library.

* * *

Camp Life of a Volunteer; a Campaign in Mexico; or, a Glimpse of Life in Camp, by One Who Has Seen the Elephant. *Philadelphia,* n.d. [1847]. (Described in a literary article in the CINCINNATI GAZETTE for Dec. 7, 1876, as "a vigorous defence of Indiana troops at Buena Vista.")

How Soldiers Were Made; or, the War as I Saw It Under Buell, Rosencrans, Thomas, Grant and Sherman. *New Albany,* n.d. [1887].

SEEGMILLER, WILHELMINA: 1866–1913.

Wilhelmina Seegmiller, daughter of Frederick and Dolena Gordon Seegmiller, was born in Fairview, Ont., Canada, on Dec. 6, 1866. She had her elementary instruction in the public schools of Goderich, Canada; took art training in studios in Toronto; trained for teaching in Grand Rapids, Mich., and graduated from Pratt Institute, Brooklyn, in 1899. From 1895 until her death, May 14, 1913, she was director of art instruction in the Indianapolis public schools. She was author of several textbooks in addition to the titles listed here.

> Information from *Who Was Who in America* and the Indianapolis Public Library.

* * *

Little Rhymes for Little Readers; Il. by Ruth M. Hallock. *Chicago,* 1903.

Suggestions in Handwork. *Chicago,* 1904.

A Hand Clasp. *Chicago,* 1911.

Other Rhymes for Little Readers. *Chicago,* 1911.

Sing a Song of Seasons; Illustrated by the Author. *Chicago,* 1914.

New Garden of Verses for Children. (Edited by Frances G. Wickes.) *Chicago,* 1925.

SELMAN, SQUIRE H.: ?–1873.

Squire H. Selman, one of the so-called "Indian Doctors," was a son-in-law of the greatest of this school of healing—the fabulous "Dr." Richard Carter of Kentucky.

Young Selman, believed to have been reared in Kentucky, married a Carter daughter evidently after 1825, and studied under Carter. Selman settled in Columbus, Ind., after he had presumably absorbed what he considered a sufficiency of Carter's learning, and began to practice. During the Thirties he traveled from town to town in Indiana and surrounding states, advertising in the newspapers and treating the ailments of the communities visited for two or three weeks at a time.

Dr. Richard Carter's fame in Kentucky had been spread by the publication of his famous *Valuable Vegetable Medical Prescriptions for the Cure of All Nervous and Putrid Disorders* in Frankfort, Ky., in 1815. It was to be expected that his son-in-law, Selman, would make a similar bid toward establishing his scholarship as soon as an opportunity offered. He brought out his book, *The Indian Guide To Health,* in 1836, and in it he used many of Carter's prescriptions, with full credit therefor. He also praised his preceptor father-in-law in sincere, if ambiguous, terms in his preface, as a man "on whom all powers of ratiocination in possession of the faculty [by which he referred to regularly educated medical men] were expended without effect."

An increasing enlightenment of the public had made a general toning-down of the Carter formulae advisable, and neither Selman nor any other could expect to equal Carter in the color of his footnotes and the frankness of his comment. Selman's book is, nevertheless, a good example of its species.

Selman died at Columbus in 1873.

* * *

The Indian Guide to Health, or, a Valuable Vegetable Medical Prescription, for the Cure of All Disorders Incident to This Climate. Designed as a Guide to Families and Young Practitioners. *Columbus, Ind.,* 1836.

SEMBOWER, CHARLES JACOB: 1871–

Charles Jacob Sembower, son of Henry Frank and Sarah Ann Lackey Sembower, was born in Newburg, W. Va., on Apr. 3, 1871, and graduated from Indiana University in 1892, receiving the Ph.D. degree from the University of Pennsylvania in 1909. On June 26, 1901, he married Lois Alta Brunt.

In 1892 he became an instructor in English at Indiana University, from 1895 to 1897 was an assistant in English at Cornell, and after 1897 was again a member of the faculty of Indiana University, serving, successively, as assistant professor of English, associate professor, and, after 1909, as professor.

Information from *Who's Who in America.*

* * *

The Life and Poetry of Charles Cotton. *New York,* 1911.

SEWALL, MRS. MAY WRIGHT (MRS. THEODORE L.): 1844–1920.

"May Eliza Wright Sewall (May 27, 1844-July 22, 1920), feminist, was born in Milwaukee, Wis., the daughter of Philander Montague and Mary Weeks (Brackett) Wright. A precocious child, she was reading Milton at the age of seven. After studying in the public schools and with her father she taught in Waukesha, Wis., to earn money for a college education. Graduated from Northwestern University in 1866, she taught in Corinth, Miss., Plainville, Mich., and Frankfort, Ind. In Frankfort she married Edwin Thompson, the principal of the school, and with him removed to Indianapolis, where both of them taught in the high school until Mr. Thompson's death, about 1876. On Oct. 30, 1880, she married Theodore Lovett Sewall, a graduate of Harvard who had established a classical school for boys in Indianapolis. Not long after, she established with him the Girls' Classical School; after his death she was its principal for many years.

"A feminist from the beginning of her life, she began as soon as she went to Indianapolis to gather groups together to work for public purposes. She was a charter member of many Indianapolis clubs and a founder of the Indiana Association for Promoting Woman's Suffrage. Following the visit of Pundita Ramabai to America, she formed the Ramabai Circle to assist in freeing the women of India from their ancient bondage. One of the first members of the Association of Collegiate Alumnae when it was organized in 1882, she helped in 1883 to organize the Western Association of Collegiate Alumnae, which later joined with the older association. From the outset of her association with these university women she had a vision of a world federation which in 1919 came to completion. From 1883 to 1912 she assisted in suffrage campaigns from Nebraska to Wisconsin and was for many years chairman of the committee which arranged and carried through the first meeting of the National Council of Women in Washington, where she presented a plan for forming an International

Council as well; from 1888 to 1899 she held various offices in the National Council. In 1891-92 she traveled abroad to awaken an interest in the World's Congress of Representative Women, at which she presided, held in Chicago in 1893 as a part of the program for the Columbian Exposition. From that time she was a prominent figure in the International Council of Women. She had been a delegate to its meetings in 1889 and in 1899 she became its president, succeeding Lady Aberdeen. She assisted in the formation of fifty women's clubs of various sorts; in 1889, when the Federation of Women's Clubs was formed, she rightly became its first president. . . Soon after her husband's death in 1895 she became profoundly interested in psychical research. In 1920 she published *Neither Dead Nor Sleeping,* an account of her personal experiences. . ."

> Condensed from L. K. M. R., *Dictionary of American Biography,* Vol. XVI.

* * *

The Domestic and Social Effects of the Higher Education of Women. 1887.

Women, World War, and Permanent Peace. *San Francisco,* 1915.

Genesis of the International Council of Women, and the Story of Its Growth, 1888-1893. *Indianapolis,* 1919.

Neither Dead nor Sleeping; with an Introduction by Booth Tarkington. *Indianapolis,* 1920.

SHAFER, SARA ANDREW (MRS. CARLTON): ?-1913.

Sara Andrew, daughter of Dr. George Lafferty and Catherine Piatt Andrew, was born in LaPorte, Ind., and was educated privately. She was married to Carlton Shafer on Nov. 19, 1884, and died in 1913.

> Information from *Who Was Who in America.*

* * *

The Day Before Yesterday. *New York,* 1904.

Beyond Chance of Change. *New York,* 1905.

A White-Paper Garden. *Chicago,* 1910.

SHARPE, MARY ELLEN GRAYDON (MRS. JOSEPH KINNE): 1825-1914.

Mary Ellen Graydon, daughter of Alexander Graydon, a Pennsylvania abolitionist and a friend of William Lloyd Garrison and Wendell Phillips, was born in Harrisburg in 1825. She was educated at Mount Joy Seminary near Philadelphia. In 1843 she came to Indianapolis and in 1847, in a ceremony conducted by Henry Ward Beecher, was married to Joseph Kinne Sharpe. She and her husband were active in church, social, and charitable work in Indianapolis.

Mrs. Sharpe began writing at an early age. In addition to her books she also had work published in the ATLANTIC MONTHLY, CENTURY, INDEPENDENT, ST. NICHOLAS, and other magazines. She died in 1914.

> Information from Dunn—*Indiana and Indianans,* Vol. III, and the Indianapolis Public Library.

* * *

A Family Retrospect. *Indianapolis,* 1909.

As The Years Go By. *Indianapolis,* 1913.

SHAW, JAMES BYRNIE: ?-

James Byrnie Shaw, a Civil War veteran, apparently spent most of his life in Remington, Ind. His wife was the former Martha Jane Morgan, and they were the parents of James Byrnie Shaw, college professor and author of several mathematical textbooks.

> Information from *Who's Who in America.*

* * *

History of the Tenth Regiment, Indiana Volunteer Infantry, Three Months and Three Years Organizations. *Lafayette, Ind.,* 1912.

SHERIDAN, WILBUR FLETCHER: 1863-1920.

Wilbur Fletcher Sheridan, son of the Rev. Andrew Jackson and Mary Anne Merrill Sheridan, was born in Rossville, Ind., on Dec. 5, 1863, and graduated from De Pauw University in 1885, receiving the A.M. degree in 1888. He was ordained to the Methodist Episcopal ministry in 1887. In 1891 he received the S.T.B. degree from Boston University.

The Rev. Mr. Sheridan was pastor of churches in Indiana and other states until 1912, when he became general secretary and executive of the Epworth League of the Methodist Church, a position he held until his death in Winnetka, Ill., on Mar. 10, 1920. In addition to his books he was a frequent contributor to magazines and to the church press.

He married Effie L. Lamar of Richmond, Ind., on June 21, 1893.

> Information from De Pauw University's *Alumnal Record, 1920,* and *Who Was Who in America.*

* * *

Talks to Probationers. *Cincinnati,* 1900.

The Sunday Night Service: a Study in Continuous Evangelism. *Cincinnati,* 1903.

The Life of Bishop Isaac Wilson Joyce. *New York,* 1907.

The Experimental Note. *Cincinnati,* 1911.

Methodism in the Making, an Inside Survey of the Epworth League. *Chicago,* 1916.

SHIEL, ROGER.: 1843–?

Of Roger R. Shiel, author of the intriguing title, *Twenty Years in Hell with the Beef Trust,* little is known. He was born in the old Indian village of Strawtown, Ind., in 1843, served in the Civil War and moved to Indianapolis in 1892, while still maintaining his home in Strawtown. In 1882, he married Julie Elizabeth Pope.

Information from the Indiana State Library.

* * *

"Early to Bed and Early to Rise." *Indianapolis,* 1908.

"Early to Bed and Early to Rise." Twenty Years in Hell with the Beef Trust. "Facts, Not Fiction." *Indianapolis,* 1909.

Comparative Discussion on the Lack of Improvement in Agriculture, Live Stock, Poultry, Etc. For the Commission on Country Life (with others). *Indianapolis,* 1918.

SHIELDS, CHARLES WOODRUFF: 1825–1904.

"Charles Woodruff Shields (Apr. 4, 1825-Aug. 26, 1904), clergyman, university professor, author, was born at New Albany, Ind., the son of James Read and Hannah (Woodruff) Shields. . . He was prepared for college at the Newark Academy, graduated from the College of New Jersey in 1844, and from Princeton Theological Seminary in 1847. On Nov. 22, 1848, he married Charlotte Elizabeth Bain of Galway, N. Y. . . . on Nov. 8, 1849, he was ordained to the Presbyterian ministry and became pastor of a church at Hempstead, Long Island. The year following he accepted a call to the Second Presbyterian Church, Philadelphia, in the service of which he remained for fifteen years. His first wife died in 1853, and in 1861 he married Elizabeth Kane, of Philadelphia, sister of the Arctic explorer, Elisha Kent Kane. . .

"In 1861 he published a little book, *Philosophia Ultima,* which changed the course of his life. All his subsequent writing and lecturing was really an effort to substantiate the challenge uttered in the pages of that pamphlet. It advocated as an attainable and desirable object of intellectual endeavor the production of a work which should be a survey of the whole field of science, a statement of Christian theology, and a reconcilement of their apparent conflicts. This project attracted much attention . . . in 1865, he was made professor of the harmony of science and religion in the College of New Jersey, at Princeton. The subject had been taught more or less irregularly in many institutions, but the chair was new and created expressly for Shields. His lectures were finished literary productions, and it was not long before they took shape as a book, *The Final Philosophy* (1877). . .

"His two great ideals, the reconcilement of science with revealed religion, and the reunion of Protestantism on a basis of ancient practices, Shields pursued with a passion which could not be discouraged. Though he frequently conducted the plain religious services which were traditional in the college chapel, he found ritual more congenial, and on Dec. 14, 1898, he was ordained deacon of the Protestant Episcopal Church, and on May 28, 1899, priest. He held his active professorship from 1865 to 1903, when he became professor emeritus. For thirteen years, 1869-82, he conducted courses in history, while continuing to lecture in philosophy.

". . . He died at his summer home in Newport, R. I., survived by two sons and a daughter; his second wife had died in 1869. . ."

Condensed from G. M. H., *Dictionary of American Biography,* Vol. XVII.

* * *

Philosophia Ultima. *Philadelphia,* 1861.

The Directory for Public Worship and the Book of Common Prayer, Considered with Reference to the Question of a Presbyterian Liturgy. *Philadelphia,* 1863.

Liturgia Expurgata, or the Book of Common Prayer Amended According to the Presbyterian Revision of 1661. *New York,* 1864.

Religion and Science in Their Relation to Philosophy. *New York,* 1875.

Book of Remembrance. *Philadelphia.*

The Final Philosophy, or System of Perfectible Knowledge Issuing from the Harmony of Science and Religion. *New York,* 1877. (Republished with two additional volumes, 1888-1905, under the title Philosophia Ultima.)

The Order of the Sciences: Essay on the Philosophical Classification and Organization of Human Knowledge. *New York,* 1882.

The Historic Episcopate: an Essay on the Four Articles of Church Unity Proposed by the American House of Bishops and the Lambeth Conference. *New York,* 1894.

The United Church of the United States. *New York,* 1895.

Church Unity: Lectures (with others). *New York,* 1896.

The Reformer of Geneva: an Historical Drama. *New York,* 1898.

The Scientific Evidences of Revealed Religion. *New York,* 1900.

Essays on Christian Unity.

The Question of Unity.

General Principles of Church Unity.

SHIPP, MAY LOUISE: ?–

May Louise Shipp was an Indianapolis resident who contributed to newspapers and periodicals in, at least, the Nineties.

> Information from Williams—*Indiana Authors* and the Indiana State Library.

* * *

The Outcomings of Addisonville: a Story (with Mary Jameson Judah). *Indianapolis,* 1892.

SHIRTS, AUGUSTUS FINCH: 1824–?

Augustus Finch Shirts, son of George Shirts, was born in Hamilton County, Ind., on Nov. 26, 1824. The second child in a large and poor family, he had to work from an early age until he was fifteen years old to support himself and help his family. Following the death of his father he was apprenticed to a farmer. He married Nancy Barnhill in 1849.

From 1854 to 1856 he was engaged in the cattle business, and from 1856 to 1860 he ran a store. In 1858 he began the study of law, starting his practice in 1861.

Mr. Shirts wrote many articles on pioneer history.

> Information from the Noblesville Public Library.

* * *

A History of the Formation, Settlement and Development of Hamilton County, Indiana. From the Year 1818 to the Close of the Civil War. n.p., 1901.

SHIVELL, PAUL: 1874–

Born in Indianapolis on Sept. 25, 1874, Paul Shivell was educated in the public schools of Dayton and Springfield, O., and at Phillips Academy, Andover, Mass. During the Columbian Exposition in 1893 he acted as special guide and lecturer on fine arts criticism. He was lay pastor of the Methodist Episcopal Church, Broad Cove, Me., in 1901-02 and spent the years

1903-15 in farming at Pleasant Hill, O. He was known as a lecturer, a reader and interpreter of poetry, and a designer and maker of handmade books.

> Information from *Who's Who in America* and the Indianapolis Public Library.

* * *

Poems and Fragments. *Springfield, O.,* 1896.

Ashes of Roses. *Dayton, O.,* 1898.

Stillwater Valley Pastorals. *Pleasant Hill, O.,* 1908.

Stillwater Pastorals, and Other Poems. *Boston,* 1915.

By the Banks of Stillwater. *Dayton, O.,* 1919.

The Little Valley. 1930.

The Spring—Brook in the Dell. 1940.

SIHLER, ERNEST GOTTLIEB: 1853–1942.

Ernest Gottlieb Sihler, son of the Rev. William S. and Susannah Kern Sihler, was born in Fort Wayne, Ind., on Jan. 2, 1853. He studied at Concordia College (Ind.), Concordia Lutheran Seminary at St. Louis and at the universities of Berlin and Leipzig, 1872-75. He received his Ph.D. in Greek from Johns Hopkins University in 1878 and the Litt.D. from Lafayette College in 1915. He married Emily Birkner on Sept. 5, 1881.

After teaching the classics in New York from 1879 to 1891, he became a member of the Concordia College (Wis.) faculty. The following year (1892) he joined the New York University faculty, where he remained as a professor of Latin and a lecturer in the graduate school until 1923. He resided in Mt. Vernon, N. Y.

Dr. Sihler died on Jan. 7, 1942.

> Information from *Who Was Who in America.*

* * *

A Complete Lexicon of the Latinity of Caesar's Gallic War. *Boston,* 1891.

New York University and Her Sons. *Boston,* 1899.

History of New York University. (Co-author.) 1901.

Memorial Volume of Hall of Fame of New York University (with Chancellor MacCracken). *New York,* 1901.

Testimonium Animae; or, Greek and Roman Before Jesus Christ. *New York,* 1908.

The Annals of Caesar, a Critical Biography with a Survey of the Sources. *New York,* 1911.

Cicero of Arpinum; a Political and Literary Biography; Being a Contribution to the History of Ancient Civilization and a Guide to the Study of Cicero's Writings. *New Haven, Conn.,* 1914.

Hellenic Civilization (with G. W. Botsford). *New York,* 1915.

From Augustus to Augustine. *Cambridge, Eng.,* 1923.

From Maumee to Thames and Tiber; the Life-Story of an American Classical Scholar. *New York,* 1930.

SIMS, CHARLES N.: 1835–1908.

Charles N. Sims, president of Valparaiso College (1860-62) and the chancellor of Syracuse University (1881-93), was born in Fairfield, Ind., on May 18, 1835. His parents were John and Irene Allen Sims.

After attending local schools he enrolled in Indiana Asbury (now De Pauw) University, from which he graduated in 1859, having taught in his home county and at Thorntown, (Ind.) Academy at intervals during his study. He married Eliza A. Foster, of Tippecanoe County, Ind., on Aug. 12, 1858.

He was made president of Valparaiso College in 1860 but left after a short time and took up active work as a Methodist minister, first in Indiana and Illinois, and later in Maryland, New Jersey, and New York.

He became chancellor of Syracuse University in 1881 and succeeded, during his twelve years in office, in putting it in a sound financial position. He resigned in 1893 and accepted the pastorate of the Meridian Street Methodist Episcopal Church in Indianapolis, which he held for two years.

The Rev. Mr. Sims died at Liberty, Ind., on Mar. 27, 1908.

Information from the *Dictionary of American Biography.*

* * *

The Temperance Problem. 1872.

The Life of the Rev. Thomas M. Eddy, D.D. *New York,* 1879.

Itinerancy Time Limit. 1879.

Address on William Ellery Channing. *Brooklyn,* 1879.

Address at the General Christian Conference, Montreal, Canada. 1888.

Annals of the Family of John Sims. *New York,* 1893.

SIMS, NEWELL LEROY: 1878–

Newell LeRoy Sims was born near Fremont, Ind., on December 3, 1878, the son of Charles Newhook and Elizabeth McClew Sims.

He attended local schools, entered Tri-State College and received the A.B. degree in 1901: he received a second A.B. from the University of Kentucky in 1905 and studied at the College of the Bible, Lexington, Ky. He received the A.M. in 1910 and the Ph.D. in 1912 from Columbia University and the B.D. from Union Theological Seminary in the latter year.

Dr. Sims married Florence Anna McNutt on Sept. 25, 1912.

He had been ordained a minister of the Christian Church in 1904 and, before he took up his teaching career, occupied pulpits in Carthage, Mo. (1905-08), Scarsdale, N. Y. (1912-14), and Columbus, O. (1914-15). He became head of the department of sociology and political science at the University of Florida in 1915, professor of sociology at the Massachusetts Agricultural College in 1920 and head of the department of sociology at Oberlin College in 1924. He received many distinctions in his field of interest.

Information from *Who's Who in America.*

* * *

A Hoosier Village; a Sociological Study with Special Reference to Social Causation. *New York,* 1912.

Ultimate Democracy and Its Making. *Chicago,* 1917.

Society and Its Surplus; a Study in Social Evolution. *New York,* 1924.

Elements of Rural Sociology. *New York,* 1928.

The New Russia. (Co-author.) 1933.

Social Problems and Social Processes. 1933.

The Problem of Social Change. *New York,* 1939.

SKINNER, HUBERT MARSHALL: 1855–1916.

Hubert Marshall Skinner, son of John N. and Joanna Marshall Skinner, was born in Valparaiso, Ind., on Jan. 15, 1855, and was graduated from De Pauw University in 1874, receiving the A.M. degree in 1877. He was awarded the Ph.D. degree by Chattanooga University in 1902 and by Valparaiso University in 1907.

From 1874 to 1880 he was a teacher and journalist, and he served as superintendent of the Brookville, Ind., schools from 1880 to 1883, when he became Deputy State Superintendent of Public Instruction of Indiana. From 1886 until 1911 he was associated with the American Book Company.

He married Emily S. Ogden in 1880 and died on June 4, 1916.

In addition to the books listed below, he was the author of several texts.

Information from *Who Was Who in America* and De Pauw University's *Alumnal Record, 1920*.

*   *   *

A History of Indiana; from the Earliest Times to the Present Day. *Valparaiso, Ind., 1876.*

Biographical Sketches of the Superintendents of Public Instruction of the State of Indiana. *Indianapolis, 1884.*

The Life and Public Services of Thomas A. Hendricks (with John W. Holcombe). *Indianapolis, 1886.*

Readings in Folk-Lore; Short Studies in the Mythology of America, Great Britain, the Norse Countries, Germany, India, Syria, Egypt, and Persia; with Selections from Standard Literature Relating to the Same. *New York, 1893.*

The Story of the Britons. *Chicago, 1903.*

The Story of the Letters and Figures. *Chicago, 1905.*

Saint Patrick: Monograph in Paragraphs. *Chicago, 1908.*

Government Revenue, Taxation, Tariffs. *Chicago, 1910.*

Discussion of School Gardens at the N. E. A. Meeting at San Francisco, Calif., July, 1911. [*Hammond, Ind.*], 1911.

Story of Michigan. *Dansville, N. Y., 1913.*

Story of Minnesota. *Dansville, N. Y., 1913.*

Story of Wisconsin. *Dansville, N. Y., 1913.*

Practical Agriculture. 1915.

Centennial History of Indiana, for Schools and for Teachers' Institutes. *Chicago, 1916.*

SMART, JAMES HENRY: 1841–1900.

James Henry Smart was a son of Dr. William H. and Nancy Farrington Smart, prosperous residents of Center Harbor, N. H. He was born on June 30, 1841.

After graduating from Concord (N. H.) High School he taught for four years and served on the staff of THE JOURNAL OF EDUCATION. He came west and became superintendent of the Fort Wayne, Ind., schools in 1865, marrying Mary H. Swan on July 21, 1870.

He was made president of Purdue University in 1883 and saw that institution through some of its most difficult years. Purdue had been a plaything of the Indiana Legislature in its first years (see sketch of Richard Owen) and, while Smart found it a going concern, he left it a distinguished one.

He was active in teachers' and educational associations throughout his life, serving in 1880 as president of the National Education Association. He died on February 21, 1900.

Information from *Who Was Who in America* and the *Dictionary of American Biography*.

*   *   *

On the Best System of Schools for a State. *Indianapolis, 1880.*

Commentary on the School Law of Indiana. *Indianapolis, 1881.*

An Ideal School System for a State.

The Institute System for the United States.

The Schools of Indiana.

SMILEY, AMANDA JANE: ?–

"Amanda Jane Smiley was a teacher in the Lafayette, Ind., public schools for many years."

de Hart—*Past and Present of Tippecanoe County, 1909.*

*   *   *

Literary Appreciations, Little Life Stories. *Lafayette, Ind., 1908.*

SMITH, BENJAMIN WILSON: 1830–1921.

Benjamin Wilson Smith, son of Abel Timothy and Deborah Spencer Wilson Smith, was born in Harrison County, Va. (now W. Va.) on January 19, 1830. He was educated in the common schools and in 1846 moved to Indiana, where he began teaching school in White County. He later taught in Jasper, Warren, and Fountain counties. In 1851 he entered De Pauw University, receiving the A.B. degree in 1855 and the A. M. in 1858.

For two years after his graduation he taught at Cornell College in Iowa, then returned to Indiana as head of Manchester Collegiate Institute. From 1858 to 1860 he was superintendent of schools at Aurora, Ind., and during this time was licensed to preach by the Methodist Church. In 1862 he became professor of ancient languages in Valparaiso Male and Female College and two years later was made president of the institution. From 1867 to 1869 he was a Methodist pastor in Terre Haute, being forced to retire because of ill health.

He moved to Brookston, Ind., in 1877, where he took charge of the academy and preached. For several terms he served as a member of the Indiana State Legislature, and from 1890 to 1893 he was postmaster at Lafayette, Ind. In 1909 he was state examiner of public accounts.

Mr. Smith married Ruth Ann Rankin of Greencastle, Ind., on Nov. 27, 1855.

Information from *Representative Men of Indiana,* Vol. II, and De Pauw University's *Alumnal Record, 1920*.

*   *   *

Sketch of the Battle of Tippecanoe, Fought Nov. 7, 1811. *Indianapolis*, 1911.

SMITH, CHARLES W.: 1846–1921.

Born at Hendricks City, Ind., on Feb. 3, 1846, Charles W. Smith, son of Morgan Lewis and Margaret Iliff Smith, grew up on his father's farm, attended the common schools and Danville (Ind.) Academy, and graduated from Indiana Asbury (now De Pauw) University in 1867. He received the A.M. degree from the same institution in 1870. He was an officer in the Union Army during the Civil War.

Graduating from Indiana Law School in Indianapolis in 1868, he was admitted to the bar in the same year and practiced law in Indianapolis until his death in 1921. He was a member of the faculty of Indiana Law School from 1895 to 1898. In 1869 Mr. Smith married Mary E. Preston of Greencastle, Ind.

> Information from Dunn—*Indiana and Indianans,* Vol. V, and De Pauw University's *Alumnal Record, 1920.*

* * *

Some Current Criticism of Courts and Lawyers. n.p., 1910.

Essays and Sketches. n.p., n.d. (pub. after the author's death).

SMITH, FREDERICK GEORGE: 1880–

Born in 1880, Frederick George Smith became attached to the Church of God as a young man and served both as editor of THE GOSPEL TRUMPET (published at Anderson, Ind.) and as editor-in-chief of all publications in English of the Church of God.

> Information from Indiana University manuscript bibliography of Indiana authors.

* * *

The Revelation Explained: Exposition, Text by Text of the Apocalypse of St. John. *Anderson, Ind.,* 1908.

Evolution of Christianity; or, Origin, Nature and Development of the Religion of the Bible. *Anderson, Ind.,* 1911.

What the Bible Teaches; a Systematic Presentation of the Fundamental Principles of Truth Contained in the Holy Scriptures. *Anderson, Ind.,* 1914.

Missionary Journeys Through Bible Lands; Italy, Greece, Egypt, Palestine, Syria, Asia Minor and Other Countries, Including a Description of Religious and Social Conditions in Palestine and Syria, Personal Missionary Experiences, and a Discussion of Missionary Methods. *Anderson, Ind.,* 1915.

The Last Reformation. *Anderson, Ind.,* 1919.

Brief Sketch of the Origin, Growth, and Distinctive Doctrine of the Church of God Reformation Movement. *Anderson, Ind.,* 1926.

Heart of the Money Problem. *Anderson, Ind.,* n.d.

Prophetic Lectures on Daniel and the Revelation. *Anderson, Ind.,* 1941.

SMITH, FREDERICK MILLER: 1870–

Frederick Miller Smith, son of James W. and Abbie F. Miller Smith, was born in Richmond, Ind., on June 16, 1870, and graduated from Indiana University in 1899.

From 1900 to 1905 he was assistant editor of WOMAN'S HOME COMPANION. After 1910 he was a member of the faculty of Cornell University as, successively, instructor in English, assistant professor, and, after 1931, professor. He contributed to magazines.

> Information from *Who's Who in America.*

* * *

The Stolen Signet. *New York,* 1909.

Eight Essays. *Ithaca, N. Y.,* 1927.

Some Friends of Dr. Johnson. *London,* 1931.

SMITH, GEORGE W.: ?–

George W. Smith was a resident of Indianapolis in 1855. According to a testimonial by Gov. Joseph A. Wright, in his second book, the governor had "known Elder George W. Smith for a number of years; he is a respectable man, a quiet, orderly good citizen, his statements may be relied upon. He is worthy of the support of all good men."

In Smith's preface he mentions a trip to Texas in 1851 to bring a "venerable old man home" [John Proctor, Sen.] to "his son's in Elkhart county Indiana." He says that he kept notes of the journey "and was solicited to publish the Journal, which I did in 1852. It was badly printed, but it sold. . ." He adds that he has written the following work in the hope of selling enough copies to finance a trip to Washington with "the venerable old man" for the purpose of getting a pension for him.

> Information from Smith's second book.

* * *

Journal to Texas. (An earlier book written by the author and mentioned in Smith's second book. No copy located.)

Incidents of Travel from the Pencil Notes of the Author . . . *Indianapolis,* 1855.

SMITH, HUBBARD MADISON: 1820–1907.

"Dr. Hubbard Madison Smith was born at Winchester, Ky., Sept. 6, 1820, and educated in the schools of that county.

"He left school at fourteen and learned the saddler's trade, which he followed for five or six years, and then took up the study of medicine. In 1844 he attended the medical department of Transylvania University. He practiced at New Liberty and at Warsaw, Ky. He then entered Starling Medical College at Columbus, O., from which he graduated with honors in 1849. Immediately upon leaving this college he came to Vincennes, where he remained. In 1846 he married Nannie W. Pendleton of Clark County, Ky. Three sons and two daughters were born to them. In 1861 he was appointed postmaster by President Lincoln and held that office until 1869. He was on the board of trustees of Vincennes University. Having a taste for literary pursuits, he wrote much for periodicals, and in 1898 he published a little volume of poems, entitled *At Midnight and Other Poems*. Later he wrote a history of Vincennes. He was a Republican and a member of the Presbyterian Church. He died on Dec. 23, 1907. Two daughters, Miss Mary and Miss Alice Smith survived him many years."

From Hodge—*Vincennes in Picture and Story.*

* * *

At Midnight and Other Poems. *Indianapolis,* 1898.
Historical Sketches of Old Vincennes Founded in 1732. Its Institutions and Churches, Embracing Collateral Incidents and Biographical Sketches of Many Persons and Events Connected Therewith. *Vincennes, Ind.,* 1902.

SMITH, ISAAC: ?–?

Of Isaac Smith, author of one of the most rare and valuable works on the Mexican War and the Rio Grande Valley, no biographical information has as yet been located.

From the fact of his having enlisted in the Indiana Brigade of Volunteers for service in that war, and from the fact of his having published at least one book in Indiana in 1844 and another after his return from the war, it may be assumed that his residence in the state was of a substantial length.

Information from Walker—*The Beginnings of Printing in the State of Indiana*; McMurtrie—*Indiana Imprints, 1804-1849*; and Littell Auction Sale Catalog—*The Distinguished Collection of Americana.*

* * *

A Brief Inquiry into the Banking System; Containing Some Historical Facts, Gathered from the Most Authentic Sources. *Indianapolis,* 1844.
Reminiscences of a Campaign in Mexico: an Account of the Operations of the Indiana Brigade on the Line of the Rio Grande and the Sierra Madre. And a Vindication of the Volunteers Against the Aspersions of Officials and Unofficials [sic]. *Indianapolis,* 1848.
Political Chart of Indiana . . . *Indianapolis,* [1849]. (2nd ed.)

SMITH, JAMES C.: 1809–?

James C. Smith was born on Apr. 17, 1809, in Madison County, Ky. He accompanied his family to Indiana in 1820, settling near Madison; there he received his early education in country subscription schools and at the academy kept in Madison by Beaumont Park.

Becoming a Methodist minister in 1830, he occupied a pulpit in 1834 in Bloomington, where he studied for a time at Indiana University. He continued his ministry in Indianapolis, Greencastle and other Indiana towns for many years.

Information from Nowland—*Sketches of Prominent Citizens of 1876.*

* * *

Reminiscences of Early Methodism in Indiana. *Indianapolis,* 1879.

SMITH, JAMES M.: 1819–?

Born in Fayette County, Ky., on Oct. 19, 1819, James M. Smith was a son of William and Margaret Smith. The family moved to Shelby County, Ind., in 1827, where, as Smith says, he "grew up to be a very wicked young man, without religious training."

In 1841 he changed his way of life and joined the Baptist Church. He was ordained a minister in 1844, afterwards studying at Franklin College for two years, teaching and preaching meanwhile. He preached in Indiana about twenty years, the same in Iowa and for about ten years in Missouri. His service to the church ended with his retirement in 1893.

James Smith married Elizabeth [?] in 1840. They were the parents of six children.

Information from Smith—*Work on Revivals, Sermons and Sketches . . .*

* * *

Work on Revivals, Sermons and Sketches in the Life and Preaching of Elder J. M. Smith, a Baptist Minister for Thirty-Five Years. *Indianapolis,* 1893. (3rd ed., enlarged)

SMITH, JEREMIAH: 1805–1874.

Jeremiah Smith was born in South Carolina in 1805. He came to Indiana with his family in 1817, settling in what was later to become Winchester. He had already received a thorough grammar school education, and he now studied surveying and read law, practicing as an attorney for thirty years and acting as county surveyor, prosecuting attorney and, for eight years, judge of the circuit court of Randolph County. By 1858 he had become active in railroad promotion, being then president of both the Cincinnati, Union & Fort Wayne and the Evansville, Indianapolis & Cleveland railroads.

Mr. Smith died in 1874.

Information from Smith—*Early Indiana Trials and Sketches.*

* * *

Is Slavery Sinful? *Indianapolis,* 1863.

SMITH, JOHN LAWRENCE: 1860–

John Lawrence Smith was born at Bridgeport, Conn., Nov. 30, 1860, the son of John and Mary Elizabeth Smith. His father was killed while serving with the Union Army in 1865, and his mother died in New York in 1866.

The two children, John Lawrence and Kate, were taken to the House of Refuge and later, with a number of others, were sent west to Williamsburg, Wayne County, Ind. The two Smith children were taken by a young lawyer of that town but were soon separated, John being sent to a baker and soon after to live on a farm. Here the boy's life was one of extreme hardship. He remained for a number of years but ran away when he was sixteen.

In order to attend school he worked for room and board, eventually entering the Indiana State Normal School at Terre Haute, Ind. After a short period of teaching he began his newspaper work as publisher and editor of the Dana DAILY NEWS. He was postmaster for a time and was later connected with newspapers in Richmond and Winchester, Ind. In 1887 he married Kate Jordan of Vermillion County, Ind.

He contributed verse and prose to THE FORUM and other magazines, as well as to state and local newspapers. In 1896-97 he served as secretary of the Western Association of Writers.

Information from Roll—*Indiana,* Vol. IV, and Smith and Driver—*Past and Present of Randolph County.*

* * *

Past and Present of Randolph County, Indiana (with Lee-otis L. Driver). *Indianapolis,* 1914.

SMITH, JOHN THOMAS: ?–1908.

John Thomas Smith received the LL.B. degree from De Pauw University in 1860. During the Civil War, from 1861 to 1865, he served in the Union Army and was mustered out a full colonel. From 1865 to 1870 he was clerk of the Greene County (Ind.) Circuit Court. He married Mary C. Armstrong of Greene County on Nov. 30, 1854, and died at Bowling Green, Ind., on Feb. 28, 1908.

Information from De Pauw University's *Alumnal Record, 1920.*

* * *

A History of the Thirty-First Regiment of Indiana Volunteer Infantry in the War of the Rebellion. *Cincinnati,* 1900.

SMITH, LAURA ALEXANDRINE: ?–1935.

Laura Alexandrine Smith was born in Waterloo, N. Y., but spent most of her life in Indianapolis, where she wrote feature articles for the INDIANAPOLIS NEWS and the INDIANAPOLIS STAR. She also contributed poetry and essays to magazines. During the first World War she worked with the American Committee for Devastated France, and following the war she was Washington correspondent for the INDIANAPOLIS STAR for some years. She died in 1935.

Information from the Indianapolis Public Library.

* * *

The Music of the Waters. A Collection of the Sailors' Chanties, or Working Songs of the Sea, of All Maritime Nations . . . *London,* 1888.
Through Romany Songland. *New York,* 1889.

SMITH, OLIVER HAMPTON: 1794–1859.

Oliver Hampton Smith has, besides his good record as a citizen and statesman, one distinction not at all common to writers of books about their contemporaries: his work, *Early Indiana Trials and Sketches,* appears immediately to the reader to be a faithful recording of the whole truth, hurt though it may.

Most such works, written by retired gentlemen in their last years, charitably gloss over the eccentricities and errors of their fellow men. Not so with Oliver H. Smith. If one of his contemporaries, a distinguished citizen in later life, had erred in his youth in the matter of appropriating a horse not his own, Smith says (in effect): "He was an excellent father and husband; he was a successful business man and a leader in the church, but in his eighteenth year he was indicted as a horse-thief." After the fulsome praise of one and all in other such works, Smith's manner is a bright relief to the reader.

According to the *Dictionary of American Biography*:

"Oliver Hampton Smith (Oct. 23, 1794-Mar. 19, 1859), lawyer, representative and senator, was of Quaker descent. His ancestors accompanied William Penn to America; his grandparents occupied Smith's Island in the Delaware River about twelve miles above Trenton; and here, in Bucks County, Pa., Oliver, the son of Thomas and Letitia Smith, was born. He had six brothers and two sisters. He obtained an elementary education at a neighboring country school. When he was in his nineteenth year his father died, and Oliver soon lost the small fortune which he had inherited. In 1816 he set out for the West, and at Pittsburgh engaged to take two coal boats to Louisville. He struck a snag and lost one of them, but succeeded, in the spring of 1817, in reaching Rising Sun, Ind., where he engaged in a small business with seventy-five dollars as his capital. A year later he was in Lawrenceburg, studying law, and in Mar. 1820 he was admitted to the bar.

"He commenced to practice at Versailles, but soon removed to Connersville, where he rapidly rose to prominence. In Aug. 1822 he was elected to the Indiana House of Representatives. He was made chairman of the judiciary committee and served until 1824, when the governor appointed him prosecuting attorney for the third judicial district. During two years of service in this capacity he successfully prosecuted four notorious frontiersmen charged with the murder of Indians. [See the sketch of Sandford Cox.] In 1826 he was elected to Congress as a Jackson Democrat. He rode to Washington on horseback and took his seat at the opening of the Twentieth Congress, Dec. 3, 1827. He was a member of the committee on Indian affairs, and on Feb. 19, 1828, made a vigorous plea for an Indian policy 'marked with justice, humanity, and a magnanimity of purpose, that will atone, as far as

possible, for the great injustice which we have done them.' In another address, Jan. 28, 1829, he presented cogent arguments in favor of appropriations for the construction of the Cumberland Road. Defeated for re-election to Congress, he was engaged in the practice of law and in farming when, in Dec. 1836, the General Assembly elected him as a Whig to a seat in the U. S. Senate. He was a member of the committee on the militia in 1837, and of the committee on the judiciary in 1839, and was made chairman of the important committee on public lands in 1841. His principal speeches in the Senate were on measures relative to the public lands, banking, bankruptcy, the Cumberland Road, and the abolition of slavery in the Territories. He rose to leadership in evolving a federal land policy in the interest of the actual settlers . . . and supported the Whig plan for the federal assumption of state debts to the extent of the proceeds of the sales of the public lands within the states.

"Failing of re-election to the Senate, Smith retired to private life in Indianapolis, projected the Indianapolis & Bellefontaine Railroad, became its first president, and subsequently participated in a project for a line from Indianapolis to Evansville. In July 1857 he commenced writing for the INDIANAPOLIS DAILY JOURNAL a series of sketches and reminiscences of frontier life in Indiana which in the following year was published in book form . . . Although crude in style, the volume is a vivid presentation of various phases of early Indiana history.

"Smith was a rough-hewn frontiersman, five feet ten inches in height, with standing black hair, shaggy eyebrows and a strong voice; he was diffuse but convincing in speech, and one of the most respected of Indiana pioneers. He married Mary Bramfield, a Quaker, in 1821, and they had three children. He died in Indianapolis and was buried in Crown Hill Cemetery."

From the *Dictionary of American Biography,* Vol. XVII, and Smith—*Early Indiana Trials and Sketches.*

* * *

Early Indiana Trials and Sketches. *Cincinnati,* 1858.

SMITH, ORLANDO JAY: 1842–1908.

Orlando J. Smith was born near Terre Haute, Ind., June 14, 1842, and died in 1908. He was educated in rural schools and at De Pauw University.

Enlisting in the Union forces for the Civil War as a private, he rose through the ranks and, at the time of his discharge, held a commission as major.

Returning to Terre Haute after the war, he edited the TERRE HAUTE MAIL and the TERRE HAUTE EXPRESS. Later he became editor of the CHICAGO EXPRESS. He was a great influence for the development of the American press along sound and responsible lines and was instrumental in the organization of the American Press Association.

> Information from the Emmeline Fairbanks Memorial Library, Terre Haute, Ind.

* * *

A Short View of Great Questions. *New York,* 1899.

The Coming Democracy. *New York,* 1900.

A Way to Abolish Bosses and Bossism, to Break Up Political Machines, and to Establish Efficient and Honest Government in Our Cities. *New York,* 1900.

Eternalism: a Theory of Infinite Justice. *Boston,* 1902.

Balance the Fundamental Verity. *Boston,* 1904.

The Agreement Between Science and Religion. *New York,* [1906].

SMITH, WILLIAM C.: 1809–1886.

William C. Smith was born near Richmond, Indiana Territory, on Sept. 14, 1809.

He married Phoebe E. King on July 17, 1828, upon which event she was disowned by the Society of Friends, Smith being a Methodist.

Smith was licensed to preach in 1839 and held pastorates in many southern Indiana towns, becoming a distinguished member of his denomination. After his retirement he lived in Martinsville, Ind., and toward the end of his life he lived with his children.

The Rev. William C. Smith died on Apr. 27, 1886.

> Information from the Indiana State Library.

* * *

Indiana Miscellany, Consisting of Sketches of Indian Life, the Early Settlement, Customs, and Hardships of the People . . . Together with Biographical Notices of the Pioneer Methodist Preachers of the State. *Cincinnati,* 1867.

SMITH, WILLIAM HENRY: 1839–1935.

William Henry Smith, son of William Carlyle and Phoebe King Smith, was born at Noblesville, Ind., on Dec. 17, 1839. His father was a Methodist minister.

Before the Civil War he became a printer and reporter and reported one or more of the speeches made by Lincoln in his first campaign. For about a year during the war he served with the 11th Indiana Volunteers, the Zouave regiment commanded by Lew Wallace; for the remainder of the war he was engaged in secret service work and in training recruits at Camp Morton.

After the war he returned to newspaper work. He published the LOGANSPORT STAR in the late Seventies and about 1880 removed to Indianapolis, where he was connected at various times with the JOURNAL, TIMES, NEWS, and SENTINEL. For a number of years he was Indiana correspondent for the CINCINNATI COMMERCIAL GAZETTE.

Mr. Smith was active in state politics and was one of those who had charge of the campaign of Benjamin Harrison in 1888. He was Harrison's biographer for the campaign, as he was later for Charles Fairbanks when Fairbanks ran for the vice-presidency. He served as secretary of the Indiana State Senate about 1876 and was chief clerk of the Indiana House of Representatives in 1886. During Harrison's administration he was in the Postoffice Department and was active in helping organize the ocean mail postal system. Later he represented Fitzgerald and Vajen, Indianapolis pension attorneys, in Washington.

About 1894 he returned to his newspaper work on the COMMERCIAL GAZETTE in Cincinnati. He then edited an Indiana periodical, THE INDIANIAN, and engaged in newspaper work in Indianapolis until 1905, when he returned to Washington. He was active in newspaper and magazine work until he was ninety-three years of age, writing for the WASHINGTON POST, the WASHINGTON STAR, several New York papers, the INDIANAPOLIS NEWS, the CHICAGO TRIBUNE, and others. His last article to attract attention was on Lincoln and was written when he was ninety-three.

Smith's mother had come to the state in a covered wagon when she was a child, and his paternal grandparents had settled there even earlier. On a trip back to Indianapolis (for the purpose of voting) in 1932, when he was ninety-four years old, Mr. Smith fell down stairs at the English Hotel, and an account of the mishap in an Indianapolis paper (the INDIANAPOLIS STAR, Nov. 8, 1832) comments that the most serious injury was to the cane he carried.

He was twice married: first to Clara Innes Wolff, who died in 1888, and second to Minnie Frybarger, who survived him by about a year. Mr. Smith died on Feb. 12, 1935.

In addition to his books, he was the author of many short stories for magazines and newspapers (under the pen name of "Randolph Wharton"). He also wrote a chapter for John Jay Knox's *History of Banking*, several chapters for Marshall Cushing's *Story of Our Post Office*, and a chapter for *Historic Towns of the Middle West*. He prepared most of the material for four of the seven volumes of the encyclopedia of *Information for Farmers*.

> Information from the William Henry Smith Memorial Library of The Indiana Historical Society.

* * *

History of the State of Indiana from the Earliest Explorations by the French to the Present Time; Containing an Account of the Principal Civil, Political and Military Events from 1763 to 1903. *Indianapolis,* [1897]. 2 vols.

The Life and Speeches of Hon. Charles Warren Fairbanks, Republican Candidate for Vice-President. *Indianapolis,* 1904.

History of the Cabinet of the United States of America; from President Washington to President Coolidge; an Account of the Origin of the Cabinet, a Roster of the Various Members with the Term of Service, and Biographical Sketches of Each Member, Showing Public Offices Held by Each. *Baltimore,* 1925.

Speakers of The House of Representatives of the United States, with Personal Sketches of the Several Speakers, with Portraits. *Baltimore,* 1928.

SMITH, WILLIAM WRIGHT: 1845–?

William Wright Smith, careful custodian of Owensville, Ind., statistics, left no biographer to preserve a record of his own life. Minnie P. Boren, of the Owensville Carnegie Library, says that he lived alone in Owensville for almost all of his life, that he had no near relatives and that he did common labor for a living.

Perhaps it was his own lack of home and family which attracted his interest toward the births, deaths and marriages of those who lived around him, and to the storms, fires, accidents and other events which affected their lives. At any rate his little book (the original date of publication of which is not known) went through four editions and is prized as an accurate local history.

> Information from the Owensville Carnegie Library.

* * *

A True Record; of the Marriages, Deaths, Accidents, Fires, Storms, Etc. of Owensville and Its Vicinity. *Owensville, Ind.*

SMYTHE, GONZALVO CORDOVA: 1836–1897.

Born in Putnam County, Ind., on Oct. 31, 1836, Gonzalvo Cordova Smythe graduated from De Pauw University in 1858, receiving the A.M. degree in 1861, and graduated from Rush Medical College in 1863.

From 1863 until his death on Feb. 9, 1897, he practiced medicine in Greencastle, Ind. He was for several years a professor at Central College of Physicians and Surgeons in Indianapolis and served as dean of the same institution. In 1890-91 he was president of the Indiana State Medical Society.

Dr. Smythe was first married to Margaret Allen, who died in 1870, then to Janie F. Black, who died in 1874, and, in 1876, to Jennie Hartley.

> Information from De Pauw University's *Alumnal Record, 1920.*

* * *

Medical Heresies Historically Considered; . . . Sketch and Review of Homeopathy Past and Present. *Philadelphia,* 1880.

SNEDEKER, CAROLINE DALE PARKE (MRS. CHARLES HENRY): 1871–

Caroline Dale Parke, daughter of Charles Augustus and Nina Dale Owen Parke and granddaughter of Robert Dale Owen, was born at New Harmony, Ind., on Mar. 23, 1871. She graduated from the College of Music in Cincinnati and before her marriage was a concert pianist and an instructor of music. She married Charles Henry Snedeker on Apr. 29, 1903. In her writing she used the pen names Caroline Dale and Caroline Dale Owen.

> Information from *Who's Who in America.*

* * *

The Coward of Thermopylae. *Garden City, N. Y.,* 1911. (Reissued in 1912 as The Spartan.)

Seth Way: a Romance of the New Harmony Community. *Boston,* 1914.

The Perilous Seat. *Garden City, N. Y.,* 1923.

Theras and His Town. *Garden City, N. Y.,* 1924.

Downright Dencey. *Garden City, N. Y.,* 1927.

The Beckoning Road. *Garden City, N. Y.,* 1929.

The Black Arrowhead; Legends of Long Island. *Garden City, N. Y.,* 1929.

The Town of the Fearless. *Garden City, N. Y.,* 1931.

The Forgotten Daughter. *Garden City, N. Y.,* 1933.

Uncharted Ways. *Garden City, N. Y., 1935.*
The White Isle. *Garden City, N. Y., 1940.*

ville, Missouri, March 7-10, 1916. *Unionville, Mo.,*
1916.
The Fight of Faith. *Indianapolis, 1918.*

SNOW, JOHN F.: 1854–1933.

Born at Portland, Ind., in 1854, John F. Snow was
a graduate of Ridgeville College. He was a teacher
and lawyer and died at Decatur, Ind., in 1933.

Information from the Barry Ms.

* * *

History of Adams County, Indiana. *Indianapolis, 1907.*

SOMMER, DANIEL: 1850–1940.

Born near Baltimore, Md., in 1850, the Rev. Daniel Sommer moved to Indianapolis in 1894. From
1887 to 1939 he was editor of the AMERICAN CHRIS-
TIAN REVIEW. He retired after sixty-nine years in the
ministry of the Church of Christ and died in Indianapolis on Feb. 18, 1940.

Information from the Barry Ms.

* * *

Hydrophobia and Its Cures; by One Who Was a Victim.
    Indianapolis, 1895.
Hector Among the Doctors. *Indianapolis, 1896.*
Rachel Reasoner; or, A Scriptural Daughter, Wife and
    Mother. *Indianapolis, 1900.*
Plain Sermons.
Jehenne Lefevre; or, a Miner's Daughter! *Indianapolis,*
    n.d.

SOMMER, DANIEL AUSTEN: 1878–

Daniel Sommer, son of the Rev. Daniel Sommer,
was born in Chester County, Pa., in 1878, and lived
in Indiana for nearly fifty years. An evangelist and
author, he was also the publisher of MACEDONIAN
CALL, a religious periodical.

Information from the Barry Ms.

* * *

Meditations in Bible Lands. *Indianapolis, 1910.*
The Church of Christ. *Indianapolis, 1913.*
Guide Through Bible History; for Private Study. *In-*
    dianapolis, 1915.
Wright-Sommer Debate, Between J. Roy Wright, of
    Unionville, Missouri, and D. Austen Sommer, of In-
    dianapolis, Indiana; Questions Discussed—Instrumental
    Music and the Societies; Held at Livezey Hall, Union-

SPAHR, JOHN: ?–

The chatty, frank county history, *Early Life and*
Times in Boone County, Indiana, was written and
compiled by "Harden & Spahr, Lebanon, Ind." Otherwise the authors do not identify themselves (although
Harden is known to be Samuel Harden, then of Anderson, Ind., the author of at least two other books).
Casual mention in the text states that the first brick
house built in Boone County was owned in 1886 by
John H. Spahr. It is presumed that both men resided
in Boone County at the time of writing.

Information from Harden and Spahr—*Early Life*
and Times in Boone County . . .

* * *

Early Life and Times in Boone County, Indiana, Giving
    an Account of the Early Settlement of Each Locality,
    Church Histories, County and Township Officers from
    the First Down to 1886; Histories of Some of the
    Pioneer Families of the County. Biographical Sketches
    of Some of the Prominent Men and Women. Communi-
    cations from Well-Informed Citizens Throughout the
    County; List of Soldiers Who Went to the Late War
    of 1861-5 (with Samuel Harden). *Lebanon, Ind., 1887.*

SPANGLER, WILLIAM WESLEY: 1855–1922.

Born near Auburn, Ind., on Nov. 15, 1855, William
Wesley Spangler graduated from Indiana University
in 1880, receiving the A.M. degree in 1886. On June
10, 1885, he married Ida Smell.

Associated with Indiana University, he was librarian from 1880 to 1893, registrar from 1884 to 1889,
and secretary of the board of trustees from 1880 to
1891. He also served as assistant director of five
European tramping tours.

Mr. Spangler died on June 26, 1922, and was
buried at Auburn, Ind.

Information from The University Libraries, Indiana University.

* * *

Indiana University Outing for 1887. 1887.

SPARLING, SAMUEL EDWIN: 1866–1941.

"Mr. Sparling was the son of Joseph B. and Adda-
line (Hammond) Sparling who came to Rensselaer

in an early day from Ohio and settled on a tract of land that is now a part of the St. Joseph College property. It was there that Samuel was born.

"As a farm boy, he attended Rensselaer High School. Following his graduation, he sought higher education and after being graduated from Indiana University [in 1892] he taught school for a time in Rensselaer High School. He later studied at the University of Berlin and then returned to America . . .

"The name of Sparling once shone brightly among the educational leaders as a member of the faculty of the University of Wisconsin, where he was an instructor for many years. Closing his teaching career, he returned to Rensselaer for a brief stay and after disposing of his property interests, he located in Alabama near Gallion on a plantation where he resided until his death April 18, 1941 . . ."

> From THE RENSSELAER REPUBLICAN, April 24, 1941.

* * *

Introduction to Business Organization. *Chicago,* 1906.

SPRINGER, REBECCA RUTER (MRS. WILLIAM MCKENDREE): 1832–1904.

Rebecca Ruter, daughter of Calvin W. and Harriet C. Ruter, was born in Indianapolis, on Nov. 8, 1832. From 1840 to 1848 she was educated in private schools in New Albany, Ind., and she graduated from Wesleyan College, O., in 1850. On Dec. 15, 1859, she was married to William McKendree Springer. Mrs. Springer died in Washington, D. C., in 1904.

> Information from *Who Was Who in America.*

* * *

Beechwood. *Philadelphia,* 1873.
Self. *Philadelphia,* 1881.
Songs by the Sea and Other Poems. *New York,* 1889.
Intra Muros. *Chicago,* 1899.
Marcus and Miriam: Story of Jesus. *Elgin, Ill.,* 1908.

SPRUNGER, JOHN A.: 1852–1911.

John A. Sprunger, son of Abraham B. and Elisabeth Zuercher Sprunger, was born in Raeh, Switzerland, Aug. 12, 1852. With his parents, brothers and sisters he emigrated to the U. S. in 1854, the family settling in Adams County, Ind. John was married to Katherine Sprunger on Feb. 15, 1880.

As a young man Mr. Sprunger engaged in various business enterprises but later entered the Mennonite ministry and became active in various spheres of Christian service. He traveled widely on evangelistic missions, both in this country and in Switzerland, founded a deaconess home and an orphanage, and also founded the Light and Hope Publishing Company of Cleveland, O.

The Rev. Mr. Sprunger died near Birmingham, O. —then site of the orphanage he had founded—in Oct., 1911. He was buried at Berne, Ind.

> Information from the Berne, Indiana, Public Library.

* * *

The Gospel in Types. *Berne, Ind.,* 1900. (Published in German as Das Evangelium in Vorbildern.)
Outline on Prophecy. *Cleveland, O.,* 1903.

SPRUNGER, SAMUEL FERDINAND: 1848–1923.

Samuel Ferdinand Sprunger, son of Abraham and Magdalena Rüffenacht Sprunger, was born near Muensterberg, Canton Bern, Switzerland, on Oct. 19, 1848. His mother died fifteen months after his birth. With his father and a number of relatives he came to the U. S. in 1852 and settled in Berne, Ind. His young manhood was spent at farming.

In the early years the ministers of the Mennonite Church at Berne were elected by lot, the last election of its kind being held on Aug. 23, 1868. In a songbook was placed a slip of paper on which was written in German, "Lord, who knowest all hearts, designate whom Thou hast chosen." As the young men passed by a table each one picked up a book. When young Samuel Sprunger passed by, something prompted him to exchange books; his final selection changed the entire course of his life as well as the future history of the Mennonite Church at Berne, for by selecting the second book he was chosen as the new minister.

Samuel Sprunger had had little opportunity for study, and he now insisted on more education. The church did not believe in an educated ministry, and most of the church members did not approve of his plans, but the retiring minister upheld him in his desire. After a few years in the Mennonite School at Wadsworth, O., he returned to Berne and began his Christian ministry. All told, he served the Mennonite Church at Berne more than thirty-three years.

Mr. Sprunger was married on Oct. 2, 1872, to Katharine, daughter of Peter and Barbara Steiner Luginbill. They became the parents of ten children.

The Rev. Samuel Sprunger died on Nov. 16, 1923, and his wife on Nov. 18, 1945.

Information supplied by Eva F Sprunger, daughter.

* * *

Geschlechts und Namens-Register der Familie Sprunger (with Abraham J. Sprunger). *Berne, Ind.,* 1890.

STARBUCK, EDWIN DILLER: 1866–

Edwin Diller Starbuck, son of Samuel and Luzena Jessup Starbuck, was born at Bridgeport, Ind., on Feb. 20, 1866, and graduated from Indiana University in 1890, receiving the A.M. degree from Harvard University in 1895 and the Ph.D. from Clark University in 1897. In 1904-05 he studied at the University of Zurich. He married Anna M. Diller on Aug. 5, 1896.

From 1891 to 1893 he was a professor of mathematics at Vincennes University, from 1897 to 1904 assistant professor of education at Stanford University, and from 1904 to 1906 professor of education at Earlham College. He was professor of philosophy at the State University of Iowa from 1906 to 1930, serving as head of the department from 1927 to 1930 and as director of the Institute of Character Research from 1923 to 1930. From 1930 to 1939 he was professor of philosophy and director of character research at the University of Southern California, becoming, in 1939, professor of psychology. From 1912 to 1914 Dr. Starbuck was consulting psychologist for the Beacon Press.

The many works which he compiled and edited are not listed here.

Information from *Indiana University, 1820-1904,* and from *Who's Who in America.*

* * *

The Psychology of Religion: an Empirical Study of the Growth of Religious Consciousness. (Introduction by William James.) *London,* 1899.
Moral Education in the Public Schools, 1904.
Religious Education in the New World-View. *Boston,* n.d.
Guide to Literature for Character Training (with F. K. Shuttleworth and Bernice Bauercamper). *New York,* 1928 and 1930. 2 vols. (Vol. I—Fairy Tale, Myth and Legend; Vol. II—Fiction.)
Life—A Symbol (with M. H. Farbridge). Manchester, Eng., 1930.
Look to This Day! *Los Angeles,* 1945.

STEALEY, ORLANDO OSCAR: 1842–1928.

Orlando Oscar Stealey, son of John O. and Mary A. Stealey, was born at Jeffersonville, Ind., on Jan. 4, 1842, and was educated in the common schools of the state. He married Lollie Sherley on Dec. 8, 1874.

For forty years Mr. Stealey was a member of the staff of the Louisville COURIER-JOURNAL, filling, during that time, all chairs at the home office except that of editor-in-chief and serving after 1881 as Washington correspondent of the paper. At the time of his death, which occurred on Dec. 29, 1928, he had been retired on a pension.

Information from *Who Was Who in America.*

* * *

Twenty Years in the Press Gallery: a Concise History of Important Legislation from the 48th to the 58th Congress. *Washington, D. C.,* 1906.
130 Pen Pictures of Live Men. *Washington, D. C.,* 1910.

STECHHAN, OTTO: 1851–1922.

Born in Prussia in 1851, Otto Stechhan came with his family to Indianapolis in 1857. He was a resident of that city until about 1920, when he went to California to live with his son.

He was a furniture upholsterer and manufacturer and was for a time a member of the city council and a representative in the Indiana State Legislature. While a member of the latter body he introduced and saw passed a law making possible the establishment of trade schools as part of the public school system.

Mr. Stechhan died in California in 1922.

Information from the Barry Ms.

* * *

I Fear Thee Not, and Other Poems. *Indianapolis,* 1893. (Translated into German as Lieben Und Leben: Gedichte. *Chicago,* 1894.)
Rudder, Rod and Gun: Poems of Nature. *Indianapolis,* 1898.
Unrequited Love: a Novel. *New York,* 1900.
Whither Are We Drifting? *New York,* 1901.

STEIN, EVALEEN: 1863–1923.

Evaleen Stein, artist, poet and writer of stories for children, was born at Lafayette, Ind., on Oct. 12, 1863. Her father, John Andrew Stein, a native of Pennsylvania, came to Lafayette in 1851 at the age of nineteen, became a successful lawyer and participated prominently in public affairs. He was a member of the Indiana Senate in 1869, where he introduced the act that established Purdue University. Later he became a trustee of that institution and was secretary of the board during its formative years. Miss Stein's mother was Virginia Tomlinson of Logansport, a cultured woman, and both she and her husband wrote verse, essays and stories that were published in local newspapers. A brother, Orth Harper Stein, also had considerable literary gifts, which he exercised in the field of journalism. He is credited with being one of the first to obtain extensive fame as a columnist.

Miss Stein was educated in the local schools, graduating from the Lafayette High School at the age of seventeen. Later she attended classes at the Chicago Art Institute, as her first interest was in this field, and she became an able illuminator, a form of decorative design then much in vogue. Just when she began to turn her attention to poetry is not certainly known, but her first verses appeared in print in 1886, chiefly in Indianapolis and Lafayette newspapers. Her first book of verse appeared early in 1897 and was entitled *One Way to the Woods*. Five years later it was followed by *Among the Trees Again*. Her only other volume of original verse, the collection called *Child Songs of Cheer*, appeared in 1918.

She wrote also a long narrative poem commemorating the Battle of Tippecanoe (1911) and in 1916 the centennial ode entitled *Indiana*. There also exist a few unpublished poems. Two other volumes of verse consist of English versions of poems by foreign authors, *Poems of Giovanni Pascoli*, 1923, from the Italian, and *Little Poems from Japanese Anthologies*, 1922.

Her original poetry deals largely with nature, of which she was a keen and accurate observer, describing with meticulous detail its varying moods and the great variety of form and color the seasons bring. She confined herself to traditional forms of rhythm and rhyme and made extensive use of alliteration. She could, on occasion, stir the deeper emotions or take the mind on broad flights of fancy, but for the most part she preferred to portray the softer and less spectacular features of nature and of human life. She was remarkably skilled in versification, on a lower level and for her friends only, turning out with the greatest of ease verses on anniversaries, accompanying or in acknowledgement of gifts, or giving humorous descriptions of current news and events. She was also an effective reader of her own poetry and that of others.

James Whitcomb Riley was an admirer of her poetry and gave both advice and encouragement. In May 1907 he, together with George Ade, Meredith Nichol-son and Charles Major, gave a benefit reading for Miss Stein on the campus of Purdue University. The proceeds of this reading, together with other gifts from friends, enabled her and her mother to spend several happy months in her beloved France, visiting the scenes and reliving the events which she used with such effect in her stories. She left an unpublished manuscript on her travels describing her visits to various scenes and shrines in romantic France.

While continuing throughout her life to compose in verse, she developed about 1900 a third talent which was to become her major interest, namely story telling for children. This first took the form of short stories, which were published in 1903 under the title of *Troubadour Tales*. From that time until her death a new story appeared on the average of every two years. They were not novels but rather long short stories. They took their subject matter and their atmosphere chiefly from European sources and mainly from those romantic regions of France, Normandy and Provence. The most successful of her stories were *Gabriel and the Hour Book*, *The Little Count of Normandy* and the *Christmas Porringer*. Three books appeared after her death, *Pepin: A Tale of Twelfth Night*, *Children's Stories* and *The Circus Dwarf Stories*.

In her poetry Miss Stein was realistic and spontaneous. Her phrasing and choice of words were remarkable, and she showed great descriptive power. Her observations of nature were of necessity colored by human emotions and attitudes, but they remained essentially and even scientifically true, being sometimes almost microscopic in their accuracy. But she preferred nature in its higher, more peaceful and joyous manifestations and for the most part ignored the "tooth and claw" aspects.

As a story teller, however, she chose to live in an unreal world. She was fascinated by the romantic tales and legends of periods remote in time and of places remote in space from those in which she lived. In this she was a part of that romantic movement in literature that in Indiana produced *Ben Hur*, *When Knighthood Was In Flower*, *Monsieur Beaucaire* and other popular works. In the case of other writers this was but a phase through which they passed or was a case of making the supply meet the demand. But with Miss Stein it was not a passing mood but amounted almost to a consecration of her powers to the re-creation for modern readers of the far distant past. Her stories have a vital and imaginative quality that sustains the interest of the reader. Perhaps one must admit that her books are *about* children rather than *for* children, as they are equally suited for adult reading. They are not great stories, but they produce an effect of reality and are true to the circumstances of the times and the people about whom they were written.

Miss Stein was not one of the top flight authors of Indiana, but her talents were of a high order and her fame has not been commensurate with the quality of her output. She died at Lafayette on Dec. 11, 1923. Good collections of her books may be found at the Indiana State Library, the Lafayette Public Library and the Tippecanoe County Historical Museum, the last two named having also considerable collections of clippings, letters, unpublished poems and other memorabilia.

By William Murray Hepburn, Librarian Emeritus, Purdue University.

* * *

One Way to the Woods. *Boston,* 1897.

Among the Trees Again. *Indianapolis,* n.d. [1902].

Troubadour Tales. *Boston,* n.d. [1903].

Gabriel and the Hour Book. *Boston,* 1906.

A Little Shepherd of Provence. *Boston,* 1910.

The Little Count of Normandy; or, the Story of Raoul. *Boston,* 1911.

The Christmas Porringer. *Boston,* 1914.

Our Little Norman Cousin of Long Ago; Being the Story of Normandy in the Time of William the Conqueror. *Boston,* 1915.

Our Little Frankish Cousin of Long Ago; Being the Story of Rainolf, a Boy in the Court of Charlemagne. *Boston,* 1917.

Rosechen and the Wicked Magpie. *Boston,* n.d. [1917].

Child Songs of Cheer. *Boston,* n.d. [1918].

Our Little Celtic Cousin of Long Ago; Being the Story of Ferdiad, a Boy of Ireland, in the Time of Brian Born. *Boston,* 1918.

Our Little Crusader Cousin of Long Ago; Being the Story of Hugh, the Page to King Richard of England, in the Third Crusade. *Boston,* 1921.

When Fairies Were Friendly. *Boston,* 1922.

Pepin: a Tale of Twelfth Night. *Boston,* 1924.

Children's Stories. *Boston,* n.d. [1926].

The Circus Dwarf Stories. *Boston,* n.d. [1927].

STEIN, THEODORE: 1858–1927.

Born in Indianapolis on Nov. 7, 1858, Theodore Stein was the eldest of the five sons of E. C. Frederick and Catherine Elizabeth Stein. He attended the German-English Independent School, then started in business as bookkeeper and manager of a lumber business. In 1887 he created an abstract of title company, which was the nucleus of the Indiana Title Guarantee and

Loan Company, and he became one of the leaders in this work. At one time his efforts were responsible for saving the German Fire Insurance Company of Indiana from financial ruin, and he later became president of the company. Mr. Stein died July 17, 1927.

Information from Dunn—*Indiana and Indianans,* Vol. V, and the Indianapolis Public Library.

* * *

Historical Sketch of the German-English Independent School of Indianapolis, "Our Old School." *Indianapolis,* 1913.

STEMPFEL, THEODORE: 1863–1935.

Theodore Stempfel was born in Ulm, Wurttemberg, Germany, Sept. 20, 1863. He attended school in Germany and became a clerk in the Ulm bank; but after completing his military service and becoming assistant cashier in the bank, he decided to come to the U. S. to study banking methods and came to Indianapolis in June, 1883. He was connected with the Indiana Trust Company, the American National Bank, and the Fletcher-American National Bank. Among his other interests were civil service reform in government and assistance in the Americanization of foreigners. He was president of the North American Gymnastic Union and served on the board of school commissioners from 1916 to 1920. He published many pamphlets and contributed to leading magazines. Mr. Stempfel died in Indianapolis on Dec. 24, 1935.

His first wife, Flora Koster, died in 1900, and five years later he married Anna Lieber.

Information from the Indianapolis Public Library.

* * *

Fünfzig Jahre Unermüdlichen Deutschen Strebens in Indianapolis: Festschrift zur Feier der Vollendung des Deutschen Hauses in Indianapolis. *Indianapolis,* 1898.

Americanization; Read Before the Indianapolis Literary Club, April 19, 1920. n.p., n.d. [1920].

Ghosts of the Past. *Indianapolis,* 1936.

STEPHENS, DAN VOORHEES: 1868–1939.

Dan Voorhees Stephens, son of Richard Lewis and Martha Lamkins Stephens, was born in Bloomington, Ind., on Nov. 4, 1868, and attended Valparaiso University in 1886-87. He married Hannah Boe on June 24, 1890.

In 1889 Mr. Stephens went to Nebraska, where he spent the remainder of his life. He was in business in

Fremont, Nebr., in 1889 and served as county superintendent of schools for Dodge County from 1890 to 1894. He was connected with various Nebraska business firms. He served three terms in the U. S. House of Representatives and in 1933 was a member of the Board of Public Works for Nebraska.

He died on Jan. 13, 1939.

Information from *Who Was Who in America.*

* * *

Silas Cobb; A Story of Super Vision. *Fremont, Nebr.,* 1901.

Phelps and His Teachers. *Fremont, Nebr.,* 1902. (2nd ed.)

Cottonwood Yarns; being Mostly Stories Told to Children about Some More or Less Wild Animals that Live at the Cottonwoods on the Elkhorn River in Nebraska. *Fremont, Nebr.,* 1935.

STEPHENSON, ANDREW: 1856–

Born at Metamora, Ill., on Sep. 26, 1856, Andrew Stephenson graduated from De Pauw University in 1882, receiving the A.M. degree in 1885, and received the Ph.D. degree from Johns Hopkins University in 1890. He married Julia Root on Aug. 17, 1883.

After serving as principal of the public schools of Sparland, Ill., and teaching at Upper Iowa University and Wesleyan University (Conn.), in 1894 Dr. Stephenson returned to Indiana to become professor of history at De Pauw University, a position he held until 1913.

Information from De Pauw University's *Alumnal Record, 1920.*

* * *

A Syllabus of Lectures in European History. *Middletown, Conn.*

A Syllabus of Lectures in European History from the Fall of Rome to 1890. *Terre Haute, Ind.,* 1897.

A Syllabus of Lectures and Library Guide in Church History. *Greencastle, Ind.,* 1900.

History of Roman Law, with a Commentary on the Institutes of Gaius and Justinian. *Boston,* 1912.

STEPHENSON, CORA ESTELLA BENNETT (MRS. FRED CLARE): 1872–

Born in Jeffersonville, Ind., on Nov. 2, 1872, Cora Estella Bennett graduated from De Pauw University in 1894. She married Fred Clare Stephenson on Jan. 24, 1899.

From 1894 to 1898 she taught Latin in the Marion, Ind., High School, in 1910-11 she was a teacher of

biology in the University of Porto Rico, and in 1913-14 she was principal of the Modern School Settlement. From 1914 to 1917 Mrs. Stephenson was an editorial writer for and a contributor to SMART SET. She served as head of the biology department in a Louisville high school from 1917 to 1919.

Information from De Pauw University's *Alumnal Record, 1920.*

* * *

The Hand of God. *Boston,* 1909.

STEPHENSON, HENRY THEW: 1870–

Henry Thew Stephenson was born in Cincinnati, O., Apr. 22, 1870, the son of Reuben Henry and Louisa Wright Stephenson.

He received the B.S. degree from Ohio State University in 1894, the A.B. from Harvard University in 1898 and the M.A. from Indiana University in 1911. He married Agnes Reynolds, of Richmond, Ind., on Nov. 28, 1900.

He joined the Indiana University faculty as an instructor in 1895 and became head of the English department in 1919.

Information from *Who's Who in America.*

* * *

Patroon Van Volkenberg: a Tale of Old Manhattan in the Year Sixteen Hundred and Ninety-nine. *Indianapolis,* n.d. [1900].

The Fickle Wheel: a Tale of Elizabethan London. *Indianapolis,* 1901.

Shakespeare's London. *New York,* 1905.

The Elizabethan People. *New York,* 1910.

A Handbook of Shakespeare. *New York,* 1914.

The Study of Shakespeare. *New York,* 1915.

Shakespeare's England. 1915.

Christie Bell of Goldenrod Valley. *Indianapolis,* 1918.

The Goldenrod. 1918.

Narrative Writing. *New York,* 1929.

The Mystery of the Murdered Bridegroom. 1931.

Elizabethan Manners and Customs.

Elizabethan London: a Topographical Description.

STEVENS, WARDER W.: 1845–1927.

Warder W. Stevens, son of Henderson and Catharine Hayden Stevens, was born Sept. 30, 1845, at Cecilia, Hardin County, Ky. He was educated in the common schools and at Corydon, Ind., High School, and received the bachelor of laws degree from Indiana

University in 1867. In the same year he located at Salem, Ind., and in 1868 he was appointed deputy auditor and later was elected prosecuting attorney. He purchased the SALEM DEMOCRAT, which he edited for twelve years. He was president of the State Board of Agriculture in 1899 and the Indiana State Horticultural Society for four years. On May 1, 1879, he married Alice Caspar of Salem: they were the parents of two children. He died in 1927.

Information from the Salem Public Library.

* * *

Swine Husbandry. *Indianapolis,* 1899.

The Centennial History of Washington County, Indiana. *Indianapolis,* 1916.

STEVENSON, AUGUSTA: ?–

Born in Patriot, Ind., Augusta Stevenson moved with her family to Indianapolis when she was a child. After attending Butler University she became a teacher in the Indianapolis public schools. She was a pioneer in the writing of dramatizations of historical events for children. For twelve years she lived in the East, working for the Houghton Mifflin publishing company, but she returned to Indianapolis and taught again in the schools until she retired from teaching in June, 1941.

Information from the Indianapolis Public Library.

* * *

Children's Classics in Dramatic Form. *Boston,* 1908-12. 5 vols.

Plays for the Home. *Boston,* 1913.

Puppet Princess; or, the Heart That Squeaked; a Christmas Play for Children. *Boston,* 1915.

Dramatized Scenes from American History. *Boston,* 1916.

Romantic Indiana: a Dramatic Pageant; Seven Episodes with Prologue and Tableaux. *Indianapolis,* 1916.

Abe Lincoln, Frontier Boy; Stories Children Can Read. *Indianapolis,* 1932.

Red Shoes, and Other Plays. *Boston,* 1938.

The White Canoe, and Other Plays. *Boston,* 1938.

Hole in the Dike, and Other Plays. *Boston,* 1938.

Scenes from American History. *Boston,* 1938.

An Indian Boy's Pet, and Other Plays. *Boston,* 1939.

Black Pearl, and Other Plays. *Boston,* 1940.

Ben Franklin, Printer's Boy. *Indianapolis,* 1941.

Andy Jackson, Boy Soldier. *Indianapolis,* 1942.

George Washington, Boy Leader. *Indianapolis,* 1942.

Daniel Boone, Boy Hunter. *Indianapolis,* 1943.

George Carver, Boy Scientist. *Indianapolis,* 1944.

Sam Houston, Boy Chieftain. *Indianapolis,* 1944.

Kit Carson, Boy Trapper. *Indianapolis,* 1945.

Clara Barton, Girl Nurse. *Indianapolis,* 1946.

Paul Revere, Boy of Old Boston. *Indianapolis,* 1946.

STEWART, JAMES HERVEY: 1809–1876.

James Hervey Stewart, long time resident of Carroll County, Ind., published one of the good "early crop" of Indiana county histories.

Information from the Indiana State Library and from D. S. A. in the CINCINNATI GAZETTE, Dec. 7, 1876.

* * *

Recollections of the Early Settlement of Carroll County, Indiana. *Cincinnati,* 1872.

STICKNEY, IDA STEARNS: ?–1932.

Born in New Hampshire, Mrs. Ida Stearns Stickney came to Indianapolis when she was a girl. After graduating from Shortridge High School and the old Indianapolis city normal school, she taught school in Indianapolis for fifty years before she retired from service in 1928. She died Nov. 9, 1932.

Information from the Indianapolis Public Library.

* * *

Pioneer Indianapolis. *Indianapolis,* 1907.

STONE, RICHARD FRENCH: 1844–1913.

Born near Sharpsburg, Ky., in 1844, Richard French Stone came with his parents to Indiana when he was eight years old. His mother, whose maiden name was Sally Lane, was a sister of Henry S. Lane, first Republican governor of Indiana. Young Stone attended the common schools and Bainbridge, Ind., Academy.

In 1863 he entered Rush Medical College but in 1864 tendered his services to the U. S. Government and was appointed a medical cadet. He later attended the University of Pennsylvania and received the M.D. degree.

After serving a time as assistant surgeon general in the U. S. Army, he established himself in southern Indiana, removing to Indianapolis in 1880. Until 1886 he served as a professor in the Central College of Physicians and Surgeons.

Dr. Stone died on Mar. 3, 1913.

Information from the Indiana State Library.

* * *

Elements of Modern Medicine, Including Principles of Pathology and Therapeutics. *New York*, 1885.

STORMONT, GILBERT R.: 1843–1930.

Gilbert R. Stormont was born in Gibson County, Ind., in 1843. His father was William Stormont, who came from South Carolina in 1832. His early life was spent on the farm. He enlisted for the Civil War in Company B, 58th Indiana Infantry, in October, 1861.

After the war he was engaged in teaching in Oakland City and Princeton. In 1873 he moved to Albion, Ill., bought old equipment and founded the ALBION JOURNAL. This venture, though at first it did not appear very promising, proved to be a financial success. After three years Mr. Stormont sold the JOURNAL plant and returned to Princeton, and in 1877, he bought the PRINCETON CLARION, which he continued to publish for nearly twenty-five years. In addition to his newspaper work, Mr. Stormont engaged in other work of literary character.

Mr. Stormont was married to Kate Keys in Princeton on Mar. 16, 1870.

Information from the Princeton, Indiana, Public Library.

* * *

Pencil Sketches of a Trip Down South. *Princeton, Ind.,* 1882.

Gibson County in the Civil War. *Princeton, Ind.,* n.d. [1912].

Centennial of the United Presbyterian Church, Princeton, Indiana. *Princeton, Ind.,* 1917.

STOTSENBURG, JOHN HAWLEY: 1830–1909.

Born at Wilmington, Del., on Dec. 13, 1830, John Hawley Stotsenburg graduated from Trinity College (Conn.) in 1850 and studied law for three years at Wilmington. In 1854 he came to New Albany, Ind.

From 1856 to 1859 he served as city attorney, and in 1861 he was elected to the Indiana General Assembly. From 1879 to 1881 he was one of the commissioners appointed to revise the Indiana laws. For twenty-two years he was city commissioner of New Albany.

In addition to his books (one is on law—not listed here) Mr. Stotsenburg wrote for newspapers and for religious and scientific publications. He was married

to Jane F. Miller. He died at New Albany on June 7, 1909.

Information from the New Albany Public Library.

* * *

An Impartial Study of the Shakespeare Title. *Louisville,* 1904.

STOTT, ROSCOE GILMORE: 1880–

Roscoe Gilmore Stott, son of William Taylor and Arabella Ruth Tracy Stott, was born at Franklin, Ind., on Oct. 29, 1880, and graduated from Franklin College in 1904, receiving an honorary A.M. degree in 1916. He also received degrees from Lenox College, Ia., and from the University of Chicago. He married Isabel Porter on Oct. 2, 1907.

After teaching at Drury College and at Michigan Agricultural College, in 1910 he became head of the English department at Eastern Kentucky State Teachers College, a position he held until 1916. After 1910 he was a lyceum and Chautauqua lecturer and after 1917 an extension lecturer for Lenox College. From 1930 to 1933 he served as a member of the faculty of the Ohio School of the Air.

In addition to his books he is known as a writer of songs and magazine articles.

Information from *Who's Who in America.*

* * *

The Man Sings. *Cincinnati,* 1914.

Selling Since Adam.

The Smiths Discover America—the Story of Americanization at Work. *Chicago,* 1920.

Walking Shadows; a Book of Poetic Portraits. *Cynthiana, Ky.,* 1929.

How to Win Boys; a Book of Information and Inspiration for the Sunday School Worker. *Cincinnati,* 1938.

Somebody's Little Gray Shadow.

Doorway to Dawn. *Grand Rapids, Mich.,* 1940.

Standard Temperance Day Book No. 1. *Cincinnati,* 1940.

When Boys Ask Questions; a Book of Humanized Information Concerning a Boy's Own Life. *Cincinnati,* 1941.

Dear Shut-In; Information and Inspiration for the Valiant who March the Road to Recovery. *Cynthiana, Ky.,* 1943.

STOTT, WILLIAM TAYLOR: 1836–1918.

William Taylor Stott, son of the Rev. John and Elizabeth Vawter Stott, was born in Vernon, Ind., on May 22, 1836, and grew up on a farm near the town. He was educated in an academy at Sardinia, entered Franklin College, and graduated in 1861.

When the Civil War broke out he enlisted as a private with the 18th Indiana Regiment, serving for three and a half years and being discharged with the rank of captain. He then entered Rochester Theological Seminary, from which he graduated in 1868, and was ordained to the Baptist ministry in the same year. He married Arabella Ruth Tracy on May 21, 1868.

In 1868-69 the Rev. Mr. Stott served as pastor at Columbus, Ind., in 1869-70 as acting president of Franklin College, and in 1870-72 as professor of natural sciences at Franklin. From 1872 to 1905 he was president of Franklin. He died on Nov. 1, 1918.

> Information from *Who's Who in America* and Dunn—*Indiana and Indianans.*

* * *

Indiana Baptist History, 1798-1908. *Franklin, Ind., 1908.*

STOUT, ANDREW PEARCE: 1844–1905.

Andrew P. Stout, for many years an evangelist in the Christian Church, was born at Eagletown, Hamilton County, Ind., on Dec. 11, 1844. His parents were Robert and Jane Pearce Stout.

After attending local schools and studying with Dr. Pair of Jolietville, Ind., he was engaged in the drug business for a time but eventually began study for the ministry and was ordained at the age of thirty-four. He engaged in evangelistic work throughout the entire West.

He was married in 1864 to Eliza A. Bowman of Hamilton County, Ind. He spent his last years in Sheridan, Ind., where he died in 1905.

> Information from the Indiana State Library.

* * *

Chronology of Christ's Life. *Indianapolis, 1885.*
Chronological Arrangement of the Gospel. n.p., 1885.
The Trials and Crucifixion of Christ. *Cincinnati, 1886.*
The Jerusalem Tragedy. *Nashville, Tenn., 1895.*
Creeds Outgrown. *Sheridan, Ind., 1902.*
The Walks and Works of the Master, n.p., n.d.

STOUT, J. W.: ?–?

D. S. A., writing in the CINCINNATI GAZETTE for Dec. 7, 1876, in describing the collection of

books by Indiana authors belonging to Daniel Hough, mentions J. W. Stout as an Indiana man who had seen service in the Mexican War. Hough had not then been able to purchase a copy of his book, which was described as "a spirited and racy account of the services of the Fourth Indiana [Regiment] while serving in Mexico."

> FROM D. S. A. in the CINCINNATI GAZETTE, Dec. 7, 1876.

* * *

Notes from My Knapsack.

STRAIN, RODNEY: 1841–1910.

Rodney Strain, son of Dr. William A. and Mary Gettys Strain was born in London, O., Feb. 14, 1841. As a young boy he helped in his father's office and later learned the drug business. During the Civil War he enlisted in an Ohio company.

In 1866 he went to Logansport, Ind., and opened a drug store, in which business he continued until 1885. He then became a mortician and continued until his death in 1910.

Mr. Strain was married to Susan McMillen of Logansport in 1867.

When Mr. Strain first went to Logansport, he transferred his membership to the First Presbyterian Church of his chosen city. He was elected trustee and later was made an elder, being Clerk of the Session at the time of his death.

As clerk, Mr. Strain realized the need of a church history which would be available as a record for present and future generations. With untiring effort he searched records, and by correspondence and personal contacts with older church members and citizens collected materials. When this was organized and published, the First Presbyterian Church of Logansport was provided an authentic record of its past.

> Information supplied by the Logansport Public Library.

* * *

History of the First Presbyterian Church of Logansport, Ind. *Logansport, 1898.*

STRAUSE, ISAAC RICE: 1859–1934.

Isaac Rice Strause, son of Samuel and Mary Frances Baker Strause, was born at Rockville, Ind., on Dec. 12, 1859, and was educated in the Rockville public schools.

At the age of sixteen he entered the office of the INDIANA PATRIOT (now the ROCKVILLE TRIBUNE), of which he later became owner and editor. For eight years he was associated with John H. Beadle in the ownership and management of the paper and at the end of that time purchased Beadle's interest and became sole proprietor.

As a member of the State Hospital Board in 1907 Mr. Strause has been credited with the establishment of the Indiana Tuberculosis Hospital at Rockville, and he was always interested in its welfare and management. He also served as a trustee for the Indiana Institute for the Blind and as collector of internal revenue for the Terre Haute district.

During the first World War he was a captain of Company E of the First Indiana Infantry.

On Dec. 22, 1881, Mr. Strause married Juliet Virginia Humphries, well-known Indiana writer and journalist.

He was a contributor of articles on history and education to eastern papers and to magazines.

He died on Dec. 5, 1934.

Information from Dunn—*Indiana and Indianans.*

* * *

Parke County Memorial. 1916.

STRAUSS, JULIET VIRGINIA HUMPHRIES (MRS. ISAAC): 1863–1918.

Juliet Virginia Humphries, whose easy humor and common sense eventually made her famous as "The Country Contributor," was born in Rockville, Ind., on Jan. 7, 1863. She was the daughter of William and Susan Humphries and received her education in the local schools of the town in which she was born and spent her life.

On Dec. 22, 1881, she married Isaac Strause, editor and publisher of the ROCKVILLE TRIBUNE—whose name she insisted upon spelling as in the original German, after she had taken it, although her husband continued to use the anglicized form.

Juliet Strauss taught school and contributed to THE INDIANAPOLIS JOURNAL, as well as to the family paper, her writing for the latter eventually taking the form of a column, "Squibs and Sayings." In 1908 she began the series of articles for THE INDIANAPOLIS NEWS signed "The Country Contributor," which, with her articles for the WOMAN'S HOME COMPANION and THE LADIES HOME JOURNAL ("The Ideals of a Plain Country Woman") gained national attention. Her book was a collection of her articles from the latter periodical.

Mrs. Strauss continued as associate editor of THE ROCKVILLE TRIBUNE and as writer of her Saturday feature in THE INDIANAPOLIS NEWS until her death. In her later years she enjoyed a highly successful career as a lecturer.

The best of her work coincided with the greatest fame of Tarkington, Ade and Kin Hubbard, and she made an entirely appropriate fourth in interpreting Hoosierdom to the world.

Mrs. Strauss died on May 22, 1918.

Information from the Rockville Public Library.

* * *

The Ideals of a Plain Country Woman. *Philadelphia,* 1906.

STREIGHTOFF, FRANCES ELIZABETH DOAN (MRS. FRANK HATCH): ?–

Frances Elizabeth Doan, born at Westfield, Ind., about 1885, was married on June 10, 1915, to Frank Hatch Streightoff, who was, successively, a member of the faculties of De Pauw, Butler and Indiana universities. The couple resided in Indianapolis.

Information from the Indianapolis Public Library.

* * *

Indiana, a Social and Economic Survey; with a Chapter on Charities and Corrections by Cecil Clare North (with Frank Hatch Streightoff). *Indianapolis,* 1916.

STREIGHTOFF, FRANK HATCH: 1886–1935.

Frank Hatch Streightoff was born in Brooklyn, N. Y., on Feb. 23, 1886, the son of C. Frank and Jennie D. Hatch Streightoff. He received his A.B. and A.M. degrees from Wesleyan University, Conn., in 1909 and 1910 and his Ph.D. from Columbia University in 1913. After serving on the faculties of De Pauw University and the College of Emporia, he came to Indianapolis in 1920 as a member of the staffs of Butler and Indiana Universities. On June 10, 1915, he married Frances Elizabeth Doan. He died in Indianapolis on Jan. 13, 1935.

Information from *Who Was Who in America* and the Indianapolis Public Library.

* * *

Standard of Living among the Industrial People of America. *Boston,* 1911.

Distribution of Incomes in the United States. *New York,* 1912.

SULGROVE, BERRY ROBINSON: 1828–1890.

Born in Indianapolis on Mar. 16, 1828, Berry R. Sulgrove, the son of James Sulgrove, was educated in private schools and at the old Marion County Seminary. For a time he worked for his father in the harness and saddle making business, then entered Bethany College (now W. Va.), from which he graduated in 1848. He read law and from 1851 to 1855 practiced in partnership with John Caven. In 1855 he took charge of the editorial department of the Indianapolis JOURNAL, having previously written for newspapers, usually under the name of "Timothy Tugmutton." He soon acquired a major financial interest in the JOURNAL but sold out in 1863 with the intention of going to Europe. The Civil War prevented his departure, so he stayed on as editor of the paper.

During the war he acted as Gov. Oliver P. Morton's private secretary, and in the fall of 1865 he went with Morton to Europe, returning to Indianapolis in the early part of 1867 to resume his work as head of the editorial department of the JOURNAL. Mr. Sulgrove contributed to other papers and for several years was Indiana editor of the CINCINNATI GAZETTE. He died in 1890.

> Information from Nowland—*Sketches of Prominent Citizens of 1876* and the Indianapolis Public Library.

* * *

History of Indianapolis and Marion County, Indiana. *Philadelphia,* 1884.

SULLIVAN, MARY E.: ?–

Mary E. Sullivan, daughter of Jeremiah H. and Catherine Kenny Sullivan, was born in Greencastle, Ind., and moved with her family to South Bend when she was a child. She taught school for many years in South Bend.

> Information from the South Bend Public Library.

* * *

Picture Action Method in Reading and Phonics for Non-English and English Speaking Children Both Normal and Defective. *South Bend, Ind.,* 1915.

SUTTON, GEORGE: 1812–1886.

Born in London, England, on June 16, 1812, George Sutton emigrated with his parents to the U. S. when he was seven years old. The family lived in Cincinnati until the spring of 1820, when they removed to a farm in Franklin County, Ind.

George attended a country school and in 1828 entered Miami University. His mother had died in 1827, and in 1832 his father moved to Cincinnati, where two years later George began the study of medicine. In 1836 he graduated from Ohio Medical College and began his practice in Aurora, Ind. He married Sarah Folbre of Aurora on June 7, 1838.

In addition to handling a large practice, Dr. Sutton engaged in medical research, contributed papers on his findings to various journals, and was a student of geology, on which he often lectured. During the Civil War he was elected mayor of Aurora. He also served as president of the Indiana State Medical Society. For over thirty years he kept a meteorological journal and furnished the Smithsonian Institution with regular meteorological observations.

Dr. Sutton's purely technical medical books are not listed here.

> Information from *Representative Men of Indiana,* Vol. I.

* * *

On the Danger of Dissolution of the Union from the Question of Slavery.

Report on Cholera in Indiana. n.p., 1868.

On Man's Power Over Nature and Medicine as Means by which He Aids and Controls the Law of Life. *Indianapolis,* 1870.

Report to the Indiana State Medical Society on Asiatic Cholera as It Prevailed in this State in 1849-1852. *Indianapolis,* 1854.

A Review of the Epidemics that Have Occurred in Southeastern Indiana during the Last Fifty Years.

SUTTON, JOHN EDWARD: 1863–1900.

"John E. Sutton, son of Andrew J. and Barbara Horn Sutton, was born in Fulton County, Ind., on Oct. 21, 1863. He was educated in the public schools of Logansport and served as city editor of the LOGANSPORT PHAROS for three years. After this experience in journalism he went West, worked on many metropolitan papers and became publisher of the REAL ESTATE REPORTER in Los Angeles. In 1887 he married May Stanley of Los Angeles and they had two children, Psyche and Lindley. He returned to

Logansport and, on Oct. 1, 1889, founded the LOGANS-
PORT REPORTER. Later he also published the GALVES-
TON SUN and the LOGANSPORT ADVANCE.

"While on a trip abroad he wrote a series of
letters for the LOGANSPORT REPORTER and these
were afterwards published in book form under the
title *Across the Sea.* He died Jan. 6, 1900."

From Powell—*History of Cass County,* 1913.

* * *

Across the Sea. *Logansport, Ind.,* 1895.

SWAFFORD, MARTHENA FUNKHOUSER (MRS. BENJAMIN F.): 1845–1913.

Marthena Funkhouser was born in Indiana in 1845
and married Dr. Benjamin F. Swafford of Terre
Haute on May 8, 1862. A writer of poetry, she was
a charter member and one of the foremost workers of
the Western Association of Writers. In her work she
often used the pen name Belle Bremer.

She died in Indianapolis in 1913 and was buried in
Terre Haute.

Information from Parker and Heiney—*Poets and
Poetry of Indiana* and *Representative Men of Indiana,* Vol. II.

* * *

Wych-Elm, Poems, by Belle Bremer. *Buffalo,* 1891.

SWAIN, JOSEPH: 1857–1927.

Joseph Swain, son of Woolston and Mary A. Swain,
was born at Pendleton, Ind., on June 16, 1857, and
graduated from Indiana University in 1883, receiving
the M.S. degree in 1895. He was later awarded the
LL.D. degree by Wabash College, Lafayette, the
University of Pennsylvania, Indiana University, and
Swarthmore College. He married Frances M. Morgan
on Sept. 22, 1885.

From 1883 to 1891 he was associated with the
mathematics department of Indiana University, and
from 1891 to 1893 he was professor of mathematics
at Leland Stanford Junior University. He returned
to Indiana in 1893 to become president of Indiana
University, a position he held until 1902, when he
became president of Swarthmore. He served in the
latter capacity until 1921.

Dr. Swain died on May 19, 1927.

Information from *Indiana University, 1820-1904,*
and *Who Was Who in America.*

* * *

Inaugural Address at Indiana University, 1893. *Bloomington, Ind.,* 1893.

Higher Education and the State. *Bloomington, Ind.,* 1898.

Inaugural Address at Swarthmore College. *Swarthmore,
Pa.,* 1902.

Address to Alumni of Swarthmore College, 1903. *Swarthmore, Pa.,* 1903.

SWEENEY, ZACHARY TAYLOR: 1849–1926.

Zachary Taylor Sweeney, son of G. E. and Talitha
Campbell Sweeney, was born at Liberty, Ky., on Feb.
10, 1849. He graduated from Scottville Seminary
(Ill.) and studied at Eureka College (Ill.) and De
Pauw University. On Mar. 10, 1875, he married
Linnie Irwin.

A school teacher in 1866, he was from 1869 to 1897
a minister of the Christian Disciples Church, occupying a pulpit in Paris, Ill., from 1869 to 1871 and in
Columbus, Ind., from 1871 to 1896. From 1889 to
1893 he served as U. S. consul general at Constantinople. After 1897 he was a lyceum lecturer.

He died on Feb. 4, 1926.

Information from *Who Was Who in America.*

* * *

Under Ten Flags. *Cincinnati,* 1888.

Pulpit Diagram Charts. *Cincinnati,* 1899.

The Spirit and the Word; a Treatise on the Holy Spirit
in the Light of a Rational Interpretation of the Word
of Truth. *Cincinnati,* 1919.

Should Churches of Christ Receive the Unimmersed into
Formal Membership. *Cincinnati,* n.d.

SWEETSER, DELIGHT (MRS. FRANCIS FLEURY PRENTISS): 1873–1903.

Delight Sweetser, daughter of James Vermilyea
and Emma Harter Sweetser, was born at Hartford
City, Ind., on Jan. 21, 1873.

She was a student at Wellesley College, studied
drawing and music in Boston, and lived in Europe for
several years where she studied languages. In 1897
she made a trip around the world.

In addition to her books, she was a translator and
wrote for Chicago and Indianapolis newspapers.

She married Francis Fleury Prentiss on Jan. 3, 1900,
and died in 1903.

Information from *Who Was Who in America.*

* * *

One Way Round the World. *Indianapolis,* 1898.

One Way Around South America. *Indianapolis,* 1905.

SWIFT, LUCIUS BURRIE: 1844–1929.

Lucius Burrie Swift was born on a farm in Orleans County, N. Y., July 31, 1844. He received his early education at Yates Academy near his home. At the opening of the Civil War, when he was only sixteen years old, he enlisted in a New York regiment and served for three years, being twice a prisoner of war. He returned to school after his discharge and prepared for college. Upon his graduation from the University of Michigan in 1870 he returned to Medina, N. Y., where he spent two years in a law office, then he came to LaPorte, Ind., as a teacher in the public schools. While he taught, and subsequently when he was superintendent of schools, he continued to read law in his leisure time, and in 1879 he came to Indianapolis, passed the bar examination, and began the practice of law.

Becoming interested in civil service reform, he took an active part in politics. He started publication of the CIVIL SERVICE CHRONICLE and was counsel, then vice-president, of the National Civil Service Reform League. His support of Theodore Roosevelt led to a lifetime friendship between them. In 1919 he received an honorary LL.D. degree from his alma mater for his work for civic betterment. He died July 3, 1929.

> Information from Nicholson—*Old Familiar Faces* and the Indianapolis Public Library.

* * *

Civil Service Reform; an Address . . . January 18, 1885. *Indianapolis, 1885.*

American Feudalism; an Address . . . at Bloomington, April 24, 1888. n.p., n.d.

Military Situation of the United States; Read Before the Economics Club of Indianapolis, May 25, 1915. *Indianapolis, 1915.*

Germans in America. *Indianapolis, 1915.*

Outline Pamphlet on the Foundations of American Liberty; "No Taxation Without Representation." *Indianapolis, 1920.*

William Dudley Foulke of Indiana in the Contest for the Merit System; an Address Delivered . . . November 20, 1925. *Indianapolis, 1927.*

How We Got Our Liberties. *Indianapolis, 1928.*

SWIGART, FRANK: 1840–1912.

"Frank Swigart was born in Ohio in 1840. When he was two years old his family moved to Cass County, Ind., where he grew to manhood. In 1865 he married Margaret I. Cline and they had five children. He enlisted with the 46th Indiana Regiment during the

Civil War and rose to the rank of captain. He was a presidential elector in 1888 and chief of the law division of the Treasury Department from 1889 to 1893. He also served as referee in bankruptcy for eight years. He died in 1912. He was the author of many short stories and articles for the NATIONAL TRIBUNE and New York and Philadelphia papers . . ."

> From Powell—*History of Cass Country*, 1913.

* * *

A History of the Forty-Sixth Regiment Indiana Volunteer Infantry. September, 1861—September, 1865. Compiled by Order of the Regimental Association (with Thomas H. Bringhurst). n.p. [*Logansport*], 1888.

Mary Lawson. *Boston, 1909.*

SWINDLER, MARY HAMILTON: 1884–

Mary Hamilton Swindler, daughter of Harrison Turley and Ida M. Hamilton Swindler, was born in Bloomington, Ind., on Jan. 1, 1884, and graduated from Indiana University in 1905, receiving the A.M. degree in 1906 and LL.D. in 1941. In 1912 she received the Ph.D. degree from Bryn Mawr College. Miss Swindler also studied in Berlin and Athens.

After 1912 she was on the faculty of Bryn Mawr College, serving as professor of classical archaeology after 1931. In 1938 she was a visiting professor at the American School of Classical Studies in Athens. She was also a contributor to and editor-in-chief of the AMERICAN JOURNAL OF ARCHAEOLOGY.

> Information from *Who's Who in America.*

* * *

Cretan Elements in the Cults and Ritual of Apollo. *Bryn Mawr, Pa., 1913.*

Ancient Painting, from the Earliest Times to the Period of Christian Art. *New Haven, Conn., 1929.*

T

TALBOT, JOHN WILLIAM: 1863–1937.

John William Talbot, son of Peter William and Johanna Mary Talbot, was born in South Bend, Ind., on Dec. 12, 1863. He read law in the office of Warren Woodbury in Detroit, Mich., and was admitted to the Michigan bar in 1892. On Sept. 24, 1894, he married Minnie E. O'Brien. From 1893 until his death on Dec. 14, 1937, he practiced law in South Bend, Ind.

> Information from *Who Was Who in America.*

* * *

Jim Connors. 1915.
Game Laws and Game. 1917.
Old Maid Ryan. 1920.
The Doll. 1926.
The Pigeon.

TARKINGTON, JOHN STEVENSON: 1832–1923.

John Stevenson Tarkington, son of the Rev. Joseph and Maria Slauson Tarkington and father of Newton Booth Tarkington, was born in Centerville, Ind., on June 24, 1832. He was educated at Indiana Asbury (now De Pauw) University, receiving the degrees of A.B. in 1852 and A.M. in 1855.

In 1855 he began the practice of law in Indianapolis and in 1863 was a member of the Indiana House of Representatives. He also served as judge of the 7th Judicial Circuit in 1870-72. During the Civil War he was a captain in the 132nd Indiana Infantry.

Mr. Tarkington was twice married: first to Elizabeth Booth, the mother of Newton Booth and Mary Booth Tarkington Jameson, and after her death to Linda Schulz. He wrote under the name of John Stevenson. He died in Indianapolis Jan. 30, 1923.

> Information from *Who Was Who in America* and the Indianapolis Public Library.

* * *

The Hermit of Capri. *New York,* 1910.
The Auto-Orphan. *Boston,* 1913.

TARKINGTON, JOSEPH: 1800–1891.

Joseph Tarkington, son of Jesse and Mary Tarkington and grandfather of Newton Booth Tarkington, was born in Nashville, Tenn., on Oct. 30, 1800.

In 1815 he moved with his family to Harrison's Blockhouse (now Edwardsport, Ind.) and in 1816 to Stanford, Ind., west of Bloomington. As a young man he farmed with his father. He was converted at a camp meeting in 1820 and in 1824 was licensed to preach.

From 1825 to 1838 he was a circuit preacher in Indiana and Illinois, in 1838 was located at Lawrenceburg, Ind., in 1839 served as pastor at Richmond, and then occupied several stations until 1843, when he was appointed presiding elder for Centerville District. From 1845 to 1853 he occupied pulpits successively in Brookville, Vincennes, and Greensburg. For two years, from 1855 to 1857 he acted as agent for Indiana Asbury (now De Pauw) University, from 1857 to 1862

he was again occupied as a minister, and in 1862 he retired to his home near Greensburg.

Mr. Tarkington married Maria Slauson on Sept. 21, 1831.

> Information from *Representative Men of Indiana,* Vol. I.

* * *

Autobiography of Rev. Joseph Tarkington, one of the Pioneer Methodist Preachers of Indiana . . . *Cincinnati,* 1899.

TARKINGTON, NEWTON BOOTH: 1869–1946.

Of all writers Booth Tarkington most nearly interpreted the American scene from the beginning of this century through the Twenties as the average American saw it.

Tarkington's interest lay in the people whom he and most other Americans knew well. He was at his best on North Meridian Street (his "National Avenue") in Indianapolis, or with the people who had prospered to a chill eminence above that thoroughfare, or, as in the case of the family of Alice Adams, had slipped below it. He did well, too, on the streets neighboring to Meridian and progressively less impressive, and he knew what went on in the residential streets which fed the ebony glitter of the colored folks' main-stem, Indiana Avenue.

Mostly, though, he knew the Indiana middle class and he put them down, in his notably careful and beautiful script, for future generations and for the world at large to meet. They were by no means all nice people; there was always the leavening of Alice Adams' bootlegging brother, the nastiness of some of the Magnificent Ambersons, but the proportion of good, near-good, wishfully-good and pure bad was about right. There was neither the high romance of George Barr McCutcheon nor the grimy realism of Theodore Dreiser: Tarkington's people lived.

Every town in American had its Magnificent Ambersons, and a doting Adams mother and a frustrated Adams daughter kept up a pretense of gentility in most American towns and cities. Penrod was easily recognizable to any citizen who was a boy in Penrod's day, and to most parents of any age, there were half a dozen prototypes of *The Gentleman from Indiana*. There have been Willie Baxters ever since boys began to reach the shaving age, and Willies will always be with us as long as civilization maintains.

Tarkington, to average citizens, was not only a great Indiana author, but to many he will always be *the* great

Indiana author, regardless of the manifestos which critics may issue on the literary virtues of Dreiser and the others.

Newton Booth Tarkington was born in Indianapolis on July 29, 1869, into the very sort of background he wrote of best—comfortably prosperous middle class. His father was Judge John Stevenson Tarkington and his mother was Elizabeth Booth Tarkington. They named the baby for a distinguished uncle, Newton Booth, early governor of California.

Tarkington was sent to Phillips Exeter Academy for his college preparation and, upon graduation, he entered Purdue University. In spite of the genial companionship of George Ade and John T. McCutcheon, he transferred to Princeton after two years but left without a degree. He was active in Princeton literary and dramatic affairs. He also stood well in his classes, although he later said, "No doubt I imbibed some education there, though it seems to me that I tried to avoid that as much as possible." It was no matter—he was to receive academic honors enough in later life.

His first ambition was to become an illustrator: he made the old LIFE with a drawing in 1895 and then received thirty-one consecutive rejections. Thereafter he stuck to writing but with little more immediate encouragement. Finally a publishing house bought *Cherry*—and put it away among its other presumed errors in judgment—but the purchase price was paid. It was $22.50, and that sum, according to Tarkington, was the gross return from five years of writing. Publishing it after the establishment of Tarkington's fame, the buyer realized a handsome profit, even including storage charges.

Success was coming, however, and it was not far away. Having had no luck with short stories (even *Monsieur Beaucaire* had made the rounds and collected its share of rejection slips), he decided to try a novel. He laid it in Indiana, he peopled it with Indianians whom he knew, and *The Gentleman from Indiana* resulted. It was an immediate best-seller, and it remained near the top of the list for an amazing length of time.

Monsieur Beaucaire and other previously rejected manuscripts came out of Tarkington's desk drawer and were viewed in a different light by publishers. The young man leaped from a $1000 or so annual income (received from the rentals he had bought with his Uncle Newton Booth's bequest) to a total of $27,000 in 1900. In 1919 he was awarded the Pulitzer Prize for literature for *The Magnificent Ambersons*; he won it again with *Alice Adams* in 1922, and later the American Institute of Arts and Letters awarded him its medal for distinguished fiction.

Tarkington was always one to enjoy his living—at Purdue and at Princeton and, after he became a notable literary figure, in the spots in North America and Europe most likely to furnish entertainment. Between times, though, he returned to Indianapolis, even from the beloved summer home of his later years in Kennebunkport, Me. In his gaudy younger days, in his mellow and intelligently socially-conscious middle life and in his contented old age he was a Hoosier.

Tarkington did not always write great books, but he always wrote good ones. Writing, for him, was a very serious business—fifteen and sixteen hour stretches in his study with his meals sent in. Probably, as time goes on, it will be realized increasingly that the best of his efforts are important social documents, that the lightest of them have a Mark Twain quality of surviving freshness and that they are all good entertainment.

Tarkington was happy in his choice of male associates throughout his life. The friendship of Ade, the McCutcheons, Harry Leon Wilson, Julian Street, and all the others could make any life an enjoyable one. With women, however, he was less at home. He had the reputation at Princeton of being something of a wallflower in mixed company; perhaps those occasions furnished documentary material for the agonies of Willie Baxter and Ramsey Milholland.

His first wife was Laurel Louisa Fletcher, daughter of a highly successful Indianapolis banking family of whom recognizable portraits appear in Tarkington's writing. Their divorce was followed shortly and tragically by the death of their one daughter of pneumonia. His second wife, Susannah Robinson of Dayton, O., whom he married on Nov. 6, 1912, survived him. She was always interested in his writing and aided him in its continuance and development.

Tarkington's later years were plagued by ill health: by a heart ailment which brought orders to slow down and by an eye trouble which brought about almost complete blindness (although he made every effort to conceal the fact). In spite of the suffering from these disabilities, and even more from the inactivity they enforced, he kept up his interest in the affairs of the world. He maintained until the last an urbane and only slightly detached attitude toward the life to which he had contributed so much.

Booth Tarkington died at his Indianapolis home, 4270 North Meridian Street, on May 19, 1946.

Information from friends of Tarkington; newspapers and miscellaneous sources.

* * *

The Gentleman from Indiana. *Garden City. N. Y.,* 1899.

Monsieur Beaucaire. *Garden City, N. Y.,* 1900.

The Two Vanrevels. *Garden City, N. Y.,* 1902.

Cherry. *New York,* 1903.

In the Arena: Stories of Political Life. *Garden City, N. Y.,* 1905.

The Conquest of Canaan. *New York,* 1905.

The Beautiful Lady. *Garden City, N. Y.,* 1905.

The Guardian (with Harry Leon Wilson). *New York,* 1907.

His Own People. *Garden City. N. Y.,* 1907.

The Man from Home (with Harry Leon Wilson). *New York,* 1908.

The Guest of Quesnay. *Garden City, N. Y.,* 1908.

Beasley's Christmas Party. *New York,* 1909.

Beauty and the Jacobin: an Interlude of the French Revolution. *New York,* 1912.

The Flirt. *Garden City, N. Y.,* 1913.

Penrod. *Garden City, N. Y.,* 1914.

Harlequin and Columbine. *New York,* 1914.

The Turmoil; a Novel. *New York,* 1915.

Penrod and Sam. *Garden City, N. Y.,* 1916.

Seventeen; a Tale of Youth and Summer Time and the Baxter Family, Especially William. *New York,* 1916.

The Country Cousin. A Comedy (with Julian Street). *New York,* 1916.

The Magnificent Ambersons. *Garden City, N. Y.,* 1918.

Ramsey Milholland. *Garden City, N. Y.,* 1919.

The Gibson Upright (with Harry Leon Wilson). *New York,* 1919.

Intimate Strangers; a Comedy in 3 Acts. *New York,* 1921.

Clarence; a Comedy in 4 Acts. *New York,* 1921.

Alice Adams. *Garden City, N. Y.,* 1921.

The Wren; a Comedy in Three Acts. *New York,* 1922.

Gentle Julia. *New York,* 1922.

The Fascinating Stranger, and Other Stories. *New York,* 1922.

Ghost Story; a One Act Play. *Cincinnati,* 1922.

The Trysting Place; a Farce in One Act. *Cincinnati,* 1923.

The Collector's Whatnot (with K. L. Roberts and H. M. Kahler). *Boston,* 1923.

Tweedles; a Comedy (with Harry Leon Wilson). *New York,* 1924.

The Midlander. *Garden City, N. Y.,* 1924.

Women. *Garden City, N. Y.,* 1925.

Looking Forward, and Others. *Garden City, N. Y.,* 1926.

Bimbo, the Pirate; a Comedy. *New York,* 1926.

Selections from [His] Stories, Arranged by Lilian Holmes Strack. *Boston,* 1926.

Station YYYY. *New York,* 1927.

The Travelers. *New York,* 1927.

Dolling, a Story from Women. *Garden City, N. Y.,* 1927.

The Plutocrat; a Novel. *Garden City, N. Y.,* 1927.

Growth. *Garden City, N. Y.,* 1927. (A combination of The Magnificent Ambersons, The Turmoil, and The Midlander.)

The World Does Move. *Garden City, N. Y.,* 1928.

Claire Ambler. *Garden City, N. Y.,* 1928.

Young Mrs. Greeley. *Garden City, N. Y.,* 1929.

Penrod Jashber. *Garden City, N. Y.,* 1929.

Mirthful Haven. *Garden City, N. Y.,* 1930.

How's Your Health? A Comedy in Three Acts (with Harry Leon Wilson). *New York,* 1930.

The Complete Penrod. *Garden City, N. Y.,* 1931. (Combining the three Penrod books.)

Wanton Mally. *Garden City, N. Y.,* 1932.

Mary's Neck. *Garden City, N. Y.,* 1932.

The Works of Booth Tarkington. *Garden City, N. Y.,* 1922-32. 27 vols.

Presenting Lily Mars. *Garden City, N. Y.,* 1933.

Little Orvie. *Garden City, N. Y.,* 1934.

Help Each Other Club. *New York,* 1934.

Mr. White, the Red Barn, Hell and Bridewater. *Garden City, N. Y.,* 1935.

Mr. Antonio: a Play in Four Acts. *New York,* 1935.

The Lorenzo Bunch. *Garden City, N. Y.,* 1936.

Rumbin Galleries. *Garden City, N. Y.,* 1937.

Some Old Portraits; a Book About Art and Human Beings. *Garden City, N. Y.,* 1939.

The Heritage of Hatcher Ide. *Garden City, N. Y.,* 1941.

The Fighting Littles. *Garden City, N. Y.,* 1941.

Kate Fennigate. *Garden City, N. Y.,* 1943.

Image of Josephine. *Garden City, N. Y.,* 1945.

The Show Piece: with an Introduction by Susannah Tarkington. *Garden City, N. Y.,* 1947.

TAYLOR, FRANK BURSLEY: 1860–1938.

Frank Bursley Taylor, son of Robert Stewart and Fanny Wright Taylor, was born in Fort Wayne, Ind., on Nov. 23, 1860. He graduated from high school in 1881 and attended Harvard University for a time. On Apr. 24, 1899, he married Minnetta A. Ketchum of Mackinac Island, Mich.

In 1900 Mr. Taylor was employed in the Michigan Geological Survey. From 1900 to 1916 he was employed in the U. S. Geological Survey, Glacial Division, and in 1908-09 in the Canadian Geological Survey. He published numerous papers relating to the history of the Great Lakes and Niagara Falls and to the glacial and postglacial geology of the lake region, both in the U. S. and Canada. Those of his works which were published by various governments are not listed here.

Information from *Who's Who in America.*

* * *

An Endogenous Planetary System. A Study in Astronomy. *Fort Wayne, Ind.*, 1898.

The Planetary System (with F. Leveret). *Fort Wayne, Ind.*, 1903.

The Fort Wayne Route. The Michigan and Erie Ship Canal . . . *Fort Wayne, Ind.*

The Growth of the Planetary System as Revealed in Its Vestiges (with F. Leveret). 1919.

Ancient Strait at Nipissing. n.p., n.d.

TAYLOR, HENRY WILLIAM: 1841–1901.

Born in Lexington, Va., in 1841, Henry William Taylor studied medicine after the Civil War and practiced in Sullivan, Ind. In addition to his poetry he wrote essays and medical papers. He died in Sullivan on Jan. 29, 1901.

> Information from Parker and Heiney—*Poets and Poetry of Indiana.*

* * *

The Romantic Story of Wickly's Woods. *Chicago,* 1888.

The White Druse, and Other Poems. *Anderson, Ind.*, 1904.

TAYLOR, JAMES WALTER: 1822–1888.

James W. Taylor, whose autobiography, *Uncle Jimmy,* was published in 1909, began dictating the book to his children while he lived in Perrysville, Ind., in 1867. His son, the Rev. A. M. Taylor, had the book published while he was minister of Zion A. M. E. Church in South Bend, Ind.

> Information from the South Bend Public Library.

* * *

Uncle Jimmy. *South Bend, Ind.,* 1909.

TAYLOR, NEWTON MARSHALL: 1847–1920.

Born at Attica, Ind., on Oct. 3, 1847, Newton Marshall Taylor graduated from Indiana Asbury (now De Pauw) University in 1873, receiving the M.S. degree in 1876. He graduated from the Bloomington Law School in 1875. On Aug. 11, 1875, he married Lou Ensey.

Mr. Taylor engaged in the practice of law in Indianapolis until his death on Apr. 14, 1920. From 1880 to 1882 he served as prosecuting attorney for the 19th Judicial Circuit, and from 1911 to 1915 he was judge of the Marion County Juvenile Court.

Information from De Pauw University's *Alumnal Record, 1920.*

* * *

Elements of Taxation. *Philadelphia,* 1905.

TAYLOR, TUCKER WOODSON: 1854–1901.

Born in Greencastle, Ind., on Dec. 22, 1854, Tucker Woodson Taylor graduated from Indiana Asbury (now De Pauw) University in 1878 and in 1878-79 was a tutor in Forest Academy, Kentucky. He was later private secretary to W. C. De Pauw and John Clark Ridpath. He first wrote poetry in 1887. He used the pen names of "William T. Hunter" and "Civis Americanus."

> Information from Parker and Heiney—*Poets and Poetry of Indiana* and Federal Writers Project— *Indiana Authors,* 1937.

* * *

Songs of Old Sileural; a Potpourri of Poetical Putnam. *Greencastle, Ind.,* 1897.

TEAL, ANGELINE GRUEY (MRS. NORMAN): 1842–1913.

Born on a farm in southern Ohio on Aug. 28, 1842, Angeline Gruey moved with her family to Noble County, Ind., when she was three years old. She grew up on a farm and was educated in the common schools and at Miss Griggs' Seminary at Wolcottville, Ind.

On Jan. 1, 1866, she married Dr. Norman Teal of Kendallville, Ind. A member of the Western Writers' Association, she wrote poems, children's stories, and short stories which were published in various magazines. She was a resident of Kendallville from her marriage until her death, which occurred on Sept. 3, 1913.

> Information from Dunn—*Indiana and Indianans,* Vol. III.

* * *

John Thorn's Folks: Study of Western Life. *Boston,* 1884.

Muriel Howe. *New York,* 1892.

The Rose of Love. *New York,* 1893.

The Speaker of the House; a Novel. *Chicago,* 1894. (Reissued in 1897 as Lillian's Lovers.)

TEST, CHARLES H.: ?–?

Charles H. Test, son of Judge John Test, early Indiana jurist and Congressman, was born in or near

Brookville, Ind. According to O. H. Smith: "He was a young man of fine talents and great energy of character. At quite an early age he took a high position among the ablest of the profession . . . He held the offices of President Judge of the Circuit and Secretary of State many years, and then returned to the county of Wayne, where he now [1857] resides . . ."

Judge Test later returned to Indianapolis, where he was residing in 1876 when D. S. A., writing of Indiana authors in the CINCINNATI GAZETTE of Dec. 7, 1876, says of him: "Several works belonging to this department [fiction] of Indiana literature are missing [from the collection of Daniel Hough], notably, 'The Novice,' by Judge Test . . . When applied to for a copy by Mr. Hough, he replied, 'I know of but one copy in the State, and I know thee'll not get that.'"

Charles H. Test was an uncle of Gen. Lew Wallace.

> Information from Smith, O. H.—*Early Indiana Trials and Sketches;* CINCINNATI GAZETTE for Dec. 7, 1876; and the INDIANA MAGAZINE OF HISTORY, Vol. 13.

* * *

The Novice.

THIEME, HUGO PAUL: 1870–1940.

Hugo Paul Thieme, son of Frederick John and Clara Hanna Thieme, was born in Fort Wayne, Ind., on Feb. 12, 1870. He was a student at Concordia College in Fort Wayne until 1890 and graduated from Johns Hopkins University in 1893, receiving the Ph.D. degree in 1897. In 1894-95 he studied in Paris and Berlin. On Sept. 6, 1899, he married Evaleth Mabel Thurston.

He was an assistant in French literature at Johns Hopkins from 1895 to 1897, acting head of the modern language department at Earlham College in 1897-98, and on the faculty of the University of Michigan after 1898 as, successively, assistant professor, junior professor, and professor of French and chairman of the Romance language department. He also served as American correspondent of LA REVUE D'HISTOIRE LITTÉRAIRE DE LA FRANCE.

He died on June 2, 1940.

French classics edited by him, and his textbooks, are not listed.

> Information from *Who Was Who in America.*

* * *

La Littérature Française au XIXᵉ Siècle. *Paris,* 1897.
The Technique of the French Alexandrine (with J. R. Effinger). *Ann Arbor,* Mich., 1899.

Women of Modern France (with J. R. Effinger). *Philadelphia,* 1907.
Guide Bibliographique de la Littérature Française de 1800-1905. *Paris,* 1907.
Notes on Victor Hugo's Versification (with W. A. McLaughlin). 1911.
Essai sur L'Histoire du Vers Français (with J. R. Effinger). *Paris,* 1916.
La Civilisation Française. *Paris,* 1924.
Essais sur la Civilisation Française. *Paris,* 1933.
Bibliographie de la Littérature Française de 1800 à 1930 (with W. A. McLaughlin). *Paris,* 1933. 3 vols.

THIEME, THEODORE F.: 1857–

Theodore F. Thieme, son of Frederick J. and Clara Weitzman Thieme, was born in Fort Wayne, Ind., on Feb. 7, 1857, and was educated at Concordia College in Fort Wayne and Columbia University. On Jan. 18, 1894, he married Bessie Loring.

After spending twelve years in the drug business, in 1891 he organized the Wayne Knitting Mills. He served as president and director of various companies and was founder of the Fort Wayne Art School and Museum.

> Information from *Who's Who in America.*

* * *

Municipal Sidelights. 1910.
A Modern System of Municipal Government. *Fort Wayne, Ind.,* 1911.
Business System of City Government Charter. *Fort Wayne, Ind.,* 1912.
What Ails Us? *Fort Wayne, Ind.,* 1913.
A New Constitution for Indiana. *Fort Wayne, Ind.,* 1914.
Liquor and Public Utilities in Indiana Politics. *Fort Wayne, Ind.,* 1915.
Home Rule for Cities. *Fort Wayne, Ind.* 1916.
Germans in Politics. *Fort Wayne, Ind.,* [1916].
Municipal Ownership, the Salvation of Our Cities. 1916.
A Business System of City Government by Professional Experts as Used Throughout the World Versus American System of Spoils, Politicians and Amateurs; a Treatise with Excerpts of Letters from Mayors of Leading Cities of the World. *Fort Wayne, Ind.,* 1934.

THOMPSON, GEORGE B.: 1862–1930.

George B. Thompson, son of John and Catherine Costello Thompson, was born in Aurora, Ind., on Sept. 24, 1862, and attended Battle Creek College in 1885-86.

In 1893 he was ordained to the ministry of the Seventh Day Adventist Church and from 1893 to 1896 served as a missionary in Africa. He was in charge of church work in West Virginia in 1897-98, in New York from 1898 to 1903, and secretary of Sunday School work for the world from 1904 to 1912. From 1912 to 1918 he was general secretary of Seventh Day Adventist church work in North America and from 1918 to 1926 field secretary for the world. The Rev. Mr. Thompson traveled and preached in India, Egypt, Great Britain, Scandinavia, and other countries of Europe and the Far East.

He was twice married—first to Delia A. Hicks, who died in 1914, then to Stella M. Slaten.

He died on June 21, 1930.

Information from *Who Was Who in America.*

* * *

Ministry of the Spirit. *Washington, D. C.,* 1914.
Soul Winning. *Washington, D. C.,* 1916.
In His Name. *Washington, D. C.,* 1918.
What Think Ye of Christ? *Washington, D. C.,* 1919.
Modern Spiritualism. *Washington, D. C.,* n.d.

THOMPSON, JAMES MAURICE: 1844–1901.

James Maurice Thompson (the name had become simply Maurice Thompson long before his signature was important to anyone but himself) was the possessor of a wide variety of talent which he employed in the shaping of careers in six widely separate fields—most successful of which was literature.

He was born in the small eastern Indiana community of Fairfield on Sept. 9, 1844, to the Rev. Mathew Grigg and Diantha Jaeggar Thompson. The senior Thompson was a Southerner by birth and, at the time of the birth of Maurice, pastor of the Baptist church in Fairfield; in the pursuit of his calling he was soon called upon to remove, first to Missouri and shortly thereafter to Kentucky.

Something occurred shortly before 1854 to bring about a radical change in Mathew Grigg Thompson's career: whether he experienced some profound spiritual upheaval or merely inherited some land and some slaves, he had deserted the pulpit by that year and was established as a planter in the Coosawattee valley of upper Georgia.

Mathew Grigg Thompson must have either inherited upon a rather generous scale or have found his years in the pulpit a good apprenticeship for the profitable management of slaves and good red soil, for he was able to hire competent tutors to educate his sons (the younger, Will Henry Thompson, had been born in Missouri in 1846) in the classical languages, literature, French and mathematics. Quiet, thoughtful young Maurice was given an extra measure of the latter, since his youthful fancy lit upon civil engineering as a career.

In addition to formal education there was also learning in woodcraft, still pleasingly and painlessly obtainable in north Georgia. Those remarkable people, the Cherokees, had been driven from the country only a generation before and there were still plenty of men about, white and black, who had learned their peculiar way in the woods and who liked nothing better than to pass it on.

Maurice and Will Thompson took full advantage of both academic and extra-curricular opportunities and acquired both an abiding love for the outdoors and a sound scientific knowledge of its components. Eventually this love would furnish ample subject matter for the best of the writing which made Maurice a prominent literary figure of the last quarter of the Nineteenth century.

The Civil War interrupted this pleasant life and both young men enlisted in the Confederate army, Maurice in 1862, before his eighteenth birthday, and Will shortly after.

The brothers served the Confederacy well but the end of the war saw most Georgia planters only a cut above penniless, with the Thompson family no exception. After being mustered out, Maurice went to Calhoun, Ga., to continue his studies in surveying and engineering and, as further insurance of a future livelihood, to read law. Little is known of his supposed two years of residence in that town except that he is believed to have done his first serious writing there: contributions of verse to some of those ephemeral Southern "literary journals" which had survived the war or were endeavoring to temper the gloomy days of Reconstruction by beginning publication.

In 1867, his studies either completed or forsaken as unpromising, Maurice Thompson began a botanical, zoological and ornithological survey of Lake Okeechobee, in Florida, of the Okeefinokee Swamp and of some other regions of similar interest in the deep South.

While natural history surveys may have been good rehabilitation measures for a young man recently fresh from the wars, they could not have been very remunerative; and neither, apparently, was any other pursuit likely to appeal to educated young Georgians of the day. The Thompson brothers rightly guessed that they would probably be elderly Georgians before conditions improved. Finally they decided upon a course which must have appeared singular indeed to most of their fellow veterans: the South was certainly overrun with undesired and undesirable Northerners; why should not this be an auspicious time for a few Southerners to go North? Packing their belongings in knapsacks and cutting a couple of walking sticks, they set out.

Some weeks later they arrived in Crawfordsville, Ind., a town as rabidly Union as might be found in the Midwest and the sanctuary of four recently retired Union generals. The Thompsons had no purpose in view, no acquaintance in the town.

Almost immediately it became evident that their unlikely choice was wise. A railroad was being built through the country. John Lee, in charge of construction, could use young engineers and Maurice and Will Thompson soon had jobs. The people of Crawfordsville must have been more tolerant of recent enemies than might have been anticipated (although Maurice Thompson was as agreeable and as urbane an enemy as one might meet) for within a year Alice, daughter of John Lee, had married him and he had settled as a permanent resident of the town. A few years later Will Thompson married Ida, sister of Alice.

In 1871, as soon as he had his feet on the ground financially, Thompson gave up engineering and opened a law office in partnership with his brother. The firm was never remarkably successful but both men were reasonably competent and their practice earned them comfortable livings. More important, law practice allowed Maurice time to resume his writing. As an evidence of the popular acceptance of the Thompson brothers in their new home, it must be noted that Maurice was elected to the Indiana State Legislature in 1879—certainly an honor not visited upon many in the Midwest who had borne hostile arms only fifteen years earlier.

In 1873 the ATLANTIC MONTHLY published one of his contributions and, encouraged, he redoubled his efforts. An early result was a series of articles on the then-neglected subject of archery which brought about his general recognition as a writer and also created a nation-wide craze for the sport. The knowledge of archery which both Maurice and Will Thompson possessed was a product of the plantation days and had been acquired, according to Meredith Nicholson's *The Hoosiers,* "from a hermit who lived in the midst of a pine forest near his home."

In 1875 Thompson's first book appeared. It was *Hoosier Mosaics,* a collection of charming sketches of incidents in the Indiana small town scene. Thompson drew the backgrounds of Colfax and Jamestown sharply and accurately and the incidents reported in

at least two of the sketches are as readable as the current and reminiscent examples in which the NEW YORKER specializes. Two novels, *His Second Campaign* and *A Tallahassee Girl,* were published in 1882; and the latter, enjoying a fair sale in both the Northern and Southern states, encouraged him to give up the law. With the exception of serving as Indiana state geologist and chief of the department of natural history between 1885 and 1889 (the duties of which office were not particularly exacting at the time) he continued until his death as a prosperous literary man and lecturer.

Thompson's novels continued to appear with some regularity but with no great success until, in 1885, his first work in the field of nature study made its appearance. It was *By-Ways and Bird Notes* and the writing of it was probably inspired by the ready acceptance which periodicals gave to his contributions on the subject. It was followed, at intervals of one or two novels, by *The Boys' Book of Sports,* 1886; *Sylvan Secrets, in Bird Songs and Books,* 1887; *Stories of the Cherokee Hills,* 1889; and *My Winter Garden,* 1900. These, with the early *Witchery of Archery* and *Alice of Old Vincennes,* are the chief basis of his fame as a writer of books. His place as a critic and a poet is yet to be finally evaluated and will be based chiefly upon his voluminous contribution to the periodical press of the Eighties and Nineties, but it was undoubtedly as an essayist, and more specifically as an essayist on the subject of the outdoors, that he excelled.

It is logical to give Maurice Thompson a considerable share of credit for arousing, through his books and his writing for periodicals, the interest of his literate fellow citizens in nature study and the outdoor life.

Thompson is remembered by his neighbors as rather diffident and self-effacing, but as an unfailingly pleasant and hospitable man. His wife, Alice Lee Thompson, was a woman of great charm and their beautiful home, Sherwood Place, on the east edge of Crawfordsville, was always open to their friends, and those of their three children—and to anyone at all who might be interested in nature, literature, the classics or, particularly, in archery. The family always wintered in their beloved South.

In this pleasant life Thompson grew in stature in the contemporary world of letters. After 1888 he served as non-resident literary editor of the INDEPENDENT, read papers and spoke widely. Finally, in 1900, he achieved his life-long ambition—he wrote a tremendously successful novel.

The book is *Alice of Old Vincennes.* Its scene is the

old French village on the lower Wabash and its plot concerns the capture of the town by hard-bitten young Gen. George Rogers Clark and the manner in which he used it to control the Old Northwest. It is an excellent historical novel of the days before the formula for the historical novel had been standardized with a ratio of at least four conquests in the boudoir to one on the battlefield. The incidental characters are real, and their activities are historically authentic. Even Alice, the heroine, is a character not entirely of his own imagining, according to Thompson's foreword. Her "romantic life, as brokenly sketched in Mr. Roussillon's letter" written in 1788 and preserved by a Louisiana Creole family, was authenticated by the author's research.

Throughout his writing career, Thompson had always returned hopefully to the novel at intervals in his more successful efforts at the essay, criticism and verse. He had published at least nine novels, only two or three of which were even moderately successful. Perhaps his recurrent efforts were inspired by the fact that Lew Wallace, a neighbor only two blocks down Pike Street, had produced a record American best seller in 1880 with a book called *Ben Hur*. Modest as he was, Thompson must have recognized that his own literary touch was both lighter and surer than that of his friend Gen. Wallace and that he lacked only a bit of good fortune and equally appealing subject matter in order to create a *Ben Hur* of his own. In the matter of appealing subject matter he could have had no great hope of a permanent triumph—Wallace had already appropriated the Christ and his early followers—but the career of Gen. George Rogers Clark and the town of Vincennes had lately attracted considerable notice through the publication of Capt. William H. English's *Conquest of the Country Northwest of the Ohio River 1778-1783* and *Life of Gen. George Rogers Clark*. Thompson wrote by far his most workmanlike novel and the good fortune took care of itself.

Alice of Old Vincennes was a best seller of 1900 and it began 1901 with even more promise. In the first weeks of that year there appeared no reason why the record of Gen. Wallace, down street, should not soon be equalled. The prospect must have been pleasing even to the unenvious spirit of Maurice Thompson, for the General was a bit arrogant in his own success and there had been some rather dismal failures among Thompson's earlier novels.

As it turned out, *Ben Hur*, with the world-wide interest in its subject and setting, continued to sell in

tens of thousands after the four or five year boom in sales of *Alice of Old Vincennes* had settled to a few thousand copies a year. By that time it made little difference to James Maurice Thompson, for he had died quietly at Sherwood Place on Feb. 15, 1901—at exactly the summit of his popularity.

Hoosier Mosaics. *New York,* 1875.

The Witchery of Archery—a Complete Manual of Archery with Many Chapters of Adventure by Field and Flood, Etc. (with Will Henry Thompson). *New York,* 1878.

How to Train in Archery: Being a Complete Study of the York Round (with Will Henry Thompson). *New York,* 1879.

A Tallahassee Girl. *Boston,* [1881].

Songs of Fair Weather. *Boston,* 1883.

His Second Campaign. *Boston,* 1883.

By-Ways and Bird Notes. *New York,* 1885.

At Love's Extremes. *New York,* 1885. (Reissued in 1901, as Milly: At Love's Extremes: a Romance of the Southland.)

A Red-Headed Family. *New York,* 1885.

A Banker of Bankersville: a Novel. *New York,* 1886.

The Boys' Book of Sports and Outdoor Life (with others.) *New York,* 1886.

Sylvan Secrets, in Bird-Songs and Books. *New York,* 1887.

Sunshine and Song, or, Southern Literature. *Nashville, Tenn.,* 1887.

A Fortnight of Folly: a Novel. *New York,* 1888.

The Story of Louisiana. *Boston,* 1888.

Poems. *Boston,* 1892.

The King of Honey Island: a Novel. *New York,* 1893.

The Ethics of Literary Art: the Carew Lectures for 1893, Hartford Theological Seminary. *Hartford, Conn.,* 1893.

Lincoln's Grave: the Harvard Phi Beta Kappa Poem of 1893. *Cambridge, Mass.,* 1894.

The Ocala Boy: a Story of Florida Town and Forest. *Boston,* 1895.

Stories of Indiana. *Cincinnati,* 1898.

Stories of the Cherokee Hills. *Boston,* 1898.

How to Study History, Literature, Fine Arts (with A. B. Hart and C. M. Fairbanks). *Meadville, Pa.*

My Winter Garden: a Nature Lover under Southern Skies. *New York,* 1900.

Alice of Old Vincennes. *Indianapolis,* 1900.

Sweetheart Manette. *Philadelphia,* 1901.

Rosalynde's Lovers. *Indianapolis,* n.d. [1901].

Toxophilus in Arcadia.

Genius and Morality: a Curious but Sincere Appreciation of Poe the Man, in a Letter Written by . . . *Ridley Park, Pa.,* 1934.

THOMPSON, RICHARD WIGGINTON: 1809–1900.

Dick Thompson was a stormy figure on the Indiana and the national scene for some sixty-five years. Hero or villain, depending upon the viewpoint, he was in the thick of every Indiana controversy: he was always a partisan, never a neutral, be the question religious, political, ethical or economic.

Richard Wigginton Thompson was born on June 9, 1809. His parents were William Mills and Catherine Wigginton Broadus Thompson, of Culpepper County, Va. They gave their son a sound education, which evidenced itself in the literary merit and the polish of his speeches and voluminous writing.

About 1831 young Thompson came west to Louisville, Ky. He taught school for a time in Lawrence County, Ind., read law, was admitted to the Indiana bar in 1834, hung out his shingle in Bedford, Ind., and the same year was elected to represent his new home in the state Legislature. Hoosiers loved orators in those days; Thompson was one of the best, and his comparatively short residence in the town seems to have been no political handicap at all. He served in the Indiana House and Senate from Lawrence County from 1834 to 1838. He was congressman from the district in 1841-43 and again 1847-49. He moved his residence to Terre Haute in 1843.

Of his national political career W. E. S., writing in the *Dictionary of American Biography*, says:

"Presidents Taylor, Fillmore, and Lincoln made him proffers of offices, but he declined. He was active in the secession controversies and during the Civil War served as provost marshal for the Terre Haute district. He was a delegate to Republican National Conventions in 1868, 1876, and 1892, and in the last named nominated Benjamin Harrison for the presidency. In 1877 he was appointed Secretary of the Navy in the Hayes administration . . . It has been affirmed that this was the only major appointment made by Hayes that was 'dictated entirely by political considerations and it was the only bad one' . . . While holding this post he took the chairmanship of the American Committee of the Panama Canal Company at a salary of $25,000 yearly, thinking this no bar to retaining his post in the cabinet, whereupon Hayes notified him 'that his resignation (unoffered) had been accepted' . . . Extremely partisan in politics, intolerant in religion, a lobbyist for railroads, Thompson was throughout his active life a figure about whom angry controversy swirled. Few of his contemporaries among public men were so frequently attacked on ethical grounds . . ."

Richard Thompson married Harriet Eliza Gardiner on May 5, 1836. She died in 1888, he on Feb. 9, 1900, at Terre Haute, Ind.

> Information from the *Dictionary of American Biography*; Woollen—*Representative Men of Indiana*; Smith—*Early Indiana Trials and Sketches*; and Roll—*Colonel Dick Thompson*.

* * *

Speech . . . Upon the Political Aspects of the Slavery Question . . . *Terre Haute, Ind.,* 1855.

Address on Masonry . . . Delivered in Terre Haute, Ind., Dec. 27, 1865. *Terre Haute, Ind.,* 1866.

Address on Masonry . . . Delivered . . . in Indianapolis May 29, 1867. *Indianapolis,* 1867.

The Papacy and the Civil Power. *New York,* 1876.

Rights of the People to the Sunday Rest, . . . Addresses (with others). *New York,* 1880.

The History of Protective Tariff Laws. *Chicago,* 1888.

Recollections of Sixteen Presidents from Washington to Lincoln. *Indianapolis,* 1894. 2 vols.

The Footprints of the Jesuits. *Cincinnati,* 1894.

THOMPSON, WILL HENRY: 1846–1918.

Will Henry Thompson, brother of Maurice and son of the Rev. Grigg and Diantha Jaeggar Thompson, was born in Missouri, on March 10, 1846. (The year 1848 is sometimes given.) He was educated by private tutors, at Calhoun Academy, and at Georgia Military Institute. (See also, sketch of James Maurice Thompson for details of early life.)

During the Civil War he served in the Fourth Georgia Infantry of the Confederate Army, taking part in the campaigns of the Wilderness, Spottsylvania Court House, Cold Harbor, and Petersburg.

In 1868, with his brother Maurice, he came to Crawfordsville, Ind., and from 1868 to 1871 was employed as a civil engineer occupied with building railroads in western Indiana. In 1871 he was admitted to the bar and opened a law office in partnership with his brother which continued until he removed to Seattle in 1889. From 1896 to 1904 he served as western attorney for the Great Northern Railway System.

Will Henry Thompson and Maurice Thompson were responsible, through their writings, for creating a nation-wide interest in the sport of archery. Both had hunted with the bow during plantation days in the South. Will Henry Thompson was champion archer of America in 1879, 1884, 1888, 1901, and 1908.

He married Ida Lee of Crawfordsville, Ind., on June 11, 1874. In addition to his books, Thompson contributed to CENTURY MAGAZINE. He is best known for his poem, "High Tide at Gettysburg."

He died in 1918.

> Information from *Who's Who in America* and Burke and Howe—*American Authors and Books, 1640-1940.*

* * *

The Witchery of Archery—A Complete Manual of Archery with Many Chapters of Adventure by Field and Flood, Etc. (with Maurice Thompson). *New York,* 1878.

How to Train in Archery: Being a Complete Study of the York Round (with Maurice Thompson). *New York,* 1879.

THORP, ABNER: 1840–?

Abner Thorp was born in Lawrenceburg, Ind., in 1840. He was the author of at least two books of the Sunday School genus, the first of which was published in New York by the Methodist Book Concern.

> Information from the Federal Writers Project— *Indiana Authors,* 1937.

* * *

A Child of Nature. *Cincinnati,* 1896.
Effie's Conquest.

THORPE, ROSE HARTWICK (MRS. EDMUND CARSON): 1850–1939.

Among the greatest contributions to the repertoire of the elocutionist, whose art thrilled the front parlor gatherings and church sociables of America in the late Nineteenth century, was that sterling composition "Curfew Must Not Ring To-night." Many an amateur well-nigh blinded himself with eye-rolling and wrecked his vocal cords in the changes of pace attendant upon its rendition. It was a classic of its kind and it was written by a daughter of Mishawaka, Ind.

She was Rose Hartwick, daughter of William and Mary Hartwick, born in Mishawaka, Ind., on July 18, 1850. She was graduated in 1868 from the high school in Litchfield, Mich., where her family had moved when she was ten years old.

Miss Hartwick's literary career began at its very pinnacle, with the writing of "Curfew Must Not Ring

To-night" in her twentieth year. The poem was published in a Detroit newspaper in 1870 and attracted immediate attention. She married Edmund Carson Thorpe on Sept. 11, 1871, and continued with her writing. By 1881 she was editing three Sunday-school papers in Chicago and she continued as editor and later contributor to journals and magazines from 1880 until her death on July 19, 1939.

Mrs. Thorpe's last years were spent with her family in San Diego, Calif.

> Information from *Who Was Who in America* and *Appletons' Cyclopaedia of American Biography,* Vol. VI.

* * *

The Yule-Log: Cluster of Christmas Selections for Holiday Times. *Chicago,* 1881.

Fred's Dark Days. *New York,* 1881.

Curfew Must Not Ring To-Night. *Boston,* 1882.

The Fenton Family; or, for Mother's Sake. *Philadelphia,* 1884.

Nina Bruce; or, a Girl's Influence. *Philadelphia,* 1886.

The Chester Girls. *Philadelphia,* 1887.

Ringing Ballads; Including Curfew Must Not Ring To-Night. *Boston,* 1887.

Temperance Poems. *Pentwater, Mich.,* 1887.

The Year's Best Days for Boys and Girls. *Boston,* 1889.

Sweet Song Stories. *Chicago,* 1898.

White Lady of La Jolla. *San Diego,* 1904.

Poetical Works of Rose Hartwick Thorpe. *New York,* 1912.

From California. 1914.

In Sunset Land. 1927.

TIPPY, WORTH MARION: 1866–

Worth Marion Tippy, son of Oren and Mary Isabel Carder Tippy, was born in Larwill, Ind., on Nov. 8, 1866, and graduated from De Pauw University in 1891, receiving the D.D. degree in 1907. He also studied at Cornell University and at Sage School of Philosophy. On May 16, 1895, he married Zella B. Ward.

Ordained to the Methodist Episcopal ministry in 1893, he served as pastor in New Jersey, Indiana (Lafayette, Oxford, Terre Haute, and Indianapolis), Ohio, and New York until 1917. From 1917 to 1937 he was executive secretary of the Commission on the Church and Social Service of the Federal Council of Churches of Christ in America. He was also a lecturer and university preacher.

> Information from *Who's Who in America.*

* * *

The Church, a Community Force; a Story of the Development of the Community Relations of Epworth Memorial Church, Cleveland, Ohio. *New York,* 1914.

The Church and the Great War. *New York,* 1918.

A Methodist Church and Its Work (with P. B. Kern). *New York,* 1919.

How to Select and Judge Motion Pictures. *New York,* n.d. [1934].

TODD, MARY GENEVIEVE: 1863–1896.

Born in Vevay, Ind., in 1863, Mary Genevieve Todd entered the Catholic Church on Sept. 19, 1886, and entered the Community of Sisters of Providence at Saint-Mary-of-the-Woods, Ind., on Jan. 10, 1890. She died in 1896.

Information from the Barry Ms.

* * *

Poems, with Pious Thoughts and Practices in Honor of Our Divine Master. *New York,* 1897.

Poems, with Other Selections from the Writings of . . . *New York,* 1897.

TOMPKINS, ARNOLD: 1849–1905.

Arnold Tompkins was born on a farm near Paris, Ill., on Sept. 10, 1849. His parents were Henry and Delilah Williams Tompkins.

Tompkins attended Indiana and Butler universities, at intervals teaching in Illinois, and finally graduated from Indiana State Normal at Terre Haute in 1880. He married Miss Jennie Snyder on Dec. 23, 1875.

After teaching in Worthington and Franklin, Ind., he became a member of the De Pauw University faculty in 1885, of the Indiana State Normal in 1890, and of the University of Illinois. He served as president of Illinois Normal University in 1899 and of Chicago Normal School, 1900-05.

He died on Aug. 12, 1905, in Georgia.

Information from the *Dictionary of American Biography,* Vol. XVIII, the De Pauw University *Alumnal Record,* and the Indiana State Library.

* * *

The Philosophy of Teaching. *Boston,* n.d. [1891].

The Philosophy of School Management. *Boston,* 1895.

Literary Interpretations; or a Guide to the Teaching and Reading of Literature. *Boston,* 1896.

TOPH, OLLAH PERKINS: 1862–

Born in Rushville, Ind., in 1862, Ollah Perkins Toph was educated in the public schools of Indianapolis.

She began writing at the age of fourteen, and her first appearance in print was the publication of an essay in the CHRISTIAN STANDARD. In addition to poems and stories printed in GOOD HOUSEKEEPING, COSMOPOLITAN, HOME MAKER, and other magazines, she was a regular contributor to and on the staff of Chicago religious papers. Mrs. Toph, a resident of Indianapolis, was also known as a musician and a lecturer.

Information from the Indianapolis Public Library.

* * *

Lazarus. *Indianapolis,* 1895.

TRAHEY, JAMES J.: 1875–1906.

Born at Michigan City, Ind., in 1875, James J. Trahey was ordained a priest in the Roman Catholic Church in 1903 and died in 1906. He contributed articles on Latin to the Catholic University BULLETIN.

Information from the Barry Ms.

* * *

Dujarie Hall. 1900.

De Sermone Ennodiano. *Notre Dame, Ind.,* 1904.

Brothers of Holy Cross. *Notre Dame, Ind.,* 1905. (2nd ed.)

TRUEBLOOD, BENJAMIN FRANKLIN: 1847–1916.

"Benjamin Franklin Trueblood (Nov. 25, 1847-Oct. 26, 1916), educator, publicist, and professional worker for international peace, was born in Salem, Ind., and adhered throughout his life to the Quaker principles of his parents, Joshua and Esther (Parker) Trueblood. After graduating from Earlham College in 1869, he began his educational work as professor of classics at Penn College, Iowa. From 1874 to 1890 he served as president of Wilmington College, O., and of Penn College . . . On July 17, 1872, he married Sarah H. Terrell of New Vienna, O. In 1890 he broadened his educational activity by becoming a professional worker for international peace. A year abroad as agent for the Christian Arbitration and Peace Society provided an opportunity for studying European conditions and for becoming acquainted with leaders in the peace movement . . . From 1892 until 1915 he served as secretary of the American Peace Society and as editor of its periodical, the ADVOCATE OF PEACE . . . As a result of his tireless activity in organizing branch peace societies, of writing not only for peace periodicals but for other magazines, and of lecturing on innumerable occasions, he played a responsible part in the rapid expansion of the peace movement . . .

"As editor of the ADVOCATE OF PEACE he set a new standard for pacifist journalism. Without sacrificing the moral, ethical, and religious elements that had given so much impetus to pacifism, he interpreted the peace movement and the forces promoting war with realism as well as vision. His analyses of contemporary events were characterized by shrewdness, insight, and literary merit. Himself an uncompromising foe of all wars, militarism, and violence, he believed it was necessary to enlist the support of every shade of opinion if pacifism and internationalism were to be translated into actualities . . ."

Condensed from M. E. C., *Dictionary of American Biography*, Vol. XIX.

* * *

Secrecy and Citizenship; Prize Essays (with I. J. Lansing and D. W. Sleuth). *Boston, 1897.*

The Federation of the World. *Boston, 1899.*

The Development of the Peace Idea, and Other Essays. *Boston, 1932.*

Pamphlets published by the American Peace Society, *Washington, D. C.*:

   A Stated International Congress.
   Washington's Anti-Militarism.
   William Penn's Holy Experiment in Civil Government. *Boston, 1906.*
   The Christ of the Andes.
   A Periodic Congress of the Nations. *Boston, 1907.*
   International Arbitration at the Opening of the Twentieth Century. *Boston, 1909.*
   Case for Limitation of Armaments. *Boston, 1909.*
   How the Sunday Schools May Aid the Peace Movement. *Washington, D. C., 1911.*
   The Historic Development of the Peace Idea. *Washington, D. C., 1913.* (4th ed.)
   History of the American Peace Society and Its Work.
   Women in the Peace Movement. *Washington, D. C.,* n.d.
   The Cost of War. *Washington, D. C.*
   Results of the Second Hague Conference. *Washington, D. C.*
   The Two Hague Conferences and Their Results. *Washington, D. C., 1914.*

TRUEBLOOD, NEWTON A.: ?–

Newton A. Trueblood was a member of the branch of the noted North Carolina Quaker family which settled in Indiana. He had a good education, engaged in

business in Kokomo, Ind., for many years, and later lived in Knightstown. He wrote under the pen name of "Frank Winter."

Information from Parker and Heiney—*Poets and Poetry of Indiana.*

* * *

Religious Essays. *Chicago, 1883.*

TRUSLER, THOMAS JAMES: 1838–1909.

Born in Fayette County, Ind., on Feb. 11, 1838, Thomas James Trusler attended Miami University. He served as school examiner in Fayette County for several years and practiced law in Liberty and Connersville before coming to Indianapolis in 1856, where he served as a deputy in the Secretary of State's office for eight years. He then established a law practice in Indianapolis and for fourteen years he had the responsibility of preparing the acts of the Indiana Legislature for the printer. He died on Mar. 5, 1909.

Information from the Indiana State Library.

* * *

Poems. *Indianapolis, 1907.*

TURNER, TIMOTHY G.: 1817–1904.

Timothy G. Turner, newspaper editor and early business statistician, was born in Waitsfield, Vt., in 1817. He was educated in the local schools and read law in New York.

As a young man he went to Cleveland, O., then a thriving lake port, served for a time as the editor of the CLEVELAND HERALD and helped to reorganize the old TRUE DEMOCRAT as the CLEVELAND LEADER.

He married L. Olivia Morrell in 1847, and in 1855 the couple moved to South Bend, Ind., where they stayed a few years before returning to Ohio. Turner enlisted in the Union forces during the Civil War. He served for two years, was captured and was held at Libby Prison for four months.

In 1867 he returned to South Bend and remained there until his death on Aug. 3, 1904. He compiled and published the South Bend city directories from 1871 through 1880.

Information from the South Bend Public Library and the Northern Indiana Historical Society.

* * *

Gazetteer of the St. Joseph Valley, Michigan and Indiana, with a View of Its Hydraulic and Business Capacities. *Chicago, 1867.*

Turner's Guide from the Lakes to the Rocky Mountains, via Cleveland and Toledo, Michigan, and Southern and Northern Indiana, Chicago and Northwestern and the Union Pacific Railroads; also from Missouri Valley, via the Pacific and Sioux City Railroad and the Steamboats of the Northwest Transportation Company; Including a Historical and Statistical Account of the Railroads of the Country, Towns and Cities Along the Route, and Notices of the Connecting Roads and Routes (with C. E. Turner). *Chicago, 1868.*

TURPIE, DAVID: 1829–1909.

David Turpie, destined to play an important part in Indiana politics during almost half a century, was born in Hamilton County, O., on July 8, 1829.

He graduated from Kenyon College in 1848, removed to Logansport, Ind., and was admitted to the bar in the following year. In 1854, at the age of twenty-five, he was appointed judge of the Court of Common Pleas. He became judge of the Circuit Court in 1856 but resigned. He served as a member of the Indiana State Legislature in 1853 and again in 1858.

Turpie was a candidate for the office of lieutenant governor in 1860 but was defeated by Oliver P. Morton, who became wartime governor of the state when Henry S. Lane resigned the office to accept a seat in the U. S. Senate. Turpie did serve in the U. S. Senate from Jan. to Mar., 1863, filling the term of Jesse D. Bright, who was expelled in 1862. He was later elected and served from 1887 to 1899.

He died in 1909.

> Information from *Who Was Who in America* and Turpie—*Sketches of My Own Times.*

* * *

Address Upon the Life and Public Services of Hon. Thomas A. Hendricks. *Indianapolis, 1890.*

Sketches of My Own Times. *Indianapolis, 1903.*

Speculative Evidence. *Indianapolis, n.d.*

TUTTLE, JOSEPH FARRAND: 1818–1901.

Joseph Farrand Tuttle, for thirty years president of Wabash College and a leader in educational and religious affairs in Indiana, was born in Bloomfield, N. J., on Mar. 12, 1818.

The Tuttles had long been well known in the East, and his father, the Rev. Jacob Tuttle, was a prominent New Jersey minister. His mother's maiden name was Elizabeth Ward.

Joseph Farrand Tuttle had private instruction until his tenth year, when he was enrolled in Newark Academy. After four years of study he was taken by his parents to Ohio, where he spent the next four years on his uncle's farm.

In 1837 he entered Marietta College as a freshman and graduated with first honors in the spring of 1841. In the same year he enrolled in Lane Theological Seminary in Cincinnati, where Lyman Beecher made a considerable impression on him. He spent 1843 as a tutor in Marietta College and was licensed as a minister of the Presbyterian Church in 1844, receiving the A.M. from Lane in the same year.

In 1845 he accepted his first pastorate, that of the Second Presbyterian Church in Delaware, O., and married Susan Caroline King, whose father, Dr. Barnabas King, was also a minister, of Rockaway, N. J.

In 1847 the Rev. Mr. Tuttle was called as assistant pastor to the Presbyterian Church in Rockaway, N. J. It was not common for young ministers in Ohio to be employed by East Coast churches in those days, and Tuttle may have owed his good fortune in part to his wife's and his own family connections: whatever the case, he continued at Rockaway, speaking and writing for the religious and secular press, until his election to the presidency of Wabash College in 1861.

It is possible that Lyman Beecher, who like his brother, Henry Ward Beecher, had long been an active supporter of Wabash College, had a hand in the selection of Dr. Tuttle to fill the presidential vacancy created by the death of Dr. Charles White.

At Crawfordsville, Dr. Tuttle found Wabash flourishing as an educational institution but in little better financial condition proportionately than it had been two decades before. The years of President White's tenure had seen almost uniform annual deficits.

President Tuttle worked to remedy this difficulty for thirty years, beginning during the Civil War, when the only able-bodied students on the campus were those who had enrolled for a semester or so between enlistments or while recovering from duty-incurred wounds or illness.

Wabash survived the war, and the president, building on the foundation that had been laid before 1861, added to endowment, increased and improved the faculty and secured funds for buildings and equipment. When he resigned, at the end of three decades of service and at the first half century mark of the college, Wabash was well established.

Even after his resignation Dr. Tuttle continued to teach at the college, to write and to speak, in Crawfordsville and out, on religion, history, current events and whatever other subject seemed in demand. He kept his intellectual and human interests bright until his death in 1901.

Information from Kennedy—*History of Montgomery County, Indiana* and Osborne and Gronert—*Wabash College: The First Hundred Years.*

* * *

Relations of the Church to the Young, n.p., n.d. [1850].

Life of William Tuttle. *New York,* 1852.

Self-Reliance. *Philadelphia,* 1853.

Popular Rights in New Jersey Previous to the Revolution. n.p., n.d. [1853].

The Penalty of the Law . . . (Sermon.) *New York,* 1853.

An Address in Behalf of the Society for the Promotion of Collegiate and Theological Education at the West. Delivered October 26, 1853. *New York,* 1854.

Inaugural Discourse. *New York,* 1862.

"This One Thing I Do." Baccalaureate Sermon Preached Before the Class of 1862 . . . *Cincinnati,* 1862.

The Late Dr. Lyman Beecher . . . *New York,* 1863.

Moses and Washington. A Discourse Delivered to the Students of Wabash College, February 21st, 1864 . . . *Cincinnati,* 1864.

The Christian College in Its Relations to the Institutions of a New Country. Delivered to the Class of 1863 . . . *New York,* 1865.

The Perfection of Beauty. *Crawfordsville, Ind.,* 1867.

Who Shall Be Your Advisers? n.p., 1868.

Courage, Love, and a Sound Mind. *Indianapolis,* 1869.

The Early History of Morris County, New Jersey . . . *Newark, N. J.,* 1870.

The Way Lost and Found, a Book for the Young, Especially Young Men. *Philadelphia,* 1870.

The Higher Culture: Its Nature, Position, Method and Patrons . . . Delivered at Wabash College . . . June 23rd, 1872. *Newark, N. J.,* 1872.

What Is the Mission of Wabash College? *Crawfordsville, Ind.,* [1873].

A Visit to Four Eastern Colleges. *Crawfordsville, Ind.,* [1873].

William Tuttle of New Haven: an Address Delivered at the Tuttle Gathering, New Haven, Conn., September 3d, 1873 . . . *Newark, N. J.,* 1873.

Physical Science and Christianity . . . Delivered at Wabash College . . . June 22, 1873. *Newark, N. J.,* 1873.

"Because and Therefore." . . . Delivered at Wabash College . . . June 21, 1874. *Newark, N. J.,* 1874.

God's Work in the World the Last Fifty Years. n.p., n.d. [1874].

The Education of Moses . . . Delivered Before the Class of '75 . . . *Newark, N. J.,* 1875.

The Believer's Victory Over Death . . . *Cincinnati,* 1875.

The Origin and Growth of Wabash College. . . . To the Class of 1876 . . . *Logansport, Ind.,* 1876.

Annals of Morris County, New Jersey. n.p., n.d. [1876?].

The Greek or the Christ! Delivered Before the Class of '77 . . . *Crawfordsville, Ind.,* 1877.

"Forty-four Years Ago This Morning." n.p., n.d. [1877].

Our Dead Brothers. *Crawfordsville, Ind.,* 1878.

Address at Dedication of Peck Scientific Hall. *Crawfordsville, Ind.,* 1878.

Caleb Mills and Indiana Common Schools. n.p., n.d. [1879].

Memorial Address to Abraham Lincoln and James A. Garfield, the Assassinated Presidents . . . *Crawfordsville, Ind.,* 1881.

Statues to the Deserving. n.p., n.d. [1881].

The University for Religion, Delivered June 19, 1881. *Crawfordsville, Ind.,* 1881.

Wabash College. Its History, Plans and Prospects . . . n.p., n.d.

Our Half Century: an Oration Before the Alumni of Marietta College, June 24, 1891. n.p., [1891].

The Race. Baccalaureate Sermon to the Class of '92, June 12, 1892. *Crawfordsville, Ind.,* 1892.

U

ULLMAN, ALICE WOODS: 1871–

Born in Goshen, Ind., in 1871, Mrs. Alice Woods Ullman was educated at the Girls' Classical School of Indianapolis and studied at the New York School of Art and at art schools in Paris.

Information from the Barry Ms. and the Indiana State Library.

* * *

Edges. *Indianapolis,* 1902.

Gingham Rose. *Indianapolis,* 1904.

Fame Seekers. *New York,* 1912.

The Thicket. *New York,* 1913.

Hairpin Duchess. *New York,* 1924.

Gilded Caravan. *New York,* 1927.

V

VAN METRE, THURMAN WILLIAM: 1884–

Born in Florida, Ind., on Oct. 28, 1884, Thurman William Van Metre, son of Isaac Newton and Margaret Guisinger Van Metre, received the A.B. (1910) and A.M. (1911) degrees from Indiana University and the Ph.D. (1913) from the University of Pennsylvania. On Sept. 9, 1913, he married Mildred Stonex, who died in 1932.

After teaching in Indiana public schools, 1902-09, he became an instructor in transportation at the University of Pennsylvania in 1913. In 1916 he joined the staff of the School of Business, Columbia University, and continued there, becoming a full professor in 1922.

Information from *Who's Who in America*.

* * *

Outline of the Development of the Internal Commerce of the United States, 1789-1900. *Baltimore, 1913.*

History of Domestic and Foreign Commerce of the United States (with E. R. Johnson, G. G. Huebner, and D. S. Hanchett). *Washington, D. C., 1915.*

Principles of Railroad Transportation (with E. R. Johnson). *New York, 1916.*

Economic History of the United States. *New York, 1921.*

Early Opposition to the Steam Railroad. *New York, 1924.*

A Course in the Economic History of the United States. *New York, 1924.*

Trains, Tracks and Travel. *New York, 1926.*

Tramps and Liners. *Garden City, N. Y., 1931.*

Transportation in the United States. *Chicago, 1939.*

VAWTER, CLARA: 1875-1900.

Clara Vawter, daughter of Dr. Louis A. and Emma Mary Dameron Vawter, was born in Boone County, Va., in 1875. When she was a child, she moved with her family to Greenfield, Ind., which was her home until one year before her death, when she moved to Indianapolis.

Clara Vawter was a sister of Will Vawter, Brown County, Ind., artist, who illustrated her book.

She died in 1900.

Information from the Greenfield Public Library.

* * *

Of Such Is the Kingdom: for Children and Grown Folk Alike: a Book of Stories and Rhymes. *Indianapolis, 1899.* (Reissued in 1902 as The Rabbit's Ransom, and Other Stories.)

VEIBY, JOHN: 1860–

John Veiby was born in Norway, July 29, 1860. After having graduated from a military school for under officers, he came to the U. S. in 1883. He worked for a watch company at Elgin, Ill., for a number of years and wrote for Norwegian publications.

In 1906 he published a book *Sunday Labor*, in English under the pen name of Thorleif. That year he came to South Bend, Ind., and worked for the South Bend Watch Company until 1929. During those years he wrote and published several other books.

Information from the South Bend Public Library.

* * *

Sunday Labor. *Mount Morris, Ill., 1906.*

Beyond Marriage. *South Bend, Ind., 1914.*

Utopian Way. *South Bend, Ind., 1917.*

Direct Action; a One Act Play. *South Bend, Ind., 1920.*

Utopian Essays. *South Bend, Ind., 1923.*

Jingo. *South Bend, Ind.,* [1927].

VOORHEES, DANIEL WOLSEY: 1827-1897.

Daniel Wolsey Voorhees, U. S. Senator from Indiana, was born in Butler County, O., on Sept. 26, 1827. He was two months old when his parents, Stephen and Rachel Elliott Voorhees, moved to a farm in Fountain County, Ind., about ten miles from Covington.

In 1845 he entered Indiana Asbury (now De Pauw) University, from which he graduated in 1849 with the A.B. degree, receiving the A.M. in 1852 and the LL.D. in 1884. On July 18, 1850, he married Anna Hardesty of Greencastle, Ind.

Following his graduation he entered the law office of Lane and Wilson in Crawfordsville, Ind., where he read law, and was admitted to the bar in 1851. He began his practice in Covington, Ind. He was associated with E. A. Hannegan, former U. S. senator, and in 1853 he served out the term of Lew Wallace, who had resigned as prosecuting attorney of the Circuit Court. In 1856 he was an unsuccessful candidate for Congress.

Voorhees moved to Terre Haute, Ind., in 1857, and this became his permanent home. In 1858 President Buchanan appointed him U. S. district attorney for the state of Indiana. In 1859, at the request of Gov. Willard of Indiana, he acted as defense attorney for Col. John E. Cook, Willard's brother-in-law and comrade of John Brown in the raid on Harper's Ferry, and although he lost the case and Cook was hanged, his speeches at the trial made him nationally known.

He was a successful candidate for Congress in 1860, 1862, 1868, and 1870. His congressional record was one of opposition to the war government, criticism of its "tyrannies," and an almost equal hatred of secession and abolitionism. He introduced the resolution unqualifiedly endorsing President Johnson's reconstruction policy.

He was appointed in 1877 to succeed Gov. Oliver P. Morton in the U. S. Senate, was elected to the Senate in 1878, and served until 1897. Here he followed the Democratic line of opposition to high tariffs and represented the Midwest agrarian policy of cheap money and distrust of Eastern financial interests. However, he led the fight for the repeal of the Sherman Silver Purchase Act in 1893 and supported the Wilson

Tariff bill in 1894. He is chiefly remembered as a great orator—"The Tall Sycamore of the Wabash."

He died in Washington, D. C., on Apr. 10, 1897, and was buried in Terre Haute.

> Information from *Representative Men of Indiana,* Vol. II; *Dictionary of American Biography,* Vol. XIX; and De Pauw University's *Alumnal Record, 1920.*

* * *

Speech Delivered in Fountain Circuit Court, July, 1857. *Covington, Ind.,* 1857.

Speeches; Compiled by C. S. Voorhees, with a Biographical Sketch. *Cincinnati,* 1875.

Address . . . to the Jury in the Case of Kilbourn vs. Thompson, Delivered in the Supreme Court of the D. C., April 21, 1882. *Washington, D. C.,* 1882.

Speech, June 23, 1885, in Defence of Capt. Edward T. Johnson, Indicted for the Murder of Maj. Edwin Henry. *Washington, D. C.,* 1885.

Forty Years of Oratory: Lectures, Addresses, and Speeches; Compiled and Edited by His Three Sons and His Daughter, Harriet Cecilia Voorhees; with a Brief Sketch of His Life by Judge Thomas B. Long. *Indianapolis,* 1898. 2 vols.

Defense of John E. Cook on the Welfare of the Nation.

Greeley as the Democratic Candidate for President.

VOORHEES, JAMES PAXTON: ?–

James Paxton Voorhees was the son of Daniel W. Voorhees, statesman, attorney and orator, called "The Tall Sycamore of the Wabash."

Young Voorhees spent his boyhood in Terre Haute, Ind., and Washington, D. C., studied law and served as his father's secretary during the later years of the parent's political career. He was interested in the arts, trying his hand with some success at writing for periodicals and as a sculptor and actor.

Mr. Voorhees was also a resident of Greencastle and later Plainfield, Ind.

> Information from the Indiana State Library and the Barry Ms.

* * *

The Tale of Wealth: Being the Personal Narrative of Chambers Rundel. *Washington, D. C.,* 1890.

Wissy: a True Tale of Modern Theatrical Bohemia. *Washington, D. C.,* 1897.

Caverns of Dawn. *Plainfield, Ind.,* 1910.

A Dwarf's Humility. *Indianapolis,* 1919.

"Flaws"; a Story of the Outlaws of Old Hoosierland in Association with Another Tale. *Plainfield, Ind.,* 1925.

The Unknown Quantity. *Plainfield, Ind.,* n.d.

VOTAW, ALBERT HIATT: 1850–1931.

Albert Hiatt Votaw, son of Isaac and Anna Maria Hiatt Votaw, was born at Richmond, Ind., on Feb. 19, 1850, and graduated from Earlham College in 1874. He married Phebe Nicholson in 1891.

From 1877 to 1902 Mr. Votaw was an instructor of Latin at Westtown School in Pennsylvania, and from 1908 to 1929 served as secretary of the Pennsylvania Prison Society. He was also editor of THE PRISON JOURNAL.

He died on Feb. 21, 1931.

> Information from *Who Was Who in America.*

* * *

County Prisons of Pennsylvania. *Philadelphia,* 1914.

Penal Legislation of 1915 in the Commonwealth of Pennsylvania; Employment of Prisoners. *Philadelphia,* 1915.

Prison Efficiency. *Philadelphia,* 1916.

Review of the County Jails of Pennsylvania. *Philadelphia,* 1920.

VOTAW, CLARENCE E.: 1853–?

Clarence E. Votaw was born near Chester, Wayne County, Ind., on Nov. 12, 1853 and attended the Society of Friends High School at Webster and Richmond, Ind. In 1884 he married Catherine Smith, who died in 1940.

Mr. Votaw engaged in farming and fruit raising until 1881, when he was appointed to the Railway Mail Service, where he served until his retirement in 1920. From 1921 to 1929 he was associated with the Friends Central Office in Richmond, Ind. In 1929 he became a resident of Fountain City, Ind.

> Information from Clarence E. Votaw.

* * *

Jasper Hunnicut of Jimpsonhurst. *Chicago,* 1907.

Patriotism; a Story of the Civil War in America. *Philadelphia,* 1941.

W

WADE, FRANK BERTRAM: 1875–

Frank Bertram Wade, born in New Bedford, Mass., in 1875, became head of the science department at Shortridge High School in Indianapolis in 1903. He became a nationally recognized authority on gems and is the author of several textbooks not listed here.

> Information from the Indianapolis Public Library.

* * *

A Teacher's Handbook. 1915.

Diamonds; a Study of the Factors That Govern Their Value. *New York, 1916.*

How to Buy Diamonds Wisely. 1921.

Facts in Regard to Industrial Diamond Setting. 1923.

The Teaching of Science and the Science Teacher (with H. Brownell). *New York, 1925.*

WALK, CHARLES EDMONDS: 1875–

"Charles Edmonds Walk was born Mar. 18, 1875, in Memphis, Tenn., the son of a Methodist minister. He was educated in Indianapolis, and in 1893 he married Mary H. Hamilton of Kokomo, Ind. In 1908 they moved to Cass County, Indiana."

From Powell—*History of Cass County, 1913.*

* * *

The Silver Blade. *Chicago,* 1908.

The Yellow Circle. *Chicago,* 1909.

The Paternoster Ruby. *Chicago,* 1910.

The Time Lock. *Chicago,* 1912.

The Crimson Cross (with Millard Lynch). *Chicago,* 1913.

The Green Seal. *Chicago,* 1914.

WALKER, CHARLES MANNING: 1834–1920.

Born in Athens, O., Dec. 25, 1834, Charles Manning Walker was educated at the University of Ohio. He came to Indianapolis about 1855, where he taught in the Institute for the Blind and studied law. From 1861 to 1869 he was connected with the U. S. Treasury Department, but he returned to Indianapolis as associate editor of the INDIANAPOLIS JOURNAL and later worked on the INDIANAPOLIS TIMES and the INDIANAPOLIS NEWS. He died in 1920.

Information from *Who's Who in America* and the Indianapolis Public Library.

* * *

History of Athens County, Ohio, and Incidentally of the Ohio Land Company, and the First Settlement of the State at Marietta. *Cincinnati,* 1869. 2 vols.

Sketch of the Life, Character, and Public Services of Oliver P. Morton. Prepared for the INDIANAPOLIS JOURNAL by Charles M. Walker. *Indianapolis,* 1878.

Hovey and Chase. Life of Alvin P. Hovey . . . Together with a Sketch of Ira J. Chase. *Indianapolis,* 1888.

WALKER, GUY MORRISON: 1870–

Guy Morrison Walker was born in Fort Wayne, Ind., Jan. 24, 1870. His parents were the Rev. Wilbur F. and Mary Florence Morrison Walker.

Mr. Walker received the A.B. from De Pauw University in 1890, the LL.B. in 1891 and the A.M. in 1893. He married Minnie L. Royse, of Terre Haute, Ind., on Dec. 15, 1891. He was admitted to the Indiana bar in 1891.

He spent some time in China and was regarded as an expert on Chinese affairs, acting as editor of Chinese material for LESLIE'S WEEKLY after the Boxer outbreaks and as a consultant to President McKinley. He organized the Terre Haute (Ind.) Trust Company in 1894 and the Security Trust Company of Toledo (O.) in 1898. He removed to New York in the latter year.

His business career was chiefly devoted to the reorganization of trust organizations and public utilities.

Information from *Who's Who in America.*

* * *

Railroads and Wages. *New York,* 1902.

The Why and How of Interurban Railways. *Chicago,* 1904.

Record of Phi Kappa Psi. *New York,* 1906.

The Spirit of Indiana. *New York,* 1907.

Fundamental Education. *New York,* 1912.

Measure of Civilization. *New York,* 1917.

Railroad Rates and Rebates. *New York,* 1917.

The Things That Are Caesar's—A Defense of Wealth. *New York,* 1919.

The English Language and the People Who Speak It. *New York,* 1920.

The Man Who Can, and Other Addresses. *New York,* 1920.

Skeletons (A Claim Agent's Stories). *Boston,* 1921.

Gods of the Nation. *New York,* 1921.

Can We Escape War with Japan? *New York,* 1921.

WALL, LEE WESLIE: ?–1899.

"Lee Weslie Wall was a printer living in Logansport, Ind., for many years. He died in that city on July 10, 1899. He is the author of a religious book . . . consisting of quotations from the Bible with appropriate poetical accompaniment . . ."

From Powell—*History of Cass County, 1913.*

* * *

Words of Comfort. *Logansport, Ind.,* 1896.

WALLACE, LEWIS: 1827–1905.

Lewis (Lew) Wallace (Apr. 10, 1827-Feb. 15, 1905) went through life as an amateur—a singularly gifted one at times—of half a dozen professions. He is best known as a writer, the author of the long-time best seller *Ben Hur; a Tale of the Christ* (1880). But as he makes clear in his posthumous *Autobiography* (1906), he wrote as an avocation and for pleasure rather than as a serious business. He liked to dream; he was an incurable romantic and his novels are the setting down of his fantasies. When he dealt with a concrete theme, as in the case of his *Autobiography*, he adopted a fairly easy-flowing, almost conversational style in contrast to the consciously "literary" style of the more pretentious works.

In addition to the two titles mentioned, Wallace wrote *The Fair God* (1873), a fictionization of the Spanish conquest of Mexico under Cortez; *The Life of Benjamin Harrison* (1888), a hastily compiled campaign biography; *The Boyhood of Christ* (1888); *The Prince of India, or Why Constantinople Fell* (1893); and the volume (1898) containing the poem *The Wooing of Malkatoon* and the tragedy *Commodus*, written at an earlier date.

Wallace's second career was as a soldier. From earliest youth a lover of adventure, he tried to run away from home at the age of thirteen and join the Texans in their war for independence. He later participated in the Mexican War (1846-47).

Wallace saw the Civil War coming and knew that it would not only be a long and bitter conflict but, as he says in his autobiography, "that it would also be crowded with opportunities for distinction not in the least inconsistent with patriotism." Acting on this foresight, he organized in 1856 a military company in Crawfordsville, Ind., officially called the Montgomery Guards but better known as the Zouaves because of the uniforms they wore.

With the coming of war in 1861 the Zouaves enlisted in the Union army almost to a man and Wallace was called by Gov. O. P. Morton to be adjutant-general of Indiana. He was given full charge of raising his state's quota of regiments, exceeded the quota, and was given command of the Eleventh Indiana Regiment.

Wallace saw action at Fort Donelson, Shiloh, and Monocacy. He served with distinction and rose to the rank of major general.

His impetuosity and lack of tact cost him the good will of Gen. Halleck and he was twice relieved of his command, perhaps in consequence, only to be restored to it again by direction of higher authority.

Near the end of the Civil War, Wallace was active in helping the Mexicans in their uprising against the French Emperor Maximilian.

For many years a cloud hung over Wallace's military career as a result of a misunderstanding with Grant at Shiloh. Grant bitterly criticized Wallace for his route of march which caused him to arrive too late for the first day's battle. Grant subsequently somewhat grudgingly modified his observations. Wallace was deeply hurt by this criticism and many years later we find him writing to his wife of "the old wound at Shiloh," a wound to the spirit.

He served on the courts martial that tried Lincoln's assassins and investigated conditions at Andersonville Prison.

Lew Wallace was also a lawyer, although he does not appear to have let the law interfere with his other interests. He read law in his father's office in Indianapolis, failed the bar examination in 1846 in his haste to be off to the Mexican War, was admitted to practice before the circuit court the following year, and ultimately, in 1849, redeemed himself before the Indiana Supreme Court and was fully admitted to the bar. While he had carried on a modest practice in Indianapolis during the years he was studying for the bar, he opened his first real law office in Covington, Ind., shortly after receiving his license from the Indiana Supreme Court. He served two terms as prosecuting attorney in Covington (1850-53) and in 1853 resigned to move to Crawfordsville, where his wife's parents lived. In 1852 he had married Susan Elston, third daughter of Maj. Isaac C. Elston. In Crawfordsville he continued the practice of law off and on for the greater part of his life.

Closely connected with his legal career was Wallace's interest in politics, although he never achieved elective public office higher than state senator (1856).

Wallace started out in politics as a Whig. His father had been a Whig before him and had been elected governor of Indiana with that party's support. But when the Whigs nominated Zachary Taylor president in 1848 Wallace could not go along with the party. He despised Taylor because of the latter's treatment of Wallace's unit in the Mexican War, so he bolted to the Democratic ranks. Soon he found himself in a political dilemma. The controversy over the admission to the union of states as "free" states or "slave" states found him torn between his dislike of the abolitionists and his repugnance to human slavery. He wound up by becoming a Douglas Democrat with the principle that each new state should determine its own status on the slavery issue. But events led Wallace away from this position and he was ultimately convinced, after hearing Lincoln debate Douglas, that the Democrats were the party not only of slavery but of secession. In 1860 he moved into the

Republican camp. It was a Republican president, Hayes, who appointed him governor of New Mexico Territory in 1878 and another Republican, Garfield, who appointed him minister to Turkey in 1881.

In both of the last assignments Wallace came on the scene in periods of excitement. The reign of terror of "Billy the Kid" occurred while he was governor of New Mexico, and the notorious Abdul Hamid II was sultan during Wallace's tour of duty in Constantinople.

Around the edges of the varied careers Wallace found time to play the violin and to paint pictures. He even dabbled in modeling clay.

Lew Wallace's formal education was of the skimpiest. He was sent from school to school and along the way spent a scant two months in the preparatory department of Wabash College, but formal education apparently did not take. His greatest source of real education was his father's library.

It has been ventured before now that a contributing psychological factor to the readiness of the South for an unnecessary and tragic war was the popularity of romantic fiction, particularly the Waverley Novels of Walter Scott. If the young manhood of the slaveholding class regarded themselves as feudal seigneurs or highland chieftains, a highly debatable contention, they certainly had a northern counterpart in Lew Wallace.

It was noted above that Wallace was a romantic in his writing; but his romanticism went deeper than that and tinged almost every phase of his life. From his first attempt to run away and be a hero he was committed to the dramatic, the fanciful, and the heroic. He dressed his military company in the baggy trousers and gay tasselled sash of the Algerian Zouaves of France. He saw in the coming Civil War a chance to rise to fame. He ordered the men of the Eleventh Indiana Regiment to fall upon their knees, raise their right hands and publicly swear a mighty oath to remember the humiliation of the Indiana forces at Buena Vista in the Mexican War and to wipe out that shame in battle.

Gen. Grant may have been weak on his facts as to what occurred before Shiloh but he knew his man when he observed in the CENTURY MAGAZINE, "I presume his idea was that by taking the route he did, he would be able to come around on the flank or rear of the enemy, and thus perform an act of heroism that would redound to the credit of his command, as well as to the benefit of his country."

The romantic tendency can be noted in Wallace's painting of the conspirators planning the assassination of Lincoln. They are shown in a range of poses from furtive to poetic before a classical ruin, a favorite stage property of the artists who revolted against the logic and reason of the classical age.

Again we find the love of the colorful in his description of the Turkish sultan: "The commander of the faithful wears the uniform of an army officer, without ornament other than a slight dress sword. His bearing is kingly, his face thin and colorless, eyes black and keen as a falcon's. He rides a milk-white Arabian, which he manages with skilful and delicate hand."

In the last years of his life, Lew Wallace caused to be built in the garden of his Crawfordsville, Ind., home a study which he described as "a pleasure-house for my soul." It is unfortunate that this tangible evidence of Wallace's choice of an ideal setting for himself as a writer and a man of the world remains for us to see. It is better to think of him as the restless adventure-seeker, the striker of picturesque attitudes that his writings and the events of his life reveal him. There is little of the commonplace in that portrait. It comes as something of a shock, then, to see preserved in this little building, now maintained as a memorial, the standard trappings and artistic clichés of an era when aesthetic judgment in the English-speaking world was at its nadir.

By John D. Forbes, Wabash College.

* * *

The Fair God; or, the Last of the 'Tzins: a Tale of the Conquest of Mexico. *Boston*, 1873.

Commodus. An Historical Play. *Crawfordsville, Ind.*, [1876].

Ben-Hur: a Tale of the Christ. *New York*, 1880.

The Life of General Benjamin Harrison. *Philadelphia*, 1888.

The Boyhood of Christ. *New York*, 1888.

Ben-Hur in Dramatic Tableaux and Pantomime Arranged by the Author. *New York*, 1891.

Life and Public Services of Benjamin Harrison . . . with a Choice Biographical Sketch of Whitelaw Reid . . . *Cincinnati*, n.d.

The Prince of India: or, Why Constantinople Fell. *New York*, 1893.

The Story of American Heroism (with others). *Akron, O.*, 1896.

The Wooing of Malkatoon; Commodus: Two Poems. *New York*, 1898.

The First Christmas; from Ben-Hur. *New York*, 1899.

Lew Wallace, an Autobiography. *New York*, 1906. 2 vols. (Brought down to the end of the Civil War by Wallace, this was completed by Susan Elston Wallace and Mary Hannah Krout.)

Chariot-Race From Ben-Hur. *New York,* 1908.
The Boy's Ben-Hur: a Tale of the Christ. *New York,*
[1880-1928].

WALLACE, SUSAN ARNOLD ELSTON (MRS. LEW): 1830-1907.

Susan Arnold Elston, daughter of Maj. Isaac C. and Maria E. Aiken Elston, was born in Crawfordsville, Ind., on Dec. 25, 1830. She was educated at home and at Poughkeepsie, N. Y., completing her course there in 1849. She married Lew Wallace in 1852 and, except for the years of his government service, made her home in Crawfordsville until her death.

In addition to her books, she contributed to newspapers and periodicals and acted as editor and critic of her husband's writing. She took pleasure in encouraging the literary efforts of all young people, and especially those of Mary Hannah Krout, who was a protégé from childhood. It has been suggested that the literary taste of Mrs. Wallace was somewhat superior to that of her illustrious husband and that his work could have been improved, in style and structure, by even more of her editing than it received.

Mrs. Elston died on Oct. 1, 1907.

> Information from *Who Was Who in America* and from the ms. notes and scrap-books of Mary Hannah Krout.

* * *

The Storied Sea. *Boston,* 1883.
Ginevra; or, the Old Oak Chest: a Christmas Story; Illustrated by Lew Wallace. *New York,* 1886.
The Land of the Pueblos. *New York,* 1888.
The Repose in Egypt: a Medley. *New York,* 1888.
Along the Bosphorus, and Other Sketches. *Chicago,* 1898.
Travel Sketches. *New York, n.d.*
The City of the King: What the Child Jesus saw and Heard. *Indianapolis,* 1903.
Child-Life Abroad (with others). *Evanston, Ill., n.d.*

WALLACE, WILSON DEWITT: 1838-1901.

Wilson DeWitt Wallace, son of James and Sarah A. Marquam Wallace, was born in Lafayette, Ind., on November 19, 1838. He attended the Lafayette grade schools, the Waveland (Ind.) Academy, and received the A.B. degree from Jefferson College, Pa., in 1861. On Nov. 19, 1861, he married Anna M. Shields.

He served in the Union army until wounded and was discharged with the rank of captain in 1863. After his discharge he studied in the law office of John A. Stein (father of Orth Harper and Evaleen Stein) and was admitted to the Tippecanoe County bar in 1864. He was elected judge of the Superior Court in 1894 and held the position until his death on Jan. 28, 1901.

Judge Wallace wrote a great deal of both prose and verse during his life and enjoyed association with others of similar tastes.

> Information from de Hart—*Past and Present of Tippecanoe County, Indiana,* and *Combination Atlas Map of Tippecanoe County, Indiana.*

* * *

Love's Ladder; a Novel. *Chicago,* 1886.
Idle Hours. *New York,* 1890.

WALSER, GEORGE HENRY: 1834-?

Except for the fact that George Henry Walser was born in Dearborn County, Ind., in 1834, no information on his life has been located. The places of publication of his first two books (both probably printed for the author) would seem to indicate that he moved west in middle life.

> Information from Federal Writers Project—*Indiana Authors,* 1937.

* * *

Poems of Leisure. *Lamar, Mo.,* 1890.
The Bouquet; a Poetic Treasury of Flowers, Their Classics and Vocabulary, *Lincoln, Nebr.,* 1897.
Life and Teachings of Jesus. *Boston,* 1908.
Floral Tribute.

WAREING, ERNEST CLYDE: 1872-1944.

Ernest Clyde Wareing, son of James and Sarah Wilson Wareing, was born in Volga, Ind., on May 29, 1872, lived in Huntingburg, Ind., in his youth, and graduated from the Huntingburg High School. He received the A.B. degree from De Pauw University in 1898, the D.D. in 1914 and the S.T.B. from Boston University in 1909. He also received degrees from Ohio Northern University, Evansville College, and McKendree College. On May 7, 1896, he married Mary Alcinda Matlock.

Ordained to the Methodist Episcopal ministry in 1901, he served as a pastor in Indiana (at Plainfield, Williamsport, Plymouth, and Brazil) from 1901 to 1912. From 1912 to 1915 he was associate editor

and from 1916 to 1932 editor of the WESTERN
CHRISTIAN ADVOCATE, with headquarters in Cincinnati. He was a pastor in Fort Wayne, 1932-33,
and in Chattanooga, Tenn., 1933-36. From 1936 to
1939 he acted as superintendent of the church's Chattanooga district, and from 1939 until his death he was
pastor of the Red Bank Methodist Church.

He died on Feb. 4, 1944.

> Information from *Who's Who in America* and
> *Wilson's History Notes,* Vol. 20.

* * *

Knights of the White Shield. 1906.
The Building of a Great Sunday School. 1911.
The Evangelism of Jesus; Six Studies. *New York,* 1918.
Critical Hours in the Preacher's Life. *New York,* 1923.
The Other Shepherd; a Tale of the First Christmas
    Among the Shepherds of Bethlehem. *New York,* 1929.
The Spiritual Force of the Epworth League Institute.

WARRUM, HENRY: 1867–1939.

Born in Greenfield, Ind., in 1867, Henry Warrum
spent most of his life in Indianapolis and Washington.
He died in 1939.

> Information from Indianapolis Public Library.

* * *

Some Religious Weft and Warp. *Indianapolis,* 1915.

WASON, ROBERT ALEXANDER: 1874–

Robert Alexander Wason, son of Robert Alexander
and Gertrude Louise Paddock Wason, was born in
Toledo, O., on Apr. 6, 1874. Removing to Indiana
as a boy, he attended high school in Delphi for one
year. On May 11, 1911, he married Emma Louise
Brownell of Peru, Ind.

For eight years he was a clerk in a general store—
at the same time making several trips to the West.
During the Spanish-American War he served nine
months in the Fifth U. S. Artillery.

In addition to his books he has written vaudeville
sketches, a comic opera, and short stories.

> Information from *Who's Who in America.*

* * *

Babe Randolph's Turning Point. 1904.
The Wolves: Fable with a Purpose. *Chicago,* 1908.
Nachette (with Ned Nye). *New York,* 1909.
Happy Hawkins. *Boston,* 1909.
The Steering Wheel. *Indianapolis,* 1910.

The Knight-Errant: a Novel of To-Day. *Boston,* 1911.
Friar Tuck; Being the Chronicles of the Reverend John
    Carmichael, of Wyoming, U. S. A., as Set Forth and
    Embellished by His Friend and Admirer Happy Haw-
    kins and Here Recorded by Robert Alexander Wason.
    Boston, 1912.
And Then Came Jean. *Boston,* 1913.
The Dog and the Child and the Ancient Sailor Man.
    Boston, n.d. [1913].
Happy Hawkins in the Panhandle. *Boston,* 1914.
Knute Ericson's Celebration, in the Grim Thirteen. 1917.
Spoilers of the Valley. 1921.

WASSON, JOHN MACAMY: 1810–?

John Macamy Wasson, author of a very well written
historical pamphlet which he published anonymously,
was born in Wayne County, Ind., in 1810, the son
of Archibald Wasson.

The family moved to Richmond, Ind., in 1829,
and young Wasson married Anna Moore.

He began to gather notes on the early history of the
county and about 1870 he began to jot down his
own recollections of the early days. These were collected and published after his death.

> Information from Young—*History of Wayne
> County* and the Indiana State Library.

* * *

Annals of Pioneer Settlers on the Whitewater and Its
    Tributaries in the Vicinity of Richmond, Indiana, from
    1804 to 1830. [Anonymous.] *Richmond, Ind.,* 1875.

WATERMAN, LUTHER DANA: 1830–1918.

Luther Dana Waterman was born in Wheeling, Va.
(now W. Va.), on Nov. 21, 1830. From 1832 to
1855 he was a resident of Ohio, where he attended
Miami University, taught school, and graduated from
the Medical College of Ohio at Cincinnati in 1853. In
1855 he came to Kokomo, Ind. During the Civil
War he was with the army for three years as surgeon
of the 39th Regiment, Indiana Volunteers, and he
spent two months as a prisoner of war at Macon, Ga.,
and Charleston, S. C. After the war he settled in
Indianapolis, where he lived until his death.

Dr. Waterman was a charter organizer of the old
Indiana Medical College and taught there for a
number of years. In 1878 he was president of the
Indiana Medical Society. At the time of his death,
June 30, 1918, he was professor emeritus of medicine
in the Indiana University School of Medicine. He
will be remembered chiefly for his gift of $100,000 to

Indiana University for the establishment of the "Luther Dana Waterman Institute for Scientific Research."

Information from Dunn—*Indiana and Indianans*, and the Indianapolis Public Library.

* * *

Phantoms of Life; Poems. *New York*, 1883.
The Economy and Necessity of a State Board of Health.

WEATHERLY, ULYSSES GRANT: 1865–1940.

Ulysses Grant Weatherly, son of William A. and Lydia Dix Weatherly, was born at West Newton, Ind., on Apr. 21, 1865, and graduated from Colgate University in 1890. In 1894 he received the Ph.D. degree from Cornell, in 1910 the Litt.D. from Colgate, and in 1911 the A.M. from Indiana University. He also studied at the universities of Heidelberg, Leipzig, and Columbia. On Dec. 24, 1890, he married Alice M. Burgess.

In 1894-95 he was an instructor at Central High School in Philadelphia. After 1895 he served on the faculty of Indiana University, first as assistant professor, then associate professor of history and, after 1899, as professor of economics and sociology. From 1907 to 1910 he was joint-editor of the Economic Bulletin. He was also a member of various state boards and commissions.

He died on July 18, 1940.

Information from *Who Was Who in America* and *Indiana University, 1820-1904*.

* * *

Louis VI, the Founder of the French Monarchy. *Hamilton, N. Y.*, 1891.
Comparative Politics. *Albany, N. Y.*, 1895.
Outlines of Sociology. *Indianapolis*, 1906.
Social Progress, Studies in the Dynamics of Change. *Philadelphia*, 1926.

WEBSTER, MARIE DAUGHERTY (MRS. GEORGE, JR.): 1859–

Born in Wabash, Ind., in 1859, Marie Daugherty moved to Marion, Ind., in 1884, when she became the wife of George Webster, Jr. She was a resident of Marion for many years, later moving to Princeton, N. J.

Information from the Marion Public Library.

* * *

Quilts: Their Story and How to Make Them. *Garden City, N. Y.*, 1915.

WEIGLE, ELIZA DANA (MRS. CHARLES): ?–

According to de Hart's *Past and Present of Tippecanoe County*, published in 1909, "Mrs. Eliza Dana Weigle has been a resident of Lafayette since the time of her marriage to Mr. Charles Weigle . . ."

de Hart—*Past and Present of Tippecanoe County*, 1909.

* * *

In an Old-Time Garden, and Bits of Nature Verse. *Brandon, Vt.*

WEIK, JESSE WILLIAM: 1857–

Jesse William Weik, son of Louis and Katharine Smith Weik, was born in Greencastle, Ind., on Aug. 23, 1857.

He received the A.B. degree from Indiana Asbury (now De Pauw) University in 1875 and the A.M. in 1883. He read law and was admitted to the bar but did not practice.

On Dec. 1, 1890, he married Frances A. Hays, of Portland, Ind.

After his graduation from college Weik spent several years in and around Springfield, Ill., where he began to form the collection of Lincolniana from which much of his writing on Lincoln's life was developed and which eventually became one of the finest collections of Lincoln letters and manuscripts.

Forming a working connection with William H. Herndon, Lincoln's former law partner, he began collecting additional material in the form of interviews with contemporaries in Springfield, in the Indiana Lincoln country and in Kentucky. Their joint work, *Herndon's Lincoln: the True Story of a Great Life*, appeared in 1889 and enjoyed an enormous sale.

Weik served with the U. S. Pension Bureau, 1882-85 and 1891-94, and spent the majority of his remaining years in Greencastle, where he served as president of the local telephone company.

Information from *Who's Who in America* and De Pauw University's *Alumnal Record, 1920*.

* * *

Herndon's Lincoln: the True Story of a Great Life (with William H. Herndon). *Chicago*, 1886-89. 3 vols.
History of the Republican Party. 1908.
History of Putnam County, Indiana. *Indianapolis*, 1910.
The Real Lincoln; a Portrait. *Boston*, 1922.

WEIR, LEBERT HOWARD: 1878–

Born on a farm near Scottsburg, Ind., on Sept. 20, 1878, Lebert Howard Weir attended the country grade schools and graduated from Scottsburg High School. In 1903 he received the A.B. degree from Indiana University. He was a student at Stanford University in 1903 and at the University of Cincinnati in 1907. He also studied in Europe in 1933 and in 1936.

Mr. Weir was a teacher in 1903-04 and served as assistant secretary of the Associated Charities of Cincinnati in 1904-05. From 1905 to 1910 he was chief officer of the Juvenile Court of Cincinnati and Hamilton County, O. From 1910 to 1919 he was associated with the National Recreation Association as field secretary and park and recreation planner.

In addition to his books he was the author of numerous magazine and newspaper articles.

Information from the Scottsburg Public Library.

* * *

A Practical Recreation Manual for Schools (with Stella Walker Durham). *Salem, Ore.,* 1914.

Summary of a Recreation Survey of Minneapolis, Minnesota. *Minneapolis,* 1915.

Survey of Vocational Recreation. 1918.

The Buffalo Recreation Survey. *Buffalo, N. Y.,* 1925.

Recreation Survey of Providence and Environs, Rhode Island. 1936.

Europe at Play; a Study of Recreation and Leisure Time Activities. *New York,* 1937.

Summary of Recreation Survey of Minneapolis. *Minneapolis,* 1944.

WELLS, HELEN WESTON (MRS. OTTO): ?–

Helen Weston Wells, a native of Indiana, was graduated from De Pauw University. She married Otto Wells and resided in Fairmount, Ind.

From about 1907 to the Twenties she contributed short stories of Indiana life of a half century before to various women's magazines, usually under the pseudonym of Forest Blake. She was the author of one published novel.

Information from Ramsey, Lenore P., in the INDIANA MAGAZINE OF HISTORY, March, 1947.

* * *

Saint Joseph. *New York,* 1909.

WELSH, JOSEPH S.: ?–

One of the most interesting among Indiana literary figures is Dr. Joseph S. Welsh, a physician by profession and a teacher by vocation.

Except for the fact that he chose west central Indiana as a place of residence, probably during his early middle life, little biographical information is available. That little was set down by Hiram W. Beckwith, lawyer and amateur historian who lived within a few miles of Dr. Welsh's sphere of activity. Beckwith, writing in 1881, says:

"Few persons in private life, dying, have been mourned by a wider circle of warm and admiring friends than was Dr. Joseph S. Welsh. He died on Coal Creek [Fountain County, Ind.] about the year 1846, having lived there presumably sixteen or eighteen years. It is much to be lamented that more is not known of his early life, his education and training . . . The industry with which he attended to the medical profession did not prevent his giving attention to general literature, and he wrote many poems and prose sketches of merit . . . he published a small volume of poems, entitled *Harp of the West,* which indicates the goings of his mind. Some of them are devotional; some breathe a spirit of high patriotism. The imagery is not always well chosen, and the versification is sometimes faulty, but many of them have high merit in various ways. They are rich in knowledge of Indian, as well as general history. He excelled rather as a prose writer . . . Reading his descriptions of natural scenery, the movement of armies and military engagements, one cannot help thinking what a war correspondent he would have been had he lived during the war of the rebellion . . .

"His conversational powers were even more remarkable . . . As a teacher he had few equals. Youth looked up to him with wonder and admiration while he discoursed to them in a strain too high for their full comprehension, but which held in their hearts and memories, their awakened curiosity, and enlarged understanding, sooner or later made clear. Of himself he wrote: 'My highest ambition is to plant in the bosoms of the rising generation, the youth of our favored land, the great, the good, and ennobling principles of morality, virtue, and patriotism.'

"His life, then, was a magnificent success. Truth regulated all his actions and guided his words."

From Beckwith—*History of Fountain County,* 1881.

* * *

Harp of the West. *Cincinnati,* 1839.

WELTY, CORA GOTTSCHALK (MRS. B. F.): ?–

Cora Gottschalk was born in Berne, Ind., attended the public schools and was graduated from the Indiana State Teachers' College. After teaching for a short time she married B. F. Welty, an attorney of Lima, O., and made her home in that place.

Information from the Berne, Ind., Public Library.

* * *

The Masquerading of Margaret. *Boston, 1908.*

WELTY, MELBA MILDRED: 1890–

Melba Mildred Welty, daughter of Alonzo and Lottie Welty was born at Sharon, Ind. in 1890. She was educated in the public schools of Carroll County and Logansport, Ind., and attended the Terre Haute Normal School. She resides in Young America, Ind.

Information supplied by the Logansport Public Library.

* * *

Memories of Youth. *Logansport, Ind., 1911.*

WENGER, CHRISTIAN M.: 1849–1926.

Christian M. Wenger, son of Martin Light and Christiana Studebaker Wenger, was born at South Bend, Ind., May 24, 1849, and was married to Mary E. Longley Sept. 17, 1872. He died Apr. 25, 1926. His little book, published in 1898, contains his father's memoirs and a wealth of local historical information.

Information from the South Bend Public Library.

* * *

Wenger Memoirs and Autobiography of Martin Light Wenger and His Wife Christiana Studebaker. Together with the Home History and Genealogy of Their Posterity to the Present Time. *South Bend, Ind., 1898.*

WENGER, MARTIN D.: 1841–1901.

Born in Lancaster County, Pa., on Mar. 24, 1841, Martin D. Wenger moved with his parents to Waterloo County, Ont., Canada, in 1856 and later in the same year moved to Elkhart, Ind.

He started to work for the Mennonite Publishing Company in Elkhart in 1867. He was later editor of the HEROLD DER WAHRHEIT and of the German children's paper, DER CHRISTLICHE JUGENDFREUND. Because of ill health he retired from the publishing company in 1881 and moved to his farm south of Elkhart, but in 1900 he returned to town.

Mr. Wenger married Nancy K. Stayrook on Apr. 30, 1876, and died on Sept. 22, 1901.

Information from Goshen College Library.

* * *

History of the Descendants of Christian Wenger . . . (with Jonas G. Wenger and Joseph H. Wenger). *Elkhart, Ind., 1903.*

WHALLON, EDWARD PAYSON: 1849–1939.

Edward Payson Whallon, son of the Rev. Thomas and Harriet Bickle Whallon, was born at Putnamville, Ind., on Mar. 30, 1849.

He was educated at Hanover College and at McCormick Theological Seminary, graduating from the latter in 1872. He received the Ph.D. degree from the University of Wooster in 1885, the D.D. in 1892, and the LL.D. from Hanover College in 1925. He married Margaret E. Kitchell on Nov. 17, 1873.

He was ordained to the Presbyterian ministry in 1871 and occupied pulpits in Indiana, Kentucky and Ohio. He was editor of CHURCH AT WORK, 1886-88, HERALD AND PRESBYTER, 1888-1925, and THE PRESBYTERIAN, from 1925 until shortly before his death in his ninetieth year.

The Rev. Mr. Whallon was active in Masonic Lodge work. During his later years he resided in Wyoming, and in Cincinnati, O.

He died June 3, 1939.

Information from *Who Was Who in America.*

* * *

History of the Presbytery of Vincennes. *Indianapolis, 1888.*

The Foursquare Christian. *Cincinnati, 1905.*

Pastoral Memories. *Cincinnati, 1907.*

Christian College. n.p., n.d.

Some Family Records . . . Partial Histories of the Whallon, Hagaman, Bickle, Bridgeland, Kitchell, Pierson, Ball, Bruen, Crist, Hughes, Vincent, Bloodgood, Jans, Farrand and Tuttle Families. *Cincinnati, 1934.*

WHITAKER, LYDIA: ?–

No information as to the date and place of birth of Lydia Whitaker is available. She received the A.B. degree from Indiana University in 1900 and was for several years a teacher of Latin in the Terre Haute public schools.

Information from the Emmeline Fairbanks Memorial Library, Terre Haute, Ind.

* * *

The Prophet of St. Pierre. *New York,* 1904.
The Prophet of Martinique. *New York,* 1906.

WHITCOMB, JAMES: 1795–1852.

Though he was a colorful figure in Indiana politics and though he had the distinction of a namesake—James Whitcomb Riley, who was to produce in his verse the very quintessence of Hoosierdom—James Whitcomb had little writing published except currently in newspapers and in reprints of political speeches.

A few extracts from the excellent sketch which appears in the *Dictionary of American Biography* give a clear enough picture of his life. According to this account he was the son of

". . . John and Lydia (Parmenter) Whitcomb . . . born in Rochester, Windsor County, Vt. . . . In 1806 the family moved to the neighborhood of Cincinnati, O. James, studious, and a poor farmer, is said to have worked his way through Transylvania University, Lexington, Ky., but there is no record of his attendance. He studied law, and in 1822 was admitted to the bar of Fayette County, Ky. From 1824 to 1836 he practised law at Bloomington, Ind., and from 1826 to 1829 was prosecuting attorney . . . He was elected to the state Senate for the sessions 1830-31 and from 1832 to 1836, standing with the Democratic party as party lines became definitely drawn. In 1836 he was appointed commissioner of the general land office by President Jackson, serving until the end of Van Buren's term, and mastering both French and Spanish for use in his work. In 1841 he established a law office at Terre Haute, Ind., where he soon developed a large and lucrative practise. In the campaign of 1843 he wrote a popular treatise, *Facts for the People,* one of the most effective arguments ever written against a protective tariff. Whitcomb was elected governor . . . and took office in December 1843. In 1846 he was re-elected . . .

"As governor, Whitcomb contributed decisively toward the adjustment of the staggering indebtedness incurred by the state in the building of roads, railroads, and especially canals . . . and in the failure of most of the canal system . . . Whitcomb vigorously promoted popular education and the development of benevo-

lent institutions. The office of superintendent of common schools was created in 1843; a school for the deaf was developed by the state in 1844; a state hospital for the insane was provided for in 1845 and received patients in 1848; and in 1847 the Indiana Institute for the Education of the Blind was created. He was an ardent supporter of the national administration in the War with Mexico . . .

"On Mar. 24, 1846, he married Martha Ann (Renwick) Hurst . . . of Pickaway County, O. Mrs. Whitcomb died the following year after the birth of a daughter . . . In the election of U. S. senator by the General Assembly for the term beginning in March 1849, Whitcomb defeated the incumbent, Edward Allen Hannegan. In failing health . . . he took little part in the Senate proceedings in the critical years 1849-52, and died in New York City, after a surgical operation . . ."

Condensed from C. B. C., *Dictionary of American Biography,* Vol. XX.

* * *

Facts for the People in Relation to a Protective Tariff; Embracing a Brief Review of the Operation of Our Tariff Laws Since the Organization of the Government, Including That of 1842. By an Indianian. *Indianapolis,* 1843.

WHITE, CHARLES: 1795–1861.

Charles White, president of Wabash College from 1841 to 1861, was born in New England on Dec. 28, 1795, and graduated from Dartmouth College in 1821. He studied theology at Andover. On Mar. 8, 1825, he married Martha Carter.

From 1834 to 1841 he served as pastor in Oswego, N. Y., and in 1841 was called to the presidency of Wabash College in Crawfordsville, Ind. He was president of the college until his death on Oct. 29, 1861, at Crawfordsville.

Information from Gronert and Osborne—*Wabash College: The First Hundred Years* and *Appletons' Cyclopaedia of American Biography,* Vol. VI.

* * *

An Address, at His Inauguration as President of Wabash College. *Indianapolis,* 1842.
The Duties of Educated Young Men of the West . . . July 20, 1842. *Indianapolis,* 1842.
Independence of Mind: a Baccalaureate Address . . . July 19, 1843. *Indianapolis,* 1843.
Goodness an Essential Element of True Greatness; a Baccalaureate Address July 17, 1844. *Indianapolis,* 1844.

A Pure and Sound Literature: a Baccalaureate Address . . . July 22, 1845. *Indianapolis, 1845.*

Political Rectitude; a Baccalaureate Address July 23, 1846. *New York, 1846.*

Discourse Delivered at the Interment of the Remains of Tilghman Ashurst Howard, at Rockville, Ind., June 2, 1847. *Indianapolis, 1848.*

Contributions of Intellect to Religion; a Baccalaureate Address, July 20, 1848. *New York, 1849.*

Essays in Literature and Ethics. *Boston, 1853.*

WHITE, ESTHER GRIFFIN: ?–

Esther Griffin White, Richmond, Ind., newspaper woman, critic, poet and feature writer, was educated in the Richmond schools and attended Earlham College from 1887 to 1892. She was at various times connected with the RICHMOND PALLADIUM, SUN-TELEGRAM, EVENING ITEM and MORNING NEWS.

Information from the Richmond Public Library.

* * *

Indiana Bookplates. *Richmond, Ind.,* 1910.

Things as They Sometimes Are. *Richmond, Ind.,* 1912.

In the Orchestra. n.p. [*Richmond, Ind.*], 1915.

In the Garden. *Richmond, Ind.,* 1936.

Poems About Richmond. *Richmond, Ind.,* 1937.

Passion's Jewels. *Centerville, Ind.,* 1939.

Sonnets of the Senses. *Centerville, Ind.,* 1939.

WHITE, GEORGE WASHINGTON: 1858–1940.

George Washington White, son of David Wesley and Lydia Emmeline Taylor White, was born at Valparaiso, Ind., on Feb. 18, 1858, and graduated from Cornell College in Iowa in 1883, receiving the A.M. degree in 1886 and the D.D. in 1896. In 1930 he was awarded an LL.D. degree by the University of Southern California. He married Celia Villette Hutchins on Jan. 24, 1885.

Entering the Methodist Episcopal ministry in 1877, he was a pastor in Iowa until 1883, when he spent a year as business agent for Cornell College and then became a pastor in southern California. From 1892 to 1895 he was superintendent of the Los Angeles District of the Methodist Episcopal Church, from 1895 to 1899 president of the University of Southern California. From 1903 to 1916 he was a pastor in San Francisco and Oakland, Calif., and from 1916 until his retirement in 1924 superintendent of the San Francisco District.

He died on Dec. 1, 1940.

Information from *Who Was Who in America.*

* * *

The Historic Christ. 1910.

WHITSON, JOHN HARVEY: 1854–1936.

John Harvey Whitson, son of Aaron F. and Tacy McNamee Whitson, was born in Seymour, Ind., on Dec. 28, 1854.

Admitted to the Indiana bar in 1876, he practiced law at Seymour until 1897. In 1897 he formed connections with eastern publishing houses and writing under the pen name of "Lieut. A. K. Sims" he turned out a great many books of the dime novel stamp. He was ordained to the Baptist ministry in 1898.

From 1920 to 1923 he taught Biblical history and literature at Ward-Belmont College in Nashville, Tenn., and he was at one time head of the department of religious education at Hardin College in Mexico, Mo.

He married Flora Josselyn in 1900 and died on May 2, 1936.

Information from *Who Was Who in America* and Burke and Howe—*American Authors and Books.*

* * *

Captain Cactus. 1888.

Huckleberry, the Foot Hills Detective. 1888.

Signal Sam. 1890.

The Rival Rustlers. 1891.

The Doctor Detective in Texas. 1893.

The King-Pin of the Leadville Lions. 1894.

The Young Ditch Rider. *Elgin, Ill.,* 1899.

With Frémont the Pathfinder; or, Winning the Empire of Gold, *Boston, 1903.*

Barbara—a Woman of the West. *Boston, 1903.*

A Courier of Empire. *Boston, 1904.*

The Rainbow Chasers. *Boston, 1904.*

Campaigning with Tippecanoe. *New York, 1904.*

Justin Wingate, Ranchman. *Boston, 1905.*

The Castle of Doubt. *Boston, 1907.*

Filibusters. 1910.

The Edgewood Enigma. 1912.

Wings of Mars. 1914.

Mystery at Greenacres. 1916.

The Castle Empire.

WHITSON, ROLLAND LEWIS: 1860–1928.

Rolland Lewis Whitson, son of David M. V. L. and Verlinda Jay Whitson, was born at Jonesboro,

Ind., on May 7, 1860. He lived in Marion, Ind., where he did some occasional journalistic work.

At the time of his death he had worked for seven years on a history of the Quaker settlement in Grant County. This history was to have been completed by a Friends minister, but Whitson's notes were burned along with other discarded possessions after his death on Oct. 26, 1928.

Information from the Marion Public Library.

* * *

Rolinda, a Tale of the Mississinewa. *Columbus, O.*

WHITTEN, ROBERT HARVEY: 1873–1936.

Robert Harvey Whitten, son of William M. and Margaret Milliken Whitten, was born in South Bend, Ind., on Oct. 9, 1873, and graduated from the University of Michigan in 1896, receiving the Ph.D. degree from Columbia University in 1898. On Dec. 6, 1900, he married Elizabeth Gilbert.

From 1898 to 1907 he was reference librarian and editor of the YEARBOOK OF LEGISLATION for the New York State Library, from 1907 to 1914 he was with the New York State Public Service Commission, and from 1914 to 1917 he was secretary of the committee on the city plan and zoning commission of New York. He then spent three years as consultant for the City Plan Commission of Cleveland, O., six years with the Boston City Planning Board, and after 1934 was a consultant for the National Resources Committee and the New York State Planning Board.

He died on June 6, 1936.

Information from *Who Was Who in America.*

* * *

Public Administration in Massachusetts; the Relation of Central to Local Activity. *New York, 1898.*

Trend of Legislation in the United States. *Albany, N. Y., 1900.*

Taxation of Corporations in New York, Massachusetts, Pennsylvania and New Jersey. *Albany, N. Y., 1901.*

Political and Municipal Legislation, 1899-1903. *Philadelphia.*

Designing a Complete System of City Thoroughfares. *New York.*

Economic Utilization of Land in City Building. *New York.*

Valuation of Public Service Corporations; Legal and Economic Phases of Valuation for Rate Making and Public Purchase. *New York, 1912.*

Regulation of Public Service Companies in Great Britain, with Supplemental Chapters on the Boston Sliding

Scale and Toronto Auction Sale and Maximum Dividend Plans. *New York, 1914.*

The Cleveland Thoroughfare Plan. 1920.

Atlanta Zone Plan. *Atlanta, 1922.*

Regional Zoning. 1923.

Providence Zone Plan; Report Outlining a Tentative Zone Plan for Providence, R. I. *Providence, 1923.*

Cranston Zone Plan; Report to the Ordinance Committee of the City Council Outlining a Tentative Zone Plan for Cranston, R. I. (with C. F. Fisher). *Cleveland, O., 1923.*

Woonsocket Zone Plan; Report to the City Zoning Commission Outlining a Tentative Zone Plan for Woonsocket, R. I. *Woonsocket, R. I., 1923.*

West Hartford Zoning; Report to the Zoning Commission on the Zoning of West Hartford, Connecticut. *West Hartford, Conn., 1924.*

Providence Thorofare Plan. 1926.

Research into the Economics of Land Subdivision; with Particular Reference to a Complete Neighborhood Unit for Low or Medium Cost Housing. *New York, 1927.*

Boston Thorofare Plan. 1930.

Neighborhoods of Small Homes; Economic Density of Low-Cost Housing in America and England (with Thomas Adams). *Cambridge, Mass., 1931.*

Model Laws for Planning Cities, Counties, and States (with others). *Cambridge, Mass., 1935.*

WILE, FREDERIC WILLIAM: 1873–1941.

Frederic William Wile, author, newspaper columnist and editorial writer, was born in LaPorte, Ind., Nov. 30, 1873. His parents were Jacob and Henrietta Guggenheim Wile.

As a young man Wile attended the University of Notre Dame, receiving the LL.D. from that institution in 1924 and the same from Ursinus in 1929. He married Ada Shakman on May 14, 1901.

Wile acted as correspondent for the CHICAGO RECORD and the CHICAGO DAILY NEWS in London and Berlin during the Boer War and as Berlin correspondent for the LONDON DAILY MAIL, NEW YORK TIMES and CHICAGO TRIBUNE from 1906 to 1914. During the first World War he was attached to the Intelligence Section, G.H.Q., A.E.F.

In 1919 he became chief of the Washington bureau of the Philadelphia PUBLIC LEDGER and later an editorial staff writer for the WASHINGTON EVENING STAR. From 1923 to 1928 he was political analyst for the National Broadcasting Company, and he occupied the same position for the Columbia Broadcasting System from 1929 to 1938. He was the first radio commentator on transatlantic news events, broadcasting from the London Naval Conference in 1930 and the World Disarmament Conference at Geneva in 1932. Frederic William Wile died Apr. 7, 1941.

Information from *Who Was Who in America*.

* * *

Our German Cousins. 1909.

Men Around the Kaiser; the Makers of Modern Germany. *London,* 1913.

The Assault; Germany before the Outbreak and England in War-Time; a Personal Narrative. *Indianapolis,* 1916.

Who's Who in Hunland. *London,* 1916.

Explaining the Britishers; the Story of England's Mighty Effort in Liberty's Cause as Seen by an American. *New York,* 1919.

Emile Berliner, Maker of the Microphone. *Indianapolis,* 1926.

News Is Where You Find It; Forty Years' Reporting at Home and Abroad. *Indianapolis,* 1939.

WILEY, HARVEY WASHINGTON: 1844–1930.

Dr. Harvey W. Wiley, through his research, writing, speaking and fighting of all comers, succeeded, well-nigh single handed, in arousing the consciousness of the American public to the dangers of impure and adulterated foods and in securing the passage of the national Food and Drugs Act.

The *Dictionary of American Biography* says of him, in part, that he was born Oct. 18, 1844

". . . in a log cabin at Kent, Jefferson County, Ind., the sixth of the seven children of Preston Pritchard and Lucinda Weir (Maxwell) Wiley, both descendants of Scotch-Irish pioneers who had fought in the Revolution. Young Wiley had his early training in a log schoolhouse, in neighboring district schools, and in his home. In 1863 he entered Hanover College (A.B., 1867). His studies were interrupted in 1864 by the Civil War, in which he served as corporal with the 137th Indiana Volunteers. After teaching for a year (1868), he entered the Medical College of Indiana in Indianapolis, from which he was graduated with the degree of M.D. in 1871. Coincident with his medical studies he taught Greek and Latin at Northwestern Christian University (later Butler College). He received the degree of B.S. at Harvard in 1873, and returned to Indianapolis to assume professorships of chemistry at Butler and the Medical College of Indiana. After a temporary breakdown that obliged him to discontinue all work, he became professor of chemistry at Purdue University, Lafayette, Ind. (1874-83), serving also as state chemist of Indiana. He spent a year

in Germany (1878), largely at the University of Berlin in the study of chemistry . . . His studies of food adulteration, begun under Sell of the German Imperial Health Office, he energetically continued after his return to Purdue.

"In 1883 he accepted an appointment as chief chemist of the United States Department of Agriculture and remained in this position until 1912. This was a period of active productivity along three principal lines. The first was a chemical study of the sugar and sirup crops of the United States, in which he performed technological work upon the application of diffusion to the extraction of sugar from sugar cane . . . The second was his work in agricultural chemical analysis, for which he devised many new pieces of apparatus and originated many new methods of procedure. The third, his greatest achievement, was his public service in the campaign against food adulteration. The analyses of American food products, which he began immediately after his appointment as chemist of the Department of Agriculture, revealed a shocking state of adulteration, and Wiley gave the rest of his life to correcting this evil. In the face of prolonged opposition he finally secured in 1906 the passage by Congress of the Food and Drugs Act. Confronted with an even more determined resistance, he then began the administration of this Act under difficulties that would have discouraged a less resolute reformer. When he investigated the effect of benzoate of soda and other food preservatives upon the health of his assistants (his famous 'Poison Squad'), his damaging reports aroused so much criticism that President Theodore Roosevelt appointed the Remsen Referee Board to reconsider the question. Although the conclusions of the board differed from Wiley's, public sentiment generally was upon his side, and the use of food preservatives has in consequence diminished.

"In Mar. 1912, after having completely vindicated himself against unjust charges of maladministration, Wiley resigned his office as chief of the bureau of chemistry. In his twenty-nine years of service he built up an organization from six to more than five hundred employees. During this period he originated many lines of chemical research in such fields as soils, milk products, road construction, and standardization of apparatus that afterwards led to the establishment of separate bureaus. Until 1914 he continued to hold the position of professor of agricultural chemistry at George Washington University which he had assumed in 1899. He devoted the rest of his life to writing and lecturing in the interest of pure food. He accepted a position (1912-30) as director of the bureau of foods, sanitation, and health of the GOOD HOUSEKEEPING magazine, for which he wrote monthly articles and conducted a question box . . .

"Wiley had great natural gifts as a wit, poet, and public speaker. His commanding presence, unfailing humor, and courageous expression of opinion held the attention of every audience. His public services won for him many degrees, medals, decorations, and honorary memberships in societies both at home and abroad . . . On Feb. 27, 1911, he married Anna Campbell Kelton, by whom he had two sons. His activity in promoting the cause of pure food continued almost to the day of his death, which occurred in Washington. He was buried in Arlington Cemetery . . ."

His scores of government bulletins and scientific papers are not listed here.

Condensed from C. A. B., *Dictionary of American Biography*, Vol. XX.

* * *

Songs of an Agricultural Chemist. 1892.

Principles and Practice of Agricultural Analysis. *Easton, Pa.,* 1894-1897. 3 vols.

Foods and Their Adulteration. *Philadelphia,* 1907.

1001 Tests of Foods, Beverages and Toilet Accessories, Good and Otherwise; Why They Are So. *New York,* 1914.

Not by Bread Alone: the Principles of Human Nutrition. *New York,* 1915.

The Lure of the Land; Farming After Fifty. *New York,* 1915.

Health Reader; Physiology—Hygiene. *Chicago,* 1916.

Beverages and Their Adulteration; Origin, Composition, Manufacture, Natural, Artificial, Fermented, Distilled, Alkaloidal and Fruit Juices. *Philadelphia,* 1919.

History of a Crime Against the Food Law; the Amazing Story of the National Food and Drugs Law Intended to Protect the Health of the People, Perverted to Protect Adulteration of Foods and Drugs. *Washington, D. C.,* 1929.

Harvey W. Wiley—an Autobiography. *Indianapolis,* 1930.

WILLIAMS, IRVING: 1873–

Irving Williams, son of Dr. Thomas George and Adella Coe Williams, was born in Watertown, Wis., Aug. 4, 1873. He was educated at the Indianapolis High School and at Purdue University and, after a brief time spent in the lumber business, settled in Indianapolis in 1897, where he was associated with an insurance journal, ROUGH NOTES, of which he became editor and vice-president.

Information from *Who's Who in America* and the Indianapolis Public Library.

* * *

Insurance Definitions. A Serio-Comic Dictionary of Insurance Terms. *Indianapolis,* 1903.

Mistah Robinson's Remembery Book. *Indianapolis,* 1913.

Big Wallace. *New York,* 1914.

Joe Manning. *New York,* 1915.

Bruce Wright. *New York,* 1916.

Insurance Policy and Forms Analyses Service. *Indianapolis,* 1929-33.

Insurance Coverages Applicable to Over 400 Specific Risks. *Indianapolis,* n.d.

WILLIAMS, OSCAR HARRISON: 1874–

Oscar Harrison Williams was born at Fairfield, Ind., in 1874 and attended Indiana University, receiving the A.B. degree in 1905. During his career as an educator he served as school principal in various Indiana towns, was with the State Board of Public Instruction (1917-24), and served on the faculties of Indiana, DePauw, Illinois and Ohio Universities, and Kent College. In 1940 he retired as dean of the college of liberal arts at Kent College and returned to his home in Bloomington, Ind.

Information supplied by the Indiana State Library.

* * *

History of Indiana. *Boston,* 1916.

Syllabus of European History. *New York,* 1918.

WILLIAMS, WILBUR HERSCHEL: 1874–1935.

Born in North Manchester, Ind., in 1874, Wilbur Herschel Williams, son of John Wesley and Elizabeth Kohser Williams, was a student at Northwestern University and at Denver University.

He began his newspaper career as a reporter on the DENVER POST, was with the DETROIT FREE PRESS from 1898 to 1902, and became literary editor on the staff of the DETROIT JOURNAL in 1903, a position he resigned to write the story of the St. Louis Fair for Laird and Lee, Chicago publishers. In 1911 he was employed by Atkinson, Mentzer and Grover, publishers, New York, and from 1911 until 1916 he was northeastern manager for the Prang Company, Boston. After 1916 he engaged in syndicate work.

He died on Sept. 15, 1935.

Information from *Who Was Who in America.*

* * *

Uncle Bob and Aunt Becky's Strange Adventures at the World's Great Exposition. *Chicago,* 1904.

Fairy Tales from Folklore. *New York,* 1908.

My Chums in Caricature. *Chicago, 1909.*

Uncle Bob and Aunt Becky's Exciting Trip and the Strange Romance of Tom and Ruth. *Chicago, 1909.*

Making Faces: a Study in Facial Expressions. *Chicago, 1910.*

My Advice Book. *Chicago, 1910.*

Young People's Story of Massachusetts. *New York, 1916.*

The Merrymakers in New York. *Boston, 1919.*

The Merrymakers in Chicago. *Boston, 1920.*

The Jolly Old Whistle and Other Tales. *New York, 1927.*

Children of the Clouds; a Phantasy and Play for Boys and Girls of All Ages. *New York, 1929.*

The Traveling Tingles. *Boston, 1931.*

WILLIAMS, WILLIAM: 1763–1824.

William Williams, distinguished minister of the Society of Friends in Indiana, was born in Chatham County, N. C., on Oct. 7, 1763. He was educated by his mother, his father having died in his early youth, and was apprenticed to a Friend who, he says, strengthened his feeling for the church.

He married Rachel Kemp on Mar. 16, 1786, and they settled in Tennessee. He joined the Lost Creek Quarterly Meeting and became a minister about 1799 or 1800. In 1804 he toured Georgia, North Carolina, and South Carolina, and in 1807 he made a tour of Ohio. In 1808 he removed to Blount County, O., where he helped to organize a new congregation.

In 1814 he removed to the White Water Valley, in eastern Indiana, and remained there as a minister until his death on Aug. 25, 1824.

His one book is important as a description of the life of the day in what are now the middle southern and middle western states. It is considered by collectors to be an item of considerable importance.

> Information from Williams, William—*Journal of the Life, Travels, and Gospel Labours, of William Williams . . .*

* * *

Journal of the Life, Travels, and Gospel Labours, of William Williams, Dec. A Minister of the Society of Friends Late of White-Water, Indiana. *Cincinnati, 1828.*

WILLSON, BYRON FORCEYTHE: 1837–1867.

Forceythe Willson was born at Little Genesee, Allegany County, N. Y., on Apr. 10, 1837. His father, Hiram Willson, was a native of Vermont, a patron of liberal education and an early abolitionist. His mother was Ann Calvin Ennis, who had been born in Rhode Island.

In about 1846 the family started west, flatboating to Maysville, Ky., where they remained about a year before moving on to Covington, Ky. Forceythe Willson had his first formal schooling in Maysville, continuing in Covington. In 1852 the family again moved, this time to New Albany, Ind.

Here Hiram Willson conducted a prosperous lumber business until his death in 1859, three years after his wife had passed away. Although he left eight children, of whom Forceythe was the eldest, there was property enough to render them all comfortable.

Young Forceythe had already spent a year at Antioch College in Ohio, which was then under the direction of Horace Mann. He continued for a year or two at Harvard, but left because of ill health and returned to New Albany.

He became interested in spiritualism when that belief enjoyed a vogue in New Albany around 1858. He soon left the company of the more avid followers of the sect but continued in his faith in his own psychic powers—of which he gave a demonstration to Lowell, Longfellow and James R. Gilmore during his later resident at Cambridge.

After his father's death he lived alone—apparently in a house apart from his younger brothers and sisters—and began his serious writing. When the Civil War began, he took somewhat more interest in it than might have been anticipated after his recent apparent renunciation of things worldly. He began to write editorials for the LOUISVILLE JOURNAL, and raised (and, according to tradition, equipped at his own expense) a company of Union volunteers. He did not serve in the war himself, although he was said to have been offered a commission.

His first poem to attract attention, "The Old Sergeant," was published anonymously as the "carrier's New Year's address" of the LOUISVILLE JOURNAL on Jan. 1, 1863. It was supposed to have been based on fact, one of the characters being a New Albany man. It was said to have appealed to Abraham Lincoln: certainly Oliver Wendell Holmes approved it, read it frequently in his wartime lectures, and made continued efforts to locate the author.

In 1863 Willson married Elizabeth Conwell Smith of Laurel, Ind., a twenty-one-year-old student in De Pauw College for Women at New Albany, and the two moved to Cambridge, Mass., purchasing a house near that of James Russell Lowell. Elizabeth Willson died the next year, leaving a few poems of her own which her husband printed privately a year or two later.

Willson remained in Cambridge until 1866, but he made no effort to become acquainted with Lowell, Holmes, or the other New England literateurs who were his neighbors. Before he left, however, they found him out, and after his death Holmes wrote of him: "He came amongst us as softly and silently as a bird drops into his nest. His striking personal appearance had attracted the attention of the scholars and poets who were his neighbors, long before they heard his name or condition. It was impossible to pass without noticing the tall and dark young man with long curled locks, and large, dreamy, almond-shaped eyes . . ."

In the autumn of 1866 he suffered a recurrence of his old illness—evidently tuberculosis. He recovered somewhat for a few weeks but died in Alfred, N. Y., on Feb. 2, 1867, and was buried beside his wife at Laurel, Ind.

> Information from Piatt, John James—"An Ohio Valley Poet" in *The Hesperian Tree*, 1900, and Nicholson—*The Hoosiers*.

* * *

The Old Sergeant and Other Poems. *Boston, 1867.*

WILLSON, ELIZABETH CONWELL SMITH (MRS. BYRON FORCEYTHE): 1842–1864.

Elizabeth Conwell Smith was born at Laurel, Ind., on June 26, 1842. She attended De Pauw College for Women in New Albany, where she met and married Byron Forceythe Willson in the fall of 1863.

The young couple removed to Cambridge, Mass., soon after their marriage, where they made a home for themselves and for Willson's brother, then a student in Harvard College.

Mrs. Willson died in Cambridge on Oct. 13, 1864, only a year after her marriage. She was buried at Laurel, Ind. After her death her husband gathered together a few of her poems and published them privately.

> Information from Piatt, John James—"An Ohio Valley Poet" in *The Hesperian Tree*, 1900.

* * *

Poems. *Cambridge, 1866.*

WILSON, ALMA WINSTON: 1855–1932.

Alma W. Wilson was born in New Albany, Ind., Mar. 6, 1855, and was brought to Indianapolis as a baby. She taught in the schools and became librarian of one of the first branch libraries of the city and later became an assistant at the Central Library. For many years she was state historian of the Philip Schoff chapter of the Daughters of 1812. She died in 1932.

> Information from Indianapolis Public Library.

* * *

Beside the Old Brass Andirons; Sketch of the Life of Mrs. Mary Barbee Wilson. *Indianapolis, 1906.*

WILSON, GEORGE ROBERT: 1863–1941.

George Robert Wilson, son of Michael and Elizabeth Chilton Wilson, was born at Cannelton, Ind., on Aug. 15, 1863. Both of his parents were English. In 1868 the family moved to Dubois County, Ind., where George grew up and spent many years of his life.

When he was eleven years old, he went to work in the coal mines near Jasper, Ind., working there for four years and studying at home in his leisure time. He then taught school for nine years—during the last two serving as principal of the high school at Ireland, Ind.—and at the same time took a course in civil engineering and held the position of Dubois County surveyor. In 1889 he became superintendent of schools for Dubois County and reorganized the school system. He resigned in 1903 to become Indiana manager of the State Life Insurance Company of Indianapolis.

Mr. Wilson held the degree of bachelor of law but never practiced. He helped reorganize the Indiana Association of Life Underwriters and served as its president. He also served on many state boards. He was considered an authority on pioneer surveys in Indiana.

In 1893 he married Caroline L. Kuebler.

> Information from *Indiana and Indianans*, Vol. III.

* * *

History and Art Souvenir of Dubois County. *Jasper, Ind., 1896.*

Titles, Deeds and Surveys. *Indianapolis, 1897.*

Battlefields in Time of Peace. *Indianapolis, 1897.*

History of Dubois County from Its Primitive Days to 1910; Including Biographies of Capt. Toussaint Dubois and the Very Rev. Joseph Kundeck. *Jasper, Ind., 1910.*

Observations. *1914.*

Dubois County Settlement Stone. *[Indianapolis], 1919.*

The Buffalo Trail Marker. *1926.*

The Buffalo Trace (with Gayle Thornbrough). *Indianapolis, 1946.*

Handbook of the Dubois County Schools.

George H. Proffit, His Day and Generation. n.p., n.d.

WILSON, LILLIAN PAMPELL (MRS. J. WOOD): ?–

Lillian Pampell, at one time a teacher in the public schools of Wabash, Ind., was married to J. Wood Wilson, a financier of Marion, Ind. She was a resident of Marion at the time of publication of her collection of one-act plays. Following the death of her husband she was married to Dr. John Vaughan, surgeon and explorer. Subsequently they moved to New York, where Dr. Vaughan died.

Information from the Marion Public Library.

* * *

Fruit of Toil and Other One-Act Plays. *Indianapolis,* 1916.

WILSON, WOOD LEVETTE: 1865–1945.

Born in Indianapolis on Aug. 20, 1865, Wood Levette Wilson was an Indianapolis journalist all of his life. He was with the Associated Press until 1892, when he became copy editor (the first in Indianapolis) for the INDIANAPOLIS NEWS. He was later an associate editor of the NEWS, until his retirement in 1938. He married Belle Closser.

Mr. Wilson was a regular contributor to PUCK, JUDGE, and the original LIFE. Hilton U. Brown, of the INDIANAPOLIS NEWS, writes that he "was a humorist of fine quality, retiring in personality, a naturalist and gardener and an accurate scholar." Mr. Wilson died on Apr. 23, 1945.

Information from Hilton U. Brown, of the INDIANAPOLIS NEWS.

* * *

The End of Dreams. *New York,* 1909.

WILSTACH, JOHN AUGUSTINE: 1824–1897.

Born in Washington, D. C., on July 14, 1824, John Augustine Wilstach moved to Lafayette, Ind., in 1842. He was educated in a military institute and at Cincinnati College, studied law, and was admitted to the bar in 1850.

From 1852 to 1862 he was a master in chancery, in 1867 he acted as commissioner for Indiana at the Paris Exposition, and from 1870 to 1875 he was commis-

sioner of immigration for Indiana. During his later years he studied philology, lectured, and wrote on literature and history.

He married Elbra Cecilia Patti.

He died at Lafayette on July 24, 1897.

Information from Houghton Mifflin Company— *A Catalogue of Authors,* 1899, and *Appletons' Cyclopaedia of American Biography,* Vol. VI.

* * *

The Imperial Period of National Greatness. A Lecture on the Destiny of the West. *Lafayette, Ind.,* 1855.

Cities, States, Nations and Their Relations. *Lafayette, Ind.,* 1876.

The Virgilians. 1884.

Dante, the Danteans, and Things Dantean. 1889.

The Battle Forest, a Poem. *New York,* 1890.

The Angel and the King, and Other Poems. 1893.

WILSTACH, JOSEPH WALTER: 1857–

Joseph Walter Wilstach, son of John Augustine and Elbra Cecilia Patti Wilstach, was born in Lafayette, Ind., on June 28, 1857, and was educated at St. John's College in Fordham, N. Y. He studied law and practiced in Lafayette.

Information from de Hart—*Past and Present of Tippecanoe County, Indiana.*

* * *

Montalembert: a Biographical Sketch. *New York,* 1885.

WILSTACH, PAUL: 1870–

Paul Wilstach, son of John Augustine and Elbra Cecilia Patti Wilstach, was born in Lafayette, Ind., on July 1, 1870, and graduated from St. Viator's College in Illinois in 1889.

During the first World War he served as a lieutenant commander in the U. S. Naval Reserve, going on the inactive list in April of 1919.

He was a contributor to SCRIBNER'S, NATIONAL GEOGRAPHIC, and ATLANTIC magazines and to the *Dictionary of American Biography.* His plays, most of which, while produced, were not published, are not all listed here.

Information from *Who's Who in America.*

* * *

Richard Mansfield, the Man and the Actor. *New York,* 1908.

Thais: the Story of a Sinner Who Became a Saint and a Saint Who Sinned: a Play in Four Acts, Founded on Anatole France's Novel. *Indianapolis*, 1911.

Fifty Games of Solitaire with Cards. *Indianapolis*, 1891.

Mount Vernon, Washington's Home and the Nation's Shrine. *Garden City, N. Y.*, 1916.

Potomac Landings. *Garden City, N. Y.*, 1921.

Along the Pyrenees. *Indianapolis*, 1925.

Jefferson and Monticello. *Garden City, N. Y.*, 1925.

Islands of the Mediterranean; a Holiday. *Indianapolis*, 1926.

Along the Mediterranean. 1926.

Patriots Off Their Pedestals. *Indianapolis*, 1927.

An Italian Holiday. *New York*, 1928.

Tidewater Virginia. *Indianapolis*, 1929.

Tidewater Maryland. *Indianapolis*, 1931.

Hudson River Landings. *Indianapolis*, 1933.

WINGER, OTHO: 1877–1946.

Son of John M. and Mary Smith Winger, Otho Winger was born near Marion, Ind., on Oct. 23, 1877.

A member of the Church of the Brethren—whose intelligent friendship for the American Indian has been a tradition for generations—it was natural that young Winger should conceive a liking for, and an interest in, the remnant of the Indiana Miamis who lived in his neighborhood while he was still a youth.

Young Winger attended the county schools and took his college preparatory work in the Academy of Manchester College. He received his A.B. degree from Indiana University in 1905 and his M.A. degree from the same institution in 1907. In 1918 he received the LL.D. degree from Mount Morris College.

After acting as teacher and administrator of various Indiana schools he returned to Manchester College as professor of history and philosophy in 1907 and became president of that institution in 1911, serving in that capacity until his retirement in 1941. He died Aug. 13, 1946.

Information from Manchester College.

* * *

The Life of Elder R. H. Miller. *Elgin, Ill.*, 1910.

History of the Church of the Brethren in Indiana. *Elgin, Ill.*, 1917.

History and Doctrines of the Church of the Brethren. *Elgin, Ill.*, 1919.

Letters from Foreign Lands to the Home Folks. *Elgin, Ill.*, 1928.

The Frances Slocum Trail. *North Manchester, Ind.*, 1933.

The Ke Na Po Co Mo Co; Eel River, the Home of Little Turtle. *North Manchester, Ind.*, 1934.

The Last of the Miamis; Me-Shin-Co-Me-Sia, the Last Tribal Chief of the Miamis. *North Manchester, Ind.*, 1935.

Brief Centennial History of Wabash County, 1835-1935. *North Manchester, Ind.*, 1935.

The Lost Sister Among the Miamis. *Elgin, Ill.*, 1936.

A Pioneer Experiment in Teaching Agriculture. *North Manchester, Ind.*, 1939.

The Potawatomi Indians. *Elgin, Ill.*, 1939.

Memories of Manchester. *Elgin, Ill.*, 1940.

Little Turtle, the Great Chief of Eel River. *North Manchester, Ind.*, 1942.

WINTER, WILLIAM HENRY: 1819–1879.

The following sketch of William Henry Winter was prepared by his youngest son, De Winter, in 1937. Mr. De Winter's manuscript, insofar as the biographical section is concerned, is given as it was written except for the addition of correct information as to his father's college course which has been taken from the Wabash College archives. William Henry Winter's book, written with Overton Johnson, commands the highest price from collectors of any Indiana production. Further information regarding it will be found in the sketch of Overton Johnson.

"William Henry Winter was born in 1819 in Vigo County, Ind. His father, William Winter, is supposed to have been born in Virginia, his mother in Massachusetts. Her maiden name was Arnold. William Winter was her second husband. One of the daughters by her first marriage married Maj. Elston of Crawfordsville. A daughter of Maria Elston married Senator Henry S. Lane; another married Gen. Lew Wallace, author of *Ben-Hur*. William Winter died in early middle life, and his widow married a man named Crawford, after whom Crawfordsville was named. [This is incorrect: Crawfordsville had been named many years before and for a Secretary of the Treasury, who made Government Land Office appointments]. W. H. Winter was brought up in and around that town. In 1834 he enrolled in the preparatory department of Wabash College, Crawfordsville, and continued through 1835-36. He was enrolled there again in 1839-40.

"In 1843 Winter joined an expedition to the Pacific coast. It started from Independence, Mo., went up the Platte River, by Fort Laramie, on to Fort Hall, Id., and into Oregon. At Willamette Falls, the company divided, one party remaining in Oregon, the other going down into California. Winter was with the California party. In May 1844, his party left Sutter's Fort, crossed Nevada into Idaho, and joined the Oregon party at Soda Springs. There Winter turned over to Overton Johnson the notes he had made on the entire route and on the scenery and resources of Oregon and California. Johnson took them back to Indiana and published a book there, based on the notes, which gave a full description of the expedition. The book was published in 1846. This book is very rare and a valuable item of Californiana.

"How W. H. Winter spent the first year or so after he left the company is not certain. Probably he explored the Sacramento and San Joaquin Valleys more fully than he had before. In the winter of 1845-46 he was employed as a carpenter at the rancho of Gen. Vallejo in Sonora. He must have helped erect some of the old buildings now there. He left Sonora shortly before the Bear Flag Incident, and went to Sutter's Fort.

"In July, 1846, he left Sutter's Fort on muleback to return to Indiana. He rode south into Sonora, Mexico, and across to Vera Cruz on the Gulf, about 2,000 miles. He went by boat to New Orleans and up the Mississippi and Ohio Rivers to his home. He had been away a year and a half. [An obvious error].

"In April, 1849, he left St. Joseph, Mo., as captain of a company bound for the California mines. They came into California by the Yuba pass. He and James A. Kleiser ran a store on the Mokelumne River, three miles above the Mexican camp of Rancha Plana. Their camp was called Winter's Bar. Late in the fall of 1850 he and Kleiser left Winter's Bar, took their gold dust to San Francisco and boarded a steamer for Panama. They crossed the Isthmus, went by boat to New Orleans, sold their gold dust at the mint, and went up the river home. They had been away nearly two years.

"Sometime early in 1851, Capt. Winter married Sarah Armstrong, of Waveland, Ind. The first of their six sons, Isaac Henry Winter, was born during the first year of their marriage. Capt. Winter engaged in cattle-raising a year or so, then sold out, headed a company, and for the third time started west. His second son, William Nebraska Winter, was born near the Platte River, in an ox-wagon. They had some trouble with the Indians, but no fighting. In California Capt. Winter first tried western Colusa County, then Lake County, then Sonoma County, and finally settled in 1856 in Huichica Creek, half-way between Sonoma and Napa. There he bought 1280 acres of land, part of the grant made by Gov. Alvarado in 1836 to Salvador Vallejo, brother of Gen. Vallejo.

"Capt. Winter made money fast on the Huichica in stock, grapes, and grain, and built a good house, a dairy, a wine-cellar, and a distillery. In company with A. J. Cook he had a stock ranch on the Eel River. He also bought a wheat ranch of 1480 acres at Crow's Landing on the San Joaquin River. He drove large bands of stock into Nevada for pasturage on the Humboldt River. On a similar drive to Idaho in 1872, he and Cook saw Fall River in Shasta County, and bought the land around the falls at the confluence with Pit River. From this time, Capt. Winter's energies were given mainly to the Fall River project. He bought out Cook, he bought more land, built a flour mill, a saw mill, a planing mill, and practically made the town of Fall River Mills. In 1875 he moved his family from the Huichica Ranch to Fall River. He built a house on an island in the rapids where Fall and Pit River met and made it his home. His wife died there in July, 1879, and he was buried beside her less than six weeks later."

De Winter ms. in the Wabash College Archives.

* * *

Route Across the Rocky Mountains, with a Description of Oregon and California; Geographical Features. Their Resources, Soil, Climate, Productions, Etc., Etc. *Lafayette, Ind.,* 1846.

WISHARD, JOHN G.: 1863–1940.

Son of John O. and Mary Fisher Wishard, John G. Wishard was born in Danville, Ind., Sept. 19, 1863. He was graduated from Central Normal (now Canterbury) College in 1885, received his M.D. from the Indiana Medical College in 1888, a second M.D. from the Faculté de Medicine in Constantinople in 1889, and the A.M. degree from Wabash College in 1903.

On Dec. 28, 1893, he married Annabette Bryan, who died in Persia in 1899. He married Harriet J. Wishard on Dec. 23, 1902, and after her death in 1937 he married Blanche Wakefield Pollock on Nov. 26, 1938.

From 1889 to 1909 Dr. Wishard acted as a medical missionary in Persia and, after 1910, as a practicing physician in Wooster, O. He died on July 15, 1940.

Information from *Who Was Who in America.*

* * *

Twenty Years in Persia. *Chicago,* 1908.
Reminiscences of a Doctor. *Wooster, O.,* 1935.

WISHARD, SAMUEL ELLIS: 1825–1915.

Samuel Ellis Wishard, son of Col. John and Agnes Henderson Oliver Wishard, was born in Johnson County, Ind., on Dec. 18, 1825, and graduated from Wabash College in 1853, receiving the A.M. degree in 1856. He graduated from Lane Theological Seminary in 1856 and received the D.D. degree from Centre College in 1884. On Feb. 13, 1857, he married Sophie Evarts.

For twenty years following his ordination in 1857 he was a pastor in various communities—Rushville, Ill., Tecumseh and Battle Creek, Mich., and Franklin, Ind. He engaged in evangelistic work from 1877 to 1880, was a pastor in Chicago from 1880 to 1883, was superintendent of home mission work in Kentucky from 1883 to 1887, and was a pastor in Des Moines, Ia., from 1887 to 1890. He then became superintendent of home mission work in Utah, a position he held until 1906, when he resumed preaching. Dr. Wishard wrote a letter every week for thirty-two years to the HERALD AND PRESBYTER.

He died on Nov. 11, 1915.

Information from *Who Was Who in America*.

* * *

In Memoriam . . . Rev. Frederick R. Gallaher. Sketch of His Life, with Funeral Services and Memorial Sermon. *Hartford*, 1870.

History of the Half Century Celebration of the Organization of the First Presbyterian Church of Franklin, Indiana. *Cincinnati*, 1874.

The Divine Law of Marriage; or, the Bible Against Polygamy. *New York*, 1888.

The Mormons. *New York*, 1904.

The Old, Old Story. *Cincinnati*, 1908.

The Testimony of the Bible Concerning Assumptions of Destructive Criticism. *Cincinnati*, 1909.

The Passion Play in the Light of Our Protestant Faith and the Word of God.

The Story of a Pilgrim, an Autobiographical Sketch. *New York*, 1912.

WISSLER, CLARK: 1870–1947.

Clark Wissler was born in Wayne County, Ind., on Sept. 18, 1870. His parents were Benjamin Franklin and Sylvania Needler Wissler.

Wissler received the A.B. degree from Indiana University in 1897 and the A.M. in 1899. In the same year he married Etta Viola Gebhart and began work toward his doctorate at Columbia University, where he received the Ph.D. in 1901. In 1929 he received the honorary LL.D. from Indiana University.

After completing his work at Columbia he joined the faculty of New York University. He was an instructor in 1901-1902, an assistant in anthropology (which became the field in which he was to gain his greatest reputation) from 1903 to 1906 and in the latter year he became curator of the American Museum of Natural History. In 1924 he became professor of anthropology at Yale University.

His work in the field of the study of the American Indian—especially of the costume of the Plains Indians—has been of greatest distinction. Besides the works listed, Dr. Wissler had some scores of contributions published in learned journals, bulletins, serials, etc.

Dr. Wissler died Aug. 25, 1947.

Information from the Richmond Public Library; additional material from *Who's Who in America*.

* * *

North American Indians of the Plains. *New York*, 1912.

The American Indian; an Introduction to the Anthropology of the New World. *New York*, 1917.

Man and Culture. *New York*, 1923.

Adventurers in the Wilderness (with C. L. Skinner and William Wood). *New Haven, Conn.*, 1925.

The Relation of Nature to Man in Aboriginal America. *New York*, 1926.

An Introduction to Social Anthropology. *New York*, 1929.

Population Changes Among the Northern Plains Indians. *New Haven, Conn.*, 1936.

Indian Cavalcade; or, Life on the Old-Time Indian Reservations. *New York*, 1938.

The Indians of the United States; Four Centuries of Their History and Culture. *New York*, 1940.

WOOD, AARON: 1802–?

Born Oct. 15, 1802, in Virginia, Aaron Wood moved with his family to Ohio in 1805, where he secured a good education. As a Methodist minister he traveled circuits in Ohio, Indiana, and Illinois, serving in Indiana on the Connersville circuit in 1823-24, the Madison circuit in 1824-25, and the Corydon circuit in 1829-30. He also served churches in Vincennes, Bloomington, Terre Haute, Lafayette, and Michigan City. He was agent for Indiana Asbury (now De Pauw) University in 1844-45 and agent for the American Bible Society from 1846 to 1851. In 1868 he was appointed moral instructor in Northern Indiana State Prison.

Information from Dunn—*Indiana and Indianans;* INDIANA MAGAZINE OF HISTORY, Vol. xxiii; Littell Auction Catalog; *The Distinguished Collection of Americana;* and the Indiana State Library.

* * *

Address Before Philisonian Society . . . *Greencastle, Ind.,* 1853.

Annals of the Methodist Episcopal Church in the State of Indiana. *Indianapolis,* 1854.

Sketches of Things and People in Indiana. *Indianapolis,* 1883.

WOOD, FLORA WILLIAMS: ?–

Flora Williams Wood, a resident of Elkhart, Ind., contributed verse to newspapers and periodicals.

Information from the Federal Writers Project, *Indiana Authors,* 1937, and from the Indiana State Library.

* * *

Reflections. *Elkhart, Ind.,* 1912.

WOOD, JOHN ANDERSON: 1865–1926.

John Anderson Wood, son of William Smith and Louisa Hamilton Anderson Wood, was born in Cleveland, O., on Aug. 14, 1865, and graduated from Indiana State Normal School in 1889. In 1897 he received the A.B. degree from Indiana University, in 1901 the A.M., and in 1903 received the Ps.D. degree from the Chicago School of Psychology. He also studied at Clark University and Columbia. On June 24, 1891, he married Louise Meyer.

From 1889 to 1896 he was principal of the high school in Frankfort, Ind., from 1897 to 1909 superintendent of the city schools of LaPorte, Ind., and from 1909 to 1912 superintendent in South Bend. After 1912 he was professor of religious education and dean of Biblical Seminary in New York.

He died on Apr. 4, 1926.

Information from *Who Was Who in America.*

* * *

Heating, Ventilating and Fuel for School Buildings. *LaPorte, Ind.,* 1903.

WOOD, WILLIAM ALLEN: 1874–1927.

Born in Covington, Ind., Sept. 25, 1874, William Allen Wood, son of Samuel Fletcher and Mary Allen

Wood, was educated at Covington High School and Indiana University.

After teaching school in the South for a short time, he came to Indianapolis where he practiced law until illness forced his retirement in 1920. He contributed to newspapers and magazines—principally editorials on political and social subjects—and was editor of the ILLUSTRATED INDIANA WEEKLY. He was also on the editorial staffs of the INDIANAPOLIS NEWS and INDIANAPOLIS SENTINEL. He was active in the affairs of the Indiana Society, Sons of the American Revolution. He died in Indianapolis on May 8, 1927.

Information from *Who's Who in America* and the Indianapolis Public Library.

* * *

Modern Business Corporations; Including the Organization and Management of Private Corporations, with Financial Principles and Practices, and Summaries of Decisions of the Courts Elucidating the Law of Private Business Corporations, and Explanations of the Acts of Promoters, Directors, Officers and Stockholders of Corporations . . . Forms of Procedure Illustrative of the Formation, Organization, Operation and Consolidation of Corporations (with Louis R. Ewbank). *Indianapolis,* 1906.

The Investment Guide and Record . . . *Indianapolis,* 1913.

Review of William Jennings Bryan's Bible Talks, and Other Articles. *Boston.*

WOODBURN, JAMES ALBERT: 1856–1943.

James Albert Woodburn, son of James and Martha Jane Hemphill Woodburn, was born in Bloomington, Ind., on Nov. 30, 1856. He graduated from Indiana University in 1876, receiving the A.M. degree in 1885, and received the Ph.D. from Johns Hopkins University in 1890. He also received honorary degrees from Indiana, Colgate, and Wabash. On Nov. 30, 1893, he married Caroline Louise Gelston.

Dr. Woodburn was professor of American history at Indiana University from 1890 to 1924 and professor emeritus from 1924 until his death on Dec. 12, 1943. He contributed to periodicals and encyclopedias and, in addition to his other books, was the author and joint-author of numerous textbooks and the editor of several works not listed here.

Information from *Who's Who in America.*

* * *

Causes of the American Revolution. *Baltimore,* 1892.

A Study of the American Commonwealth (As Reflected by

Orations of Burke and Webster) (with Cyrus Wilburn Hodgin). *Boston,* 1893.

The Making of the Constitution: a Syllabus of Madison's Journal of the Constitutional Convention, Together with a Few Outlines Based on the Federalist. *Chicago,* 1898.

The American Republic and Its Government: an Analysis of the Government of the United States with a Consideration of Its Fundamental Principles and of Its Relations to the States and Territories. *New York,* 1903.

American Politics. Political Parties and Party Problems in the United States: a Sketch of American Party History and of the Development and Operations of Party Machinery, Together with a Consideration of Certain Party Problems in Their Relation to Political Morality. *New York,* 1903.

American History and Government (joint-author). 1906.

Scotch-Irish Presbyterians in Monroe Co., Ind. 1910.

The Life of Thaddeus Stevens; a Study in American Political History, Especially in the Period of the Civil War and Reconstruction. *Indianapolis,* 1913.

The Citizen and the Republic. 1918.

The History and Government of Indiana (with Thomas F. Moran). *New York,* 1920.

The American Community (joint-author). 1924.

Since the Beginning: a Retrospect. *Bloomington, Ind.,* 1924.

The High School Teacher in Indiana History.

Finders and Founders of the New World (joint-author). 1925.

Studies in American History. *Bloomington, Ind.,* 1926.

Introduction to American History; the European Background (joint-author). 1926.

Makers of America (joint-author). 1926.

Active Citizenship (with Thomas F. Moran). *New York,* 1928.

Our United States (with Thomas F. Moran and H. C. Hill). *New York,* 1930.

Our Country; a United States History for City Boys and Girls. *New York,* 1938. 3 vols.

History of Indiana University, 1820-1902. *Bloomington, Ind.,* 1940.

WOODWARD, WALTER CARLETON: 1878–1942.

Walter Carleton Woodward, son of Ezra Hinshaw and Amanda Maris Woodward, was born near Mooresville, Ind., on Nov. 28, 1878.

Removing to Oregon, he attended the Friends Pacific Academy at Newberg and received the A.B. degree from Pacific College, in the same town, in 1898. A year later he received the B.L. degree from Earlham

College and earned his M.A. and Ph.D. degrees at the University of California in 1908 and 1910.

He married Catherine Hartman and spent the years 1900-1907 as associate editor of a Newberg newspaper and as an instructor in history and political science at Pacific College. Between 1910 and 1915 he was a member of the Earlham College faculty and in 1917 he became editor of THE AMERICAN FRIEND, residing in Richmond, Ind. He died in April, 1942.

Information from the Richmond Public Library.

* * *

The Rise and Early History of Political Parties in Oregon, 1843-1868. *Portland, Ore.,* 1913.

The Indiana Centennial.

The Pageant in Quest of Freedom (with Edna Johnson and Mrs. Mary H. Flanner). *Richmond, Ind.,* 1916.

The Pageant of Earlham College, in Quest of Freedom. Presented on the College Campus June, 1922. [*Richmond,* 1922.]

Friendly Tales of Foreign Trails. *Richmond, Ind.,* 1923.

Pageant of Richmond. *Richmond, Ind.,* 1924.

Timothy Nicholson—Master Quaker. *Richmond, Ind.,* 1927.

WOOLLEN, EVANS: 1864–1942.

Evans Woollen, son of William Watson and Mary Allen Evans Woollen, was born in Indianapolis on Nov. 28, 1864. After graduating from Yale in 1886 and receiving the A.M. degree in 1889, he began the practice of law in Indianapolis. Mr. Woollen was a founder and president of the Fletcher Trust Company and was active in numerous civic affairs. In 1928 he was a candidate for the Democratic presidential nomination. He died on May 20, 1942, at his home in Indianapolis.

Information from *Who's Who in America* and the Indianapolis Public Library.

* * *

Benjamin Franklin. *Indianapolis,* 1906.

After the War. n.p. [*Indianapolis*], n.d. [1917].

The Federal Reserve Act. n.p. [*Indianapolis*], n.d.

WOOLLEN, WILLIAM WATSON: 1838–1921.

William Watson Woollen, son of Milton and Sarah Black Woollen, was born in Indianapolis on May 28, 1838. He grew up on his father's farm, attended the district schools, and graduated from the law department of Northwestern Christian (now Butler) University in 1860. On Apr. 1, 1861, he was admitted to the Indianapolis bar, and at the time of his death he was the senior member both in age and continuous practice.

Mr. Woollen was active in civic affairs and will be remembered largely for his interest in and knowledge of natural history. He founded the Nature Study Club of Indiana, was president of the Indiana Audubon Society, and presented Buzzard's Roost, a tract of ground set apart for bird and flower study, to the city of Indianapolis. He died in Indianapolis on Mar. 26, 1921. He edited and annotated several law books not listed here.

> Information from Dunn—*Indiana and Indianans* and the Indianapolis Public Library.

* * *

Birds of Buzzard's Roost. *Indianapolis,* 1907.

Inside Passage to Alaska, 1792-1920; with an Account of the North Pacific Coast from Cape Mendocino to Cook Inlet, from the Accounts Left by Vancouver and Other Early Explorers, and from the Author's Journals of Explorations and Travel in that Region; Ed. from His Original Manuscripts by Paul L. Haworth. *Cleveland,* 1924. 2 vols.

Marion County Bar. *Indianapolis,* 1918.

WOOLLEN, WILLIAM WESLEY: 1828–1902.

William Wesley Woollen, the eldest son of Edward and Anna Wheeler Woollen, was born June 21, 1828, in Dorchester County, Md. Until he was sixteen years old he lived on his father's farm, attended the district schools, and worked in a dry-goods house. In 1844 he came to Madison, Ind., where he taught school for a time, then entered Hanover College. After he left Hanover, he held county offices of auditor and treasurer and studied law on the side. For two years he was editor and part owner of the MADISON BANNER, and in 1857, with Capt. John Marsh, he opened the banking house of John Marsh & Co. He moved to Franklin, Ind., in 1860 and was associated with banking there.

In 1865 he came to Indianapolis, where he spent the remainder of his life. He helped found the Indiana Banking Company, was a co-founder of the banking house of Woollen, Webb, & Co., and was associated with insurance companies in Indianapolis. For years he contributed to the editorial columns of the Indianapolis SENTINEL and the JOURNAL. He died in 1902.

> Information from *Representative Men of Indiana,* Vol. II; the Barry Ms.; and the Indianapolis Public Library.

* * *

Madison from 1844 to 1852: a Lecture. n.p. [*Indianapolis*], n.d. [1879].

Biographical and Historical Sketches of Early Indiana. *Indianapolis,* 1883.

William McKee Dunn, Brigadier-General, U. S. A. *New York,* 1892.

Representative Men of Indiana (author and editor). *Indianapolis,* 1880.

WRAY, NEWTON: 1854–1933.

Newton Wray, son of Isom and Miami Bower Wray, was born Oct. 30, 1854, in Shelby County, Ind.

He received the A.B. degree from De Pauw University in 1875, the B.D. from Drew Theological Seminary in 1887, and the D.D. from Taylor University in 1912. He married Mary Alma Gilbert of Bainbridge, N. Y., on Nov. 15, 1892.

From 1877 to 1879 he practiced law in Greenfield, Ind. He was ordained to the Methodist Episcopal ministry in 1880 and occupied pulpits in various Indiana and New York cities, with one academic year of teaching, until 1905.

In 1906 he joined the faculty of Asbury (Ky.) College, removing to Taylor University, Upland, Ind., in 1909. There he taught theology, Bible history, the Greek New Testament and Christian apologetics until 1929.

Dr. Wray died in 1933.

> Information from *Who's Who in America.*

* * *

Fun and Finance: a Discussion of Modern Church Novelties in Connection with the Subject of Christian Giving. *Boston,* 1890.

Must the Bible Go? Some Plain Words About Higher Criticism. *Chicago,* 1916.

The Book of Job, a Biblical Masterpiece Interpreted and Explained. *Boston,* 1929.

Things That Count—Studies in Life and Character. 1930.

Century Message to the Churches.

Church Finance.

WRIGHT, EDWARD DANVILLE: 1859–

Born in Wayne County, Ind., in 1859, Edward Danville Wright was reared in that locality and was apparently a resident there until at least middle age.

> Information from the Federal Writers Project, *Indiana Authors,* 1937, and from the Indiana State Library.

* * *

Poetical Compositions . . . Comprising Poems of Boyhood Days, Voices of the Heart, Religious, Sentimental, and Comical Poems. Also, the Federal Spy, Deception's Prey, and Others. *Richmond, Ind.,* 1888.

WRIGHT, WILLIAMSON SWIFT: 1857–1923.

"Williamson Swift Wright, son of Williamson Wright, was born Jan. 11, 1857, at Logansport, Ind. He was graduated from Wabash College with the class of 1877 and later received the A.M. degree at the same institution. He studied and practiced law at Logansport and was editor and proprietor of the LOGANSPORT JOURNAL from 1888 to 1898. He was a lieutenant in the U. S. Signal Corps during the Spanish-American War. He served as deputy postmaster 1889 to 1893 and Deputy Secretary of the State of Indiana in 1894 . . ." He died in 1923.

From Powell—*History of Cass County,* 1913.

* * *

Pastime Sketches, Scenes and Events at "The Mouth of Eel" on the Historic Wabash. *Logansport, Ind.,* 1907.

WYLIE, ANDREW: 1789–1851.

"Andrew Wylie (Apr. 12, 1789-Nov. 11, 1851), educator, first president of Indiana University, was born at Washington, Pa., the son of Adam Wylie who emigrated from Antrim, Ireland, about 1776 and became a farmer in Fayette County, Pa. He was educated at home and in local schools until the age of fifteen, when he entered Jefferson College, Canonsburg, Pa., supporting himself by tutoring and odd jobs until his graduation, with first honors, in 1810. For the next two years he was a tutor and at twenty-three succeeded to the principalship of the college. This office he ably administered for four years, resigning only as the result of dissatisfaction over his approval of plans for the consolidation of Jefferson College with Washington College, Washington, Pa. Soon after his resignation, April, 1816, he was named president of Washington College. He resigned, Dec. 9, 1828, to become the first president of Indiana College, which had been established by act of legislature, Jan. 24, 1828, as successor to the Indiana Seminary at Bloomington. He held this office until his death. When Wylie assumed office the faculty consisted of himself (as professor of moral and mental philosophy, political economy, and polite literature), two instructors, and sixty students. In 1838 the college became Indiana University and in 1842 a school of law was opened. Wylie's work as an educator was distinguished by the introduction of a system of study called 'specialization by rotation,' in which the student devoted himself to one subject at a time, mastering it before going to the next. His administration was marked by a slow but steady growth.

"In early life Wylie embraced the tenets of Presbyterianism, was licensed to preach by the Presbytery of Ohio, Oct. 12, 1812, and was pastor of a church at Millers Run, Pa., for several years after 1813. But the Presbyterian doctrine became unsatisfactory to him because of its extreme 'sectarianism,' and in 1841 he united with the Protestant Episcopal Church. In December he was ordained deacon and in May 1842 priest. He was described as 'tolerant and patient to a fault of everything but meanness and duplicity,' for the most part affable but occasionally brusque in manner . . . He was married in May 1813 to Margaret Ritchie, who survived him . . ."

Condensed from P. D. J., *Dictionary of American Biography,* Vol. XX.

* * *

An Address Delivered at Bloomington, Oct. 29, 1829. *Indianapolis,* 1829.

Blessedness of the Pious Dead; a Sermon Preached April 12, 1829 . . . *New York,* 1829.

Religion and State, Not Church and State; a Sermon Delivered July 4, 1830, at Bloomington, Ind. n.p., n.d.

A Discourse on Education Delivered before the Legislature of the State of Indiana. *Indianapolis,* 1830.

An Address Delivered to the Graduates in Indiana College. *Bloomington, Ind.,* 1833.

The Sabbath, a Sermon . . . *Indianapolis,* 1833.

Baccalaureate Delivered at the Fifth Commencement of Indiana College, September 24, 1834. *Bloomington, Ind.,* 1834.

Sermon on the Subject of the Union of Christians for the Conversion of the World. *Madison, Ind.,* 1834.

An Eulogy on Lafayette. *Cincinnati,* 1835.

Baccalaureate Delivered to the Senior Class, in the Chapel of Indiana College, on the 25th of September, 1836. *Terre Haute, Ind.,* 1836.

Address on the Subject of Common School Education, . . . January 3, 1837. *Indianapolis,* 1837.

The Danger and Duty of the Young; a Sermon Preached to the Senior Class on the Sabbath Previous to Commencement, . . . Indiana College. *Pittsburgh,* 1837.

The Propriety of Retaining Greek and Roman Classics in Their Place as a Part of Study Necessary in the Course of a Liberal Education. An Address Delivered at Crawfordsville, Ind., July, 1838. *Bloomington, Ind.,* 1838.

Address on the Importance and Best Method of Cultivating the Moral Faculties Delivered before the

Education Convention of Indiana, December 26, 1837. *Indianapolis*, 1838.

An Address Delivered before the Philomathean Society of the Wabash College . . . July 10, 1838. Published by the Society. *Bloomington, Ind.*, n.d. ([1838?].

Baccalaureate Address . . . to Senior Class of Indiana University . . . September 25, 1839. *Bloomington, Ind.*, 1839.

The Perfect Man; a Sermon occasioned by the Death of Jonathan Nichols. *Bloomington, Ind.*, 1839.

Sectarianism Is Heresy. *Bloomington, Ind.*, 1840.

Address to the Citizens of Monroe County . . . *Bloomington*, 1840.

Baccalaureate, Addressed to the Senior Class of Indiana University, at the Late Commencement, September, 1841. *Bloomington, Ind.*, 1841.

Baccalaureate, Addressed to the Senior Class, on the Day of Commencement, 1843. *Bloomington, Ind.*, 1843.

Baccalaureate, Addressed to the Senior Class of Indiana University, at the Late Commencement, September, 1845. *Bloomington, Ind.*, 1845.

Baccalaureate, Addressed to the Senior Class of 1846, of Indiana University. *Bloomington, Ind.*, 1846.

Energy and Refinement in Woman. A Sermon Preached before the Pupils and Teachers of St. Mary's Seminary, Indianapolis . . . *Indianapolis*, 1846.

Baccalaureate, Addressed to the Senior Class of Indiana University, at the Late Commencement, September, 1847. *Bloomington, Ind.*, 1847.

Baccalaureate, Addressed to the Senior Class . . . September, 1848. *Bloomington, Ind.*, 1848.

Baccalaureate, Addressed to the Senior Class of Indiana University, at the Late Commencement, August, 1850. *Bloomington, Ind.*, 1850.

Justice: a Discourse to the Students of the Law Department of the Indiana University . . . February 26, 1850. *Bloomington, Ind.*, 1850.

The Individual: a Baccalaureate Delivered to the Class of Seniors at the Commencement of the Indiana University, Aug. 13, 1851. *Indianapolis*, 1851.

Y

YOST, M. EDITH (MRS. ?): 1863–

Born in Mt. Summit, Ind., in 1863, Mrs. Yost was the author of a book of poems.

Information from the Federal Writers Project— *Indiana Authors*, 1937.

* * *

A Summer Tale, and Other Poems.

YOUNG, CLAIBORNE ADDISON: 1843–1912.

Claiborne Addison Young, Unitarian clergyman, was born in Boone County, Ind., in 1843. After attend-

ing local schools he graduated from Wabash College in 1869.

He married Lucy C. Farnham on May 8, 1890, and died in Lafayette, Ind., in 1912.

Information from *Who's Who in America* and the Wabash College Archives.

* * *

Way Songs and Wanderings. *Boston*, 1897.

In the Red Man's Land, and Other Poems. *Crawfordsville, Ind.*, 1915.

Z

ZAHM, JOHN AUGUSTINE: 1851–1921.

Born at New Lexington, Perry County, O., on June 14, 1851, John Augustine Zahm was the son of Jacob M. and Mary Braddock Zahm. He received the A.B. degree from the University of Notre Dame in 1871 and in the same year entered the Order of the Holy Cross. He was in charge of the scientific department of Notre Dame, president of the board of trustees, curator of the Museum, and a lecturer at other schools. He died in 1921.

Information from the University of Notre Dame Library.

* * *

The Catholic Church and Modern Science. *Notre Dame, Ind.*, 1883.

Colorado, Its Past, Present and Future. 1883.

The Great Southwest, Its Attractions, Resources and People. *Notre Dame, Ind.*, 1883.

Alaska: the Country and the People. 1886.

Letters from the Hawaiian Islands. 1887.

Souvenirs of Travel: 1883-87.

Sound and Music. *Chicago*, 1892.

Catholic Science and Catholic Scientists. *Philadelphia*, 1893.

De la Necessité de Developper les Etudes Scientifiques dans les Seminaires Ecclesiastiques. 1894.

Bible, Science and Faith. *Baltimore*, 1894.

Evolution and Dogma. *Chicago*, 1896.

Scientific Theory and Catholic Doctrine. *Chicago*, 1896.

Science and the Church. *Chicago*, 1896.

What the Church Has Done for Science. *Notre Dame, Ind.*, n.d.

Science and Doctrine. *New York*.

Following the Conquistadores Up the Orinoco and Down the Magdalena. *New York*, 1910.

Following the Conquistadores Along the Andes and Down the Amazon. *New York*, 1911.

Woman in Science with an Introductory Chapter on Woman's Long Struggle for Things of the Mind. *New York,* 1913.

Following the Conquistadores Through South America's Southland, with an Account of the Roosevelt Scientific Expedition to South America. *New York,* 1916.

Great Inspirers. *New York,* 1917.

The Quest of El Dorado: the Most Romantic Episode in the History of South American Conquest. *New York,* 1917.

From Berlin to Bagdad and Babylon. *New York,* 1922.

Hawaii and the Hawaiians.

Art and Life: Syllabus. *Chicago.*

British Municipal Life: Syllabus. *Chicago.*

Common Life: Syllabus. *Chicago.*

Elements and Structure of Society; Syllabus. *Chicago.*

Prophets of Social Morality: Syllabus. *Chicago.*

Religion and the Church. *Philadelphia.*

Social Reform in Fiction: Syllabus. *Chicago.*

Twentieth Century City: Syllabus. *Chicago.*

Unity of Faith: Syllabus. *Chicago.*

Value of Ethical Organizations. *Philadelphia.*

Work and Wealth: Syllabus. *Chicago.*

ZUEBLIN, CHARLES: 1866–1924.

Charles Zueblin, sociologist, was born in Pendleton, Ind., the son of John E. and Henrietta Follett Zueblin, on May 4, 1866. He attended the University of Pennsylvania from 1883 to 1885, received the Ph.B. degree from Northwestern University in 1885, the D.B. degree from Yale in 1889 and studied at the University of Leipzig from 1889 to 1891.

He married Miss Rho Fisk on June 18, 1892. In 1891 he founded the Northwestern University Settlement and in 1892 he became the first secretary of the Chicago Society for University Extension and assisted in the Extension Division of the University of Chicago. Between 1892 and 1908 he was, successively, instructor, assistant professor, associate professor and professor of sociology on the University of Chicago faculty. He edited the TWENTIETH CENTURY MAGAZINE in 1911-12 and devoted the rest of his life to writing and lecturing. He died Sept. 15, 1924, at his home in Winchester, Mass.

Information from *Who Was Who in America.*

* * *

English Fiction and Social Reform; Syllabus. *Chicago,* 1892.

Chicago Ghetto. 1895.

American Municipal Progress; Chapters in Municipal Sociology. *New York,* 1902.

A Decade of Civic Improvement. *Springfield, O.,* 1903.

A Decade of Civic Development. *Chicago,* 1905.

Democracy and the Overman. *New York,* 1910.

The Religion of a Democrat. *New York,* 1908.

ZUVER, JOHN HENRY: 1873–

John Henry Zuver, son of Henry and Julia A. Kuhns Zuver, was born at Amboy, Mich., on July 29, 1873. He was educated in the public schools of Amboy and the high school of Pioneer, O., going from the latter to Hillsdale College in 1889. In 1893 he graduated from the Detroit College of Law, was admitted to the bar, and began practicing in Jackson, Mich. From 1897 to 1905 he was associated with a law publishing house at Jackson and Battle Creek, Mich. He married Mary C. Campbell of Detroit on June 19, 1895.

From 1905 until 1908 he was identified with the BATTLE CREEK MOON, from 1908 to 1911 with the JOURNAL, and in 1911 was a political writer for the GRAND RAPIDS HERALD. In 1912 he became a resident of South Bend, Ind., where he was on the staff of the NEWS-TIMES, becoming editor of this paper in 1914. After 1924 he was editor of the SOUTH BEND MIRROR.

Information from Dunn—*Indiana and Indianans.*

* * *

The Earthly Pilgrimage of John Jay. *Battle Creek, Mich.,* 1902.

Get Ready To Lead. *South Bend, Ind.,* 1917.

Scribblings of a Scribe; Selected Editorials That Appeared in the South Bend Mirror, 1938. *South Bend,* 1938.

The Spirit of Helpfulness.

Analysis of the League of Nations Covenant. 1920.

Civilized Christianity. 1925.